Lorrha-Stowe M True Worshi

As used in the

Ancient Divine Prayers: Lorrha-Stowe Missal:
Mass (Offering, or Divine Liturgy); Baptism and Chrismation;
Anointing of the Sick; St. Gall Confession;
Antiphonary of Bangor, Hours of Prayer of the Day and Night:
Vespers, Beginning of Night, Midnight, Matins,
Second Hour, Third Hour, Sixth Hour, Ninth Hour;
Breviary Rules to say the Psalms
of Saints Brendan, Mael Ruain, and Columbanus;
Hours of Holy and Great Friday; Cross Vigil;
Paschal Liturgy; Mass of the Holy Cross and Adoration;
Mass of St. Patrick; Traditio of St. Ambrose;
Hymns: Gallican Hymn of St. Hilary; Apostles' Forty-fold Kyrie;
Deers-Cry; Paschal Hymns; Abecedarian Hymns:
Altus Prosator by St. Colum cille; Audite omnes for St. Patrick;
Litanies; Visitation of Sick; Departure; Wake; Funeral; Burial;
Lectionary through the Year; Complete Psalter;
Notes; Creeds; Desert Meditations on Virtues and Faults.

Translations and Notes: † MAELRUAIN (Kristopher Dowling)
Editing and Notes: Deaconess Elizabeth Dowling

Copyright and Acknowledgments

Translation of the Sacraments of Holy Communion, Baptism and Chrismation, Unction from the Lorrha-Stowe Missal, with an Irish Confession and Absolution from St. Gall, translated from Latin and given rubrics, and a translation of the prayers and hymns of the Hours (the Breviary) from Latin of the Antiphonary of Bangor, © 1996 + Maelrúain Kristopher Dowling, All Rights Reserved, copyright through the Library of Congress. Much of the outline for the structure of the Breviary is drawn from the well-researched book, *The Antiphonary of Bangor,* by Michael Curran. However, this translation from Latin into English and arrangement into the Hours is © 1996 by Bishop Maelruain (Kristopher Dowling). My sincere thanks to Dionysios Redington and Professor Karen Rae Keck, who brought the Lorrha-Stowe Missal Latin critical text to my attention. Translation and notes made public on the Feast of the Ascension of our Lord Jesus Christ, 1995 (amended January1996, October 2004, edited into one book: 2008).

ISBN: 978-0-557-00229-0

This Missal, Ordinary and the Propers therein are approved for all Orthodox Christians of the Celtic Tradition of our jurisdiction. +Maelrúain, Céle Dé, Celtic Orthodox Christian Church. (The Celtic Orthodox Christian Church is a recognized tax-exempt Church with Orthodox Apostolic Succession and Doctrine.) Those outside of the Celtic Orthodox Christian Church seeking permission to use this Missal must apply to their own Bishops for permission to use any of the services herein.

This Missal, together with the Celtic Propers and Lections, is the exact translation of a Divine Liturgy in use in the undivided Orthodox Catholic Church, is complete in content, and was known among Celtic, Gallican, and many other peoples, including those in North America around 600 A.D. These prayers are meant for anybody, not just one nationality or ethnicity. However, using non-Celtic Propers or Lections with the Celtic Missal, such as Byzantine or Roman Propers through the year, would be inappropriate, and would constitute a change in this Divine Liturgy. Celtic Propers for the Mass through the entire year and the Sacrament of Holy Orders are in a separate book: apply to Ap. Ep. MAELRUAIN. Those clergy outside of the Celtic Orthodox Christian Church who use this Divine Liturgy occasionally in the commemoration of a particular Feast may do so, but the Celtic Propers through the year for the great Feasts, all Sundays and Saint days, connect the teachings of Scripture with the Presence of the Holy Trinity in the Mass.

Ap. Ep. Maelrúain (Dowling), Celtic Orthodox Christian Church
P.O. Box 72102, Akron, OH 44372 USA. Phone: 1-330-622-6359
Homepage: www.CelticChristianity.org   e-mail: espmaelruain@ CelticChristianity.org

This book has pre-schism sources, before the churches of Rome in the West and the Byzantine East split in theology and administration over a thousand years ago. The Sacraments of the *Lorrha-Stowe Missal* and prayers of the *Antiphonary of Bangor* embody the central prayers of the Church, having ancient sources from the Apostles. This book is copyrighted, and we respect the copyrights of others who have translated Celtic Marriage rites. (Other modern translators have provided a few early occasional prayers. Many of the books of "Celtic Prayers" commonly available have post-schism sources, written after the Irish were not allowed to join their own monasteries, i.e., contemporary with or after Henry II of England.) The pre-schism Celtic prayers more directly teach the literal and spiritual truths of Jesus Christ and the Apostles and Saints, including St. Patrick, St. Columbanus, St. Brendan, St. Mael Ruain (Maelruain), St. John Cassian and the desert Fathers of Egypt who taught in early 5th century southern France, and with whom St. Patrick studied. The Celtic Missal includes many essential prayers missing from other Liturgies; these follow early theological writings and the "Ecumenical Councils." Portions of Celtic prayers can be found in the Byzantine Rite and Roman Rite. The Church is one and continuous, so this Missal is more than an effort at "Liturgical Archeology." Those Saints who used and approved these prayers are not dead, but alive in Christ. These prayers are a living tradition.

Contents

Copyrights, Acknowledgments, Note on Accuracy, Pre-Schism Sources	2
Rules of Fasting	8
Rite of Reconciliation (St. Gall. Confession, Counseling, Absolution)	9
Ordinary of the Mass, the Lorrha-Stowe Mass. (Not all parts are in the Contents.)	
Opening Prayers; Litany of the Saints	11
Prayer of St. Ambrose; Vesting Prayer of St. Augustine	13
Preparation of Water, Bread, and Wine	15
Old Testament Reading (If any, substitute from the Lectionary)	15
Introductory Collect (Substitute Propers through the year)	16
Angelic Hymn (Gloria) (music page 17)	16
Collect Before the Epistle (Substitute Propers through the year)	18
Epistle (Substitute the Proper Lectionary Epistle)	19
Gradual and Alleluia (Psalm) (From Psalm order through year)	20
Litany of Supplication by St. Martin of Tours	20
Censing prayers and Censing	22
Prayer of St. Gregory over the Gospel (Offering prayer)	22
Holy Gospel (Substitute the Proper Lectionary Gospel)	22
Sermon (Based on Gospel, Epistle, Propers of the day)	23
Creed; Elevation	23
Collect of the Preface (Substitute Proper Secret or Ad Pacem)	24
Lift up our Hearts; Dignum, Contestatio, or Immolacio (Proper Preface)	25
Sanctus (Holy Holy Holy)	27
The Sovereign Canon of Pope Gelasius (like a Litany)	28
Commemoration of the Living (Inside the Gelasian Canon)	28
Proper Communicantes (if any)	28
Post Sanctus from the Gothic Missal (if any)	29
The Most Dangerous Prayer (Words of Institution)	30
Commemoration of the Departed	31
Examination and Fraction and Prayers of the Fraction	32
Proper Post Secreta or Post Mysterium (Epiklesis)	33
Our Father (The Lord's Prayer)	33
The Peace; Proper Blessing of the Day (if Bishop is present)	34
Confraction (begins here)	34
Psalms sung during the Confraction	37
Holy Communion	41
Post Communion (Substitute Proper Prayer)	43
Thanksgiving Prayer, Ending Prayers, and Final Benediction	44
Final Gospel, usually the beginning of St. John's Gospel	45
(Notes on the Missal, Sacraments, and Breviary, are after the Litanies.)	
Hymns Sung During Communion (if time)	
Sancti Venite "Ye Holy Ones" (always sung) (musical setting next page)	46
The Beatitudes; Similitudes	49
Hymn to St. Michael the Archangel (always Sunday Sixth Hour)	49
The Magnificat	50
The Cross Vigil from the Rule of Tallaght of St. Mael Ruain	51
(Hymns of the Cross Vigil may be used at Holy Communion.)	
Psalms 118, 119, 120, 121	438
Antiphonary of Bangor Hymn 2 by St. Hilary of Poitiers	52
Unitas (Unity in Trinity)	55
Hymn to Mary	56
Shrine of Piety (which may follow or precede a Liturgy)	57

Other Hymns Which may be inserted at Holy Communion, or Seasonal Hymns	
Deers Cry, the Breastplate of St. Patrick	58
Hymn of the Apostles: Antiphonary of Bangor Hymn 3, 40-fold Kyrie	59
Abecedarian Hymns: Altus Prosator by St. Colum cille	63
Abecedarian Hymns: Audite omnes, (about St. Patrick) by St. Secundinus	67
Seasonal (Other Hymns: See Matins; Resurrection Vigil, etc.) O Come Emmanuel	71
Notes on Paschal Hymns: Angelic Hymn of the Candle	72
Fiery Creator of Fire Antiphonary of Bangor Hymn 9	74
Paschal Salutations and other Salutations	75
Continuous Prayers ("Pray without ceasing." 1 Thess. 5:17.); Deus in adjutorium	75
Jesus Prayer; Angelic Salutation ("Hail Mary")	76
Occasional Prayers: Prayer of St. Ephraim the Syrian; Prayers at Meals-Informal	77
Prayers at Meals- Formal, in a monastic community	78
Hours of Night and Day from the Antiphonary of Bangor	
Short Introduction to the Daylight Psalms of St. Brendan	80
Vespers (sunset, beginning of day, Gen. 1:5), (Gloria and Antiphons page 83)	80
The Hour of the Beginning of Night (mid-evening, around 9:00 P.M.)	84
The Hour of Midnight	87
Matins (Hour of the Resurrection, after midnight to dawn) Notes (also p 342-361)	89
Beginning of Matins: Psalms (In Matins: See notes pages 345, 346, 349)	91
Collects (Note: only read the Collects specified for the day.)	92
1st Canticle of Moses AB 1 Deut. 32:1-43 Advent-Epiphany	93
Blessing of Saint Zacharias Lk 1:68-80 Other Sundays	96
Antiphons before the Second Canticle of Moses	96
2nd Canticle of Moses AB 5 (Exodus 15:1-19) Always said	97
Collects and Antiphons	98
Song of the Three Youths AB 6 (Daniel 3:57-88a), and Collects	99
Psalms of Praise: Psalms 148, 149, 150	100
Collects after Psalms of Praise	101
Thrice-Holy Hymn, Irish "Trisagion" [AB 123, 128, 90, 93, 125]	102
Resurrection Gospel; or in Lent, Old Testament; Collects	103
Te Deum	104
Gloria AB 116 with Antiphons	107
Hymn and Procession to the Cross: AB 12 "Spirit of Divine glorious Light, Look upon me, O Lord..." Sundays	108
Hymn and Procession to the Cross: AB 11 "Most Holy Martyrs of the Most High God..." Saturdays and Saints' Days	109
Hymn and Procession to the Cross Daily AB 2	110
(Other Saint day or Seasonal Hymns inserted here.)	
Prayer of the Community of the Brethren: Long form	113
Credo (Creed); Divine Prayer (Lord's Prayer, the "Our Father")	116
(A shorter Community of the Brethren may be substituted, p 463.)	
Intercessory Prayer of Matins for the Martyrs	116
Shrine of Piety	117
Second Hour (just after dawn: about 7:00 A.M.)	118
Third Hour (mid-morning: 9:00 A.M.)	121
Sixth Hour (noon)	122
Ninth Hour (3:00 P.M.)	123
The Hours of Holy and Great Friday, the portion existing in Lections	125
Note on the full Harmony of the Gospels (Instead of the Psalms)	126
Vespers and Beginning of Night combined on Holy and Great Friday	127
Midnight on Holy and Great Friday	134
Matins on Holy and Great Friday	137
Second Hour on Holy and Great Friday	141

Third Hour on Holy and Great Friday	145
Sixth Hour on Holy and Great Friday	148
Ninth Hour, the most Holy Hour of the Crucifixion	152
Holy Saturday Matins Gospel and Psalm (See Cross Vigil page 51)	155
The Resurrection of our Lord Jesus Christ (Notes p. 156.) Very long Service	158
Some Hymns of the Resurrection (used in Paschaltide etc.):	
The Song of the Three Youths (entire chapter of Daniel 3:1-100)	168
Hymn of the Candle at the Resurrection	174
Fiery Creator of Fire (Antiphonary of Bangor Hymn 9)	176
Byzantine Paschal Hymns and Salutations	206
(Within the Vigil: Baptism p. 216 Resuming the Liturgy p. 178)	
Rogation Prayers and Procession, last days before Ascension	212
Minor Healings and Blessings from the Lorrha-Stowe Missal	216
The Rite of Baptism from the Lorrha-Stowe Missal; (short note)	216
Preparation, Baptism, Chrismation, Mandatum, First Communion	217
Visitation of the Sick from the Ambrosian Rite	229
Holy Unction, the Anointing of the Sick from the Lorrha-Stowe Missal	230
(For healing of those who are sick, not only for the dying.)	
(Note: See Copyright and Acknowledgments regarding Marriage and Holy Orders.)	
Emergency Rites	234
Prayers for the Dying and Funeral from the Ambrosian Rite	235
Prayers [Before] the Soul Goes Forth From the Body (with Unction)	235
Commending the Soul When it Goes Forth from the Body	235
Funeral After the Soul Goes Forth From the Body	
Preparation of the Body and Psalms	236
Wake for the Dead, the 150 Psalms, or a few Psalms here	238
Psalms for When the Body is Carried to the Church	239
Chants for When the Body is Carried to the Church	240
Requiem Mass (from the Ordinary, with these prayers)	240
When the Body is Taken from the Church to the Tomb	241
At the Tomb	241
After the Burial	243
Litanies translated by Charles Plummer (from later Celtic sources) Notes	244
Of the Savior	244
Of the Virgin and All Saints	245
Of the Trinity	246
Of St. Michael	249
Of Jesus I	250
Of Jesus II	252
Of the Virgin	253
Metrical Litany of the Virgin Mary	255
Of the Irish Saints I	256
Of the Irish Saints II	257
Of the Virgins	263
Of Confession	264
Notes on the Missal and Breviary	
Discussion of Symbols of the Mass contemporary with the Missal	269
The Mass: The Meaning of "Liturgy" and "Eternity"	271
Early Church Services, and the Mass	272
Dating and history of the Lorrha-Stowe Missal, the Celtic Rite	273
The Suppression of the Celtic Rite after 1171, the finding of the Missal	274
This Liturgy is Approved; the Orthodox Saints are always Saints	274

What Theological Problems Were Avoided by the Celtic Rite?	275
Heresies pertaining to God	275
Heresies pertaining to our Faith and Response to God	277
The Celtic Rite Focuses on True Worship	278
Details on the Manuscript Itself: Folio Problems, Abbreviations	279
Some specifics on the Mass: Liturgy of Word and Faith together	281
Some specifics on the Mass: Correct Celtic Propers; Bread	281
Word Usage: Essential-Substantial; Word Usage: And the Holy Spirit	282
Clergy in the Mass; Rubrics (Gestures and Directions)	282
Penitential Prayers and Gestures; Sounds of the Mass	283
The Beginning of the Mass, Offering Not Before the Beginning	284
Censing; Gospel and Sermon	284
The Creed: Complete Nicene, and Two Other Apostolic Creeds	284
Complete Orthodox Nicene Creed in the Lorrha-Stowe Missal	285
Apostles' Creed from the Antiphonary of Bangor (8th C.)	285
Another Apostles' Creed from the Bobbio Missal	285
Celtic Preface and Sanctus, a Masterpiece of Catechism and Praise	286
The Canon and Litanies in the Mass	286
Consecration, Fraction, Epiklesis	286
Both Species, Intinction	287
Unity, Eternity, the Mass in the Confraction and Litany of the Saints	287
Confraction Prayers before Communion affirm the Eucharist	288
Corporate Holy Communion	289
Dismissal and Final Gospel	289
Notes on Baptism, Chrismation, First Communion and Command	289
The Lorrha-Stowe Missal, a Chain of Charity	290
(What is not in the Missal: Marriage, Holy Orders, a Few Services)	291
An Essay About the Cross in the Mass (in Response to a Question)	292
The Celtic Lectionary, and Psalms in the Graduals and Alleluias of the Mass	293
Examples of Propers (short note)	302
Propers for The Feast of the Finding of the True Cross (as an example)	303
Adoration of the Holy Cross and two Hymns "Before Thy Cross"	305
Propers for St. Patrick	306
The Traditio: Symbols of Gospels and Creed	308
Prayer: The Our Father, Divine Prayer, The Lord's Prayer: four kinds of prayer	312
Salve Sancta Parens of Caelius Sedulius (St. Siadal), in Carmen Paschal	314
Meditations on Psalms, and Examination of Faults and Virtues in the Hours	314
The Term "Sin" in the Psalms, Deficiency versus Active Sin	314
"Flesh" and "Spirit" may be good or bad in context, not dual	314
Layers of Meaning in Scripture and Psalms, Not Nationalism	315
Virtue overcoming sin through the Hours of Prayer, from God	315
The Cross is the Greatest Sign of Virtue Which Comes From God	316
God's Many Virtues together in the Church	316
Psalms Cure the Wild Beast, St. Basil: Holy Spirit, Music, Seven	317
Names of God and the Virtues of Faith, Hope, and Charity	317
Our Response to the Virtues of Faith, Hope, and Charity	318
Word, Thought, and Deed of God and our Response	318
Two Commandments	319
Twelve Virtues: St. Antony, Abbot Pinufius (St. John Cassian)	319
List of Eight Sins and Virtues from an Irish Penitential	324
Overcoming Faults and Learning Virtues in the Hours of Prayer (note)	332
Hours, Virtues, Overcoming Faults	333
The Beatitudes, A Possible Inner Meaning of Ten Commandments	339
Conclusion, comparing the Desert Fathers to modernism, further study	341

Notes on the Hours	342
Prayer; Psalm designations for Sundays, Saint days, Weekdays	342
Eight Times a Day	342
What are the Psalms of the Hours (Hours of the Day and Night)?	342
Greater than a Local Irish Usage, Sources of other Usages	343
Blessing and Care of an Elder; the Sacraments, Word, Thought, and Deed	343
Melodies and Singing Aloud; How to Do the Prayers of the Church	343
Seasonal and Daily Collects and Prayers, Especially Matins	344
Prayer of the Community of the Brethren, Short or Long Forms	344
The Creed and the Our Father in the Hours	344
Psalm Numbering, Rules, Gospels, Canticles, Psalm Names, The Psalms	345
Psalm Numbering in Greek: Early Christian, not Hebrew numbering	345
Psalm Reading According to the Monastery of Bangor	345
An "All-Night Vigil" using Beginning of Night and Midnight with Matins	346
No Psalms on Holy and Great Friday, and Adjustments in Holy Week	346
A Few Solitaries Practice 150 Psalms in a Day, with Permission	346
Rule of St. Mael Ruain: Psalms at the Beginning of Night and Midnight	347
Psalm table of St. Mael Ruain which specified the Psalms by name	347
Rule of St. Columbanus: Psalms at Matins (Vigil)	349
The Holy Nights (any night) preceding Saturday and Sunday	350
On other nights in Matins (Monday to Friday)	350
Alternate Psalm Usages; Byzantine Psalm Readings	351
Resurrection Gospels for Sunday Matins in the (Celtic) Ten Week Cycle (Notes)	351
Matins Resurrection Gospels (Notes:)	352
During Lent and Paschaltide – Gospels are replaced by other Lections.	352
Holy Gospels in Matins – First Edition Arrangement in the Breviary	352
Holy Gospels in Matins - Variant Order of Gospels from Paschaltide	352
Resurrection Gospels (in order of the four Gospels, not the ten weeks)	353
Byzantine Eleven Matins Resurrection Gospels.	360
Some Canticles (Note)	360
Canticles in the order of the Antiphonary of Bangor, and Others	360
Nine Odes of the Byzantine Rite	362
Russian 151st Psalm by the Prophet David	362
Psalm Names in Latin and English in Greek Numbering	362
Psalter: The 150 Psalms in Greek Numbering, and St. Mael Ruain's Divisions	
Sunday (modern Saturday night.) Beginning of Night Psalms 1-13	366
Sunday Midnight Psalms 14-25	372
Monday (modern Sunday night.) Beginning of Night Psalms 26-37	380
Monday Midnight Psalms 38-50	388
Tuesday (modern Monday night.) Beginning of Night Psalms 51-63	396
Tuesday Midnight Psalms 64-75	402
Wednesday (modern Tues. night.) Beginning of Night Psalms 76-87	411
Wednesday Midnight Psalms 88-100	419
Thursday (modern Wed. night) Beginning of Night Psalms 101-112	426
Thursday Midnight Psalms 113-124	435
Friday (modern Thursday night) Beginning of Night Psalms 125-137	448
Friday Midnight Psalms 138-150	452
Ending Prayers for Hours: Community of the Brethren Prayers Long Form	459
Short Form of the Community of the Brethren Prayers; Creed and Our Father	463

Rules for Fasting in Monastic and Lay Usage

The Irish fasting rules are ideal, because these follow the Rules of the ancient desert fathers.

Before the Mass, no food or drink is taken from the evening before the Mass. (An exception is given to those with medical conditions, for medicines, or other medical needs.)

Periods of fasting in the monastery of Bangor (traditional early fasts):

The forty day fasts are called "Moses fasts," because these correspond to the forty fast days Moses was in Mt. Sinai receiving the Law, and the forty years in the desert. Forty day fasts are still called "Moses fasts" in traditional usages.

Forty days before Christmas (earlier than from St. Andrew's Feast). Six weeks was the standard Advent fast everywhere until late. Other than the Celtic Rite, the six week Advent fast is still practiced in all the Byzantine churches and in the Roman Patriarchate of Milan, which follows the Ambrosian Rite. The Martyrology of Tallaght and Oengus's Speckled Book both state that Advent begins November 13th, and the first Sunday in Advent is the first Sunday after November 13th. This may be proven another way: St. Martin's day, November 11th, was treated as a carnival in all of Europe, i.e., a day of eating meat before a fast. (Note: Old Calendar date of the beginning of Advent is Nov. 26th, usually after the American Thanksgiving, which is derived in menu and herbs from the St. Martin's day goose. Laity may begin the Advent fast afterwards.)

Forty days before Pascha (Lent). Actually fasting begins in Pre-Lent, two weeks before the beginning of Lent, or may extend from the post-Epiphany fast through Lent.

Forty days after Pentecost (not variable in number of days).

Non-Moses Fast: The Jesus Fast, January 7/ 20 through February 14/27: This fast marks the time Jesus spent in the desert after His Baptism: Winter Fast which starts the day after Epiphany and becomes part of the Lenten fast. But, if the only food that is available is dried or preserved meat, this fast is not in force. The purpose of this fast is to make certain that food is shared with all people during these cold months, which were called the "terror time" by the Irish. (Some people have claimed recently that the winter was a time of feasting and festivals. There are some Feasts during this time, but all the early church calendars talk about this winter fast, called "Jesus' fast" in the *Martyrology of Tallaght* and Oengus' *Speckled Book*, because it is special to Jesus, but is not quite a forty day fast, or it may run into the Lenten fast and become about twice as long as the other fasts. The purpose of "boxing day" and the celebration of St. Stephen's day immediately after Christmas is to make certain that all the poor had a supply of food, blankets, and heat through the winter. To quote Oengus' Speckled Book for the close of this fast, the Feast day February 15/ 28, "Sing a Sunday's celebration..." [say a Mass, i.e., an important Feast day in the year;] "the Son of God's victory over His enemy." And in the gloss, "The devil tempts Christ and then flees from His presence." ending, or making a pause, in this fasting season. The same lection is done on the Monday of the first week in Lent, and corresponds to fleeing from reductions in the faith, and holding fast to the truth.)

One meal per day at Ninth hour was allowed during fasting periods, and during fasts, no wine, beer or milk. Meat and fish would not be eaten. In a monastery, in fast seasons, flour for bread was made with the entire wheat plant, including the stalks: very high in fiber. Absolute fasting was practiced on Wednesdays and Fridays (no food). Fasting rules were suspended or relaxed when non-monastic guests were present. Milk was allowed to travelers, sick and aged at Bangor. Two meals per day were allowed during non-fasting periods. In non-fasting periods monks were allowed to eat: vegetables, sea-weed, bread, water, whey, wine, beer. Fish, either scale or shell-fish, was allowed on feasts. Other monastic disciplines included continuous prayer, work, sleeping on stones without heat, etc., each monastery had their own rule. St. Finian, Abbot and teacher of many other monastic missionary Saints, was noted for extreme discipline, following the Rule of Scetis, Egypt, but more extreme due to the cold and damp winter in Ireland.

Rite of Reconciliation

[St. Gallen Manuscript F.F. iii, *a Celtic Confession*]

Dost thou believe in the Father, the Son and the Holy Spirit?
R. I believe.

Dost thou believe that these same three Persons, as we say, the Father, and the Son and the Holy Spirit, **are** three and **is** one God? R. I believe.

Dost thou believe that thou shalt arise in this very same flesh in which thou art now on the day of Judgment and receive the good or ill which thou hast given? R. I believe.

Dost thou desire to forgive those who have committed all manner of sin against thee, as has been said by the Lord: "If ye will not forgive men their sins, neither will your Father in Heaven forgive your sins?"
R. I forgive them.

> *Inquire after the person's sins and ask if they are willing to stop their persistence in them. Make them confess all of their sins and at the end they are to say:*

R. **Many are my sins in deeds, in words, and in thoughts**.

> *Then give them a penance and say this prayer over them:*

Let us pray: Protect this Thy servant -N- O Lord through Thy mercy and quickly blot out all of his (her) iniquities by Thy pardon, through our Lord Jesus Christ Who reigneth with Thee and the Holy Spirit throughout all ages of ages. R. Amen.

Let us pray: Harken unto our prayers O Lord and spare from sins those who confess unto Thee, and may the clemency of Thy Fidelity absolve those whose guilt of conscience accuses them, through our Lord Jesus Christ Who reigneth with Thee and the Holy Spirit throughout all ages of ages.
R. Amen.

> *And the like. If there is sufficient time, do as in the Sacramentary [i.e.: administer a Penance] (if one does not have sufficient time this is sufficient) and if this is for an intelligent person, give them counseling that they come at the appointed time unto you or another Priest at the Lord's Supper as set forth in the Sacramentary. [This service is done in two parts: 1) The Confession of sins and assignment of Penance and 2) the Prayer of Reconciliation before the Liturgy at the appointed time]. Whoever does not receive reconciliation while they remain in the body cannot do so after parting from the flesh. If they were truly without intellect, for they did not understand, one can reconcile them in one session.*
>
> *Holding the hand over, but not touching their head, say the Prayer for person about to begin penance:*

Grant O Lord, we beseech Thee, The worthy fruits of penitence to this servant, that through the pursuit and attainment of pardon of his (her) sinning, he (she) may be restored innocent unto Thy Holy Church, from whose completeness he (she) has wandered through sinning. This we ask through our Lord Jesus Christ Who reigneth with Thee and the Holy Spirit throughout all ages of ages. **R.** Amen.

> *If they are seriously ill, one ought to reconcile them [to the Body and Blood of the Lord] immediately. [Perform the Service of Unction, if possible. The following Prayers of Reconciliation are said before the Liturgy of the appointed day. The form of the Lord's Prayer is from the Rite of Unction. None except those who have met the conditions for reconciliation should approach a Priest for this office. Those who require further counseling and time to resolve their difficulties should discuss this in private before the day of the Liturgy. This Our Father is a half-century old English translation from Greek and Church Slavonic; same as St. Jerome's Latin, Greek New Testament, and the Lorrha-Stowe Missal.]*

Priest: O Lord, regard us Thy servants, that praying with confidence, we may be worthy to say:

All together: Our Father, Who art in the Heavens, hallowed be Thy Name. Thy Kingdom come. Thy will be done on earth as it is in Heaven. Give us this day our daily bread and forgive us our debts as we forgive our debtors and lead us not into temptation but deliver us from evil.

Priest: Deliver us O Lord from every evil and preserve us in all good, O Jesus Christ, the Author of all that is good, Who reigneth unto ages of ages.
R. Amen.

> *The following Absolution prayers from folio 291 of the Bobbio Missal is repeated for each penitent received:*
> *With the right hand on the head of the penitent, [the Priest should] say:*

Beloved Brethren, let us beseech God, the Almighty and Merciful, Who doth not desire the death of a sinner, but that he be converted and live. May God be appeased and grant His servant -N- the dispensation of mercy unto the right way of Life. In that this person incurred the wounds of his (her) guilt after the sacred washing in the Waters, it is appropriate that he (she) be cleansed in the esteemed [act of] public confession, so that no scars remain to condemn him (her), through our Lord Jesus Christ Who reigneth with the same unoriginate Father and the Holy Spirit throughout all ages of ages.
R. Amen.

Priest: O our Savior and Redeemer, Thou dost grant the gift of Thy Favor and Mercy not only to sinners but to all that desire to come before [Thee]. We Thy suppliants beseech Thee that Thou bring this Thy servant -N- unto the dispensation of Communion of Thy Body and Blood by Thy pardoning Heavenly blessing. We ask this through Thee Who reignest with Thine unoriginate Father and the Holy Spirit throughout all ages of ages.
R. Amen.

Ordinary of the Mass

[The Rite of Reconciliation is completed as the Song of the Three Children is sung. The Shrine of Piety from the Breviary may be done just before the Mass. In the ancient custom, the women stand to the left of the center aisle, the men to the right of the aisle. Where there is a cross sign (+), the Sign of the Cross should be made. In the original Latin, this was indicated by a capital letter or the sign "+", which sometimes appeared in the middle of a sentence.]

The Litany of the Saints

[A Deacon in amice, alb, stole and Chasuble (or Celebrant in cassock) begins the Mass in the middle of the nave. According to the Rule of Tallaght: there is no kneeling on Sundays; the congregation should stand instead wherever the text says "kneel." On other days, follow the instructions to stand and kneel given here. This Litany is not optional. If there is no Deacon, the Celebrant must say it. Repeated names are different Saints; see the Litany in Baptism.]

STAND

Deacon (or Celebrant) (V.): + O God come to my assistance.

People (R.): O Lord make haste to help me.

V. Glory be to the Father, and to the Son, and to the Holy Spirit, as it was in the beginning, is now, and ever unto ages of ages.

R. Amen.

KNEEL [or STAND on Sundays]. [The following prayer is said for all that are present.] **Deacon (or Celebrant):**

We have sinned, O Lord, we have sinned: remit our sins and save us. Hear us, O Thou Who didst guide Noah upon the waves of the Flood, and didst recall Jonah from the abyss by Thy Word; free us. O Thou Who didst offer a hand to Peter as he was sinking; bear us up, O Christ, Son of God. Thou didst perform wonders among our fathers, O Lord: stretch forth Thy hand from on high to answer our necessities.

V. Free us, O Christ:

R. Hear us, O Christ.   **V.** Hear us, O Christ: **R.** Hear us.

Kyrie eleison. [**R.** Christe eleison. **V.** Deo Gratias.] *[St. Patrick's ending assumed.]*

[chanted on one note or going up and down:]

Saint Mary	**R.** Pray for us.
Saint Peter:	**R.** Pray for us.
Saint Paul:	**R.** Pray for us.
Saint Andrew:	**R.** Pray for us.
Saint James:	**R.** Pray for us.
Saint John:	**R.** Pray for us.
Saint Bartholomew:	**R.** Pray for us.
Saint Thomas:	**R.** Pray for us.
Saint Matthew:	**R.** Pray for us.

Saint James:	℟. Pray for us.
Saint Thaddeus:	℟. Pray for us.
Saint Matthias:	℟. Pray for us.
Saint Philip:	℟. Pray for us.
Saint Simon:	℟. Pray for us.
Saint Mark:	℟. Pray for us.
Saint Luke:	℟. Pray for us.
Saint Stephen:	℟. Pray for us.
Saint Martin:	℟. Pray for us.
Saint Jerome:	℟. Pray for us.
Saint Augustine:	℟. Pray for us.
Saint Gregory:	℟. Pray for us.
Saint Hilary:	℟. Pray for us.
Saint Patrick:	℟. Pray for us.
Saint Ailbe:	℟. Pray for us.
Saint Finian:	℟. Pray for us.
Saint Finian:	℟. Pray for us.
Saint Keiran:	℟. Pray for us.
Saint Keiran:	℟. Pray for us.
Saint Brendan:	℟. Pray for us.
Saint Brendan:	℟. Pray for us.
Saint Columba:	℟. Pray for us.
Saint Columba:	℟. Pray for us.
Saint Comgall:	℟. Pray for us.
Saint Cainnech:	℟. Pray for us.
Saint Finbarr:	℟. Pray for us.
Saint Nessan:	℟. Pray for us.
Saint Fachtna:	℟. Pray for us.
Saint Lua:	℟. Pray for us.
Saint Lacten:	℟. Pray for us.
Saint Ruadhan:	℟. Pray for us.
Saint Carthage:	℟. Pray for us.
Saint Kevin:	℟. Pray for us.
Saint Mochon:	℟. Pray for us.
Saint Brigid:	℟. Pray for us.
Saint Ita:	℟. Pray for us.
Saint Scetha:	℟. Pray for us.
Saint Sinecha:	℟. Pray for us.
Saint Samthann:	℟. Pray for us.

All you Saints: ℟. Pray for us.

V. Be Gracious: **R.** Spare us, O Lord...
V. Be Gracious: **R.** Free us, O Lord...
V. From all evil: **R.** Free us, O Lord...
V. Through Thy Cross: **R.** Free us, O Lord...
V. We sinners en-treat Thee: **R.** Hear us, O Son of God.
V. We en-treat Thee: **R.** Hear us, and grant us peace.

V. We en-treat Thee: **R.** Hear us.

V. O Lamb of God Who takest away the sins of the world:

R. Have mercy on us. **V.** Christ hear us: **R.** Christ hear us: **V.** Christ hear us.

STAND

[If the Celebrant did not chant the Litany, he now enters the church with the Subdeacon and stands at the rear of the Church. If there is no center aisle the Celebrant and Subdeacon stand just before the Sacristy. The Subdeacon stands at the Celebrant's left hand. The Celebrant is wearing only a cassock. The Subdeacon is vested in amice, alb and has said the prayer of vesting as noted below. The Deacon goes to the Celebrant and stands at the Celebrant's right hand. The Celebrant accompanied by the two ministers goes to the foot of the altar and says:]

Prayer of Saint Ambrose

Celebrant: O God, I who presume to invoke Thy Holy Name, stand in the presence of Thy Divine Majesty: have mercy upon me, a man: a sinner smeared by the foulness of inherent impurity; forgive the unworthy priest in whose hand this oblation is seen offered: Spare O Lord one polluted by sins: in faults the foremost, in comparison to all others, and do not enter into judgment with Thy servant, for no one living is justified in Thy sight. It is true that we are weighed down in the faults and desires of our flesh: remember, O Lord, that we are flesh and there is no other help besides Thee. Yea, in Thy sight not even those in Heaven are much more cleansed than we earthly humans, of whom, the Prophet said, "all of our righteous acts are like unto a menstrual rag." [Isaiah 64:6, Latin and Hebrew.] We are unworthy O Jesus Christ, but that we may be living, O Thou Who dost not will the death of a sinner: grant forgiveness unto us who were created in the flesh, so that by penitential acts we may come to enjoy eternal life in the Heavens; through our Lord Jesus Christ Who reigneth with Thee and the Holy Spirit throughout all ages of ages.
R. Amen.

Vesting Prayer of Saint Augustine

[THE CONGREGATION MAY SIT.] [Vestments listed are based on vestments found on the relics of St. Cuthbert. Note that the Subdeacon and Deacon have vested before the Litany, saying this prayer, but omitting all text between the †s. The Celebrant now vests, standing in the middle of the nave, saying:]

I pray Thee, O God of Sabaoth, most high, Holy Father, be pleased to arm me with the tunic of Chastity,
> *[Put on **amice** and **alb**.]*

and gird my loins with the cincture of Love of Thee,
> *[Tie **cincture**.]*

and furthermore, be pleased to inflame the reins of my heart with the fire of Thy Charity
> *[Put on **stole**. Note: Subdeacons do not wear stoles.]*

enabling me to make an intercession for my sins †
> *[Put on **right cuff**.]*

and earn remission of the sins of these people who are present,
> *[Put on **left cuff**.]*

and moreover sacrifice the peace-making offering of each one.†
> *[Put on **Maniple**.]*

Also do not abandon me, nor permit me to die when I boldly approach Thee, but permit me to wash, vest and calmly undertake this service.
> *[The Servers then **pour** water over the hands of the Celebrant, using pitcher and basin. The servers help the Celebrant put on the **Chasuble**. (The Celebrant may stand with arms to the sides in the form of a Cross, while the servers put the Chasuble on him.) If the Celebrant serves alone he may go to the Credenza or a portable table to wash and vest, and he may put on the Chasuble before he washes his hands.]*

[For a Bishop only: *Putting on the Rationale, he says:* Permit us to hold Thy Truth resolutely, O Lord, and worthily open the Doctrine of Truth to Thy People.]

Celebrant: Grant this through our Lord Jesus Christ, Who reigneth with Thee and the Holy Spirit throughout all ages of ages. **R.** Amen.

> *[The **Deacon** and **Subdeacon** go to the Credenza which is on the Epistle side of the Altar. The **Deacon** takes the **Corporal** from the Credenza and unfolds it upon the Altar, and then stands in front of the Epistle side of the Altar, facing the Crucifix.]*
> *[The **Subdeacon** takes the **Chalice** (with **Pall**, folded **veil** and **Purificator** on top of it) in his left hand and the **Paten** with the **Host** upon it in his right hand. He gives the Chalice and the linens to the Deacon, and waits in front of the Epistle side of the Altar, behind the Deacon. (No cleric of rank lower than Subdeacon may carry the Chalice, Host and Paten.)]*
> *[The **Celebrant ascends to the Altar**, and **kisses the open Corporal** (the only Procession). The **Celebrant** faces the Crucifix, praying with the Congregation.]*
> *[**Servers** bring the cruets, and wait to the Epistle side of the Altar.]*
> *[The **Celebrant** takes the **Chalice and Purificator** from the Deacon.*
> *The **Celebrant** holds the Chalice and wipes its interior with the Purificator. He gives the Purificator to the Subdeacon. [The **Celebrant** makes the **Sign of the Cross** with the Chalice over the Corporal and sets the Chalice on the Corporal.]*

> The Altar is the image of the inflicted persecution. The Chalice is the image of the Church which has been set and built upon the persecution of the Prophets and of others. [Notes on the meaning of the images of the Mass are in the end of the original text].

STAND [OR SIT].
> *[The Celebrant **blesses the water in the cruet** with the **Sign of the Cross** and takes water cruet.] **Water** is poured first into the Chalice by the Celebrant:*

Celebrant: I pray to Thee, O Father; I ask intercession of Thee, O Son; I appeal to Thee, O Holy Spirit.
> *[The water cruet is given back to the server.]*
> *This is an image of the People which are "poured into" the Church.*

> *[The Celebrant takes the **Paten with the Host** upon it; makes the **Sign of the Cross** with the Paten over the Corporal; and tips the Paten, allowing the] **Host** to slip on to the center of the Corporal in front of the Chalice, saying:*

Celebrant:

Jesus Christ, Alpha and Omega: this is the First and the Last.
> *[The Celebrant then gives the **Paten** to the Subdeacon who returns it to the Credenza and covers it with the purificator. If the Celebrant serves alone, the Celebrant places the Paten under the right edge of the Corporal and covers the Paten with the Purificator.]*
> *The setting of the Host upon the Altar is His Conception. This is an image of Christ's Body which has been set in the linen sheet of Mary's womb.*

> *[The Celebrant takes the **wine cruet**.] The Celebrant then adds **Wine** to the Chalice:*

Celebrant:

May the Father remit, may the Son pardon, may the Holy Spirit have mercy.
> *This is Christ's Godhead with His humanity that comes upon the People at the time of His Conception.*

> *[The cruet is given back to the server, who places the cruets on the Credenza. The Celebrant takes the **Pall** sets it on the Chalice, and covers both the Chalice and the Host on the Corporal with the **veil**. **Optional:** before the Gifts are covered, a small censing: bless the censer, then cense only the Veil and Gifts, not the Altar and congregation at this time (part of the Offering).]*

STAND. *[ALL WHO ARE PRESENT **STAND LOOKING UPON THE CRUCIFIX**.]*
> *[No person, especially the Celebrant, may have their back to the Cross. The Celebrant lifts his eyes to the Crucifix, extends and lifts his hands with palms upward so that they are just above and to the sides of the gifts and says:]*

This prayer is to be chanted at all Masses: *[May hold the censer, optional.]*

Celebrant: Let our prayer ascend to the Throne of Thy Renown, O Lord, lest emptiness be returned to us in response to our petitions. This we ask through our Lord Jesus Christ Who reigneth with Thee and the Holy Spirit throughout all ages of ages.   R. Amen.
> *[If the censer was used, return it to its stand.] All the text of the Mass from now up to the Epistle and the Gradual is an image of the establishment of the Knowledge of Christ in the law of nature through the Members of His Body and by His own deeds.*

[SIT].   *[Note: Requiem Lections are on page 240.]*

[Old Testament Reading
*In the manuscript of the Lorrha-Stowe Missal, there is no Old Testament Reading. In the Bobbio Missal, the Old Testament Reading is before the Introductory Collect; then the **Collect after the Prophecy** is said, if any. Before the Old Testament reading: "A reading from the Book of [Isaiah]," Then: "At that time..." or, "Thus saith the Lord..."]*

[STAND OR KNEEL].

INTRODUCTORY COLLECT

*[Called the **"Praefatio"** in the Bobbio and Gothic Missals]*
The "Collect of the Day" from the Propers of this Missal is to be used in place of the following: *[Substitute one of the prayers below for Saint days etc., or use the Proper for the day. See the Proper Prayers for movable and fixed days.]*

In Solemnities of Peter and Christ:

O God, Who to Blessed Peter Thine Apostle didst bestow by the keys of the Heavenly Kingdom, the power to bind and loosen souls, and didst give the office of High Priest, receive our prayers of propitiation and his intercession. We ask O Lord for help that we may be freed from the bonds of our sins through our Lord Jesus Christ Who reigneth with Thee and the Holy Spirit throughout all ages of ages. **R.** Amen.

In the Mass of Apostles, Martyrs and Holy Virgins:

O God the Father, God the Son and God the Holy Spirit, the one and only Lord of Lords and King of Kings and glory of all to come, we faithfully implore Thee, by the clear laws and judgments of the Patriarchs, by the glorious prophecies of the Prophets, through the holy examples of the Apostles, by the witness of the martyrs, by the fidelity of the Confessors, by the sanctity of Virgins, by the contemplative lives of the Anchorites, by the spiritual silence of the monks, by the dependable continuous orations of the Bishops, Abbots and Catholic Princes, and especially by the suffrage of the Saints (or Holy Virgins) whose solemnity is celebrated by us; that this offering of Thy servants which we offer unto the Holy Trinity in honor of -N- may be acceptable to God and also be profitable unto Salvation; through our Lord Jesus Christ Who reigneth with Thee and the Holy Spirit throughout all ages of ages. **R.** Amen.

In the Mass for Living Penitents:

Being faithful to Thine Exalted Divine Fatherhood, and in trembling supplication before Thy great majesty, we beseech Thee on behalf of Thy servants, to give them a pure mind, perfect charity, sincerity in acts, purity of heart, virtue in work, discipline in habit, and to restore them in the fear of Thy Justice. For these, **-NN-**, we offer the intention of our devotion unto Thee that they may come to know Thy fidelity. Through our Lord Jesus Christ Who reigneth with Thee and the Holy Spirit throughout all ages of ages.
R. Amen.

In the Mass of the Dead:

Grant, we beseech Thee, Almighty and Merciful God, that the souls of Thy servants -NN- may obtain forgiveness of sins and perpetual joy of Light, through our Lord Jesus Christ Who reigneth with Thee and the Holy Spirit throughout all ages of ages. **R.** Amen.

[STAND].

The Angelic Hymn

[Then in the middle of the Altar the Celebrant extends his hands, and bowing, says:] *[**Chanted**; musical setting may be used, see separate pages.]*

Glory to God in the Highest,   *[Still bowing, the Celebrant joins his hands:]*
and on earth peace to men of good will. We praise Thee; we bless Thee; we worship Thee; we glorify Thee; we magnify Thee; we give thanks to Thee for Thy great mercy. O Lord heavenly King, God the Father Almighty; O Lord, the Only Begotten Son of God, Jesus Christ; O Holy Spirit of God, and all of us say, Amen. O Lord the Son of God the Father: Lamb of God Who takest away the sin of the world, have mercy upon us. Receive our prayers; Thou Who sittest at the right-hand of God the Father: Have mercy upon us, for Thou only art holy, Thou only art the Lord, Thou only art the Lord, Thou only art glorious; with the + Holy Spirit in the glory of God the Father. **R.** Amen.

[An example of Scottish music for the Angelic Hymn "Gloria" is below.]
*[**All join in singing:** (The Missal did not specify the Celebrant here.)]*

Glory to God in the High-est,

[Still bowing, the Celebrant joins his hands:]

and on earth peace to men of good will.

We praise Thee; we bless Thee; we wor-ship Thee;

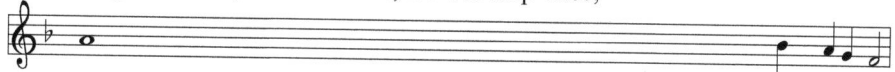

we glorify Thee; we magnify Thee; we give thanks to Thee for Thy great mer- cy.

O Lord heaven-ly King, God the Father Al-might-y;

O Lord, the Only Begotten Son of God, Je - sus Christ;

O Holy Spirit of God, and all of us say, A - men.

O Lord the Son of God the Fa - ther:

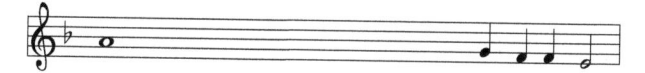

Lamb of God Who takest away the sin of the world,

have mercy up - on us. Re - ceive our prayers;

Thou Who sittest at the right-hand of God the Fa - ther:

Have mer-cy up-on us, for Thou on-ly art ho-ly,

Thou on-ly art the Lord, Thou on-ly art the Lord,

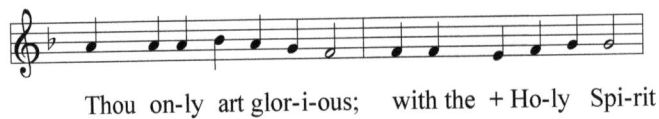

Thou on-ly art glor-i-ous; with the + Ho-ly Spi-rit

in the glo-ry of God the Fa - ther. ℟. *A - men.*

[The Celebrant continues bowed and with joined hands:]

Celebrant: O God Who didst prepare unseen good things for those who are devoted to Thee, send forth an attitude of love of Thee into our hearts, that we may follow Thee in all things, and above all things pursue Thine attentive promises which surpass all expectations. Through our Lord Jesus Christ Who reigneth with Thee and the Holy Spirit throughout all ages of ages. ℟. Amen.

KNEEL (except on Sundays):

COLLECTS BEFORE THE EPISTLE:

[The Collects of the observance, of the season and of lesser commemorations are to be inserted here. Use the Proper Collect from the Lorrha-Stowe Missal first.]

In the Mass of Apostles, Martyrs, and Holy Virgins.

We give Thee thanks O our Lord and God Jesus Christ, splendor of the Father's glory, and day of eternal clarity, for being pleased to illumine Thy twelve Apostles by the Fire of the Holy Spirit as the twelve hours of the day are illuminated by the light of the Sun; unto whom Thou didst say "ye are the light of the world" and again, "Are there not twelve hours of the daylight? If one walks in the light of day, he shall not stumble." Descend on us, O our Lord and God Jesus Christ the Sun of Righteousness; in Whose wings is well-being for those that fear Thee, that we may walk in the Light. Therefore we have the Light, that we may be sons of the Light. O Thou Who didst illumine the Apostles as Thy proxies and the other Saints as their proxies like lamps unto this world: endowed with the Grace of the Holy Spirit and the Doctrines, dispel the darkness of ignorance and send forth the light of Thy righteousness through the patronage of those -N- whose festivities we honor today. That we may remain always in Thee and through Thee, Who reignest with Thine unoriginate Father and the Holy Spirit throughout all ages of ages, ℟. Amen.

In the Mass for Living Penitents.

O Lord, pardon us Thy penitents, Thy pretentious servants, that with untroubled mind we may be able to offer this Sacrifice for -NN-, that by the dictates of Faith, they may obtain forgiveness and health, through Thee O Holy Father. May Thy followers be able to make the offering and attain to the Salvation of eternal grace by Thine aid. Through our Lord Jesus Christ Who reigneth with Thee and the Holy Spirit throughout all ages of ages. ℟. Amen.

In the Mass of the Dead.
We beg Thee, O Lord, grant us Thy mercy, that the souls of Thy servants -NN- may await the future Resurrection, forgiven of all faults and freed of all cares under Thy protection, through our Lord Jesus Christ Who reigneth with Thee and the Holy Spirit throughout all ages of ages. **R.** Amen.

*[**Other collects** may be said after the Lorrha-Stowe Collect. Use the Proper for the Season, then the Collect against persecution or for the chief Bishop or from the Proper for the Saint of the day Ad Libitum.]*

*The following prayer, "Who is offended by faults" is said in **daily** Masses [weekdays]: [The Celebrant extends and joins his hands, as he says:]*
Celebrant: O God Who is offended by faults and appeased by penitence, consider the groans of the afflicted, and mercifully avert the evils which Thou dost justly impose, through our Lord Jesus Christ Who reigneth with Thee and the Holy Spirit throughout all ages of ages. **R.** Amen.

The portion of the Mass from the Epistle and gradual to the uncovering of the Chalice is a recounting of the law Letter which prophesies Christ, but what is prefigured is not yet known. The Gospel, Alleluia, and prayers chanted from the half-uncovering of the Host and the Chalice until the prayer "May these Gifts" is a recounting of the Law of the Prophets which specifically foretold Christ, but the significance of the Prophecy is unknown until His Incarnation.
[SIT].

EPISTLE

*This is said louder [by the **Subdeacon**, or higher clergy, who reads or chants the Epistle at the foot of the altar facing the Oblations:]*
   The Lesson of Paul the Apostle to the [Corinthians] begins:
Or
   The General Epistle of <Name> the Apostle begins:
Or
   The Lesson from the Acts of the Apostles begins:

*[The **Lesson of the day is to be substituted for the following**, which is provided as a general Lection only. See the Propers and Lections through the year. (Translation from the Latin of the original Celtic Lorrha-Stowe Missal):]*
   [Note: Requiem Lections are on page 240.]

[I Cor. 11:26-32] Brethren: for as often as you shall eat this Bread, and drink the Chalice, you shall show the death of the Lord, until He come. Therefore whosoever shall eat this Bread, or drink the Chalice of the Lord unworthily, shall be guilty of the Body and of the Blood of the Lord. But let a man prove himself: and so let him eat of that Bread, and drink of the Chalice. For he that eateth and drinketh unworthily, eateth and drinketh judgment to himself, not discerning the Body of the Lord. Therefore there are those many weak, sickly [and imbecile] among you, and many sleep. But if we would judge ourselves, we should not be judged. But when we are judged, we are chastised by the Lord, that we be not condemned with this world.

[After the reading of the Epistle, the Congregation makes no response at this time. The Celebrant extends and joins his hands, saying with raised voice immediately:]
Celebrant: O God Who savest us by guidance and justifiest us by forbearance, rescue us from the tribulations of this time and bestow joy upon us through our Lord Jesus Christ Who reigneth with Thee and the Holy Spirit throughout all ages of ages. **R.** Amen.

[KNEEL OR STAND].
  [The Celebrant bows and says:]
Celebrant: Almighty, eternal God, Who didst redeem Thy people by the blood of Thine Only-Begotten Son, destroy the works of the devil, break the chains of sin, that those who have attained to eternal life in the confession of Thy Name may be bound by no thing to the author of death, through our Lord Jesus Christ Who reigneth with Thee and the Holy Spirit throughout all ages of ages. **R.** Amen.

[STAND OR SIT].
The Gradual and Alleluia, Tract, or Sequence
*[The Gradual of the day is **substituted for the following**, which is a general Lection only. Through the year, all one hundred fifty Psalms are used, see the Lectionary in the notes.]*

(Psalm 104: 1-4) Seek the Lord and his strength; seek his Face evermore. O give thanks unto the Lord; call upon his Name. Seek the Lord and his strength; seek his Face evermore.

[Afterwards, the Celebrant, with hands joined upon the Altar, bows and asks:]
Celebrant: Let these gifts by which the mysteries are celebrated be pleasing to Thee O Lord, unto our freedom and life: through our Lord Jesus Christ Who reigneth with Thee and the Holy Spirit throughout all ages of ages. **R.** Amen.

[In the case of a Psalm or other text used as a Tract or Sequence there might be no Gradual, but the preceding prayer is read before the Tract or Sequence.]
*[The Alleluia, Tract or Sequence of the day is **substituted for the following**, which is a general Lection only. See Propers and Lections through the year.]*

Alleluia, Alleluia. The Lord is my strength and my praise and He is become my Salvation. Alleluia.

[Afterwards, the Celebrant, hands joined upon the Altar, bows slightly and asks:]
Celebrant: O Lord we beg Thee to graciously attend these sacrificial offerings here present that our devotions may be profitable to salvation through our Lord Jesus Christ Who reigneth with Thee and the Holy Spirit throughout all ages of ages.

  The Congregation responds:
R. Amen. Thanks be to God.

The Litany of Supplication by Saint Martin (of Tours)
Deacon (or Celebrant): Let us all say, Lord hear and have mercy:

R. Lord have mercy.   *[Examples of music for convenience.]*
Deacon (or Celebrant) (V): From our whole heart and our whole mind, O Thou Who dost look over all the earth and make it to tremble, Let us pray: **R. Lord have mercy.**

V: For the greatest peace and tranquillity of our times, for the holy Catholic Church which is from the borders, yea unto the ends of the earth: Let us pray:
R. Lord have mercy.

V: For the Shepherd and Bishop -N-, and for all the Bishops and Priests and Deacons and all the clergy: Let us pray: **R. Lord have mercy.**

V: For this place and those living in it, for pious *leaders* and all our military: Let us pray: **R. Lord have mercy.**

V: For all who are under the sublime Rule, for virgins, widows and orphans: Let us pray: **R. Lord have mercy.**

V: For pilgrims and those who travel by land and water [and air and space]; for penitents, catechumens and captives: let us pray: **R. Lord have mercy.**

V: For these who in the holy Church give forth the fruits of mercy, O Lord God of virtues listen to our petitions: let us pray: **R. Lord have mercy.**

V: That we be mindful of the Saints, Apostles and Martyrs, that by their prayers for us we may merit forgiveness: let us pray: **R. Lord have mercy.**

V: Permit a Christian and peaceful end: we ask of the Lord, *[Or]*

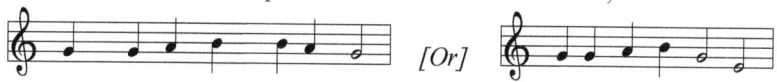

R. Grant it, O Lord, grant it.

V: And the divine influence to remain with us, a holy chain of Charity: we ask the Lord:
R. Grant it, O Lord, grant it.

V: To preserve sanctity and purity of the Catholic Faith: we ask the Lord:
R. Grant it, O Lord, grant it.

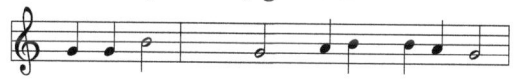

V: Let us say: **R. Lord have mer - cy.**

[The Celebrant extends his hands and looks to heaven, saying:]
Celebrant: O Lord graciously attend the celebration of this Sacrifice unto Thee, which cleanses us from the fault of our condition, and restores us to acceptability by Thy Name, through our Lord Jesus Christ, Who reigneth with Thee and the Holy Spirit throughout all ages of ages. **R. Amen.**

[THE CELEBRANT STANDS
[Bowing deeply, with hands joined, the Celebrant says:]
Celebrant: O Lord before Thine eyes I defend myself while accused by the witness of a guilty conscience. I do not dare to petition for others because I am unworthy to accomplish it. However, Thou knowest, O Lord, all which has been done among us of which we are ashamed to confess. It is because of this that we do not fear to admit that we obey Thee in words: but we lie in our hearts. We say we are willing; we prove we are unwilling by our acts. Spare, O Lord, the insolent; forgive sinners; have mercy on those who call to Thee. Since in Thy Sacrament my thoughts are refuted: Grant O Lord, Who dost not receive our words with a hard heart, that, by Thyself, Thou mayest bestow forgiveness, through our Lord Jesus Christ, Who reigneth with Thee and the Holy Spirit throughout all ages of ages.. **R. Amen.**

ALL STAND: [The Chalice and Host] are half uncovered.
*[The Celebrant folds back the veil of the Chalice and Host to expose the Host and the front of the Chalice. **Incense is set in the thurible and blessed. The Celebrant censes the Offerings on the Altar in the form of a Cross three times,** each Cross from east to west, then north to south, i.e., over the Gifts toward him and over the Gifts from left to right, then repeat twice more], saying three times:*

Let my prayer be set forth in Thy sight as incense
and the lifting of my hand be an evening sacrifice.

*[**The Celebrant** moves the **censer in two counter-clockwise circles and then one clockwise circle around the Offerings**, for each circle saying:] This prayer is recited **thrice**:*

Come, O Lord, the Almighty Sanctifier and bless this Sacrifice prepared unto Thee. ℟. Amen.

*[Then the Celebrant continues to **cense the Altar and congregation**. The altar is censed with three swings over the Offerings on the altar, then one swing before the altar; then walking a quarter of the way around the altar to the right, then facing the alter (facing north), one swing toward the altar; walking a quarter of the way around the altar to the right and facing the altar (facing west), one swing, then walking a quarter of the way around the altar to the right and facing the altar (facing south) one swing, then walking a quarter of the way around the altar to the right to face the altar and making three swings over the Offerings again. Then, he walks around the Congregation, **censing each person**.]*

The Prayer of St. Gregory over the Gospel

Celebrant: *Then the Celebrant **censes the Gospel with three more swings** of the censer, or three Crosses and three circles, saying once over the Gospel:]*

We beseech Thee, O Lord Almighty God, that Thou most mercifully accept our offerings which are sacrificed to Thee, and that Thou stretch forth Thy right hand unto our defense, through our Lord Jesus Christ, Who reigneth with Thee, and the Holy Spirit throughout all ages of ages. ℟. Amen.

*[When the Celebrant completes the censing of the Gospel, he hands the Thurible to the server or **replaces the censer** on the stand if serving alone. **Servers or others hold lights**.]*

GOSPEL

The Deacon (or Celebrant) goes to the foot of the altar and reads the Gospel facing the Oblations. Deacon or Celebrant: [Requiem Lections on p. 240.]

The Lesson of the Gospel according to [John] **begins:** [℟. Glory be to Thee, O Lord.]

*[The Gospel of the day is to be **substituted for the following**, which is provided as a general Lection only. See the Propers and Lections through the year.*
(Translation from the Latin original Celtic Lorrha-Stowe Missal) Jn 6:51-57:]

Our Lord Jesus Christ said; 'I am the living Bread which came down from heaven. If any man eat of this Bread, he shall live forever; and the Bread that I will give is my Flesh, for the life of the world.' The Jews therefore strove among themselves, saying, 'how can this man give us his flesh to eat?' Then Jesus said unto them: 'Amen, amen, I say unto you: Except you eat the Flesh of the Son of man, and drink His Blood, you shall not have life in you. He that eateth my Flesh, and drinketh my Blood, hath everlasting life: and I will raise him up in the last day. For my Flesh is meat indeed: and my Blood is drink indeed. He that eateth my Flesh and drinketh my Blood, abides in me, and I in him.'

[Afterwards, the congregation responds (according to the Rule of Tallaght):

Pray for us, and lift up the Gospel towards us.

Then the Celebrant blesses then with the Gospel Book. In Paschaltide:

May He Whose Dominion and Kingdom remain without end, be pleased to sustain us unto ages of ages. ℟. Amen.

[or, another blessing by the Celebrant, and then:
R. Praise be to Thee, O Christ.
[Then the congregation may approach and kiss the Gospel book.]

[SIT]
(SERMON)

[A sermon is said about the Feast, Gospel and Epistle. Only the Bishop, Priest, or Deacon may read the Gospel and give the Sermon.]

[The Congregation may be seated. In the time of the Lorrha Missal, the Congregation brought folding chairs or carpets for this purpose. It is noted that only the Doorkeeper or the Cook of a community was allowed to be absent during the Sermon, or the beginning of the Mass.]

*[**Notices** and **Banns** (announcements and engagements) having been duly read, all present profess the Creed. The Creed below is an accurate translation of the Lorrha-Stowe Creed, not adding, omitting, or changing any words or phrases in the text.]*

STAND.

The Creed

I believe in one God, the Father Almighty, maker of heaven and earth and of all things visible and invisible. And in one Lord Jesus Christ, the Only-Begotten Son of God. Born of the Father before all ages. Light of light, true God of true God. Born, not made, of one Substance with the Father: through Whom all things were made. Who for us men, and for our Salvation descended from heaven. And was Incarnate of the Holy Spirit and the Virgin Mary: And was born man. And was crucified also for us: under Pontius Pilate; He suffered and was buried. And He rose on the third day, according to the Scriptures. And ascended into heaven: and sitteth at the right hand of God the Father. And He shall come again with glory to judge both the living and the dead: Whose Kingdom shall have no end. And I believe in the Holy Spirit, the Lord and Giver of life: Who proceedeth from the Father. Who with the Father and the Son together is worshiped and glorified: Who spake by the Prophets. And in one, Holy, Catholic, and Apostolic Church. I confess one Baptism for the remission of sins. And I look for the resurrection of the dead. + And the life of the world to come. Amen.

*Fully uncovered: [**The veil and Pall of the Chalice are removed.** Standing erect, the Priest extends his hands, raises them and joins them, and lifting his eyes to heaven and lowering them, says:]*
*This prayer is recited **thrice**:*

Celebrant: Show us Thy Mercy O Lord, and grant us Thy Salvation.

The Elevation

[The Chalice is elevated, and all look at it.]

Celebrant: O Lord, may these gifts which are offered be sanctified, and cleanse us from the blots of our sins, through our Lord Jesus Christ, Who reigneth with Thee, and the Holy Spirit, throughout all ages of ages.
R. Amen.

The elevation of the Chalice, after the full uncovering, during the prayer "May these gifts" is the commemoration of Christ's Birth and of His Glory through the signs and miracles.
*[The **Chalice is replaced** on the Corporal and is covered by the **Pall**.]*

Celebrant: We, Thy servants, beseech Thee, O Lord, that Thou benignly receive these Offerings of our devotion, through this glorious Sacrifice and our purified hearts, through our Lord Jesus Christ, Who reigneth with Thee, and the Holy Spirit, throughout all ages of ages. **R.** Amen.

Celebrant: O Lord, we sacrifice these oblations and sincere offerings unto Thee, O Jesus Christ Who suffered for us and rose on the third day from the dead, for the souls of our loved ones -N- and -N-, whose names we recite, and also of those whose names we do not recite but whose names are recited by Thee in the Book of Life Eternal. Of Thy mercy, rescue them, O Thou Who reignest unto ages of ages. **R.** Amen.

*[A **Post Nomina** of the day, if any, may be inserted here.]*
[KNEEL].

COLLECT OF THE PREFACE

*[The **"Secret"** said audibly, called the "Ad Pacem" in the Bobbio Missal. The Proper Collect (Ad Pacem) of the day may be substituted for one of the following. Use one of the Collects of the Preface from the Lorrha-Stowe Missal below, and also the Collect of the day from the Propers through the year.]*

Celebrant: May this oblation of Thy servants be pleasing unto Thee, which we offer unto Thee in honor of our Lord Jesus Christ, and in commemoration of Thy blessed Apostles, and Thy Martyrs and Confessors, of whom we especially remember -N-, and those whose feast is celebrated today, and for the souls of all our Bishops, and our Priests, and our Deacons, and our loved ones, and our children, and our penitents. May all of this be profitable unto salvation, through our Lord Jesus Christ Who reigneth with Thee and the Holy Spirit throughout all ages of ages. **R.** Amen.

In the Mass of Apostles, Martyrs and Holy Virgins.

O God, Who dost surround and protect us by the intercessions of the most blessed Spirits of Angels, and Archangels, the Principalities, and Powers, Dominations, Virtues, Cherubim and Seraphim, Patriarchs, Prophets, Apostles, Martyrs, Confessors and Virgins, Anchorites, Cenobites, and of all the Saints and citizens of Heaven, grant we beseech Thee that Thou make use of them and our imitation of them, to guard us by setting them between us and dangers, and by the assembly of the interceding Saints, defend us from dangers; through Thy Son, our Lord Jesus Christ Who reigneth with Thee and the Holy Spirit throughout all ages of ages. **R.** Amen.

In the Mass for Living Penitents.

Almighty God, again we make our entreaties in the presence of Thy majesty, especially for Thy servants -NN-. We offer these Oblations for their sins in honor of Thy Saints: Mary, Peter, Paul, John and all of Thy Saints. Perfect these offerings so that their petitions may arise to Thy compassionate ears, and that a pious blessing may descend upon them, that they may be protected in all things beneath Thy wings. May our prayers of propitiation unto Thee for them be not rejected from the Presence of Thy Faith, but be pleased to help and defend them in all things, through our Lord Jesus Christ Who reigneth with Thee and the Holy Spirit throughout all ages of ages. **R.** Amen.

In the Mass of the Dead.

Attend, O Lord, the gifts which we bring to Thine Altar in commemoration for (Thy Saints) [Thy faithful who have fallen asleep] -NN- and which we sacrifice for our offenses, through our Lord Jesus Christ Who reigneth with Thee and the Holy Spirit throughout all ages of ages. **R.** Amen.

[Continue here:]

℟. Amen. **Celebrant:** Let us lift up our hearts.

℟. We have un-to the Lord.

Celebrant: Let us give thanks un-to our Lord God.

℟. It is worth-y and just.

The Preface, Dignum, Contestatio, or Immolacio

*The usual Preface is **always said** before any other: [Called the **"Dignum"** in the Lorrha Missal, or the **"Contestatio"** or **"Immolacio"** in other Celtic sources.]*

Celebrant: Truly it is worthy and just and right and unto Salvation for us now and here, always and everywhere to give thanks, through Christ our Lord, unto Thee, Holy Lord Almighty and Eternal God. Thou Who with Thine Only-Begotten and the Holy Spirit, O God, art One and Immortal God, Incorruptible and Immutable God, Unseen and Faithful God, Marvelous and Praise-worthy God, Honorable and Mighty God, the Highest and Magnificent God, Living and True God, Wise and Powerful God, Holy and Exemplary God, Great and Good God, Terrible and Peaceful God, Beautiful and Correct God, Pure and Benign God, Blessed and Just God, Pious and Holy, not in one singularity of person but One Trinity of One Substance. Thee we believe; Thee we bless; Thee we adore; and we praise Thy Name unto eternity and unto ages of ages: Thou through Whom is the Salvation of the world; through Whom is the Life of men; through Whom is the Resurrection of the dead.

Here insert the Proper Preface for the Day (after the usual Preface above).

*[In addition to the Preface that is always said in the Lorrha-Stowe Missal, there are special **Prefaces for Festal days and movable Sundays.** The Celtic Propers are from sources such as the* Bobbio Missal *and* Gothic Missal *("Contestatio" or "Immolacio").]*

*[In Masses of Saints, in fasting seasons, or for the Departed, **also say one of the following** Prefaces for Saints, Penitents or the Dead:]*

Proper Prefaces ("Dignum" from the Corrba Missal):

... FOR THE HOLY MARTYRS

O Lord Almighty God Who dost test Thy Saints with a measure and glorifies without measure, Whose precepts have a goal and rewards have no end, hear our prayers through the Martyrs and by their examples and tribulations. May their patronage encourage us: to the perfection of Faith, the fruition of good works, to the good of prosperity and of good health, to religious zeal, and to the increasing of divine fear. May the Holy Martyrs pray for us, and for our dead, and for our herds, and the abundant crops of our land, and for all residing in this place.   * The innumerable multitudes of the Heavenly and earthly creatures, of Thy Saints and of the Choir of Angels unceasingly proclaim Thee, Almighty God saying:

... OF THE APOSTLES AND ALL THE SAINTS

It is Truly worthy, and right, and just, and Glorious for us to give Thee thanks all the days of our life, O Lord God Almighty, but in this day of love and abundance we ought to be grateful with the Joyful Holy Spirit in the solemnity of -N- the Apostle (or Saints, etc.). Grant us, therefore, Almighty God: Faith, Hope and Charity, a Catholic ending, and peacefulness, through the example and the commemoration of Thy Saint -N- in whose honor today's oblation is offered, that altogether it may profit unto salvation,   * through our Lord Jesus Christ, by Whom all the Angels, Archangels, Prophets and Apostles, Martyrs and Confessors, Virgins, and All of the Saints, with a perpetual hymn and unwearied praises, with the four beasts and the twenty four elders *[Re.4:4-11, 5:8-14]* harmonize, saying:

... FOR LIVING PENITENTS   *[or in fasting Seasons]*

It is truly Worthy, through our Lord Jesus Christ Thy Son, Whose Power is to intercede, Whose Mercy is to entreat, Whose Faith is all-encompassing. who else is there, who is able to ponder the marvels of all Thy power, or to hear with human ears, or to attain with human mind, or to discover by human estimation how much Thou hast prepared for Thine elect? Yet, let us be able to be abundantly ashamed of all that is earthly and lacking in self-control; of Thy mercy, grant a favor of forgiveness and of refuge for Thy suppliants. Furthermore, in commemoration of the Saints through whose intercessions we hope for forgiveness and petition, that Thou grant unto Thy servants, - NN- , remission of their sins, that Thou perfect their works, and that Thou answer their needs. Finally, by Thy servants, the Saints who intercede for them, give these people healing of their souls, since we beg that Thou fulfill their professed needs. O Almighty, grant Thy suppliants pardon, Thy petitioners forgiveness, those who cry unto Thee fulfillment of their longing. 'May the Lord hear thee in the day of tribulation: may the Name of the God of Jacob protect thee. May He send thee help from the Sanctuary: and defend Thee out of Sion. May He be mindful of all thy sacrifices: and may thy whole burnt offering be made fat' (Ps 19:1-3). By these things, give those who petition a divine yearning, and establish their assembly in that which is good, that the hearts of those who petition may be restored to life by Thee,   * through Christ our Lord, through Whom, unto Thy Majesty, the Angels give praise, the Dominations Worship, the Powers of the Heavens tremble, and the heavenly Virtues and the Blessed Seraphim together with exaltation celebrate. With Whom, we beseech Thee, bid that our voices also be admitted, with suppliant confession saying:

... OF THE DEAD

It is truly worthy that we await Him Whose promises are the fulfillment of eternal good things, in Whom the promises are made known, in Whom we know the promises are left here with us: our Lord Jesus Christ, Who truly is the Life of those who believe, and is the Resurrection of Thy servants - **NN.** Of these, for whom we offer this Sacrifice, we make our entreaties, that Thou willingly admit those who were cleansed in the font of regeneration and excluded from temptation, to be counted among the Saints. Command that those whom Thou hast made participants by adoption, may share in Thy legacy, through our Lord Jesus Christ, Thy Son*

> *The Preface continues here if the text does not contain this or a similar ending. Otherwise the prayer continues at the Sanctus.*

* Through Whom, unto Thy Majesty, the Angels give praise, the Dominations Worship, the Powers of the Heavens tremble, and the heavenly Virtues and the Blessed Seraphim together with exaltation celebrate. With Whom, we beseech Thee, bid that our voices also be admitted, with suppliant confession saying:

THE SANCTUS

[Chanted, musical setting may be used; see page below for an example.]

Holy, Holy, Holy Lord, God of Sabaoth. Heaven and the whole earth are full of Thy glory, Hosanna in the highest. Blessed is He that cometh in the Name of the Lord. Hosanna in the highest.

[Example of music: The version below is the Paschal Sanctus from Liber Usualis, which is an ancient melody, and may be Gallican.]

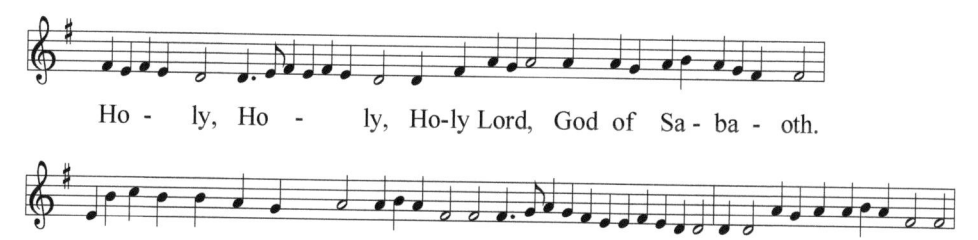

Ho - ly, Ho - ly, Ho-ly Lord, God of Sa - ba - oth.

Hea-ven and the whole earth are full of Thy glo- ry, Hosan-na in the highest.

Bless-ed is He that com-eth in the Name of the Lord.

Ho - san - na in the high - est.

Celebrant:

Blessed is He Who cometh from heaven that He might enter the world, and didst become man unto the blotting out of the sins of the flesh, and became a Victim that through suffering He might give eternal life to those that believe; through the same Lord Jesus Christ, Who reigneth with Thee and the Holy Spirit throughout all ages of ages. ℟. Amen.

The Sovereign Canon of Pope Gelasius

*[All prayers from this point until the Antiphon and Psalms before Communion are said by the Celebrant. All responses are as indicated. **The Canon is never omitted or reduced.** **The Celebrant extending then joining his hands, raising his eyes to heaven and at once lowering them, bowing profoundly before the Altar, with his hands placed upon it, says:]***

Therefore, most clement Father, through Jesus Christ Thy Son our Lord, we humbly beseech and pray Thee, *[he kisses the Altar and with hands joined before his breast, says:]* that Thou accept and bless these gifts, these offerings, these holy and unspotted sacrifices, *[with extended hands he proceeds:]* which, first, we offer unto Thee for Thy holy Catholic Church: that Thou graciously keep her in peace, to guard, unify, and govern her throughout the whole world: together with Thy Servants, the Orthodox Patriarchs, the Bishops of the Apostolic See and all who hold the Orthodox and Apostolic faith, [and our Metropolitan -N-,] Abbot-Bishop -N-, Bishop -N-. Yea, remember, O Lord, Thy servants and handmaids -N- and -N-, *(Here the names of the living are recited)* and all who are present here, whose faith and devotion unto Thee are known and manifest, who offer unto Thee this sacrifice of praise, for themselves, and for all of theirs: for the redemption of their souls; for their body of elders; for the purity of all ministers; for the integrity of virgins and the continence of widows; for mildness of weather, fruitfulness of the lands; for the returning of peace and an end to division; for the safety of our leaders and peace of the people, and the rescue of captives, and for the prayers of those here present; for the commemoration of martyrs; for the remission of our sins, and the correction of culprits; for repose for the dead; and good fortune of our journey; for the Lord Patriarch Bishop and all the Bishops and the priests and all in Holy Orders; for the whole world, and all Christian leaders; for our brothers and sisters; for the brethren who follow the straight way; for the brethren whom the Lord deemed worthy to call from the dimness of this world, from this darkness, may eternal Divine Faith of the Highest and peaceful light take them up; for brethren afflicted by various sorrows of their lot, may Divine Faith be pleased to cure them; for the hope of salvation and safety; for those who pay their vows unto Thee, the eternal, living and true God in communion with

Proper Communicantes: *of the day is inserted here:*

In the Nativity of the Lord. *[or of the Octave]*
and celebrating the most sacred day *[or time]* on which inviolate virginity brought forth the Savior into this world,

Circumcision
and celebrating the most sacred day of the circumcision of our Lord Jesus Christ,

Epiphany *[or of the Octave]*
and celebrating the most sacred day *[or time]* on which Thine Only-Begotten Son, God coeternal with Thee and Thy majesty, appeared visibly and bodily to the magi who had come from afar,

The institution of the Cup of our Lord Jesus Christ *[Maundy Thursday]*
and celebrating the most sacred day on which our Lord Jesus Christ was betrayed,

Pascha   *[Easter or of the Octave]*
and celebrating the most sacred night or day   *[or time]* of the Resurrection of our Lord Jesus Christ,

In the giving up of Easter   *[the day before the Ascension]*
and celebrating this most sacred day of the end of the Passover of our Lord Jesus Christ,

Ascension   *[or of the Octave]*
and celebrating the most sacred day   *[or time]* of the Ascension to heaven of our Lord Jesus Christ,

Pentecost   *[or of the Octave]*
and celebrating the most sacred day   *[or time]* of the Pentecost of our Lord Jesus Christ on which the Holy Spirit descended upon the Apostles,

---
[The prayer continues here:]
and venerating the memory first, of the glorious ever-virgin Mary the Birthgiver of our God and Lord Jesus Christ, and of Thy blessed Apostles and martyrs: Peter and Paul, Andrew, James, John, Thomas, James, Philip, Bartholomew, Matthew, Simon and Thaddeus, Linus, Ancletus, Clement, Xixtus, Cornilius, Cyprian, Lawrence, Crysoginus, John and Paul, Cosmas and Damian and of all Thy Saints by whose examples and prayers mayest Thou grant that, in all things, we may be ever strengthened by the help of Thy protection *[joins hands]* through our Lord Jesus Christ Who reigneth with Thee and the Holy Spirit throughout all ages of ages. **R.** Amen.

[The Celebrant extends his hands, palms down, above the Offerings:]
Therefore we offer this oblation of our service and of Thy whole family, which we offer unto Thee in honor of our Lord Jesus Christ, and in commemoration of Thy blessed martyrs in this church, which Thy servants built in honor of Thy glorious Name. We beseech Thee graciously take it under Thy protection. Moreover, rescue them and all of the people from the cult of idols and turn them unto Thyself, the True God , the Father Almighty. Also order our days in Thy peace, save us from eternal damnation, and number us among Thine elect; *[He joins his hands.]* through our Lord Jesus Christ Who reigneth with Thee and the Holy Spirit throughout all ages of ages.   **R.** Amen.

The Celebrant makes the Sign of the Cross once over the oblations:
Which oblation do Thou, O God, we beseech Thee, be pleased in all things to make Blessed, + approved, ratified, reasonable and acceptable: that unto us it may become the Body and Blood of Thy most dearly beloved Son, our Lord Jesus Christ,

*[The **Post Sanctus** of the Day from the Gothic Missal, may be inserted, **without omitting the previous prayer**. From the Lorrha-Stowe Missal:]*
IN MASSES OF THE APOSTLES, MARTYRS, SAINTS OR VIRGINS, BEFORE THE MOST DANGEROUS PRAYER:
Truly Holy, Truly Blessed, Truly Wondrous in His Saints, is our God Jesus Christ, Who Himself bestowed virtue and fortitude to His servants. Blessed be God Whom we bless in the Apostles, and in all His Saints who have striven to appease Him from the Beginning of the age, through the Same our Lord Jesus Christ,
THE CONGREGATION KNEELS OR PROSTRATES:
When the prayer "Who, the day before He suffered, took Bread..." begins, the Celebrant bows three times in repentance of his sins. He offers the Oblations to God, and while this is done: **and there must be no other voice lest it disturb the Priest,** *for his mind must not separate from God while he chants this lesson. For this reason, its name is* **The Most Dangerous Prayer.**

The Most Dangerous Prayer

The Celebrant bows three times. [The Words of Institution:]

Who the day before He suffered,   *[he takes the Host]*
took bread into His Holy and venerable Hands,
[he lifts up his eyes to heaven]
and with His eyes lifted up to heaven to Thee, God, His Almighty Father,   *[he bows his head]*
gave thanks to Thee,   *[setting the Host on the Corporal, he signs over it]*
He + Blessed, He broke, and gave to His disciples, saying:
[Holding the Host with the right hand between the thumb and forefinger, he utters the Words of Institution distinctly and attentively over the Host.]

Take and eat from this all of you, for this is my Body.
[The Host is raised to eye-level. A bell may ring. Offered and set again in its place upon the Corporal. He bows or genuflects, stands and then removes the Pall from the Chalice.]

In a similar manner after the supper,
[he takes the Chalice in both hands]
He took this excellent Chalice in His Holy and venerable Hands:
[he bows his head]
also giving thanks to Thee,
[setting the Chalice on the Corporal, he signs over it]
He + Blessed, and gave to His disciples, saying:
[He utters the Words of Institution over the Chalice distinctly and attentively, holding it slightly raised.]

Take and drink from this all of you,
for this is the Chalice of my Blood,
of the new and eternal testament:
the mystery of faith: which is shed for you and for many unto the remission of sins.
[The Chalice is raised to eye-level. A bell may ring. Offered and set again in its place upon the Corporal. He bows or genuflects, stands, and covers the Chalice with the Pall.]

Whenever you do these things, you shall do them unto my memory: you will praise my Passion; you will proclaim my Resurrection; you will hope on my coming until I come again to you from heaven.
[With extended hands he proceeds:]
Wherefore, O Lord, we Thy servants, together with Thy holy people, are mindful of the Blessed Passion of the same Holy Christ Thy Son our Lord, as also His Resurrection from hell and glorious Ascension into heaven: we offer unto Thine excellent majesty of Thine own gifts and bounty, a pure [+] Host, a Holy [+] Host, a spotless [+] Host, the Holy [+] Bread of eternal life and the Chalice of everlasting salvation.

Upon which graciously look with a favorable and gracious countenance: and to accept them, even as Thou didst graciously accept the gifts of Thy just child Abel, and the sacrifice of our Patriarch Abraham: and the Holy Sacrifice, the spotless Host, which Thy high priest Melchizedek offered unto Thee.

We humbly beseech and pray to Thee, Almighty God: command Thou these things to be brought by the hands of Thy Holy Angel to Thine Altar on high, in the presence of Thy Divine majesty: that, as many of us as shall receive from the *[kisses altar]* Altar of Sanctification the most sacred Body and Blood of Thy Son, may be fulfilled with all heavenly benediction and grace.

[THE CONGREGATION MAY STAND:]
The Commemoration of the Departed
Remember also O Lord the names of those who preceded us with the sign of faith and rest in the sleep of peace: -N- and -N-.

With all those in the whole world who offer the Sacrifices in spirit unto God the Father, and the Son, and the Holy Spirit, our senior, the Priest [*if a Bishop* Highpriest], -N- [*Celebrant*] with the holy and venerable Priests, offers for himself, for his own, and for all the rest of the Catholic Church assembly; and for the commemoration of the wrestling of the Patriarchs, Prophets, Apostles and Martyrs, and of all the Saints, that they may be pleased to entreat the Lord our God for us:

Abel, Seth, Enoch, Noah, Melchizedek, Abraham, Isaac, Jacob, Joseph, Job, Moses, Josuah, Samuel, David, Elijah, Elisah, Isaiah, Jeremiah, Ezechial, Daniel, Ester, Hosea, Joel, Amos, Obidiah, Jonah, Micah, Nahum, Habacuc, Zephaniah, Hagai, Zachariah, Malachi, Tobit, Ananias, Azarias, Mishael, the Machabees,
also Holy Innocents, John the Baptist, Virgin Mary, Peter, Paul, Andrew, James, John, Philip, Bartholomew, Thomas, Matthew, James, Simon, Thaddeus, Matthias, Mark, Luke, Stephen, Cornelius, Cyprian and all other Martyrs, Paul, Anthony and other Fathers of the hermitages of Sceti,

and also the Bishops Martin, Gregory, Maximus, Felix, Patrick, Patrick, Secundinus, Auxilius, Iserninus, Cerbanus, Erc, Carthage, Ibar, Ailbe, Conleth, MacNissi, Moinenn, Senan, Finbarr, Colman, Cuan, Aiden, Laurentius, Mellitus, Justus, Etto, Dagan, Tigernach, Mochti, Ciannan, Buite, Eugene, Declan, Carthain, Mel, Ruadhan.
[*Other departed Bishops may be inserted:* Maelrúain, Gregory, Dionisij, Polikarp, Nikanor, Mstyslav, Hryhorij, Hennadij, Andrew]
also the Priests Finian, Kieran, Oengus, Enda, Gildas, Brendan, Brendan, Cainnech, Columba, Columba, Colman, Comgall, Comghan,
[*Other departed Priests may be inserted.*]
and all of those at rest who pray for us in the Lord's peace, from Adam unto this day, whose names God has called and renewed. Unto them O Lord and to all who rest in Christ, we entreat Thee to grant a place of refreshing light and peace.

The Celebrant, Deacon and Subdeacon take three steps backward, pause briefly, and take three steps forward.
The three steps backward and three steps forward is the three ways in which everyone sins: in word, in thought, in deed. These are also the three means by which one is renovated and by which one is moved to Christ's Body.

To us sinners also, Thy servants, hoping for the multitude of Thy mercies, graciously grant some part and fellowship with Thy Holy Apostles and Martyrs: with Peter, Paul, Patrick; John, Stephen, Matthias, Barnabas, Ignatius, Alexander, Marcellinus, Peter, Perpetua, Agnes, Cecilia, Felicitas, Anastasia, Agatha, Lucy and with all Thy Saints: within whose fellowship we beseech Thee admit us, not weighing our merit, but granting us forgiveness through our Lord Jesus Christ, through Whom, O Lord Thou dost ever + create, + Sanctify, + Enliven, + Bless, and bestow all these good things upon us.

THE EXAMINATION AND FRACTION

[KNEEL].

The Examination of the Chalice and Host, and the effort with which the Celebrant attempts to break it is an image of the rejection, punches, lashings and the Arrest of Christ.

[He genuflects and bows profoundly, rises and uncovers the Chalice:]

It is through + Him, with + Him, and in + Him, within the unity of the Holy + Spirit, that unto Thee, God the Father + Almighty,

*It is here that the principle **Host is lifted up over the Chalice, elevating both:***

is all honor and glory, through all ages of ages. ℟. Amen.

*[The Subdeacon takes the **Paten, Purificator and knife** from the Credenza. (The knife must never be placed on the Altar). He gives the Paten and the Purificator to the Deacon who **wipes** the Paten with the Purificator. The Paten may be on the Altar.]*

This is said thrice *as the **Host is submerged halfway in the Chalice:***

Let Thy mercy be upon us even as we have hoped on Thee.

*[After the Celebrant has withdrawn the Host from the Chalice, the Deacon holds the **Paten under the Host**. The Celebrant **places the Host upon the Paten**, takes the Paten and Host from the Deacon and **sets them on the Corporal** before the Chalice.]*

The Host on the Paten is Christ's Flesh upon the tree of the Cross.

The Fraction *It is here that the Bread is broken:*

The Fraction of the Host upon the Paten is the breaking of Christ's Body with nails on the Cross. [A Celebrant Priest and Priest concelebrant break the Host together over the Paten with right hands only. A Priest serving alone or a Bishop uses both hands, saying:]

They have known the Lord - Alleluia -
in the Fraction of the Bread - Alleluia.
The Bread which we break is the Body of our Lord Jesus Christ - Alleluia -
The Chalice which we bless - Alleluia -
is the Blood of our Lord Jesus Christ - Alleluia -
in remission of our sins - Alleluia.
Let Thy mercy be upon us - Alleluia -
even as we have hoped on Thee - Alleluia.
They have known the Lord. - Alleluia.

The two halves of the Host are submerged totally in the Chalice.

*[After the Celebrant has withdrawn the Host from the Chalice, the Deacon holds the **Paten under the Host**. The Paten and Host are **set on the Corporal** before the Chalice.]*

*[The following prayer, **always said**, is a **"Post Secreta"** or **"Post Mysterium"** of the Gothic Missal. Other Post Secreta or Post Mysterium may follow.]*

We believe, O Lord. We believe we have been redeemed in this Fraction of the Body, and the pouring forth of the Blood; and we shall rely on the consumption of this Sacrifice for fortification: that which we now hold in hope, we may enjoy in truth by Heavenly fruition, through our Lord Jesus Christ Who reigneth with Thee and the Holy Spirit throughout all ages of ages. ℟. Amen.

[For Apostles, Bishops, and the Virgin Mary, this prayer resembles the Byzantine Epiklesis. The "Post Mysterium" on the Feast of the Throne of St. Peter at Rome, always said in the Celtic Orthodox Church:]

We who serve, offer these prescribed Holy Gifts of our Salvation, that Thou may be pleased to send Thy Holy Spirit upon this Sacrifice so that it may be changed into a legitimate Eucharist for us in the Name of Thee, Thy Son and the Holy Spirit, in the transformation of the Body and Blood of our Lord Jesus Christ; and may it be unto us who eat and drink, Life eternal and the eternal Kingdom. Through Himself, Christ Our Lord who reigneth with Thee and the Holy Spirit throughout all ages of ages. Amen.

[Another Post Secreta or Post Mysterium may be added also.]
[The halves are placed together on the Paten. A small candle may be lit on the Altar now.]
The reunion of the two halves after the Fraction is the affirmation of the wholeness of Christ's Body after His Resurrection. The submersion of the two halves in the Blood are an affirmation that at His Crucifixion, Christ's Body was covered in Blood.

[The Proper Collect of the day before the Our Father may replace the introduction:]

Taught by Divine instruction, and shaped by Divine institution, we dare to say:

[All together:]

Our Father, Who art in the Heavens, hallowed be Thy Name. Thy Kingdom come. Thy will be done on earth as it is in Heaven. Give us this day our daily bread and forgive us our debts as we forgive our debtors and lead us not into temptation but deliver us from evil.

[**Celebrant:**] Free us O Lord from every evil: past, present, and to come, and by the intercessions for us of Thy blessed Apostles Peter, Paul and Patrick, give us favorable peace in our time, that helped by the strength of Thy mercy we may be always free of sin and secure from all turmoil, through our Lord Jesus Christ Who reigneth with Thee and the Holy Spirit throughout all ages of ages. ℟. Amen.

*[Proper **Collect after the Our Father** from the Gothic Missal may be substituted for this.]*

The Peace

[Celebrant turns to the people, and makes the Sign of the Cross, saying:]

The + Peace and Charity of our Lord Jesus Christ, and the Communion of all the Saints be always with us.

R. And with thy spirit.

[This response keeps focus on the Peace; it is only found at this place.]
[Turning to the Altar, he continues:]

Thou didst command peace; Thou didst give peace; Thou didst leave peace: bestow, O Lord, Thy peace from heaven and make this day peaceful, and establish all the remaining days of our life in Thy peace, through Thee Who reignest with Thine unoriginate Father and the Holy Spirit throughout all ages of ages. **R. Amen.**

[Exchange of the Pax]

*[If there is a Deacon the Celebrant exchanges the **Pax** with him, bowing. The Deacon then continues the Pax to the Congregation. **The Celebrant must not shake hands with any person at this time, as his hands are purified in order to handle the Holy Eucharist.** If serving alone, the Celebrant may bow to each person, because each person is made in the image of God, and they would return the bow. If the Deacon will be performing the Ablutions later, he also may not shake hands.]*

*[The **Proper Blessing of the Day** from the Pontificale of Egbert, or the Gothic Missal, is given here, **only by a Bishop when he is present**, celebrating or non-celebrating at this Mass. A non-Celebrating Bishop may also cut the Particle and drop it into the Chalice if his hands have been purified at the vesting.]*

*[The Pax being completed, the Celebrant (or Bishop) turns again to the Altar, takes the knife from the Subdeacon, **cuts a Particle** from the bottom of the left hand portion of the Host and **rejoins the two halves of the Host on the Paten**. The Celebrant (or Bishop) gives the knife to the Deacon. The Deacon wipes it with the Purificator and gives it to the Subdeacon who returns it to the Credenza. The Celebrant (or Bishop) **drops the Particle into the Chalice**.]*

May the commixture of the Body and Blood of our Lord Jesus Christ be for us live-giving unto life eternal. **R. Amen.**

The Particle that is cut from the Bottom of the half which is on the Priest's left hand is the wounding with the Lance in the Armpit of the right side; for Christ was facing Westward as He hung upon the Cross: Facing the City, and Longinus faced Eastward, so what was left to Christ was right to him.

THE CONFRACTION

[KNEEL]

Turning to the people, holding a Particle of the Host over the Paten, the Celebrant says: *[St. John 1:29]*

Behold the Lamb of God. Behold, O Thou Who takest away the sins of the world.

[The Congregation may respond with the prayer of the Centurion at this point:]
[Lord, I am not worthy that Thou shouldest come under my roof, but speak the word only, and my soul shall be healed. *(thrice)*]

[THE CONGREGATION MAY STAND].
*[The Celebrant **turns to the altar** and if serving alone, begins the verses. Then the Celebrant continues to perform the **Confraction** according to the number required for the day, breaking the Host and placing the Particles in correct formation upon the Paten; while the Celebrant or other clergy say the verses, and choir or congregation sing the Psalms (sing slowly at Easter, Christmas, and Pentecost). At all Masses, these **words are said clearly and in order**, not at the same time as other verses. Holy Communion occurs after these verses are completed. If it is a very large congregation, the door wardens may help them line up to receive Communion, but otherwise they should wait until after the Confraction.]*

There are seven kind of Confraction, that is: *[For the five through thirteen Particles, the images below are from Irish Crosses, but it is possible also to do simple Crosses of a similar shape to the five or seven. For the sixty-five Particles, the exact form is described in the Missal. Notes are within the Lorrha-Stowe Missal, with bracketed clarification.]*

5 Particles for Daily Mass.
Five Particles of the Daily Host as the image of the five senses of the soul;

7 Particles for Saints and Virgins.
[The Particle where the bars cross is the Celebrant's Particle.] Seven Particles of the Host of Saints and Virgins except the most important ones as the image of the Seven Gifts of the Holy Spirit;

8 Particles for the Virgin Mary and Holy Martyrs.
[The Upper Central Particle is for the Celebrant.] Eight Particles of the Host of the Holy Martyrs as an image of the octonary New Testament; [This has two meanings: 1) The Eighth Day of Creation, the Resurrection of the Dead. 2) The Eight Fold New Testament according to St. Athanasius: four Gospels; Acts and Epistles (together); Revelation; The Didache; and Pastor of Hermas. Since the time of this Missal, the last two have been deleted from the Bible.]

9 Particles for Sundays and Ferias of Lent.
Nine Particles of the Host of a Sunday [and also of the Proper Ferias of Lent] is an image of the nine Households of Heaven and the nine Grades of the Church;

11 Particles for the Holy Apostles.
Eleven Particles of the Host of the Apostles is an image of the incomplete number of the Apostles due to the Sin of Judas;

12 Particles for the Lord's Circumcision and Holy Thursday.
Twelve Particles of the Host of the Circumcision and of Holy Thursday are in memory of the complete number of the Apostles;

13 Particles for Low Sunday and Christ's Ascension.
Thirteen Particles of the Host of Low Sunday and the Feast of the Ascension, is an image of Christ with His twelve Apostles; it is not usual to distribute from all thirteen Particles.

65 Particles for Easter, Christmas and Pentecost.
Added together, five, seven, eight, nine, eleven, twelve and thirteen come to sixty-five which is the number of Particles of the Host of Easter, Christmas and Pentecost. For all of them are comprised in Christ. All of the Confraction is set upon the Paten in the form of the Cross, and the upper Particle is moved down to the left side as reminder us that "Bowing His head, He gave up the ghost." [Note later on when to do this.] **The arrangement of the Confraction at Easter and Christmas is:** [one center Particle], fourteen Particles in the upright of the Cross, fourteen Particles in the crosspiece, twenty Particles in its circlet: five pieces in each quarter [of the circlet]; sixteen pieces to the Crosses: four to each one [of the Crosses]. **Arrangement of the Church in the Particles:** One Particle, for the Celebrant of the Mass is in the middle as the image of the Secrets kept in the heart. The upper part of the shaft of the Cross is for the Bishops, the left portion of the crosspiece is for Priests; the right portion of the crosspiece is to the grades lower than Priest; the lower portion of the stem is to monastics and penitents; the upper left quadrant is for young clerics; the upper right quadrant is to children; the lower left is for those who are truly repentant; the lower right is for those who are married and those who have never before received Communion. [For further information, see the note after the Mass.]

The Celebrant or Deacon continuing [The following verses before the Psalms are said aloud, without any omissions, before arranging the Particles. Then the Celebrant pauses while arranging the Particles to say the prayers between the Psalms.]

The Prayers of the Confraction:

℣. My peace I give to you - Alleluia - my peace I leave you Alleluia. *[John 14:27]*

℣. Abundant peace is for those who are attentive to Thy Law, O Lord - Alleluia - and there is no scandal in them - Alleluia. *[Psalm 118:165]*

℣. For the King of Heaven with peace - Alleluia *[Lk 19:38, Zch. 9:9-10]*
Who is full of the promise of life - Alleluia - *[John 10:10, 11:25-26]*
Sing Ye a new song - Alleluia - *[Psalms 95:1; 149:1; Is 42:10]*
All of ye holy ones come forth – Alleluia. *[Jn 5:29, 11:43]*

℣. Come, eat my Bread - Alleluia - and drink the Wine which has been mixed for you - Alleluia. *[Jn. 21:12]*

[Full Psalms may be said by Reader or Congregation. The Septuagint or Latin Douay-Rheims translation and Psalm numbering is used. Chant antiphonally, alternating verses between groups or readers. Do these slowly on Pascha, Christmas, and Pentecost, when the Particles will be arranged into sixty-five.]

Psalm 22

The Lord shepherds me I shall not want*
  He hath made me dwell in a place of green pasture.
He hath made me rest beside the still water.*
  He hath converted my soul.
He hath led me on the paths of justice,*
  for His own Name's sake.
For though I should walk in the midst of the shadow of death,*
  I will fear no evils, for Thou art with me.
Thy rod and Thy staff,*
  they have comforted me.
Thou hast prepared a table before me *
  against them that afflict me.
Thou hast anointed my head with oil;*
  and my chalice which inebriateth me, how goodly is it!
And Thy mercy will follow me*
  all the days of my life.
And that I may dwell in the house of the Lord*
  unto length of days.

℣. Whosoever eateth my Body and drinketh my Blood - Alleluia -
  Such a one abideth in me and I in him - Alleluia. *[St. John 6:56]*

Psalm 23

The earth is the Lord's and the fullness thereof: *
  the world, and all they that dwell therein.
For He hath founded it upon the seas;*
  and hath prepared it upon the rivers.
Who shall ascend into the mountain of the Lord?*
  or who shall stand in His holy place?

The innocent in hands, and clean of heart, who hath not taken his soul in vain,*
 nor sworn deceitfully to his neighbor.
He shall receive a blessing from the Lord,*
 and mercy from God his Savior.
This is the generation of them that seek Him,*
 of them that seek the Face of the God of Jacob.
Lift up your gates, O ye princes, and be ye lifted up, O eternal gates:*
 and the King of Glory shall enter in.
Who is this King of Glory? *
 the Lord Who is strong and mighty: the Lord mighty in battle.
Lift up your gates, O ye princes, and be ye lifted up, O eternal gates:*
 and the King of Glory shall enter in.
Who is this King of Glory?*
 the Lord of hosts, He is the King of Glory.

℣. This is the Bread of Life which cometh down from Heaven - Alleluia -
 whosoever eateth of It shall live unto eternity - Alleluia. *[St. John 6:50, 54, 58.]*

Psalm 24

To Thee, O Lord,*
 have I lifted up my soul.
In Thee, O my God, I put my trust; let me not be ashamed.*
 Neither let my enemies laugh at me:
For none of them that wait on Thee shall be confounded.*
 Let all them be confounded that act unjust things without cause.
Show, O Lord, Thy ways to me,*
 and teach me Thy paths.
Direct me in Thy truth, and teach me; for Thou art God my Savior;*
 and on Thee have I waited all the day long.
Remember, O Lord, Thy bowels of compassion;*
 and Thy mercies that are from the beginning of the world.
The sins of my youth *
 and my ignorances do not remember.
According to Thy mercy remember Thou me:*
 for Thy goodness' sake, O Lord.
The Lord is sweet and righteous:*
 therefore He will give a law to sinners in the way.
He will guide the mild in judgment: *
 He will teach the meek His ways.
All the ways of the Lord are mercy and truth,*
 to them that seek after His covenant and His testimonies.
For Thy Name's sake, O Lord,*
 Thou wilt pardon my sin: for it is great.
Who is the man that feareth the Lord?*
 He hath appointed him a law in the way he hath chosen.
His soul shall dwell in good things: *
 and his seed shall inherit the land.
The Lord is a firmament to them that fear Him:*
 and His covenant shall be made manifest to them.
My eyes are ever towards the Lord:*
 for He shall pluck my feet out of the snare.
Look Thou upon me, and have mercy on me;*
 for I am alone and poor.

The troubles of my heart are multiplied: *
   deliver me from my necessities.
See my abjection and my labor; *
   and forgive me all my sins.
Consider my enemies for they are multiplied,*
   and have hated me with an unjust hatred.
Keep Thou my soul, and deliver me:*
   I shall not be ashamed, for I have hoped in Thee.
The innocent and the upright have adhered to me:*
   because I have waited on Thee.
Deliver Israel, O God, *
   from all his tribulations.

℣. The Lord gave the Bread of Heaven to them - Alleluia -
   Man ate the Bread of the Angels - Alleluia.   *[Psalm 77:24-25]*

   [This may be done antiphonally between Celebrant and congregation if the Confraction is complete:]

Psalm 42

Judge me, O God, and distinguish my cause from the nation that is not holy; *
   Deliver me from the unjust and deceitful man.
For Thou art God, my strength:*
   why hast Thou cast me off? and why do I go sorrowful, whilst the enemy afflicteth me?
Send out Thy light and Thy truth: they have conducted me *
   and brought me unto Thy holy hill, and into Thy tabernacles.
And I will go in to the Altar of God: *
   to God Who giveth joy to my youth.
To Thee, O God, my God,*
   I will give praise upon the harp:
Why art thou sad, O my soul?*
   and why dost thou disquiet me?
Hope in God, for I will still give praise to Him:*
   the salvation of my countenance, and my God.

[KNEEL OR STAND].
   [The following verses are always said for the nine kinds of Communicants:]
℣. Eat, O my friends - Alleluia -
   and be intoxicated, O beloved - Alleluia.   *[Song of Songs 5:1]*

℣. This sacred Body and Blood of the Lord and Savior - Alleluia -
   take you unto yourselves unto life eternal. - Alleluia.   *[St. John 6:54]*

℣. Upon my lips will I practice the hymn - Alleluia -
   which Thou didst teach me - Alleluia-
   and I shall respond in righteousness - Alleluia.   *[Psalm 118:171-172]*

℣. I shall bless the Lord at all times - Alleluia -
   His praise shall ever be in my mouth - Alleluia.   *[Psalm 33:1]*

℣. Taste and see - Alleluia -
   how sweet the Lord is – Alleluia.   *[Psalm 33:8]*

℣. Wherever I go - Alleluia -
there He shall be and minister unto me - Alleluia.
[Psalm 138:6-10, Psalm 22:4, St. Matthew 28:20]

℣. Suffer the little ones to come unto me - Alleluia -
and do not desire to forbid them - Alleluia -
of such is the kingdom of Heaven - Alleluia.   [St. Matthew 19:14]

℣. Devote yourselves to penitence - Alleluia -
for the kingdom of Heaven is at hand - Alleluia.   [St. Matthew 3:2]

℣. The kingdom of Heaven tolerates sieges - Alleluia -
and the forceful take it - Alleluia.   [Matt. 11:12, Latin and Greek.]

*[**Blessed Bread:** After the Confraction is completed, other loaves of bread, already broken or cut into pieces on a tray and kept on the Credenza, are brought by the Subdeacon to the Deacon or Celebrant, who blesses and passes them over the Paten. This bread will be taken by the Communicants immediately after they have received Holy Communion, to be certain all of the Communion is swallowed. **Wine** may also be blessed in the same way. This blessed but unconsecrated bread and wine must never be set on the Altar.]*

*Still facing the Altar, the Celebrant **moves the Particle** immediately above the center Particle slightly to the right (his left) and downward. The upper Particle is moved down to the left side as reminder us that "Bowing His head, He gave up the ghost". [The Confraction is completed.]*

[KNEEL]

*The Celebrant then turns to the people, **and shows the people the completed Confraction,** holding the Paten lowered and at a slight angle, saying:*

[ALL PRESENT LOOK AT THE COMPLETED CONFRACTION.]
Celebrant:

Come Forth and take possession of the kingdom of My Father - Alleluia -
which hath been prepared for ye from the beginning of the world - Alleluia -   [St. Matthew 25:34]

Glory be to the Father and to the Son and to the Holy Spirit: Come forth!
As it was in the beginning is now and ever unto ages of ages. Amen. Come forth!

("Moel Caich wrote this." note in the Lorrha Missal) [Jn 5:29, 11:43]

[A note in the Antiphonary of Bangor says about the Hymn, Sancti Venite:*"When the Clergy receives Holy Communion." During Holy Communion, starting from the Priest's Communion through Ablutions, the choir should sing **Communions Hymns**.*

HOLY COMMUNION

*The Celebrant turns back to the Altar, and **Communicates himself**, saying, [The Body is soaked, and he also drinks of the Chalice:]*

May the Body and Blood of our Lord Jesus Christ be to me unto life eternal. Amen.

[May the Blood of our Lord Jesus Christ be to me unto life eternal. Amen.]

*[A large **Communion Cloth** (at least three feet long) is either held by two servers or set upon the floor where Communion is to be given. This cloth is not to be stepped or kneeled upon by the Celebrant or congregation.]*

[Those who have not been Baptized and Confirmed need these Sacraments before participation in Holy Communion. Adults and older children who intend to join the Church must also have Catechism (instruction).]

Those who are Baptized and Confirmed, including infants, and prepared to receive Holy Communion now line up at the Communion Cloth in the following order:

Bishops, Priests, lower Holy Orders, Monastics, penitents, clerics, babes in arms with their parents or godparents, children, unmarried adults, married persons, and new Communicants.

[THOSE WHO WILL RECEIVE: KNEEL AT THE COMMUNION CLOTH].
The Celebrant turns and goes to the Communion Cloth, holding the Paten.

The Distribution for Confractions of Nine or More Particles

Bishops.

Clerics   *Children*

Priests   *Celebrant*   *Lower Holy Orders*

Unmarried adults   *Married adults*
New Communicants

Monastics
Penitents

The Distribution for Confractions of Less than Nine Particles

[This is inserted for the sake of convenience; it is not in the original text.]

Bishops.

Priests & lower   *Celebrant*   *Monastics,*
Holy Orders   *penitents, and clerics*

Children, All adults
New Communicants

[The Celebrant administers the Body and Blood from the Paten, saying:]

[From the Sacrament of Baptism:
May the Body and Blood of our Lord Jesus Christ be to thee unto life eternal. ℟. Amen.*]*

[Or, from the Sacrament of Unction:
May the Body and Blood of our Lord Jesus Christ, the Son of the living and most high God, be to thee unto life eternal. ℟. Amen.*]*

[The Chalice is administered with the words:
May the Blood of our Lord Jesus Christ be to thee unto life eternal. ℟. Amen.

*[The **caim**, a circle, is made with the chalice about the head of each communicant after they have received, and they may kiss the Chalice.]*

[Infants *may be communicated with a spoon from the Chalice, but all others receive from the Bread and Wine on the Paten, which the Celebrant administers with the **first two fingers of his right hand on their tongue** (not touching the tongue with his fingers).* **No person receives the Holy Communion in their hands, including clergy other than the Celebrant.** *Only the Celebrant or another Bishop, Priest or Deacon may administer the Holy Communion from one Paten, using Holy Communion Consecrated at this Mass.]*

*[**A server holds the tray of blessed bread** for those who have just received Holy Communion, or a movable table may hold the blessed bread and blessed wine.]*

[If Holy Communion is to be reserved for a Pre-Sanctified Mass or sick call, a piece of the upper Particle is reserved: see the note on the Confraction into 13 parts. The Confraction usually produces fewer Particles than there are people; the Particles are subdivided further during the administration of Communion.]

This is what God has declared worthy, that the mind be upon the Symbols of the Mass, and that this be your mind: that portion of the Host which you receive is a portion of Christ from His Cross, and that there may be a Cross in the labor of each in his own life since it is that Cross which unites each one of us to the Crucified Body of Christ. It is not proper to swallow the Particle without having tasted it, just as it is improper to not bring savor into God's Mysteries. It is improper for it to be chewed by the back teeth for such an act symbolizes rumination over God's Mysteries, for it is by such rumination that heresy is increased. It is ended. Amen. Thanks be to God. *[End of the Lorrha Missal commentary, as found in Gaelic and Latin.]*

[The Deacon or another Priest may perform the Ablutions, if their hands have been purified at the beginning of the Mass. *(The directions given are for a Celebrant serving alone.)*
After all have been Communicated who intended to receive, **Ablutions** are performed. The Celebrant consumes all of the remaining Body and Blood. The Chalice is set on the Altar to the Epistle side of the Corporal. The Knife and spoon are washed with water then wine over the Chalice and dried with the Purificator. If the Paten has no raised edge caution must be now observed. The Celebrant holds the Paten over the Chalice and pours wine over the Paten into the Chalice. He then dislodges any adhering Particles of the Sanctissimus with his forefinger or thumb, and then pours the wine from the Paten into the Chalice. This action may be repeated if necessary, turning the Paten so that no Particles remain. Then he pours water onto the Paten turning it so that its entire surface is washed, and pours the water from the Paten into the Chalice. The

Paten is then dried with the purificator. The Celebrant then drinks the wine and water. He then holds the Chalice with both hands so that the fingers which came into contact with the Body and the Blood are over the top. Wine and then water is poured over the fingers of the Celebrant into the Chalice by the servers to make certain that no Particles or Blood of Christ that had been on his fingers remain.

Any other clergy who have touched the Holy Eucharist such as a Bishop if he dropped the Particle into the Chalice after the Peace, or Celebrant if Deacon is performing the Ablutions, also have wine and water poured over their fingers into the Chalice.

*The Celebrant drinks the water and wine. Wine is poured into the Chalice. The wine in the Chalice is then drunk by the Celebrant who turns the Chalice, making certain that no Particles or Blood of the Lord remain. (Additional washings may use water alone.) The inside of the Chalice is **dried with the Purificator**. The **Purificator** is put on top of the **Chalice** and both are covered with the **Pall**. **The Paten and the Chalice are returned to the Credenza by the Subdeacon and covered with the veil**. The **Corporal** is now folded by the Deacon (or the Celebrant) and returned to the Credenza. The **Communion Cloth** is folded and returned to the Credenza.]*

POSTCOMMUNION PRAYER

[The Proper Postcommunion Prayer of the day (a Proper below and for the Sunday or Feast, see Propers through the year) may be substituted for or inserted before the following:]

Grant, O Lord, that those whom Thou hast satisfied with the Heavenly gift may be cleansed of all that is hidden, and that we may be freed from the snares of our enemies.
R. Amen.

In the Mass of Apostles, Martyrs, and Holy Virgins
We have consumed, O Lord, the Heavenly Sacrifice celebrated at the solemnity of Thy Saints. We beseech Thee grant that we may earn eternal joy by that which we do but briefly in life, through our Lord Jesus Christ Who reigneth with Thee and the Holy Spirit throughout all ages of ages. R. Amen.

In the Mass for Living Penitents
O God, Who purifies the hearts which confide in Thee and absolves those who reproach their consciences from all their iniquities: grant forgiveness to the sinners, and bestow healing to the injured, that having received remission in Thy Sacraments of all sins, they may remain sincere and devoted, and sustain nothing detrimental to eternal salvation.
R. Amen.

In the Mass of the Dead.
Let us pray, most beloved brethren, for our beloved -NN- who have already proceeded into the Lord's peace; whose ending was destined and course of crossing concluded; that God, the Almighty Father of our Lord Jesus Christ, command their flesh and their soul and their spirit to be received in a place of light, in a place of refreshment, in the bosom of Abraham and Isaac and Jacob. May He also dismiss whatsoever incorrectness by which they sinned through ignorance, or because of the hidden enemy and may He be pleased to refresh them by the spirit of His mouth, through our Lord Jesus Christ, Who reigneth with Thee, the unoriginate Father, and the Holy Spirit throughout all ages of ages. R. Amen.

The **Thanksgiving** *is always said:*

We give Thee thanks, O Lord, Holy Father, Almighty and eternal God, Who has satisfied us by the Communion of the Body and Blood of Christ Thy Son, and we humbly apply for Thy mercy: that this Thy Sacrament, O Lord, may not be unto our condemnation unto punishment: but may it be unto intercession of Salvation unto forgiveness; may it be unto the washing away of wickedness; may it be unto strengthening of the weak; a mainstay against the dangers of the world; may this Communion purge us of all guilt; and may it bestow the Heavenly joy of being partners, through our Lord Jesus Christ, Who reigneth with Thee and the Holy Spirit throughout all ages of ages. **R.** Amen.

[STAND]. [The Celebrant faces the congregation:]

The Mass has been given in Peace. *(During Paschaltide:* Alleluia.)
R. Thanks be unto God. *(During Paschaltide:* **Alleluia.***)*

The Closing Prayers

[The closing prayers for the Mass are from the Sacrament of Unction after Holy Communion, supplied as the ending.]
[KNEEL OR BOW].

For He hath satisfied the empty soul and hath filled the hungry soul with good things - Alleluia, Alleluia. *[Ps 104:9]* Visit us, O God, in Thy Salvation - Alleluia. *[Ps 105:4]* The Lord is my strength and my praise, and He is become my Salvation - Alleluia. *[Ps 117:14]* I will take the Chalice of Salvation, and I will call upon the Name of the Lord - Alleluia. *[Ps 115:13]* Refreshed by the Body and Blood of Christ, may we ever say unto Thee, O Lord - Alleluia. O Praise the Lord, all ye nations, praise him all ye people. For His mercy is confirmed upon us and the truth of the Lord remaineth for ever. *[Ps 116]* Offer up the Sacrifice of justice and trust in the Lord. *[Ps 4:6]* O God, we give Thee thanks, O Thou through Whom we have celebrated the Holy Mysteries, and we claim the gift of Holiness from Thee Who reigneth unto ages of ages. **R.** Amen.

The Final Benediction

[THE CONGREGATION BOWS PROFOUNDLY OR KNEELS:]
[The Celebrant extends both hands, palms outwards, fingers forming the Sign ICXC (according to both older Roman and Byzantine usage), over the heads of the Congregation:]

May the Lord bless you and protect you. May the Lord reveal His face unto you and have mercy. May the Lord turn His Face to you and give you peace. **R.** Amen.

Then signing the Congregation with his right hand, says:

You are marked with the Sign + of the Cross of Christ. Peace be with you unto life eternal.
R. Amen.

Thus ends the Order of Communion. [Note found at the end of Unction].

[The Final Gospel, *traditionally the beginning of the Gospel of St. John to verse 15 or 18 as in the Christmas Prophecies. It may be replaced by a displaced Gospel of the day. The complete Gospel of St. John was bound together with the Lorrha-Stowe Missal, and therefore the Lorrha-Stowe Missal is also called "The Gospel of St. Maelruain." A different Lection for a Requiem is on page 240.]*

[ALL STAND]

[In the beginning was the Word, and the Word was with God, and the Word was God. The same was in the beginning with God. All things were made by Him: and without Him was not any thing made that was made: in Him was life, and the life was the light of men: and the light shineth in darkness, and the darkness comprehended it not.

There was a man sent from God, whose name was John. The same came for a witness, to bear witness of the light, that all men through him might believe. He was not that light, he was sent to bear witness of that light.

That was the true Light, which lighteth every man that cometh into the world. He was in the world, and the world was made by Him, and the world knew Him not. He came unto His own, and His own received Him not. But as many as received Him, to them gave He power to become the sons of God, even to them that believe on His Name: which were born, not of blood, nor of the will of the flesh, nor of the will of man, but of God. *[all genuflect]* And the Word was made flesh, *[all rise]* and dwelt among us: and we beheld His glory, the glory as of the Only-begotten of the Father, full of grace and truth.

John beareth witness of Him, and crieth out, saying: This was He of whom I spoke: He that shall come after me, is preferred before me: because He was before me.

And of His fulness we all have received, and grace for grace. For the law was given by Moses; grace and truth came by Jesus Christ. No man hath seen God at any time: the Only-begotten Son who is in the bosom of the Father, He hath declared Him.

℟. Thanks be to God.]

*[Afterwards the Celebrant **unvests in the midst of the Church**, unless there is a special procession such as a funeral. He does not carry the Chalice out. The clergy may lead the Congregation in other Thanksgiving Prayers or Hymns; on some days a veneration of the Cross or other blessing. The Congregation kisses the blessing Cross.]*

+ + +

Hymns to be inserted at Communion:

*[During Holy Communion, starting from the Priest's Communion continuously through Ablutions, the choir should sing Communion Hymns, starting with the Sancti Venite. **A note in the Antiphonary of Bangor says about the Sancti Venite: "When the Clergy receives Holy Communion"** If the clergy finishes their Communion before the Hymn ends, continue singing Sancti Venite during the Communion of the Congregation and Ablutions. Continue singing other Hymns until Ablutions is over, ending at the end of a Hymn. As well as Sancti Venite, **on Sundays at the Sixth Hour, from the Antiphonary of Bangor, chant the Beatitudes, Hymn to Saint Michael and Hymn AB 2 in the Cross Vigil ("The Community of the Brethren"). On other days: Beatitudes and Magnificat.** May also do Deer's Cry and other Hymns appropriate to the Feast day.]*

Sancti Venite - Communion Hymn

Ye Holy Ones come forth: Eat ye the Body of Christ,
Drink ye the Holy Blood, Ye who are redeemed.
      S*anc*ti uenite *chris*ti corpus sumite. sanctum bibentes quo redempti sanguine "*.*,

For the Body and Blood of Christ the Savior
From which we are fed, let us give praises to God.
      Saluati *chris*ti corpore et sanguine a quo refecti laudes dicamus deo...,

By the Sacrament of the Body and Blood,
All are drawn out of the jaws of Hell.
      Hoc sacromento corporis et sanguinis omnes exuti ab inferni faucibus..,

The bestower of Salvation, Christ, the Son of God,
Hath saved the world through the Cross and Blood.
      Dator salutis *chris*tus filius dei mundum saluauit per crucen et sanguinem ".

For the Universe, the Lord was sacrificed,
He Himself, ariseth: the Priest and Victim.
      Pro uniuersis immolatus d*omi*nu*s*. ipse sacerdos existit et hostia..,

Under the Law of the Precepts were victims sacrificed
Which foreshadowed the Divine Mystery.
      Lege praecept*um* immolari hostias. qua adumbrantur diuina misteria ".

The bestower of Light and Savior of all,
Hath poured forth excellent Grace upon the Saints.
      LUcis indultor et saluator omnium praeclaram sanctis largitus est gratia*m* ".

All those approach who believe with pure mind;
They consume the eternal Custodian of Salvation.
      Accedunt omnes pura mente creduli sumant aeternam * salutis custodiam ".

The Guardian of the Saints, both guide and Lord,
Doth pour Life Eternal upon those who believe.
      S*anc*torum custos rector quoq*ue* d*omi*nus uitae perennis largitur credentibus..,

Heavenly Bread He giveth to the hungry,
From the Living Font supplies those who thirst.
      Caelestem panem dat esurientibus de fonte uiuo praebet sitientibus.

Alpha and Omega Himself, Christ the Lord,
came and will come to judge men.
      Alfa et ω ipse *chris*tus d*omi*nus uenit uenturus iudicare homines...,

A musical setting (© *Elizabeth Dowling, with a quote from Irish chant.*)

Ye Ho-ly Ones come forth: Eat ye the Bo-dy of Christ,

Drink ye the Ho-ly Blood, Ye who are re-deemed.

For the Bo-dy and Blood of Christ the Sa-vior

From which we are fed, let us give prais-es to God.

By the Sa-cra-ment of the Bo-dy and Blood,

All are drawn out of the jaws of Hell.

The be-stow-er of Sal-va-tion, Christ, the Son of God,

Hath saved the wor-ld through the Cross and Blood.

For the Un-i-verse, the Lord was sa-cri-ficed,

He Him-self, a-ris-eth: the Priest and Vic-tim.

Un-der the Law of the Pre-cepts were vic-tims sa-cri-ficed

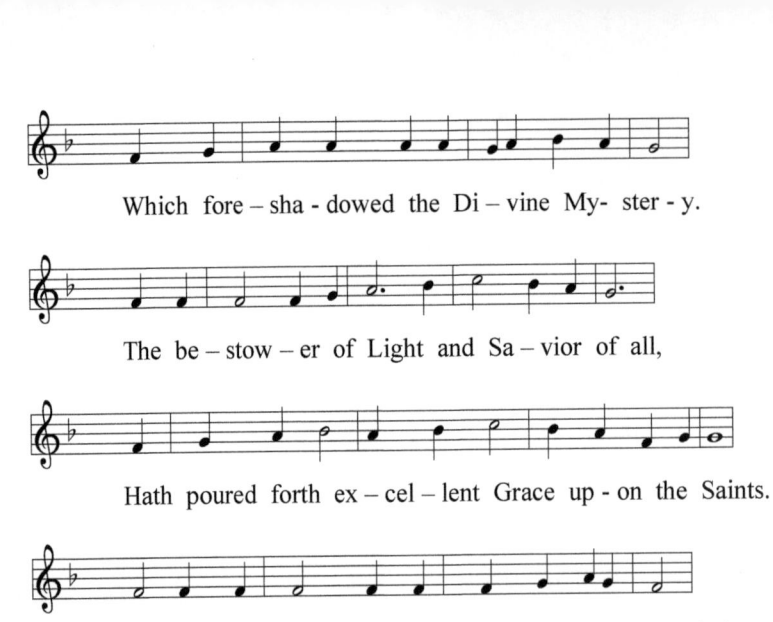

Which fore-sha-dowed the Di-vine My-ster-y.

The be-stow-er of Light and Sa-vior of all,

Hath poured forth ex-cel-lent Grace up-on the Saints.

All those ap-proach who be-lieve with pure mind;

They con-sume the e-ter-nal Cus-to-di-an of Sal-va-tion.

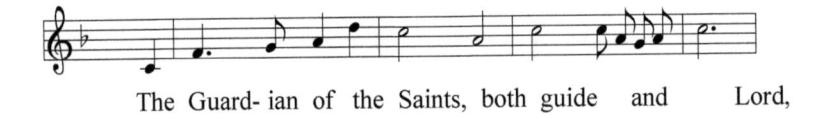

The Guard-ian of the Saints, both guide and Lord,

Doth pour Life e-ter-nal up-on those who be-lieve.

Heav-en-ly Bread He giv-eth to the hun-gry,

From the Liv-ing Font sup-plies those who thirst.

Al-pha and O-me-ga Him-self, Christ the Lord,

came and will come to judge men.

[At Pascha: return to p. 206.]

The Beatitudes (St. Matthew 5: 3-12a)

[After Hours, Holy Communion, meals. Music: repeat notes as needed:]

Blessed are the poor in spirit; for theirs is the kingdom of   heaven.
Blessed are the meek; for they shall possess the land.
Blessed are they that mourn; for they shall be comforted.
Blessed are they that hunger and thirst after justice; for they shall have their fill.
Blessed are the merciful; for they shall obtain mercy.
Blessed are the clean of heart; for they shall see God.
Blessed are the peacemakers; for they shall be called the children of God.
Blessed are they that suffer persecution for justice' sake; for theirs is the kingdom of heaven.
Blessed are ye when they shall revile you and persecute you and speak all that is evil against you, untruly, for my sake;
Be glad and rejoice, for your reward is very great in heaven;
[for so they persecuted the prophets that were before you.]

The Similitudes

[The Similitudes may also have been said at meals. .Matt. 5:13-16.]

You are the salt of the earth. But, if the salt lose its savour, wherewith shall it be salted?
It is good for nothing any more but to be cast out and to be trodden on by men.
You are the light of the world. A city seated on a mountain cannot be hid.
Neither do men light a candle and put it under a bushel, but upon a candlestick, that it may shine to all that are in the house. So let your light shine before men that they may see your good works and glorify your Father Who is in heaven.

A Hymn to St. Michael the Archangel

*[After meals. Sixth Hour Sunday in the Rule of Tallaght: this and Hymn AB 2
in the Cross Vigil replace the Magnificat. Music for convenience only.]*

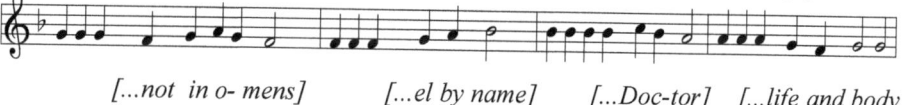

[...not in o- mens]   [...el by name]   [...Doc-tor]   [...life and body]

In the Trinity is my hope set, not in omens:
and I beseech Archangel Michael by name.

That he be ready and sent to me by God, the Doctor,
At the hour I leave this life and body.

May the aid of Michael, the Archangel, attend me
In the hour when the just and Angels rejoice.

I ask that he not leave me to the savage host of the enemy,
but that he lead me to where there is the repose of the kingdom.

May Saint Michael help me day and night
That he may put me in the company of the good Saints.

May Saint Michael, worthy aid, intercede for me
For I am a sinner in acts and am weak.

May Saint Michael defend me by his powers
When the soul goes forth with the armies of Saints.

May Saint Gabriel, Saint Raphael, all the angels,
and the Archangels Intercede for me forever.

May they be able to answer for me in the eternal courts of the
King's kingdom, that I might seize the joys of Paradise with Christ.

Glory to the Father and the Son and the Holy Spirit
Together.

Help us Archangel and Most Worthy Saint Michael whom God most high sent to save
souls.   *[Repeat the first line, add ending instead:]*

In the Trinity is my hope set, not in omens,   and I beseech Archangel Michael by name.

The Magnificat (St. Luke 1:46-55) *[music ad libitum]*

[After meals. Also said after or before the Hours, with the Beatitudes.]

My soul doth mag-ni- fy the Lord: And my spirit hath rejoiced in God my Saviour.
Because He hath regarded the humility of His handmaid;
    for, behold, for henceforth all generations shall call me blessed.
Because He that is mighty hath done great things to me;
    and Holy is His Name.
And His mercy is from generation unto generations,
    to them that fear Him.
He hath shewed might in His arm;
    He hath scattered the proud in the conceit of their heart.
He hath put down the mighty from their seat
    and hath exalted the humble.
He hath filled the hungry with good things;
    and the rich He hath sent empty away.
He hath received Israel His servant,
    being mindful of His mercy.
As He spoke to our fathers;
    to Abraham and to His seed for ever.

Other Communion Hymns

St. Mael Ruain states that Hymn AB 2 "The congregation of the Brethren," from the Cross Vigil may be done during Holy Communion. "Unitas" and "Hymn to Mary" are also appropriate, or, the ancient Kyrie which is Hymn AB 3. Or, on certain days: The Deer's Cry, Abcedarian Hymns, Paschal Hymns, Hymns found in Matins in the Antiphonary of Bangor, and Hymns for Saints. "The Shrine of Piety" may be done before or after the Mass.

The Cross Vigil
from the Rule of St. Mael Ruain

[The Psalms 118, 119, 120, and 121 use Greek numbering. These are written out in the Psalter. There are 200 verses, and the Cross Vigil is traditionally the time when 100 prostrations are done (at every other verse, starting with even verses of Psalm 118, *; an optional practice). This is difficult, and must be done with moderation, according to medical condition. A little bow may replace these prostrations. The verses may also be sung Antiphonally, that is, one chanter or group sings one verse, and another chanter or group sings the next verse, alternating. After the opening prayers and Psalms 118 through 121, the Rule of Mael Ruain says to do Hymn AB 2, "The Congregation of the Brethren," "Unitas," the "Hymn to Mary," and "The Shrine of Piety." The Cross Vigil may be done modern Friday evening (the beginning of Saturday after Vespers), especially just after Holy and Great Friday in Holy Week, when the words to the "Hymn to Mary" seem to match some of the ancient music for that day. These same three Psalms are the last three Psalms sung in the Season of Pentecost. This entire Vigil is in the Rule of the Cele De.]

V. + O God come to my assistance.

R.: O Lord make haste to help me.

V. Glory be to the Father, and to the Son, and to the Holy Spirit, as it was in the beginning, is now, and ever unto ages of ages. **R.** Amen.

Read Psalms 118, 119, 120, and 121 from the Psalter (p. 438).

On Holy and Great Saturday (modern Friday night in Holy Week) in Parish usage: Sing Psalm 64 here (page 402).

To complete the "Cross Vigil," do: Hymn AB 2, "The Congregation of the Brethren," "Unitas," "Hymn to Mary," and "The Shrine of Piety."

Hymn AB 2 by St. Hilary of Poitiers

[Also as Communion Hymns or ending Sunday's Sixth Hour; after the Beatitudes and Hymn to Michael, in the Rule of Tallaght. May also do other Hymns or AB3.]

The congregation of the Brethren sing the hymn
They sonorously sing the music of the Hymn
Unto Christ the King, harmoniously
Let us give due praise

O Thou Word from the heart of God.
Thou Way, Thou Truth,
Thou art called the branch of Jesse.
We recite, Thou art the Lion.

At the right hand of the Father, Mount and Lamb,
Thou art the cornerstone,
Bridegroom, or dove,
Flame, shepherd, door.

Thou wast proclaimed by the Prophets:
Born into our world,
Who wast before all worlds:
Maker of the first world.

Maker of Heaven, maker of earth:
Thou Gatherer of the seas
and Thou Maker of all things
that the Father commanded be made.

Received by the Virgin's womb,
Heralded by Gabriel,
Her womb swelled with Holy child:
Let us be taught to believe

A new thing not seen before
That the Virgin bore a Son.
Then Magi, following the Star
were first to worship the newborn

Offering incense and gold:
Offerings worthy of a king.
Soon it is reported to Herod,
It is distasteful to his authority

Who then commands the children slain:
He made all of them martyrs.
The child was born away, hidden.
None of Him in that flood spilled.

He was borne back after Herod's death:
The Heavenly one was raised in Nazareth
As a child and as an adult
He wrought many signs

Which remain and are documented
By many witnesses:
The promises given by the heavenly Kingdom
He fulfills by deeds:

He makes the infirm strong.
He illumines the blind.
By words, He cleanses the disease of the Lepers.
He raises the dead.

Into wine, because it had failed,
He commanded the water in the jars
to be made, which the wedding party
esteemed to be drunk unmixed by the people.

With five loaves and two fish
He feeds five thousand.
The fragments of the meal
Fill twelve baskets.

The gathering of all that dined
Gives forth perpetual praise.
He accepts twelve men
Through whom life is learned.

Of whom one is found,
Judas, the betrayer of Christ.
Those sent out by Annas
Are prompted by the traitor's kiss.

He Who is innocent, captive is held,
And Who does not resist, is led away.
He is arrested falsely, Those who deliver
[Him] to Pilate, berate [Him].

The governor dismisses the charges
He finds no guilt.
But with the assembly of the Jews
For the regard of Caesar

Say Christ is rebellious.
The Holy One is handed to the crowd
With impious words they rage at Him.
He endures spitting, stripes.

He is commanded to mount the Cross,
Innocent, for ills.
By the death of the flesh which He bore
He conquers the death of all.

Then, hanging, with a great shout,
Calls to God the Father.
Death took hold of the frame of Christ
He looses the tight chains.

The veil of the Temple hangs ripped
Night obscures the world.
Corpses once closed up
Are raised up from the tombs.

Blessed Joseph comes:
The Corpse is coated with myrrh
And wrapped in rough cloth
with sorrow he preserves it.

Annas, the leader, directs
Soldiers to guard the Corpse:
That he might see if Christ would prove
What He declared.

They tremble before the Angel of God,
Vested in a white cloak,
Which cloth exceeds
silk in brightness.

He rolls the stone away from the tomb:
Christ arises unconquered.
Lying Judea sees this:
They deny, having seen.

The women learn first
That the Savior liveth.
Those whom He greets in sorrow,
He fills rejoicing with joy.

Afterwards, they announce
that He, raised From the dead
by the Paternal right hand,
Had returned on the Third day.

Soon He is seen by the blessed
Brethren whom He had tried.
He answers those that doubted,
Entering while the doors were barred.

He teaches the precepts of the Law,
He gives the Divine Spirit:
The perfect Spirit of God:
The chain of the Trinity.

He commandeth that throughout the World
Believers be Baptized:
Calling upon the Name of the Father:
Confiding in the Son.

By the Holy Spirit, He reveals
Mystic Faith to the Baptized:
Those immersed in the Font
Are remade: made sons of God.

Before the dawn, let us the Gathering
Of the brethren hymn in concert the Glory:
By which we are taught we will be
In the eternal age.

The crowing of the cock, the flapping of the cock,
Says that day is nigh,
We, singing and litanizing
What we believe will be.

The Majestic and immense,
Hymn we together:
Before the dawn we proclaim
Christ the King unto the age.

Before the dawn we proclaim
Christ the King unto the age.
Who in Him rightly believe
That we will reign with Him.

Glory to the Father, Unbegotten,
Glory to the Onlybegotten,
Likewise to the Holy Spirit
Unto eternal ages.

Unitas

[musical setting © Elizabeth Dowling 2006.]

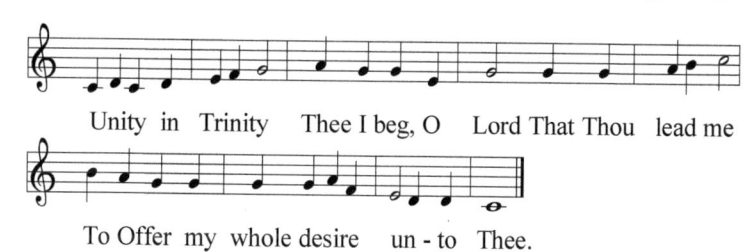

Unity in Trinity Thee I beg, O Lord That Thou lead me
To Offer my whole desire un - to Thee.

On Holy and Great Saturday in Parish usage: Stand, and read the **Holy Passion Gospel**. St. Matthew 27: 61-66 (on page 156).

A Hymn to Mary   From the *Liber Hymnorum*

[Music is of the Myrrh-bearing women on Holy Saturday in the Byzantine Rite.]

Let us sing to God all day, harmonizing and chanting
In unison the worthy hymn of Mary.

Twice by this chorus and again, let us praise Mary,
That the voice may knock at all ears through obedient praise.

Mary of the Tribe of the Jews, highest Mother of the Lord,
Gave suitable medicine unto sick mankind.

Gabriel bore the Word which from the first was in the Paternal bosom:
Which was conceived and nurtured by the maternal womb.

This is the highest and holy, venerable Virgin,
Who didst not shy but stood fast.

Unto this Mother, neither before, at the time, nor after
Is found the like among the generations of human origin.

Through a woman and wood the world first fell.
Through the virtue of a woman, it is returned to health.

Mary, wondrous Mother, gave birth to her Father,
through Whom, all the far world endowed by water believes.

She conceived the pearl: those are not vain dreams
For which sane Christians sell all that they have.

The Mother made Christ's tunic woven throughout
Which by lot remained intact at Christ's death.

Let us assume the armor of Light: the breastplate and the helm,
That we may be perfected by God and protected by Mary.

Amen Amen: we swear by the qualities of the Birthgiver
That the flames of the dread pyre cannot deceive us.

We call upon the Name of Christ: under witnessing Angels:
That we may enjoy and be inscribed in Heavenly script.

We implore the most worthy example of Mary
That we may be worthy to dwell in the highest Throne.   *[Repeat first line.]*

The Shrine of Piety in the Cross Vigil

(Paragraph 6, Teaching of Mael Ruain of Tallaght)

Standing facing the East with both hands raised to Heaven and clear of vesture say:

The Divine Prayer AB 36

Our Father, Who art in the Heavens, hallowed be Thy Name. Thy Kingdom come. Thy will be done on earth as it is in Heaven. Give us this day our daily bread and forgive us our debts as we forgive our debtors and lead us not into temptation but deliver us from evil. Amen.

O God come to my assistance, O Lord make haste to help me.
O God come to my assistance, O Lord make haste to help me.
O God come to my assistance, O Lord make haste to help me.

Make the Sign of the Cross with the right hand to the East.
Turn and repeat the prayers and Cross to each of the other three directions.

After again turning to the East, repeat the Divine Prayer and the three repetitions of "O Lord come to my assistance..." for all four directions with face bent down toward the ground, standing erect only to make the Sign of the Cross in each direction.

After again turning to East, repeat the Divine Prayer and the three repetitions of "O Lord come to my assistance..." for all four directions with face raised to Heaven, looking ahead only to make the Sign of the Cross in each direction.

Therefore the Divine Prayer is repeated twelve times, "O Lord come to my assistance..." is repeated thirty six times and the Sign of the Cross is made twelve times.

(The Shrine of Piety may end an Hour, the Cross Vigil, or be done just before a Liturgy.)

THE DEER'S CRY
(Breastplate of St. Patrick)

St. Patrick composed this hymn in the time of Loegaire son of Niall. The cause of its composition, however, was to protect St. Patrick and his monks against deadly enemies that lay in wait for the clerics. This is a breast-plate of faith for the protection of body and soul against devils and men and vices. When anyone shall repeat it every day with diligent intentness on God, devils shall not dare to face him; it shall be a protection to him against every poison and envy; it shall be a defense to him against sudden death; it shall be a breast-plate to his soul after his death. St. Patrick sang this hymn when ambushes were laid against his coming by Loegaire, that he might not go to Tara to sow the Faith. Those who were lying in ambush saw wild deer (St. Patrick and the monks), with a fawn (St. Benen) following them carrying the books, and let them pass. St. Patrick arrived at Tara; his Easter fire was the first spring light, conquering darkness. [Music is late.]

I arise today through a mighty strength, the invocation of the Trinity,
through belief in the Threeness,
through confession of the Oneness of the Creator of creation.

I arise today through the strength of Christ with His Baptism,
through the strength of His Crucifixion with His Burial
through the strength of His Resurrection with His Ascension,
through the strength of His descent for the Judgment of Doom.

I arise today through the strength of the love of Cherubim
in obedience of Angels, in the service of the Archangels,
in hope of resurrection to meet with reward,
in prayers of Patriarchs, in predictions of Prophets,
in preachings of Apostles, in faiths of Confessors,
in innocence of Holy Virgins, in deeds of righteous men.

I arise today, through the strength of Heaven:
light of Sun, brilliance of Moon,
splendour of Fire, speed of Lightning,
swiftness of Wind, depth of Sea,
stability of Earth, firmness of Rock.

I arise today, through God's strength to pilot me:
God's might to uphold me, God's wisdom to guide me,
God's eye to look before me, God's ear to hear me,
God's word to speak for me, God's hand to guard me,
God's way to lie before me, God's shield to protect me,
God's host to secure me: against snares of devils, against temptations of vices,
    against inclinations of nature, against everyone who shall wish me ill,
      afar and anear, alone and in a crowd.

I summon today all these powers between me (and these evils):
against every cruel and merciless power that may oppose my body and my soul,
    against incantations of false prophets, against black laws of heathenry,
    against false laws of heretics, against craft of idolatry,
    against spells of women [any witch] and smiths and wizards,
    against every knowledge that endangers man's body and soul.

Christ to protect me today
    against poison, against burning, against drowning, against wounding,
    so that there may come abundance of reward.

Christ with me, Christ before me, Christ behind me,
Christ in me, Christ beneath me, Christ above me,
Christ on my right, Christ on my left,
Christ in breadth, Christ in length, Christ in height,
Christ in the heart of every man who thinks of me,
Christ in the mouth of every man who speaks of me,
Christ in every eye that sees me,
Christ in every ear that hears me.

I arise today through a mighty strength, the invocation of the Trinity,
through belief in the Threeness,
through confession of the Oneness
of the Creator of creation.

Salvation is of the Lord.
Salvation is of the Lord.
Salvation is of Christ.
May Thy Salvation, O Lord, be ever with us.

AB 3 Hymn of the Apostles

(Notice that the last verse implies that the words "Kyrie eleison" or "Lord have mercy" have been said after each verse except for the first and last verses which end with "Alleluia." This "Kyrie" has been reduced either to nine verses in the Tridentine Roman Rite or forty repeats of "Kyrie eleison" in the Byzantine Rite at Compline, equivalent to Beginning of Night. This seems to be one of the oldest of the Hymns.)

Let us beg the Father
The Almighty King
And Jesus Christ
and also the Holy Spirit.
Alleluia

God in one
Perfect Substance
Triune in Three
Adored Persons   (R: Lord have mercy...)

Of the universes,
The luminous brightness of the font
of the Aethereals
and sphere of lights. (R: Lord have mercy...)

This truly is the day
As the firstborn of heaven
flashed from the great vault
of the world. (R: Lord have mercy...)

Thus the Word was made
Flesh, the Light from the
Beginning sent by
the Father into the world (R: Lord have mercy...)

And He that first
took away the powers from chaos
Drove off night from
The unsuspecting world. (R: Lord have mercy...)

Thus, this opposing
lethargy being subdued,
He breaks down the Pole
unto the chains of death. (R: Lord have mercy...)

The shadows were
above and before the abyss
Whence shown the
First day of Days. (R: Lord have mercy...)

He went forth,
The True Light,
[He] joined the highest hearts
To mortal ignorance. (R: Lord have mercy...)

The same day
The so-called Red Sea
Flowing behind,
Israel is freed. (R: Lord have mercy...)

Through this we are taught
to reject the works of the world
and take up virtue
in the desert. (R: Lord have mercy...)

Fierce Pharaoh submerged
who strove jealously with God,
Lead by fire
They sing praises. (R: Lord have mercy...)

Thus freed and our
Confident enemies driven away
May we likewise be appointed
to praise God. (R: Lord have mercy...)

And thus He who
Made the beginning of Light
Also and here
Makes the beginning of Salvation. (R: Lord have mercy...)

The first is set forth
In the beginning of the day,
The Second in the true
Fervor of Faith. (R: Lord have mercy...)

At the end of the world
After so great a Mystery
The Savior comes
With great clemency. (R: Lord have mercy...)

Just as bare,
the elements set forth,
what mouths of poets
lucidly celebrate. (R: Lord have mercy...)

Born as a man
in mortal flesh
Not absent from Heaven
Remaining in the Trinity (R: Lord have mercy...)

Swaddled in cloth
Adored by the Magi
He shown among the stars
Adored in the Heavens (R: Lord have mercy...)

His size was held
By a common manger
Whose fist can
Contain the world. (R: Lord have mercy...)

And the first sign
of water turned
into sweetest wine
Portends to the Disciples. (R: Lord have mercy...)

Then is quickly fulfilled
What was said through
The Prophets: The lame
goeth forth like a stag. (R: Lord have mercy...)

And the tongue of the mute
speaks plainly,
the chains being broken,
by the commanding Lord. (R: Lord have mercy...)

The deaf, the blind
And Lepers are healed.
Death is thrust aside
the Dead are raised. (R: Lord have mercy...)

Likewise, He divides
Five loaves to content
the discomfort of the thousands,
so close to doubt. (R: Lord have mercy...)

After so much abundance
of Divine clemency
This stimulates the
Beginning of envy. (R: Lord have mercy...)

He who wishes
for enemies
stretches forth to envy
and to hate the soul. (R: Lord have mercy...)

Council is begun
Against Him
Who is called
The messenger of good Council. (R: Lord have mercy...)

They come upon Him
as upon a thief with swords.
The thief will give up
eternal coins. (R: Lord have mercy...)

Then He is dragged
to a human court
The perpetual is condemned
by a mortal king. (R: Lord have mercy...)

He who is fixed to the Cross,
O wonder, shook the Pole
and blotted out the
Light of the Sun at the Third hour. (R: Lord have mercy...)

Boulders were split
The veil of the temple was rent
The dead came forth,
living, from the tombs. (R: Lord have mercy...)

He frees him
who was gnawed
by bonds of thousands of years
of death of the lower old man. (R: Lord have mercy...)

The first-formed [is freed]
from the scandalous child of evil,
grasping death by
raging avenger. (R: Lord have mercy...)

By His return,
He clemently restores
each who of old
dwelled in Paradise. (R: Lord have mercy...)

Raising the head of
the body of the universe
in the Trinity
He calls to the Church (R: Lord have mercy...)

In this the Heavenly One
Commands the ancient gates
to open for the King and
His eternal retinue. (R: Lord have mercy...)

He seeks from on High
The one who has strayed
Bearing back on shoulders
to the sheep fold. (R: Lord have mercy...)

Him we await,
Who will come
judging the just
To redeem His handiwork (R: Lord have mercy...)

I ask how
and with how much offerings
will we be able to repay
such a recompense? (R: Lord have mercy...)

How are we,
mortals of the small word,
to narrate anything
which no one dares declare? (R: Lord have mercy...)

We only pray
this same maxim:
O our eternal Lord,
have mercy.
    Alleluia.

"Abecedarian" Hymns – Latin Alphabet begins verses:
A,B,C,D,E,F,G,H,I,K,L,M,N,O,P,Q,R,S,T,U,X,Y,Z, subject.

In an abecedarian Hymn, consecutive letters of the alphabet begin each stanza. In usual Hymns or Litanies, the first line or subject is repeated.. In an abecedarian Hymn, this last line usually is after the last letter of the alphabet, and the first letter of the verse begins the word that is the subject or object of the Hymn. For example, the last verse of the abecedarian Hymn of St. Patrick by St. Secundinus begins with St. Patrick's name, using the letter P.

The *Altus Prosator* or another abecedarian Hymn is used to Consecrate a Church, and at other important times, such as for All Saints and All Souls. In an Irish Litany of the Saints, it says that St. Patrick himself chanted an abecedarian Hymn (similar to Altus Prosator) as a Consecration of a church. In the Pontificale of St. Egbert, for a Church Consecration, it says to sing an abecedarian hymn while the Bishop writes the letters on the floor of the Church with his Pastoral staff. In the York Pontificale, this consecration is reduced to writing the Greek and Latin alphabets on the floor of the church by the Consecrating Bishop, the instructions to sing the abecedarian assumed. The Byzantines only have a procession around the Church after consecrating the altar table at a Church Consecration. In Latin the term for "alphabet" is "elements" or "parts" (literally translated). There are many other Abecedarian Hymns. Later than the Irish used this form of Hymn, the Greeks used Abecedarian Hymns called Kontakion.

There is much alliteration and rhythm in the text that is lost in translation. The Latin used is very much influenced by Gaelic, and would be difficult to understand for most classical Latin readers. These are translated because languages must be clearly understood in prayers.

Altus Prosator
St. Colum cille

Altus Prosator is the abecedarian Hymn of the Creation and history of the universe of St. Colum cille. The original is in Latin. This translation is by Bernard, D.D., and Atkinson, LL.D., London, 1898. The later *Dies Irae*, which resembles it, talks about the Last Judgment, but only begins at the letter R of this Hymn. The last verse, after the completion of the alphabet, begins with the letter "D" (DEUM) for the subject of the Hymn: God. This Hymn is used for Church Consecrations and All Saints Day.

A *[Altus]*
The High Creator, Ancient of Days, and Unbegotten
was without origin of beginning and without end; He is and shall be to infinite ages of ages
with Whom is Christ the only begotten and the Holy Spirit,
coeternal in the everlasting glory of the Godhead.
We set forth not three gods, but we say there is One God,
saving our faith in three most glorious Persons.

B *[Bonos]*
He created good Angels, and Archangels, the orders
of Principalities and Thrones, of Authorities and Powers,
that the Goodness and Majesty of the Trinity might not be inactive
in all offices of bounty,
but might have creatures in which
it might richly display heavenly privileges by a word of power.

C *[Caeli]*
From the summit of heaven's kingdom, from the brightness of angelic station,
from the beauty of the splendor of his form,
through pride Lucifer, whom He had made, had fallen;
and the apostate angels too by the same sad fall
of the author of vainglory and stubborn envy,
the rest remaining in their principalities.

D *[Draco]*
The Dragon, great, most foul, terrible, and old,
which was the slimy serpent, more subtle than all the beasts
and fiercer living things of earth,
drew with him the third part of the stars into the abyss
of the infernal regions and of divers prisons,
apostate from the True Light, headlong cast by the parasite.

E *[Excelsus]*
The Most High, foreseeing the frame and order of the world
had made the heaven and earth. The sea and waters He established;
likewise the blades of grass, the twigs of shrubs;
sun, moon, and stars; fire and necessary things;
birds, fish, and cattle; beasts and living things:
and lastly man first-formed to rule with prophecy.

F *[Factis]*
So soon as the stars, the lights of the firmament, were made,
the angels praised for His wondrous handywork
the Lord of the vast mass, the Builder of the heavens,
with praise giving proclamation, meet and unceasing;
and in noble concert gave thanks to the Lord,
of love and choice, not from endowment of nature.

G *[Grasatis]*
Our first two parents having been assailed and seduced,
the Devil falls a second time, with his satellites;
by the horror of whose faces and the sound of whose flight
frail men, stricken with fear, should be affrighted,
being unable with carnal eyes to look upon them;
who now are bound in bundles with the bonds of their prison-houses.

H *[Hic]*
He, removed from the midst, was cast down by the Lord
The space of the air is closely crowded
with a disordered crew of his rebel satellites; invisible,
lest men infected by their evil examples and their crimes,
no screens or walls ever hiding them,
should openly defile themselves before the eyes of all.

I *[Inuehunt]*
The clouds carry the wintry floods from the fountains of the sea--
the three deeper floods of Ocean --
to the regions of heaven in azure whirlwinds,
to bless the crops, the vineyards and the buds;
driven by the winds issuing from their treasure houses;
which drain the corresponding shallows of the sea.

K *[Kaduca]*
The tottering and despotic and momentary glory
of the kings of this present world is set aside by the will of GOD!
Lo! the giants are recorded to groan beneath the waters
with great torment, to be burned with fire and punishment;
and, choked with the swelling whirlpools of Cocytus,
overwhelmed with Scillas, they are dashed to pieces with waves and rocks.

L *[Ligatas]*
The waters that are bound up in the clouds the Lord ofttime droppeth,
lest they should burst forth all at once, their barriers being broken
from whose fertilizing streams as from breasts,
gradually flowing through the regions of this earth,
cold and warm at divers seasons,
the never failing rivers ever run.

M *[Magni]*
By the divine powers of the great GOD is suspended
the globe of earth, and thereto is set the circle of the great deep,
supported by the strong hand of GOD Almighty;
promontories and rocks sustaining the same,
with columns like to bars on solid foundations,
immoveable like so many strengthened bases.

N *[Nulli]*
To no man seemeth it doubtful that hell is in the lowest regions,
where are darkness, worms, and dread beasts,
where is fire of brimstone blazing with devouring flames,
where is the crying of men, the weeping and gnashing of teeth,
where is the groaning of Gehenna, terrible and from of old
where is the horrid, fiery, burning of thirst and hunger.

O *[Orbem]*
Under the earth, as we read, there are dwellers, we know,
whose knee ofttimes bendeth in prayer to the Lord;
for whom it is impossible to unroll the written book --
sealed with seven seals, according to the warnings of Christ --
which He Himself had opened, after He had risen victorious,
fulfilling the prophetic presages of His Advent.

P *[Plantatum]*
That Paradise was planted by the Lord from the beginning
we read in the noble opening of Genesis;
from its fountain four rivers are flowing,
and in its flowery midst is the Tree of Life,
whose leaves for the healing of the nations fall not;
its delights are unspeakable and abounding.

Q *[Quis]*
Who hath ascended to Sinai, the appointed mountain of the Lord,
Who hath heard the thunders beyond measure pealing,
Who the clang of the mighty trumpet resound,
Who hath seen the lightnings gleaming round about,
Who the flashes and the thunderbolts and the crashing rocks,
Save Moses the judge of Israel's people?

R *[Regis]*
The day of the Lord, the King of Kings most righteous, is at hand:
a day of wrath and vengeance, of darkness and cloud;
a day of wondrous mighty thunderings,
a day of trouble also, of grief and sadness,
in which shall cease the love and desire of women
and the strife of men and the lust of this world.

S *[Stantes]*
Trembling we shall be standing before the judgment seat of the Lord,
and shall give account of all our deeds;
seeing also our crimes set before our eyes,
and the books of conscience open before us,
we shall break forth into most bitter cries and sobs,
the necessary opportunities of action being withdrawn.

T *[Tuba]*
As the wondrous trumpet of the First Archangel soundeth,
the strongest vaults and sepulchres shall burst open,
thawing the (death) chill of the men of the present world;
the bones from every quarter gathering together to their joints,
the ethereal souls meeting them
and again returning to their proper dwellings.

U *[Uagatur]*
Orion wanders from his culmination the meridian of heaven,
the Pleiades, brightest of constellations, being left behind,
through the bounds of Ocean, of its unknown eastern circuit;
Vesper circling in fixed orbits returns by her ancient paths,
rising after two years at eventide;
(these), with figurative meanings, (are) regarded as types.

X *[Xristo]*
When Christ, the most High Lord, descendeth from heaven,
before Him shall shine the most brilliant sign and standard of the Cross;
and the two chief luminaries being darkened,
the stars shall fall to the earth, as the fruit from a figtree,
and the surface of the world shall be like a fiery furnace.
Then shall the hosts hide themselves in the caves of the mountains.

Y *[Ymnorum]*
By chanting of hymns continually ringing out,
by thousands of angels rejoicing in holy dances,
and by the four living creatures full of eyes,
with the four and twenty happy elders,
casting down their crowns beneath the feet of the Lamb of GOD,
the Trinity is praised with eternal threefold repetition.

Z *[Zelus]*
The raging fury of fire shall consume the adversaries,
unwilling to believe that Christ came from GOD the Father;
but we shall forthwith fly up to meet Him,
and so shall we be with Him in divers orders of dignities
according to the everlasting merits of our rewards,
to abide in glory, for ever and ever.

DEUM *[God]*
Who can please GOD in the last time,
when the glorious ordinances of truth are changed?
Who but the despisers of this present world?

Audite omnes, an abecedarian hymn on St. Patrick, Teacher of the Irish by St. Secundinus

This is a literal translation by Esp. Maelruain Kristopher Dowling from the Latin of the Antiphonary of Bangor. A non-literal translation such as the one by Ludwig Bieler may lead one away from the original doctrine of the Irish Church: for example, Bieler replaces "with Christ" with "in union with Christ" in verse five. In the eighth verse the term "stigmata" is used in the original text. This Hymn is the only source on the life of St. Patrick which suggests stigmata, but it is contemporary, and should not be translated "marks." The twenty-fourth verse was completely omitted in Bieler's translation, perhaps because the stanza is after the last letter of the Latin alphabet. (It begins with the letter P, for Patrick.) It is an acclamation and a prayer for intercessions, and belongs in the text. Without this last verse asking the Saint to pray for us and with us, we would be saying that contemplation of the merits or qualities of the life of St. Patrick would be sufficient for our salvation, i.e., the modern Roman view of "merits." (Esp. Maelruain's literal translation is in italics.)

The following notes are paraphrased from Bieler: The original text is found in the Antiphonary of Bangor, called *Audite omnes*. Secundinus came from the continent (probably known to St. Patrick when he studied in Gaul), and wrote this hymn contemporary with St. Patrick. Muirchu states in his Life of Patrick that St. Patrick was granted the favor that all persons who sang this hymn on their last day would be saved by St. Patrick's intercession. Tirechan states in the Book of Armagh that "his canticle" should be sung throughout the triduum of his dormition, that is, from the 17th to the 19th of March. In the Genair Patraic (which Bieler says is 800 A.D. because footnotes and margin notes are later, but is probably contemporary with St. Patrick) the hymn of Secundinus is called a protection, a lorica (breast-plate) or prayer of special power, as is the *"Deer's Cry."*

The music here is only for convenience; the original text probably had a much more complicated chant to go with these words.

A [Audite omnes amantes]
Hear ye all, lovers of God, the | holy merits
Of the man blessed in Christ, Pa - | trick the bishop,
How for his good ways he is likened to the an - | gels,
And because of his perfect life is deemed equal to | the Apostles.

B [Beata Christi]
Christ's holy precepts he keeps | in all things,
His works shine | bright among men,
And they follow his holy and wondrous exam - | ple,
And thus *magnify* God the Father | *in the heavens*.

C [Constans]
Constant in the fear of God and steadfast | in his faith,
Upon whom the Church is built | as on Peter;
And his Apostleship has he received from | God --
The gates of Hell will not pre - | vail against him.

D [Dominus]
The Lord has chosen him to teach the barbar - | ian tribes,
To fish with the nets | of his teaching,
And to draw from the world unto grace the believ - | ers,
Men who would follow the Lord to His | heavenly seat.

E [Electa]
He sells the choice talents of | Christ's Gospel
And collects them among the Irish hea - | thens with usury;
As a reward for the great labor of his *voy* - | *age*,
He will come into possession of joy *with Christ in the* heavenly kingdom.

F [Fidelis]
God's faithful *minister* and His distinguished am - | bassador,
He gives the good an Apostolic ex - | ample and model,
Preaching as he does to God's people in words as well as in | deeds,
So that him whom he converts not with words he inspires with good conduct.

G [Gloriam]
Glory has he with Christ, honor | in the world,
He who is venerated by all as an | angel of God.
God has sent him, as He sent Paul, an Apostle to the gen - | tiles,
To offer men guidance to the | kingdom of God.

H [Humilis]
Humble is he of mind and body because of his | fear of God;
The Lord *abides upon him* because | of his good deeds;
In his *righteous flesh* he bears the *stigmata* of | Christ;
In His Cross alone, his sole comfort, | he glor - ies.

I [Impiger]
Untiringly he feeds the faithful from the heaven - | ly banquet,
Lest those who are with Christ | faint on the way;
Like bread he gives to them the words of the Gos - | pel,
Which are multiplied like manna | in his hands.

K [Kastam]
He preserves his body chaste for love | of the Lord;
This body he has prepared as a temple for the | Holy Spirit,
And he keeps it such by purity in all his act - | ions;
He offers it as a living sacrifice, acceptable | to the Lord.

L [Lumenque]
Enflaming light of the world, *great one* | *of the* Gospel,
Lifted up on a candlestick, shining *un* - | *to all the age* -
The fortified city of the King, *founded upon* a moun - | tain,
Wherein there is great abundance | of the Lord.

M [Maximus]
Greatest indeed will be called in the kingdom | of heaven
The man who fulfills with good deeds the holy | words he teaches,
Who by his good example is a leader and model to the faith - | ful,
Who in *purity* of heart has con - | fidence in God.

N [Nomen]
Boldly he proclaims the Name of the Lord to | the heathens,
And gives them eternal grace in the bath | of salvation.
He prays to God daily for their | sins,
For them he offers sacrifices, worthy in | the eyes of God.

O [Omnem]
For the sake of God's law he despises all | worldly glory;
Compared to His table he considers all | else as trifling;
He is not moved by the violence of this | world,
But, suffering for Christ, he rejoices in | adversity.

P [Pastor]
A good and faithful shepherd of the flock won for | the Gospel,
God has chosen him to watch o - | ver God's people
And to feed with divine teaching His | folk,
For whom, following Christ's example, he | gives *forth his soul.*

Q [Quem]
Who for his merits the Savior has raised him to the dignity of a | *pontifex,*
In heavenly things he instructs the army | *of* the clergy,
Providing them with heavenly rations, besides vest - | ments -
The rations of divine | and sacred *texts*.

R [Regis]
He is the King's herald, inviting the faithful | to the wedding.
He is richly clad in a | wedding garment,
He drinks heavenly wine from heavenly | cups
And gives God's people the spiritual | cup   to drink.

S [Sacrum]
He finds a holy treasure in the Sa - | cred Volume
And perceives the Savior's divinity | in   His flesh.
It is a treasure he purchases with holy and perfect | works.
ISRAEL his soul is called -- | "see - ing God."

T [Testis]
A faithful witness of the Lord in the Ca - | tholic Law,
His speech is spiced with divine | *revelations*,
That human flesh may not decay, eaten by | worms,
But be salted with heavenly savor | for sacrifice.

U [Verus]
A true and renowned tiller of the | Gospel field,
His seeds | are Christ's Gospels.
These he sows from his God-inspired mouth into the ears of the | wise,
And cultivates their hearts and minds with the | Holy Spirit.

X [Xps *(Greek for Christos)*]
Christ chose him to be His vi - | car on earth.
He frees captives from a two-fold | ser - vitude:
The great numbers whom he liberates from bondage to | men,
These countless ones he frees from the yoke | of the devil.

Y [Ymnos]
Hymns, and the Apocalypse, and the Psalms of | God he sings,
And explains them for the edification | of God's people.
He believes the law in the Trinity of the holy | Name,
And he teaches one Substance | in Three Persons.

Z [Zona]
Girt with the Lord's girdle | day and night,
He prays unceasingly | to God the Lord.
He will receive the reward for his immense la - | bor -
With the Apostles will he reign, holy, over | Is - rael.

subject verse [Patricius]
May Bishop Patrick pray for | *all of us,*
That the sins which we have committed be blotted out | *immediately,*
May we ever sing Patrick's prais - | *es,*
That we may ever | *live   with him.*   [*Amen.*]

Seasonal Hymns and Services

It would be nice to include in this book Propers at least, Christmas through Epiphany, the Mass of the Institution of the Eucharist on Holy Thursday, Bright Week, Ascension, and Pentecost, etc. and the rest of the year, but there isn't room. It was decided that the one Mass that could not be omitted from this book is the Vigil of the Resurrection of our Lord Jesus Christ. Other services: The "Traditio" is a catechism, necessary at the beginning of Holy Week. The Propers for the Holy Cross and the Adoration of the Holy Cross, and for St. Patrick are also given to show examples of some Propers.

O Come Emmanuel *(not Celtic, but a familiar Advent Hymn)*

The words of the ancient Roman "O Antiphons," one verse said each day during the week before Christmas, are also found in the Byzantine Rite in the Christmas Canon. This Carol is in reverse order of the "O Antiphons." English translation by John M. Neale, 1851, music is 15th century.

O come, O come, Emmanuel,
And ransom captive Israel,
That mourns in lonely exile here
Until the Son of God appear.
    Rejoice! Rejoice! *(Refrain)*
    Emmanuel shall come to thee, O Israel.

O come, Thou Wisdom from on high,
Who orderest all things mightily;
To us the path of knowledge show,
And teach us in her ways to go. *(Refrain)*

O come, Thou Rod of Jesse, free
Thine own from Satan's tyranny;
From depths of hell Thy people save,
And give them victory over the grave. *(Refrain)*

O come, Thou Day-spring, come and cheer
Our spirits by Thine advent here;
Disperse the gloomy clouds of night,
And death's dark shadows put to flight. *(Refrain)*

O come, Thou Key of David, come,
And open wide our heavenly home;
Make safe the way that leads on high,
And close the path to misery. *(Refrain)*

O come, O come, great Lord of might,
Who to Thy tribes on Sinai's height
In ancient times once gave the law
In cloud and majesty and awe. *(Refrain)*

O come, Thou Root of Jesse's tree,
An ensign of Thy people be;
Before Thee rulers silent fall;
All peoples on Thy mercy call. *(Refrain)*

O come, Desire of nations, bind
In one the hearts of all mankind;
Bid Thou our sad divisions cease,
And be Thyself our King of Peace. *(Refrain)*

Paschal Hymns

During Paschaltide, from the Vigil of the Resurrection to Ascension, some of the Paschal Hymns may be sung. These are found in the Vigil of the Resurrection. These include "**The Hymn of the Candle;**" "**Fiery Creator of the Light giving Light**" which is *Antiphonary of Bangor* Hymn 9; and also the Byzantine Hymn in many languages and settings; "**Christ is Risen from the dead**, trampling on death by death, and on those in the tombs bestowing life."

There are also special Paschal Salutations in many languages which mean, "**Christ is Risen! He is truly risen!**" These are all written in full in the Vigil of the Resurrection. Some notes about these Hymns are below.

The "**Song of the Three Youths**" from Daniel Chapter 3 is used at the office of Matins, but the entire chapter (verses 1-100) is used at the Vigil of the Resurrection, and it is written out in full in this book because many Bibles have cut verses. (We use the complete *Douay-Rheims* version.)

In the Vigil of the Resurrection, there is "**The Hymn of the Candle**," which is found within the Mass of Pascha.

Modern Roman musical setting:

Or, in the traditional Mode of Tone 6 for the Resurrection (Greek Hypolydian and Dorian modes):

Now let the Angelic host of the heavens rejoice: let the divine mysteries rejoice:
and for the victory of the great King   let the trumpet of salvation sound forth.
-

Let that of which is illumined,   by the great lightning flashes, be glad:
and enlightened and washed,   by the splendour of the eternal King,
-

let all the world sense,   that she hath cast away darkness.
Let our mother the Church rejoice, adorned with the lightening of the light:
-

and let this courtyard resound,   with great voices of peoples.
Wherefore, you who are standing here,   dearly beloved brethren,
-

in the wondrous clearness of this holy light,   join with me, I beseech you,
in calling upon the mercy,   of Almighty God.
-

That He who was pleased to graft us,   through the grace of His light, being poured,
may He admonish us,   unto the completing of the praise of this Candle.

Another version of the "Hymn of the Candle" is below:

The **Byzantine Hymn of the Candle Procession**, which is Tone 6 (Hypolydian mixed with Dorian modes in the correct Greek modes), Troparion for Ordinary Sundays in their eight week cycle, also used on the Vigil of the Resurrection. Notice the similarity to the Celtic and Roman Hymn of the Candle in the Vigil of the Resurrection, although this does not have all the verses of the Hymn of the Candle, and must be repeated several times in Byzantine procession at the Vigil of Pascha:

Angelic Powers did stand above Thy tomb,
And they that guarded were as dead, And
Mary stood at Thy grave searching for Thy precious body.
Thou didst conquer Hades, and was not tempted thereby.
Thou didst meet the Virgin and didst bestow life. O
Thou that art Risen from the dead, O Lord glory to Thee.

Another Hymn used at the Vigil of the Resurrection is "**Fiery Creator of the Light giving Light**," *Antiphonary of Bangor* Hymn 9. which is one of the Matins blessings of the candle of the Resurrection. The themes of light, fire, and the honeycomb are directly from the Vigil of the Resurrection. The Byzantine Rite "Phos hilarion" ("Joyful light") is a Vespers Hymn, referring more to the Creation rather than the Resurrection, and therefore it is possible that "Fiery Creator of the Light..." has other uses such as at Sunday Vespers, modern Saturday evening. Both "Phos hilarion" and "Fiery Creator of the Light giving Light" are very old, earlier than the first Ecumenical Council. Note that this very early Hymn refers to "cells" of the heart, filled with the Word.

Hymn AB 9, Fiery Creator of Fire

Fiery creator of fire,
Light and the bestower of light,
Life and the author of life,
Giver of Salvation and Salvation.

Indeed the vigil lamp set loose
the joys of this night,
O Thou Who dost not will that men die,
Set a light within our hearts.

To those leaving Egypt,
Thou gavest a two-fold Grace.
Thou sent forth a cover of cloud
Thou offered light by night.

As a pillar of cloud by day
Thou didst protect the traveling crowd.
As a pillar of fire at evening,
Thou dispelled the night with Light.

Out of the flame Thou challenged Thy Servant
Thou didst not reject the spiny bush,
and with the burning fire
Thou didst not consume what Thou illuminated.

Time, with a red destroying haze,
Having purged impurity
Through the fervent Holy Spirit:
Flesh is illumined like wax:

Thou stream of Divine sweet honey
having made the treasury of the honeycomb
Cleansing the inmost parts of the heart
Hast refilled the cells with the Word.

The swarm, like a newborn
having abandoned its burdens
tries, on wings of joy, to obtain
the Heaven preached by the mouth of the Spirit.

Glory to the Father Unbegotten
Glory to the Son Only-Begotten
Likewise to the Holy Spirit
Unto endless ages.   [Amen. Or repeat the first verse.]

Paschal Season salutations in a few languages:

Iar túaslucud anman, asréracht Íssu a brú thalman.	*[Old Irish]*
[Having loosed souls, Jesus has arisen from the womb of the earth.]	
Tá Críost éirithe! Go deimhin, tá sé éirithe!	*[Irish Gaelic]*
Tha Crìosd air èiridh! Gu dearbh, tha e air èiridh!	*[Scots' Gaelic]*
Atgyfododd Crist! Yn wir atgyfododd!	*[Cymru (Welsh)]*
Dassoret eo Krist! E wirionez dassoret eo!	*[Breton]*
Taw Creest Ereen! Taw Shay Ereen Guhdyne!	*[Manx]*
Asréracht Críst! Asréracht Hé-som co dearb!	*[Old Irish]*
Christ is Risen! He is Truly Risen!	*[English.]*
Christus surrexit! Vere surrexit!	*[Latin.]*
Christós aneste! Alithós aneste!	*[Greek.]*
Christ est Ressuscité! En Vérité, Il est Ressuscité!	*[French]*
Cristo ha resucitado. En verdad ha resucitado.	*[Spanish]*
Christo Ressuscitou! Em Verdade Ressuscitou!	*[Portugese]*
Christ ist auferstanden! Der ist wirklicht auferstanden!	*[German.]*
Christos voskresia! Voistinu voskresia!	*[Slavonic.]*
Al Masih qam! Haq am qam!	*[Arabic.]*

Orthodox Salutations at other times:

Christmas: **Christ is Born! Glorify Him!**
At any time: **Christ is among us! He is and ever shall be!**

Continuous Prayers:

[1 Thess. 5:17], "Pray without ceasing." Always remembering Christ: "This is the work of God, that you believe in Him whom He hath sent." [John 6:29]. "But other fell into good ground, and brought forth fruit, some an hundredfold, some sixtyfold, some thirtyfold." [Mt 13:8] St. Ignatius of Antioch: "And pray ye without ceasing in behalf of other men; for there is hope of the repentance, that they may attain to God." Jer. 8:4, "Thus saith the Lord: Shall not he that falleth, rise again? And he that is turned away; shall he not turn again?" The Pastor of Hermas, commandment IX, "Prayer must be made to God without ceasing and with unwavering confidence... Wherefore do not cease to make the request of your soul, and you will obtain it. But if you grow weary and waver in your request, blame yourself, and not Him who does not give to you. Consider this doubting state of mind, for it is wicked and senseless, and turns many away entirely from the faith, even though they be very strong."

Realize that only meditating on God, Who is the Cross and Center of our spiritual life, will bring any sort of virtue. Christ's salvation is explained in the Hours of Holy and Great Friday, especially the Third, Sixth, and Ninth Hours, where we contemplate God in truth and not mocked in the Third Hour, and participate in His saving Grace in the Sixth Hour, and in the full impact of the completion of His Work and the beginning of Resurrection in the Ninth Hour, the "greatest Hour of the Crucifixion." See also prayer under the Virtue of Intercession of Saints; and the discussion of the need for continuous prayer by Abbot Abraham in the XXIV Conference, on Mortification, Chapter 6, of St. John Cassian.

Deus in adjutorium:

This prayer is said continuously in the deserts of Scete, as found in the writings of St. John Cassian (fourth century), the beginning of Psalm 69, asking God to come to us, and also that we do not forget, hesitate, doubt or waver in our faith in God. This prayer helps us to be attentive to God, and begins all prayer. The desert fathers said it is the only prayer permitted in places of uncleanness, because this prayer should never cease.

"O God, come to my assistance; O Lord, make haste to help me."

The Jesus Prayer:

On Mt. Athos, a few sketes practice a recitation of the Jesus Prayer, thousands of times a day, using a set of 100 beads instead of the recitation of the Breviary. The initials of the early Greek word for fish (ichthus), is an abbreviation of this prayer (I. Ch. Th. U. S.), because Jesus, like a fish, was able to survive the waters of death.

Saying Jesus's Name is especially healing as it is a direct prayer to God: St. Mark 2:17, "They that are well have no need of a physician, but they that are sick. For I came not to call the just, but sinners." St. Luke 9:48-50 "...And John, answering, said: Master, we saw a certain man casting out devils in thy name, and we forbade him, because he followeth not with us. And Jesus said to him: Forbid him not; for he that is not against you, is for you." St. Matthew 10:41-42, "He that receiveth a prophet in the name of a prophet, shall receive the reward of a prophet: and he that receiveth a just man in the name of a just man, shall receive the reward of a just man. And whosoever shall give to drink to one of these little ones a cup of cold water only in the name of a disciple, amen I say to you, he shall not lose his reward." St. Matthew 12:21 "And in His name the Gentiles shall hope." St. Matthew 18:20 "For where there are two or three gathered together in my name, there am I in the midst of them." (The desert fathers who spoke to St. John Cassian said, the two or three gathered together may also be our minds, hearts, and and bodies, gathered in faith and synergy with God, not works alone.) Some repeat the Jesus Prayer through the day:

"Lord Jesus Christ God's Son, Savior, have mercy on me a sinner."

The Angelic Salutation to the Blessed Virgin Mary:

This was used as an early Byzantine prayer [from St. Luke 1:28 and 1:42. The Council of Ephesus in 431, refering to arguments of St. John Cassian, upheld the Greek term "Theotokos," in Latin "Deigenetrix," which means: "Birthgiver of God."]

The Rosary, also called by some "the Psalter" (or rather, *instead* of the Psalter which is the book of Psalms), a series of prayers based on the Angelic Salutation to the Blessed Virgin Mary ("Hail Mary"), was composed in the eighth or ninth century in Europe for those who did not have a Breviary. It used one hundred fifty repetitions of the "Hail Mary" prayer with meditations on the life of Christ and the Blessed Virgin Mary, a very short set of prayers. The Rosary was often practiced in America by Roman Catholic monastics, especially nuns, who were issued Missals but not Brevaries, and therefore the Rosary replaced the Office and Psalms in such an emergency. The Breviary with the 150 Psalms is the traditional prayer of the Christian Church. In the Passion Gospels, it states that after the Institution of the Last Supper, Christ and the Apostles sang a hymn before going to the Garden of Gethsemane, St. Mark 14:26; the Scriptural hymns are the Psalms or a few other Canticles. The 150 Psalms prophesy the life of Jesus Christ, the Apostles, and the Blessed Virgin Mary. The "God of the Old Testament" is the same God as the "God of the New Testament," and although the Dominicans who promoted the Rosary prayers were fighting a heresy which divided the one true God, they should not have agreed with the heretics to the extent of re-naming the Psalter and repudiating the Psalms. Byzantine and also Western European practice uses a Breviary. But, the use of the Angelic Hymn and the Rosary is a beautiful prayer that may be encouraged, not as a replacement, but in addition to other prayers. This prayer is often repeated through the night in Byzantine monastic practice.

This short prayer is also used in the Byzantine Rite continuously, especially at night:
"Hail! Mary, full of grace, the Lord is with thee, O Virgin Birthgiver of God: Blessed art thou among women, and blessed is the fruit of thy womb, for thou hast borne Jesus Christ, the Savior of our souls."

Later version with the ending from Europe from the 15th century:
"Hail! Mary full of grace, the Lord is with Thee. Blessed art thou among women, and blessed is he fruit of thy womb Jesus. Holy Mary, mother of God, pray for us sinners, now and at the hour of our death."

Occasional Prayers:
(Note that the Cross Vigil and Litanies are also occasional prayers.)

Prayer of St. Ephraim the Syrian (Prostrate after each sentence):
O Lord and Master of my life, take from me the spirit of sloth, despondency, ambition, and faint heartedness.

But rather bestow upon Thy servant a spirit of chastity, humility, patience and love.

Yea, O Lord and King, grant me to see my failings and not condemn my brother; for blessed art Thou unto the ages of ages. Amen.

Hymn to Christ by St. Clement of Alexandria

Bridle of untamed colts, Wing of unwandering birds, sure Helm of babes, Shepherd of royal lambs, assemble Thy simple children to praise holily, to hymn guilelessly with innocent mouths, Christ the guide of children. O King of saints, all-subduing Word of the most high Father, Ruler of wisdom, Support of sorrows, that rejoicest in the ages, Jesus, Saviour of the human race, Shepherd, Husbandman, Helm, Bridle, Heavenly Wing of the all-holy flock, Fisher of men who are saved, catching the chaste fishes with sweet life from the hateful wave of a sea of vices,-Guide [us], Shepherd of rational sheep; guide unharmed children, O holy King, O footsteps of Christ, O heavenly way, perennial Word, immeasurable Age, Eternal Light, Fount of mercy, performer of virtue; noble [is the] life of those who hymn God, O Christ Jesus, heavenly milk of the sweet breasts of the graces of the Bride, pressed out of Thy wisdom. Babes nourished with tender mouths, filled with the dewy spirit of the rational pap, let us sing together simple praises, true hymns to Christ [our] King, holy fee for the teaching of life; let us sing in simplicity the powerful Child. O choir of peace, the Christ-begotten, O chaste people, let us sing together the God of peace.

There are many other prayers and Hymns available; but not enough space for all.

Before and after meals when alone:
+ O God come to my assistance, O Lord make haste to help me.
Glory to the Father, and to the Son, and to the Holy Spirit, now and ever and unto ages and ages. Amen.

The Lord's Prayer ("Pater Noster" or "Our Father") may be done:
Our Father, Who art in the Heavens, hallowed be Thy Name. Thy Kingdom come. Thy will be done on earth as it is in Heaven. Give us this day our daily bread and forgive us our debts as we forgive our debtors and lead us not into temptation but deliver us from evil. Amen.
and:
Let those who hunger eat and be satisfied, and let them praise the Lord who seek Him. May their hearts live unto the age of the age. Taste and see how sweet the Lord is. Blessed is the man who hopes in Him. Fear the Lord, all ye His saints, for there is no emptiness in the fear of Him. The eyes of all hope in Thee, O Lord, and Thou givest them their food in due season. Thou openest Thy hand and satisfiest all living creatures with blessing. Let all Thy gifts which are from Thy bounty be blessed to us, O Lord, which we will receive, through Christ our Lord, Who reignest with the Father and the Holy Spirit unto ages of ages. Amen.

OR *[From a Roman prayerbook:]*
Bless us, O Lord, and these Thy gifts, which we are about to receive from Thy bounty. Through Christ our Lord. Amen.

(After meals: the Beatitudes, Magnificat, Hymn to St. Michael. See note at the "Twelfth Hour" concerning different times for meals in different places.)

To be said Before a meals in a Monastic Community:

[The teaching of Mael Rúain, a Céli Dé Rule, set out prayers before and after meals. These prayers are for a monastic community, but they may also be used at home. The Celtic Chrismation (Confirmation) anoints the right hand of every Christian so that they can bless themselves and bless their food.]

*A **bell** is sounded, usually the handle of a knife against a dish cover.*
*The **Pater Noster (Our Father)** is sung,*

Our Father, Who art in the Heavens, hallowed be Thy Name.
Thy Kingdom come. Thy will be done on earth as it is in Heaven.
Give us this day our daily bread
and forgive us our debts as we forgive our debtors
and lead us not into temptation but deliver us from evil. Amen.

Alleluia *is sung.*
   Then chanted:
Who giveth food to all flesh: for his mercy endureth for ever.
   Then chanted:
Let us confess to the God of heaven: for his mercy endureth for ever.

Then: **The Gloria. AB 116**
   Glory to God in the Highest, and on earth peace to men of good will. We praise Thee; we bless Thee; we worship Thee; we glorify Thee; we magnify Thee; we give thanks to Thee for Thy great mercy. O Lord heavenly King, God the Father Almighty; O Lord, the Only Begotten Son of God, Jesus Christ; O Holy Spirit of God, and all of us say, Amen. O Lord the Son of God the Father: Lamb of God Who takest away the sin of the world, have mercy upon us. Receive our prayer; Thou Who sittest at the right-hand of God the Father: Have mercy upon us, for Thou only art holy, Thou only art the Lord, Thou only art the Lord, Thou only art glorious; with the Holy Spirit in the glory of God the Father. [Amen.]

Collect (all may say together):
   Let those who hunger eat and be satisfied, and let them praise the Lord who seek Him. May their hearts live unto the age of the age. Taste and see how sweet the Lord is. Blessed is the man who hopes in Him. Fear the Lord, all ye His saints, for there is no emptiness in the fear of Him. The eyes of all hope in Thee, O Lord, and Thou givest them their food in due season. Thou openest Thy hand and satisfiest all living creatures with blessing. Let all Thy gifts which are from Thy bounty be blessed to us, O Lord, which we will receive, through Christ our Lord, Who reignest with the Father and the Holy Spirit unto ages of ages.
R. Amen. *[All say:]* Bid Lord, a blessing.

   Abbot or Abbess, (or Senior), the blessing:
May the King of eternal glory make us participants of the eternal banquet. May the Lord bless all this. **R.** Amen.

   *Then the **Pater Noster (Our Father)** is sung again.*

   The Senior [S] who is present, or presiding monk, would say:
Next? [Immanaire] *His Junior [J] would respond:* Leave is given.
S: Amen.

J: Next? **S**: Bless. **J**: God be with you. **S**: Amen.

J: Next? **S**: Leave is given. **J**: Bless. **S**: God be with you. **J**: Amen.

*All this time, no one present would speak except the two. The Senior would break the bread, dividing it into small pieces, and a piece was placed in the palm of each person. They said the **Our Father** before eating it. This is the first thing they would eat after taking their seats. Then they would [stand and] bless the drink. Another knell was struck, then they said,*
Let all Thy works, O Lord, praise Thee: and let Thy Saints bless Thee.

Collect (all may say together):
Let those who hunger eat and be satisfied, and let them praise the Lord who seek Him. May their hearts live unto the age of the age. Taste and see how sweet the Lord is. Blessed is the man who hopes in Him. Fear the Lord, all ye His saints, for there is no emptiness in the fear of Him. The eyes of all hope in Thee, O Lord, and Thou givest them their food in due season. Thou openest Thy hand and satisfiest all living creatures with blessing. Let all Thy gifts which are from Thy bounty be blessed to us, O Lord, which we will receive, through Christ our Lord, Who reignest with the Father and the Holy Spirit unto ages of ages.
R. Amen. Bid Lord, a blessing.

Abbot or Abbess, (or Senior), the blessing:
May the King of eternal glory make us participants of the eternal banquet. May the Lord bless all this. **R.** Amen.

During the meal, a lector would read one Gospel per season: In spring: St. Matthew; in summer: St. Mark; in autumn: St. Luke; in winter: St. John. It is possible that they heard one chapter from the Gospel per night before beginning to eat, and then sat. Also read Life of the Saints, or Rules, i.e.: St. John Cassian on the Eight Principal Faults.

Psalm 68   *[Starting at Verse 14; may be said before meals.]*
14. But as for me, my prayer is to Thee, O Lord; for the time of Thy good pleasure, O God. In the multitude of Thy mercy hear me, in the truth of Thy salvation.
15. Draw me out of the mire, that I may not stick fast: deliver me from them that hate me, and out of the deep waters.
16. Let not the tempest of water drown me, nor the deep swallow me up: and let not the pit shut her mouth upon me.
17. Hear me, O Lord, for Thy mercy is kind; look upon me according to the multitude of Thy tender mercies.
18. And turn not away Thy Face from Thy servant: for I am in trouble, hear me speedily.
19. Attend to my soul, and deliver it: save me because of my enemies.
20. Thou knowest my reproach, and my confusion, and my shame.
21. In Thy sight are all they that afflict me; my heart hath expected reproach and misery. And I looked for one that would grieve together with me, but there was none: and for one that would comfort me, and I found none.
22. And they gave me gall for my food, and in my thirst they gave me vinegar to drink.
23. Let their table become as a snare before them, and a recompense, and a stumbling block.
24. Let their eyes be darkened that they see not; and their back bend Thou down always.
25. Pour out Thy indignation upon them: and let Thy wrathful anger take hold of them.
26. Let their habitation be made desolate: and let there be none to dwell in their tabernacles.
27. Because they have persecuted him whom Thou hast smitten; and they have added to the grief of my wounds.
28. Add Thou iniquity upon their iniquity: and let them not come into Thy justice.
29. Let them be blotted out of the book of the living; and with the just let them not be written.
30. But I am poor and sorrowful: Thy salvation, O God, hath set me up.
31. I will praise the Name of God with a canticle: and I will magnify Him with praise.
32. And it shall please God better than a young calf, that bringeth forth horns and hoofs.
33. Let the poor see and rejoice: seek ye God, and your soul shall live.

34. For the Lord hath heard the poor: and hath not despised His prisoners.
35. Let the heavens and the earth praise Him; the sea, and every thing that creepeth therein.
36. For God will save Sion, and the cities of Juda shall be built up. And they shall dwell there, and acquire it by inheritance.
37. And the seed of His servants shall possess it; and they that love his Name shall dwell therein.

After Meals in a Community:

Do the Beatitudes, Magnificat, and Hymn to St. Michael (see above).

Hours of Prayer Day and Night

Please see the notes on the Breviary for directions in saying the Hours.

Daylight Psalms of St. Brendan of Clonfert:

The Liturgical Day starts at Vespers, so that Sunday begins on modern Saturday evening at sundown (from Genesis 1:5, "...And there was evening and morning one day."). Although Vespers starts the day, it is considered to be the end of the Daytime Hours, although it is counted among the Hours of what we would call the "next" day. The "day-time" hours are the Second Hour (around 7:00 A.M.), Third Hour (around 9:00 A.M.), Sixth Hour (Noon), Ninth Hour (around 3:00 P.M.), and Vespers (around 6:00 P.M.)

The "night-time" Hours are the Beginning of Night around 9:00 P.M., earlier or later, when fully dark, even in summer. In Latin this is called "Compline" or "after dinner," but in the Irish and the early desert monasteries in Alexandria, Jerusalem, Greece, and Mt. Athos, the dinner is at the Ninth Hour (around 3:00 P.M.), and therefore the Irish call the Hour after Vespers the Beginning of Night instead. The other night Hours are Midnight (in the middle of the night), and Matins (the "All Night Vigil" between midnight and dawn, the Hour of the Resurrection).

The daytime Psalms are three per Hour, and are fixed, but the night time Psalms are variable, much more numerous, and are sung as a "Vigil" or "watch," for the Lord Who comes "as a thief in the night" and rose from the dead at night. The Navigatio of St. Brendan, which describes his exploration of America before 583, states the order of the Psalms during the daylight Hours. On some of the islands he passed, the birds were singing the Psalms for the time of day, and he lists what Psalms they sang (and said that the birds sang the correct melodies), thereby giving us the order of Psalms as practiced at that time. Other Celtic sources do not list the daytime Psalm numbers or titles. The Daylight Psalms (Douay or Greek numbering), from the *Navigatio* of St. Brendan of Clonfert, are: Second Hour: 50, 62, 89; Third Hour: 46, 53, 114; Sixth Hour: 66, 69, 115; Ninth Hour: 129, 132, 147; Vespers: 64, 103, 112. Although the daytime Psalms are fixed, Collects and Prayers are variable (see notes on the Breviary).

Daytime Psalms in Hebrew or King James Version (but different wording): Second Hour: 51, 63, 90; Third Hour: 47, 54, 116 verses 1-9; Sixth Hour: 67, 70, 116 verses 10-19; Ninth Hour: 130, 133, 147 verses 12 - 20; Vespers: 65, 104, 113.

Vespers, Daily Prayer

(Approximately 6 p.m., at sunset, beginning the *[next]* day.)

[V. ✠ O God come to my assistance. R.: O Lord make haste to help me.

V. Glory be to the Father, and to the Son, and to the Holy Spirit, as it was in the beginning, is now, and ever unto ages of ages. R. Amen.]

Antiphon: A hymn, O God, becometh Thee in Sion: and a vow shall be paid to Thee in Jerusalem. (Ps: 64,2)

Psalm 64

2. A hymn, O God, becometh Thee in Sion: and a vow shall be paid to Thee in Jerusalem.
3. O hear my prayer: all flesh shall come to Thee.
4. The words of the wicked have prevailed over us: and Thou wilt pardon our transgressions.
5. Blessed is he whom Thou hast chosen and taken to Thee: he shall dwell in Thy courts. We shall be filled with the good things of Thy house: holy is Thy temple,
6. wonderful in justice. Hear us, O God our Saviour, Who art the hope of all the ends of the earth, and in the sea afar off.
7. Thou Who preparest the mountains by Thy strength, being girded with power:
8. Who troublest the depth of the sea, the noise of its waves. The Gentiles shall be troubled,
9. And they that dwell in the uttermost borders shall be afraid at Thy signs: Thou shalt make the outgoings of the morning and of the evening to be joyful.
10. Thou hast visited the earth, and hast plentifully watered it: Thou hast many ways enriched it. The river of God is filled with water: Thou hast prepared their food: for so is its preparation.
11. Fill up plentifully the streams thereof; multiply its fruits: it shall spring up and rejoice in its showers.
12. Thou shalt bless the crown of the year of Thy goodness: and Thy fields shall be filled with plenty.
13. The beautiful places of the wilderness shall grow fat: and the hills shall be girded about with joy,
14. The rams of the flock are clothed; and the vales shall abound with corn: they shall shout; yea, they shall sing a hymn.

Antiphon: A hymn, O God, becometh Thee in Sion: and a vow shall be paid to Thee in Jerusalem. (Ps: 64,2)

Psalm 103

1. Bless the Lord, O my soul: O Lord my God, Thou art exceedingly great. Thou hast put on praise and beauty:
2. And art clothed with light as with a garment. Who stretchest out the heaven like a pavilion:
3. Who coverest the higher rooms thereof with water. Who makest the clouds Thy chariot: Who walkest upon the wings of the winds.
4. Who makest Thy angels spirits: and Thy ministers a burning fire.
5. Who hast founded the earth upon its own bases: it shall not be moved for ever and ever.
6. The deep like a garment is its clothing: above the mountains shall the waters stand.
7. At Thy rebuke they shall flee: at the voice of Thy thunder they shall fear.
8. The mountains ascend: and the plains descend into the place which Thou hast founded for them.
9. Thou hast set a bound which they shall not pass over: neither shall they return to cover the earth.
10. Thou sendest forth springs in the vales: between the midst of the hills the waters shall pass.
11. All the beasts of the field shall drink: the wild asses shall expect in their thirst.
12. Over them the birds of the air shall dwell: from the midst of the rocks they shall give forth their voices.
13. Thou waterest the hills from Thy upper rooms: the earth shall be filled with the fruit of Thy works:
14. Bringing forth grass for cattle, and herb for the service of men. That Thou mayst bring bread out of the earth:

15. And that wine may cheer the heart of man. That he may make the face cheerful with oil: and that bread may strengthen man's heart.
16. The trees of the field shall be filled, and the cedars of Libanus which he hath planted:
17. There the sparrows shall make their nests. The highest of them is the house of the heron:
18. The high hills are a refuge for the harts: the rock for the hares.
19. He hath made the moon for seasons: the sun knoweth His going down.
20. Thou hast appointed darkness, and it is night: in it shall all the beasts of the woods go about:
21. The young lions roaring after their prey, and seeking their meat from God.
22. The sun ariseth, and they are gathered together: and they shall lie down in their dens.
23. Man shall go forth to his work: and to his labour until the evening.
24. How great are Thy works, O Lord! Thou hast made all things in wisdom: the earth is filled with Thy riches.
25. So is this great sea, which stretcheth wide its arms: there are creeping things without number, creatures little and great:
26. There the ships shall go. This sea-dragon which Thou hast formed to play therein:
27. All expect of Thee that Thou give them food in season.
28. What Thou givest to them they shall gather up: when Thou openest Thy hand, they shall all be filled with good.
29. But if Thou turnest away Thy Face, they shall be troubled: Thou shalt take away their breath, and they shall fail, and shall return to their dust.
30. Thou shalt send forth Thy spirit, and they shall be created: and Thou shalt renew the face of the earth.
31. May the glory of the Lord endure for ever: the Lord shall rejoice in His works.
32. He looketh upon the earth, and maketh it tremble: He troubleth the mountains, and they smoke.
33. I will sing to the Lord as long as I live: I will sing praise to my God while I have my being.
34. Let my speech be acceptable to Him: but I will take delight in the Lord.
35. Let sinners be consumed out of the earth, and the unjust, so that they be no more: O my soul, bless Thou the Lord.

Antiphon: A hymn, O God, becometh Thee in Sion: and a vow shall be paid to Thee in Jerusalem. (Ps: 64,2)

Psalm 112

1. Praise the Lord, ye children: praise ye the Name of the Lord.
2. Blessed be the Name of the Lord: from henceforth now and for ever.
3. From the rising of the sun unto the going down of the same, the Name of the Lord is worthy of praise.
4. The Lord is high above all nations: and His glory above the heavens.
5. Who is as the Lord our God, Who dwelleth on high,
6. And looketh down on the low things in heaven and in earth?
7. Raising up the needy from the earth: and lifting up the poor out of the dunghill:
8. That he may place him with princes; with the princes of His people.
9. Who maketh a barren woman to dwell in a house; the joyful mother of children.

Antiphon: A hymn, O God, becometh Thee in Sion: and a vow shall be paid to Thee in Jerusalem. (Ps: 64,2)

Gloria (with Antiphons) AB 116

(1) Glory to God in the Highest, and on earth peace to men of good will. We praise Thee; we bless Thee; we worship Thee; we glorify Thee; we magnify Thee;
(2) we give thanks to Thee for Thy great mercy.
(3) O Lord heavenly King, God the Father Almighty; O Lord, the Only Begotten Son of God, Jesus Christ; O Holy Spirit of God, and all of us say, Amen.
(4) O Lord the Son of God the Father: Lamb of God Who takest away the sin of the world, have mercy upon us.
(5) Receive our prayer; Thou Who sittest at the right-hand of God the Father:
(6) Have mercy upon us,
(7) for Thou only art holy,
(8) Thou only art the Lord,
(9) Thou only art the Lord,
(10) Thou only art glorious;
(11) with the Holy Spirit
(12) in the glory of God the Father.

Antiphon 1: Every day will we bless Thee, and we will praise Thy Name forever and unto ages of ages.
Antiphon 2: Be pleased, O Lord to keep us sinless today.
Antiphon 3: Blessed art Thou, O Lord, God of our Fathers, and may Thy Name be laudable and glorious unto the ages. Amen.
Antiphon 4: Have mercy on us, O Lord, have mercy on us.
Antiphon 5: Give ear, O Lord, to my words, understand my cry. Hearken to the voice of my prayer, O My King and my God. (Ps. 5:2-3)
Antiphon 6: And in the morning hear my voice.
Antiphon 7: In the morning shall my prayer come before Thee, O Lord.
Antiphon 8: Throughout days and nights, hours and moments, have mercy upon us, O Lord.
Antiphon 9: By the prayers and examples of the Saints, have mercy upon us, O Lord.
Antiphon 10: By the prayers and examples of the Angels, Archangels, Patriarchs, and Prophets, have mercy upon us, O Lord.
Antiphon 11: By the prayers and examples of the Apostles, Martyrs and Confessors, have mercy upon us, O Lord.
Antiphon 12: Glory and honor to the Father and to the Son and to the Holy Spirit, now and ever, and unto ages of ages. Amen.

> *[**Sunday** (modern Saturday evening) only: in honor of the Resurrection, it is possible to do the Hymn AB 9 "**Fiery creator of fire, Light and the bestower of light, Life and the author of life, Giver of Salvation and Salvation...**" This Hymn venerates the lighting of the Paschal Candle, and is therefore about Resurrection, more than a commemoration of Creation and the lighting of the lamps of evening.]*

Collects

AB 21 Daily Collect (for any season): O Lord we call upon Thee at this time of Evening: Grant our prayers; deny our sins: Who reignest unto the ages. Amen.

AB 31 Evening Before a Liturgy Collect: May our Evening prayer ascend to the ears of Thy divine Majesty and may Thy Blessing descend upon us, O Lord, for we have hoped in Thee: Who reignest unto the ages. Amen.

The Prayers of the *Community of the Brethren*, long or short form are said. These are written out at the end of the Psalter. Also Credo and Our Father.

Beginning of Night

("when fully dark") **Notes on the Beginning of Night**

Gospels, Acts, variable Readings at night, Psalm Readings

First, read the group of twelve or thirteen Psalms for the Beginning of Night. The Psalms are in the Psalter; see the table below, and the more extensive notes on the Breviary.

Then, according to the Rule of Tallaght: The Gospel according to Saint John is read one week and the Book of Acts is read the next. [Read the first four Chapters of Acts on the Saturday afternoon before Pascha, and the first three Chapters of the Gospel of St. John on the Sunday, modern Saturday night, of St. Thomas Sunday.] Verses of the Book of Acts are read at the Vigil of the Resurrection, and Acts is read Holy Saturday in the Byzantine Rite.

St. Mael Ruain said, in a Rule of Tallaght that, **"It is an old custom to say or read a portion for each night for a week from the Gospel of St. John, and a portion for each night for another week from the Book of Acts. It is not our custom to decrease this amount. We prohibit anything to the contrary."** Although Lent does not have Matins Gospel readings, in Lent the cycle of the Gospel of St. John and the Book of Acts continues during the Hour of the Beginning of Night in the Rule of Tallaght. These readings are never changed, except the Gospel of St. John in Holy Week, towards the end of Holy Week, doing the skipped readings before Holy Thursday earlier in the week in the evening services following Palm Sunday. The Irish Christians considered themselves the Church of St. John the Apostle, and all the Apostles, and they understood that the Lord is always with us, and the Resurrection is always with us. To be practical, because the Beginning of Night readings are always done, it is required that at times a lay-person, monk or nun, or person blessed by a Priest may also read the Gospel of St. John. However, during a Mass (a Divine Liturgy), no person with less rank than Deacon may read a Gospel.

Beginning of Night, Daily Prayer

[**V.** ✠ O God come to my assistance. **R.:** O Lord make haste to help me.

V. Glory be to the Father, and to the Son, and to the Holy Spirit, as it was in the beginning, is now, and ever unto ages of ages. **R.** Amen.]

The Reading of the Psalms According to St. Mael Ruain
This antiphon preceding only the first Psalm at an Hour is recorded in the Navigatio.

Antiphon: We have acted wrongfully, we have done iniquity. Thou O Lord, Who are our faithful Father, spare us. In peace in the selfsame I will sleep, and I will rest: For Thou, O Lord, singularly hast settled me in hope.

[Paraphrase of Psalm 102:12-13, and Psalm 105:6, 7-8; Psalm 4:9-10]

Greek, Latin, and Douay numbering:	Beginning of Night	Midnight
[night before] **Sunday** (modern Saturday night.)	1-13	14-25
[night before] **Monday** (modern Sunday night.)	26-37	38-50
[night before] **Tuesday** (modern Monday night.)	51-63	64-75
[night before] **Wednesday** (modern Tues. night.)	76-87	88-100
[night before] **Thursday** (modern Wed. night)	101-112	113-124
[night before] **Friday** (modern Thursday night)	125-137	138-150

This Cycle ends Friday Midnight according to St. Mael Rúain's rule. The Cross Vigil may be done [night before] Saturday (modern Friday night).

After each group of 12 or 13 Psalms for the Hour, GENUFLECT, then say the *"Our Father."* *Psalm pages in this book for the Beginning of Night:*

Our Father, Who art in the Heavens, hallowed be Thy Name. Thy Kingdom come. Thy will be done on earth as it is in Heaven. Give us this day our daily bread and forgive us our debts as we forgive our debtors and lead us not into temptation but deliver us from evil. Amen.

Antiphon (whispered after each Psalm, and after the "Our Father"):
O God come to my assistance. O Lord make haste to help me.

Gospel of St. John or Book of Acts Readings

The Gospel according to Saint John is read one week and the Book of Acts is read the next, beginning in Pre-Lent. These continue through Lent, although Lent does not have Matins Gospel readings.

On Weeks with Readings of The Gospel of St. John:

Quinquagesima Sunday and during the week, 2nd and 4th Sundays in Lent and during their weeks, Palm Sunday and Holy Week, 1st, 3rd, and 5th Sundays after Pascha and during their weeks (St. Thomas Sunday is the 1st Sunday after Pascha), Pentecost and its week, 2nd, 4th, 6th, 8th, 10th, 12th, 14th, 16th, 18th, 20th, 22nd, 24th Sundays after Pentecost and during their weeks (whenever the Season of Pentecost ends), then continue alternating weeks for the last week in Pentecost, weeks of Advent, Christmas, Epiphany and Throne of Peter.

ALL STAND FOR THE HOLY GOSPEL:

Vigil of Sunday (Saturday evening):   St. John, Chapters 1 through 3.
Vigil of Monday (Sunday evening):   St. John, Chapters 4 through 6.
Vigil of Tuesday (Monday evening):   St. John, Chapters 7 through 9.
Vigil of Wednesday (Tuesday evening): St. John, Chapters 10 through 12.
Vigil of Thursday (Weds. evening): St. John, Chapters 13 through 15.
Vigil of Friday (Thursday evening):   St. John, Chapters 16 through 18.
Vigil of Saturday (Friday evening):   St. John, Chapters 19 through 21.

On Weeks with Readings of the Book of Acts:

Sexagesima Sunday and during its week, 1st, 3rd, 5th Sundays and during their weeks in Lent, Vigil of Pascha (Holy Saturday afternoon in anticipation) and through the week of Pascha, 2nd, 4th Sundays after Pascha and during their weeks, Sunday after Ascension and during its week, First Sunday after Pentecost (All Saints) with its week, 3rd, 5th, 7th, 9th, 11th, 13th, 15th, 17th, 19th, 21st, 23rd etc. Sundays after Pentecost and during their weeks (whenever the Season of Pentecost ends), then continue alternating weeks for the last week in Pentecost, weeks of Advent, Christmas, Epiphany, and the Throne of Peter.

SITTING IS ALLOWED:

Vigil of Sunday (Saturday evening.):   Acts, Chapters 1 through 4.
Vigil of Monday (Sunday evening):   Acts, Chapters 5 through 8.
Vigil of Tuesday (Monday evening):   Acts, Chapters 9 through 12.
Vigil of Wednesday (Tuesday evening):   Acts, Chapters 13 through 16.
Vigil of Thursday (Wednesday evening): Acts, Chapters 17 through 20.
Vigil of Friday (Thursday evening):   Acts, Chapters 21 through 24.
Vigil of Saturday (Friday evening):   Acts, Chapters 25 through 28.

Collects

Daily Collect AB 22: We pass the time of night in Thy praises, O Christ: have pity on all who beseech Thee from the heart: Who reignest unto the ages. Amen.

Night before Liturgy Collect AB 32: O God, Who illumines the chaotic darkness of the nights, and brightens the thickness of gloom, we pray to Thee: preserve our hearts in the works of Thy statutes: Who reignest unto the ages. Amen.

Night before Liturgy Collect AB 33: We beseech Thy mercy throughout the times of day which have unfolded and the times of night which have overtaken them, O God, that filled with Divine thoughts we may be able to reject the works of darkness: Who reignest unto the ages. Amen.

Peace (said every Night) AB 34

Antiphon: We have acted unjustly, we have wrought iniquity. (Ps. 105:6b)
Collect: Thou hast redeemed, O Lord, us by Thy Holy Blood: now encourage us in all things, O Jesus Christ Who reignest unto the ages. Amen.
Antiphon: Abundant peace is for those who are attentive to Thy Law, O Lord and there is no scandal in them. (Ps. 118:165)
Collect: May Thy peace, O Lord, King of Heaven, always pervade our vitals, so that we may not fear the terror by night: Who reignest unto the ages. Amen.

[The Prayer for the Community of the Brethren is not designated for the Beginning of Night in the Antiphonary of Bangor, but continue with the Creed and the Our Father.]

Credo

Complete Creed from The Lorrha-Stowe Missal

I believe in one God, the Father Almighty, maker of heaven and earth and of all things visible and invisible. And in one Lord Jesus Christ, the Only-Begotten Son of God. Born of the Father before all ages. Light of light, true God of true God. Born, not made, of one Substance with the Father: through Whom all things were made. Who for us men, and for our Salvation descended from heaven. And was Incarnate of the Holy Spirit and the Virgin Mary: And was born man. And was crucified also for us: under Pontius Pilate; He suffered and was buried. And He rose on the third day, according to the Scriptures. And ascended into heaven: and sitteth at the right hand of God the Father. And He shall come again with glory to judge both the living and the dead: Whose Kingdom shall have no end. And I believe in the Holy Spirit, the Lord and Giver of life: Who proceedeth from the Father. Who with the Father and the Son together is worshiped and glorified: Who spake by the Prophets. And in one, Holy, Catholic, and Apostolic Church. I confess one Baptism for the remission of sins. And I look for the resurrection of the dead. + And the life of the world to come. Amen.

The Divine Prayer AB 36

Our Father, Who art in the Heavens, hallowed be Thy Name. Thy Kingdom come. Thy will be done on earth as it is in Heaven. Give us this day our daily bread and forgive us our debts as we forgive our debtors and lead us not into temptation but deliver us from evil. Amen.

Here Ends the Hour. There is no "Community of the Brethren" prayer. *May do Beatitudes, Magnificat, and Shrine of Piety.*

Midnight, Daily Prayer

V. ✠ O God come to my assistance. **R.:** O Lord make haste to help me.
V. Glory be to the Father, and to the Son, and to the Holy Spirit, as it was in the beginning, is now, and ever unto ages of ages. **R.** Amen.

12 - 13 Psalms

Psalms in Greek, Latin, or Douay numbering, for Midnight:
[night before] **Sunday** 14-25; [night before] **Monday** 38-50; [night before] **Tuesday** 64-75; [night before] **Wednesday** 88-100; [night before] **Thursday** 113-124; [night before] **Friday** 138-150. *(Cross Vigil night before Saturday, at Beginning of Night.)*

Antiphon *(same as at the Beginning of Night)*:
We have acted wrongfully, we have done iniquity. Thou O Lord, Who are our faithful Father, spare us. In peace in the selfsame I will sleep, and I will rest: For Thou, O Lord, singularly hast settled me in hope.

"O God come to my assistance, O Lord make haste to help me." *(Whispered after Psalms.)*
End the group with "Our Father." The Divine Prayer AB 36

Our Father, Who art in the Heavens, hallowed be Thy Name. Thy Kingdom come. Thy will be done on earth as it is in Heaven. Give us this day our daily bread and forgive us our debts as we forgive our debtors and lead us not into temptation but deliver us from evil. Amen.

Hymn of the Bridegroom AB 10

At the time of Midnight,
The prophetic Voice admonishes
us to ever sing praises to God
the Father and the Son

And also to the Holy Spirit.
The perfect Trinity and
one in Substance
is ever praised by us.

This hour holds terror
Thereon the destroying angel
brought death to Egypt
slaying the first-born.

This hour is healing to the Just
because the angel dared
not to punish where the
the Sign of Blood was formed.

Egypt mourned mightily
at the dreadful death of so many;
Israel alone rejoiced
protected by the blood of the Lamb.

We are the true Israel.
We rejoice in Thee, O Lord
rejecting the enemy and defended
from evil by the Blood of Christ.

At this time itself, comes to pass
what by voice of the Gospel is
believed: the Bridegroom comes:
the maker of the heavenly Kingdom.

Then Holy virgins hasten
to attend the arrival
bearing bright lamps
Rejoicing with great joy.

The foolish ones remain,
with their extinct lamps
Frustratedly pounding doors:
The Palace of the King being closed.

Therefore let us watch soberly,
bearing gleaming minds,
May we worthily hasten to
attend the arrival of Jesus.

And at the time of Midnight
both Paul and Silas, chained
in prison praising Christ,
were set free of bonds.

This world is a prison to us:
We praise Thee, O Christ God:
Break the chains of our sins:
In Thee, O Holy One is our Faith.

Make us worthy of glory,
Holy King of the Kingdom
that will be, that we may
acclaim Thee with eternal praises.

Glory to the Father Unbegotten
Glory to the Only Begotten
Likewise to the Holy Spirit
Unto endless ages. Amen.

Collects

Daily Collect AB 23:
O Jesus, mercifully visit those who pray at Midnight just as by Divine power the chains of Peter were severed: Who reignest unto the ages. Amen.

Night before Liturgy Collect AB 37:
Through the Hour of Midnight the Angels rejoiced at the Birth of our Lord Jesus Christ, likewise, we ought to rejoice in Thy Peace, O Almighty God: Who reignest unto the ages. Amen.

Fast day Collect AB 57:
Let a shout go out at Midnight that we may be found prepared for the Bridegroom: Who reigneth unto the ages. Amen.

Credo **Complete Creed from** The Lorrha-Stowe Missal

I believe in one God, the Father Almighty, maker of heaven and earth and of all things visible and invisible. And in one Lord Jesus Christ, the Only-Begotten Son of God. Born of the Father before all ages. Light of light, true God of true God. Born, not made, of one Substance with the Father: through Whom all things were made. Who for us men, and for our Salvation descended from heaven. And was Incarnate of the Holy Spirit and the Virgin Mary: And was born man. And was crucified also for us: under Pontius Pilate; He suffered and was buried. And He rose on the third day, according to the Scriptures. And ascended into heaven: and sitteth at the right hand of God the Father. And He shall come again with glory to judge both the living and the dead: Whose Kingdom shall have no end. And I believe in the Holy Spirit, the Lord and Giver of life: Who proceedeth from the Father. Who with the Father and the Son together is worshiped and glorified: Who spake by the Prophets. And in one, Holy, Catholic, and Apostolic Church. I confess one Baptism for the remission of sins. And I look for the resurrection of the dead. + And the life of the world to come. Amen.

The Divine Prayer AB 36

Our Father, Who art in the Heavens, hallowed be Thy Name. Thy Kingdom come. Thy will be done on earth as it is in Heaven. Give us this day our daily bread and forgive us our debts as we forgive our debtors and lead us not into temptation but deliver us from evil. Amen.

Here Ends the Hour *There are no "Community of the Brethren" prayers for Midnight in the Antiphonary of Bangor. May do Beatitudes, Magnificat, Shrine of Piety.*

Notes on Matins
(Approximately 3 a.m, or an All-Night Vigil after Midnight to dawn.)

The other Hours need little preparation, but for Matins it is necessary first to know whether there is a Sunday Divine Liturgy or special Feast in the morning, what season and day in the season it is, which week in Matins it is, what day of the week it is, before the prayers are started. Matins is long, but not difficult.

The Night before a Liturgy

Matins includes many parts that are specifically for preparation before a Sunday Divine Liturgy, since Sunday is the day of the Resurrection. For Sundays the First Canticle of Moses is sung. The Second Canticle of Moses and the Song of the Three Youths are sung on all days. Then there are Psalms of Praise and Collects of Praise, including the great Irish Trisagion. On Sundays a Gospel of the Resurrection is sung, the Te Deum (Sundays only), Gloria, Hymns of St. Hilarion and Procession to the Cross, and an Antiphon for the Martyrs. Finally ending Matins, the Shrine of Piety blesses all directions, similar in this to St. Patrick's prayer known as "The Deer's Cry." (It may also end other Hours.) If a Mass is to begin immediately (as in a monastery), the Shrine of Piety is followed by the Litany of the Saints of the Stowe-Lorrha Missal. (Russian monastic usage in the Byzantine Rite also bows to the four quarters at the start of the Divine Liturgy.) If there is to be an immediate Divine Liturgy in monastic usage, it is not necessary to do all the Hours of daylight, but the ending Hymns of the Hours such as the Beatitudes, Hymn to St. Michael, and the Magnificat are convenient to use as Communion Hymns after the Sancti Venite.

Collects in Matins

The sets of Collects found in Matins cover: Sundays (Easter, Sundays after Easter, Pentecost, Sundays after Pentecost after the Apostles' fast and before

Advent, and Sundays after Christmas before Lent), Daily at these seasons, Sundays in Lent (and fasting seasons), Daily in Lent (and fasting seasons), for a Vigil of a Feast of Jesus Christ, for a Vigil of a Feast of a Saint or for the Departed, and two sets of Collects which were appended to the Antiphonary from another source: for monastic tonsure and for exorcism.. During the Hours, the Gloria is only sung at Vespers and Matins. Do not read all the Collects every day, but only the Collects appropriate to the day. Some Collects are "before" Psalms, Canticles, or the Gospel, and some Collects are "after" Psalms, Canticles, or the Gospel. Just do the ones listed for a particular day; in practice these Collects help to focus on the day or season. For example; either do "Daily" Collects or "Night before a Liturgy" Collects, not both in one day.

For the Psalms of Matins see the notes on the Breviary concerning the Rule of St. Columbanus used in Irish monasteries such as Bangor, or instead, spreading the Rule of St. Mael Ruain to include Matins.

The cycle of Ten Weeks in the Antiphons and Gospels:

Matins Antiphons that say "Week I," etc. are in a cycle of ten weeks. Do not read all ten weeks every day. For example, in Week X, read the Antiphons for the Second Canticle of Moses and the Song of the Three Youths that say "Week X," but do not read the other Antiphons for other weeks. Since Sunday is considered the first day of the week, the Antiphons that would be for Week X are read on Sunday early morning in Matins, and every day at Matins during that week. Then on the next week, in Sunday Matins, begin the cycle again with Week I. The Matins Resurrection Gospel selection goes with the Antiphon readings. However, the Matins Resurrection Gospel (or other reading) is usually only read in Sunday Matins, not during the week. (In Lent, however, there is a different Old Testament reading for every day of the week.) On days without the Matins Gospel or other reading, the correct week's Antiphons for the Canticle of Moses and Song of the Three Youths are sung.

There are seasons when the Matins Gospel is not done, but is replaced by another reading. Old Testament readings for Matins in Lent are listed in the Lectionary. During Paschaltide through the day of Pentecost, the Gospel of the Mass of the day is read at Matins instead of the Matins Gospel cycle. On Holy and Great Friday, there are no Psalms or Glorias, and there are both Old Testament and Gospel readings for every Hour following an Irish Harmony of the Gospels, written out in this book. During the rest of the year, there are ten Matins Resurrection Gospels. One of these is read every Sunday and on specific days. (Remember, Sunday begins at modern Saturday evening at Vespers.) On Feast days which are not observed by a Divine Liturgy (a Minor Feast day, if daily Masses are not being observed), or on days when the Irish Pre-Sanctified Matins service is done, the Gospel of the Mass of the Feast day is read. On weekdays there is not a Matins Resurrection Gospel unless it is a major Feast or titular.

The Matins Gospels cycle is on the movable calendar. The cycle of Matins Gospels begins at the same time as the Byzantine Matins Gospels: one week after Pentecost. However, since the Antiphons for Second Canticle of Moses and the Song of the Three Youths still continue during Lent, the weeks are listed starting in Pre-Lent, not for the Gospel readings, but for the Antiphons. For example, Pentecost uses Week X in Matins, concerning the instruction to "Feed my sheep," although it uses the Gospel of Pentecost in place of the Matins Resurrection Gospel. (Using Roman Numerals for the ten weeks: I, II, III, IV, V, VI, VII, VIII, IX, X):

V Sexagesima, VI Quinquagesima, VII 1st Lent, VIII 2nd Lent, IX 3rd Lent, X 4th Lent, I 5th Lent, II Palm Sunday (6th Sunday in Lent), III Pascha, IV (St. Thomas Sunday is the 1st Sunday after Pascha), V 2nd Pascha, VI 3rd Pascha, VII 4Th Pascha, and VIII 5th Sunday after Pascha, IX Sunday after Ascension, X Pentecost, I First Sunday after Pentecost (All Saints), II 2nd, III 3rd, IV 4th, V 5th, VI 6th, VII 7th, VIII 8th, IX 9th, X 10th, I 11th, II 12th, III 13th, IV14th, V 15th, VI 16th,

VII 17th, VIII 18th, IX 19th, X 20th, I 21st, II 22nd, III 23rd, IV 24th Sundays after Pentecost (whenever the Season of Pentecost ends), then continue in the weeks for the last week in Pentecost, weeks of Advent, Christmas, Epiphany and Throne of Peter. The reason that Pre-Lent starts on Week V is so that the Sunday after Pentecost is week I, and also to show some passage of time, although the time is different every year, between Christmas-Epiphany and Pre-Lent. Unless deciding on the 25th and last Sunday after Pentecost always being Week V, otherwise it is necessary every year to arrange an Advent-Christmas-Epiphany-Throne of Peter calendar for the Matins Gospels.

The Matins Resurrection Gospels resemble the Byzantine Matins Gospels, except that there are ten, not eleven. The arrangement below has been checked against the content of the Matins Antiphons of the Canticles of Moses and the Song of the Three Youths. They also are in the order of the Ten Commandments. (Unlike the daylight Psalms which were recorded by St. Brendan of Clonfert in the *Navigatio*, these Gospels are referred to as the "ten Resurrection Gospels of Matins," but the order and verse numbers is not given. There is a variant order of Matins Gospels from the first week in Paschaltide with one from Mid-Pascha. See the Resurrection Gospels toward the back of this volume page 352.)

(List of Gospels in first edition:)
Week I St. John 20:1-18.
Week II St. Luke 24:1-12.
Week III St. Mark 16:9-20.
Week IV St. Luke 24:12-35.
Week V St. Matthew 28:1-10.
Week VI St. Mark 16:1-8.
Week VII St. Luke 24:36-53.
Week VIII St. John 20:19-31.
Week IX St. Matthew 28:11-20.
Week X St. John 21:1 to end.

(Variant: Gospels from Paschaltide:)
Week I Matthew 28:1-20
Week II Luke 24:1-12 , [13-35]
Week III Mark 15:47-16:11
Week IV Mark 16:12-20
Week V John 11:1-45
Week VI John 20:1-9
Week VII John 20:11-18
Week VIII John 21:1-14, [15-25]
Week IX John 20:19-31
Week X Luke 24:36-48

Matins, Daily Prayer
The All-Night Vigil, after Midnight, before Dawn

[V. ✠ O God come to my assistance. R.: O Lord make haste to help me.
V. Glory be to the Father, and to the Son, and to the Holy Spirit, as it was in the beginning, is now, and ever unto ages of ages. R. Amen.]

Psalms

These vary with the day and season in the Rule of Columbanus:
(See notes on the Breviary (p. 345, 346, 349); tables for this Rule have not been included in this edition. If a monastery or home is not able to do all these Psalms, the Psalms in the Hours of Beginning of Night and Midnight may be combined with Matins to supply the Psalms, completing the Psalter within a week.)

Columbanus's Rule: On Holy nights before dawn of Saturdays and Sundays:
November 1 through January 31----- 75 Psalms
February 1 through April 30--------- decrease 3 Psalms per week until 36
May 1 through June 24 --------------- 36 Psalms
June 25 through October 31: add 3 Psalms per week until back to 75

Columbanus's Rule On nights before dawn of other days:
September 25 through March 24 ---- 36 Psalms
March 25 through September 24----- 24 Psalms

Antiphon said before each Psalm:
Praise ye the Lord All His Angels: Praise ye Him, all His Hosts.

[Psalm 148:2, paraphrase, from the Navigatio.]

Collects

*[Remember: **only** do the prayers for a particular day, whether the prayers appear before or after a Canticle. "Daily" means days other than Sundays, Saturdays, fast days, etc.]*

Daily Collect AB 24
O God, give aid to those who praise Thee, Holy Three, and confess Thee One, by holy songs: Who reignest unto the ages. Amen.

Daily AB 25
Collect: At cock-crow, we beseech Thee with resounding song, O Christ, as by the tearful cries of Peter. Answer our prayer: Who reignest unto the ages. Amen.

Daily AB 26
Collect: O God, Who hast banished darkness and bestowed light to the day: pour out the True Light which is coming upon Thy Servants: Who reignest unto the ages. Amen.

Morning of Liturgy AB 38
Collect: Thou art, O Lord, the Illuminator of the darkness, Creator of the elements, Remitter of sins. Thy great mercy, O Lord, is upon those who seek Thee with their whole heart. May Thy Majesty, O Lord, hear us in the Morning, and forgive our offenses which are not hidden from Thee: Who reignest unto the ages. Amen.

Morning of Liturgy Collect AB 39:
Thou art hope and Salvation; Thou art life and strength; Thou art a helper in tribulation. Thou art the defender of our souls, O God of Israel, in all things: Who reignest unto the ages. Amen.

Fast Days Collect AB 58:
O God, our God, we ought to watch for Thee from dawn: raise up our souls from deepest slumber, and free them from stupor, so that we may be goaded in our beds, and be worthy to be mindful of Thee: Who reignest unto the ages. Amen.

Fast Days Collect AB 59:
Thou art hope and Salvation; Thou art life and strength; Thou art a helper in tribulation. Thou art the defender of our souls, O God of Israel, in all things: Who reignest unto the ages. Amen.

Fast Days Collect AB 60:
We beseech Thee from the depth of our hearts, O Thou Who dwellest in the heights, and in heaven hast regard unto humility, and in earth, in sea, and in all the abysses, that Thou strengthen our hands unto battle and our fingers unto war, that in the morning we may be able to destroy all the sinners in our land and we may be worthy to be Thy completed Holy Temple, O Christ: Who reignest unto the ages. Amen.

Collects before the Canticles of Moses

Daily Collect AB 68:
O God, Who absolved Thy people from the daily yoke of Egyptian servitude, and when the enemy had been thoroughly beaten, led Thy people through the spiritual washing into the Promised Land; give us victory over the assaults of corrupters, and lead us from our conquered darknesses into the Sanctuary, the inheritance which Thy hands have made, O Savior of the world, Who with the Eternal Father and the Holy Spirit, reigneth unto the ages. Amen.

Collect for Feasts of our Lord AB 71:

O God, Who beat down impious Egypt with ten plagues, and by the parting of the sea granted level ground to the people, we beseech Thee hear our prayers and save us in that same manner, O Savior of the world: Who reignest unto the ages. Amen.

Collect for Monastic Vows and Tonsure AB 91:

We chant to Thee, O lord of Hosts, praying that just as Thou didst redeem Thy Chosen People from the yoke of the most cruel captivity, showed them the way by means of a column of smoke throughout the day and similarly the same of fire throughout the night: the sea being split into separate parts to the right and to the left: stopped in its course, the water, was solidified into separated heaps: Thy people navigated the sea on solid grounds: O Marvelous thing! Neither horse nor ship was able to follow their course. Mary beat the drum, this hymn was sung, the herd of sheep watched. In this manner, free us from the pursuit of the old enemy, and from all the dangers of this world, O Savior of the world: Who liveth, guideth and reigneth with the eternal Father, at one with the eternal Holy Spirit unto ages of ages. Amen.

Collect when Exorcism is performed AB 94:

O Lord, Who protected the fleeing two sixes of the Tribes from the Pharaoh, Cinchrim, during their hardships on that difficult route, first by driving back the floods into two towering mountains on both sides, as dry, looming walls and dry land, and then producing water from the rock: we beseech Thee, that just as at the prayer of those pious ones, let the charioteers which are the conversation and activity of the eternal enemy sink down and be swallowed up with the quick wit of Pharaoh, O King, Who saved the True Israel from that flood so that she might sing hymns to Christ throughout the ages: Who liveth and reigneth with the Father and the Holy Spirit throughout ages of ages. Amen.

On Sundays of Advent and the Feasts of the Circumcision and Epiphany:
The First Canticle of Moses AB 1
Deuteronomy 32:1-43

Hear, O ye heavens, the things I speak: let the earth give ear to the words of my mouth.
Let my doctrine gather as the rain, let my speech distill as the dew: as a shower upon the herb, and as drops upon the grass:
Because I will invoke the Name of the Lord: give ye magnificence to our God.
The works of God are perfect, and all His ways are judgments:

Hear, O ye heavens, the things I speak: let the earth give ear to the words of my mouth.

God is faithful and without any iniquity; he is just and right.
They have sinned against Him, and are none of His children in their filth: they are a wicked and perverse generation.
Is this the return thou makest to the Lord, O foolish and senseless people? Is not He thy Father, that hath possessed thee, and made thee, and created thee?

Hear, O ye heavens, the things I speak: let the earth give ear to the words of my mouth.

Remember the days of old: think upon every generation. Ask thy father, and he will declare to thee: thy elders and they will tell thee. Hear, O ye heavens, the things I speak: let the earth give ear to the words of my mouth.

Hear, O ye heavens, the things I speak: let the earth give ear to the words of my mouth.

When the Most High divided the nations, when He separated the sons of Adam: He appointed the bounds of people according to the number of the children of Israel.
But the Lord's portion is His people: Jacob the lot of His inheritance.
He found him in a desert land, and in a place of horror, and of vast wilderness. He led him about, and taught him: and he kept him as the apple of his eye.

Hear, O ye heavens, the things I speak: let the earth give ear to the words of my mouth.

As an eagle enticing her young to fly, and hovering over them, He spread His wings: and hath taken him and carried him on His shoulders.
Hear, O ye heavens, the things I speak: let the earth give ear to the words of my mouth.

The Lord alone was his leader: and there was no strange god with him.
He set him upon high land: that he might eat the fruits of the fields, that he might suck honey out of the rock, and oil out of the hardest stone,

Hear, O ye heavens, the things I speak: let the earth give ear to the words of my mouth.

Butter of the herd, and milk of the sheep with the fat of lambs, and of the rams of the breed of Basan. And goats with the marrow of wheat: and might drink the purest blood of the grape.

Hear, O ye heavens, the things I speak: let the earth give ear to the words of my mouth.

The beloved grew fat, and kicked: he grew fat, and thick and gross. He forsook God Who made him, and departed from God his Savior.
They provoked him by strange gods: and stirred Him up to anger, with their abominations.

Hear, O ye heavens, the things I speak: let the earth give ear to the words of my mouth.

They sacrificed to devils and not to God: to gods whom they knew not: that were newly come up, whom their fathers worshipped not.
Thou hast forsaken the God that begot thee: and hast forgotten the Lord that created thee.
The Lord saw, and was moved to wrath: because His own sons and daughters provoked Him.
And He said: I will hide my face from them, and will consider what their last end shall be.

Hear, O ye heavens, the things I speak: let the earth give ear to the words of my mouth.

For it is a perverse generation, and unfaithful children.
They have provoked me with that which was no god, and have angered me with their vanities. And I will provoke them with that which is no people and will vex them with a foolish nation.

Hear, O ye heavens, the things I speak: let the earth give ear to the words of my mouth.

A fire is kindled in my wrath, and shall burn even to the lowest hell: and shall devour the earth with her increase, and shall burn the foundations of the mountains.

Hear, O ye heavens, the things I speak: let the earth give ear to the words of my mouth.

I will heap evils upon them: and will spend mine arrows among them.
They shall be consumed with famine, and birds shall devour them with a most bitter bite.
I will send the teeth of beasts upon them, with the fury of creatures that trail upon the ground, and of serpents.

Hear, O ye heavens, the things I speak: let the earth give ear to the words of my mouth.

Without, the sword shall lay them waste, and terror within: both the young man and the virgin, the suckling child with the man in years.

Hear, O ye heavens, the things I speak: let the earth give ear to the words of my mouth.

I said: Where are they? I will make the memory of them to cease from among men. But for the wrath of the enemies I have deferred it: lest perhaps their enemies might be proud and should say: Our mighty hand, and not the Lord, hath done all these things.

Hear, O ye heavens, the things I speak: let the earth give ear to the words of my mouth.

They are a nation without counsel, and without wisdom.
O that they would be wise and would understood, and would provide for their last end! How should one pursue after a thousand, and two chase ten thousand?

Hear, O ye heavens, the things I speak: let the earth give ear to the words of my mouth.

Was it not, because their God had sold them, and the Lord had shut them up?
For our God is not as their gods: our enemies themselves are judges.

Hear, O ye heavens, the things I speak: let the earth give ear to the words of my mouth.

Their vines are of the vineyard of Sodom, and of the suburbs of Gomorrah: their grapes are grapes of gall, and their clusters most bitter.
Their wine is the gall of dragons, and the venom of asps, which is incurable.

Hear, O ye heavens, the things I speak: let the earth give ear to the words of my mouth.

Are not these things stored up with me, and sealed up in my treasures?
Revenge is mine, and I will repay them in due time, that their foot may slide.

Hear, O ye heavens, the things I speak: let the earth give ear to the words of my mouth.

The day of destruction is at hand, and the time makes haste to come.
The Lord will judge His people, and will have mercy on His servants.

Hear, O ye heavens, the things I speak: let the earth give ear to the words of my mouth.

He shall see that their hand is weakened, and that they who were shut up have also failed, and they that remained are consumed.
And He shall say: Where are their gods, in whom they trusted?

Hear, O ye heavens, the things I speak: let the earth give ear to the words of my mouth.

Of whose victims they ate the fat, and drank the wine of their drink-offerings. Let them arise and help you, and protect you in your distress.

Hear, O ye heavens, the things I speak: let the earth give ear to the words of my mouth.

See ye that I alone am, and there is no other God besides me: I will kill and I will make to live. I will strike, and I will heal; and there is none that can deliver out of my hand.

Hear, O ye heavens, the things I speak: let the earth give ear to the words of my mouth.

I will lift up my hand to heaven; and I will say: I live for ever.
If I shall whet my sword as the lightning, and my hand take hold on judgment: I will render vengeance to my enemies, and repay them that hate me.
I will make my arrows drunk with blood, and my sword shall devour flesh; of the blood of the slain and of the captivity, of the bare head of the enemies.

Hear, O ye heavens, the things I speak: let the earth give ear to the words of my mouth.

Praise His people, ye nations; for He will revenge the blood of His servants, and will render vengeance to their enemies: and He will be merciful to the land of His people.

Hear, O ye heavens, the things I speak: let the earth give ear to the words of my mouth.

On Other Sundays:
The Blessing of Saint Zacharias AB 4
St. Luke 1:68-80

Blessed be the Lord God of Israel; because He hath visited and wrought the redemption of His people;
And hath raised up an horn of salvation to us, in the house of David His servant.
As He spoke by the mouth of His holy prophets, who are from the beginning:
Salvation from our enemies and from the hand of all that hate us;
To perform mercy to our fathers and to remember His holy testament.
The oath, which He swore to Abraham our father, that He would grant to us;
That, being delivered from the hand of our enemies, we may serve Him without fear,
In holiness and justice before Him, all our days.
And thou, child, shalt be called the prophet of the Highest; for thou shalt go before the Face of the Lord to prepare His ways:
To give knowledge of salvation to His people unto the remission of their sins;
Through the bowels of the mercy of our God in which the Orient from on High hath visited us:
To enlighten them that sit in darkness and in the shadow of death; to direct our feet into the way of peace.
And the child grew and was strengthened in spirit; and was in the deserts until the day of his manifestation to Israel.

Always said:
The Second Canticle of Moses

[Only one Antiphon verse is sung per week, matching the Matins Gospel of the week;.see the notes above. The antiphon alternates with the verses.]

AB 99 Antiphon *
Week I Antiphon Being lead out of Egypt and walking through the Red Sea, our Fathers, gave the praise unto our Lord:
Week II Antiphon The children of the Hebrews crossed: The Israelites went across: Through the dry sea, giving the praise:
Week III Antiphon He is Glorious in the Saints, Marvelous in Majesty: working wonders:
Week IV Antiphon Moses looked to the right and then the left: He lead the People out onto the royal road: He lead them through to the shore:
Week V Antiphon Pharaoh sunk into the Red Sea: Moses trod through the dry Sea, Singing unto God:
Week VI Antiphon Thou didst guide, O Lord, Thy People through the Red Sea:

Week VII Antiphon O Lord, Thou reignest unto eternity, and unto ages of ages and beyond.
Week VIII Antiphon The Lord stamps down war: The Lord is his Name.
Week IX Antiphon + Let us sing to the Glorious Lord for He is certainly magnified.
Week X Antiphon The children of Israel walked on dry land through the midst of the Sea.

AB 5 (Exodus 15:1-19)

1. Let us sing to the Lord, for He is gloriously magnified: the horse and the rider He hath thrown into the sea.
2. The Lord is my strength and my praise: and He is become salvation to me. He is my God and I will glorify Him: the God of my father, and I will exalt Him.
3. The Lord is as a man of war: Almighty is His Name.
4. Pharaoh's chariots and his army He hath cast into the sea: his chosen captains are drowned in the Red Sea.
5. The depths have covered them: they are sunk to the bottom like a stone.
6. Thy right hand, O Lord, is magnified in strength: Thy right hand, O Lord, hath slain the enemy.
7. And in the multitude of Thy glory Thou hast put down Thy Adversaries: Thou hast sent Thy wrath, which hath devoured them like stubble.
8. At the blast of Thy anger the waters were gathered together. The flowing water stood: the depths were gathered together in the midst of the sea.
9. The enemy said: I will pursue and overtake; I will divide the spoils, my soul shall have its fill. I will draw my sword; my hand shall slay them.
10. Thy wind blew and the sea covered them: they sunk as lead in the mighty waters.
11. Who is like to Thee, among the strong, O Lord? who is like to Thee, glorious in holiness, terrible and praiseworthy, doing wonders?
12. Thou stretchedst forth Thy hand: and the earth swallowed them.
13. In Thy mercy Thou hast been a leader to the people which Thou hast redeemed: and in Thy strength Thou hast carried them to Thy Holy habitation.
14. Nations rose up, and were angry: sorrows took hold on the inhabitants of Philisthiim.
15. Then were the princes of Edom troubled, trembling seized on the stout men of Moab: all the inhabitants of Chanaan became stiff.
16. Let fear and dread fall upon them, in the greatness of Thy arm; let them become unmoveable as a stone, until Thy people, O Lord, pass by: until this Thy people pass by, which Thou hast possessed.
17. Thou shalt bring them in, and plant them in the mountain of Thy inheritance, in Thy most firm habitation which Thou hast made, O Lord: Thy Sanctuary, O Lord, which Thy hands have established.
18. The Lord shall reign for ever and ever.
19. For Pharaoh went in on horseback with his chariots and horsemen into sea: and the Lord brought back upon them the waters of the sea. But the children of Israel walked on dry ground in the midst thereof.

Collects after Canticle of Moses

Sunday Collect:

O God Who divided the sea for those departing from the people of Egypt, commanding the streams to stand on either side as if they were vertical walls, be pleased to free our souls from the flood of sins: that we may have the strength to traverse the depths of our faults, contemptuous of the adversary, O Savior of the World, Who liveth, guideth and reigneth with the eternal Father, at one with the eternal Holy Spirit unto ages of ages. Amen.

Collect for Feasts of Saints and Departed AB 76:

When Pharaoh drowned in the sea, Israel was freed: we beseech Thee that through the Grace of Baptism and the Triumph of the Cross, we may be freed from all evil, Through Thee, O Christ.

Sunday Collect during Great Lent AB 81:
O Christ God Who was the helper and protector unto the salvation of Thy People, Israel, which Though didst lead through the dry land of the sea out of Egypt, save us in this way from the yoke of sin, Who reigneth unto the ages. Amen.

Collects before The Song of the Three Youths

Daily Collect AB 69:
Holy and Glorious Lord, the worker of wonders and virtuous deeds: Who during their prayers was the fourth man Who stood by them; for Whom it is simple to alter the created nature of the fires, and coerce the power of the conflagration of flame, that they might rejoice cool and singing hymns to Thee, with the great victory: O Lord, let the same gifts of Thy power free us and protect us, O Savior of the World.

Daily Collect during Great Lent AB 88:
The people of Israel in prefiguring us were freed in passing through the sea; therefore free us through the grace of Baptism from the destructions of the world: Who reigneth unto the ages. Amen.

Collect for Monastic Vows and Tonsure AB 92:
The Hebrews, venerable in number, sustained by the sacrament, young of age, but solid of robust faith, because of love of divine religion, were loath to love the king's idol; naturally, they were contemptuous of the king himself, who being filled with wrath commanded that the oven be heated seven times with pitch and hemp. The men at arms were set ablaze by balls of fire. Heaven itself blushed red with this alien fire. Into that, they were thrust and in that very place they found Thee for Whom they were thrust into that place, O Christ. In such a manner, be pleased to free us from the madness of intellectual tyranny and from our natural fire, O Savior of the world, Who reignest with the Father and the Holy Spirit unto ages of ages. Amen.

The Song of the Three Youths

AB 99 Antiphon *
[Only one Antiphon verse is sung per week, matching the Matins Gospel of the week, and alternating with the verses; see the note at the Matins Gospel.]

Week I Antiphon: The three youths were cast into the furnace and did not fear the tongues of fire: they gave praise unto our Lord:

Week II Antiphon: The three youths were praying to Thee: From the midst of the fire they cried to Thee: With one voice they chanted the hymn:

Week III Antiphon: Let us bless God the Father, and the Son and the Holy Spirit: the Lord:

Week IV Antiphon: The youths were contemptuous of the flames of the furnace: They perpetually made offering to Christ: They abandoned the way of iniquity:

Week V Antiphon: The youths were thrust into the furnace, at the word of the vain iniquitous king: They sang this hymn unto the Lord King:

Week VI Antiphon: The three youths chanted with one voice from the midst of the intense tongues of fire:

Week VII Antiphon: Ye Saints and humble of heart of the Lord: bless the Lord:

Week VIII Antiphon: All ye works of the Lord, bless ye the Lord:

Week IX Antiphon: Praise Him and exalt Him above all forever:

Week X Antiphon: Let us bless the Father, and the Son and the Holy Spirit: the Lord:

The Song of the Three Youths AB 6 (Daniel 3:57-88a)

[Repeat notes as needed.]

57. All ye works of the Lord, bless the Lord: praise and exalt Him above all forever.
58. O ye angels of the Lord, bless the Lord: praise and exalt Him above all forever.
59. O ye heavens, bless the Lord: praise and exalt Him above all forever.
60. O all ye waters that are above the heavens, bless the Lord: praise and exalt Him above all forever.
61. O all ye powers of the Lord, bless the Lord: praise and exalt Him above all forever.
62. O ye sun and moon, bless the Lord: praise and exalt Him above all forever.
63. O ye stars of heaven, bless the Lord: praise and exalt Him above all forever.
64. O every shower and dew, bless ye the Lord: praise and exalt Him above all forever.
65. O all ye spirits of God, bless the Lord: praise and exalt Him above all forever.
66. O ye fire and heat, bless the Lord: praise and exalt Him above all forever.
67. O ye cold and heat, bless the Lord: praise and exalt Him above all forever.
68. O ye dews and hoar frosts, bless the Lord: praise and exalt Him above all forever.
69. O ye frost and cold, bless the Lord: praise and exalt Him above all forever.
70. O ye ice and snow, bless the Lord: praise and exalt Him above all forever.
71. O ye nights and days, bless the Lord: praise and exalt Him above all forever.
72. O ye light and darkness, bless the Lord: praise and exalt Him above all forever.
73. O ye lightenings and clouds, bless the Lord: praise and exalt Him above all forever.
74. O let the earth bless the Lord: let it praise and exalt Him above all forever.
75. O ye mountains and hills, bless the Lord: praise and exalt Him above all forever.
76. O all ye things that spring up in the earth, bless the Lord: praise and exalt Him above all forever.
77. O ye fountains, bless the Lord: praise and exalt Him above all forever.
78. O ye seas and rivers, bless the Lord: praise and exalt Him above all forever.
79. O ye whales, and all that move in the waters, bless the Lord: praise and exalt Him above all forever.
80. O all ye fowls of the air, bless the Lord: praise and exalt Him above all forever.
81. O all ye beasts and cattle, bless the Lord: praise and exalt Him above all forever.
82. O ye sons of men, bless the Lord: praise and exalt Him above all forever.
83. O let Israel bless the Lord: let them praise and exalt Him above all forever.
84. O ye priests of the Lord, bless the Lord: praise and exalt Him above all forever.
85. O ye servants of the Lord, bless the Lord: praise and exalt Him above all forever.
86. O ye spirits and souls of the just, bless the Lord: praise and exalt Him above all forever.
87. O ye holy and humble of heart, bless the Lord: praise and exalt Him above all forever.
88. O Ananias, Azarias, and Misael, bless ye the Lord: praise and exalt Him above all forever.

Let us bless the Father and the Son and the Holy Spirit, The Lord: Let us chant the hymn and exalt Him above all unto the ages. Amen.

Collects after The Song of the Three Youths

Sunday Collect AB 63:
Hear our prayer, Almighty God, and grant that as we pursue the repetition of the hymn of the youths by blessed custom; thus by Thine aid, freed from the snares of our sins, we may not by engulfed in eternal burning fire, Who with the Father livest and reignest with the Holy Spirit throughout all ages of ages. Amen.

Collect for Feasts of our Lord AB 72:
O God, Who by Faith made the flames of the fiery furnace cool for the youths, and wast the fourth man who stood by them as they triumphed and death was thwarted; we beseech

Thee, grant virtue unto us who are scorched by the burning of the flesh, through Thee O Christ, Who reignest unto ages of ages. Amen.

Collect for Feasts of Saints and Departed AB 77:
O God, Who delivered the three youths from the furnace, likewise deliver us from the torments of Hell, Who reignest unto the ages. Amen.

Sunday Collect during Great Lent AB 82:
Therefore, by edict, we bless Thee, Almighty God; Thou Who freed the three youths from the fire, also rescue us from the torment of eternal death because of Thy mercy; Who reignest unto the ages. Amen.

Daily Collect during Great Lent AB 89:
As Thou didst save the three youths in the flames by the descent of the heavenly messenger into the furnace, be pleased to free us from the fires of Hell through the Angel of Good Counsel: Who reigneth unto the ages. Amen.

Collects before Psalms of Praise

Daily Collect AB 70:
Let them praise the Lord, Who is praised by all the elements: Whose testimony is Holy in Heaven and earth and in His possession, Sion: Sing a new hymn you who thunder: Ye under sentence unto torment, shout with diverse modes of spiritual melody, that your spirits may praise Christ in concert through all the ages. Who liveth and reigneth with the Father and the Holy Spirit throughout all ages of ages. Amen.

Collect AB 126:
By Rule we praise Thee, O Father of all things.
In all places, we confess and acclaim Thee.
We minister unto Thee in spontaneous service.
Hear us, and grant that which we ask:
Who reignest unto the ages. Amen.

Psalms of Praise
Psalm 148

Antiphon AB 100:
Praise the Lord from the Heavens, offer pleasant chants, Praise him with sound of trumpet.

1. Praise ye the Lord from the heavens: praise ye Him in the high places.
2. Praise ye Him, all His angels: praise ye Him, all His hosts.
3. Praise ye Him, O sun and moon: praise Him, all ye stars and light.
4. Praise Him, ye heavens of heavens: and let all the waters that are above the heavens,
5. Praise the Name of the Lord. For He spoke, and they were made: He commanded, and they were created.
6. He hath established them for ever, and for ages of ages: He hath made a decree, and it shall not pass away.
7. Praise the Lord from the earth, ye dragons, and all ye deeps:
8. Fire, hail, snow, ice, stormy winds, which fulfill His word:
9. Mountains and all hills, fruitful trees and all cedars:
10. Beasts and all cattle: serpents and feathered fowls:
11. Kings of the earth and all people: princes and all judges of the earth:
12. Young men and maidens. Let the old with the younger praise the Name of the Lord:
13. For His Name alone is exalted.
14. The praise of Him is above heaven and earth: and He hath exalted the horn of His people.

A hymn to all His saints: to the children of Israel, a people approaching to Him. Alleluia.

AB 100 Antiphon: Praise the Lord from the Heavens, offer pleasant chants, Praise him with sound of trumpet.

Psalm 149

1. Sing ye to the Lord a new canticle: let His praise be in the church of the saints.
2. Let Israel rejoice in Him that made him: and let the children of Sion be joyful in their King.
3. Let them praise His Name in choir: let them sing to him with the timbrel and the psaltery.
4. For the Lord is well pleased with His people: and He will exalt the meek unto salvation.
5. The saints shall rejoice in glory: they shall be joyful in their beds.
6. The high praises of God shall be in their mouth: and two-edged swords in their hands:
7. To execute vengeance upon the nations; chastisements among the people:
8. To bind their kings with fetters, and their nobles with manacles of iron:
9. To execute upon them the judgment that is written: this glory is to all His saints. Alleluia.

Antiphon AB 100:
Praise the Lord from the Heavens, offer pleasant chants, Praise him with sound of trumpet.

Psalm 150

1. Praise ye the Lord in His holy places: praise ye Him in the firmament of His power.
2. Praise ye Him for His mighty acts: praise ye Him according to the multitude of His greatness.
3. Praise Him with the sound of trumpet: praise Him with psaltery and harp.
4. Praise Him with timbrel and choir: praise Him with strings and organs.
5. Praise Him on high sounding cymbals: praise Him on cymbals of joy: let every spirit praise the Lord. Alleluia.

Antiphon AB 100:
Praise the Lord from the Heavens, offer pleasant chants, Praise him with sound of trumpet.

Collects after Psalms of Praise

Sunday Collect AB 64:
Let us praise Thee from the Heavens, let us be worthy to sing a new song unto Thee. We beseech Thee, O Lord, Who art venerable among Thy Saints, that Thou accept our petitions, forgive our sins, O Savior of the world, Who reignest unto the ages. Amen.

Collect for Feasts of our Lord AB 73:
We adore our God, God of all souls, grant that we may persevere in this assigned vigil of the solemnity until the time that our iniquity be transformed in Light just as the Sun becomes brighter at midday, O Savior of the world: Who reignest unto ages. Amen.

Collect for Feasts of Saints and Departed AB 78:
We praise Thee O Lord, with Thy Saints, that Thou mayest be pleased to receive our prayers: Who reignest unto ages of ages. Amen.

Sunday Collect during Great Lent AB 83:
Most high God, King of the Angels, O God, Praise of all the elements, O God, Glory and exultation of the Saints, Preserve the souls of Thy servants: Who reignest unto the ages. Amen.

Irish "Trisagion"

[Note: AB 123, 128, and 125 with the ending, are purposely repeated. On Sundays, all three Collects are said. These Collects represent an Irish form of the "Trisagion." In Greek, the Trisagion is: "'Agios ó Theos, 'Agios Ischyros, 'Agios Athanatos, eleison ymas," or "Holy God, Holy Mighty, Holy Immortal, have mercy on us." "Eleison" is related in derivation to being anointed with oil, the receiving of God's grace. Apocalypse 4:8, "...And they rested not day and night, saying: Holy, Holy, Holy, Lord God Almighty, Who was, and Who is, and Who is to come." In the margin, a later copyist added the "Filioque" to Collect AB 125. A photographic facsimile shows that the placement, script, and style of the "Filioque" is of a much later date than the rest of the book.]

Sunday Collect AB 123:
We adore Thee, eternal Father, We call to Thee, eternal Son,
and we confess Thee O Holy Spirit, abiding the one Divine Substance.
Let us return due praise and thanks to Thee, one God in Trinity, that we may be worthy to praise Thee with unceasing voices, through eternal ages of ages. Amen.

All days Collect AB 128:
We adore Thee, eternal Father, We call to Thee, eternal Son,
and we confess Thee O Holy Spirit, abiding the one Divine Substance.
Let us return due praise and thanks to Thee, one God in Trinity, that we may be worthy to praise Thee with unceasing voices, through eternal ages of ages. Amen.

Daily Collect during Great Lent AB 90:
O God, Whom the army of heaven sings,
And Whom the Church of the Saints praises,
Whom the Spirit of the Universals hymns,
Have mercy, I beseech Thee, on all of us:
Who reignest unto ages of ages. Amen.

Collect for Monastic Vows and Tonsure AB 93:
Let the Angels, Virtues, Thrones, and Powers praise Thee, O Lord, and let those who owe their origin to Thee rejoice in the office of Thy praise so that through harmony of the universe, expanding unto Thee in consonance, Thy will be done in Heaven and also on earth. We beseech Thee, O Lord, be at peace with Thy people that by Thy praises which are found in their mouths, there may remain, in every one of them, the defense of Thy Word, by which Thou doest teach and the Truth of our Life by which Thou doest ever regard us, and well-being by which Thou doest exalt the meek. For Thy many great deeds, we praise Thee, O Lord by thanks offerings of show of praise through the Psalms, mortification through the drum, by group worship through the chorus, exultation through the organ, jubilation through the cymbals that we deserve to have thy mercy, O Christ, Savior of the world.

Collect AB 125:
We adore Thee, eternal Father, We call to Thee, eternal Son,
and we confess Thee O Holy Spirit, abiding the one Divine Substance.
To Thee, O Trinity, we return praise and thanks
To Thee, O God, we recite unceasing praise
Thee, Father, unbegotten Thee, Son, Only Begotten,
Thee O Holy Spirit from Father proceeding, we believe in our hearts.
We give Thee thanks, Inestimable, Incomprehensible,
Almighty God, Who reignest unto the ages. Amen.

Sunday Gospel of the Resurrection or Proper Lection, or of a Major Feast

The Gospel is read by a Deacon or Priest [or Abbot, or rarely Abbess if blessed, see the hour of the Beginning of Night.]:(Remember, Sunday begins Saturday evening at Vespers. On weekdays there is not a Matins Resurrection Gospel unless it is a Feast or titular. For more notes see page 352.)

During Lent and Paschaltide, these Gospels are **not** read now, but other readings replace them: see the Lectionary. (In Lent, the readings at the Beginning of Night do not change.)

ALL STAND. (The Holy Gospels are before the Psalter, page 352.)

(List of Gospels in first edition of Breviary:)
- Week I St. John 20:1-18.
- Week II St. Luke 24:1-12.
- Week III St. Mark 16:9-20.
- Week IV St. Luke 24:12-35.
- Week V St. Matthew 28:1-10.
- Week VI St. Mark 16:1-8.
- Week VII St. Luke 24:36-53.
- Week VIII St. John 20:19-31.
- Week IX St. Matthew 28:11-20.
- Week X St. John 21:1 to end.

(Variant: Gospels from Paschaltide:)
- Week I Matthew 28:1-20
- Week II Luke 24:1-12, [13-35]
- Week III Mark 15:47-16:11
- Week IV Mark 16:12-20
- Week V John 11:1-45
- Week VI John 20:1-9
- Week VII John 20:11-18
- Week VIII John 21:1-14, [15-25]
- Week IX John 20:19-31
- Week X Luke 24:36-48

[Then, next week is Week I again.]

At the conclusion of the Gospel, all say,

Pray for us, and lift up the Gospel to us.

*And the Priest or Deacon blesses everyone with the Holy Gospel (Tallaght Rule). He may say the Roman formula, "**By the words of the Holy Gospel may our sins be blotted out.**" as he blesses everyone with the Book of the Gospels, using the Sign of the Cross.*

In Great Lent, there are Old Testament readings instead of the Matins Resurrection Gospels (see the Lectionary). In Lent, there is a different reading for each day. These are listed at the end of the book in Appendix III. On Holy and Great Friday, there are both Old Testament and Gospel readings for every Hour, and these follow an Irish Harmony of the Gospels, written out at the back of this book.

Collects after the Reading

Sunday Collect AB 65:

Rejoicing with joy for what has been returned to us by the Light of This day, let us raise up praise and thanks unto Almighty God. That He may be pleased to grant unto us who very solemnly celebrate the day of the Lord's Resurrection, Peace, tranquillity, and joy, that, protected from morning until night by the favor of His clemency, we may, exultant, rejoice with eternal joy, through our Lord Jesus Christ, Who reigneth with the unoriginate Father and the Holy Spirit, unto ages of ages. Amen.

Collect for Feasts of our Lord AB 74:

Venerating the Lord Who is the beginning of our Resurrection, let us with one mind give deserved praise and thanks to our God, the Trinity, imploring His mercy, that He concede participation in the Resurrection of our Lord and Saviour as much to the spirit as to the body, who with the Father liveth and reigneth unto ages of ages. Amen.

Collect for Feasts of Saints and Departed AB 79:

At this dawn, let us beseech the Risen Lord, that we might arise into eternal life, throughout all ages of ages. Amen.

Sunday Collect during Great Lent AB 84:
O Christ, let us sing with pleasure together unto Thee hymns with spiritual lyrics, by which Thy majesty is able to be pleased with spiritual offerings of praise Who liveth with the Father and the Holy Spirit, unto ages of ages. Amen.

Vigil of the Sunday of the Resurrection (only) AB 85:
With the dawn of light and the Author arisen, Let us rejoice in the Lord, by Whom, since death is overthrown, we may be able to confront our sins, and let us walk in newness of life, Who livest and reignest with the Father and the Holy Spirit unto ages of ages. Amen.

On Sundays only: Te Deum

Antiphon AB 7: *[Antiphonary of Bangor words.]*
O Youths praise ye the Lord: praise the Name of the Lord.

[Sing three notes together as a triplet; the font had no notation for triplets.]

1. O God, we praise Thee: we con-fess Thou art the Lord.

2. O e-ter-nal Fa-ther, all the earth wor-ships Thee

3. Un-to Thee, all the An-gels, un-to Thee, the Hea-vens and all the pow-ers,

4. Un-to Thee, the Cherubim and Seraphim, with unceasing voice cry:

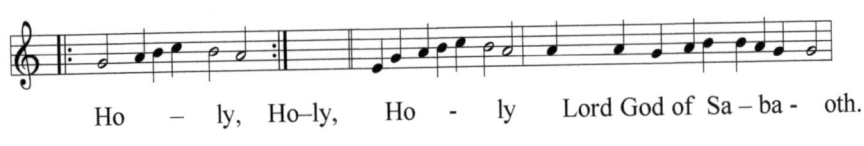

Ho – ly, Ho–ly, Ho - ly Lord God of Sa – ba - oth.

6. The Hea-vens and all the earth are full of the tri-bute to Thy Glo-ry.

7. Thee, the choir of the glor – i - ous A – pos - tles,

8. Thee, the throng of the ven – er – a - ble Pro - phets,

9. Thee, the white-clad ar-my of mar-tyrs praise.

10. Thee, the Ho-ly Church con-fess-es, through-out the en-tire world:

11. The Fa-ther of im-mense Ma-jes-ty;

12. Thy ven-er-a-ble, true, and On-ly-Be-got-ten Son;

13. And al-so the Ho-ly Spir-it, the Com-fort-er.

14. Thou art the King of Glo-ry, O Christ.

15. Thou art the e-ter-nal Son of the Fa-ther.

16. Thou didst take up hu-man na-ture un-to the li-ber-a-tion of the world.

Thou didst not dis-dain the Vir-gin's womb.

17. Thou, when the sting of death was bound,

open-ed the Hea-ven-ly King-dom to those who be-lieve.

18. Thou art seat-ed at the right hand of God, in the Glo-ry of the Fa-ther.

19. Thou art be-lieved [that Thou art] com-ing to be Judge.

20. Thee, there-fore we be-seech,

help thy ser-vants whom Thou hast re-deemed by Pre-cious Blood.

21. Make num-bered with the Saints in e-ter-nal Glo-ry.

22. Save Thy peo-ple, O Lord, and bless Thine in-her-i-tance,

23. And rule them and ex-alt them un-to the a-ges.

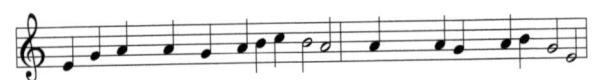

24. Each day we bless Thee,

25. And we praise Thy Name un-to e-ter-ni-ty, and un-to a-ges of a-ges. A-men.

26. Let Thy mer-cy, O Lord, be up-on us,

in that we have hoped on Thee. *[At Pascha: return to p. 186.]*

Collect AB 24:
O God, give aid to all those who praise Thee O Holy Three and to those who confess Thee One in offerings of the singing of songs: Who reignest unto the ages. Amen.

Prayer over those afflicted by devils AB 96

O Lord, Holy Father, Almighty and eternal God, expel the devil and his kin from this person: from the head, from the hair, from the crown of the head, from the brain, from the brow, from the eyes, from the ears, from the nostrils, from the lips, from the mouth, from the tongue, from beneath the tongue, from the throat, from the passages of the throat, from the neck, from the heart, from the entire body, from the joints of his (her) members, with in and without, from the bones, from the veins, from the nerves from the blood, from the senses, from the thoughts, from the words, from all of his (her) the deeds, and from all developments now and in the future. But may there be worked in thee the power of Christ in Him Who suffered that we might achieve eternal life through the same our Lord Jesus Christ, Who reignest with the Father and the Holy Spirit throughout ages of ages. Amen.

Gloria AB 116 *with Antiphons. [A musical setting is in the Mass.]*

(1) Glory to God in the Highest, and on earth peace to men of good will. We praise Thee; we bless Thee; we worship Thee; we glorify Thee; we magnify Thee;
(2) we give thanks to Thee for Thy great mercy.
(3) O Lord heavenly King, God the Father Almighty; O Lord, the Only Begotten Son of God, Jesus Christ; O Holy Spirit of God, and all of us say, Amen.
(4) O Lord the Son of God the Father: Lamb of God Who takest away the sin of the world, have mercy upon us.
(5) Receive our prayer; Thou Who sittest at the right-hand of God the Father:
(6) Have mercy upon us,
(7) for Thou only art holy,
(8) Thou only art the Lord,
(9) Thou only art the Lord,
(10) Thou only art glorious;
(11) with the Holy Spirit
(12) in the glory of God the Father.

[The Antiphons may be either placed within the Gloria if a group is singing antiphonally, or sung after it is completed.]

Antiphon 1: Every day will we bless Thee, and we will praise Thy Name forever and unto ages of ages.
Antiphon 2: Be pleased, O Lord to keep us sinless today.
Antiphon 3: Blessed art Thou, O Lord, God of our Fathers, and may Thy Name be laudable and glorious unto the ages. Amen.
Antiphon 4: Have mercy on us, O Lord, have mercy on us.
Antiphon 5: Give ear, O Lord, to my words, understand my cry. Hearken to the voice of my prayer, O My King and my God. (Ps. 5:2-3)
Antiphon 6: And in the morning hear my voice.
Antiphon 7: In the morning shall my prayer come before Thee, O Lord.
Antiphon 8: Throughout days and nights, hours and moments, have mercy upon us, O Lord.
Antiphon 9: By the prayers and examples of the Saints, have mercy upon us, O Lord.
Antiphon 10: By the prayers and examples of the Angels, Archangels, Patriarchs, and Prophets, have mercy upon us, O Lord.
Antiphon 11: By the prayers and examples of the Apostles, Martyrs and Confessors, have mercy upon us, O Lord.
Antiphon 12: Glory and honor to the Father and to the Son and to the Holy Spirit, now and ever, and unto ages of ages. Amen.

Collects before the Hymn

Sunday Collect AB 66:
Holy Lord, Illumination and true Salvation unto those who believe: Lordly Resurrection of brightness, Light of our hearts, let us be worthy to be, by the knowledge of the Trinity and perception of the Unity: children of Light, and members of Christ, and a temple of the Holy Spirit. Who reignest unto ages of ages. Amen.

Hymn and Procession to the Cross Sundays AB 12

Spirit of Divine glorious Light,   Look upon me, O Lord.

God of Truth, Lord God of Sabaoth, God of Israel,   Look upon me, O Lord.

Light from Light, Let us repay the Son of the Father
And the Holy Spirit one in Substance,   Look upon me, O Lord.

Only Begotten and First begotten,
From Thee we gain
Our Redemption,   Look upon me, O Lord.

Thou wast born by the Holy Spirit
From the Virgin Mary.
Through this, live those born
to Thee from the font
into the adoption of Sons.   Look upon me, O Lord.

Heirs and coheirs
Of Thy Christ, in Whom
And through Whom Thou created all,
as fore-ordained from all ages unto us,
is God Jesus, O Thou Who now commences: Look upon me, O Lord.

By the Only-begotten from the Dead:
From God, the corpse obtains God's brightness
remaining unto ages of ages.
O King of the eternals: Look upon me, O Lord.

For now begins He Who ever was,
Of Thy Nature, the Son,
Of Divine light of Thy Glory
Who was formed and was filled
With the fullness of Thy Divinity: Look upon me, O Lord.

Person, only begotten And Firstbegotten He Who is all of all
We call Thee Light of Light   Look upon me, O Lord.

And True God from True God Himself. We confess To Three Persons in one Substance. Look upon me, O Lord.

Sunday Collect during Great Lent AB 86:
Thine Only Begotten was made the dawn's first light in days of old, Who came to wash away our sins through the Cross. Who reigneth with Thee and the Holy Spirit unto ages of ages. Amen.

Other Hymns

*Hymns for Saints on their Feasts or Titulars, or for intercession at any time. Examples of Hymns: for St. Patrick (***Audite Omnes** *by St. Secundinus,); for the* ***Blessed Virgin Mary*** *(in the Cross Vigil, etc.); for* ***St. Martin of Tours****; Feasts of* ***the Lord*** *or the* ***Apostles*** *(the* **Apostle's Hymn, AB3***,);* ***All Saints Day*** *and* ***Church Consecration*** *(***Altus Prosator** *by St. Colum cille,).*

Hymn and Procession to the Cross Saturdays and Saints' Days AB 11

Most Holy Martyrs of the Most high God Most strong warriors of Christ the King
Most mighty generals of God's army Victors in the Heavens singing to God: Alleluia.

Most excellent Christ, God of the Heavens,
Of the Cherubim: Unto Whom, seated with the Holy Father,
The Chorus of Angels and shining martyrs, Unto Thee, the Saints proclaim: Alleluia.

O Magnificence, Thou first, for all [Thou] died on the Cross,
Who, when death was trod down, illumined the world.
Thou didst ascend unto the Heavens unto the right hand of God
 Unto Thee, the Saints proclaim: Alleluia.

As a spiritual army with strengthened heart, The Holy Apostles followed Thee,
Who with the Cross itself cast out death: Unto Thee, the Saints proclaim: Alleluia.

Christ, Thou art the mighty aid of the Martyrs Who fight for Thy Holy Glory
Who with the victor go forth from this age. Unto Thee, the Saints proclaim: Alleluia.

O Lord, Thy brilliant praised power
Which through the Holy Spirit strengthens the Martyrs
Which confounds the devil and conquers death, Unto Thee, the Saints proclaim: Alleluia.

Protected by the high hand of the Lord,
They stand strengthened against the devil
Servants to faith of the eternal Trinity.
 Unto Thee, the Saints proclaim: Alleluia.

Truly they reign with Thee, O Christ God,
Who by merit of suffering have crowns
And filled with the fruits of eternity they rejoice.
Unto Thee, the Saints proclaim: Alleluia.

Let us, suppliants implore the Grace of Christ God
That we may be perfect in His glory
And in the Holy City, Jerusalem of God
The Trinity, with the Saints, we may say: Alleluia.

AB 80 Collect for Feasts of Saints and Departed:
Let us venerate Thy Resurrection O Christ, through which we may be worthy to be saved unto eternity, throughout all ages of ages. Amen.

Hymn and Procession to the Cross Daily AB 2

The congregation of the Brethren sing the hymn
They sonorously sing the music of the Hymn
Unto Christ the King, harmoniously
Let us give due praise

O Thou Word from the heart of God.
Thou Way, Thou Truth,
Thou art called the branch of Jesse.
We recite, Thou art the Lion.

At the right hand of the Father, Mount and Lamb,
Thou art the cornerstone,
Bridegroom, or dove,
Flame, shepherd, door.

Thou wast proclaimed by the Prophets:
Born into our world,
Who wast before all worlds:
Maker of the first world.

Maker of Heaven, maker of earth:
Thou Gatherer of the seas
and Thou Maker of all things
that the Father commanded be made.

Received by the Virgin's womb,
Heralded by Gabriel,
Her womb swelled with Holy child:
Let us be taught to believe

A new thing not seen before
That the Virgin bore a Son.
Then Magi, following the Star
were first to worship the newborn

Offering incense and gold:
Offerings worthy of a king.
Soon it is reported to Herod,
It is distasteful to his authority

Who then commands the children slain:
He made all of them martyrs.
The child was born away, hidden.
None of Him in that flood spilled.

He was borne back after Herod's death:
The Heavenly one was raised in Nazareth
As a child and as an adult
He wrought many signs

Which remain and are documented
By many witnesses:
The promises given by the heavenly Kingdom
He fulfills by deeds:

He makes the infirm strong.
He illumines the blind.
By words, He cleanses the disease of the Lepers.
He raises the dead.

Into wine, because it had failed,
He commanded the water in the jars
to be made, which the wedding party
esteemed to be drunk unmixed by the people.

With five loaves and two fish
He feeds five thousand.
The fragments of the meal
Fill twelve baskets.

The gathering of all that dined
Gives forth perpetual praise.
He accepts twelve men
Through whom life is learned.

Of whom one is found,
Judas, the betrayer of Christ.
Those sent out by Annas
Are prompted by the traitor's kiss.

He Who is innocent, captive is held,
And Who does not resist, is led away.
He is arrested falsely, Those who deliver
[Him] to Pilate, berate [Him].

The governor dismisses the charges
He finds no guilt.
But with the assembly of the Jews
For the regard of Caesar

Say Christ is rebellious.
The Holy One is handed to the crowd
With impious words they rage at Him.
He endures spitting, stripes.

He is commanded to mount the Cross,
Innocent, for ills.
By the death of the flesh which He bore
He conquers the death of all.

Then, hanging, with a great shout,
Calls to God the Father.
Death took hold of the frame of Christ
He looses the tight chains.

The veil of the Temple hangs ripped
Night obscures the world.
Corpses once closed up
Are raised up from the tombs.

Blessed Joseph comes:
The Corpse is coated with myrrh
And wrapped in rough cloth
with sorrow he preserves it.

Annas, the leader, directs
Soldiers to guard the Corpse:
That he might see if Christ would prove
What He declared.

They tremble before the Angel of God,
Vested in a white cloak,
Which cloth exceeds
silk in brightness.

He rolls the stone away from the tomb:
Christ arises unconquered.
Lying Judea sees this:
They deny, having seen.

The women learn first
That the Savior liveth.
Those whom He greets in sorrow,
He fills rejoicing with joy.

Afterwards, they announce
that He, raised From the dead
by the paternal right hand,
Had returned on the Third day.

Soon He is seen by the blessed
Brethren whom He had tried.
He answers those that doubted,
Entering while the doors were barred.

He teaches the precepts of the Law,
He gives the Divine Spirit:
The perfect Spirit of God:
The chain of the Trinity.

He commandeth that throughout the World
Believers be Baptized:
Calling upon the Name of the Father:
Confiding in the Son.

By the Holy Spirit, He reveals
Mystic Faith to the Baptized:
Those immersed in the Font
Are remade: made sons of God.

Before the dawn, let us the Gathering
Of the brethren hymn in concert the Glory:
By which we are taught we will be
In the eternal age.

The crowing of the cock, the flapping of the cock,
Says that day is nigh,
We, singing and litanizing
What we believe will be.

The Majestic and immense,
Hymn we together:
Before the dawn we proclaim
Christ the King unto the age.

Before the dawn we proclaim
Christ the King unto the age.
Who in Him rightly believe
That we will reign with Him.

Glory to the Father, Unbegotten,
Glory to the Onlybegotten,
Likewise to the Holy Spirit
Unto eternal ages. [Amen.]

Collects after the Hymn AB2

Collect for Feasts of our Lord AB 75:
Hearken to our prayers, O Lord, Who has visited our human infirmities to bestow Thy Sanctification and Immortality on us: Who reignest unto the ages. Amen.

Prayer of the Community of the Brethren: Long form
(There are prayers which follow these prayers in Matins, so the text is in full here.)

Antiphon AB 40: Remember not our former iniquities; let Thy mercies speedily prevent us, for we have become exceedingly poor. (Ps 78:8)
Prayer: Help us, O God of our Salvation, for the Glory of Thy Name's sake.
Prayer: O Lord free us and forgive our sins because of Thy Name.
Prayer: Give not the soul of one who trusts in Thee over to the beasts.
Prayer: Forget not the souls of Thy poor ones unto the end.
Prayer: Respect Thy promises, O Lord: Who reignest unto the ages. Amen.

For Our Sins (Ps. 69:2)
Antiphon AB 40': O God, come to my assistance: O Lord, make haste to help me.
Prayer: Hasten, O Lord to free us from all of our sins: Who reignest unto the ages. Amen.

For the Baptized
Antiphon AB 41: Save, O Lord, Thy People and bless Thine inheritance: and rule them and exalt them for ever. (Ps. 27:9).
Prayer: Have mercy, O Lord, On Thy Catholic Church, which Thou didst ransom by Thy Holy Blood: Who reignest unto the ages. Amen.

For the Priests
Antiphon AB 41': Arise, O Lord into Thy resting place, Thou and Thine ark, which Thou hast sanctified. (Ps. 131:8)
Antiphon: Let Thy priests be clothed with justice and let Thy Saints rejoice. (Ps. 131:9)
Prayer: May all Thy Saints rejoice in Thee O Lord, they who hope upon Thee in all Truth: Who reignest unto the ages. Amen.

For the Abbot
Antiphon AB 42: The Lord preserve him and give him life, and make him blessed upon the earth. (Ps. 40:3a)
Antiphon: May the Lord keepeth thee from all evil: may the Lord keep thy soul. (Ps. 120:7)
Antiphon: May the Lord keep thy coming in and thy going out; from henceforth now and forever. (Ps. 120:8)

For the Brethren
Antiphon AB 43: Keep us, O Lord as the apple of Thine eye; protect us under the shadow of Thy wing. (Ps. 16:8b)
Prayer: Be pleased to protect and sanctify all of them, O Almighty God Who reignest unto the ages. Amen.

For the Brotherhood
Antiphon AB 44: Thou, O Lord wilt preserve us and keep us from this generation forever. (Ps. 11:8)
Prayer: Hear our prayers for our brethren, that Thou wilt have mercy upon them O God: Who reignest unto the ages. Amen.

For Peace of Peoples and Kingdoms
Antiphon AB 45: The Lord will give strength to His people: the Lord will bless His people with peace. (Ps. 28:11)
Prayer: Be pleased to grant peace to all, Almighty God: Who reignest unto the ages. Amen.

For Blasphemers
Antiphon AB 46: Thy mercy, O Lord, endureth forever: O despise not the works of Thy hands. (Ps. 137:8)
Prayer: O Lord God of Virtues, do not let those here remain in sin: Who reignest unto the ages. Amen.

For the Impious
Antiphon AB 47: Judge them, O God. Let them fall from their devices: according to the multitude of their wickednesses cast them out: for they have provoked Thee, O Lord.
(Ps. 5:11b)
Prayer: May they who trust in themselves be confounded, O Lord, but not we who trust in Thee: Who reignest unto the ages. Amen.

For those who Journey
Antiphon AB 48: O Lord, save me: O Lord, give good success. (Ps. 117:25)
Prayer: Grant a successful journey to Thy servants: Who reignest unto the ages. Amen.

For Grace unto Pilgrims
Antiphon AB 49: Let all Thy works, O Lord, praise Thee, and let Thy Saints bless Thee.
(Ps. 144:10)

Prayer: Our souls give Thee thanks for Thine innumerable good works, O Lord: Who reignest unto the ages. Amen.

For the Charitable
Antiphon AB 50: He hath distributed, He hath given to the poor: His justice remaineth forever and ever. His horn shall be exalted in glory. (Ps 111:9)
Prayer: O Lord, repay those who gave alms in this world in Thy Holy Kingdom: Who reignest unto the ages. Amen.

For the Infirm
Antiphon AB 51: And they cried to the Lord in their tribulation: and He delivered them out of their distresses. (Ps. 106:6)
Prayer: Grant, O Lord, Thy servants health of mind and body: Who reignest unto the ages. Amen.

For Captives
Antiphon AB 51': Arise, O Lord, help us and redeem us for Thy Name's sake.
(Ps. 43:26)
Antiphon: Our help is in the Name of the Lord. (Ps. 123:8)
Prayer: Be pleased to save us through the invocation of Thy Name: Who reignest unto the ages. Amen.

For Martyrs
Antiphon AB 101: After fires and swords, crosses and beasts the Saints are borne with great triumph into the Kingdom and rest.
Antiphon AB 102: These are the ones who came forth in great tribulation and washed their stoles and made them white in the Blood of the Lamb.
Prayer AB 52: O God, Who hast bestowed the crown of martyrdom unto Thy Saints and Elect, we beseech Thee, O Lord, that through their examples, we who have not earned such glory may obtain forgiveness: Who reignest unto the ages. Amen.

For those who are in Tribulations
Antiphon AB 53: Unto Thee will I cry, O Lord; O my God, be not silent to me.
(Ps. 27:1a)
Antiphon: The Lord of virtues is with us; the God of Jacob is our protector. (Ps. 45:8)
Prayer: O Our Helper, the God of Jacob, have mercy upon us, O Lord Who reignest unto the ages. Amen.
Collect AB 54: Holy among the Saints, the spotless Lamb: Glorious in the Heavens, Marvelous upon the Earth, grant us, O Lord, according to Thy Great Mercy that for which we petition and pray to Thee, O God: Who reignest unto the ages. Amen.

For Martyrs
Antiphon AB 103: In memory of Thy Martyrs, O Lord, harken to the prayer of Thy servants, O Christ.
Antiphon AB 104: In the invocation of Thy Holy Martyrs, have mercy, O God, upon Thy Suppliants.
Prayer AB 55: We pray the eternal Name of Thy Virtue, Almighty God, that Thou makest us to be equal to the Martyrs and all of Thy Saints: companions in example, similar in Faith, vigorous in devotion, alike in suffering, and fruitful in the Resurrection: Who reignest unto the ages. Amen.

For Penitents
Antiphon AB 56: Have mercy on me, O God, according to Thy great mercy. (Ps. 50:3)

Prayer: Grant, O Lord, forgiveness to those who out of Faith are penitent unto Thee, according to Thy great mercy, O God: Who reignest unto the ages. Amen.

Credo Complete Nicene Creed (Lorrha-Stowe Missal)

I believe in one God, the Father Almighty, maker of heaven and earth and of all things visible and invisible. And in one Lord Jesus Christ, the Only-Begotten Son of God. Born of the Father before all ages. Light of light, true God of true God. Born, not made, of one Substance with the Father: through Whom all things were made. Who for us men, and for our Salvation descended from heaven. And was Incarnate of the Holy Spirit and the Virgin Mary: And was born man. And was crucified also for us: under Pontius Pilate; He suffered and was buried. And He rose on the third day, according to the Scriptures. And ascended into heaven: and sitteth at the right hand of God the Father. And He shall come again with glory to judge both the living and the dead: Whose Kingdom shall have no end. And I believe in the Holy Spirit, the Lord and Giver of life: Who proceedeth from the Father. Who with the Father and the Son together is worshiped and glorified: Who spake by the Prophets. And in one, Holy, Catholic, and Apostolic Church. I confess one Baptism for the remission of sins. And I look for the resurrection of the dead. + And the life of the world to come. Amen.

The Divine Prayer AB 36

Our Father, Who art in the Heavens, hallowed be Thy Name. Thy Kingdom come. Thy will be done on earth as it is in Heaven. Give us this day our daily bread and forgive us our debts as we forgive our debtors and lead us not into temptation but deliver us from evil. Amen.

(Or do the Community of the Brethren Short Form, see the back of this book.)

The Intercessory Prayers of Matins for the Martyrs

[All day of week or season is specified.]

Antiphon AB 101:
After fires and swords, crosses and beasts, the Saints are borne with great triumph into the Kingdom and rest.

Collect AB 61:
O Lord Almighty God Who dost test Thy Saints with a measure and glorifies without measure, Whose precepts have a goal and rewards have no end, hear our prayers through their examples, and grant that they help us by their patronage: unto the perfection of Faith, unto the fruition of good works, unto the good of prosperity, unto the reward of wholesomeness, unto the refinement of religion, unto the increase of fear of the Divine; Through our Lord Jesus Christ, Thy Son, Who is the King of Kings and Lord of Lords, and glory of those to come, reigning and remaining, One with [Thee and] the Holy Spirit unto ages of ages. Amen.

Antiphon AB 102:
These are the ones who came forth in great tribulation, and washed their stoles, and made them white in the Blood of the Lamb.

Sunday Collect AB 67:
These were, O Lord, those who with joy were awash with blood while rejecting the enticing allurements of this world, by glorious suffering: they conquered death by death; and reflecting that all hidden from that Light will be thrown down in the end, they tasted life from suffering, and from death, victory. We ask Thee, O Christ, that we may be worthy to be helped by their prayers: the prayers of those whose like we are unable to be, through Thee, O Christ, Who liveth, guidest and reignest with the Father and the Holy Spirit unto ages of ages. Amen.

Antiphon AB 103:
In memory of Thy Martyrs, O Lord, harken to the prayer of Thy servants, O Christ.

Sunday Collect during Great Lent AB 87:
Remembering the triumphs of Thy Martyrs, who endured the darts of suffering of Thee, we implore Thee, that through their examples, we may be worthy of forgiveness of our sins. Who reignest unto the ages. Amen.

Antiphon AB 104:
In the invocation of Thy Holy Martyrs, have mercy, O God, upon Thy Suppliants.

Collect when Exorcism is performed AB 97:
O God, Who hast lavished Thy kingdom upon Thy martyrs, be pleased to grant us sinners forgiveness. By suffering for the Faith, these were worthy of their Crown. We, however, beg of Thee, remission of our iniquities and prevarication's and we beg of Thee mercy, Through Thee, O Jesus Christ Who reignest unto the ages. Amen.

Collect AB 124:
O Holy and glorious, wondrous and powerful martyrs whose works please the Lord, and in whose assembly He is joyful, the best intercessors and mightiest protectors, remember us always in the sight of the Lord, that we be worthy of help by the Lord, Who reigneth with the Father and the Holy Spirit unto ages of ages. Amen.

The Shrine of Piety
(Paragraph 6 Teaching of Maelruain of Tallaght)
*Standing **facing the East** with both hands raised to Heaven and clear of vesture say:*

The Divine Prayer AB 36
Our Father, Who art in the Heavens, hallowed be Thy Name. Thy Kingdom come. Thy will be done on earth as it is in Heaven. Give us this day our daily bread and forgive us our debts as we forgive our debtors and lead us not into temptation but deliver us from evil. Amen.

O God come to my assistance, O Lord make haste to help me.
O God come to my assistance, O Lord make haste to help me.
O God come to my assistance, O Lord make haste to help me.

Make the Sign of the Cross with the right hand to the East.

Turn and repeat to each of the other three directions.

*After again turning to the East, repeat the Divine Prayer and the three repetitions of "O Lord come to my assistance..." for all four directions with **face bent down toward the ground**, standing erect only to make the Sign of the Cross in each direction.*

*After again turning to East, repeat the Divine Prayer and the three repetitions of "O Lord come to my assistance..." for all four directions with **face raised to Heaven**, looking ahead only to make the Sign of the Cross in each direction. Therefore the Divine Prayer is repeated twelve times, "O Lord come to my assistance..." is repeated thirty six times and the Sign of the Cross is made twelve times. [Note: when the face is up, breathe deeply and lean back a bit so that the neck is not cramped.]*

Here Ends the Hour. *May do the Beatitudes and Magnificat.*

Second Hour, Daily Prayer

(approximately 7 a.m.)

V. ✠ O God come to my assistance. **R.**: O Lord make haste to help me.

V. Glory be to the Father, and to the Son, and to the Holy Spirit, as it was in the beginning, is now, and ever unto ages of ages. **R.** Amen.

Saturday Antiphon AB 106:
Look upon Thy servants and Thy works, O Lord.   (Ps. 89:16a)

Sunday Antiphon AB 105:
✠ Return O Lord, how long? and be entreated in favor of Thy servants.   (Ps. 89:13)

Daily Antiphon AB 108:
And let the brightness of the Lord our God be upon us.   (Ps. 89:17)

Fastdays' Antiphon AB 107:
We are filled in the morning with Thy mercy.   (Ps. 89:14)

Christmas Antiphon AB 98:
✠ For today night is diminished, days are enlarged, shadows are shattered, illumination is increased and the loss of night is translated into a wealth of Light.

Psalm 50

3. Have mercy on me, O God, according to Thy great mercy. And according to the multitude of Thy tender mercies, blot out my iniquity.
4. Wash me yet more from my iniquity: and cleanse me from my sin.
5. For I know my iniquity: and my sin is always before me.
6. To Thee only have I sinned, and have done evil before Thee: that Thou mayst be justified in Thy words, and mayst overcome when Thou art judged.
7. For, behold, I was conceived in iniquities: and in sins did my mother conceive me.
8. For, behold, Thou hast loved truth: the uncertain and hidden things of Thy wisdom Thou hast made manifest to me.
9. Thou shalt sprinkle me with hyssop, and I shall be cleansed: Thou shalt wash me, and I shall be made whiter than snow.
10. To my hearing Thou shalt give joy and gladness: and the bones that have been humbled shall rejoice.
11. Turn away Thy face from my sins: and blot out all my iniquities.
12. Create a clean heart in me, O God: and renew a right spirit within my bowels.
13. Cast me not away from Thy face: and take not Thy Holy Spirit from me.
14. Restore unto me the joy of Thy salvation: and strengthen me with a perfect spirit.
15. I will teach the unjust Thy ways: and the wicked shall be converted to Thee.
16. Deliver me from blood, O God, Thou God of my salvation: and my tongue shall extol Thy justice.
17. O Lord, Thou wilt open my lips: and my mouth shall declare Thy praise.
18. For if Thou hadst desired sacrifice, I would indeed have given it: with burnt-offerings Thou wilt not be delighted.
19. A sacrifice to God is an afflicted spirit: a contrite and humbled heart, O God, Thou wilt not despise.
20. Deal favourably, O Lord, in Thy good-will with Sion: that the walls of Jerusalem may be built up.
21. Then shalt Thou accept the sacrifice of justice, oblations and whole burnt-offerings: then shall they lay calves upon Thy altar.

Saturday Antiphon AB 106:
Look upon Thy servants and Thy works, O Lord.   (Ps. 89:16a)
Sunday Antiphon AB 105:
✠ Return O Lord, how long? and be entreated in favor of Thy servants.   (Ps. 89:13)
Daily Antiphon AB 108:
And let the brightness of the Lord our God be upon us.   (Ps. 89:17)
Fastdays' Antiphon AB 107:
We are filled in the morning with Thy mercy.   (Ps. 89:14)
Christmas Antiphon AB 98:
✠ For today night is diminished, days are enlarged, shadows are shattered, illumination is increased and the loss of night is translated into a wealth of Light.

Psalm 62

2. O God, my God, to Thee do I watch at break of day. For Thee my soul hath thirsted. For Thee my flesh, O how many ways!
3. In a desert land, and where there is no way and no water: so in the sanctuary have I come before Thee, to see Thy power and Thy glory.
4. For Thy mercy is better than lives: Thee my lips shall praise.
5. Thus will I bless Thee all my life long: and in Thy Name I will lift up my hands.
6. Let my soul be filled as with marrow and fatness: and my mouth shall praise Thee with joyful lips.
7. If I have remembered Thee upon my bed, I will meditate on Thee in the morning:
8. Because Thou hast been my helper. And I will rejoice under the covert of Thy wings.
9. My soul hath stuck close to Thee: Thy right hand hath received me.
10. But they have sought my soul in vain, they shall go into the lower parts of the earth:
11. They shall be delivered into the hands of the sword, they shall be the portions of foxes.
12. But the king shall rejoice in God; all they shall be praised that swear by Him: because the mouth is stopped of them that speak wicked things.

Saturday Antiphon AB 106:
Look upon Thy servants and Thy works, O Lord.   (Ps. 89:16a)
Sunday Antiphon AB 105:
✠ Return O Lord, how long? and be entreated in favor of Thy servants. (Ps. 89:13)
Daily Antiphon AB 108:
And let the brightness of the Lord our God be upon us.   (Ps. 89:17)
Fastdays' Antiphon AB 107:
We are filled in the morning with Thy mercy.   (Ps. 89:14)
Christmas Antiphon AB 98:
✠ For today night is diminished, days are enlarged, shadows are shattered, illumination is increased and the loss of night is translated into a wealth of Light.

Psalm 89

1. Lord, Thou hast been our refuge: from generation to generation.
2. Before the mountains were made, or the earth and the world was formed: from eternity and to eternity Thou art God.
3. Turn not man away to be brought low: and Thou hast said: Be converted, O ye sons of men.
4. For a thousand years in Thy sight are as yesterday, which is past. And as a watch in the night;
5. Things that are counted nothing shall their years be.
6. In the morning man shall grow up like grass; in the morning he shall flourish and pass away: in the evening he shall fall, grow dry, and wither.

7. For in Thy wrath we have fainted away: and are troubled in Thy indignation.
8. Thou hast set our iniquities before Thy eyes: our life in the light of Thy countenance.
9. For all our days are spent: and in Thy wrath we have fainted away. Our years shall be considered as a spider:
10. The days of our years in them are threescore and ten years. But if in the strong they be fourscore years: and what is more of them is labour and sorrow. For mildness is come upon us: and we shall be corrected.
11. Who knoweth the power of Thy anger: and for Thy fear
12. Can number Thy wrath? So make Thy right hand known: and men learned in heart, in wisdom.
13. Return, O Lord: how long? And be entreated in favour of Thy servants.
14. We are filled in the morning with Thy mercy: and we have rejoiced, and are delighted all our days.
15. We have rejoiced for the days in which Thou hast humbled us: for the years in which we have seen evils.
16. Look upon Thy servants and upon their works: and direct their children.
17. And let the brightness of the Lord our God be upon us: and direct Thou the works of our hands over us; yea, the work of our hands do Thou direct.

Saturday Antiphon AB 106:
Look upon Thy servants and Thy works, O Lord.   (Ps. 89:16a)
Sunday Antiphon AB 105:
✠ Return O Lord, how long? and be entreated in favor of Thy servants.   (Ps. 89:13)
Daily Antiphon AB 108:
And let the brightness of the Lord our God be upon us.   (Ps. 89:17)
Fastdays' Antiphon AB 107:
We are filled in the morning with Thy mercy.   (Ps. 89:14)
Christmas Antiphon AB 98:
✠ For today night is diminished, days are enlarged, shadows are shattered, illumination is increased and the loss of night is translated into a wealth of Light.

Collects

Sunday Collect AB 16:
Be our protector this day, O Lord, Holy Father Almighty, eternal God, Who feels pity: the bestower of mercy, our helper, leader and Illuminator of our hearts. Guard, O Lord, our thoughts, conversations, and acts that we may be able, O Lord, to be pleasing in Thy sight, obedient to Thy will and walk in the correct way for the rest of our life: Who reignest unto the ages. Amen.

Sunday Collect AB 17:
We pray Thee, Most High, show forth the light of the sun, Christ, Who is called Orient; be with us, O Lord: Who reignest unto the ages. Amen.

Fast days Collect AB 27:
O Lord, hear us Thy suppliants who repay Thee with thanks in this first hour of the day, O our Lord God, Who redeemed us by Thy Holy Blood, accept our prayers and petitions as the first fruits that are offered Who reignest unto the ages. Amen.

Daily Collect AB 122:
O Lord, Holy Father, Almighty, Eternal God, Who illuminates the day and lights by light, O Lord, take not Thy mercy from us: restore unto us the joy of Thy Salvation, and confirm us by Thine original Spirit, that the Bearer of Light might be born in our hearts, through Thee, O Jesus Christ: Who reignest unto the ages. Amen.

The Prayers of the *Community of the Brethren*, long or short form are said. These are written out at the end of the Psalter. Also Credo and Our Father.

Third Hour, Daily Prayer

(approximately 9 a.m.)

V. ✠ O God come to my assistance. **R.:** O Lord make haste to help me.
V. Glory be to the Father, and to the Son, and to the Holy Spirit, as it was in the beginning, is now, and ever unto ages of ages. **R.** Amen.

Antiphon: Sing praises to our God, sing ye: sing praises to our King, sing ye wisely.
(Ps. 46:7)

Psalm 46

2. O clap your hands, all ye nations: shout unto God with the voice of joy,
3. For the Lord is high, terrible: a great King over all the earth.
4. He hath subdued the people under us: and the nations under our feet.
5. He hath chosen for us His inheritance: the beauty of Jacob which He hath loved.
6. God is ascended with jubilee: and the Lord with the sound of trumpet.
7. Sing praises to our God, sing ye: sing praises to our King, sing ye.
8. For God is the King of all the earth: sing ye wisely.
9. God shall reign over the nations: God sitteth on His holy Throne.
10. The princes of the people are gathered together, with the God of Abraham: for the strong gods of the earth are exceedingly exalted.

Antiphon: Sing praises to our God, sing ye: sing praises to our King, sing ye wisely.
(Ps. 46:7)

Psalm 53

3. Save me, O God, by Thy Name, and judge me in Thy strength.
4. O God, hear my prayer: give ear to the words of my mouth.
5. For strangers have risen up against me; and the mighty have sought after my soul: and they have not set God before their eyes.
6. For, behold, God is my helper: and the Lord is the protector of my soul.
7. Turn back the evils upon my enemies: and cut them off in Thy truth.
8. I will freely sacrifice to Thee, and will give praise, O God, to Thy Name: because it is good:
9. For Thou hast delivered me out of all trouble: and my eye hath looked down upon my enemies.

Antiphon: Sing praises to our God, sing ye: sing praises to our King, sing ye wisely.
(Ps. 46:7)

Psalm 114

1. I have loved, because the Lord will hear the voice of my prayer.
2. Because He hath inclined His ear unto me: and in my days I will call upon Him.
3. The sorrows of death have compassed me: and the perils of hell have found me. I met with trouble and sorrow:
4. And I called upon the Name of the Lord. O Lord, deliver my soul:
5. The Lord is merciful and just, and our God sheweth mercy.
6. The Lord is the keeper of little ones: I was humbled, and He delivered me.
7. Turn, O my soul, into thy rest: for the Lord hath been bountiful to thee.
8. For He hath delivered my soul from death: my eyes from tears, my feet from falling.
9. I will please the Lord in the land of the living.

Antiphon: Sing praises to our God, sing ye: sing praises to our King, sing ye wisely.
(Ps. 46:7)

Collects

Sunday Collect AB 18:
Through the Third Hour let us beg for the clemency of Christ, that He grant us His perpetual Grace: Who reigneth unto the ages. Amen.

All other Days Collect AB 28:
We who rely upon Thee, bow in prayer to Thee, O Lord Christ, Who sent the Holy Spirit at the Third Hour of the day unto the praying Apostles: Mandate for us, who beg Thee, participation in the same grace of forgiveness: Who reignest unto the ages. Amen.

The Prayers of the *Community of the Brethren*, long or short form are said. These are written out at the end of the Psalter. Also Credo and Our Father.

Sixth Hour, Daily Prayer
(Noon)

V. ✠ O God come to my assistance. **R.:** O Lord make haste to help me.

V. Glory be to the Father, and to the Son, and to the Holy Spirit, as it was in the beginning, is now, and ever unto ages of ages. **R.** Amen.

Antiphon: Cause the Light of Thy Countenance to shine upon us, O Lord, and have mercy on us.   (paraphrase of: Psalm 66:2)

Psalm 66

2. May God have mercy on us, and bless us: may He cause the light of His countenance to shine upon us; and may He have mercy on us.
3. That we may know Thy way upon earth: Thy salvation in all nations.
4. Let people confess to Thee, O God: let all people give praise to Thee.
5. Let the nations be glad and rejoice: for Thou judgest the people with justice and directest the nations upon earth.
6. Let the people, O God, confess to Thee: let all the people give praise to Thee:
7. The earth hath yielded her fruit. May God, our God bless us,
8. May God bless us: and all the ends of the earth fear him.

Antiphon: Cause the Light of Thy Countenance to shine upon us, O Lord and have mercy on us.

Psalm 69

2. O God, come to my assistance: O Lord, make haste to help me.
3. Let them be confounded and ashamed that seek my soul:
4. Let them be turned backward, and blush for shame that desire evils to me: Let them be presently turned away blushing for shame, that say to me: 'Tis well, 'tis well.
5. Let all that seek Thee rejoice and be glad in Thee; and let such as love Thy salvation say always: The Lord be magnified.
6. But I am needy and poor: O God, help me. Thou art my helper and my deliverer: O lord, make no delay.

Antiphon: Cause the Light of Thy Countenance to shine upon us, O Lord and have mercy on us.

Psalm 115

10. I have believed, therefore have I spoken: but I have been humbled exceedingly.
11. I said in my excess: Every man is a liar.
12. What shall I render to the Lord for all the things that he hath rendered to me?
13. I will take the chalice of salvation: and I will call upon the Name of the Lord.
14. I will pay my vows to the Lord before all His people:
15. Precious in the sight of the Lord is the death of His saints.
16. O Lord, for I am Thy servant: I am Thy servant, and the son of Thy handmaid. Thou hast broken my bonds:
17. I will sacrifice to Thee the sacrifice of praise: and I will call upon the Name of the Lord.
18. I will pay my vows to the Lord in the sight of all His people:
19. In the courts of the house of the Lord, in the midst of Thee, O Jerusalem.

Antiphon: Cause the Light of Thy Countenance to shine upon us, O Lord and have mercy on us.

Collects

Sunday Collect AB 19:
Spare O Christ, Thy Suppliants who pray at the Sixth Hour in as much as Thou wast lifted up upon the Cross for all: Who reignest unto the ages. Amen.

All other Days Collect AB 29:
Almighty, Eternal God, Who wrought great things for us at the Sixth Hour: ascended the Cross and illumined the darkness of the world: Be pleased to likewise illumine our hearts: Who reignest unto the ages. Amen.

The Prayers of the *Community of the Brethren*, long or short form are said. These are written out at the end of the Psalter. Also Credo and Our Father.

Ninth Hour, Daily Prayer
(approximately 3 p.m.)

V. ✠ O God come to my assistance. **R.:** O Lord make haste to help me.
V. Glory be to the Father, and to the Son, and to the Holy Spirit, as it was in the beginning, is now, and ever unto ages of ages. **R.** Amen.

Antiphon: Behold how good and how pleasant it is for brethren to dwell together in unity. (Ps: 132:1)

Psalm 129

1b. Out of the depths I have cried to Thee, O Lord:
2. Lord, hear my voice: Let Thy ears be attentive to the voice of my supplication.
3. If Thou, O Lord, wilt mark iniquities: Lord, who shall stand it?
4. For with Thee there is merciful forgiveness: and by reason of Thy law I have waited for Thee, O Lord. My soul hath relied on His word:
5. My soul hath hoped in the Lord.

6. From the morning watch even until night: let Israel hope in the Lord.
7. Because with the Lord there is mercy: and with him plentiful redemption.
8. And he shall redeem Israel from all his iniquities.

Antiphon: Behold how good and how pleasant it is for brethren to dwell together in unity. (Ps: 132:1)

Psalm 132

1. Behold how good and how pleasant it is for brethren to dwell together in unity:
2. Like the precious ointment on the head, that ran down upon the beard, the beard of Aaron, Which ran down to the skirt of his garment:
3. As the dew of Hermon, which descendeth upon mount Sion. For there the Lord hath commanded blessing, and life for evermore.

Antiphon: Behold how good and how pleasant it is for brethren to dwell together in unity. (Ps: 132:1)

Psalm 147

2. Praise the Lord, O Jerusalem: praise Thy God, O Sion.
3. Because He hath strengthened the bolts of Thy gates, He hath blessed Thy children within Thee.
4. Who hath placed peace in Thy borders: and filleth Thee with the fat of corn.
5. Who sendeth forth His speech to the earth: His word runneth swiftly.
6. Who giveth snow like wool: scattereth mists like ashes.
7. He sendeth His crystal like morsels: who shall stand before the face of His cold?
8. He shall send out His word, and shall melt them: His wind shall blow, and the waters shall run.
9. Who declareth His word to Jacob: His justices and His judgments to Israel.
10. He hath not done in like manner to every nation: and His judgments He hath not made manifest to them. Alleluia.

Antiphon: Behold how good and how pleasant it is for brethren to dwell together in unity. (Ps: 132:1)

Collects

Sunday Collect AB 20:
Hear O Christ the prayer of all who pray at the Ninth Hour, just as Thou didst attend to Cornelius by the Angel Who reignest unto the ages. Amen.

Fast Days Collect AB 30:
The Ninth Hour of the day is offered unto Thee, O Lord, with simple supplication: in that Divine wonders are shown to Thy worshippers, by imitation of them, may our hearts also be illumined: Who reignest unto the ages. Amen.

Other Days Collect AB 121:
Our dearest brethren gather for the Ninth Hour, the time at which the Thief confessed and the Kingdom of Paradise was promised to him: likewise may we confess our sins, O Lord, that we may gain the Kingdom of the Heavens and deserve eternal life: Who reignest unto the ages. Amen.

The Prayers of the Community of the Brethren, long or short form are said. These are written out at the end of the Psalter. Also Credo and Our Father.

The Hours of Holy and Great Friday

The Old Gallican Missal specifies: NO PSALMS OR GLORIAS on this day, including no daily prayers, Collects, etc. The prayers and Harmony of the Gospels below replace the entire Hours of Holy and Great Friday. *[Psalms have elements of the Resurrection in them as Prophecy, see Meditations on the Psalms and Lectionary.]*

Holy and Great Friday Lectionary Harmony of the Gospels

Matins (portion existing, part of the book was destroyed, including previous Hours):
St. Matthew 26: 72
St. John 18:26
St. Matthew 26:73-74
St. Luke 22:61-62

Second Hour:
Isaiah 52:13-53:12
St. Matthew 27:1-2a
St. John 18:28a
St. Matthew 27:2-14
St. John 18:28b-38
St. Luke 23:5a,2b,5b-15
St. Matthew 27:15-16
St. Luke 23:19
St. Matthew 27:17-23
St. Luke 23:22
St. Matthew 27:23b
St. Luke 23:23
St. Matthew 27:24-26

Third Hour:
Jer: 11:15-20, 12:7-9
St. Matthew 27:27-28a
St. John 19:2b
St. Matthew 27:28b-29
St. John 19:3b
St. Matthew 27:30
St. John 19:4-16
St. Matthew 27:31a
St. John 19:16b-17a
St. Mark 15:20b, 25a
St. Matthew 27:32
St. Luke 23:26b-32
St. Matthew 27:33-34

Sixth Hour:
Amos 8:4-11
St. Matthew 27:35a
St. John 19:19-24
St. Matthew 27:36
St. John 19:25-27
St. Matthew 27:38
St. John 19:18b
St. Mark 15:28
St. Luke 23:34a
St. Matthew 27:39-43
St. Luke 23:39-43

Ninth Hour:
Zach: 8:14-16, 12:10-12
St. Matthew 27:45-55a
St. Luke 23:48-49a
St. Matthew 27:55-56
St. John 19:31-37
St. Matthew 27:57
St. Mark 16:44
St. Matthew 27:58
St. John 19:39-40a
St. Matthew 27: 60-61
Holy Saturday
Matins *(which may be done within the Cross Vigil)*:
St. Matthew 27: 61-66

The Harmony of the Gospels of Holy and Great Friday written out in full:

The Harmony of the Gospels of Holy and Great Friday for Vespers, Midnight, and the beginning of Matins has been destroyed. All the books were ripped: the Lectionaries of Luxeil, Bobbio, and the Gallican Rite. The same pages are always missing from the binding; i.e., the earlier usages did include a harmony of these sections. Furthermore, the special Collects of Vespers, Midnight, and Matins are also missing. (The agony in the Garden must not replace the Crucifixion and our salvation; but the agony in the Garden should not be excluded.) Therefore, a complete Harmony of the Gospels, reconstructed according to the hours, is provided below, to be placed in Vespers, Midnight and the beginning of Matins, but some of the Collects that would end the Hours are not available. The Prophecies of these Hours are found in other Celtic and traditional sources, and were not chosen "ad libitum" for this Breviary.

The usual Gospel readings for Friday at the Beginning of Night (modern Thursday evening), and Saturday at the Beginning of Night (modern Friday evening): St. John, Chapters 16 through 21, should be done earlier in the week, or on the day of Holy Thursday. The first four chapters of the Book of Acts is read Holy Saturday afternoon in anticipation of the Beginning of Night of the Vigil of the Resurrection.

Note about the general ending prayers for each Hour: There are references made to faithless Jews. Understand that this is meant in a tropological way (see the definition under "Layers of Meaning" in Meditations on the Psalms); what is meant here is faithless people who assume that they are faithful because of either inheritance or a one-time offering of prayer or decision or alms to the Lord; but who never continue to pray so that their belief is weak, or assume that others in the greater Church or in their family will pray for them so they never find the time to either pray or learn about the Lord, or do not make decisions based on the teachings of God rather than the letter of the Law, or do not continue to help the poor; i.e., each and every one of us who assumes that we are "saved" simply because we are Christians. This is also a reference to the attitude of St. John: that he was of the Tribe of Judah, and that he is in need of prayers. This is meant for us to examine ourselves, and not judge our brothers, however, the wording of these prayers has been left as is to keep the translation accurate, and because the early Christians considered themselves to be grafted on to the tree of Abraham, i.e., that we also are the Jews being directly referred to.

The first Hour of Holy and Great Friday is the longest and combines both Vespers and the Beginning of Night.

Vespers and the Beginning of Night of Holy and Great Friday Combined:

[Book of Osee at Vespers specified in old Gallican Missal, selection of chapter and verse not specified. Chapter and verses are given in the Roman Presanctified Liturgy of St. Gregory the Great, which lifts much of the material from the Hours of Gallican usage. The Gallican and Irish usages did not use the Presanctified Liturgy of St. Gregory the Great on Holy and Great Friday. At other times, occasionally a Pre-Sanctified Mass would be a part of Matins.]

Prophecy: Hosea (Osee) 6:1 - 6

In their affliction they will rise early to me: Come, and let us return to the Lord: For He hath taken us, and He will heal us: He will strike, and He will cure us. He will revive us after two days: on the third day He will raise us up and we shall live in His sight. We shall know and we shall follow on, that we may know the Lord. His going forth is prepared as the morning light and He will come to us as the early and the latter rain to the earth. What shall I do to thee, O Ephraim? What shall I do to thee, O Juda? Your mercy is as a morning cloud and as the dew that goeth away in the morning. For this reason have I hewed them by the prophets, I have slain them by the words of my mouth: and thy judgments shall go forth as the light. For I desired mercy and not sacrifice: and the knowledge of God more than holocausts.

After Old Testament reading (from the Old Gallican Missal):
R. I have heard, O Lord.

At all Hours after the Prophecy:

Collect: O God, from Whom Judas received the punishment of his guilt, and the thief the reward of his confession, grant unto us the effects of Thy propitiation: that as in His Passion Jesus Christ, our Lord, gave unto both the divers rewards of their merits; so he may take away the transgressions of our old nature, and bestow upon us the grace of His Resurrection: Who liveth and reigneth with Thee and the Holy Spirit, unto ages of ages.
R. Amen.

The Holy Passion Gospel:
STAND:

After the supper still in the house:
Jn 13:34 A new commandment I give unto you: That you love one another, as I have loved you, that you also love one another.
Jn 13:35 By this shall all men know that you are my disciples, if you have love one for another.
Lk 24 And there was also a strife amongst them, which of them should seem to be the greater.
Lk 25 And He said to them: The kings of the Gentiles lord it over them: and they that have power over them are called beneficent.
Lk 26 But you not so; but he that is the greater among you, let him become as the younger; and he that is the leader, as he that serveth.
Lk 27 For which is greater, he that sitteth at table or he that serveth? Is not he that sitteth at table? But I am in the midst of you, as He that serveth.
Lk 28 And you are they who have continued with me in my temptations;
Lk 29 And I dispose to you, as my Father hath disposed to me, a kingdom;
Lk 30 That you may eat and drink at my table, in my kingdom; and may sit upon thrones, judging the twelve tribes of Israel.
Jn 14:1 Let not your heart be troubled. You believe in God; believe also in me.
Jn 14:2 In my Father's house there are many mansions. If not, I would have told you; because I go to prepare a place for you.

Jn 14:3 And, if I shall go and prepare a place for you, I will come again and will take you to myself; that where I am, you also may be.

Jn 14:4 And whither I go you know; and the way you know.

Jn 14:5 Thomas saith to Him: Lord, we know not whither Thou goest; and how can we know the way?

Jn 14:6 Jesus saith to him: I am the way, and the truth, and the life. No man cometh to the Father, but by me.

Jn 14:7 If you had known me, you would without doubt have known my Father also; and from henceforth you shall know Him. And you have seen Him.

Jn 14:8 Philip saith to Him: Lord, shew us the Father; and it is enough for us.

Jn 14:9 Jesus saith to him: Have I been so long a time with you and have you not known me? Philip, he that seeth me seeth the Father also. How sayest thou: Shew us the Father?

Jn 14:10 Do you not believe that I am in the Father and the Father in me? The words that I speak to you, I speak not of myself. But the Father who abideth in me, He doth the works.

Jn 14:11 Believe you not that I am in the Father and the Father in me?

Jn 14:12 Otherwise believe for the very works' sake. Amen, amen, I say to you, he that believeth in me, the works that I do he also shall do; and greater than these shall he do;

Jn 14:13 Because I go to the Father; and whatsoever you shall ask the Father in my Name, that will I do; that the Father may be glorified in the Son.

Lk 31 And the Lord said: Simon, Simon, behold, Satan hath desired to have you, that he may sift you as wheat.

Lk 32 But I have prayed for thee, that thy faith fail not; and thou, being once converted, confirm thy brethren.

Jn 14:14 If you shall ask me any thing in my Name, that I will do.

Jn 14:15 If you love me, keep my commandments.

Jn 14:16 And I will ask the Father; and he shall give you another Paraclete, that He may abide with you for ever;

Jn 14:17 The Spirit of truth, Whom the world cannot receive, because it seeth Him not, nor knoweth Him. But you shall know Him; because He shall abide with you and shall be in you.

Jn 14:18 I will not leave you orphans; I will come to you.

Jn 14:19 Yet a little while, and the world seeth me no more. But you see me; because I live, and you shall live.

Jn 14:20 In that day you shall know that I am in my Father; and you in me, and I in you.

Lk 34b And He said to them:

Lk 35 When I sent you without purse and scrip and shoes, did you want anything?

Lk 36 But they said: Nothing. Then said He unto them: But now he that hath a purse, let him take it, and likewise a scrip; and he that hath not, let him sell his coat and buy a sword.

Lk 37 For I say to you that this that is written must yet be fulfilled in me: And with the wicked was He reckoned. For the things concerning me have an end.

Lk 38 But they said: Lord, behold, here are two swords. And He said to them: It is enough.

Jn 14:21 He that hath my commandments and keepeth them; he it is that loveth me. And he that loveth me shall be loved of my Father; and I will love him and will manifest myself to him.

Jn 14:22 Judas saith to Him, not the Iscariot: Lord, how is it that Thou wilt manifest Thyself to us, and not to the world?

Jn 14:23 Jesus answered and said to him: If any one love me, he will keep my word. And my Father will love him; and we will come to him and will make our abode with him.

Jn 14:24 He that loveth me not, keepeth not my words. And the word which you have heard is not mine; but the Father's who sent me.

Jn 14:25 These things have I spoken to you, abiding with you.

Jn 14:26 But the Paraclete, the Holy Ghost, Whom the Father will send in My Name, He will teach you all things and bring all things to your mind, whatsoever I shall have said to you.
Jn 14:27 Peace I leave with you; my peace I give unto you; not as the world giveth, do I give unto you: Let not your heart be troubled; not let it be afraid.
Jn 14:28 You have heard that I said to you: I go away, and I come unto you. If you loved me, you would indeed be glad, because I go to the Father; for the Father is greater than I.
Jn 14:29 And now I have told you before it come to pass; that, when it shall come to pass, you may believe.
Jn 14:30 I will not now speak many things with you. For the prince of this world cometh; and in me he hath not any thing.
Jn 14:31 But that the world may know that I love the Father; and as the Father hath given me commandment, so do I. Arise, let us go hence.

On the Mount of Olives:

Mk 14: 26 And when they had sung a hymn they went forth to the Mount of Olives.
Lk 39 And going out He went, according to His custom, to the mount of Olives. And His disciples also followed Him.

[And Jesus said:]
Jn 15:1 I am the true vine; and my Father is the husbandman.
Jn 15:2 Every branch in me that beareth not fruit, He will take away; and every one that beareth fruit, He will purge it, that it may bring forth more fruit.
Jn 15:3 Now you are clean, by reason of the word which I have spoken to you.
Jn 15:4 Abide in me; and I in you. As the branch cannot bear fruit of itself, unless it abode in the vine, so neither can you, unless you abide in me.
Jn 15:5 I am the vine; you the branches. He that abideth in me, and I in him, the same beareth much fruit; for without me you can do nothing.
Jn 15:6 If any one abide not in me, he shall be cast forth as a branch and shall wither; and they shall gather him up and cast him into the fire; and he burneth.
Jn 15:7 If you abide in me and my words abide in you, you shall ask whatever you will; and it shall be done unto you.
Jn 15:8 In this is my Father glorified; that you bring forth very much fruit and become my disciples.
Jn 15:9 As the Father hath loved me, I also have loved you. Abide in my love.
Jn 15:10 If you keep my commandments, you shall abide in my love; as I also have kept my Father's commandments and do abide in His love.
Jn 15:11 These things I have spoken to you, that my joy may be in you, and your joy may be filled.
Jn 15:12 This is my commandment, that you love one another, as I have loved you.
Jn 15:13 Greater love than this no man hath, that a man lay down his life for his friends.
Jn 15:14 You are my friends if you do the things that I command you.
Jn 15:15 I will not now call you servants; for the servant knoweth not what his lord doth. But I have called you friends; because all things, whatsoever I have heard of my Father, I have made known to you.
Jn 15:16 You have not chosen me; but I have chosen you; and have appointed you, that you should go and should bring forth fruit; and your fruit should remain; that whatsoever you shall ask of the Father in my Name He may give it you.
Jn 15:17 These things I command you, that you love one another.
Jn 15:18 If the world hate you, know ye that it hath hated me before you.
Jn 15:19 If you had been of the world, the world would love its own; but because you are not of the world, but I have chosen you out of the world, therefore the world hateth you.
Jn 15:20 Remember my word that I said to you: The servant is not greater than his master. If they have persecuted me, they will also persecute you. If they have kept my word, they will keep yours also.
Jn 15:21 But all these things they will do to you for my Name's sake; because they know not Him that sent me.

Jn 15:22 If I had not come and spoken to them; they would not have sin; but now they have no excuse for their sin.

Jn 15:23 He that hateth me hateth my Father also.

Jn 15:24 If I had not done among them the works that no other man hath done, they would not have sin; but now they have both seen and hated both me and my Father.

Jn 15:25 But that the word may be fulfilled which is written in their law: They hated me without cause.

Jn 15:26 But when the Paraclete cometh, Whom I will send you from the Father, the Spirit of truth, Who proceedeth from the Father, He shall give testimony of me.

Jn 15:27 And you shall give testimony, because you are with me from the beginning.

Jn 16:1 These things have I spoken to you that you may not be scandalized.

Jn 16:2 They will put you out of the synagogues; yea, the hour cometh that whosoever killeth you will think that he doth a service to God.

Jn 16:3 And these things will they do to you; because they have not known the Father nor me.

Jn 16:4 But these things I have told you, that when the hour shall come you may remember that I told you of them.

Jn 16:5 But I told you not these things from the beginning, because I was with you. And now I go to Him that sent me, and one of you asketh me: Whither goest Thou?

Jn 16:6 But because I have spoken these things to you, sorrow hath filled your heart.

Jn 16:7 But I tell you the truth; it is expedient to you that I go. For if I go not, the Paraclete will not come to you; but if I go, I will send Him to you.

Jn 16:8 And, when He is come, He will convince the world of sin and of justice and of judgment.

Jn 16:9 Of sin; because they believed not in me.

Jn 16:10 And of justice; because I go to the Father; and you shall see me no longer.

Jn 16:11 And of judgment; because the prince of this world is already judged.

Jn 16:12 I have yet many things to say to you; but you cannot bear them now.

Jn 16:13 But when He, the Spirit of truth, is come, He will teach you all truth. For He shall not speak of Himself; but what things soever He shall hear, He shall speak. And the things that are to come, He shall shew you.

Jn 16:14 He shall glorify me; because He shall receive of mine and shall shew it to you.

Jn 16:15 All things whatsoever the Father hath are mine. Therefore I said that He shall receive of mine and shew it to you.

Jn 16:16 A little while, and now you shall not see me; and again a little while, and you shall see me; because I go to the Father.

Jn 16:17 Then some of His disciples said one to another: What is this that He saith to us: A little while, and you shall not see me; and again a little while, and you shall see me, and, Because I go to the Father?

Jn 16:18 They said therefore: What is this that He saith, A little while? We know not what He speaketh.

Jn 16:19 And Jesus knew that they had a mind to ask Him. And He said to them: Of this do you inquire among yourselves, because I said: A little while, and you shall not see me: and again a little while, and you shall see me?

Jn 16:20 Amen, amen, I say to you, that you shall lament and weep, but the world shall rejoice; and you shall be made sorrowful, but your sorrow shall be turned into joy.

Jn 16:21 A woman, when she is in labor, hath sorrow, because her hour is come; but, when she hath brought forth the child, she remembereth no more the anguish, for joy that a man is born into the world.

Jn 16:22 So also you now indeed have sorrow; but I will see you again and your heart shall rejoice. And your joy no man shall take from you.

Jn 16:23 And in that day you shall not ask me any thing. Amen, amen, I say to you: If you ask the Father any thing in my Name, He will give it you.

Jn 16:24 Hitherto, you have not asked any thing in my Name. Ask, and you shall receive; that your joy may be full.

Jn 16:25 These things I have spoken to you in proverbs. The hour cometh when I will no more speak to you in proverbs, but will shew you plainly of the Father.

Jn 16:26 In that day, you shall ask in my Name; and I say not to you that I will ask the Father for you.

Jn 16:27 For the Father Himself loveth you, because you have loved me and have believed that I came out from God.

Jn 16:28 I came forth from the Father and am come into the world; again I leave the world and I go to the Father.

Jn 16:29 His disciples say to Him: Behold, now Thou speakest plainly and speakest no proverb.

Jn 16:30 Now we know that Thou knowest all things and Thou needest not that any man should ask Thee. By this we believe that Thou camest forth from God.

Jn 16:31 Jesus answered them: Do you now believe?

Jn 16:32 Behold, the hour cometh, and it is now come, that you shall be scattered every man to his own and shall leave me alone. And yet I am not alone, because the Father is with me.

Jn 16:33 These things I have spoken to you, that in me you may have peace. In the world you shall have distress. But have confidence. I have overcome the world.

Jn 17:1 These things Jesus spoke; and lifting up His eyes to heaven He said: Father, the hour is come. Glorify Thy Son, that Thy Son may glorify Thee.

Prayer for Disciples on the Mount of Olives (before entering Gethsemane):

Jn 17:1 These things Jesus spoke; and lifting up His eyes to heaven He said: Father, the hour is come. Glorify Thy Son, that Thy Son may glorify Thee.

Jn 17:2 As Thou hast given Him power over all flesh, that He may give eternal life to all whom Thou hast given Him.

Jn 17:3 Now this is eternal life: That they may know Thee, the only true God, and Jesus Christ, Whom Thou hast sent.

Jn 17:4 I have glorified Thee on the earth; I have finished the work which Thou gavest me to do.

Jn 17:5 And now glorify Thou me, O Father, with Thyself, with the glory which I had, before the world was, with Thee.

Jn 17:6 I have manifested Thy Name to the men whom Thou hast given me out of the world. Thine they were; and to me Thou gavest them. And they have kept Thy word.

Jn 17:7 Now they have known that all things which Thou hast given me are from Thee;

Jn 17:8 Because the words which Thou gavest me, I have given to them. And they have received them and have known in very deed that I came out from Thee; and they have believed that Thou didst send me.

Jn 17:9 I pray for them. I pray not for the world, but for them whom Thou hast given me; because they are Thine.

Jn 17:10 And all my things are Thine, and Thine are mine; and I am glorified in them.

Jn 17:11 And now I am not in the world, and these are in the world, and I come to Thee. Holy Father, keep them in Thy Name whom Thou hast given me; that they may be one, as We also are;

Jn 17:12 While I was with them, I kept them in Thy Name. Those whom Thou gavest me have I kept; and none of them is lost, but the son of perdition, that the scripture may be fulfilled.

Jn 17:13 And now I come to Thee; and these things I speak in the world, that they may have my joy filled in themselves.

Jn 17:14 I have given them Thy word, and the world hath hated them; because they are not of the world, as I also am not of the world.

Jn 17:15 I pray not that Thou shouldst take them out of the world, but that Thou shouldst keep them from evil.

Jn 17:16 They are not of the world, as I also am not of the world.

Jn 17:17 Sanctify them in truth. Thy word is truth.

Jn 17:18 As Thou hast sent me into the world, I also have sent them into the world.

Jn 17:19 And for them do I sanctify myself, that they also may be sanctified in truth.
Jn 17:20 And not for them only do I pray, but for them also who through their word shall believe in me.
Jn 17:21 That they all may be one, as Thou, Father, in me, and I in Thee; that they also may be one in us; that the world may believe that Thou hast sent me.
Jn 17:22 And they glory which Thou hast given me, I have given to them; that they may be one, as we also are one,
Jn 17:23 I in them, and Thou in me; that they may be made perfect in one; and the world may know that Thou hast sent me and hast loved them, as Thou hast also loved me.
Jn 17:24 Father, I will that where I am, they also whom Thou hast given me may be with me; that they may see my glory which Thou hast given me, because Thou hast loved me before the creation of the world.
Jn 17:25 Just Father, the world hath not known Thee; but I have known Thee; and these have known that Thou hast sent me.
Jn 17:26 And I have made known Thy Name to them and will make it known; that the love wherewith Thou hast loved me may be in them, and I in them.

At the end of each Hour of Holy and Great Friday, say these prayers:

[For the Church.]
Let us pray, beloved, primarily for the holy churches of God, that our God and Lord be pleased to pacify, multiply, and protect them, throughout the entire world, against principalities and powers, and grant us a peaceful and quiet life, apart from the nations, to glorify God the Father Almighty. **R.** Amen.

Let us pray. Almighty and eternal God, reveal Thy glory unto all of the nations in Christ. Protect the works of Thy mercy, that the Church spread throughout the entire world, and may it persevere stable in the Faith in the confession of Thy Name; through Our Lord Jesus Christ, Who reigneth with the Father and the Holy Spirit, unto ages of ages. **R.** Amen.

[For the Patriarchs:]
Let us pray for our blessed Patriarchs, that God Almighty that appointed them unto the Order of Bishop may preserve them in health and safety. May they guard the Holy Church unto the regulation of the holy people of God. **R.** Amen.

Let us pray. Almighty and eternal God, by Whose eternal statement the universe was founded, regard and be propitious to our prayers, and protect our elected Bishop for us by Thy Faith, that Christian peoples who are governed by such authority under so great a Pontifex, may increase in the merits of Thy Faith; through Our Lord Jesus Christ, Who reigneth with the Father and the Holy Spirit, unto ages of ages. **R.** Amen.

[For all the Clergy and the People of God:]
Let us pray for all Bishops, Priests, Deacons, Acolytes, Exorcists, Lectors, Ostiaries, Confessors, Virgins, Widows, and for all the holy people of God.

Let us pray. Almighty and eternal God, by Whose Spirit the Body of the Church is sanctified and guided, hear us suppliants, for all the clergy of the universe, that by the Gifts of Thy Grace, that from all of the grades of the Church, they may be faithfully obedient to Thee; through Our Lord Jesus Christ, Who reigneth with the Father and the Holy Spirit, unto ages of ages. **R.** Amen.

[For all Christian leaders:]
Let us pray for Christian kings [leaders], that our God and Lord subdue all barbarian nations unto them, unto our perpetual peace. **R.** Amen.

Let us pray. Almighty and eternal God, in Thy hand are the powers of all the ages, and the authorities of all kingdoms; look down and be propitious and benign to the [Christian world] *(Roman Empire)*, that all the nations which are in it may be confident in Thy fierceness, and guided by the strength of Thy right hand; through Our Lord Jesus Christ, Who reigneth with the Father and the Holy Spirit, unto ages of ages. **R.** Amen.

[For Catechumens:]
Let us pray for our Catechumens, that our God and Lord may open the ears of their innermost beings and the door of mercy, so that through the washing of regeneration, they may receive remission of all their sins, and find themselves in Christ Jesus, our Lord.

Let us pray. Almighty and eternal God, Who ever-fertilizes Thy new Church with progeny, increase the Faith and the intellect of our Catechumens, that renewed in the Font of Baptism of Thy adoption, as children they may be gathered together; through Our Lord Jesus Christ, Who reigneth with the Father and the Holy Spirit, unto ages of ages. **R.** Amen.

[For healing of mind and body, release of captives, safety in travel,]
Let us pray, beloved, to God the Father Almighty, that He purge the error from the purity of all of us, that He sweep away sickness, that He dispel famine, that He open prisons, that He break chains, that He grant travelers safe return, health to the infirm, and safe port to seamen.

Let us pray. Almighty and merciful God, consolation of those who sorrow, strength of those who labor, may the prayers of all those crying out in tribulation come unto Thee, that in their necessities they may rejoice in Thy mercy, which comes to them through Our Lord Jesus Christ, Who reigneth with the Father and the Holy Spirit, unto ages of ages. **R.** Amen.

[For heretics:]
Let us pray for heretics and schismatics, that our God and Lord uproot them from universal error and be pleased to call them back to Holy Mother the Catholic and Apostolic Church. **R.** Amen.

Let us pray. Almighty and eternal God, Who saves all, and desires that none perish, look upon the souls that are deceived by the frauds of the devil, that all depravity of heresy being set aside, they may come to their senses, and return to the stability of Thy Truth; through Our Lord Jesus Christ, Who reigneth with the Father and the Holy Spirit, unto ages of ages. **R.** Amen.

[For faithless and doubters:]
Let us pray for the faithless Jews and all doubters, that our God and Lord remove the veil from their hearts, and that they may know Christ Jesus our Lord. **R.** Amen.

Let us pray. Almighty and eternal God, Who because of Thy mercy dost not cast away those who are faithless; hear our prayers, which we give for the healing of the blindness of such people, that acknowledgment of the light of Thy Truth, which is in Christ, grow out of their darkness; through Our Lord Jesus Christ, Who reigneth with the Father and the Holy Spirit, unto ages of ages. **R.** Amen.

[For atheists and idolators:]
Let us pray for pagans and all atheists, that God Almighty remove iniquity from their hearts, and convert them to the abandonment of their idols, and unto the True God and His Only-Begotten Son, Jesus Christ. **R.** Amen.

Let us pray. Almighty and eternal God, Who ever seeks not the death of sinners, but life, be propitious and accept our prayers, and free them from the cult of idols, and gather them into Thy holy Church, unto the praise and glory of Thy Name; through Our Lord Jesus Christ, Who reigneth with the Father and the Holy Spirit, unto ages of ages. **R.** Amen.

[Vespers and the Beginning of Night combined is ended.]
[At the Hour of Vespers and Beginning of Night, the Collect for Holy and Great Friday was placed here.]

Midnight of Holy and Great Friday.

Prophecy: Lamentations 1:12, and Genesis 22:6-8

O all ye that pass by the way, attend, and see if there be any sorrow like to my sorrow: for He hath made a vintage of me, as the Lord spoke in the day of His fierce anger.

And he took the wood for the holocaust, and laid it upon Isaac his son: and he himself carried in his hands fire and a sword. And as they two went on together, Isaac said to his father: My father. And he answered: What wilt thou, son? Behold, saith he, fire and wood; where is the victim for the holocaust? And Abraham said: God will provide himself a victim for a holocaust, my son. So they went on together.

R. I have heard, O Lord.

Collect: O God, from Whom Judas received the punishment of his guilt, and the thief the reward of his confession, grant unto us the effects of Thy propitiation: that as in His Passion Jesus Christ, our Lord, gave unto both the divers rewards of their merits; so he may take away the transgressions of our old nature, and bestow upon us the grace of His Resurrection: Who liveth and reigneth with Thee and the Holy Spirit, unto ages of ages.
R. Amen.

STAND for the Holy Passion Gospel: Upon crossing the brook Cedron and entering the Garden (farm or estate) of Gethsemane:

Jn 18:1a   When Jesus had said these things, He went forth with His disciples over the brook Cedron,

Mk 32   And they came to a farm called Gethsamani. And He saith to His disciples: sit you here while I pray.

Lk 40   And, when He was come to the place, He said to them: Pray, lest ye enter into temptation.   *[The agony in the Garden: Note: the Gospel of St. John places Christ's words at the time of Christ's entering into Jerusalem on Palm Sunday. At that time, the Father speaks to Jesus, and the multitude hears Him. St. John verses 27-30. This event does not replace the Cross.]*

Mt 37a   And, taking with Him Peter and the two sons of Zebedee,

Mk 33b   James and John, with Him; and He began to fear and to be heavy.

Mt 38   Then He saith to them: My soul is sorrowful even unto death. Stay you here and watch with me.

Lk 41a   And He was withdrawn away from them a stone's cast.

Mk 35   And when He was gone forward a little He fell flat on the ground; and He prayed that, if it might be, the hour might pass from him.

Mt 39b   He fell upon His Face, praying and saying:

Mk 36   Abba, Father, all things are possible to Thee; remove this chalice from me; but not what I will, but what Thou wilt.

Lk 43   And there appeared to Him an angel from heaven, strengthening Him. And being in an agony, He prayed the longer.

Lk 44   And His sweat became as drops of blood, trickling down upon the ground.

Lk 45   And, when He rose up from prayer and was come to the disciples, He found them sleeping for sorrow.

Mt 40b   And He saith to Peter: What? Could you not watch one hour with me?

Lk 46   And He said to them: Why sleep you? Arise; pray, lest you enter into temptation.

Mt 41b   The spirit indeed is willing, but the flesh weak.

Mt 42   Again, the second time, He went and prayed, saying; My Father, if this chalice may not pass away, but I must drink it, Thy will be done.

Mk 40   And when He returned He found them again asleep (for their eyes were heavy); and they knew not what to answer Him.

Mt 44   And, leaving them, He went again; and He prayed the third time, saying the selfsame words.
Mk 41   And He cometh the third time and saith to them: Sleep ye now and take your rest. It is enough. The hour is come; behold, the Son of man shall be betrayed into the hands of sinners.
Mt 46   Rise; let us go. Behold, he is at hand that will betray me.

The Arrest

Jn 18:2   And Judas also, who betrayed Him, knew the place; because Jesus had often resorted thither together with His disciples.
Jn 18:3   Judas, therefore, having received a band of soldiers and servants from the chief priests and the Pharisees, cometh thither with lanterns and torches and weapons.
Mt 48   And he that betrayed [Jesus] gave them a sign, saying: Whomsoever I shall kiss, that is He. Hold Him fast.
Mk 45   And, when he was come, immediately going up to Him, he saith: Hail, Rabbi! And he kissed Him.
Lk 48   And Jesus said to him: Judas, dost thou betray the Son of man with a kiss?
Jn 18:4   Jesus, therefore, knowing all things that should come upon Him, went forth and said to them: Who seek ye?
Jn 18:5   They answered Him: Jesus of Nazareth. Jesus saith to them: I am He. And Judas also, who betrayed Him, stood with them.
Jn 18:6   As soon therefore as He had said to them: I am He; they went backward and fell to the ground.
Jn 18:7   Again therefore He asked them: Whom seek ye? And they said: Jesus of Nazareth.
Jn 18:8   Jesus answered: I have told you that I am he. If therefore you seek me, let these go their way.
Jn 18:9   That the word might be fulfilled which He said: Of them whom thou hast given me, I have not lost any one.
Mk 46   But they laid hands on Him and held him.
Lk 49   And they that were about Him, seeing what would follow, said to Him: Lord, shall we strike with the sword?
Jn 18:10   Then Simon Peter, having a sword, drew it and struck the servant of the high priest and cut off his right ear. And the name of the servant was Malchus.
Jn 18:11a   Jesus therefore said to Peter: Put up thy sword into the scabbard.
Mt 52b   for all that take the sword shall perish by the sword.
Jn 18:11b   The chalice which my Father hath given me, shall I not drink it?
Lk 51   But Jesus, answering, said: Suffer ye thus far. And when He had touched his ear, He healed him.
Mt 53   Thinkest thou that I cannot ask my Father, and he will give me presently more than twelve legions of angels?
Mt 54   How then shall the scriptures be fulfilled, that so it must be done?
Lk 52   And Jesus said to the chief priests and magistrates of the temple and the ancients, that were come unto Him: Are ye come out, as it were against a thief, with swords and clubs?
Lk 53   When I was daily with you in the temple, you did not stretch forth your hands against me; but this is your hour and the power of darkness.
Mt 56   Now all this was done that the scriptures of the prophets might be fulfilled. Then the disciples, all leaving Him, fled.
Mk 51   And a certain young man followed him, having a linen cloth cast about his naked body. And they laid hold on him.
Mk 52   But he, casting off the linen cloth, fled from them naked.
Jn 18:12   Then the band and the tribune and the servants of the Jews took Jesus and bound Him.
Lk 54   And apprehending Him they led him to the high priest's house. But Peter followed afar off.

At the end of each Hour of Holy and Great Friday, say these prayers:
[For the Church.]

Let us pray, beloved, primarily for the holy churches of God, that our God and Lord be pleased to pacify, multiply, and protect them, throughout the entire world, against principalities and powers, and grant us a peaceful and quiet life, apart from the nations, to glorify God the Father Almighty. **R.** Amen.

Let us pray. Almighty and eternal God, reveal Thy glory unto all of the nations in Christ. Protect the works of Thy mercy, that the Church spread throughout the entire world, and may it persevere stable in the Faith in the confession of Thy Name; through Our Lord Jesus Christ, Who reigneth with the Father and the Holy Spirit, unto ages of ages. **R.** Amen.

[For the Patriarchs:]

Let us pray for our blessed Patriarchs, that God Almighty that appointed them unto the Order of Bishop may preserve them in health and safety. May they guard the Holy Church unto the regulation of the holy people of God. **R.** Amen.

Let us pray. Almighty and eternal God, by Whose eternal statement the universe was founded, regard and be propitious to our prayers, and protect our elected Bishop for us by Thy Faith, that Christian peoples who are governed by such authority under so great a Pontifex, may increase in the merits of Thy Faith; through Our Lord Jesus Christ, Who reigneth with the Father and the Holy Spirit, unto ages of ages. **R.** Amen.

[For all the Clergy and the People of God:]

Let us pray for all Bishops, Priests, Deacons, Acolytes, Exorcists, Lectors, Ostiaries, Confessors, Virgins, Widows, and for all the holy people of God.

Let us pray. Almighty and eternal God, by Whose Spirit the Body of the Church is sanctified and guided, hear us suppliants, for all the clergy of the universe, that by the Gifts of Thy Grace, that from all of the grades of the Church, they may be faithfully obedient to Thee; through Our Lord Jesus Christ, Who reigneth with the Father and the Holy Spirit, unto ages of ages. **R.** Amen.

[For all Christian leaders:]

Let us pray for Christian kings [leaders], that our God and Lord subdue all barbarian nations unto them, unto our perpetual peace. **R.** Amen.

Let us pray. Almighty and eternal God, in Thy hand are the powers of all the ages, and the authorities of all kingdoms; look down and be propitious and benign to the [Christian world] *(Roman Empire)*, that all the nations which are in it may be confident in Thy fierceness, and guided by the strength of Thy right hand; through Our Lord Jesus Christ, Who reigneth with the Father and the Holy Spirit, unto ages of ages. **R.** Amen.

[For Catechumens:]

Let us pray for our Catechumens, that our God and Lord may open the ears of their innermost beings and the door of mercy, so that through the washing of regeneration, they may receive remission of all their sins, and find themselves in Christ Jesus, our Lord.

Let us pray. Almighty and eternal God, Who ever-fertilizes Thy new Church with progeny, increase the Faith and the intellect of our Catechumens, that renewed in the Font of Baptism of Thy adoption, as children they may be gathered together; through Our Lord Jesus Christ, Who reigneth with the Father and the Holy Spirit, unto ages of ages. **R.** Amen.

[For healing of mind and body, release of captives, safety in travel,]

Let us pray, beloved, to God the Father Almighty, that He purge the error from the purity of all of us, that He sweep away sickness, that He dispel famine, that He open prisons, that He break chains, that He grant travelers safe return, health to the infirm, and safe port to seamen.

Let us pray. Almighty and merciful God, consolation of those who sorrow, strength of those who labor, may the prayers of all those crying out in tribulation come unto Thee, that in their necessities they may rejoice in Thy mercy, which comes to them through Our Lord Jesus Christ, Who reigneth with the Father and the Holy Spirit, unto ages of ages. **R.** Amen.

[For heretics:]

Let us pray for heretics and schismatics, that our God and Lord uproot them from universal error and be pleased to call them back to Holy Mother the Catholic and Apostolic Church. **R.** Amen.

Let us pray. Almighty and eternal God, Who saves all, and desires that none perish, look upon the souls that are deceived by the frauds of the devil, that all depravity of heresy being set aside, they may come to their senses, and return to the stability of Thy Truth; through Our Lord Jesus Christ, Who reigneth with the Father and the Holy Spirit, unto ages of ages. **R.** Amen.

[For faithless and doubters:]

Let us pray for the faithless Jews and all doubters, that our God and Lord remove the veil from their hearts, and that they may know Christ Jesus our Lord. **R.** Amen.

Let us pray. Almighty and eternal God, Who because of Thy mercy dost not cast away those who are faithless; hear our prayers, which we give for the healing of the blindness of such people, that acknowledgment of the light of Thy Truth, which is in Christ, grow out of their darkness; through Our Lord Jesus Christ, Who reigneth with the Father and the Holy Spirit, unto ages of ages. **R.** Amen.

[For atheists and idolators:]

Let us pray for pagans and all atheists, that God Almighty remove iniquity from their hearts, and convert them to the abandonment of their idols, and unto the True God and His Only-Begotten Son, Jesus Christ. **R.** Amen.

Let us pray. Almighty and eternal God, Who ever seeks not the death of sinners, but life, be propitious and accept our prayers, and free them from the cult of idols, and gather them into Thy holy Church, unto the praise and glory of Thy Name; through Our Lord Jesus Christ, Who reigneth with the Father and the Holy Spirit, unto ages of ages. **R.** Amen.

The Midnight Collect was placed here.
[The Hour of Midnight is ended.]

Matins of Holy and Great Friday:

Prophecy: Isaiah 50:4-9

The Lord hath given me a learned tongue, that I should know how to uphold by word him that is weary. He wakeneth in the morning: in the morning he wakeneth my ear, that I may hear him as a master. The Lord God hath opened my ear, and I do not resist: I have not gone back. I have given my body to the strikers, and my cheeks to them that plucked them: I have not turned away my face from them that rebuked me and spit upon me. The Lord God is my helper: therefore am I not confounded. Therefore have I set my face as a most hard rock: and I know that I shall not be confounded. He is near that justifieth me. Who will contend with me? Let us stand together. Who is my adversary? Let him come near to me. Behold, the Lord God is my helper: who is he that shall condemn me? Lo, they shall all be destroyed as a garment: the moth shall eat them up.

R. I have heard, O Lord.

Collect: O God, from Whom Judas received the punishment of his guilt, and the thief the reward of his confession, grant unto us the effects of Thy propitiation: that as in His Passion Jesus Christ, our Lord, gave unto both the divers rewards of their merits; so he may take away the transgressions of our old nature, and bestow upon us the grace of His Resurrection: Who liveth and reigneth with Thee and the Holy Spirit, unto ages of ages. **R.** Amen.

STAND for the Holy Passion Gospel:

>*Before Annas and Caiphas the high priest, Peter following (Peter's third denial is in Matins):*

Jn 18:13 And they led Him away to Annas first, for he was father-in-law to Caiphas, who was the high priest of that year.

Jn 18:14 Now Caiphas was he who had given the counsel to the Jews; that it was expedient that one man should die for the people.

St. Peter's first denial:

Jn 18:15 And Simon Peter followed Jesus; and so did another disciple. And that disciple was known to the high priest and went in with Jesus into the court of the high priest.

Jn 18:16 But Peter stood at the door without. The other disciple therefore, who was known to the high priest, went out and spoke to the portress and brought in Peter.

Jn 18:17 The maid therefore that was portress saith to Peter: Art not thou also one of this man's disciples? He saith: I am not.

>*Jesus questioned, buffeted:*

Jn 18:19 The high priest therefore asked Jesus of his disciples and of His doctrine.

Jn 18:20 Jesus answered him: I have spoken openly to the world. I have always taught in the synagogue and in the temple, whither all the Jews resort; and in secret I have spoken nothing.

Jn 18:21 Why askest thou me? Ask them who have heard what I have spoken unto them. Behold, they know what things I have said.

Jn 18:22 And, when he had said these things, one of the servants standing-by gave Jesus a blow, saying: Answerest thou the high priest so?

Jn 18:23 Jesus answered him: If I have spoken evil, give testimony of the evil; but if well, why strikest thou me?

Jn 18:24 And Annas sent Him bound to Caiphas the high priest.

Mk 53b And all the priests and the scribes and the ancients assembled together.

>*Peter's second denial:*

Mt 58 And Peter followed Him afar off, even to the court of the high priest. And, going in, he sat with the servants, that he might see the end.

Jn 18:18 Now the servants and ministers stood at a fire of coals, because it was cold, and warmed themselves. And with them was Peter also, standing, and warming himself.

Mk 66 Now, when Peter was in the court below, there cometh one of the maidservants of the high priest.

Mk 67 And when she had seen Peter warming himself, looking on him, she saith: Thou also wast with Jesus of Nazareth.

Mk 68 But he denied, saying: I neither know nor understand what thou sayest. And he went forth before the court; and the cock crew.

>*Officially before Caiphas:*

False witnesses:

Mk 55 And the chief priests and all the council sought for evidence against Jesus, that they might put Him to death; and found none.

Mk 56 For many bore false witness against Him; and their evidences were not agreeing.

Mt 60b And last of all there came two false witnesses; saying:

Mk 58 We heard Him say, I will destroy this temple made with hands, and within three days I will build another not made with hands.

Mk 59 And their witness did not agree.

>*The high priest, and Jesus's answer:*

Mt 62 And the high priest, rising up, said to him: Answerest thou nothing to the things which these witness against Thee?

Mt 63 But Jesus held His peace. And the high priest said to Him: I adjure Thee by the living God, that Thou tell us if Thou be the Christ the Son of God.

Lk 67 And He saith to them: If I shall tell you, you will not believe me.

Lk 68 And If I shall also ask you, you will not answer me, nor let me go.

Lk 69 But hereafter the Son of man shall be sitting on the right hand of the power of God.
Lk 70a Then said they all: Art Thou then the Son of God? Who said: You say that I am.
Mt 64b Nevertheless I say to you, hereafter you shall see the Son of man sitting on the right hand of the power of God and coming in the clouds of heaven.
Mt 65 Then the high priest rent his garments, saying: He hath blasphemed. What further need have we of witnesses? Behold, now you have heard the blasphemy.
Lk 71b For we ourselves have heard it from His own mouth.
Mt 66 What think you? But they, answering, said: He is guilty of death.
The buffeting after the "trial:"
Lk 63 And the men that held Him mocked Him and struck Him.
Mt 67 Then did they spit in His Face and buffeted Him. And others struck His Face with the palms of their hands.
Lk 64 And they blindfolded Him and smote His Face. And they asked Him, saying: Prophesy: Who is it that struck Thee?
Lk 65 And blaspheming, many other things they said against Him.
The beginning of Peter's third denial (the third denial is in Matins):
Mk 70b And after a while they that stood by said again to Peter: Surely thou art one of them; for thou art also a Galilean.

(All lectionaries of the period are missing pages containing the beginning of the Harmony of the Passion Gospel. Great and Holy Friday Matins begins here in the Lectionary of Luxieul, but earlier Lectionaries would not have omitted the Trial of Jesus. Since St. Peter's denial is part of the Trial, the beginning of Matins is moved to the beginning of the Trial. Early Lectionaries of Holy and Great Friday, such as the Byzantine Lectionary, are very careful to not to omit anything on this great and terrible day.)

St. Matthew 26: 72

And again he denied with an oath: I know not the man.

St. John 18:26

One of the servants of the high priest (a kinsman to him whose ear Peter cut off) saith to him: Did not I see thee in the garden with him?

St. Matthew 26:73-74

And, after a little while, they came that stood by and said to Peter: Surely thou also art one of them; for even thy speech doth discover thee. Then he began to curse and to swear that he knew not the man. And immediately the cock crew.

St. Luke 22:61-62

And the Lord turning looked on Peter. And Peter remembered the word of the Lord, as He had said: Before the cock crow, thou shalt deny me thrice. And Peter, going out, wept bitterly.

At the end of each Hour of Holy and Great Friday, say these prayers:
[For the Church.]

Let us pray, beloved, primarily for the holy churches of God, that our God and Lord be pleased to pacify, multiply, and protect them, throughout the entire world, against principalities and powers, and grant us a peaceful and quiet life, apart from the nations, to glorify God the Father Almighty. **R.** Amen.

Let us pray. Almighty and eternal God, reveal Thy glory unto all of the nations in Christ. Protect the works of Thy mercy, that the Church spread throughout the entire world, and may it persevere stable in the Faith in the confession of Thy Name; through Our Lord Jesus Christ, Who reigneth with the Father and the Holy Spirit, unto ages of ages. **R.** Amen.

[For the Patriarchs:]

Let us pray for our blessed Patriarchs, that God Almighty that appointed them unto the Order of Bishop may preserve them in health and safety. May they guard the Holy Church unto the regulation of the holy people of God. **R.** Amen.

Let us pray. Almighty and eternal God, by Whose eternal statement the universe was founded, regard and be propitious to our prayers, and protect our elected Bishop for us by Thy Faith, that Christian peoples who are governed by such authority under so great a Pontifex, may increase in the merits of Thy Faith; through Our Lord Jesus Christ, Who reigneth with the Father and the Holy Spirit, unto ages of ages. **R.** Amen.

[For all the Clergy and the People of God:]

Let us pray for all Bishops, Priests, Deacons, Acolytes, Exorcists, Lectors, Ostiaries, Confessors, Virgins, Widows, and for all the holy people of God.

Let us pray. Almighty and eternal God, by Whose Spirit the Body of the Church is sanctified and guided, hear us suppliants, for all the clergy of the universe, that by the Gifts of Thy Grace, that from all of the grades of the Church, they may be faithfully obedient to Thee; through Our Lord Jesus Christ, Who reigneth with the Father and the Holy Spirit, unto ages of ages. **R.** Amen.

[For all Christian leaders:]

Let us pray for Christian kings [leaders], that our God and Lord subdue all barbarian nations unto them, unto our perpetual peace. **R.** Amen.

Let us pray. Almighty and eternal God, in Thy hand are the powers of all the ages, and the authorities of all kingdoms; look down and be propitious and benign to the [Christian world] *(Roman Empire)*, that all the nations which are in it may be confident in Thy fierceness, and guided by the strength of Thy right hand; through Our Lord Jesus Christ, Who reigneth with the Father and the Holy Spirit, unto ages of ages. **R.** Amen.

[For Catechumens:]

Let us pray for our Catechumens, that our God and Lord may open the ears of their innermost beings and the door of mercy, so that through the washing of regeneration, they may receive remission of all their sins, and find themselves in Christ Jesus, our Lord.

Let us pray. Almighty and eternal God, Who ever-fertilizes Thy new Church with progeny, increase the Faith and the intellect of our Catechumens, that renewed in the Font of Baptism of Thy adoption, as children they may be gathered together; through Our Lord Jesus Christ, Who reigneth with the Father and the Holy Spirit, unto ages of ages. **R.** Amen.

[For healing of mind and body, release of captives, safety in travel,]

Let us pray, beloved, to God the Father Almighty, that He purge the error from the purity of all of us, that He sweep away sickness, that He dispel famine, that He open prisons, that He break chains, that He grant travelers safe return, health to the infirm, and safe port to seamen.

Let us pray. Almighty and merciful God, consolation of those who sorrow, strength of those who labor, may the prayers of all those crying out in tribulation come unto Thee, that in their necessities they may rejoice in Thy mercy, which comes to them through Our Lord Jesus Christ, Who reigneth with the Father and the Holy Spirit, unto ages of ages. **R.** Amen.

[For heretics:]

Let us pray for heretics and schismatics, that our God and Lord uproot them from universal error and be pleased to call them back to Holy Mother the Catholic and Apostolic Church. **R.** Amen.

Let us pray. Almighty and eternal God, Who saves all, and desires that none perish, look upon the souls that are deceived by the frauds of the devil, that all depravity of heresy being set aside, they may come to their senses, and return to the stability of Thy Truth; through Our Lord Jesus Christ, Who reigneth with the Father and the Holy Spirit, unto ages of ages. **R.** Amen.

[For faithless and doubters:]

Let us pray for the faithless Jews and all doubters, that our God and Lord remove the veil from their hearts, and that they may know Christ Jesus our Lord. **R.** Amen.

Let us pray. Almighty and eternal God, Who because of Thy mercy dost not cast away those who are faithless; hear our prayers, which we give for the healing of the blindness of such people, that acknowledgment of the light of Thy Truth, which is in Christ, grow out of their darkness; through Our Lord Jesus Christ, Who reigneth with the Father and the Holy Spirit, unto ages of ages. **R.** Amen.

[For atheists and idolators:]

Let us pray for pagans and all atheists, that God Almighty remove iniquity from their hearts, and convert them to the abandonment of their idols, and unto the True God and His Only-Begotten Son, Jesus Christ. **R.** Amen.

Let us pray. Almighty and eternal God, Who ever seeks not the death of sinners, but life, be propitious and accept our prayers, and free them from the cult of idols, and gather them into Thy holy Church, unto the praise and glory of Thy Name; through Our Lord Jesus Christ, Who reigneth with the Father and the Holy Spirit, unto ages of ages. **R.** Amen.

The Matins Collect was placed here.
[The Hour of Matins is ended.]

Second Hour of Holy and Great Friday:
Isaiah 52:13-53:12

Behold, my servant shall understand: He shall be exalted and extolled, and shall be exceeding high. As many have been astonished at thee, so shall His visage be inglorious among men and His form among the sons of men. He shall sprinkle many nations: kings shall shut their mouth at Him. For they to whom it was not told of Him have seen: and they that heard not have beheld.

Who hath believed our report? And to whom is the arm of the Lord revealed? And He shall grow up as a tender plant before him, and as a root out of a thirsty ground. There is no beauty in Him, nor comeliness: and we have seen Him, and there was no sightliness, that we should be desirous of Him; Despised and the most abject of men, a man of sorrows and acquainted with infirmity: and His look was as it were hidden and despised. Whereupon we esteemed Him not. Surely He hath borne our infirmities and carried our sorrows: and we have thought Him as it were a leper, and as one struck by God and afflicted. But He was wounded for our iniquities: He was bruised for our sins. The chastisement of our peace was upon Him: and by His bruises we are healed.

All we like sheep have gone astray, every one hath turned aside into his own way: and the Lord hath laid on him the iniquity of us all. He was offered because it was His own will, and He opened not His mouth. He shall be led as a sheep to the slaughter and shall be dumb as a lamb before His shearer, and he shall not open His mouth.

He was taken away from distress and from judgment. Who shall declare His generation? Because He is cut off out of the land of the living: for the wickedness of my people have I struck Him. And He shall give the ungodly for His burial and the rich for His death: because He hath done no iniquity, neither was there deceit in His mouth. And the Lord was pleased to bruise Him in infirmity. If He shall lay down His life for sin, He shall see a long-lived seed: and the will of the Lord shall be prosperous in His hand.

Because His soul hath labored, He shall see and be filled. By His knowledge shall this my just servant justify many: and He shall bear their iniquities. Therefore will I distribute to Him very many, and He shall divide the spoils of the strong; because He hath delivered His soul unto death and was reputed with the wicked. And He hath borne the sins of many and hath prayed for the transgressors.

R. I have heard, O Lord.

Collect: O God, from Whom Judas received the punishment of his guilt, and the thief the reward of his confession, grant unto us the effects of Thy propitiation: that as in His Passion Jesus Christ, our Lord, gave unto both the divers rewards of their merits; so he may take away the transgressions of our old nature, and bestow upon us the grace of His Resurrection: Who liveth and reigneth with Thee and the Holy Spirit, unto ages of ages. **R.** Amen.

STAND for the Holy Passion Gospel:

St. Matthew 27:1-2a
And, when morning was come, all the chief priests and ancients of the people took counsel against Jesus, that they might put Him to death. And they brought Him bound.
St. John 18:28a
Then they led Jesus from Caiphas to the governor's hall.
St. Matthew 27:2-14
And they brought Him bound and delivered Him to Pontius Pilate the governor. Then Judas, who betrayed Him, seeing that He was condemned, repenting himself, brought back the thirty pieces of silver in the temple, he departed and went and hanged himself with an halter. But the chief priests, having taken the pieces of silver, said: It is not lawful to put them into the corbona, because it is the price of blood. And, after they had consulted together, they bought with them the potter's field, to be a burying place for strangers. For this cause that field was called Haceldama, that is, The field of blood, even to this day. Then was fulfilled that which was spoken by Jeremias the prophet, saying: and they took the thirty pieces of silver, the price of him that was prized, whom they prized of the children of Israel; And they gave them unto the potter's field, as the Lord appointed to me. And Jesus stood before the governor, and the governor asked him, saying: Art thou the king of the Jews? Jesus saith to him: Thou sayest it. And, when he as accused by the chief priests and ancients, he answered nothing. Then Pilate saith to Him: Dost not thou hear how great testimonies they allege against thee? And He answered to him never a word, so that the governor wondered exceedingly.
St. John 18:28b-38
And it was morning; and they went not into the hall, that they might not be defiled, but that they might eat the pasch. Pilate therefore went out to them, and said: What accusation bring you against this man? They answered and said to him: If he were not a malefactor, we would not have delivered him up to thee. Pilate therefore said to them: Take him you, and judge him according to your law. The Jews therefore said to him: It is not lawful for us to put any man to death. That the word of Jesus might be fulfilled, which He said, signifying what death He should die. Pilate therefore went into the hall again and called Jesus and said to Him: Art thou the king of the Jews? Jesus answered: Sayest thou this thing of thyself, or have others told it thee of me? Pilate answered: Am I a Jew? Thy own nation and the chief priests have delivered thee up to me. What hast thou done? Jesus answered: My kingdom is not of this world. If my kingdom were of this world, my servants would certainly strive that I should not be delivered to the Jews; but now my kingdom is not from hence. Pilate therefore said to Him: Art thou a king then? Jesus answered: Thou sayest that I am a king. For this was I born, and for this came I into the world, that I should give testimony to the truth. Every one that is of the truth heareth my voice. Pilate saith to Him: What is truth? And when he said this he went out again to the Jews and saith to them: I find no cause in him.
St. Luke 23:5a,2b,5b-15
But they were more earnest, saying: We have found this man perverting our nation and forbidding to give tribute to Caesar and saying that he is Christ the king. He stirreth up the people, teaching throughout all Judea, beginning from Galilee to this place. But Pilate, hearing Galilee, asked if the man were of Galilee? And when he understood that he was of Herod's jurisdiction, he sent him away to Herod, who was also himself at Jerusalem in those days. And Herod, seeing Jesus, was very glad; for he was desirous of a long time to see him, because he had heard many things of him; and he hoped to see some sign wrought by him. And he questioned him in many words. But he answered him nothing. And the chief priests and the scribes stood by, earnestly accusing Him. And Herod with his army set him at nought and mocked him, putting on Him a white garment; and sent Him back to Pilate. And Herod and Pilate were made friends, that same day; for before they were enemies one to another. And Pilate, calling together the chief priests and the magistrates and the people, Said to them: You have presented unto me this man as one that

perverteth the people. And, behold, I, having examined him before you, find no cause in this man, in those things wherein you accuse him. No, no Herod neither. For I sent you to him; and, behold, nothing worthy of death is done to him.
St. Matthew 27:15-16
Now upon the solemn day the governor was accustomed to release to the people one prisoner, whom they would. And he had then a notorious prisoner that was called Barabbas.
St. Luke 23:19
Who, for a certain sedition made in the city and for a murder, was cast into prison.
St. Matthew 27:17-23
They, therefore, being gathered together, Pilate said: Whom will you that I release to you; Barabbas, or Jesus that is called Christ? For he knew that for envy they had delivered him. And, as he was sitting in the place of judgment, his wife sent to him, saying: Have thou nothing to do with that just man; for I have suffered many things this day in a dream because of him. But the chief priests and ancients persuaded the people that they should ask Barabbas and make Jesus away. And the governor, answering, said to them: Which will you of the two to be released unto you? But they said: Barabbas. Pilate saith to them: What shall I do then with Jesus that is called Christ? They say all: Let him be crucified. The governor said to them: Why, what evil hath he done? But they cried out the more, saying: Let him be crucified.
St. Luke 23:22
And he said to them the third time: Why, what evil hath this man done? I find no cause of death in him. I will chastise him therefore and let him go.
St. Matthew 27:23b
But they cried out the more, saying, Let him be crucified.
St. Luke 23:23
But they were instant with loud voices, requiring that He might be crucified. And their voices prevailed.
St. Matthew 27:24-26
And Pilate, seeing that he prevailed nothing, but that rather a tumult was made, taking water, washed his hands before the people, saying: I am innocent of the blood of this just man. Look you to it. And the whole people answering said: His blood be upon us and upon our children. Then he released to them Barabbas; and, having scourged Jesus, delivered Him unto them to be crucified.

At the end of each Hour of Holy and Great Friday, say these prayers:
[For the Church.]

Let us pray, beloved, primarily for the holy churches of God, that our God and Lord be pleased to pacify, multiply, and protect them, throughout the entire world, against principalities and powers, and grant us a peaceful and quiet life, apart from the nations, to glorify God the Father Almighty. **R.** Amen.

Let us pray. Almighty and eternal God, reveal Thy glory unto all of the nations in Christ. Protect the works of Thy mercy, that the Church spread throughout the entire world, and may it persevere stable in the Faith in the confession of Thy Name; through Our Lord Jesus Christ, Who reigneth with the Father and the Holy Spirit, unto ages of ages. **R.** Amen.

[For the Patriarchs:]

Let us pray for our blessed Patriarchs, that God Almighty that appointed them unto the Order of Bishop may preserve them in health and safety. May they guard the Holy Church unto the regulation of the holy people of God. **R.** Amen.

Let us pray. Almighty and eternal God, by Whose eternal statement the universe was founded, regard and be propitious to our prayers, and protect our elected Bishop for us by Thy Faith, that Christian peoples who are governed by such authority under so great a Pontifex, may increase in the merits of Thy Faith; through Our Lord Jesus Christ, Who reigneth with the Father and the Holy Spirit, unto ages of ages. **R.** Amen.

[For all the Clergy and the People of God:]

Let us pray for all Bishops, Priests, Deacons, Acolytes, Exorcists, Lectors, Ostiaries, Confessors, Virgins, Widows, and for all the holy people of God.

Let us pray. Almighty and eternal God, by Whose Spirit the Body of the Church is sanctified and guided, hear us suppliants, for all the clergy of the universe, that by the Gifts of Thy Grace, that from all of the grades of the Church, they may be faithfully obedient to Thee; through Our Lord Jesus Christ, Who reigneth with the Father and the Holy Spirit, unto ages of ages. **R.** Amen.

[For all Christian leaders:]

Let us pray for Christian kings [leaders], that our God and Lord subdue all barbarian nations unto them, unto our perpetual peace. **R.** Amen.

Let us pray. Almighty and eternal God, in Thy hand are the powers of all the ages, and the authorities of all kingdoms; look down and be propitious and benign to the [Christian world] *(Roman Empire)*, that all the nations which are in it may be confident in Thy fierceness, and guided by the strength of Thy right hand; through Our Lord Jesus Christ, Who reigneth with the Father and the Holy Spirit, unto ages of ages. **R.** Amen.

[For Catechumens:]

Let us pray for our Catechumens, that our God and Lord may open the ears of their innermost beings and the door of mercy, so that through the washing of regeneration, they may receive remission of all their sins, and find themselves in Christ Jesus, our Lord.

Let us pray. Almighty and eternal God, Who ever-fertilizes Thy new Church with progeny, increase the Faith and the intellect of our Catechumens, that renewed in the Font of Baptism of Thy adoption, as children they may be gathered together; through Our Lord Jesus Christ, Who reigneth with the Father and the Holy Spirit, unto ages of ages. **R.** Amen.

[For healing of mind and body, release of captives, safety in travel,]

Let us pray, beloved, to God the Father Almighty, that He purge the error from the purity of all of us, that He sweep away sickness, that He dispel famine, that He open prisons, that He break chains, that He grant travelers safe return, health to the infirm, and safe port to seamen.

Let us pray. Almighty and merciful God, consolation of those who sorrow, strength of those who labor, may the prayers of all those crying out in tribulation come unto Thee, that in their necessities they may rejoice in Thy mercy, which comes to them through Our Lord Jesus Christ, Who reigneth with the Father and the Holy Spirit, unto ages of ages. **R.** Amen.

[For heretics:]

Let us pray for heretics and schismatics, that our God and Lord uproot them from universal error and be pleased to call them back to Holy Mother the Catholic and Apostolic Church. **R.** Amen.

Let us pray. Almighty and eternal God, Who saves all, and desires that none perish, look upon the souls that are deceived by the frauds of the devil, that all depravity of heresy being set aside, they may come to their senses, and return to the stability of Thy Truth; through Our Lord Jesus Christ, Who reigneth with the Father and the Holy Spirit, unto ages of ages. **R.** Amen.

[For faithless and doubters:]

Let us pray for the faithless Jews and all doubters, that our God and Lord remove the veil from their hearts, and that they may know Christ Jesus our Lord. **R.** Amen.

Let us pray. Almighty and eternal God, Who because of Thy mercy dost not cast away those who are faithless; hear our prayers, which we give for the healing of the blindness of such people, that acknowledgment of the light of Thy Truth, which is in Christ, grow out of their darkness; through Our Lord Jesus Christ, Who reigneth with the Father and the Holy Spirit, unto ages of ages. **R.** Amen.

[For atheists and idolators:]
Let us pray for pagans and all atheists, that God Almighty remove iniquity from their hearts, and convert them to the abandonment of their idols, and unto the True God and His Only-Begotten Son, Jesus Christ. **R.** Amen.

Let us pray. Almighty and eternal God, Who ever seeks not the death of sinners, but life, be propitious and accept our prayers, and free them from the cult of idols, and gather them into Thy holy Church, unto the praise and glory of Thy Name; through Our Lord Jesus Christ, Who reigneth with the Father and the Holy Spirit, unto ages of ages. **R.** Amen.

Collect for the Second Hour:
Commemorating, Beloved, the hour of the Lord's betrayal; when He, like unto a sheep led to the slaughter and like a lamb who does not open his mouth to the shearer, was led to the Cross, which He voluntarily ascended for us. He was led and offered because He desired it. Let us commend our souls to Christ, Lord and faithful God, Who working in a figurative manner, washes away our sins by the pure Lamb. Let us bow our heads unto the Victim Who was silent, because it was said by His keeping His peace, that He bear and destroy our iniquities which he did not have; Who reigneth with the Father and the Holy Spirit unto ages of ages.
R. Amen.   *[The Second Hour is ended.]*

Third Hour of Holy and Great Friday:
Jer: 11:15-20, 12:7-9

What is the meaning that my beloved hath wrought much wickedness in my house? Shall the holy flesh take away from thee thy crimes in which thou hast boasted? The Lord called thy name, a plentiful olive-tree, fair, fruitful, and beautiful: at the noise of a word, a great fire was kindled in it and the branches thereof are burnt. And the Lord of hosts that planted thee hath pronounced evil against thee: for the evils of the house of Israel and of the house of Juda which they have done to themselves; to provoke me, offering sacrifice to Baalim.

But Thou, O Lord, hast shown me, and I have known: then Thou showedst me their doings. And I was as a meek lamb that is carried to be a victim: and I knew not that they had devised counsels against me, saying: Let us put wood on his bread and cut him off from the land of the living, and let his name be remembered no more. But Thou, O Lord of Sabaoth, who judgest justly and triest the reins and the hearts, let me see Thy revenge on them: for to Thee have I revealed my cause.

I have forsaken my house, I have left my inheritance, I have given my dear soul into the hand of her enemies. My inheritance is become to me as a lion in the wood: it hath cried out against me. Therefore have I hated it. Is my inheritance to me as a speckled bird? Is it as a bird dyed throughout? Come ye, assemble yourselves, all ye beasts of the earth, make haste to devour.
R. I have heard, O Lord.

Collect: O God, from Whom Judas received the punishment of his guilt, and the thief the reward of his confession, grant unto us the effects of Thy propitiation: that as in His Passion Jesus Christ, our Lord, gave unto both the divers rewards of their merits; so he may take away the transgressions of our old nature, and bestow upon us the grace of His Resurrection: Who liveth and reigneth with Thee and the Holy Spirit, unto ages of ages.
R. Amen.

STAND for the Holy Passion Gospel:
St. Matthew 27:27-28a
Then the soldiers of the governor, taking Jesus into the hall, gathered together unto Him the whole band. And, stripping Him,

St. John 19:2b
platting a crown of thorns, put it upon His head; and they put on Him a purple garment.
St. Matthew 27:28b-29
They put a scarlet cloak about him. And, platting a crown of thorns, they put it upon His head, and a reed in His right hand. And, bowing the knee before Him, they mocked Him, saying: Hail, King of the Jews.
St. John 19:3b
And they gave Him blows.
St. Matthew 27:30
And, spitting upon Him, they took the reed and struck His head.
St. John 19:4-16
Pilate therefore went forth again and saith to them: Behold, I bring Him forth unto you, that you may know that I find no cause in Him. (Jesus therefore came forth, bearing the crown of thorns and the purple garment.) And he saith to them: Behold the Man. When the chief priests, therefore, and the servants had seen Him, they cried out, saying: Crucify him, Crucify him. Pilate saith to them: Take Him you, and crucify Him; for I find no cause in Him. The Jews answered him: We have a law; and according to the law he ought to die, because he made himself the Son of God. When Pilate therefore had heard this saying, he feared the more. And he entered into the hall again; and he said to Jesus: Whence art thou? But Jesus gave him no answer. Pilate therefore saith to Him: Speakest Thou not to me? Knowest thou not that I have power to crucify Thee, and I have power to release Thee? Jesus answered: Thou shouldst not have any power against me, unless it were given thee from above. Therefore he that hath delivered me to thee hath the greater sin. And from henceforth Pilate sought to release Him. But the Jews cried out, saying: If thou release this man, thou art not Caesar's friend. For whosoever maketh himself a king speaketh against Caesar. Now, when Pilate had heard these words, he brought Jesus forth and sat down in the judgment seat, in the place that is called Lithostrotos, and in Hebrew Gabbatha. And it was the parasceve [Friday] of the Pasch, about the sixth hour; and he saith to the Jews: Behold your king. But they cried out: Away with him: Away with him: Crucify him. Pilate saith to them: Shall I crucify your king? The chief priests answered: We have no king but Caesar. Then therefore he delivered Him to them to be crucified. And they took Jesus and led Him forth.
St. Matthew 27:31a
And, after they had mocked Him, they took off the cloak from Him and put on Him His own garments.
St. John 19:16b-17a
And they took Jesus and led Him forth. And, bearing His own cross, he went forth.
St. Mark 15:20b, 25a
And they led Him out to crucify Him. And it was the third hour.
St. Matthew 27:32
And, going out, they found a man of Cyrene, named Simon; him they forced to take up His cross.
St. Luke 23:26b-32
And they laid the cross on him to carry after Jesus. And there followed Him a great multitude of people and of women, who bewailed and lamented Him. But Jesus, turning to them, said: Daughters of Jerusalem, weep not over me; but weep for yourselves and for your children. For, behold, the days shall come, wherein they will say: Blessed are the barren and the wombs that have not borne and the paps that have not given suck. They shall they begin to say to the mountains: Fall upon us. And to the hills: Cover us. For if in the green wood they do these things, what shall be done in the dry?
St. Matthew 27:33-34
And they came to the place that is called Golgotha, which is the place of Calvary. And they gave Him wine to drink mingled with gall. And, when He had tasted, He would not drink.

At the end of each Hour of Holy and Great Friday, say these prayers:

[For the Church.]

Let us pray, beloved, primarily for the holy churches of God, that our God and Lord be pleased to pacify, multiply, and protect them, throughout the entire world, against principalities and powers, and grant us a peaceful and quiet life, apart from the nations, to glorify God the Father Almighty. **R.** Amen.

Let us pray. Almighty and eternal God, reveal Thy glory unto all of the nations in Christ. Protect the works of Thy mercy, that the Church spread throughout the entire world, and may it persevere stable in the Faith in the confession of Thy Name; through Our Lord Jesus Christ, Who reigneth with the Father and the Holy Spirit, unto ages of ages. **R.** Amen.

[For the Patriarchs:]

Let us pray for our blessed Patriarchs, that God Almighty that appointed them unto the Order of Bishop may preserve them in health and safety. May they guard the Holy Church unto the regulation of the holy people of God. **R.** Amen.

Let us pray. Almighty and eternal God, by Whose eternal statement the universe was founded, regard and be propitious to our prayers, and protect our elected Bishop for us by Thy Faith, that Christian peoples who are governed by such authority under so great a Pontifex, may increase in the merits of Thy Faith; through Our Lord Jesus Christ, Who reigneth with the Father and the Holy Spirit, unto ages of ages. **R.** Amen.

[For all the Clergy and the People of God:]

Let us pray for all Bishops, Priests, Deacons, Acolytes, Exorcists, Lectors, Ostiaries, Confessors, Virgins, Widows, and for all the holy people of God.

Let us pray. Almighty and eternal God, by Whose Spirit the Body of the Church is sanctified and guided, hear us suppliants, for all the clergy of the universe, that by the Gifts of Thy Grace, that from all of the grades of the Church, they may be faithfully obedient to Thee; through Our Lord Jesus Christ, Who reigneth with the Father and the Holy Spirit, unto ages of ages. **R.** Amen.

[For all Christian leaders:]

Let us pray for Christian kings [leaders], that our God and Lord subdue all barbarian nations unto them, unto our perpetual peace. **R.** Amen.

Let us pray. Almighty and eternal God, in Thy hand are the powers of all the ages, and the authorities of all kingdoms; look down and be propitious and benign to the [Christian world] *(Roman Empire)*, that all the nations which are in it may be confident in Thy fierceness, and guided by the strength of Thy right hand; through Our Lord Jesus Christ, Who reigneth with the Father and the Holy Spirit, unto ages of ages. **R.** Amen.

[For Catechumens:]

Let us pray for our Catechumens, that our God and Lord may open the ears of their innermost beings and the door of mercy, so that through the washing of regeneration, they may receive remission of all their sins, and find themselves in Christ Jesus, our Lord.

Let us pray. Almighty and eternal God, Who ever-fertilizes Thy new Church with progeny, increase the Faith and the intellect of our Catechumens, that renewed in the Font of Baptism of Thy adoption, as children they may be gathered together; through Our Lord Jesus Christ, Who reigneth with the Father and the Holy Spirit, unto ages of ages. **R.** Amen.

[For healing of mind and body, release of captives, safety in travel,]

Let us pray, beloved, to God the Father Almighty, that He purge the error from the purity of all of us, that He sweep away sickness, that He dispel famine, that He open prisons, that He break chains, that He grant travelers safe return, health to the infirm, and safe port to seamen.

Let us pray. Almighty and merciful God, consolation of those who sorrow, strength of those who labor, may the prayers of all those crying out in tribulation come unto Thee, that in their necessities they may rejoice in Thy mercy, which comes to them through Our Lord Jesus Christ, Who reigneth with the Father and the Holy Spirit, unto ages of ages. **R.** Amen.

[For heretics:]

Let us pray for heretics and schismatics, that our God and Lord uproot them from universal error and be pleased to call them back to Holy Mother the Catholic and Apostolic Church. **R.** Amen.

Let us pray. Almighty and eternal God, Who saves all, and desires that none perish, look upon the souls that are deceived by the frauds of the devil, that all depravity of heresy being set aside, they may come to their senses, and return to the stability of Thy Truth; through Our Lord Jesus Christ, Who reigneth with the Father and the Holy Spirit, unto ages of ages. **R.** Amen.

[For faithless and doubters:]

Let us pray for the faithless Jews and all doubters, that our God and Lord remove the veil from their hearts, and that they may know Christ Jesus our Lord. **R.** Amen.

Let us pray. Almighty and eternal God, Who because of Thy mercy dost not cast away those who are faithless; hear our prayers, which we give for the healing of the blindness of such people, that acknowledgment of the light of Thy Truth, which is in Christ, grow out of their darkness; through Our Lord Jesus Christ, Who reigneth with the Father and the Holy Spirit, unto ages of ages. **R.** Amen.

[For atheists and idolators:]

Let us pray for pagans and all atheists, that God Almighty remove iniquity from their hearts, and convert them to the abandonment of their idols, and unto the True God and His Only-Begotten Son, Jesus Christ. **R.** Amen.

Let us pray. Almighty and eternal God, Who ever seeks not the death of sinners, but life, be propitious and accept our prayers, and free them from the cult of idols, and gather them into Thy holy Church, unto the praise and glory of Thy Name; through Our Lord Jesus Christ, Who reigneth with the Father and the Holy Spirit, unto ages of ages. **R.** Amen.

Collect for the Third Hour:

O faithful Wisdom of the Living God, O Thou ever-living of the eternal God the Father, the Word and eternal Power, because of the eternal birth by which Thou art the eternal Son and God from the eternal Father, apart from Whom there is nothing and through Whom there is all, in Whom, all that is, stands firm, Thou Who art God above us, and man because of us: for us, Thou didst will to be what we are: give us what Thou hast promised: give us, who are unworthy, the release which Thou offerest to all in Thy community. Thy suffering is certainly our liberation, and Thy death our life, and Thy Cross our redemption, and Thy wounds our healing, and with the gift of Thy crucifixion, we arise exalted unto Thy Father with Whom Thou livest and reignest unto ages of ages. **R.** Amen.

[The Third Hour is ended.]

Sixth Hour of Holy and Great Friday:

Amos 8:4-11

Hear this, you that crush the poor and make the needy of the land to fail. Saying: When will the month be over, and we shall sell our wares: and the Sabbath, and we shall open the corn: that we may lessen the measure and increase the sickle and may convey in deceitful balances, That we may possess the needy for money and the poor for a pair of shoes and may sell the refuse of the corn? The Lord hath sworn against the pride of Jacob: Surely I will never forget all their works. Shall not the land tremble for this and every one mourn that dwelleth therein, and rise up altogether as a river, and be cast out, and run down as the river of Egypt?

And it shall come to pass in that day, saith the Lord God, that the sun shall go down at midday, and I will make the earth dark in the day of light. And I will turn your

feasts into mourning and all your songs into lamentation: and I will bring up sackcloth upon every back of yours and baldness upon every head: and I will make it as the mourning of an only son, and the latter end thereof as a bitter day. Behold, the days come, saith the Lord, and I will send forth a famine into the land: not a famine of bread, nor a thirst of water, but of hearing the word of the Lord.
R. I have heard, O Lord.

Collect: O God, from Whom Judas received the punishment of his guilt, and the thief the reward of his confession, grant unto us the effects of Thy propitiation: that as in His Passion Jesus Christ, our Lord, gave unto both the divers rewards of their merits; so he may take away the transgressions of our old nature, and bestow upon us the grace of His Resurrection: Who liveth and reigneth with Thee and the Holy Spirit, unto ages of ages.
R. Amen.

STAND for the Holy Passion Gospel:
St. Matthew 27:35a
And, after they had crucified Him, they divided His garments, casting lots; that it might be fulfilled which was spoken by the prophet.
St. John 19:19-24
And Pilate wrote a title also; and he put it upon the cross. And the writing was: JESUS OF NAZARETH, THE KING OF THE JEWS. This title therefore many of the Jews did read; because the place where Jesus was crucified was nigh to the city. And it was written in Hebrew, in Greek, and in Latin. Then the chief priests of the Jews said to Pilate: Write not: The King of the Jews. But that he said: I am the King of the Jews. Pilate answered: What I have written, I have written. The soldiers, therefore, when they had crucified Him, took His garments (and they made four parts, to every soldier a part) and also His coat. Now the coat was without seam, woven from the top throughout. They said then one to another: Let us not cut it, but let us cast lots for it, whose it shall be; that the scripture might be fulfilled, saying: They have parted my garments among them, and upon my vesture they have cast lots. And the soldiers indeed did these things.
St. Matthew 27:36
And they sat and watched Him.
St. John 19:25-27
Now there stood by the cross of Jesus, His mother and His mother's sister, Mary of Cleophas, and Mary Magdalen. When Jesus therefore had seen His mother and the disciple standing, whom He loved, He saith to His other: Woman, behold thy son. After that, He saith to the disciple: Behold thy mother. And from that hour the disciple took her to his own.
St. Matthew 27:38
Then were crucified with him two thieves; one on the right hand and one on the left.
St. John 19:18b
and Jesus in the midst.
St. Mark 15:28
And the scripture was fulfilled, which saith: And with the wicked He was reputed.
St. Luke 23:34a
And Jesus said: Father, forgive them, for they know not what they do.
St. Matthew 27:39-43
And they that passed by blasphemed Him, wagging their heads, And saying: Vah, thou that destroyest the temple of God and in three days dost rebuild it; save thy own self. If thou be the Son of God, come down from the cross. In like manner also the chief priests, with the scribes and ancients, mocking said: He saved others; himself he cannot save. If he be the king of Israel, let him now come down from the cross; and we will believe him. He trusted in God: let him now deliver him if he will have him. For he said: I am the Son of God.
St. Luke 23:39-43

And one of those robbers who were hanged blasphemed him, saying: If thou be Christ, save thyself and us. But the other, answering, rebuked him, saying: Neither dost thou fear God, seeing thou art under the same condemnation? And we indeed justly; for we receive the due reward of our deeds: but this man hath done no evil. And he said to Jesus: Lord, remember me when thou shalt come into thy kingdom. And Jesus said to him: Amen, I say to thee: This day thou shalt be with me in paradise.

At the end of each Hour of Holy and Great Friday, say these prayers:
[For the Church.]

Let us pray, beloved, primarily for the holy churches of God, that our God and Lord be pleased to pacify, multiply, and protect them, throughout the entire world, against principalities and powers, and grant us a peaceful and quiet life, apart from the nations, to glorify God the Father Almighty. **R.** Amen.

Let us pray. Almighty and eternal God, reveal Thy glory unto all of the nations in Christ. Protect the works of Thy mercy, that the Church spread throughout the entire world, and may it persevere stable in the Faith in the confession of Thy Name; through Our Lord Jesus Christ, Who reigneth with the Father and the Holy Spirit, unto ages of ages. **R.** Amen.

[For the Patriarchs:]

Let us pray for our blessed Patriarchs, that God Almighty that appointed them unto the Order of Bishop may preserve them in health and safety. May they guard the Holy Church unto the regulation of the holy people of God. **R.** Amen.

Let us pray. Almighty and eternal God, by Whose eternal statement the universe was founded, regard and be propitious to our prayers, and protect our elected Bishop for us by Thy Faith, that Christian peoples who are governed by such authority under so great a Pontifex, may increase in the merits of Thy Faith; through Our Lord Jesus Christ, Who reigneth with the Father and the Holy Spirit, unto ages of ages. **R.** Amen.

[For all the Clergy and the People of God:]

Let us pray for all Bishops, Priests, Deacons, Acolytes, Exorcists, Lectors, Ostiaries, Confessors, Virgins, Widows, and for all the holy people of God.

Let us pray. Almighty and eternal God, by Whose Spirit the Body of the Church is sanctified and guided, hear us suppliants, for all the clergy of the universe, that by the Gifts of Thy Grace, that from all of the grades of the Church, they may be faithfully obedient to Thee; through Our Lord Jesus Christ, Who reigneth with the Father and the Holy Spirit, unto ages of ages. **R.** Amen.

[For all Christian leaders:]

Let us pray for Christian kings [leaders], that our God and Lord subdue all barbarian nations unto them, unto our perpetual peace. **R.** Amen.

Let us pray. Almighty and eternal God, in Thy hand are the powers of all the ages, and the authorities of all kingdoms; look down and be propitious and benign to the [Christian world] *(Roman Empire)*, that all the nations which are in it may be confident in Thy fierceness, and guided by the strength of Thy right hand; through Our Lord Jesus Christ, Who reigneth with the Father and the Holy Spirit, unto ages of ages. **R.** Amen.

[For Catechumens:]

Let us pray for our Catechumens, that our God and Lord may open the ears of their innermost beings and the door of mercy, so that through the washing of regeneration, they may receive remission of all their sins, and find themselves in Christ Jesus, our Lord.

Let us pray. Almighty and eternal God, Who ever-fertilizes Thy new Church with progeny, increase the Faith and the intellect of our Catechumens, that renewed in the Font of Baptism of Thy adoption, as children they may be gathered together; through Our Lord Jesus Christ, Who reigneth with the Father and the Holy Spirit, unto ages of ages. **R.** Amen.

[For healing of mind and body, release of captives, safety in travel,]

Let us pray, beloved, to God the Father Almighty, that He purge the error from the purity of all of us, that He sweep away sickness, that He dispel famine, that He open prisons, that He break chains, that He grant travelers safe return, health to the infirm, and safe port to seamen.

Let us pray. Almighty and merciful God, consolation of those who sorrow, strength of those who labor, may the prayers of all those crying out in tribulation come unto Thee, that in their necessities they may rejoice in Thy mercy, which comes to them through Our Lord Jesus Christ, Who reigneth with the Father and the Holy Spirit, unto ages of ages. **R.** Amen.

[For heretics:]

Let us pray for heretics and schismatics, that our God and Lord uproot them from universal error and be pleased to call them back to Holy Mother the Catholic and Apostolic Church. **R.** Amen.

Let us pray. Almighty and eternal God, Who saves all, and desires that none perish, look upon the souls that are deceived by the frauds of the devil, that all depravity of heresy being set aside, they may come to their senses, and return to the stability of Thy Truth; through Our Lord Jesus Christ, Who reigneth with the Father and the Holy Spirit, unto ages of ages. **R.** Amen.

[For faithless and doubters:]

Let us pray for the faithless Jews and all doubters, that our God and Lord remove the veil from their hearts, and that they may know Christ Jesus our Lord. **R.** Amen.

Let us pray. Almighty and eternal God, Who because of Thy mercy dost not cast away those who are faithless; hear our prayers, which we give for the healing of the blindness of such people, that acknowledgment of the light of Thy Truth, which is in Christ, grow out of their darkness; through Our Lord Jesus Christ, Who reigneth with the Father and the Holy Spirit, unto ages of ages. **R.** Amen.

[For atheists and idolators:]

Let us pray for pagans and all atheists, that God Almighty remove iniquity from their hearts, and convert them to the abandonment of their idols, and unto the True God and His Only-Begotten Son, Jesus Christ. **R.** Amen.

Let us pray. Almighty and eternal God, Who ever seeks not the death of sinners, but life, be propitious and accept our prayers, and free them from the cult of idols, and gather them into Thy holy Church, unto the praise and glory of Thy Name; through Our Lord Jesus Christ, Who reigneth with the Father and the Holy Spirit, unto ages of ages. **R.** Amen.

Collect for the Sixth Hour:

O Christ God, Great Adonai, crucify us with Thee from this world that Thy Life may be in us, and place our sins beside Thee that they be nailed to the Cross. Draw us unto Thyself, O Thou Who wast lifted up from the earth for us so that Thou mayest rescue us from worldly adulteration. It is true that we are flesh; we are noxious fodder for the devil; we prefer to serve Thee and not him; and we desire to live under Thy rule; and we appeal to Thee to rule us, who are mortals, whom Thou desired to free and seized from Death by Thy death on the Cross. For which today's devotion is served unto Thee, and today we suppliants adore, implore and call upon Thee that Thou hasten unto us, O eternal power, God, Whose Cross is profitable unto us. Triumphing over the world in us by virtue of Thy Cross, may Thy Faith restore in us the blessing, virtue, and grace that were of old. Thou Who makest by power what was to be again in the future, what was present, similarly present again: return to us, so that Thy Passion, which is present and occurs today, may be Salvation to us; and thus today the one-time shedding of Thy Sacred Blood upon the ground from the Cross is salvation for us, and cleansing of all of the sins of our land; and mixed with the clay of our bodies, may it refashion us as Thine from the earth: reconciled unto Thee Who regnest with the Father and the Holy Spirit now, and will come to reign, O man-God Christ Jesus, King unto ages of ages. **R.** Amen.

*[The Sixth Hour is ended. The Hymn "**Before Thy Cross**" and adorations may be added here. See the **Adorations of the True Cross** after the Propers of the Finding of the True Cross. Each person may do prostrations, and kiss the Cross.]*

Ninth Hour of Holy and Great Friday: Saving Hour of the Passion, Great Ninth Hour of the greatest grace, the greatest of the Hours.

Zach: 8:14-16, 12:10-12

For thus saith the Lord of hosts: As I purposed to afflict you; when your fathers had provoked me to wrath, saith the Lord, And I had no mercy: so turning again I have thought in these days to do good to the house of Juda and Jerusalem. Fear not. These then are the things which you shall do: Speak ye truth every one to his neighbor: judge ye truth and judgment of peace in your gates:

And I will pour out upon the house of David and upon the inhabitants of Jerusalem the spirit of grace and of prayers: and they shall look upon me, Whom they have pierced. And they shall mourn for him as one mourneth for an only son: and they shall grieve over him, as the manner is to grieve for the death of the first-born. In that day there shall be a great lamentation in Jerusalem, like the lamentation of Adadremmon in the plain of Mageddon. And the land shall mourn, families and families apart: the families of the house of David apart and their women apart.

R. I have heard, O Lord.

Collect: O God, from Whom Judas received the punishment of his guilt, and the thief the reward of his confession, grant unto us the effects of Thy propitiation: that as in His Passion Jesus Christ, our Lord, gave unto both the divers rewards of their merits; so he may take away the transgressions of our old nature, and bestow upon us the grace of His Resurrection: Who liveth and reigneth with Thee and the Holy Spirit, unto ages of ages.
R. Amen.

STAND for the Holy Passion Gospel:

St. Matthew 27:45-55a
Now from the sixth hour there was darkness over the whole earth, until the ninth hour. And about the ninth hour, Jesus cried with a loud voice, saying: Eli, Eli, lamma sabacthani? That is, My God, My God, why hast thou forsaken me? And some that stood there and heard said: This man calleth Elias. And immediately one of them running took a sponge and filled it with vinegar and put it on a reed and gave him to drink. And the others said: Let be. Let us see whether Elias will come to deliver him. And Jesus, again crying with a loud voice, yielded up the ghost. And, behold, the veil of the temple was rent in two from the top even to the bottom; and the earth quaked and the rocks were rent. And the graves were opened; and many bodies of the saints that had slept arose, And, coming out of the tombs after His Resurrection, came into the holy city and appeared to many. Now the centurion and they that were with Him, watching Jesus, having seen the earthquake and the things that were done, were sore afraid, saying: Indeed this was the Son of God. And there were there many women afar off, who had followed Jesus from Galilee.
St. Luke 23:48-49a
And all the multitude of them that were come together to that sight and saw the things that were done returned, striking their breasts. And all His acquaintance,

St. Matthew 27:55-56

And there were there many women afar off, who had followed Jesus from Galilee, ministering unto Him; Among whom was Mary Magdalen, and Mary the mother of James and Joseph, and the mother of the sons of Zebedee.

St. John 19:31-37

Then the Jews (because it was the parasceve [Friday]), that the bodies might not remain upon the cross on the Sabbath day (for that was a great Sabbath day), besought Pilate that their legs might be broken; and that they might be taken away. The soldiers therefore came; and they broke the legs of the first, and of the other that was crucified with Him. But after they were come to Jesus, when they saw that He was already dead, they did not break His legs. But one of the soldiers with a spear opened His side; and immediately there came out blood and water. And he that saw it hath given testimony; and his testimony is true. And he knoweth that he saith true; that you also may believe. For these things were done that the scripture might be fulfilled: You shall not break a bone of Him. And again another scripture saith: they shall look on Him Whom they pierced.

St. Matthew 27:57

And, when it was evening, there came a certain rich man of Arimathea, named Joseph, who also himself was a disciple of Jesus.

St. Mark 15:43-44

But Pilate wondered that He should be already dead. And, sending for the centurion, he asked him if he were already dead.

St. Matthew 27:58

[Joseph of Arimathea] went to Pilate and asked the body of Jesus. Then Pilate commanded that the body should be delivered.

St. John 19:39-40a

And Nicodemus also came (he who at the first came to Jesus by night), bringing a mixture of myrrh and aloes, about an hundred pound weight. They took therefore the body of Jesus and bound it in linen cloths, with the spices,

St. Matthew 27: 60-61

And laid it in his own new monument, which [Joseph] had hewed out in a rock. And he rolled a great stone to the door of the monument and went his way. And there was there Mary Magdalen and the other Mary, sitting over against the sepulchre.

At the end of each Hour of Holy and Great Friday, say these prayers:
[For the Church.]

Let us pray, beloved, primarily for the holy churches of God, that our God and Lord be pleased to pacify, multiply, and protect them, throughout the entire world, against principalities and powers, and grant us a peaceful and quiet life, apart from the nations, to glorify God the Father Almighty. **R.** Amen.

Let us pray. Almighty and eternal God, reveal Thy glory unto all of the nations in Christ. Protect the works of Thy mercy, that the Church spread throughout the entire world, and may it persevere stable in the Faith in the confession of Thy Name; through Our Lord Jesus Christ, Who reigneth with the Father and the Holy Spirit, unto ages of ages. **R.** Amen.

[For the Patriarchs:]

Let us pray for our blessed Patriarchs, that God Almighty that appointed them unto the Order of Bishop may preserve them in health and safety. May they guard the Holy Church unto the regulation of the holy people of God. **R.** Amen.

Let us pray. Almighty and eternal God, by Whose eternal statement the universe was founded, regard and be propitious to our prayers, and protect our elected Bishop for us by Thy Faith, that Christian peoples who are governed by such authority under so great a Pontifex, may increase in the merits of Thy Faith; through Our Lord Jesus Christ, Who reigneth with the Father and the Holy Spirit, unto ages of ages. **R.** Amen.

[For all the Clergy and the People of God:]

Let us pray for all Bishops, Priests, Deacons, Acolytes, Exorcists, Lectors, Ostiaries, Confessors, Virgins, Widows, and for all the holy people of God.

Let us pray. Almighty and eternal God, by Whose Spirit the Body of the Church is sanctified and guided, hear us suppliants, for all the clergy of the universe, that by the Gifts of Thy Grace, that from all of the grades of the Church, they may be faithfully obedient to Thee; through Our Lord Jesus Christ, Who reigneth with the Father and the Holy Spirit, unto ages of ages. **R.** Amen.

[For all Christian leaders:]

Let us pray for Christian kings [leaders], that our God and Lord subdue all barbarian nations unto them, unto our perpetual peace. **R.** Amen.

Let us pray. Almighty and eternal God, in Thy hand are the powers of all the ages, and the authorities of all kingdoms; look down and be propitious and benign to the [Christian world] *(Roman Empire)*, that all the nations which are in it may be confident in Thy fierceness, and guided by the strength of Thy right hand; through Our Lord Jesus Christ, Who reigneth with the Father and the Holy Spirit, unto ages of ages. **R.** Amen.

[For Catechumens:]

Let us pray for our Catechumens, that our God and Lord may open the ears of their innermost beings and the door of mercy, so that through the washing of regeneration, they may receive remission of all their sins, and find themselves in Christ Jesus, our Lord.

Let us pray. Almighty and eternal God, Who ever-fertilizes Thy new Church with progeny, increase the Faith and the intellect of our Catechumens, that renewed in the Font of Baptism of Thy adoption, as children they may be gathered together; through Our Lord Jesus Christ, Who reigneth with the Father and the Holy Spirit, unto ages of ages. **R.** Amen.

[For healing of mind and body, release of captives, safety in travel,]

Let us pray, beloved, to God the Father Almighty, that He purge the error from the purity of all of us, that He sweep away sickness, that He dispel famine, that He open prisons, that He break chains, that He grant travelers safe return, health to the infirm, and safe port to seamen.

Let us pray. Almighty and merciful God, consolation of those who sorrow, strength of those who labor, may the prayers of all those crying out in tribulation come unto Thee, that in their necessities they may rejoice in Thy mercy, which comes to them through Our Lord Jesus Christ, Who reigneth with the Father and the Holy Spirit, unto ages of ages. **R.** Amen.

[For heretics:]

Let us pray for heretics and schismatics, that our God and Lord uproot them from universal error and be pleased to call them back to Holy Mother the Catholic and Apostolic Church. **R.** Amen.

Let us pray. Almighty and eternal God, Who saves all, and desires that none perish, look upon the souls that are deceived by the frauds of the devil, that all depravity of heresy being set aside, they may come to their senses, and return to the stability of Thy Truth; through Our Lord Jesus Christ, Who reigneth with the Father and the Holy Spirit, unto ages of ages. **R.** Amen.

[For faithless and doubters:]

Let us pray for the faithless Jews and all doubters, that our God and Lord remove the veil from their hearts, and that they may know Christ Jesus our Lord. **R.** Amen.

Let us pray. Almighty and eternal God, Who because of Thy mercy dost not cast away those who are faithless; hear our prayers, which we give for the healing of the blindness of such people, that acknowledgment of the light of Thy Truth, which is in Christ, grow out of their darkness; through Our Lord Jesus Christ, Who reigneth with the Father and the Holy Spirit, unto ages of ages. **R.** Amen.

[For atheists and idolators:]

Let us pray for pagans and all atheists, that God Almighty remove iniquity from their hearts, and convert them to the abandonment of their idols, and unto the True God and His Only-Begotten Son, Jesus Christ. **R.** Amen.

Let us pray. Almighty and eternal God, Who ever seeks not the death of sinners, but life, be propitious and accept our prayers, and free them from the cult of idols, and gather them into Thy holy Church, unto the praise and glory of Thy Name; through Our Lord Jesus Christ, Who reigneth with the Father and the Holy Spirit, unto ages of ages. **R.** Amen.

Collect for the Ninth Hour:
O saving hour of the Passion, O great Ninth Hour of the greatest grace, the greatest of the hours. This is the hour, O our beloved Bridegroom, when it is permissible to make a fuss about the Cross after the triumph of the Cross. We pray Thee, to kiss, to impart Thy salvation unto us: O marvelous Triumphant One: supreme Charioteer, Faithful God most glorious Champion. Hail Him, Greet Him, Increase in frequency and celebrate mightily, let us be strengthened to say with our hearts, 'O examiner, Christ'. Art Thou not able to do the same as Thou didst once upon a time? Thou art able; Thou art especially able, for Thou art all powerful; thou art able most beloved, able to do that of which we are incapable to even consider, since nothing is impossible for Thee, God Almighty. O Jesus, we beg Thee to kiss us, Beloved, Who returned triumphant unto the Father, with Whom Thou ever wast and remained One. For Thy kiss is sweet, and Thy tears are sweeter than wine, more aglow than the best ointments; and Thy Name, above the oil which girls loved, which the righteous whom Thou drawest unto Thee loved, whose elect are covered with flowers, whose trophy is the Cross. Thou alone Who in that Hour, red as of Edom and of tint of the vesture of Bosrus due to the Cross, the Stamper in that great wine press, ascended unto heaven. To Whom the Angels and Archangels hastened, saying, Who is this Who rises colored like the vesture of Bosra? Who asking Thee, "Why is Thy vesture red?" Thou responded: "I have stamped out the vintage and no man of the nations was with me." Truly, Savior, truly red is Thy body for us. Red is the blood of the Lamb: Thou hast washed Thy stole in wine: Thou hast washed Thy cloak in the blood of the Lamb; Thou Who art God alone, Crucified for us who for old prevarications were given over to death. He by Whose Wounds the innumerable wounds of the sins of all are healed. O Sweet Crucified Christ, redeem us by Thine own: save us, Sweet goodness, God, Who reignest with the Father and the Holy Spirit, One unto eternity and unto ages of ages. **R.** Amen.

*[The Ninth Hour of Holy and Great Friday is ended. The Hymn **"Before Thy Cross"** and **adorations** may be added here. At the end of this Hour, the Image of Christ is taken from the Cross and set on the Altar on the open Antimins, and the congregation may adore. See the **Adorations of the True Cross** after the Propers of the Finding of the True Cross. Each person may do prostrations, and kiss the Cross.]*

Holy Saturday

Evening after Ninth Hour of Holy Friday (Holy Saturday Vespers):
Cross Vigil, with prostrations (optional). *[The Cross Vigil is given in the Communion Hymns, page 51.].* The Antimins may be processed, and lifted up over the people, and the specific Gospel and Psalm for today (page 156) is said instead of the Matins Resurrection Gospel. Some of the verses from Matins Week II may also be used. Litanies may be done. **Sequence** Psalm 64 in Matins or in the Cross Vigil. The Matins Gospel for Holy Saturday also may be done as part of the Cross Vigil. Hours begin again on Saturday afternoon.

Matins Gospel on Holy Saturday: St. Matthew 27: 61-66
And there was there Mary Magdalen and the other Mary, sitting over against the sepulchre. And the next day, which followed the day of preparation, the chief priests and the Pharisees came together to Pilate, Saying: Sir, we have remembered, that that seducer said, while He was yet alive: After three days I will rise again. Command therefore the sepulchre to be guarded until the third day; lest perhaps His disciples come and steal Him away and say to the people: He is risen from the dead. And the last error shall be worse than the first. Pilate saith to them: You have a guard. God, guard it as you know. And they, departing, made the sepulchre sure, sealing the stone and setting guards.

Saturday afternoon: In anticipation of the Vigil of the Resurrection, the first four chapters of the Book of Acts are read, and Confessions are heard. The Prophecies are part of the Vigil of the Resurrection.

Paschaltide

Propers for Pascha and Paschaltide include the Vigil and Mass of the Resurrection, the Dawn Mass of the Resurrection, Bright Week, and the rest of Paschaltide. See the Lectionary in the notes. During the entire forty days of Paschaltide and through the day of Pentecost, the Gospel of the day is also done in the Hour of Matins, instead of doing the Matins Resurrection Gospel cycle of ten weeks (see the Lectionary). The Proper Prayers are necessary in the Masses. See notes. (The Matins Resurrection Gospel is replaced by an Old Testament reading during Lent; see the notes for Matins.)

The Feast of Feasts

What is the greatest Feast of the year in any Christian Church? That is easy. The Resurrection of our Lord Jesus Christ, also called Pascha, and commonly called Easter. The Celtic Rite is a very early complete Divine Liturgy of the Vigil of the Resurrection. The Paschal Mass, together with Christmas, are best written out in full in a separate book in large type. But at least Pascha, though long, should not be omitted from this book, and so most of the Prophecies and readings are only referenced, to be read out of a Bible, and the type face used here is small. There isn't room here to include all the Masses of Holy Week, including Palm Sunday and Holy Thursday, nor for Ascension and Pentecost, Christmas and Epiphany, etc. For these services see the clergy book.

Do not forget, everybody should go to Confession (the Sacrament of Reconciliation) prior to the beginning of the Vigil of the Resurrection. In Celtic usage, this means that during Holy Week the Confessions are heard at length, with penance assigned. Confession may also be heard before the Vigil begins, during the reading of the Book of Acts. So that the Church is not silent, people are assigned to read the first four or more chapters of the Book of Acts before the Vigil of the Resurrection begins (in anticipation of the Hour of Beginning of Night).

The total time of the Vigil Mass of the Resurrection is about six hours. The Vigil may begin as early as seven o'clock, or earlier, culminating with the Mass at about Midnight, because the beginning of the day according to Jewish and Christian tradition is at sunset. The Patriarchate of Jerusalem, at the Church of the Holy Sepulchre, has the descent of the Holy Fire earlier in the day, not in anticipation, but so they are the first Orthodox Church in the world where this occurs. Every year the Lord sends the Church in Jerusalem the Fire without human intervention; and although other Orthodox Churches use flint, the Holy Fire in Jerusalem at the Orthodox Resurrection Liturgy is a Divine fire. The Byzantines do some of the Prophecy and Baptism on Holy Saturday, but the readings of the Prophecy are meant to be heard at the Vigil of the Resurrection. There is also a dawn Mass for use of those who could not come at night due to employments such as healing, or their own illness, etc. There is no requirement to attend both Masses, however, clergy may Binate if necessary on this day if congregation is expected at both Masses. It is preferred that everybody, including infants and children, attend the Vigil Mass of the Resurrection, when Prophecy is heard, Holy Fire is lit, vows to Jesus Christ are renewed, and the first Mass of the Resurrection is offered. **The Vigil Mass is the most important worship service in the year.**

The Church is darkened, with only enough light to enable reading. Candles are provided to each person in the congregation, **but not yet lit**. **Until the Paschal Candle is lit, do not light any candles**.

The vesting color is red at Pascha and Christmas, from Isaiah Chapter 63:1-3, and also from the Ninth Hour on Holy and Great Friday, a hint that at that great and holy moment when the Resurrection occurred, Christ Himself was this color: "...Thou alone Who in that Hour, red as of Edom and of tint of the vesture of Bosrus due to the Cross, the Stamper in that great wine press, ascended unto heaven. To Whom the Angels and Archangels hastened, saying, 'Who is this Who rises colored like the vesture of Bosra?' Who asking Thee, 'Why is Thy vesture red?' Thou responded: 'I have stamped out the vintage and no man of the nations was with me.' Truly, Savior, truly red is Thy body for us. Red is the blood of the Lamb: Thou hast washed Thy stole in wine: Thou hast washed Thy cloak in the blood of the Lamb..."

Red-dyed eggs were used in the ancient Church to teach about the Resurrection. Traditionally, eggs dyed red, bread, and non-fasting foods in baskets are brought on this Saturday evening to be blessed and shared with all after the Vigil Mass is complete (see note after the Vigil).

The choir and readers should be instructed in chanting the Psalms at the Confraction SLOWLY, and Lectors should be assigned for the Prophecies at the beginning of the Vigil, which should NOT be read slowly. For Old Testament readings, the congregation may sit, and at the prayers after the Prophecies, they may stand and then prostrate or genuflect. Note that the Prophecies are read before the Holy Fire is lit. (Read the Old Testament from the Douay-Rheims Version, or similar version of the Old Testament, translated from the Septuagint.) All clergy participating in this Mass should review the rubrics for this Vigil Mass beforehand, and read and be familiar with, and be prepared to do the Lorrha-Stowe Missal, the Rite of Baptism, and the lighting of the Paschal fire.

When the Holy Fire and Paschal Candle are lit, everybody STAND. There is NO KNEELING from this time, although bowing is allowed at times, looking up at the Holy Eucharist, and children or infirm may sit at times.

No part of the Vigil and Mass may be omitted. (Parts of the Rite of Baptism may be omitted if a candidate for Baptism is not present, but *only* as noted in the Rite of Baptism. The Blessing of Water of Baptism is necessary at the Vigil of the Resurrection of the Lord, because some of the Baptismal water is used during the year for the blessing of homes and emergency Baptisms, and because the vows to our Lord Jesus Christ in Baptism are repeated by the entire congregation every year.)

Office of the Vigil Mass of the Resurrection of Our Lord Jesus Christ

The Celebrant, Bishop or Priest, begins without other Litanies.

[Standing in the center of the Church, the Celebrant begins the Vigil:]

Beloved Brethren, let us venerate the Author Of Light, The First Light, the Inspector of the hearts of those who believe, so that He may harken unto the voices that cry out, and illumine the coming darkness of the night with the splendor of His Light, least anything tempting or vexing be the occasion of darkness for us. May He be our protector, Who is Himself the bestower of Light, so that we who glorify Christ may ever be in His Light; through the same, Jesus Christ our Lord, Who reigneth with His unoriginate Father and the Holy Spirit throughout all ages of ages. **R.** Amen.

Guide us, O Lord, past the various vices of the times, and preserve us throughout the successions of the days and nights, so that assisted by the prayers of aid of Thy Saints we might complete this day through the vastness of Thy mercy. May we complete this night with acceptable purity of souls and bodies through the Resurrection from the dead of our Lord Jesus Christ, Thy Son, Who reigneth with Thee and the Holy Spirit throughout all ages of ages. **R.** Amen.

Priest or Deacon: + O God come to my assistance.

R. O Lord make haste to help me.

Priest or Deacon: Glory be to the Father, and to the Son, and to the Holy Spirit, as it was in the beginning, is now, and ever unto ages of ages.

R. Amen.

Prayer of Saint Ambrose

Celebrant: O God, I who presume to invoke Thy Holy Name, stand in the presence of Thy Divine Majesty: have mercy upon me, a man: a sinner smeared by the foulness of inherent impurity; forgive the unworthy priest in whose hand this oblation is seen offered: Spare O Lord one polluted by sins: in faults the foremost, in comparison to all others, and do not enter into judgment with Thy servant, for no one living is justified in Thy sight. It is true that we are weighed down in the faults and desires of our flesh: remember, O Lord, that we are flesh and there is no other help besides Thee. Yeah, in Thy sight not even those in Heaven are much more cleansed than we earthly humans, of whom, the Prophet said, "all of our righteous acts are like unto a menstrual rag." [Isaiah 64:6, Latin and Hebrew.] We are unworthy O Jesus Christ, but that we may be living, O Thou Who dost not will the death of a sinner: grant forgiveness unto us who were created in the flesh, so that by penitential acts we may come to enjoy eternal life in the Heavens; through our Lord Jesus Christ Who reigneth with Thee and the Holy Spirit throughout all ages of ages.

R. Amen.

Vesting Prayer of Saint Augustine

[THE VESTMENT COLOR IS RED.]

[Vestments listed are based on vestments found on the relics of St. Cuthbert, including cuffs in cloth or metal, especially needed tonight at the Confraction. Note that the Subdeacon and Deacon have vested before the Litany, saying this prayer, but omitting all text between the † s. The Celebrant now vests, standing in the middle of the nave, saying:]

I pray Thee, O God of Sabaoth, most high, Holy Father, be pleased to arm me with the tunic of Chastity, *[Put on **amice** and **alb**.]*

and gird my loins with the cincture of Love of Thee, *[Tie **cincture**.]*

and furthermore, be pleased to inflame the reins of my heart with the fire of Thy Charity *[Put on **stole**. Note: Subdeacons do not wear stoles.]*

enabling me to make an intercession for my sins

†and earn remission of the sins of these people who are present, and moreover sacrifice the peace-making offering of each one. †

Also do not abandon me, nor permit me to die when I boldly approach Thee, but permit me to wash, vest and calmly undertake this service.

*[The Servers **pour water** over the hands of the Celebrant, using pitcher and basin. The servers help the Celebrant put on the **Cuffs**, the **Maniple**, and then the **Chasuble**. (The Celebrant may stand with arms to the sides in the form of a Cross, while the servers put the Chasuble on him.) If the Celebrant serves alone he may go to the Credenza to wash and vest, and he may put on the outer vestments before he washes his hands.]*

(For a Bishop): *Putting on the Rationale, he says:* Permit us to hold Thy Truth resolutely, O Lord, and worthily open the Doctrine of Truth to Thy People.

Celebrant: Grant this through our Lord Jesus Christ, Who reigneth with Thee and the Holy Spirit throughout all ages of ages. **R.** Amen.

*[The **Deacon** and **Subdeacon** go to the Credenza which is on the Epistle side of the Altar. The **Deacon** takes the **Corporal** from the Credenza and unfolds it upon the Altar, and then stands in front of the Epistle side of the Altar, facing the Crucifix.]*

*[The **Subdeacon** takes the **Chalice** (with **Pall**, folded **veil** and **Purificator** on top of it) in his left hand and the **Paten** with the **Host** upon it in his right hand. He gives the Chalice and the linens to the Deacon, and waits in front of the Epistle side of the Altar, behind the Deacon. (No cleric of rank lower than Subdeacon may carry the Chalice, Host and Paten.)]*

*[The **Celebrant** ascends to the Altar, and **kisses the open Corporal** (the only Procession).]* *[The **Celebrant** faces the Crucifix, praying with the Congregation.]*
*[**Servers** bring the cruets, and wait to the Epistle side of the Altar.]*
*[The **Celebrant** takes the **Chalice and Purificator** from the Deacon.]*
*[The **Celebrant** holds the Chalice and **wipes** its interior with the Purificator. He gives the Purificator to the Subdeacon.]*
*[The **Celebrant** makes the **Sign of the Cross** with the Chalice over the Corporal and sets the Chalice on the Corporal.]*

The Altar is the image of the inflicted persecution. The Chalice is the image of the Church which has been set and built upon the persecution of the Prophets and of others. [Notes on the meaning of the images of the Mass are in the end of the original Stowe-Lorrha text].

STAND [OR SIT].

Offertory

*[The Celebrant **blesses the water in the cruet** with the **Sign of the Cross** and takes water cruet.] **Water** is poured first into the Chalice by the Celebrant:*

Celebrant: I pray to Thee, O Father; I ask intercession of Thee, O Son; I appeal to Thee, O Holy Spirit.
[The water cruet is given back to the server.]
This is an image of the People which are "poured into" the Church.

*[The Celebrant takes the **Paten with the Host** upon it; makes the **Sign of the Cross** with the Paten over the Corporal; and tips the Paten, allowing the] **Host** to slip on to the center of the Corporal in front of the Chalice, saying:*

Celebrant: Jesus Christ, Alpha and Omega: this is the First and the Last.

*[The Celebrant then gives the **Paten** to the Subdeacon who returns it to the Credenza and covers it with the purificator. If the Celebrant serves alone, the Celebrant places the Paten under the right edge of the Corporal and covers the Paten with the Purificator.]*
The setting of the Host upon the Altar is His Conception. This is an image of Christ's Body which has been set in the linen sheet of Mary's womb.

*[The Celebrant takes the **wine cruet**.]*
*The Celebrant then adds **Wine** to the Chalice:*

Celebrant: May the Father remit, may the Son pardon, may the Holy Spirit have mercy.

*[The cruet is given back to the server, who places the cruets on the Credenza. The Celebrant takes the **Pall** sets it on the Chalice, and covers both the Chalice and the Host on the Corporal with the **veil**.]*
This is Christ's Godhead with His humanity that comes upon the People at the time of His Conception.

STAND. [ALL WHO ARE PRESENT **STAND LOOKING UPON THE CRUCIFIX**.]

[No person, especially the Celebrant, may have their back to the Cross. The Celebrant lifts his eyes to the Crucifix, extends and lifts his hands with palm upward so that they are just above and to the sides of the gifts and says:]

This prayer is to be chanted at all Masses:

Celebrant: Let our prayer ascend to the Throne of Thy Renown, O Lord, lest emptiness be returned to us in response to our petitions. This we ask through our Lord Jesus Christ Who reigneth with Thee and the Holy Spirit throughout all ages of ages. ℟. Amen.

The Prophecies

*[The Congregation and Clergy may SIT during the Prophecies. **Assign Lectors**. Lectors may be members of the Congregation. **Do NOT read slowly**. The Celebrant or Deacon says the Collects before and after each Old Testament reading. During these prayers, all STAND; in the Collects after the readings, prostration or genuflexion may be done.]*

I. **Collect:** For all of us here present at the Mass of the Resurrection of our Lord Jesus Christ:

During this first solemnity of the celebrating of Pascha, let the Consecration of the offerings begin in thanksgiving for what has occurred: may we pursue the beginning of Faith in Christ Who suffered and was sacrificed for us, and pursue the beginning of confidence of the Sacred Mystery with our voices in harmony: Through the Resurrection from the dead of His only begotten Son our Lord Jesus Christ Who reigneth with Him and the Holy Spirit throughout ages of ages. **R.** Amen.

Author of the universe and Lord, we beseech Thee and implore Thee, for each one who has been mortified through discipline in this world, permit them to become a new human, to serve Thee through the Resurrection from the dead of Thy Son our Lord Jesus Christ, Who reigneth with Thee and the Holy Spirit, throughout ages of ages. **R.** Amen.

[Sit]

I. Genesis, Chapter 1:1 to Chapter 2:6   *[The Creation.]*
   STAND AFTER THE PROPHECY.
   [Prostration or genuflexion may be done during these prayers.]

Brethren, let us with supplication beseech Almighty God, the + Father and the Son and the Holy Spirit, the one Creator of the universe, in this great morning of the Sabbath of the Lord: especially for the repose of the body; that His Son, Who mercifully freed Adam from the depths of the gates of Hell, dig us out of the pollution in which we are mired. Let us cry out and pray, lest He spew us from His mouth into the pit of Hell, and although freed from sin, we may yet still be thrust in; through Christ our Lord, Who reigneth with the Father and the Holy Spirit, unto ages of ages. **R.** Amen.

Collect: O Lord Jesus Christ, sweet God, hear us and grant, we pray, that which we ask with our hearts. This we ask: that we may please Thee, that we may remain with Thee forever, that we may ever give Thee thanks; for Thou, O Lord, hast redeemed us unto eternal life from eternal death. We beseech Thee, O Thou Who descended into the pit, that Thou mayest lead those who were bound out of hell. Because of Thy piety, descend also now into our vitals, that Thou mayest free us from the chains of sin by which each one of us is constrained. Who reignest with the Father and the Holy Spirit, unto ages of ages. **R.** Amen.

II. **Collect:** For those in chains or otherwise unable to attend the Paschal Service:

Dear brethren, let us entreat the mercy of Almighty God the Father so that our God may judge unto a pure and free state those whom the envious devil has oppressed with the slavery of captivity: Through the Resurrection from the dead of His only begotten Son our Lord Jesus Christ Who reigneth with Him and the Holy Spirit throughout ages of ages. **R.** Amen.

Author of the universe and Lord, we beseech Thee and implore Thee, for each one who has been mortified through discipline in this world, permit them to become a new human, to serve Thee through the Resurrection from the dead of Thy Son our Lord Jesus Christ, Who reigneth with Thee and the Holy Spirit, throughout ages of ages. **R.** Amen.

[Sit]
II.   Genesis, Chapter 2:7 to Chapter 3:24   *[Man and Woman; The Fall.]*
     STAND AFTER THE PROPHECY.
          [Prostration or genuflexion may be done during these prayers.]
Brethren, let us with supplication beseech Almighty God, the + Father and the Son and the Holy Spirit, the one Creator of the universe, in this great morning of the Sabbath of the Lord: especially for the repose of the body; that His Son, Who mercifully freed Adam from the depths of the gates of Hell, dig us out of the pollution in which we are mired. Let us cry out and pray, lest He spew us from His mouth into the pit of Hell, and although freed from sin, we may yet still be thrust in; through Christ our Lord, Who reigneth with the Father and the Holy Spirit, unto ages of ages. ℟. Amen.

Collect: O Lord Jesus Christ, sweet God, hear us and grant, we pray, that which we ask with our hearts. This we ask: that we may please Thee, that we may remain with Thee forever, that we may ever give Thee thanks; for Thou, O Lord, hast redeemed us unto eternal life from eternal death. We beseech Thee, O Thou Who descended into the pit, that Thou mayest lead those who were bound out of hell. Because of Thy piety, descend also now into our vitals, that Thou mayest free us from the chains of sin by which each one of us is constrained. Who reignest with the Father and the Holy Spirit, unto ages of ages. ℟. Amen.

III. **Collect:** For the Clergy:
Dear brethren, let us suppliants beseech our God and Lord Jesus Christ on behalf of the Priests and Ministers of His Church so that entering into the Holy of Holies and being participants of the altars, we may be completely filled in diverse manners by the gifts of Spiritual Graces: Through the Resurrection from the dead of His only begotten Son our Lord Jesus Christ Who reigneth with Him and the Holy Spirit throughout ages of ages.
℟. Amen.

Author of the universe and Lord, we beseech Thee and implore Thee, for each one who has been mortified through discipline in this world, permit them to become a new human, to serve Thee through the Resurrection from the dead of Thy Son our Lord Jesus Christ, Who reigneth with Thee and the Holy Spirit, throughout ages of ages. ℟. Amen.

[Sit]
III. Genesis, Chapter 6:5 to Chapter 8:21 [or 22]   *[Noah and the Flood.]*
     STAND AFTER THE PROPHECY.
          [Prostration or genuflexion may be done during these prayers.]
Brethren, let us with supplication beseech Almighty God, the + Father and the Son and the Holy Spirit, the one Creator of the universe, in this great morning of the Sabbath of the Lord: especially for the repose of the body; that His Son, Who mercifully freed Adam from the depths of the gates of Hell, dig us out of the pollution in which we are mired. Let us cry out and pray, lest He spew us from His mouth into the pit of Hell, and although freed from sin, we may yet still be thrust in; through Christ our Lord, Who reigneth with the Father and the Holy Spirit, unto ages of ages. ℟. Amen.

Collect: O Lord Jesus Christ, sweet God, hear us and grant, we pray, that which we ask with our hearts. This we ask: that we may please Thee, that we may remain with Thee forever, that we may ever give Thee thanks; for Thou, O Lord, hast redeemed us unto eternal life from eternal death. We beseech Thee, O Thou Who descended into the pit, that Thou mayest lead those who were bound out of hell. Because of Thy piety, descend also now into our vitals, that Thou mayest free us from the chains of sin by which each one of us is constrained. Who reignest with the Father and the Holy Spirit, unto ages of ages.
℟. Amen.

IV. **Collect:** For Virgins [chaste monastics]:
Dear brethren let us suppliants pray to God the Almighty Father that a conception of mind be well established in our brothers and sisters who swore holy and most acceptable virginity to God: perpetually persevering and holding themselves spotless. Through the Resurrection from the dead of His only begotten Son our Lord Jesus Christ Who reigneth with Him and the Holy Spirit throughout ages of ages. ℟. Amen.

Author of the universe and Lord, we beseech Thee and implore Thee, for each one who has been mortified through discipline in this world, permit them to become a new human, to serve Thee through the Resurrection from the dead of Thy Son our Lord Jesus Christ, Who reigneth with Thee and the Holy Spirit, throughout ages of ages. ℟. Amen.

[Sit]
IV.   Genesis, 22:1-19   *[Abraham and Isaac.]*
        STAND AFTER THE PROPHECY.
                [Prostration or genuflexion may be done during these prayers.]
Brethren, let us with supplication beseech Almighty God, the + Father and the Son and the Holy Spirit, the one Creator of the universe, in this great morning of the Sabbath of the Lord: especially for the repose of the body; that His Son, Who mercifully freed Adam from the depths of the gates of Hell, dig us out of the pollution in which we are mired. Let us cry out and pray, lest He spew us from His mouth into the pit of Hell, and although freed from sin, we may yet still be thrust in; through Christ our Lord, Who reigneth with the Father and the Holy Spirit, unto ages of ages. ℟. Amen.

Collect: O Lord Jesus Christ, sweet God, hear us and grant, we pray, that which we ask with our hearts. This we ask: that we may please Thee, that we may remain with Thee forever, that we may ever give Thee thanks; for Thou, O Lord, hast redeemed us unto eternal life from eternal death. We beseech Thee, O Thou Who descended into the pit, that Thou mayest lead those who were bound out of hell. Because of Thy piety, descend also now into our vitals, that Thou mayest free us from the chains of sin by which each one of us is constrained. Who reignest with the Father and the Holy Spirit, unto ages of ages. ℟. Amen.

V. **Collect:** For those who perform works of mercy:
Let us with supplication pray to God the Father of Mercy: may His abundance pour the powers of the gifts of the Heavens into the Saints of this poor world, and may participation in society while in the flesh be capable of deserving spiritual rewards. Through the Resurrection from the dead of His only begotten Son our Lord Jesus Christ Who reigneth with Him and the Holy Spirit throughout ages of ages. ℟. Amen.

Author of the universe and Lord, we beseech Thee and implore Thee, for each one who has been mortified through discipline in this world, permit them to become a new human, to serve Thee through the Resurrection from the dead of Thy Son our Lord Jesus Christ, Who reigneth with Thee and the Holy Spirit, throughout ages of ages. ℟. Amen.

[Sit]
V.   Genesis, 27:1-40 [or 41]   *[Isaac blesses Jacob instead of Esau.]*
        STAND AFTER THE PROPHECY.
                [Prostration or genuflexion may be done during these prayers.]
Brethren, let us with supplication beseech Almighty God, the + Father and the Son and the Holy Spirit, the one Creator of the universe, in this great morning of the Sabbath of the Lord: especially for the repose of the body; that His Son, Who mercifully freed Adam from the depths of the gates of Hell, dig us out of the pollution in which we are mired. Let

us cry out and pray, lest He spew us from His mouth into the pit of Hell, and although freed from sin, we may yet still be thrust in; through Christ our Lord, Who reigneth with the Father and the Holy Spirit, unto ages of ages. ℟. Amen.

Collect: O Lord Jesus Christ, sweet God, hear us and grant, we pray, that which we ask with our hearts. This we ask: that we may please Thee, that we may remain with Thee forever, that we may ever give Thee thanks; for Thou, O Lord, hast redeemed us unto eternal life from eternal death. We beseech Thee, O Thou Who descended into the pit, that Thou mayest lead those who were bound out of hell. Because of Thy piety, descend also now into our vitals, that Thou mayest free us from the chains of sin by which each one of us is constrained. Who reignest with the Father and the Holy Spirit, unto ages of ages. ℟. Amen.

VI. **Collect:** For those who are traveling:
Let us suppliants entreat God the Father of the Heavens and the Worlds that the power of His aid protect and defend all of our brethren who are under necessity to travel: Through the Resurrection from the dead of His only begotten Son our Lord Jesus Christ Who reigneth with Him and the Holy Spirit throughout ages of ages. ℟. Amen.

Author of the universe and Lord, we beseech Thee and implore Thee, for each one who has been mortified through discipline in this world, permit them to become a new human, to serve Thee through the Resurrection from the dead of Thy Son our Lord Jesus Christ, Who reigneth with Thee and the Holy Spirit, throughout ages of ages. ℟. Amen.

[Sit]
VI.   Exodus, 12:1-50 [or 51]   *[The Passover blood and lamb of Moses.]*
        STAND AFTER THE PROPHECY.
            [Prostration or genuflexion may be done during these prayers.]

Brethren, let us with supplication beseech Almighty God, the + Father and the Son and the Holy Spirit, the one Creator of the universe, in this great morning of the Sabbath of the Lord: especially for the repose of the body; that His Son, Who mercifully freed Adam from the depths of the gates of Hell, dig us out of the pollution in which we are mired. Let us cry out and pray, lest He spew us from His mouth into the pit of Hell, and although freed from sin, we may yet still be thrust in; through Christ our Lord, Who reigneth with the Father and the Holy Spirit, unto ages of ages. ℟. Amen.

Collect: O Lord Jesus Christ, sweet God, hear us and grant, we pray, that which we ask with our hearts. This we ask: that we may please Thee, that we may remain with Thee forever, that we may ever give Thee thanks; for Thou, O Lord, hast redeemed us unto eternal life from eternal death. We beseech Thee, O Thou Who descended into the pit, that Thou mayest lead those who were bound out of hell. Because of Thy piety, descend also now into our vitals, that Thou mayest free us from the chains of sin by which each one of us is constrained. Who reignest with the Father and the Holy Spirit, unto ages of ages. ℟. Amen.

VII. **Collect:** For the Sick:
Let us entreat the Lord of the Salvation of the Universe for our brothers and sisters who are vexed by diverse infirmities and sicknesses of the flesh: that He Who alone is powerful may be pleased to attend the ill because of His tenderness. Through the Resurrection from the dead of His only begotten Son our Lord Jesus Christ Who reigneth with Him and the Holy Spirit throughout ages of ages. ℟. Amen.

Author of the universe and Lord, we beseech Thee and implore Thee, for each one who has been mortified through discipline in this world, permit them to become a new human, to serve Thee through the Resurrection from the dead of Thy Son our Lord Jesus Christ, Who reigneth with Thee and the Holy Spirit, throughout ages of ages. **R.** Amen.

[Sit]
VII. Exodus, Chapter 13:18 to Chapter 15:21   *[The Parting of the Red Sea.]*
  STAND AFTER THE PROPHECY.
    [Prostration or genuflexion may be done during these prayers.]

Brethren, let us with supplication beseech Almighty God, the + Father and the Son and the Holy Spirit, the one Creator of the universe, in this great morning of the Sabbath of the Lord: especially for the repose of the body; that His Son, Who mercifully freed Adam from the depths of the gates of Hell, dig us out of the pollution in which we are mired. Let us cry out and pray, lest He spew us from His mouth into the pit of Hell, and although freed from sin, we may yet still be thrust in; through Christ our Lord, Who reigneth with the Father and the Holy Spirit, unto ages of ages. **R.** Amen.

Collect: O Lord Jesus Christ, sweet God, hear us and grant, we pray, that which we ask with our hearts. This we ask: that we may please Thee, that we may remain with Thee forever, that we may ever give Thee thanks; for Thou, O Lord, hast redeemed us unto eternal life from eternal death. We beseech Thee, O Thou Who descended into the pit, that Thou mayest lead those who were bound out of hell. Because of Thy piety, descend also now into our vitals, that Thou mayest free us from the chains of sin by which each one of us is constrained. Who reignest with the Father and the Holy Spirit, unto ages of ages. **R.** Amen.

VIII. **Collect:** For Penitents:
Dear brethren, let us beseech the God of our Hope that He not reject the guilty, who in the fear of the mandates, turned around onto the path of righteousness due to the aspect of serenity. Nor at His Coming may He exclude them as condemned from the gates of His Kingdom. through the Resurrection from the dead of His only begotten Son our Lord Jesus Christ Who reigneth with Him and the Holy Spirit throughout ages of ages. **R.** Amen.

Author of the universe and Lord, we beseech Thee and implore Thee, for each one who has been mortified through discipline in this world, permit them to become a new human, to serve Thee through the Resurrection from the dead of Thy Son our Lord Jesus Christ, Who reigneth with Thee and the Holy Spirit, throughout ages of ages. **R.** Amen.

[Sit]
VIII. Ezechial, 37:1-11 [may read to 14]   *[The Resurrection of the Field of Bones.]*
  STAND AFTER THE PROPHECY.
    [Prostration or genuflexion may be done during these prayers.]

Brethren, let us with supplication beseech Almighty God, the + Father and the Son and the Holy Spirit, the one Creator of the universe, in this great morning of the Sabbath of the Lord: especially for the repose of the body; that His Son, Who mercifully freed Adam from the depths of the gates of Hell, dig us out of the pollution in which we are mired. Let us cry out and pray, lest He spew us from His mouth into the pit of Hell, and although freed from sin, we may yet still be thrust in; through Christ our Lord, Who reigneth with the Father and the Holy Spirit, unto ages of ages. **R.** Amen.

Collect: O Lord Jesus Christ, sweet God, hear us and grant, we pray, that which we ask with our hearts. This we ask: that we may please Thee, that we may remain with Thee forever, that we may ever give Thee thanks; for Thou, O Lord, hast redeemed us unto eternal life from eternal death. We beseech Thee, O Thou Who descended into the pit, that Thou mayest lead those who were bound out of hell. Because of Thy piety, descend also now into our vitals, that Thou mayest free us from the chains of sin by which each one of us is constrained. Who reignest with the Father and the Holy Spirit, unto ages of ages.
R. Amen.

IX. **Collect:** For the unity of the Church:
Let us beseech the Font of all Good: the Author of human Salvation: the Lord, that He be pleased to preserve inviolate the unity of the Church, so that we who are present within His protection, may deserve the reward of the eternal life to come in the future; through the Resurrection from the dead of His only begotten Son our Lord Jesus Christ Who reigneth with Him and the Holy Spirit throughout ages of ages. **R.** Amen.

Author of the universe and Lord, we beseech Thee and implore Thee, for each one who has been mortified through discipline in this world, permit them to become a new human, to serve Thee through the Resurrection from the dead of Thy Son our Lord Jesus Christ, Who reigneth with Thee and the Holy Spirit, throughout ages of ages. **R.** Amen.

[Sit.]
IX.   Isaiah, Chapter 1:1 to Chapter 5:24   *[Exhortation and Prediction of Christ.]*
    STAND AFTER THE PROPHECY.
        [Prostration or genuflexion may be done during these prayers.]

Brethren, let us with supplication beseech Almighty God, the + Father and the Son and the Holy Spirit, the one Creator of the universe, in this great morning of the Sabbath of the Lord: especially for the repose of the body; that His Son, Who mercifully freed Adam from the depths of the gates of Hell, dig us out of the pollution in which we are mired. Let us cry out and pray, lest He spew us from His mouth into the pit of Hell, and although freed from sin, we may yet still be thrust in; through Christ our Lord, Who reigneth with the Father and the Holy Spirit, unto ages of ages. **R.** Amen.

Collect: O Lord Jesus Christ, sweet God, hear us and grant, we pray, that which we ask with our hearts. This we ask: that we may please Thee, that we may remain with Thee forever, that we may ever give Thee thanks; for Thou, O Lord, hast redeemed us unto eternal life from eternal death. We beseech Thee, O Thou Who descended into the pit, that Thou mayest lead those who were bound out of hell. Because of Thy piety, descend also now into our vitals, that Thou mayest free us from the chains of sin by which each one of us is constrained. Who reignest with the Father and the Holy Spirit, unto ages of ages. **R.** Amen.

X. **Collect:** For Peace:
Let us pray with supplication to God the King of the Universe that He pour out prayerfulness, love and friendship between the kings and powers of this world and their ministers. through the Resurrection from the dead of His only begotten Son our Lord Jesus Christ, Who reigneth with Him and the Holy Spirit throughout ages of ages. **R.** Amen.

Author of the universe and Lord, we beseech Thee and implore Thee, for each one who has been mortified through discipline in this world, permit them to become a new human, to serve Thee through the Resurrection from the dead of Thy Son our Lord Jesus Christ, Who reigneth with Thee and the Holy Spirit, throughout ages of ages. **R.** Amen.

[Sit]
X.　　Josuah, Chapter 3:1 to Chapter 4:25　　*[The Parting of the Jordan River.]*
　　　STAND AFTER THE PROPHECY.
　　　　　[Prostration or genuflexion may be done during these prayers.]
Brethren, let us with supplication beseech Almighty God, the + Father and the Son and the Holy Spirit, the one Creator of the universe, in this great morning of the Sabbath of the Lord: especially for the repose of the body; that His Son, Who mercifully freed Adam from the depths of the gates of Hell, dig us out of the pollution in which we are mired. Let us cry out and pray, lest He spew us from His mouth into the pit of Hell, and although freed from sin, we may yet still be thrust in; through Christ our Lord, Who reigneth with the Father and the Holy Spirit, unto ages of ages. **R.** Amen.

Collect: O Lord Jesus Christ, sweet God, hear us and grant, we pray, that which we ask with our hearts. This we ask: that we may please Thee, that we may remain with Thee forever, that we may ever give Thee thanks; for Thou, O Lord, hast redeemed us unto eternal life from eternal death. We beseech Thee, O Thou Who descended into the pit, that Thou mayest lead those who were bound out of hell. Because of Thy piety, descend also now into our vitals, that Thou mayest free us from the chains of sin by which each one of us is constrained. Who reignest with the Father and the Holy Spirit, unto ages of ages.
R. Amen.

XI. **Collect:** For the Souls of the Dead:
Let us with supplication pray, dear Brethren, to God the Father Almighty for the commemoration of the dead, that the Lord pour out His refreshment of merciful forgiveness of the faults of sin, upon those who have passed on, who by merits deserve punishment; through the Resurrection from the dead of His only begotten Son our Lord Jesus Christ Who reigneth with Him and the Holy Spirit throughout ages of ages.
R. Amen.

Author of the universe and Lord, we beseech Thee and implore Thee, for each one who has been mortified through discipline in this world, permit them to become a new human, to serve Thee through the Resurrection from the dead of Thy Son our Lord Jesus Christ, Who reigneth with Thee and the Holy Spirit, throughout ages of ages. **R.** Amen.
[Sit]
XI.　　Jonah, Chapter 1:1 to Chapter 3:10　　*[Jonah; the Fish; Saving of Ninive.]*
　　　STAND AFTER THE PROPHECY.
　　　　　[Prostration or genuflexion may be done during these prayers.]
Brethren, let us with supplication beseech Almighty God, the + Father and the Son and the Holy Spirit, the one Creator of the universe, in this great morning of the Sabbath of the Lord: especially for the repose of the body; that His Son, Who mercifully freed Adam from the depths of the gates of Hell, dig us out of the pollution in which we are mired. Let us cry out and pray, lest He spew us from His mouth into the pit of Hell, and although freed from sin, we may yet still be thrust in; through Christ our Lord, Who reigneth with the Father and the Holy Spirit, unto ages of ages. **R.** Amen.

Collect: O Lord Jesus Christ, sweet God, hear us and grant, we pray, that which we ask with our hearts. This we ask: that we may please Thee, that we may remain with Thee forever, that we may ever give Thee thanks; for Thou, O Lord, hast redeemed us unto eternal life from eternal death. We beseech Thee, O Thou Who descended into the pit, that Thou mayest lead those who were bound out of hell. Because of Thy piety, descend also now into our vitals, that Thou mayest free us from the chains of sin by which each one of us is constrained. Who reignest with the Father and the Holy Spirit, unto ages of ages.
R. Amen.

XII. **Collect:** For those about to be Baptized:
Dear Brethren, let us implore the Mercy of God the Father for the catechumens: that the Almighty Lord reward those who come to the Font of His regeneration, with all of the assistance of His Heavenly Mercy; through the Resurrection from the dead of His only begotten Son our Lord Jesus Christ, Who reigneth with Him and the Holy Spirit throughout ages of ages. **R.** Amen.

Author of the universe and Lord, we beseech Thee and implore Thee, for each one who has been mortified through discipline in this world, permit them to become a new human, to serve Thee through the Resurrection from the dead of Thy Son our Lord Jesus Christ, Who reigneth with Thee and the Holy Spirit, throughout ages of ages. **R.** Amen.
[Sit]

XII.   Daniel, 3:1-100   *[Entire below: the Fiery Furnace; the complete Song of the Three Youths. ALL STAND and chant during the Song of the Three Youths.]*

Song of the Three Youths

Daniel 3:1-100 *(Some modern Bibles do not include all verses of Daniel.)*
    Verses 1 - 45 of the third chapter of the Book of Daniel are read the Sunday following Pascha (St. Thomas Sunday), and verses 57 to 88 are done in Matins, or just before a Liturgy. At the Paschal Liturgy, Daniel 3 verses 1 - 100 are read. The modern, not the original, King James Version of the Bible cuts out a great portion of these verses in Chapter 3, having only thirty verses, even though the 100 verses of this Chapter of the Greek and Douay Versions of the Bible are used in Liturgics. In the King James version, all the verses are skipped between the KJV 24 and 25, including verses which tell that the fire was built higher, killing some servants of the king. The Song of the Three Youths is considered a required prayer during the services of Pascha by the early Christian Church. It reminds us that even in the middle of fires of torments or personal struggles with faults, only the Lord God can save us. (For example, often anger and lust are described as "fiery darts.") For this reason, Christians pray for each other, even if we think another person's case is hopeless, or they are no longer living; because hope comes from God, who saved the three youths from the fiery furnace, and has raised the dead into eternal life.

Daniel, 3:1-100 *[Entire below: the Fiery Furnace; the complete Song of the Three Youths.
Sit during the reading at the beginning. ALL STAND and chant during the Song of the Three Youths, verses 26-45, and 52-90.]*

    [Read:]
1. King Nabuchodonosor made a statue of gold, of sixty cubits high and six cubits broad: and he set it up in the plain of Dura of the province of Babylon.
2. Then Nabuchodonosor the king sent to call together the nobles, the magistrates and the judges, the captains, the rulers and governors, and all the chief men of the provinces, to come to the dedication of the statue which king Nabuchodonosor had set up.
3. Then the nobles, the magistrates and the judges, the captains and rulers, and the great men that were placed in authority, and all the princes of the provinces, were gathered

together to come to the dedication of the statue which king Nabuchodonosor had set up. And they stood before the statue which king Nabuchodonosor had set up.

4. Then a herald cried with a strong voice: To you it is commanded, O nations, tribes, and languages:

5. That in the hour that you shall hear the sound of the trumpet and of the flute and of the harp, of the sackbut and of the psaltery and of the symphony and of all kind of music: ye fall down and adore the golden statue which king Nabuchodonosor hath set up.

6. But if any man shall not fall down and adore, he shall the same hour be cast into a furnace of burning fire.

7. Upon this therefore, at the time when all the people heard the sound of the trumplet, the flute and the harp, of the sackbut and the psaltery, of the symphony and of all kind of music: all the nations, tribes and languages fell down and adored the golden statue which king Nabuchodonosor had set up.

8. And presently at that very time some Chaldeans came and accused the Jews,

9. And said to king Nabuchodonosor: O king, live for ever.

10. Thou, O king, hast made a decree that every man that shall hear the sound of the trumpet, the flute and the harp, of the sackbut and the psaltery, of the symphony and of all kind of music shall prostrate himself and adore the golden statue:

11. And that if any man shall not fall down and adore, he should be cast into a furnace of burning fire.

12. Now there are certain Jews shom thou hast set over the works of the province of Babylon, Sidrach, Misach and Abdenago: these men, O king, have slighted thy decree. They worship not thy gods, nor do they adore the golden statue which thou hast set up.

13. Then Nabuchodonosor, in fury and in wrath, commanded that Sidrach, Misach and Abdenago should be brought: who immediately were brought before the king.

14. And Nabuchodonosor the king spoke to them and said: Is it true, O Sidrach, Misach and Abdenago, that you do not worship my gods, nor adore the golden statue that I have set up?

15. Now therefore if you be ready, at what hour soever you shall hear the sound of the trumpet, flute, harp, sackbut and psaltery and symphony and of all kind of music, prostrate yourselves and adore the statue which I have made: but if you do not adore, you shall be cast the same hour into the furnace of burning fire. And who is the God that shall deliver you out of my hand?

16. Sidrach, Misach and Abdenago answered and said to king Nabuchodonosor: We have no occasion to answer thee concerning this matter.

17. For, behold, our God, Whom we worship,is able to save us from the furnace of burning fire and to deliver us out of thy hands, O king.

18. But if He will not, be it known to thee, O king, that we will not worship thy gods nor adore the golden statue which thou hast set up.

19. Then was Nabuchodonosor filled with fury: and the countenance of his face was changed against Sidrach, Misach and Abdenago: and he commanded that the furnace should be heated seven times more than it had been accustomed to be heated.

20. And he commanded the strongest men that were in his army to bind the feet of Sidrach, Misach and Abdenago and to cast them into the furnace of burning fire.

21. And immediately these men were bound and were cast into the furnace of burning fire, with their coats and their caps and their shoes and their garments.

22. For the king's commandment was urgent and the furnace was heated exceedingly, and the flame of the fire slew those men that had cast in Sidrach, Misach and Abdenago.

23. But these three men, that is, Sidrach, Misach and Abdenago, fell down bound in the midst of the furnace of burning fire.

24. And they walked in the midst of the flame, praising God and blessing the Lord.

[Plainchant:]

25. Then Azarias standing up prayed in this manner: and, opening his mouth in the midst of the fire, he said:

26. Blessed art Thou, O Lord, the God of our fathers, and Thy Name is worthy of praise and glorious for ever:
27. For Thou art just in all that Thou hast done to us, and all Thy works are true, and Thy ways right, and all Thy judgments true.
28. For Thou hast executed true judgments in all the things that Thou hast brought upon us and upon Jerusalem the holy city of our fathers: for according to truth and judgment Thou hast brought all these things upon us for our sins.
29. For we have sinned and commited iniquity, departing from Thee: and we have trespassed in all things.
30. And we have not hearkened to Thy commandments, nor have we observed nor done as Thou hadst commanded us, that it might go well with us.
31. Wherefore all that Thou hast brought upon us and every thing that Thou hast done to us, Thou hast done in true judgment:
32. And Thou hast delivered us into the hands of our enemies that are unjust and most wicked and prevaricators, and to a king unjust and most wicked beyond all that are upon the earth.
33. And now we cannot open our mouths: we are become a shame and reproach to Thy servants and to them that worship Thee.
34. Deliver us not up for ever, we beseech Thee, for Thy Name's sake, and abolish not Thy covenant.
35. And take not away Thy mercy from us, for the sake of Abraham Thy beloved and Isaac Thy servant and Israel thy holy one:
36. To whom Thou hast spoken, promising that Thou wouldst multiply their seed as the stars of heaven and as the sand that is on the sea shore.
37. For we, O Lord, are diminished more than any nation and are brought low in all the earth this day for our sins.
38. Neither is there at this time prince or leader or prophet or holocaust or sacrifice or oblation or incense or place of first-fruits before Thee,
39. That we may find Thy mercy: nevertheless in a contrite heart and humble spirit let us be accepted.
40. As in holocausts of rams and bullocks and as in thousands of fat lambs: so let our sacrifice be made in Thy sight this day that it may please Thee: for there is no confusion to them that trust in Thee.
41. And now we follow Thee with all our heart and we fear Thee and seek Thy face.
42. Put us not to confusion, but deal with us according to Thy meekness and according to the multitude of Thy mercies.
43. And deliver us according to Thy wonderful works, and give glory to Thy Name, O Lord.
44. And let all them be confounded that shew evils to Thy servants: let them be confounded in all Thy might, and let their strength be broken.
45. And let them know that Thou art the Lord, the only God, and glorious over all the world.

[read]
46. Now the king's servants that had cast them in ceased not to heat the furnace with brimstone and tow and pitch and dry sticks.
47. And the flame mounted up above the furnace nine and forty cubits:
48. And it broke forth and burnt such of the Chaldeans as it found near the furnace:
49. But the angel of the Lord went down with Azarias and his companions into the furnace: and he drove the flame of the fire out of the furnace:
50. And made the midst of the furnace like the blowing of a wind bringing dew. And the fire touched them not at all, nor troubled them, nor did them any harm.

[STAND and chant.]
51. Then these three as with one mouth praised and glorified and blessed God in the furnace, saying:

The Song of the Three Youths

[Repeat notes as needed.]

52. Blessed art Thou, O Lord the God of our fathers:
    and worthy to be praised and glorified and exalted above all for ever:
and blessed is the holy Name of Thy glory:
    and worthy to be praised and exalted above all in all ages.
53. Blessed art Thou in the holy temple of Thy glory:
    and exceedingly to be praised and exceeding glorious for ever.
54. Blessed art Thou on the throne of Thy kingdom:
    and exceedingly to be praised and exalted above all for ever.
55. Blessed art Thou, that beholdest the depths and sittest upon the cherubims:
    and worthy to be praised and exalted above all for ever.
56. Blessed art Thou in the firmament of heaven:
    and worthy of praise and glorious for ever.
57. All ye works of the Lord, bless the Lord: praise and exalt Him above all forever.
58. O ye angels of the Lord, bless the Lord: praise and exalt Him above all forever.
59. O ye heavens, bless the Lord: praise and exalt Him above all forever.
60. O all ye waters that are above the heavens, bless the Lord:
    praise and exalt Him above all forever.
61. O all ye powers of the Lord, bless the Lord: praise and exalt Him above all forever.
62. O ye sun and moon, bless the Lord: praise and exalt Him above all forever.
63. O ye stars of heaven, bless the Lord: praise and exalt Him above all forever.
64. O every shower and dew, bless ye the Lord: praise and exalt Him above all forever.
65. O all ye spirits of God, bless the Lord: praise and exalt Him above all forever.
66. O ye fire and heat, bless the Lord: praise and exalt Him above all forever.
67. O ye cold and heat, bless the Lord: praise and exalt Him above all forever.
68. O ye dews and hoar frosts, bless the Lord: praise and exalt Him above all forever.
69. O ye frost and cold, bless the Lord: praise and exalt Him above all forever.
70. O ye ice and snow, bless the Lord: praise and exalt Him above all forever.
71. O ye nights and days, bless the Lord: praise and exalt Him above all forever.
72. O ye light and darkness, bless the Lord: praise and exalt Him above all forever.
73. O ye lightenings and clouds, bless the Lord: praise and exalt Him above all forever.
74. O let the earth bless the Lord: let it praise and exalt Him above all forever.
75. O ye mountains and hills, bless the Lord: praise and exalt Him above all forever.
76. O all ye things that spring up in the earth, bless the Lord:
    praise and exalt Him above all forever.
77. O ye fountains, bless the Lord: praise and exalt Him above all forever.
78. O ye seas and rivers, bless the Lord: praise and exalt Him above all forever.
79. O ye whales, and all that move in the waters, bless the Lord:
    praise and exalt Him above all forever.
80. O all ye fowls of the air, bless the Lord: praise and exalt Him above all forever.
81. O all ye beasts and cattle, bless the Lord: praise and exalt Him above all forever.
82. O ye sons of men, bless the Lord: praise and exalt Him above all forever.
83. O let Israel bless the Lord: let them praise and exalt Him above all forever.
84. O ye priests of the Lord, bless the Lord: praise and exalt Him above all forever.
85. O ye servants of the Lord, bless the Lord: praise and exalt Him above all forever.
86. O ye spirits and souls of the just, bless the Lord:
    praise and exalt Him above all forever.
87. O ye holy and humble of heart, bless the Lord: praise and exalt Him above all forever.
88. O Ananias, Azarias, and Misael, bless ye the Lord:
    praise and exalt Him above all for ever:

for He hath delivered us from hell and saved us out of the hand of death and delivered us out of the midst of the burning flame and saved us out of the midst of the fire.

89. O give thanks to the Lord, because He is good:
because His mercy endureth for ever and ever.
90. O all ye religious, bless the Lord, the God of gods:
praise Him and give Him thanks, because His mercy endureth for ever and ever.
[Let us bless the Father and the Son and the Holy Spirit, The Lord: Let us chant the hymn and exalt Him above all unto the ages. Amen.]

[Plainchant:]

91. Then Nabuchodonosor the king was astonished and rose up in haste and said to his nobles: Didwe not cast three men bound into the midst of the fire? They answered the king and said, True, O king.
92. He answered and said: Behold, I see four men loose and walking in the midst of the fire. And there is no hurt in them: and the form of the fourth is like the Son of God.
93. Then Nabuchodonosor came tothe door of the burning fiery furnace and said: Sidrach, Misach and Abdenago, ye servants of the most high God, go ye forth, and come. And immediately Sidrach, Misach and Abdenago went out from the midst of the fire.
94. And the nobles and the magistrates and the judges and the great men of the king, being gathered together, considered these men, that the fire had no power on their bodies and that not a hair of their head had been singed, nor their garments altered, nor the smell of the fire had passed on them.
95. Then Nabuchodonosor breaking forth said: Blessed be the God of them, to with, of Sidrach, Misach and Abdenago, who hath sent His Angel and delivered His servants that believed in Him: and they changed the king's word and delivered up their bodies that they might not serve nor adore any god, except their own God.
96. By me therefore this decree is made, that every people, tribe and tongue, which shall speak blasphemy against the God of Sidrach, Misach and Abdenago, shall be destroyed, and their houses laid waste: for there is no other God that can save in this manner.
97. Then the king promoted Sidrach, Misach and Abdenago, in the province of Babylon.
98. Nabuchodonosor the king, to all peoples, nations and tongues, that dwell in all the earth: Peace be multiplied unto you.
99. The most high God hath wrought signs and wonders toward me. It hath seemed good to me therefore to publish
100. His signs, because they are great, and His wonders, because they are mighty: and His kingdom is an everlasting kingdom, and His power to all generations.

[STAND at the beginning of the prayer, prostration or genuflexion may also be made.]

Brethren, let us with supplication beseech Almighty God, the + Father and the Son and the Holy Spirit, the one Creator of the universe, in this great morning of the Sabbath of the Lord: especially for the repose of the body; that His Son, Who mercifully freed Adam from the depths of the gates of Hell, dig us out of the pollution in which we are mired. Let us cry out and pray, lest He spew us from His mouth into the pit of Hell, and although freed from sin, we may yet still be thrust in; through Christ our Lord, Who reigneth with the Father and the Holy Spirit, unto ages of ages. **R.** Amen.

Collect: O Lord Jesus Christ, sweet God, hear us and grant, we pray, that which we ask with our hearts. This we ask: that we may please Thee, that we may remain with Thee forever, that we may ever give Thee thanks; for Thou, O Lord, hast redeemed us unto eternal life from eternal death. We beseech Thee, O Thou Who descended into the pit, that Thou mayest lead those who were bound out of hell. Because of Thy piety, descend also now into our vitals, that Thou mayest free us from the chains of sin by which each one of us is constrained. Who reignest with the Father and the Holy Spirit, unto ages of ages.
R. Amen.

[All lights are now out in the church, including all candles.]

The Paschal Fire, Lighting the Lights

[After Vespers has been said in Choir (the Prophecies) all the clergy and congregation leave the Church building in procession outside of the Church and stand before the closed doors of the Church. The congregation holds unlit candles. Meanwhile: The Priest (or Bishop), vested in Amice, Alb, Cincture, Stole, (Cuffs), stands with the Ministers, with the Cross, holy water which was the previous year's Baptismal water, and incense, before the door of the Church, if it can conveniently be done, or in the entry of the church itself. Fire is struck from a flint. (Use wax and palms). The Celebrant blesses the new fire, saying:]

O Lord God, Father Almighty, Who art light unfailing, and the author of all lights; + bless this light which hath here been sanctified and blessed by Thee, who hast enlightened the whole world: that we may be enkindled by that light, and enlightened with the fire of Thy brightness: and like as Thou didst enlighten Moses going forth from Egypt, so do Thou enlighten our hearts and understandings; that we may be found worthy to attain unto life and light everlasting. Through Christ, our Lord Who reigneth with Thee and the Holy Spirit throughout all ages of ages. **R.** Amen.

O Lord God our Almighty Father In exhaustible Light, author of all Lights: hear us Thy servants and bless this fire which is consecrated for Thy sanctification and blessing. Thou Who dost illumine every man that cometh into this world, enlighten the consciences of our heart by the fire of Thy charity so they may be kindled by Thy fire and Illumined by Thy light: Thou dost expel the darkness of sin form our hearts so that with Thee to light our way we may be worthy to come through to eternal Life. Through Christ, our Lord Who reigneth with Thee and the Holy Spirit throughout all ages of ages. **R.** Amen.

[Sprinkling the new fire with holy water, see note above on this page, he says:]

O Lord Holy Father Almighty and eternal God, Please bless and sanctify this fire which we unworthy ones presume to bless through the invocation of Thine Only Begotten Son our Lord Jesus Christ: Sanctify it with Thy sanctifying Blessing of most clement One and allow the human race to advance to perfection Through Thy Son our Lord, Jesus Christ, Who reigneth with Thee and the Holy Spirit throughout all ages of ages. **R.** Amen.

[Coals are lit and placed in the censer. The new fire is censed.

[He then blesses the five grains of incense to be placed in the Candle, saying:]

We beseech Thee O Lord, to always and everywhere protect us by the Heavenly Light so that we may discern with pure insight and perceive with pure affections O Thou who desirest Thou shall be participants of Thy mysteries.

[He then sprinkles them with Holy water.]

[Then the Deacon, vested in a Red Chasuble, takes the reed upon the top of which are three candles in the shape of a triangle. A server with a taper lit from the new fire stands with him. The servers take the censer and the five grains of incense and re-enter the church: the Subdeacon follows with the Cross, the Clergy in their order: then the Deacon with the reed, after him the Celebrant then the other clergy. The Congregation follows.

[When the Deacon enters the church, he lowers the reed, and the server lights one of the three candles placed upon it, and the Deacon, elevating the reed, genuflects, as do all others with him except the Subdeacon bearing the Cross, and sings alone:

The Light of Christ. ℟. Thanks be to God.

And proceeding to the middle of the church, another candle is lighted: and having again genuflected, he sings in a higher tone:

The Light of Christ. ℟. Thanks be to God.

For the third time he proceeds before the Altar, where the third candle is lighted: and again, having genuflected as before, he sings still higher:

The Light of Christ. ℟. Thanks be to God.

[The Celebrant then ascends to the Altar.
[The Deacon then goes to the Paschal candle and with the servers and the Subdeacon with the Cross. All rise and STAND as at the Gospel.]

Deacon [and choir] *(Chanting):* *[The Gregorian musical setting may be used; the first line given below: or use the Greek or Russian musical setting, which puts the original accidentals back into the music.]*

Modern Roman musical setting:

Or, in the traditional Mode of Tone 6 for the Resurrection (Greek Hypolydian and Dorian modes):

Now let the Angelic host of the heavens rejoice: let the divine mysteries rejoice: and for the victory of the great King let the trumpet of salvation sound forth.

-

Let that of which is illumined by the great lightning flashes, be glad: and enlightened and washed by the splendour of the eternal King,

-

let all the world sense that she hath cast away darkness.
Let our mother the Church rejoice, adorned with the lightening of the light:

-

and let this courtyard resound with great voices of peoples.
Wherefore, you who are standing here, dearly beloved brethren,

-

in the wondrous clearness of this holy light, join with me, I beseech you, in calling upon the mercy of Almighty God.

-

That He who was pleased to graft us through the grace of His light, being poured, may He admonish us unto the completing of the praise of this Candle.

℞. Amen. ℣. Let us lift up our hearts. ℞. We have un-to the Lord.

℣. Let us give thanks un-to our Lord God. ℞. It is wor-thy and just.

℣. It is worthy and just, truly it is worthy and just, that we should with the whole affection of our heart and mind, and with the service of our lips, give praise to the unseen God, the Father Almighty, and to His only-Begotten Son, our Lord Jesus Christ. Who paid for us, to the eternal Father, the debt of Adam, and wiped away the reproach of former offenses by the shedding of His dear blood. For this, is the Feast of the Passover, on which the True Lamb is slain, and by Whose Blood, the doorposts are consecrated. On which first, our fathers, the sons of Israel, were led out of Egypt, and were made to cross over the Red Sea as if on dry land. This is the night when the darkness of sins has been purged away by a pillar of illumination. This is the night when this day, throughout the entire world, those who believe in Christ are called apart from the evils of this age, and from the darkness of sins, the returning of grace, and the society of the holy. This is the night, in which the chains of death are destroyed: Christ the Victor ascends from hell. Indeed, it profiteth us nothing to be born, if it did not profit us to be redeemed. O wonder encircling us, is the honor of thy pity! O how inestimable the delight of Thy charity: That to redeem a slave, Thou gavest Thy Son! O truly necessary sin of Adam, which by the death of Christ is deleted! O happy + fault, which was counted to merit so great a Redeemer! O Blessed night, which alone was worthy to know the time and the hour in which Christ rose again from hell. This is the night, of which it is written: And the night was as illuminated as the day, and my night by illumination shall be unto my pleasures. *[Psalm 138: 11-12]* This therefore is the sanctification of the night. Evil deeds fly. Sins are washed away. Innocence is returned to the fallen; and great joy to them that mourn. Enmity flees; it prepares concord, and bows down empires.

[The Deacon fixes the five grains of incense in the Candle, placing them in the form of a Cross in this order:]

```
      1
    4 2 5
      3
```

Therefore in this grace of night, accept, O holy Father, this evening sacrifice of incense: which unto Thee, in this solemn offering of this Candle, by the hands of Thy ministers, from the works of bees, holy Church doth return to Thee. But we already know the proclamation of this pillar, which in honor of God, glowing fire doth ascend.

[The Deacon lights the Candle with one of the three candles set on the reed.]
Which, is allowed to be divided into parts of borrowed light, does not know loss, for by melting waxes, which the bee the mother hath wrought into the precious substance of this Candle.

[Here the lamps of the congregation are lighted by the Paschal candle, passing the flame from candle to candle.]

The bee who excelled the rest, who were subject to living humans, who though with smallness of body, has greatness of spirit. + She turns in narrow places of the comb. In physical strength, she is frail, but she is capable of power. She has ascertained the succession of the seasons: with the grey mornings of winter, they have been capable: they are capable with the greyness of the mornings of winter, and have swept away old ice in the moderation of the time of spring. Immediately coming out unto labor, the careful one marches out, and disperses through the fields, balanced on little wings. Suspended by its legs, it inserts part of the mouth to select the flowers. Having gathered their food, they return to their fort, and there, others by inestimable art have built up cells by tenacious glue. Others pack in liquid honey. Others turn flowers into wax. + Others shape the newborns by the mouth. Others seal up the contributions of bits of nectar. O truly blessed and marvelous bee, whom neither the masculine sex violate, whom childbirth doth not shake, nor children destroy [her] chastity. Just as the holy Virgin Mary conceived, the Virgin gave birth and remained a Virgin.

Deacon: O night truly blessed, which did spoil the Egyptians, and made rich the Hebrews! O night wherein heavenly things are joined unto earthly, things human unto things divine. We therefore pray Thee, O Lord: that this Candle, consecrated to the honor of Thy Name, may continue without ceasing to vanquish the darkness of this night. That, being accepted for a savor of sweetness, it may be mingled with the lights of heaven. May the morning star find it burning. That morning star, I say, which knoweth not his going down. That star, which, rising again from hell, steadfastly giveth light to all mankind. We therefore pray Thee, O Lord: that Thou wouldest offer to rule, govern and preserve with Thy continual protection, us Thy servants, the whole clergy and Thy most faithful people: together with our most blessed Patriarch(s) *[N.]* and our Bishop *[N.]*, granting us peaceful times in this our Paschal joy. Through the Resurrection of Jesus Christ Thy Son our Lord: Who liveth and reigneth with the Father and the Holy Spirit, God, throughout all ages of ages. **R.** Amen.

Holy Lord Almighty God Who in consideration for our darkness commanded lights to blaze forth in the shadows of this world: Grant that on that day of eternity we may hastily prepare for the meeting of Thine Only-begotten. May we walk without the blemish of sins to this light which Thou prepared against the darkness while this night passes. Through the Resurrection of Jesus Christ Thy Son our Lord: Who liveth and reigneth with the Father and the Holy Spirit, God, throughout all ages of ages. **R.** Amen.

[All the lights in the Church are lit: on the Altar, before Icons, on candle-stands, in chandeliers, etc., during the following hymn:]

Hymn for the Blessing of the Paschal Candle *[The Antiphonary of Bangor Hymn 9]*

Fiery creator of fire,
Light and the bestower of light,
Life and the author of life,
Giver of Salvation and Salvation.

Indeed the vigil lamp set loose
the joys of this night,
O Thou Who dost not will that men die,
Set a light within our hearts.

To those leaving Egypt,
Thou gavest a two-fold Grace.
Thou sent forth a cover of cloud
Thou offered light by night.

As a pillar of cloud by day
Thou didst protect the traveling crowd.
As a pillar of fire at evening,
Thou dispelled the night with Light.

Out of the flame Thou challenged Thy Servant
Thou didst not reject the spiny bush,
and with the burning fire
Thou didst not consume what Thou illuminated.

Time, with a red destroying haze,
Having purged impurity
Through the fervent Holy Spirit:
Flesh is illumined like wax:

Thou stream of Divine sweet honey
having made the treasury of the honeycomb
Cleansing the inmost parts of the heart
Hast refilled the cells with the Word.

The swarm, like a newborn
having abandoned its burdens
tries, on wings of joy, to obtain
the Heaven preached by the mouth of the Spirit.

Glory to the Father Unbegotten
Glory to the Son Only-Begotten
Likewise to the Holy Spirit
Unto endless ages. *[Amen. Or repeat the first verse.]*

AB 127 Collect: In the night Thou wast a pillar of fire, O Lord, unto the defense of Thy people from Pharaoh and his army. Therefore be pleased to send Thy Holy Spirit from Thy flaming, jeweled Throne unto the preservation of Thy people. Defend us this night with the shield of the Father, that we do not fear the terror by night: O Thou Who reignest unto the ages. **R.** Amen.

O God, the Temple of Eternal Fire, God, Truly the Habitation of the Light, God the Throne of Perpetual Clarity: Let us pray: celebrating with the solemn offerings, of this day which is finished and of this night which has just begun, unto Thee Lord, and offering temporal light by the lamps of Thine altar of incense so that Thou might pour forth Thy true and eternal Light upon Thy servants and handmaids Through the Resurrection of Jesus Christ Thy Son our Lord: Who liveth and reigneth with the Father and the Holy Spirit, God, throughout all ages of ages. **R.** Amen.

Go immediately to **The Rite of Baptism** *[page 216.]*

which is done now as part of the Vigil of the Resurrection, and follow directions for Pascha. *[This major blessing of the water of Baptism with the Paschal candle is necessary as part of the Resurrection. This is the time when Christ's New Life is given to us, and the most traditional time for candidates to enter the Church. It is better if there are candidates for Baptism, and the complete Rite may be done. All people present say the responses together whether there is a candidate or not.]*

[***Continue immediately after Baptism with the Mass:]

The Mass of the Resurrection of our Lord Jesus Christ, Holy Pascha

All the text of the Mass from now up to the Epistle and the Gradual is an image of the establishment of the Knowledge of Christ in the law of nature through the Members of His Body and by His own deeds.

[STAND. THERE IS NO KNEELING TODAY.]
Immediately, without pause, the Divine Liturgy continues at the

INTRODUCTORY COLLECT

*[Called the "**Praefatio**" in the Bobbio and Gothic Missals]*

Beloved Brethren, Freed from the darkness of the world and elected to the promise of justice and heavenly light, let us implore the inexhaustible goodness of Almighty God the Father, through Christ His Son, that His Holy Catholic Church may be spread throughout the world, that Church which He gathered unto Himself by the Passion and glorious Blood of His most beloved Son. May He guard it by the protection of His Majesty against all the insidious things of this world. May He bestow a protection and a defense, and grant it a perpetual time of tranquility, though the Risen Christ, Who reigneth with the Father and the Holy Spirit, God, throughout all ages of ages.

R. Amen.

[STAND].

The Angelic Hymn (Gloria)

[The musical setting may be the same as in the Ordinary of the Mass. (The music of the Paschal Gloria from Liber Usualis *happens to fit the Lorrha-Stowe words for the Angelic Hymn, and is probably the oldest chant and not necessarily originally associated only with Easter, but the Scottish setting is simpler.)]*

[Then in the middle of the Altar the Celebrant extends his hands, and bowing, says:]

[All join in singing: *(The Missal did not specify the Celebrant here.)]*

Glory to God in the High-est, *[Still bowing, the Celebrant joins his hands:]*
and on earth peace to men of good will.
We praise Thee; we bless Thee; we worship Thee;
we glorify Thee; we magnify Thee; we give thanks to Thee for Thy
great mercy. O Lord heavenly King, God the Father Almighty;
O Lord, the Only Begotten Son of God, Je sus Christ;
O Holy Spirit of God, and all of us say, Amen.
O Lord the Son of God the Father:
Lamb of God Who takest away the sin of the world,
have mer-cy upon us. Receive our prayers;
Thou Who sittest at the right-hand of God the Father:
Have mercy upon us, for Thou only art holy,
Thou only art the Lord, Thou only art the Lord,
Thou only art glorious; with the + Holy Spirit
in the glory of God the Father. **R.** Amen.

[The Celebrant continues bowed and with joined hands:]
Celebrant: O God Who didst prepare unseen good things for those who are devoted to Thee, send forth an attitude of love of Thee into our hearts, that we may follow Thee in all things, and above all things pursue Thine attentive promises which surpass all expectations. Through our Lord Jesus Christ Who reigneth with Thee and the Holy Spirit throughout all ages of ages. **R.** Amen.
ALL BOW:

COLLECT BEFORE THE EPISTLE:

Thou hast redeemed us, O Lord God through the washing of regeneration and the Blood of the Cross, so that the flesh which became mortal in Adam may be drawn back into heaven, through the Passion of Thy Majesty, O Savior, Who liveth and reigneth with Thine unoriginate Father and the Holy Spirit, throughout all ages of ages. **R.** Amen.

The portion of the Mass from the Epistle and gradual to the uncovering of the Chalice is a recounting of the law Letter which prophesies Christ, but what is prefigured is not yet known. The Gospel, Alleluia, and prayers chanted from the half-uncovering of the Host and the Chalice until the prayer "May these Gifts" is a recounting of the Law of the Prophets which specifically foretold Christ, but the significance of the Prophecy is unknown until His Incarnation.

[SIT].

EPISTLE

This is said louder [by the **Subdeacon** *who reads the Epistle at the foot of the altar facing the Oblations:]* I Corinthians 5:6-8

The Epistle of St. Paul to the Corinthians begins.
Brethren: Your glorying is not good. Know you not that a little leaven corrupteth the whole lump? Purge out the old leaven, that you may be a new paste, as you are unleavened. For Christ our pasch is sacrificed. Therefore let us feast, not with the old leaven, nor with the leaven of malice and wickedness; but with the unleavened bread of sincerity and truth.

[The Congregation makes no response at this time.]

[STAND]
[The Celebrant extends and joins his hands, saying with raised voice immediately:]
Celebrant: O God Who savest us by guidance and justifiest us by forbearance, rescue us from the tribulations of this time and bestow joy upon us through our Lord Jesus Christ Who reigneth with Thee and the Holy Spirit throughout all ages of ages. **R.** Amen.

[The Celebrant bows and says:]
Celebrant: Almighty, eternal God, Who didst redeem Thy people by the blood of Thine Only-Begotten Son, destroy the works of the devil, break the chains of sin, that those who have attained to eternal life in the confession of Thy Name may be bound by no thing to the author of death, through our Lord Jesus Christ Who reigneth with Thee and the Holy Spirit throughout all ages of ages. **R.** Amen.

Proper Gradual and Alleluia for the Resurrection

[St. Columbanus of Luxeiul and Bobbio specified that the Psalm of the Resurrection is Psalm 65 (Greek, Latin, and Douay numbering). Also, Psalm 150 is an appropriate Alleluia for the three most holy Feasts. The Hour of Matins has the theme of the Resurrection, and some portions should be included at the Gradual and Alleluia. These selections from Matins (Antiphonary of

Bangor), including Week III Antiphons, complement the specific content of the Immolatio (Preface) and the other Propers for the Resurrection. The Second Canticle, Exodus 15:1-19 was already read as part of the Prophecy, Antiphon AB 99 is read, with the Collects, as an antiphon with the Gradual in the Mass. Although Matins uses three Psalms of Praise: 148, 149, and 150, Psalms 148 and 149 are used for Christmas and Pentecost; Psalm 150 is done in the Alleluia for all three Feasts.

[Instead of the Alleluia, the Byzantines usually have a "Trisagion," and on the Resurrection substitute, "As many as have been Baptized into Christ, have put on Christ, Alleluia." sung three times, and it refers to the fact that Baptisms usually take place on this day. This could be added to the Irish praises which include a Trisagion, with a special verse within it for Pascha. The Celtic Collects for the Saints and Departed are for the general Resurrection of the Dead; and as we are Baptized into the Resurrection, these are for all who have been Baptized.]

[STAND OR SIT]

THE GRADUAL
Chanter, Choir, or Congregation, chanting:
Psalm 65, the Paschal Psalm of St. Columbanus of Luxeuil

℟. Shout with joy to God, all the earth: sing ye a Psalm to His Name: give glory to His praise.

Shout with joy to God, all the earth: sing ye a Psalm to His Name: give glory to His praise. Say unto God: How terrible are Thy works, O Lord! In the multitude of Thy strength Thy enemies shall lie to Thee. Let all the earth adore Thee and sing to Thee: let it sing a Psalm to Thy Name.

Come and see the works of God: Who is terrible in His counsels over the sons of men. Who turneth the sea into dry land: in the river they shall pass on foot: there shall we rejoice in Him. Who by His power ruleth for ever; His eyes behold the nations: let not them that provoke Him be exalted in themselves.

O bless our God, ye Gentiles: and make the voice of His praise to be heard. Who hath set my soul to live: and hath not suffered my feet to be moved. For Thou, O God, hast proved us: Thou hast tried us by fire, as silver is tried. Thou hast brought us into a net; Thou hast laid afflictions on our back: Thou hast set men over our heads. We have passed through fire and water: and Thou hast brought us out into a refreshment.

I will go into Thy house with burnt-offerings: I will pay Thee my vows, which my lips have uttered, And my mouth hath spoken, when I was in trouble. I will offer up to Thee holocausts full of marrow, with burnt-offerings of rams: I will offer to Thee bullocks with goats.

Come and hear, all ye that fear God; and I will tell you what great things He hath done for my soul. I cried to Him with my mouth, and I extolled Him with my tongue. If I have looked at iniquity in my heart, the Lord will not hear me. Therefore hath God heard me, and hath attended to the voice of my supplication. Blessed be God, Who hath not turned away my prayer, nor His mercy from me.

℟. Shout with joy to God, all the earth: sing ye a Psalm to His Name: give glory to His praise.

(The Matins verses of the Second Canticle of Moses for Pascha):

℟: He is Glorious in the Saints, Marvelous in Majesty: working wonders.

Celebrant: O God Who divided the sea for those departing from the people of Egypt, commanding the streams to stand on either side as if they were vertical walls, be pleased to free our souls from the flood of sins: that we may have the strength to traverse the depths of our faults, contemptuous of the adversary, O Savior of the World, Who liveth, guideth and reigneth with the eternal Father, at one with the eternal Holy Spirit throughout all ages of ages. Amen.

R: He is Glorious in the Saints, Marvelous in Majesty: working wonders.

[For all the Faithful Baptized in Christ:]
Celebrant: When Pharaoh drowned in the sea, Israel was freed: we beseech Thee that through the Grace of Baptism and the Triumph of the Cross, we may be freed from all evil, Through Thee, O Christ.

R: He is Glorious in the Saints, Marvelous in Majesty: working wonders.

[After the Gradual: the Celebrant, with hands joined upon the Altar, bows and asks:]
Celebrant: Let these gifts by which the mysteries are celebrated be pleasing to Thee O Lord, unto our freedom and life: through our Lord Jesus Christ Who reigneth with Thee and the Holy Spirit throughout all ages of ages. **R.** Amen.

THE ALLELUIA *[Psalm 150 with Antiphons: and the Celtic Trisation.]*
Psalm of Praise 150 entire:
Alleluia! Alleluia! Praise ye the Lord in His holy places: praise ye Him in the firmament of His power. Praise ye Him for His mighty acts: praise ye Him according to the multitude of His greatness. Praise Him with sound of trumpet: praise Him with psaltery and harp. Praise Him with timbrel and choir: praise Him with strings and organs. Praise Him on high sounding cymbals: praise Him on cymbals of joy: let every spirit praise the Lord.
Alleluia!

R. Praise the Lord from the Heavens, offer pleasant chants, Praise him with sound of trumpet.

Celebrant: Let them praise the Lord, Who is praised by all the elements: Whose testimony is Holy in Heaven and earth and in His possession, Sion: Sing a new hymn you who thunder: Ye under sentence unto torment, shout with diverse modes of spiritual melody, that your spirits may praise Christ in concert through all the ages. Who liveth and reigneth with the Father and the Holy Spirit throughout all ages of ages. Amen.
Alleluia.

R. Praise the Lord from the Heavens, offer pleasant chants, Praise him with sound of trumpet.

Celebrant: By Rule we praise Thee, O Father of all things.
In all places, we confess and acclaim Thee.
We minister unto Thee in spontaneous service.
Hear us, and grant that which we ask:
Who reignest unto the ages. Amen.
Alleluia.

R. Praise the Lord from the Heavens, offer pleasant chants, Praise him with sound of trumpet.

Celebrant: Let us praise Thee from the Heavens, let us be worthy to sing a new song unto Thee. We beseech Thee, O Lord, Who art venerable among Thy Saints, that Thou accept our petitions, forgive our sins, O Savior of the world, Who reignest unto the ages. Amen.
Alleluia.

℟. Praise the Lord from the Heavens, offer pleasant chants, Praise him with sound of trumpet.

[For all Faithful Baptized in Christ:]
Celebrant: We praise Thee O Lord, with Thy Saints, that Thou mayest be pleased to receive our prayers: Who reignest unto ages of ages. Amen.
Alleluia.

℟. Praise the Lord from the Heavens, offer pleasant chants, Praise him with sound of trumpet.
Alleluia.

The Celtic Trisagion from Matins. *[All sing, as written, with repeats.]*
We adore Thee, eternal Father,
We call to Thee, eternal Son,
 and we confess Thee O Holy Spirit, abiding the one Divine Substance.
Let us return due praise and thanks to Thee, one God in Trinity, that we may be worthy to praise Thee with unceasing voices, through eternal ages of ages. Amen.

We adore Thee, eternal Father,
We call to Thee, eternal Son,
 and we confess Thee O Holy Spirit, abiding the one Divine Substance.
Let us return due praise and thanks to Thee, one God in Trinity, that we may be worthy to praise Thee with unceasing voices, through eternal ages of ages. Amen.

Collect *[clergy]*: O God, Whom the army of heaven sings,
And Whom the Church of the Saints praises,
Whom the Spirit of the Universals hymns,
Have mercy, I beseech Thee, on all of us:
Who reignest unto ages of ages. Amen.
[louder:]
We adore Thee, eternal Father,
We call to Thee, eternal Son,
and we confess Thee O Holy Spirit, abiding the one Divine Substance.
To Thee, O Trinity, we return praise and thanks
To Thee, O God, we recite unceasing praise
Thee, Father, unbegotten
Thee, Son, Only Begotten,
Thee O Holy Spirit from Father proceeding, we believe in our hearts.
We give Thee thanks inestimable, incomprehensible,
Almighty God, Who reignest unto the ages. Amen.

[The Byzantine Paschal prayer for the Baptized may be added, said three times:
"As many as have been Baptized into Christ, have put on Christ, Alleluia.]

[Ending always said: the Celebrant, bows slightly with hands joined on the Altar:]
Celebrant: O Lord we beg Thee to graciously attend these sacrificial offerings here present that our devotions may be profitable to salvation through our Lord Jesus Christ Who reigneth with Thee and the Holy Spirit throughout all ages of ages.

The Congregation chants:
℟. **Amen. Thanks be to God.**

The Litany of Supplication by Saint Martin

[ALL STANDING. Led by Deacon or Celebrant, responses chanted:]
Deacon (or Celebrant) (V):
Let us all say, Lord hear and have mercy:

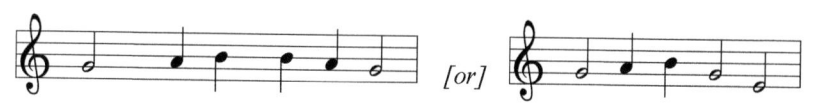

R. Lord have mercy.   *[Examples of music for convenience.]*

V: From our whole heart and our whole mind, O Thou Who dost look over all the earth and make it to tremble, Let us pray: **R. Lord have mercy.**

V: For the greatest peace and tranquillity of our times, for the holy Catholic Church which is from the borders, yeah unto the ends of the earth: Let us pray: **R. Lord have mercy.**

V: For the Shepherd and Bishop -N-, and for all the Bishops and Priests and Deacons and all the clergy: Let us pray: **R. Lord have mercy.**

V: For this place and those living in it, for pious emperors *[leaders]* and all the Roman military *[our military]*: Let us pray: **R. Lord have mercy.**

V: For all who are under the sublime Rule, for virgins, widows and orphans: Let us pray: **R. Lord have mercy.**

V: For pilgrims and those who travel by land and water [and air and space]; for penitents, catechumens and captives: let us pray: **R. Lord have mercy.**

V: For these who in the holy Church give forth the fruits of mercy, O Lord God of virtues listen to our petitions: let us pray: **R. Lord have mercy.**

V: That we be mindful of the Saints, Apostles and Martyrs, that by their prayers for us we may merit forgiveness: let us pray: **R. Lord have mercy.**

V: Permit a Christian and peaceful end: we ask of the Lord,

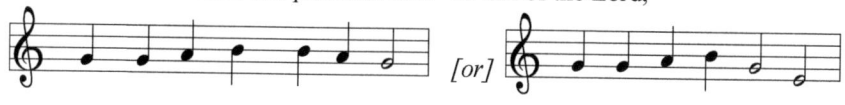

R. Grant it, O Lord, grant it.

V: And the divine influence to remain with us, a holy chain of Charity: we ask the Lord:
R. Grant it, O Lord, grant it.

V: To preserve sanctity and purity of the Catholic Faith: we ask the Lord:
R. Grant it, O Lord, grant it.

V: Let us say: **R. Lord have mercy.**

[The Celebrant extends his hands and looks to heaven, saying:]
Celebrant: O Lord graciously attend the celebration of this Sacrifice unto Thee, which cleanses us from the fault of our condition, and restores us to acceptability by Thy Name, through our Lord Jesus Christ, Who reigneth with Thee and the Holy Spirit throughout all ages of ages. **R̴.** Amen.

[THE CELEBRANT STANDS]
  [Bowing deeply, with hands joined, the Celebrant says:]
Celebrant: O Lord before Thine eyes I defend myself while accused by the witness of a guilty conscience. I do not dare to petition for others because I am unworthy to accomplish it. However, Thou knowest, O Lord, all which has been done among us of which we are ashamed to confess. It is because of this that we do not fear to admit that we obey Thee in words: but we lie in our hearts. We say we are willing; we prove we are unwilling by our acts. Spare, O Lord, the insolent; forgive sinners; have mercy on those who call to Thee. Since in Thy Sacrament my thoughts are refuted: Grant O Lord, Who dost not receive our words with a hard heart, that, by Thyself, Thou mayest bestow forgiveness, through our Lord Jesus Christ, Who reigneth with Thee and the Holy Spirit throughout all ages of ages.
R̴. Amen.

The Censing

ALL STAND:
  *[The **Chalice and Host**] are **half uncovered**: [The Celebrant folds back the veil of the Chalice and Host to expose the Host and the front of the Chalice. The **censing** is illustrated in back of the Lorrha-Stowe Missal. **Incense** is set in the thurible and **blessed**.]*
  *This prayer is recited **thrice**: [The Celebrant **censes the Offerings in the form of a Cross three times**, saying each time:]*

Celebrant:
Let my prayer be set forth in Thy sight as incense
and the lifting of my hand be an evening sacrifice.
  *This prayer is recited **thrice**: [The Celebrant moves the **censer in two anti-clockwise circles and one clockwise circle around the Offerings**, for each circle saying:]*
  Celebrant:
Come, O Lord, the Almighty Sanctifier
and bless this Sacrifice prepared unto Thee.
R̴. Amen.
  *[Then the Celebrant continues to **cense the Altar and congregation**.]*

The Prayer of St. Gregory over the Gospel

Celebrant: *[The Celebrant **censes the Gospel**, saying once over the Gospel:]*

We beseech Thee, O Lord Almighty God, that Thou most mercifully accept our offerings which are sacrificed to Thee, and that Thou stretch forth Thy right hand unto our defense, through our Lord Jesus Christ, Who reigneth with Thee, and the Holy Spirit throughout all ages of ages.
R̴. Amen. [Glory be to Thee, O Lord.] *[The response is assumed.]*

  *[When the Celebrant completes the censing, he hands the Thurible to the server or **replaces the censer** on the stand if serving alone. Servers and as many as are safely able to, hold **lights** near the Deacon or Celebrant, where they will read the Holy Gospel.]*

HOLY GOSPEL (St. Matthew 28:1-20.)

The Deacon (or Celebrant) goes to the foot of the altar and reads the Gospel facing the Oblations. [The Holy Gospel should be chanted, not read plainly. It is better to read this Holy Gospel from a Gospel Book.]

The Gospel according to St. Matthew begins:

[**R.** Glory be to Thee, O Lord.]

And in the end of the Sabbath, when it began to dawn towards the first day of the week, came Mary Magdalen and the other Mary, to see the sepulchre. And behold there was a great earthquake. For an angel of the Lord descended from heaven, and coming, rolled back the stone, and sat upon it. And his countenance was as lightning, and his raiment as snow. And for fear of him, the guards were struck with terror, and became as dead men. And the angel answering, said to the women: Fear not you; for I know that you seek Jesus who was crucified. He is not here, for His is risen, as He said. Come, and see the place where the Lord was laid. And going quickly, tell ye his disciples that He is risen: and behold He will go before you into Galilee; there you shall see Him. Lo, I have foretold it to you.

And they went out quickly from the sepulchre with fear and great joy, running to tell His disciples. And behold Jesus met them, saying: All hail. But they came up and took hold of His feet, and adored Him. Then Jesus said to them: Fear not. Go, tell my brethren that they go into Galilee, there they shall see me. Who when they were departed, behold some of the guards came into the city, and told the chief priests all things that had been done. And they being assembled together with the ancients, taking counsel, gave a great sum of money to the soldiers, Saying: Say you, His disciples came by night, and stole Him away when we were asleep. And if the governor shall hear of this, we will persuade him, and secure you. So they taking the money, did as they were taught: and this word was spread abroad among the Jews even unto this day.

And the eleven disciples went into Galilee, unto the mountain where Jesus had appointed them. And seeing Him they adored: but some doubted. And Jesus coming, spoke to them, saying: All power is given to me in heaven and in earth. Going therefore, teach ye all nations; baptizing them in the Name of the Father, and of the Son, and of the Holy Spirit. Teaching them to observe all things whatsoever I have commanded you: and behold I am with you all days, even to the consummation of the world.

R. Pray for us, and lift up the Gospel towards us.

[This response is from the Rule of Tallaght, which states that when the Gospel is read, the congregation says this, asking the Celebrant to bless them with the Gospels. He makes the Sign of the Cross over the congregation with the Book of the Gospels, saying: [From the Mass of Holy Thursday:]

May He Whose Dominion and Kingdom remain without end, be pleased to sustain us unto ages of ages. **R.** Amen.

[After this the congregation may say: **Praise be to Thee, O Christ.***]*
[The congregation may approach and kiss the Book of the Gospels.]

The Sermon

[The sermon may be shortened, or from St. John Chrysostom. The Collects after the Resurrection Gospel of Matins should be done. The Te Deum may be done.]

Collect: Rejoicing with joy for what has been returned to us by the Light of This day, let us raise up praise and thanks unto Almighty God. That He may be pleased to grant unto us who very solemnly celebrate the day of the Lord's Resurrection, Peace, tranquillity, and joy, that, protected from morning until night by the favor of His clemency, we may, exultant, rejoice with eternal joy, through our Lord Jesus Christ, Who reigneth with the unoriginate Father and the Holy Spirit, unto ages of ages. **R.** Amen.

Collect: Venerating the Lord Who is the beginning of our Resurrection, let us with one mind give deserved praise and thanks to our God, the Trinity, imploring His mercy, that He concede participation in the Resurrection of our Lord and Saviour as much to the spirit as to the body, who with the Father liveth and reigneth unto ages of ages. ℞. Amen.

[For all of us who are Baptized:]
Collect: At this dawn, let us beseech the Risen Lord, that we might arise into eternal life, throughout all ages of ages.
℞. Amen.

Vigil of the Sunday of the Resurrection:
With the dawn of light and the Author arisen, Let us rejoice in the Lord, by Whom, since death is overthrown, we may be able to confront our sins, and let us walk in newness of life, Who livest and reignest with the Father and the Holy Spirit throughout all ages of ages.
℞. Amen.

Te Deum *[Optional - see above. A music setting is in Matins, p. 104.]*
Antiphon: O Youths praise ye the Lord: praise the Name of the Lord.
1. O God, we praise Thee: we confess Thou art the Lord.
2. O eternal Father, all the earth worships Thee
3. Unto Thee, all the Angels, unto Thee, the Heavens and all the powers,
4. Unto Thee, the Cherubim and Seraphim, with unceasing voice cry:
5. Holy, Holy, Holy Lord God of Sabaoth.
6. The Heavens and all the earth are full of the tribute to Thy Glory.
7. Thee, the choir of the glorious Apostles,
8. Thee, the throng of the venerable Prophets,
9. Thee, the white-clad army of martyrs praise.
10. Thee, the Holy Church confesses, throughout the entire world:
11. The Father of immense Majesty;
12. Thy venerable, true and Only-Begotten Son;
13. And also the Holy Spirit, the Comforter.
14. Thou art the King of Glory, O Christ.
15. Thou art the eternal Son of the Father.
16. Thou didst take up human nature unto the liberation of the world. Thou didst not disdain the Virgin's womb.
17. Thou, when the sting of death was bound, opened the Heavenly Kingdom to those who believe.
18. Thou art seated at the right hand of God, in the Glory of the Father.
19. Thou art believed [that Thou art] coming to be Judge.
20. Thee, therefore we beseech, help thy servants whom Thou hast redeemed by Precious Blood.
21. Make numbered with the Saints in eternal Glory.
22. Save Thy people, O Lord, and bless Thine inheritance,
23. And rule them and exalt them unto the ages.
24. Each day we bless Thee,
25. And we praise Thy Name unto eternity, and unto ages of ages. Amen.
26. Let Thy mercy, O Lord, be upon us, in that we have hoped on Thee.

Collect: O God, give aid to all those who praise Thee, O Holy Three, and to those who confess Thee, One, in offerings of the singing of songs: Who reignest unto the ages.
℞. Amen.

Collect: Holy Lord, Illumination and true Salvation unto those who believe: Lordly Resurrection of brightness, Light of our hearts, let us be worthy to be, by the knowledge of the Trinity and perception of the Unity: children of Light, and members of Christ, and a temple of the Holy Spirit. Who reignest unto ages of ages. **R.** Amen.

[For all the Faithful Baptized.]
Collect: Let us venerate Thy Resurrection O Christ, through which we may be worthy to be saved unto eternity, throughout all ages of ages. **R.** Amen.

Collect: Hearken to our prayers, O Lord, Who has visited our human infirmities to bestow Thy Sanctification and Immortality on us: Who reignest unto the ages. **R.** Amen.

Christ is Risen! R. He is Risen indeed!

*[**Notices** and **Banns** (very brief announcements and engagements) having been duly read, all present profess the Creed. The Creed below is Orthodox, and an accurate translation of the Lorrha-Stowe Creed, not adding, omitting, or changing any words or phrases in the text.]*
STAND.

The Creed

I believe in one God, the Father Almighty, maker of heaven and earth and of all things visible and invisible.

And in one Lord Jesus Christ, the Only-Begotten Son of God. Born of the Father before all ages. Light of light, true God of true God. Born, not made, of one Substance with the Father: through Whom all things were made. Who for us men, and for our Salvation descended from heaven. And was Incarnate of the Holy Spirit and the Virgin Mary: And was born man. And was crucified also for us: under Pontius Pilate; He suffered and was buried. And He rose on the third day, according to the Scriptures. And ascended into heaven: and sitteth at the right hand of God the Father. And He shall come again with glory to judge both the living and the dead: Whose Kingdom shall have no end.

And I believe in the Holy Spirit, the Lord and Giver of life: Who proceedeth from the Father. Who with the Father and the Son together is worshiped and glorified: Who spake by the Prophets. And in one, Holy, Catholic, and Apostolic Church. I confess one Baptism for the remission of sins. And I look for the resurrection of the dead. + And the life of the world to come. Amen.

*Fully uncovered: [**The veil and Pall of the Chalice are removed.** Standing erect, the Priest extends his hands, raises them and joins them, and lifting his eyes to heaven and lowering them, says:]*
*This prayer is recited **thrice**:*
Celebrant: Show us Thy Mercy O Lord, and grant us Thy Salvation.

The Elevation

*[**The Chalice is elevated**, and all look at it.] [The following prayer is called the **"Post Nomina"** (after the Word of God and the Creed) in the Bobbio Missal, and is always said.]*

Celebrant: O Lord, may these gifts which are offered be sanctified, and cleanse us from the blots of our sins, through our Lord Jesus Christ, Who reigneth with Thee, and the Holy Spirit, throughout all ages of ages.
R. Amen.

The elevation of the Chalice, after the full uncovering, during the prayer "May these gifts" is the commemoration of Christ's Birth and of His Glory through the signs and miracles.

*[The **Chalice is replaced** on the Corporal and is covered by the **Pall**.]*

Celebrant: We, Thy servants, beseech Thee, O Lord, that Thou benignly receive these Offerings of our devotion, through this glorious Sacrifice and our purified hearts, through our Lord Jesus Christ, Who reigneth with Thee, and the Holy Spirit, throughout all ages of ages. **R.** Amen.

Celebrant: O Lord, we sacrifice these oblations and sincere offerings unto Thee, O Jesus Christ Who suffered for us and rose on the third day from the dead, for the souls of our loved ones -N- and -N-, whose names we recite, and also of those whose names we do not recite but whose names are recited by Thee in the Book of Life Eternal. Of Thy mercy, rescue them, O Thou Who reignest unto ages of ages. **R.** Amen.

POST NOMINA

Let us pray for those who offer holy Spiritual gifts for themselves and their loved ones, and for the spirits of their bodies in commemoration of the Holy Martyrs, that the Lord our God be pleased to hear their prayers. **R.** Amen.

COLLECT OF THE PREFACE
Secret (Ad Pacem):

[Said audibly:]

O Lord, receive the prayers of Thy people with this offering of Sacrifices so that the initiation into the Paschal Mystery may, by Thee working, be beneficial for us unto depths of eternity through the Risen Lord Jesus Christ, Who reigns with the Father and the Holy Spirit, God, unto the ages of ages.

R. Amen. **V.** Let us lift up our hearts. **R.** We have un-to the Lord.

V. Let us give thanks un-to our Lord God. **R.** It is wor-thy and just.

The Preface:

*The usual Preface, called the **"Dignum"** in the Lorrha Missal, is **always said** by the Celebrant before any other: [Called the **"Contestatio"** or **"Immolacio"** in other Celtic sources.]*

Celebrant: Truly it is worthy and just and right and unto Salvation for us now and here, always and everywhere to give thanks, through Christ our Lord, unto Thee, Holy Lord Almighty and Eternal God. Thou Who with Thine Only-Begotten and the Holy Spirit, O God, art One and Immortal God, Incorruptible and Immutable God, Unseen and Faithful God, Marvelous and Praise-worthy God, Honorable and Mighty God, the Highest and Magnificent God, Living and True God, Wise and Powerful God, Holy and Exemplary God, Great and Good God, Terrible and Peaceful God, Beautiful and Correct God, Pure and Benign God, Blessed and Just God, Pious and Holy, not in one singularity of person but One Trinity of One Substance. Thee we believe; Thee we bless; Thee we adore; and we praise Thy Name unto eternity and unto ages of ages: Thou through Whom is the Salvation of the world; through Whom is the Life of men; through Whom is the Resurrection of the dead.

Immolatio:

It is worthy and just, equal and just for us, here and everywhere to give Thee Thanks. To Thee we sing praises and offer sacrifice and trust in Thy mercy, O Lord Holy Father Almighty and eternal God, For Thou art great and dost wonderful things: Thou art God alone. Thou hast made the heavens in understanding. Thou didst form the land above the waters. Thou didst make great lights: the Sun to rule the day and the moon and stars to rule the night. Thou didst make us and not we, ourselves: despise not the works of Thy hands. Thine is the day and Thine is the night. In the daytime hast Thou commanded Thy mercy; and in the nighttime Thou hast declared daily vigil. In the festival of this light we celebrate: This is the night of knowledge of the saving Sacraments: the night in which Thou dost grant forgiveness unto sinners: Thou doest make new from the old man: the mature with deluding senses Thou dost return as infants whom Thou dost bring forth, reborn in a new creature from the sacred font. This night a reborn people is conceived into eternal day. The halls of the heavenly kingdom are opened and humanity is transformed by the blessed law of divine commerce. This is the night which were made the pleasures in which Thou delightest us, O Lord, in Thy works. This is the night in which hell was burst asunder, the night in which Adam was absolved, the night in which the groat that was lost is found, the night in which the lost sheep is laid upon the shoulders of the Good Shepherd, the night in which the devil was laid low, and the Sun of justice is arisen, and the bonds of hell being broken and the gates being shattered, many bodies of the Saints that had slept arose, and coming out of the tombs after the Resurrection came into the holy city.

O truly blessed night which did merit to know the time and the hour when Christ rose, of which the prophet said in the Psalm: for the night shall be light as the day: the night in which the Resurrection unto eternity arose. Thee, therefore, Almighty God, the multitude of the heavenly creatures and the innumerable choirs of Angels proclaim without ceasing:

THE SANCTUS

*[**Chanted by all**, a musical setting may be used. The version below is the Paschal Sanctus from Liber Usualis, which is an ancient melody, and may be Gallican.]*

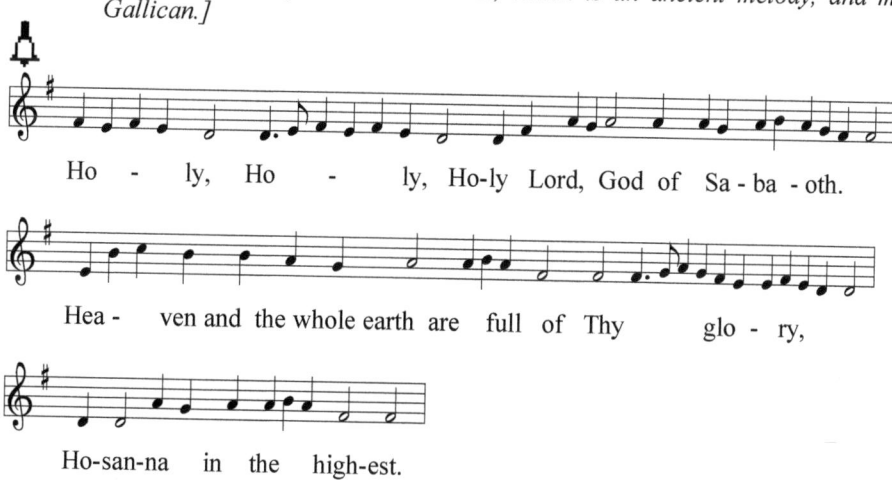

Ho - ly, Ho - ly, Ho-ly Lord, God of Sa - ba - oth.

Hea - ven and the whole earth are full of Thy glo - ry,

Ho-san-na in the high-est.

Bless-ed is He that com-eth in the Name of the Lord.

Ho - san - na in the high - est.

Celebrant: Blessed is He Who cometh from heaven that He might enter the world, and didst become man unto the blotting out of the sins of the flesh, and became a Victim that through suffering He might give eternal life to those that believe; through the same Lord Jesus Christ, Who reigneth with Thee and the Holy Spirit throughout all ages of ages.

R. Amen.

*[All prayers from this point until the Antiphon and Psalms before Communion are said by the Celebrant. All responses are as indicated. **The Canon is never omitted or reduced.** The Celebrant extending then joining his hands, raising his eyes to heaven and at once lowering them, bowing profoundly before the Altar, with his hands placed upon it, says:]*

The Sovereign Canon of Pope Gelasius

Therefore, most clement Father, through Jesus Christ Thy Son our Lord, we humbly beseech and pray Thee, *[he kisses the Altar and with hands joined before his breast, says:]* that Thou accept and bless these gifts, these offerings, these holy and unspotted sacrifices, *[with extended hands he proceeds:]* which, first, we offer unto Thee for Thy holy Catholic Church: that Thou graciously keep her in peace, to guard, unify, and govern her throughout the whole world: together with Thy Servants, the Orthodox Patriarchs, the Bishops of the Apostolic See and all who hold the Orthodox and Apostolic faith, and our Metropolitan -N-, Abbot-Bishop -N-, Bishop -N-. Yeah, remember, O Lord, Thy servants and handmaids **-N- and -N-,** *(Here the names of the living are recited)* and all who are present here, whose faith and devotion unto Thee are known and manifest, who offer unto Thee this sacrifice of praise, for themselves, and for all of theirs: for the redemption of their souls; for their body of elders; for the purity of all ministers; for the integrity of virgins and the continence of widows; for mildness of weather, fruitfulness of the lands; for the returning of peace and an end to division; for the safety of the king *[our leaders]* and peace of the people, and the rescue of captives, and for the prayers of those here present; for the commemoration of martyrs; for the remission of our sins, and the correction of culprits; for repose for the dead; and good fortune of our journey; for the Lord Patriarch Bishop and all the Bishops and the priests and all in Holy Orders; for the Roman empire *[whole world]*, and all Christian kings *[leaders]*; for our brothers and sisters; for the brethren who follow the straight way; for the brethren whom the Lord deemed worthy to call from the dimness of this world, from this darkness, may eternal Divine Faith of the Highest and peaceful light take them up; for brethren afflicted by various sorrows of their lot, may Divine Faith be pleased to cure them; for the hope of salvation and safety; for those who pay their vows unto Thee, the eternal, living and true God in communion with,

and celebrating the most sacred night or day *[or* time*]* of the Resurrection of our Lord Jesus Christ,
and venerating the memory first, of the glorious ever-virgin Mary the Birthgiver of our God and Lord Jesus Christ, and of Thy blessed Apostles and martyrs: Peter and Paul, Andrew, James, John, Thomas, James, Philip, Bartholomew, Matthew, Simon and Thaddeus, Linus, Ancletus, Clement, Xixtus, Cornilius, Cyprian, Lawrence, Crysoginus, John and Paul, Cosmas and Damian and of all Thy Saints by whose examples and prayers mayest Thou grant that, in all things, we may be ever strengthened by the help of Thy protection *[joins hands]* through our Lord Jesus Christ Who reigneth with Thee and the Holy Spirit throughout all ages of ages.

R. Amen.

[The Celebrant extends his hands, palms down, above the Offerings:]

🔔 Therefore we offer this oblation of our service and of Thy whole family, which we offer unto Thee in honor of our Lord Jesus Christ, and in commemoration of Thy blessed martyrs in this church, which Thy servants built in honor of Thy glorious Name. We beseech Thee graciously take it under Thy protection. Moreover, rescue them and all of the people from the cult of idols and turn them unto Thyself, the True God, the Father Almighty. Also order our days in Thy peace, save us from eternal damnation, and number us among Thine elect; *[He joins his hands.]* through our Lord Jesus Christ Who reigneth with Thee and the Holy Spirit throughout all ages of ages.
℟. Amen.

The Celebrant makes the Sign of the Cross once over the oblations:
Which oblation do Thou, O God, we beseech Thee, be pleased in all things to make Blessed, + approved, ratified, reasonable and acceptable: that unto us it may become the Body and Blood of Thy most dearly beloved Son, our Lord Jesus Christ,

Post Sanctus: *[Gothic Missal: **without omitting the previous prayer.**]*

At Thy command the universes were made in Heaven and Earth in Sea and in all the abysses: Unto Thee, Patriarchs, Prophets, Apostles, Martyrs, Confessors, and all of the Saints give thanks, and we implore Thee, making this spiritual offering and the first fruits of sincerity that thou gladly hear us. We pray Thee to bless this Sacrifice and pour down the dew of Thy Holy Spirit, and it may be to all a legitimate Eucharist through Christ our Lord,

When the prayer "Who, the day before He suffered, took Bread..." begins, the Celebrant bows three times in repentance of his sins. He offers the Oblations to God, and while this is done: **and there must be no other voice lest it disturb the Priest,** *for his mind must not separate from God while he chants this lesson. For this reason, its name is* **The Most Dangerous Prayer.** *[Take crying children out a few minutes.]*

The Celebrant bows three times. THE CONGREGATION BOWS VERY DEEPLY OR PROSTRATES:

The Most Dangerous Prayer

Who the day before He suffered,
> *[he **takes the Host**]*

took bread into His Holy and venerable Hands,
> *[he **lifts up his eyes** to heaven]*

and with His eyes lifted up to heaven to Thee, God, His Almighty Father,
> *[he **bows his head**]*

gave thanks to Thee,
> *[he **signs over the Host**]*

He + Blessed, He broke, and gave to His disciples, saying:

> *[**Holding the Host** with both hands between the thumbs and forefingers, he utters the Words of Institution distinctly and attentively over the Host.]*

Take and eat from this all of you, for this is my Body.

♩ *[The Host is **raised** to eye-level, **Offered** and **set again** in its place upon the Corporal. He **bows or genuflects, stands and then removes the Pall from the Chalice.**]*

In a similar manner after the supper,
> *[he takes the **Chalice** in both hands]*

He took this excellent Chalice in His Holy and venerable Hands:
> *[he **bows his head**]*

also giving thanks to Thee,
> *[holding the Chalice in his left hand, he signs over it with his right]*

He + Blessed, and gave to His disciples, saying:

> *[He utters the Words of Institution over the Chalice distinctly and attentively, **holding it slightly raised**.]*

Take and drink from this all of you, for this is the Chalice of my Blood, of the new and eternal testament: the mystery of faith: which is shed for you and for many unto the remission of sins.

♩ *[The Chalice is **raised** to eye-level, **Offered** and **set again** in its place upon the Corporal. He **bows or genuflects, stands, and covers the Chalice with the Pall.**]*

Whenever you do these things, you shall do them unto my memory: you will praise my Passion; you will proclaim my Resurrection; you will hope on my coming until I come again to you from heaven.

> *[With extended hands he proceeds:]*

Wherefore, O Lord, we Thy servants, together with Thy holy people, are mindful of the Blessed Passion of the same Holy Christ Thy Son our Lord, as also His Resurrection from hell and glorious Ascension into heaven: we offer unto Thine excellent majesty of Thine own gifts and bounty, a pure [+] Host, a Holy [+] Host, a spotless [+] Host, the Holy [+] Bread of eternal life and the Chalice of everlasting salvation.

Upon which graciously look with a favorable and gracious countenance: and to accept them, even as Thou didst graciously accept the gifts of Thy just child Abel, and the sacrifice of our Patriarch Abraham: and the Holy Sacrifice, the spotless Host, which Thy high priest Melchizedek offered unto Thee.

We humbly beseech and pray to Thee, Almighty God: command Thou these things to be brought by the hands of Thy Holy Angel to Thine Altar on high, in the presence of Thy Divine majesty: that, as many of us as shall receive from the *[kisses altar]* Altar of Sanctification the most sacred Body and Blood of Thy Son, may be fulfilled with all heavenly benediction and grace.

[THE CONGREGATION MAY STAND:]

The Commemoration of the Departed

Remember also O Lord the names of those who preceded us with the sign of faith and rest in the sleep of peace: -N- and -N-. With all those in the whole world who offer the Sacrifices in spirit unto God the Father, and the Son, and the Holy Spirit, our senior, the Priest, -N- *[Celebrant]* with the holy and venerable Priests, offers for himself, for his own, and for all the rest of the Catholic Church assembly; and for the commemoration of the wrestling of the Patriarchs, Prophets, Apostles and Martyrs, and of all the Saints, that they may be pleased to entreat the Lord our God for us:

Abel, Seth, Enoch, Noah, Melchizedek, Abraham, Isaac, Jacob, Joseph, Job, Moses, Josuah, Samuel, David, Elijah, Elisah, Isaiah, Jeremiah, Ezechial, Daniel, Ester, Hosea, Joel, Amos, Obidiah, Jonah, Micah, Nahum, Habacuc, Zephaniah, Hagai, Zachariah, Malachi, Tobit, Ananias, Azarias, Mishael, the Machabees,

also Holy Innocents, John the Baptist, Virgin Mary, Peter, Paul, Andrew, James, John, Philip, Bartholomew, Thomas, Matthew, James, Simon, Thaddeus, Matthias, Mark, Luke, Stephen, Cornelius, Cyprian and all other Martyrs,

Paul, Anthony and other Fathers of the hermitages of Sceti,

and also the Bishops Martin, Gregory, Maximus, Felix, Patrick, Patrick, Secundinus, Auxilius, Iserninus, Cerbanus, Erc, Carthage, Ibar, Ailbe, Conleth, MacNissi, Moinenn, Senan, Finbarr, Colman, Cuan, Aiden, Laurentius, Mellitus, Justus, Etto, Dagan, Tigernach, Mochti, Ciannan, Buite, Eugene, Declan, Carthain, Mel, Ruadhan, ** Maelrúain, Gregory, Dionisij, Polikarp, Nikanor, Mstyslav, Hryhorij, Hennadij, Andrew   *[** Other departed Bishops may be inserted.]*

also the Priests Finian, Kieran, Oengus, Enda, Gildas, Brendan, Brendan, Cainnech, Columba, Columba, Colman, Comgall, Comghan,
   * *[Other departed Priests may be inserted.]*

and all of those at rest who pray for us in the Lord's peace, from Adam unto this day, whose names God has called and renewed. Unto them O Lord and to all who rest in Christ, we entreat Thee to grant a place of refreshing light and peace.

The Celebrant, Deacon and Subdeacon take three steps backward, pause briefly, and take three steps forward.

The three steps backward and three steps forward is the three ways in which everyone sins: in word, in thought, in deed. These are also the three means by which one is renovated and by which one is moved to Christ's Body.

To us sinners also, Thy servants, hoping for the multitude of Thy mercies, graciously grant some part and fellowship with Thy Holy Apostles and Martyrs: with Peter, Paul, Patrick; John, Stephen, Matthias, Barnabas, Ignatius, Alexander, Marcellinus, Peter, Perpetua, Agnes, Cecilia, Felicitas, Anastasia, Agatha, Lucy and with all Thy Saints: within whose fellowship we beseech Thee admit us, not weighing our merit, but granting us forgiveness through our Lord Jesus Christ, through Whom, O Lord Thou dost ever + create, +   Sanctify, +   Enliven, +   Bless, and bestow all these good things upon us.

THE EXAMINATION AND FRACTION

The Examination of the Chalice and Host, and the effort with which the Celebrant attempts to break it is an image of the rejection, punches, lashings and the Arrest of Christ.

[STAND].

[He genuflects and bows profoundly, rises and uncovers the Chalice:]

It is through + Him, with + Him, and in + Him, within the unity of the Holy + Spirit, that unto Thee, God the Father + Almighty,

It is here that the principle Host is lifted up over the Chalice, elevating both:

is all honor and glory, through all ages of ages.

R. Amen.

*This is **said thrice** as the **Host is submerged halfway** in the Chalice:*

Let Thy mercy be upon us even as we have hoped on Thee.

*[The Subdeacon takes the **Paten, Purificator and knife** from the Credenza. (The knife must never be placed on the Altar). He gives the Paten and the Purificator to the Deacon who **wipes** the Paten with the Purificator. After the Celebrant has withdrawn the Host from the Chalice, the Deacon holds the **Paten under the Host**.]*

*[The Celebrant **places the Host upon the Paten**, takes the Paten and Host from the Deacon and **sets them on the Corporal** before the Chalice.]*

The Host on the Paten is Christ's Flesh upon the tree of the Cross.

The Fraction *It is here that the Bread is broken:*

*The Fraction of the Host upon the Paten is the breaking of Christ's Body with nails on the Cross. [The Celebrant holds the Host between the first and medius fingers and the Thumbs of both hands and **breaks it over the Paten**, saying:]*

They have known the Lord - Alleluia -
in the Fraction of the Bread - Alleluia.
The Bread which we break is the Body of our Lord Jesus Christ - Alleluia -
The Chalice which we bless - Alleluia -
is the Blood of our Lord Jesus Christ - Alleluia -
in remission of our sins - Alleluia.
Let Thy mercy be upon us - Alleluia -
even as we have hoped on Thee - Alleluia.
They have known the Lord. - Alleluia.

The two halves of the Host are submerged totally in the Chalice.

*[After the Celebrant has withdrawn the Host from the Chalice, the Deacon holds the **Paten under the Host**. The Paten and Host are **set on the Corporal** before the Chalice. The following prayer is called the **"Post Secreta"** or **"Post Mysterium"** in the Gothic Missal, and is always said.]*

We believe, O Lord. We believe we have been redeemed in this Fraction of the Body, and the pouring forth of the Blood; and we shall rely on the consumption of this Sacrifice for fortification: that which we now hold in hope, we may enjoy in truth by Heavenly fruition, through our Lord Jesus Christ Who reigneth with Thee and the Holy Spirit throughout all ages of ages. **R.** Amen.

*[**Post Mysterium** from the Gothic Missal is inserted here, without omitting the previous prayer. The oldest written form of an Epiklesis is always said in the prayers at the Fracture in the Lorrha-Stowe Missal. At the Vigil of the Resurrection, the Post Sanctus is an Epiklesis said before the Words of Institution. The following Collect is for the Resurrection Mass.]*

Collect at the Breaking of the Bread *[A Post-Mysterium.]*

Regard this Offering, Almighty God, which we offer to Thee in honor of Thy Name, for the well-being of the nations and their armies, and all who stand present here, and grant that those who eat of It may receive salvation of the spirit, integrity of body, support of health, intellect of the senses of Christ, security of hope, eternal corroboration of the faith, of the Holy Spirit, grant this through Him Who liveth and reigneth with Thee and the Holy Spirit throughout all ages of ages.

℟. Amen.

[In Masses of Apostles, Bishops, and the Virgin Mary, the Post Secreta just before the Lord's Prayer, after the Fracture, resembles the Byzantine Epiklesis. The "Post Mysterium" for the Feast of the Throne of St. Peter at Rome is added here.]

We who serve, offer these prescribed Holy Gifts of our Salvation, that Thou may be pleased to send Thy Holy Spirit upon this Sacrifice so that it may be changed into a legitimate Eucharist for us in the Name of Thee, Thy Son and the Holy Spirit, in the transformation of the Body and Blood of our Lord Jesus Christ; and may it be unto us who eat and drink, Life eternal and the eternal Kingdom. Through Himself, Christ Our Lord who reigneth with Thee and the Holy Spirit throughout all ages of ages. ℟. Amen.

[A small candle may be lit on the Altar now.]

*[**The halves are placed together on the Paten**.] The reunion of the two halves after the Fraction is the affirmation of the wholeness of Christ's Body after His Resurrection. The submersion of the two halves in the Blood are an affirmation that at His Crucifixion, Christ's Body was covered in Blood.*

Taught by Divine instruction, and shaped by Divine institution, we dare to say:
[All say together:]

Our Father, Who art in the Heavens, hallowed be Thy Name. Thy Kingdom come. Thy will be done on earth as it is in Heaven. Give us this day our daily bread and forgive us our debts as we forgive our debtors and lead us not into temptation but deliver us from evil.

[Celebrant:] Free us O Lord from every evil: past, present, and to come, and by the intercessions for us of Thy blessed Apostles Peter, Paul and Patrick, give us favorable peace in our time, that helped by the strength of Thy mercy we may be always free of sin and secure from all turmoil, through our Lord Jesus Christ Who reigneth with Thee and the Holy Spirit throughout all ages of ages.
R. Amen.

The Peace

[Celebrant turns to the people, and makes the Sign of the Cross, saying:]
The + Peace and Charity of our Lord Jesus Christ, and the Communion of all the Saints be always with us.
R. And with thy spirit.
[Turning to the Altar, he continues:]
Thou didst command peace; Thou didst give peace; Thou didst leave peace: bestow, O Lord, Thy peace from heaven and make this day peaceful, and establish all the remaining days of our life in Thy peace, through Thee Who reignest with Thine unoriginate Father and the Holy Spirit throughout all ages of ages. ℟. Amen.

[Exchange of the Pax]

*[If there is a Deacon the Celebrant exchanges the **Pax** with him, bowing. The Deacon then continues the Pax to the Congregation.* **The Celebrant and other clergy must not shake hands with any person at this time, as their hands are purified in order to handle the Holy Eucharist***. If serving alone, the Celebrant may bow to each person, because each person is made in the image of God, and they would return the bow.]*

[The **Proper Blessing of the Day** *from the Pontificale of Egbert or similar document is done here,* **only by a Bishop when he is present***, celebrating or non-celebrating at this Mass. The Bishop may also cut the Particle and drop it into the Chalice if his hands have been purified at the vesting.*

In Sabbato Sancto [The Vigil of the Resurrection]

May God, Who producing a new people from the pure womb of Thy Church, makes her ever fruitful with new progeny while her virginity remains intact; May He complete you with the gift of hope and charity, and pour forth into you the gift of His blessing. ℟. Amen.

And may He Who determined to illumine this most holy night by His Resurrection of our Redeemer make your minds abundantly shimmer brightly, cleansed of the darkness of sins. ℟. Amen.

For they who are reborn in this fashion are certain to imitate innocence. And may the vessels of your minds be illumined with the light of the present lesson. ℟. Amen.

Thus may you be able to enter in with the wise virgins, with lamps of good works, into the bridal chamber of that Bridegroom Whose Resurrection you celebrate. ℟. Amen.

May He Whose Dominion and Kingdom remain without end, be pleased to sustain us unto ages of ages. ℟. Amen.

May the blessing of God: the Father and the Son and the Holy Spirit and the peace of the Lord be ever with you. ℟. Amen.

> [Deus qui de aecclesie suae intemerato / utero novos populos producens eam virginitate manente nova semper prole fecundat fidei spei et caritatis vos munere repleat. et suae in vobis benedictionis donum infundat. Amen.
> Et qui hanc sacratissimam noctem redemptoris nostri resurrectione sua voluit inlustrare. mentes vestras peccatorum tenebris mundatas virtutum copiis faciet coruscare. Amen.
> Quo eorum qui modo renati sunt innocentiam imitari certetis. et vascula mentium vestrarum exemplo presentium luminum inlustratis. Amen.
> Ut cum bonorum operum lampadibus ad huius sponsi thalamum cuius resurrectionem celebratis. cum prudentibus virginibus intrare possitis. Amen.
> / Quod ipse prestare. Amen. Benedictio. Amen.]
> Benedictio in Die Sancto Paschae

[On the Day of the Holy Resurrection, the Dawn Liturgy]

May Almighty God bless you through the daily continuous Paschal Solemnity, and the Merciful One be pleased to defend you from all depravity. R. Amen.

And may He Who restored you to eternal life in the Resurrection of His only begotten Son, make you rejoice with the joys of immortality at His Coming. R. Amen.

And may you who completed the days of the Fasts or the days of the Lord's Passion by the joys of the Paschal Feast be present at that Feast which is not annual but continuous: Through Him Who is quick to come to the assistance to the souls that rejoice. R. Amen.

May He Whose Dominion and Kingdom remain without end, be pleased to sustain us unto ages of ages. R. Amen.

May the blessing of God: the Father and the Son and the Holy Spirit and the peace of the Lord be ever with you. R. Amen.

[Benedicat vos omnipotens deus hodierna interveniente paschali sollempnitate. et ab omni miseratus dignetur defendere pravitate. Amen.

Et qui ad aeternam vitam in unigeniti sui resurrectione vos reparat. in ipsius adventu inmortalitatis vos gaudiis letificet. Amen.

Et qui expletis ieiuniorum siue passionis dominice diebus paschalis festi gaudia celebratis ad ea festa. quae non sunt annua sed continua ipso opitulante exultantibus animis veniatis. Amen.

Quod ipse. Amen. Benedictio. Amen.]

In Pascha Ad Vesperum. Benedictio (Pascha Vespers)

O God Who art pleased by the breaking of the links of the chains of our captivity when the laws of hell had been trampled down, [be likewise pleased] to recall [us] to the reward of freedom. R. Amen.

So that any one who carries through with the considerations of their transgression, by compelling example of Thy Passion, may be recalled to life through [Baptism and Chrismation] working as an adornment [in the heart]. R. Amen.

Please incline thy ears to the petitions of the people so that they, to Thee, may ever intently lift up the realization of their salvation unto Thee.
R. Amen.

May they know Thee, may they correct themselves, may they pray to Thee, may they commend themselves, may they cherish Thee, may they arm themselves, may they please Thee, may they prepare themselves.
R. Amen.

May they preserve inviolate what they received; so that when Thou reward them they might acquire what they need. R. Amen.

May Thou be a defense around them without breach; may they be Thy possession without invasion of the enemy. R. Amen.

So that they who are reborn the font of salvation, may, hastening to the joy of blessed life, may not repeat the excess of original sin. R. Amen.

May He bless you from heaven who bought you back through the Cross of His Passion on earth; to Whom is the Power and the glory unto ages of ages. R. Amen.

May the Blessing of God the Father and the Son and the Holy Spirit descend upon you and remain with you always. R. Amen.

[Deus qui calcatis inferni legibus capti[/]vitatem nostram resoluta catenarum conpage dignatus es ad libertatis premia revocare. Amen.
Ut qui per sue transgressionis deliberationem merito compellente perierat. passionis tuae medela operante misericorditer revocatus est ad vitam. Amen.
Inclina aures tuas ad populi vota propitius. ut hinc ad te recuperatorem suum sensus semper attollat intentos. Amen.
Te cognoscat. se corrigat. te deprecetur. se commendet. te colat. se muniat. te diligat. se componat. Amen.
Inlesus custodiat quod accepit. ut adquirat te remunerante quod indiget. Amen.
Tu sis circumstantium sine interpellatione defensio. isti sint tua sine hostis invasione possessio. Amen.
/ Ut ad beate vite gaudia festinantes. qui salutari fonte renati sunt. peccati non repetant originalis excessum. Amen.
Ille vos benedicat de caelis qui per crucem passionis sue vos redimit in terris. cui est. Amen. Benedictio dei patris et filii. Amen.]

*[The Pax being completed, the Celebrant (or Bishop) turns again to the Altar, takes the knife from the Subdeacon, **cuts a Particle** from the bottom of the left hand portion of the Host and **rejoins the two halves of the Host on the Paten**. The Celebrant (or Bishop) gives the knife to the Deacon. The Deacon wipes it with the Purificator and gives it to the Subdeacon who returns it to the Credenza.*

*The Celebrant (or Bishop) **drops the Particle into the Chalice**.]*

May the commixture of the Body and Blood of our Lord Jesus Christ be for us live-giving unto life eternal.

R. Amen.

The Particle that is cut from the Bottom of the half which is on the Priest's left hand is the wounding with the Lance in the Armpit of the right side; for Christ was facing Westward as He hung upon the Cross: Facing the City, and Longinus faced Eastward, so what was left to Christ was right to him.

[A cloth used only during Holy Communion may be placed just behind the Celebrant, where the Celebrant will turn.]

THE CONFRACTION

[ALL STAND AND BOW.]
   ***Turning to the people, holding a Particle of the Host over the Paten**, the Celebrant says*:

Behold the Lamb of God.
Behold, O Thou Who takest away the sins of the world.   *[St.John 1:29]*

[The Congregation may respond with the prayer of the Centurian at this point:]
[Lord, I am not worthy that Thou shouldest come under my roof, but speak the word only, and my soul shall be healed.
   (thrice)]

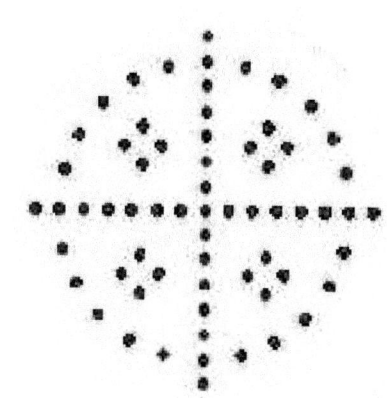

*[The Celebrant **turns to the altar** and if serving alone, begins the verses on the next page. Then the Celebrant continues to perform the **Confraction** of 65 Particles, breaking the Host and placing the Particles in correct formation upon the Paten; while the Celebrant or other clergy say the verses, and choir or congregation sing the Psalms as written between the verses. **Sing the Psalms very slowly today. Holy Communion occurs after these verses are completed**. If it is a very large congregation, the doorwardens may help them line up to receive Communion, but in most cases they should wait until after the Confraction is completed to line up.]*

[The sixty-five Particles used on this day include every day and every Feast. The Stowe-Lorrha Missal has of seven kinds of Confraction:]

Five Particles of the Daily Host as the image of the five senses of the soul;

Seven Particles of the Host of Saints and Virgins except the most important ones as the image of the Seven Gifts of the Holy Spirit;

Eight Particles of the Host of the Holy Martyrs as an image of the octonary New Testament; [This has two meanings: 1) The Eighth Day of Creation, the Resurrection of the Dead.

2) The Eight Fold New Testament according to St. Athanasius:

4 Gospels; Acts and Epistles; Revelation;

The Apostles' Creed; and Pastor of Hermas.

Since the time of this Missal, the last two have been deleted from the Bible.]

Nine Particles of the Host of a Sunday [and also of the Proper Ferias of Lent] is an image of the nine Households of Heaven and the nine Grades of the Church;

Eleven Particles of the Host of the Apostles is an image of the incomplete number of the Apostles due to the Sin of Judas;

Twelve Particles of the Host of the Circumcision and of Holy Thursday are in memory of the complete number of the Apostles;

Thirteen Particles of the Host of Low Sunday and the Feast of the Ascension, is an image of Christ with His twelve Apostles; it is not usual to distribute from all thirteen Particles.

Added together, five, seven, eight, nine, eleven, twelve and thirteen come to sixty-five which is the number of Particles of the Host of Easter, Christmas and Pentecost. For all of them are comprised in Christ.

65 Particles for Easter, Christmas and Pentecost.

The arrangement of the Confraction at Easter and Christmas is: 14 Particles in the upright of the Cross, 14 Particles in the crosspiece, twenty Particles in its circlet: five pieces to each quarter; 16 pieces to the Crosses: 4 to each one. One Particle, for the Celebrant of the Mass is in the middle as the image of the Secrets kept in the heart. The upper part of the shaft of the Cross is for the Bishops, the left portion of the crosspiece is for Priests; the right portion of the crosspiece is to the grades lower than Priest; the lower portion of the stem is to monastics and penitents; the upper left quadrant is for young clerics; the upper right quadrant is to children; the lower left is for those who are truly repentant; the lower right is for those who are married and those who have never before received Communion.

The Celebrant or Deacon continuing *The Prayers of the Confraction:*
*[The initial verses are said before arranging the Particles, spoken aloud, without any omissions.   (Use a copy of this page as an **Altar Card**.)]*

℣.* My peace I give to you - Alleluia -   my peace I leave you - Alleluia. *[St. John 14:27]*

℣. Abundant peace is for those who are attentive to Thy Law, O Lord- Alleluia
and there is no scandal in them - Alleluia.   *[Psalm 118:165]*

℣. For the King of Heaven with peace - Alleluia - *[St. Luke 19:38, Zach. 9:9-10]*
Who is full of the promise of life - Alleluia -   *[St. John 10:10, 11:25-26]*
Sing Ye a new song - Alleluia -   *[Psalms 95:1; 149:1; Isaiah 42:10]*
All of ye holy ones come forth - Alleluia.   *[Jn 5:29, 11:43]*

℣. Come, eat my Bread - Alleluia -
and drink the wine which has been mixed for you - Alleluia. *[St. John 21:12]*

[The Choir immediately starts Psalm 22, VERY SLOWLY.]

*[Altar Card: The Celebrant will say the following verses **between** the Psalms, while completing the Confraction into 65 Particles. Wait for the completion of a Psalm before saying each set of verses.]*

(First, Psalm 22 Greek numbering. Then:)

℣. Whosoever eateth my Body and drinketh my Blood - Alleluia -
Such a one abideth in me and I in him - Alleluia.   *[St. John 6:56]*

(Psalm 23 Greek numbering. Then:)

℣. This is the Bread of Life which cometh down from Heaven - Alleluia -
whosoever eateth of It shall live unto eternity - Alleluia.   *[Jn 6:50,54,58.]*

(Psalm 24 Greek numbering. Then:)

℣. The Lord gave the Bread of Heaven to them - Alleluia -
Man ate the Bread of the Angels - Alleluia.   *[Psalm 77:24-25]*

(Next is Psalm 42. By the end of Psalm 42, Confraction must be completed, then continue the Mass.)

Psalm 22   *[Psalms said by Reader, Choir, or Congregation, CHANTING **SLOWLY**.]*

The Lord shepherds me I shall not want*
   He hath made me dwell in a place of green pasture.
He hath made me rest beside the still water.*
   He hath converted my soul.
He hath led me on the paths of justice,*
   for His own Name's sake.
For though I should walk in the midst of the shadow of death,*
   I will fear no evils, for Thou art with me.
Thy rod and Thy staff,*
   they have comforted me.
Thou hast prepared a table before me *
   against them that afflict me.
Thou hast anointed my head with oil;*
   and my chalice which inebriateth me, how goodly is it!
And Thy mercy will follow me*
   all the days of my life.
And that I may dwell in the house of the Lord*
   unto length of days.

℣. Whosoever eateth my Body and drinketh my Blood - Alleluia -
Such a one abideth in me and I in him - Alleluia.   *[St. John 6:56]*

Psalm 23

The earth is the Lord's and the fullness thereof: *
  the world, and all they that dwell therein.
For He hath founded it upon the seas;*
  and hath prepared it upon the rivers.
Who shall ascend into the mountain of the Lord?*
  or who shall stand in His holy place?
The innocent in hands, and clean of heart, who hath not taken his soul in vain,*
  nor sworn deceitfully to his neighbor.
He shall receive a blessing from the Lord,*
  and mercy from God his Savior.
This is the generation of them that seek Him,*
  of them that seek the Face of the God of Jacob.
Lift up your gates, O ye princes, and be ye lifted up, O eternal gates:*
  and the King of Glory shall enter in.
Who is this King of Glory? *
  the Lord Who is strong and mighty: the Lord mighty in battle.
Lift up your gates, O ye princes, and be ye lifted up, O eternal gates:*
  and the King of Glory shall enter in.
Who is this King of Glory?*
  the Lord of hosts, He is the King of Glory.

V. This is the Bread of Life which cometh down from Heaven - Alleluia -
  whosoever eateth of It shall live unto eternity - Alleluia. *[St. John 6:50, 54, 58.]*

Psalm 24

To Thee, O Lord,*
  have I lifted up my soul.
In Thee, O my God, I put my trust; let me not be ashamed.*
  Neither let my enemies laugh at me:
For none of them that wait on Thee shall be confounded.*
  Let all them be confounded that act unjust things without cause.
Show, O Lord, Thy ways to me,*
  and teach me Thy paths.
Direct me in Thy truth, and teach me; for Thou art God my Savior;*
  and on Thee have I waited all the day long.
Remember, O Lord, Thy bowels of compassion;*
  and Thy mercies that are from the beginning of the world.
The sins of my youth *
  and my ignorances do not remember.
According to Thy mercy remember Thou me:*
  for Thy goodness' sake, O Lord.
The Lord is sweet and righteous:*
  therefore He will give a law to sinners in the way.
He will guide the mild in judgment: *
  He will teach the meek His ways.
All the ways of the Lord are mercy and truth,*
  to them that seek after His covenant and His testimonies.
For Thy Name's sake, O Lord,*
  Thou wilt pardon my sin: for it is great.
Who is the man that feareth the Lord?*
  He hath appointed him a law in the way he hath chosen.
His soul shall dwell in good things: *
  and his seed shall inherit the land.

The Lord is a firmament to them that fear Him:*
 and His covenant shall be made manifest to them.
My eyes are ever towards the Lord:*
 for He shall pluck my feet out of the snare.
Look Thou upon me, and have mercy on me;*
 for I am alone and poor.
The troubles of my heart are multiplied: *
 deliver me from my necessities.
See my abjection and my labor; *
 and forgive me all my sins.
Consider my enemies for they are multiplied,*
 and have hated me with an unjust hatred.
Keep Thou my soul, and deliver me:*
 I shall not be ashamed, for I have hoped in Thee.
The innocent and the upright have adhered to me:*
 because I have waited on Thee.
Deliver Israel, O God, *
 from all his tribulations.

℣. The Lord gave the Bread of Heaven to them - Alleluia -
   Man ate the Bread of the Angels - Alleluia.   *[Psalm 77:24-25]*

Psalm 42
Judge me, O God, and distinguish my cause from the nation that is not holy; *
 Deliver me from the unjust and deceitful man.
For Thou art God, my strength:*
 why hast Thou cast me off? and why do I go sorrowful, whilst the enemy afflicteth me?
Send out Thy light and Thy truth: they have conducted me *
 and brought me unto Thy holy hill, and into Thy tabernacles.
And I will go in to the Altar of God: *
 to God Who giveth joy to my youth.
To Thee, O God, my God,*
 I will give praise upon the harp:
Why art thou sad, O my soul?*
 and why dost thou disquiet me?
Hope in God, for I will still give praise to Him:*
 the salvation of my countenance, and my God.
   [STAND].
   [The following verses are always said for the nine kinds of Communicants:]

℣. Eat, O my friends - Alleluia -
   and be intoxicated, O beloved - Alleluia.   *[Song of Songs 5:1]*

℣. This sacred Body and Blood of the Lord and Savior - Alleluia -
   take you unto yourselves unto life eternal. - Alleluia.   *[St. John 6:54]*

℣. Upon my lips will I practice the hymn - Alleluia -
   which Thou didst teach me - Alleluia-
   and I shall respond in righteousness - Alleluia.   *[Psalm 118:171-172]*

℣. I shall bless the Lord at all times - Alleluia -
   His praise shall ever be in my mouth - Alleluia.   *[Psalm 33:1]*

℣. Taste and see - Alleluia -
how sweet the Lord is - Alleluia. *[Psalm 33:8]*

℣. Wherever I go - Alleluia -
there He shall be and minister unto me - Alleluia.
[Psalm 138:6-10, Psalm 22:4, St. Matthew 28:20]

℣. Suffer the little ones to come unto me - Alleluia -
and do not desire to forbid them - Alleluia -
of such is the kingdom of Heaven - Alleluia. *[St. Matthew 19:14]*

℣. Devote yourselves to penitence - Alleluia -
for the kingdom of Heaven is at hand - Alleluia. *[St. Matthew 3:2]*

℣. The kingdom of Heaven tolerates sieges - Alleluia -
and the forceful take it - Alleluia.
[St. Matthew 11:12, Latin and Greek text.]

*[**Blessed Bread:** After the Confraction is completed, other loaves of bread, already broken or cut into pieces on a tray and kept on the Credenza, are brought by the Subdeacon to the Deacon or Celebrant, who blesses and passes them over the Paten. This bread will be taken by the Communicants immediately after they have received Holy Communion, to be certain all of the Communion is swallowed. **Wine** may also be blessed and used in the same way. This blessed but unconsecrated bread and wine must never be set on the Altar.]*

*Still facing the Altar, the Celebrant **moves the Particle** immediately above the center Particle slightly to the right (his left) and downward.*

The upper Particle is moved down to the left side as reminder us that "Bowing His head, He gave up the ghost". [The Confraction is completed.]

*The Celebrant then turns to the people, **and shows the people the completed Confraction,** holding the Paten lowered and at a slight angle, saying:*

[BOW, then look up.]
[ALL PRESENT LOOK AT THE COMPLETED CONFRACTION.]

Celebrant:

Come Forth and take possession of the kingdom of My Father
- Alleluia -
which hath been prepared for ye from the beginning of the world
- Alleluia - *[St. Matthew 25:34]*

Glory be to the Father and to the Son and to the Holy Spirit:
Come forth!
As it was in the beginning is now and ever unto ages of ages. Amen.
Come forth!
[Jn 5:29, 11:43]
("Moel Caich wrote this." [note in the Lorrha Missal])

HOLY COMMUNION

*The Celebrant turns back to the Altar, and **Communicates himself**, saying,*

May the Body and Blood of our Lord Jesus Christ be to me unto life eternal. Amen.

*[A large **Communion Cloth** (at least three feet long) is either held by two servers or set upon the floor where Communion is to be given. This cloth is not to be stepped upon by the Celebrant or congregation.]*

[Those who have not been Baptized and Confirmed need these Sacraments before participation in Holy Communion. Adults and older children who intend to join the Church must also have Catechism (instruction).]

Those who are Baptized and Confirmed, including infants, and prepared to receive Holy Communion, now line up at the Communion Cloth in the following order, and will be Communicated in the same order from the sixty-five Particles:

Celebrant *The Center Particle is for the Celebrant.*
Bishops *The upper part of the shaft of the Cross is for the Bishops.*
Priests *The left portion of the Cross-piece is for Priests.*
lower Holy Orders *The right portion of the Cross-piece is for those in lower Holy Orders.*
Monastics *The lower portion of the shaft of the Cross is for Monastics and penitents.*
clerics *The upper left quarter is to young clerics.*
babes in arms with their godparents or parents *The upper right quarter is to children.*
unmarried adults *The lower left to unmarried adults. (those who are truly repentant)*
married persons *The lower right quarter is to married persons and new Communicants.*

[THOSE WHO WILL RECEIVE: STAND IN LINE AT THE COMMUNION CLOTH].

The Celebrant turns and goes to the Communion Cloth, holding the Paten.
[If Holy Communion is to be reserved for a sick call, a piece of the upper Particle is reserved. The Confraction usually produces fewer Particles than there are people; the Particles are subdivided further during the administration of Communion.]

*[Infants may be communicated with a spoon from the Chalice, but all others receive from the Bread and Wine on the Paten, which the Celebrant administers with the **first two fingers of his right hand on their tongue** (not touching the tongue with his fingers). **No person receives the Holy Communion in their hands**, including clergy other than the Celebrant. Only the Celebrant or another Bishop, Priest or Deacon may administer the Holy Communion from one Paten, using Holy Communion consecrated at this Mass.]*

[The Celebrant administers the Body and Blood from the Paten, saying:]
[From the Sacrament of Baptism:
May the Body and Blood of our Lord Jesus Christ be to thee unto life eternal.
R. Amen.*]*
[Or, from the Sacrament of Unction:
May the Body and Blood of our Lord Jesus Christ, the Son of the living and most high God, be to thee unto life eternal.
R. Amen.*]*

[A server holds the tray of blessed bread for those who have just received Holy Communion, or a movable table may hold the blessed bread and blessed wine.]

This is what God has declared worthy, that the mind be upon the Symbols of the Mass, and that this be your mind: that portion of the Host which you receive is a portion of Christ from His Cross, and that there may be a Cross in the labor of each in his own life since it is that Cross which unites each one of us to the Crucified Body of Christ. It is not proper to swallow the Particle without having tasted it, just as it is improper to not bring savor into God's Mysteries. It is improper for it to be chewed by the back teeth for such an act symbolizes rumination over God's Mysteries, for it is by such rumination that heresy is increased. It is ended. Amen. Thanks be to God. [End of the Lorrha Missal commentary, as found in Gaelic and Latin.]

Communion Hymns:

Sancti Venite Communion Hymn from the Bangor Antiphonary (Musical setting is on page 46.)

[The Sancti Venite begins during the Celebrant's Communion. It follows the theme of the Gospel. A musical setting is at the Ordinary of the Mass.]

Ye Holy Ones come forth: Eat ye the Body of Christ,
Drink ye the Holy Blood, Ye who are redeemed.

For the Body and Blood of Christ the Savior
From which we are fed, let us give praises to God.

By the Sacrament of the Body and Blood, All are drawn out of the jaws of Hell.

The bestower of Salvation, Christ, the Son of God,
Has saved the world through the Cross and Blood.

For the Universe, the Lord was sacrificed,
He Himself, ariseth: the Priest and Victim.

Under the Law of the Precepts were victims sacrificed
Which foreshadowed the Divine Mystery.

The bestower of Light and Savior of all,
Has poured forth excellent Grace upon the Saints.

All those approach who believe with pure mind;
They consume the eternal Custodian of Salvation.

The Guardian of the Saints, both guide and Lord,
Doth pour Life Eternal upon those who believe.

Heavenly Bread He giveth to the hungry,
From the Living Font supplies those who thirst.

Alpha and Omega Himself, Christ the Lord, came and will come to judge men.

*[During the Communion and Ablutions, the choir may chant the Orthodox Hymn, "**Christ is Risen**." This may be sung in a few languages and melodies:]*

Byzantine Paschal Season Hymn: (English, Greek, Latin, Arabic, Slavonic.)

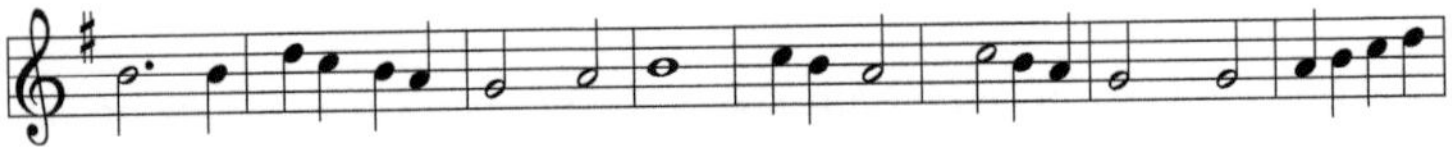

Christ is ris-en from the dead, tramp-ling down death by death, and on those in the tombs be-stow-ing life.

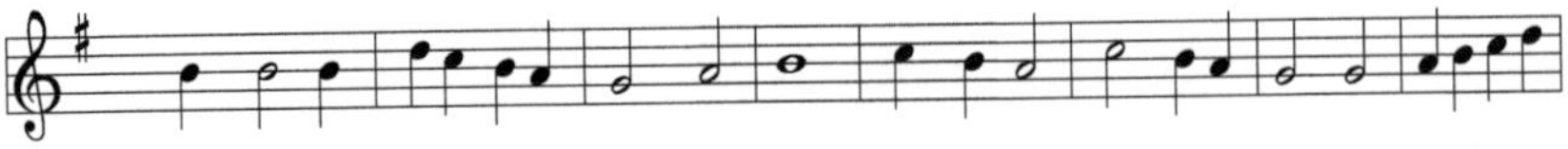

Christ-os a-nes-te ek ne-kron, than-a-tos, than-a-ton pa-ti-sas, kai tis en tis mni-ma-si zo-in, ka-ri-sa-men-os.

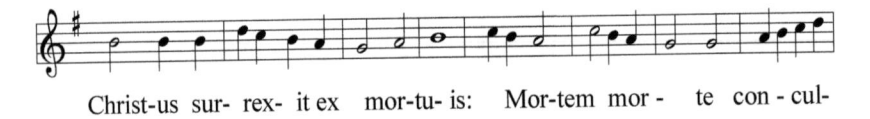

Christ-us sur-rex-it ex mor-tu-is: Mor-tem mor-te con-cul-ans, et il-lis in se-pul-chris vi-tam do-nans.

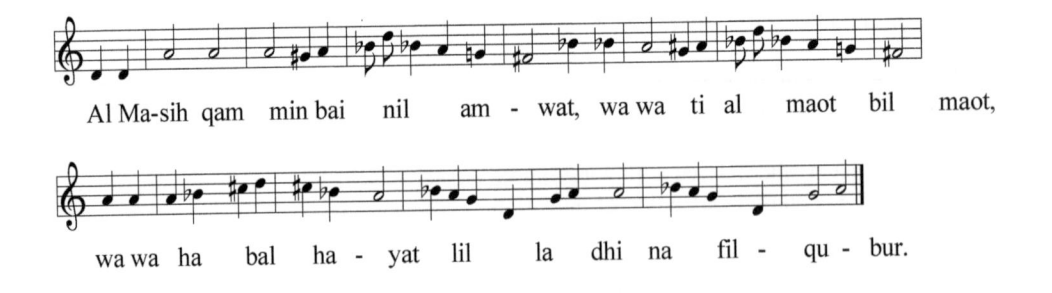

Al Ma-sih qam min bai nil am-wat, wa wa ti al maot bil maot, wa wa ha bal ha-yat lil la dhi na fil-qu-bur.

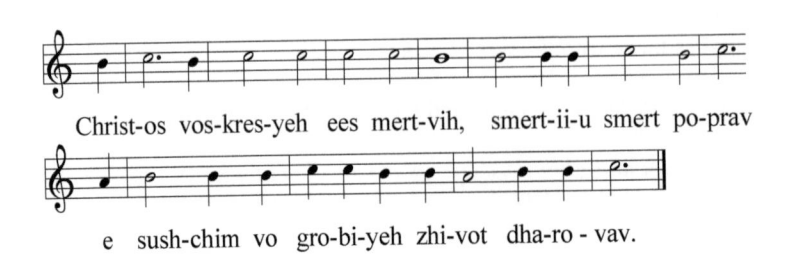

Christ-os vos-kres-yeh ees mert-vih, smert-ii-u smert po-prav e sush-chim vo gro-bi-yeh zhi-vot dha-ro-vav.

If there is time, i.e., a very large congregation, the **Hymn of the Apostles**, *(42 verses), from the Breviary (Antiphonary of Bangor Hymn 3) may be sung; this has a "Kyrie Eleison" response to each verse. After that, other hymns may be sung if time.*

Ablutions

[The Deacon or another Priest may perform the Ablutions, if their hands have been purified at the beginning of the Mass. *(The directions given are for a Celebrant serving alone.) After all have been Communicated who intended to receive,* **Ablutions** *are performed. The Celebrant consumes all of the remaining Body and Blood. The Chalice is set on the Altar to the Epistle side of the Corporal. The Knife and spoon are washed with water then wine over the Chalice and dried with the Purificator. If the Paten has no raised edge caution must be now observed. The Celebrant holds the Paten over the Chalice and pours wine over the Paten into the Chalice. He then dislodges any adhering Particles of the Sanctissimus with his forefinger or thumb, and then pours the wine from the Paten into the Chalice. This action may be repeated if necessary, turning the Paten so that no Particles remain. Then he pours water onto the Paten turning it so that its entire surface is washed, and pours the water from the Paten into the Chalice. The Paten is then dried with the purificator.]*

[The Celebrant then drinks the wine and water. He then holds the Chalice with both hands so that the fingers which came into contact with the Body and the Blood are over the top. Wine and then water is poured over the fingers of the Celebrant into the Chalice by the servers to make certain that no Particles or Blood of Christ that had been on his fingers remain. **Any other clergy who have touched the Holy Eucharist such as a Bishop if he dropped the Particle into the Chalice after the Peace, or Celebrant if Deacon is performing the Ablutions, also have wine and water poured over their fingers into the Chalice.** *The Celebrant drinks the water and wine. Wine is poured into the Chalice. The wine in the Chalice is then drunk by the Celebrant who turns the Chalice, making certain that no Particles or Blood of the Lord remain.]*
[(Additional washings may use water alone.)]

[The inside of the Chalice is **dried with the Purificator**. *The* **Purificator** *is put on top of the* **Chalice** *and both are covered with the* **Pall**. *The* **Paten** *and the* **Chalice** *are returned to the Credenza by the Subdeacon and covered with the veil. The* **Corporal** *is now carefully folded by the Deacon (or the Celebrant serving alone) and returned to the Credenza. The* **Communion Cloth** *is folded flag style and returned to the Credenza by the servers.]*

Post Communion:

[Salutations: In as many languages as you know, and at least a few people can say the response (including Gaelic, which literally means, "Christ is Risen from the dead.":]

Iar túaslucud anman, asréracht Íssu a brú thalman.   *[Old Irish]*
   [Having loosed souls, Jesus has arisen from the womb of the earth.]
Tá Críost éirithe! Go deimhin, tá sé éirithe!   *[Irish Gaelic]*
Tha Crìosd air èiridh! Gu dearbh, tha e air èiridh!   *[Scots' Gaelic]*
Atgyfododd Crist! Yn wir atgyfododd!   *[Cymru (Welsh)]*
Dassoret eo Krist! E wirionez dassoret eo!   *[Breton]*
Taw Creest Ereen! Taw Shay Ereen Guhdyne!   *[Manx]*
Asréracht Críst! Asréracht Hé-som co dearb!   *[Old Irish]*
Christ is Risen! He is Truly Risen!   *[English.]*
Christus surrexit! Vere surrexit!   *[Latin.]*
Christós aneste! Alithós aneste!   *[Greek.]*
Christ est Ressuscité! En Vérité, Il est Ressuscité!   *[French]*

Cristo ha resucitado. En verdad ha resucitado. *[Spanish]*
Christo Ressuscitou! Em Verdade Ressuscitou! *[Portugese]*
Christ ist auferstanden! Der ist wirklicht auferstanden! *[German.]*
Christos voskresia! Voistinu voskresia! *[Slavonic.]*
Al Masih qam! Haq am qam! *[Arabic.]*
Christ is Risen! ℟. **He is Truly Risen!** *[English.]*

POSTCOMMUNION PRAYERS

We beseech Thee, O Lord, enrich the holy libation of this Paschal Sacrament in us, and may it transfer us from earthly affections, to heavenly custom. ℟. Amen.

We beg Thee, O Lord, may the grace of this Paschal Sacrament, enliven our minds, and by Its gifts, may It make us worthy.
℟. Amen.

Refreshed with spiritual nourishment and renewed with the food of heaven: by the Body and Blood of the Lord; let us return proper praise and thanks to our God and Lord Jesus Christ, as we pray for His inexhaustible mercy, so that we may have the divine gifts of the Sacraments unto the increase of Faith and perfection of eternal Salvation, through our Lord Jesus Christ Who reigneth with His unoriginate Father and the Holy Spirit, unto ages of ages. ℟. Amen.

*[Do the Post Communion prayers above, and, if there has been a **Baptism**:]*
Let us pray, dear brethren, for our brother (sister) -N- who has won the Grace of the Lord, that he (she) may bear the Baptism which he (she) has received, spotless and in its entirety before the tribunal of our Lord Jesus Christ, Who reigneth with His unoriginate Father and the Holy Spirit, unto ages of ages. ℟. Amen.

*The **Thanksgiving** is always said:*
We give Thee thanks, O Lord, Holy Father, Almighty and eternal God, Who has satisfied us by the Communion of the Body and Blood of Christ Thy Son, and we humbly apply for Thy mercy: that this Thy Sacrament, O Lord, may not be unto our condemnation unto punishment: but may it be unto intercession of Salvation unto forgiveness; may it be unto the washing away of wickedness; may it be unto strengthening of the weak; a mainstay against the dangers of the world; may this Communion purge us of all guilt; and may it bestow the Heavenly joy of being partners, through our Lord Jesus Christ, Who reigneth with Thee and the Holy Spirit throughout all ages of ages. ℟. Amen.

[Then:]
O God, we give Thee thanks, O Thou through Whom we have celebrated this Holy Mystery: and we beg of Thee a gift of Thy Sanctification, through our Lord Jesus Christ Who reigneth with Thee and the Holy Spirit, unto ages of ages. ℟. Amen.

The Mass has been given in Peace. Alleluia.
℟. **Thanks be unto God. Alleluia.**

[Then, all remain for the usual ending, with Benediction and Final Gospel.]

The Closing Prayers
[BOW].

> [The following prayers are included because these prayers, including the Final Benediction, are assumed. They are written out in the office of the Sacrament of Unction. These are called the **"Consummatio Missae"** in the Gothic Missal:]

For He hath satisfied the empty soul and hath filled the hungry soul with good things - Alleluia, Alleluia. [Ps 104:9] Visit us, O God, in Thy Salvation - Alleluia. [Ps 105:4] The Lord is my strength and my praise, and He is become my Salvation - Alleluia. [Ps 117:14] I will take the Chalice of Salvation, and I will call upon the Name of the Lord - Alleluia. [Ps 115:13] Refreshed by the Body and Blood of Christ, may we ever say unto Thee, O Lord - Alleluia. O Praise the Lord, all ye nations, praise him all ye people. For His mercy is confirmed upon us and the truth of the Lord remaineth for ever. [Ps 116] Offer up the Sacrifice of justice and trust in the Lord. [Ps 4:6] O God, we give Thee thanks, O Thou through Whom we have celebrated the Holy Mysteries, and we claim the gift of Holiness from Thee Who reignth unto ages of ages.

R. Amen.

The Final Benediction

[THE CONGREGATION BOWS:]

> [The Celebrant extends both hands, palms outwards, fingers forming the Sign ICXC (according to both older Roman and Byzantine usage), over the heads of the Congregation:]

May the Lord bless you and protect you. May the Lord reveal His face unto you and have mercy. May the Lord turn His Face to you and give you peace.

R. Amen.

> Then signing the Congregation with his right hand, says:

You are marked with the Sign + of the Cross of Christ. Peace be with you unto life eternal.

R. Amen.

The Final Gospel

> [The Final Gospel of St. John (1:1-14, or 1-18) is read by a Deacon, immediately before the Celebrant unvests in the middle of the church, before the congregation leaves.]

[ALL STAND]

Deacon or Celebrant: The Gospel of St. John begins:

[**R.** Glory be to Thee, O Lord.]

In the beginning was the Word, and the Word was with God, and the Word was God. The same was in the beginning with God. All things were made by Him: and without Him was not any thing made that was made: in Him was life, and the life was the light of men: and the light shineth in darkness, and the darkness comprehended it not. There was a man sent from God, whose name was John. The same came for a witness, to bear witness of the light, that all men through him might believe. He was not that light, he was sent to bear witness of that light. That was the true Light, which lighteth every man that cometh into the world. He was in the world, and the world was made by Him, and the world knew Him not. He came unto His own, and His own received Him not. But as many as received Him, to them gave He power to become the sons of God, even to them that believe on His Name: which were born, not of blood, nor of the will of the flesh, nor of the will of man, but of God. *[all bow]* And the Word was made flesh, *[all stand]* and dwelt among us: and we beheld His glory, the glory as of the Only-begotten of the Father, full of grace and truth.

John beareth witness of him and crieth out, saying: This was he of whom I spoke: He that shall come after me is preferred before me; because he was before me. And of his fulness we all have received; and grace for grace. For the law was given by Moses; grace and truth came by Jesus Christ. No man hath seen God at any time; the only begotten Son who is in the bosom of the Father, he hath declared him.

R. Pray for us and lift up the Gospel to us. Thanks be to God.

*[Afterwards the Celebrant **unvests in the midst of the Church**, unless there is a special procession at the blessing of the foods, in which case he may wear a cope. He does not carry the Chalice out. The clergy may lead the Congregation in other Thanksgiving Prayers as the foods are blessed.]*

+   +   +

[Optional: The Sermon of St. John Chyrsostom; translation Isabel Florence Hapgood, 1906, 1922.]

If any man be devout and loveth God, let him enjoy this fair and radiant triumphant feast. If any man be a wise servant, let him rejoicing enter into the joy of his Lord. If any have labored long in fasting, let him now receive his recompense. If any have wrought from the first hour, let him today receive his just reward. If any have come at the third hour, let him with thankfulness keep the feast. If any have arrived at the sixth hour, let him have no misgivings; because he shall in nowise be deprived therefore. If any have delayed until the ninth hour, let him draw near, fearing nothing. If any have tarried even until the eleventh hour let him, also, be not alarmed at his tardiness; for the Lord, who is jealous of his honor, will accept the last even as the first; he giveth rest unto him who cometh at the eleventh hour, even as unto him who hath wrought fromt he first hour. [Mt 20:1-16] And he showeth mercy upon the last, and careth for the first; and to the one he giveth, and upon the other he bestoweth gifts. And he both accepteth the deeds, and welcometh the intention, and honoreth the acts and praiseth the offering. Wherefore, enter ye all into the joy of your Lord; and receive ye your reward, both the first, and likewise the second. Ye rich and poor together, hold ye high festival. Ye sober and ye heedless, honor ye the day. Rejoice today, both ye who have fasted and ye who have disregarded the fast. The table is full-laden; feast ye all sumptuously. The calf is fatted; let no one go hungry away. Enjoy ye all the feast of faith; Receive ye all the riches of loving-kindness. Let no one bewail his poverty, for the universal kingdom hath been revealed. Let no one weep for his iniquities, for pardon hath shone forth from the grave. Let no one fear death, for the Savior's death hath set us free. He that was held prisoner of it, hath annihilated it. By descending into Hell, he made Hell captive. [Eph 4:8] He angered it when it tasted of his flesh. And Isaiah, foretelling this, did cry: Hell, said he, was angered, when it encountered thee in the lower regions. [Is 53:7-12?] It was angered, for it was abolished. It was angered, for it was mocked. It was angered, for it was slain. It was angered, for it was overthrown. It was angered, for it was fettered in chains. It took a body, and met God face to face. It took earth, and encountered Heaven. It took that which was seen, and fell upon the unseen. O Death, where is thy sting? O Hell, where is thy victory? [I Cor 15:55] Christ is risen, and thou art overthrown. Christ is risen, and the demons are fallen. Christ is risen, and the Angels rejoice. Christ is risen, and life reigneth. Christ is risen, and not one dead remaineth in the grave. For Christ, being risen from the dead, is become the first-fruits of those who have fallen asleep. [I Cor 15:20] To Him be glory and dominion unto ages of ages. Amen.

[After the Mass is ended, distribute Holy Water, red-colored eggs (for the Resurrection, in the tradition of St. Mary Magdalene), and bless Easter baskets brought by the Congregation, sprinkling all foods with holy Paschal water. These foods break the Lenten Fast. The food is then taken to the Church hall or dining area. Everybody brings something to be blessed and shared: sweet egg and butter or oil breads, butter or rich candy in the shape of a lamb and eggs, cheese, olives, wines and spirits, meats including lamb if possible, etc. This feast is not a long or heavy feast, due to the lateness of the hour.

[EASTER AND CHRISTMAS ARE THE ONLY EXCEPTIONS IN THE YEAR TO THE FASTING AND RECEIVING HOLY COMMUNION RULES. Fasting occurs before the Vigil Mass, but not between Masses. The Congregation may attend both Masses. Clergy or others who intend to Binate should eat a modest amount at the feast. Holy Communion is allowed to all the Faithful at both Masses, but the dawn Mass is not required, being primarily for those who could not attend the Vigil Mass due to medical occupations or illness.

[Although the Church requires attendance at the Vigil Mass with the exception only of extreme illness, medical profession, or Bishop's permission, attendance at both Masses is optional for all who are not clergy. The dawn Mass includes the Confession of Faith for those in Holy Orders. There are Masses and prayers for every day in the Octave of the Resurrection, and throughout Paschaltide. Attention should be paid to these.]

+ + +

[Note: The Epistle for the Vigil Mass seems to suggest that unleavened bread was used. However, St. Paul is not referring to the bread used at the Mass, which has always been leavened, but to our attitude on this day. Just as at the Crucifixion we never forget that Christ is Resurrected from the dead, on the day of the Resurrection, we do not forget His death. The Most Dangerous Prayer shows us that Christ gives Himself to the Faithful through His one Sacrifice on the Cross. The meaning of the Mass does not change at Pascha, even though it is the Feast of the Resurrection. Red is the traditional color of this day, which is suggested by the Introductory Collect and the Collect before the Epistle: Christ was literally covered in His own Blood at His Crucifixion, and it is through this Sacrifice of His Passion that we are drawn into Heaven at His Resurrection. On Holy and Great Friday, this is specifically described. Our Sacrifice to Him today and on every day is unbloody, because God gives Himself to us once for all time. Our glory, as St. Paul says, is not a victory of pride or nationalism, but God's victory over sin; and in this we cannot glorify ourselves, but only God can take the credit. The angels may now rejoice in heaven, and we rejoice with them, but we do not rejoice in personal pride. Our justice must be mercy, or we will receive condemnation for our sins which are forgiven only by God. God enlightens us this day so that we may see His glory, not another's faults. This is not the day for quarrels, but for peace. This is not the day for the show of riches, but for charity. Today we are saved, and the whole world rejoices. Today CHRIST IS RISEN. CHRIST IS TRULY RISEN.]

Sunday Dawn: Easter Day

(Matins is incorporated into the Vigil of the Resurrection. If the beginning of the Book of Acts was not read the evening before due to lack of time, it may be read before this Divine Liturgy.) The Divine Liturgy that is incorporated into the Vigil of the Resurrection (previous pages) is considered the most important Divine Liturgy of the year. There is more than one Divine Liturgy on this day: not a repeat, but usually for the infirm. The dawn Mass of the Resurrection has its own Propers. The Lections are the same as in the Vigil on Sunday at dawn, but on the other days of this week follow the special Lections for the week. Selections are read from the Book of the Apocalypse, also called the Book of Revelation, in place of the Old Testament. Notice that in the week following Christmas, there are different Psalms each day, but in this week the Psalms do not change for the Gradual and Alleluia. *[The Sunday Dawn Liturgy and the Liturgies during this week are in another book.]*

Hymns If there is a large congregation, other Hymns may be sung as well during Holy Communion, such as Hymn 2 from the *Antiphonary of Bangor* by St. Hilary of Poitiers, "The congregation of the Brethren sing the hymn...;" Unitas; Hymn 3 from the *Antiphonary of Bangor* by the Apostles, "Let us beg the Father, the Almighty King...;" the Beatitudes (St. Matthew 5:3-12a), the Similitudes (St. Matthew 5:13-16), Hymn to St. Michael from the *Antiphonary of Bangor*; the Deer's Cry which is a protection for the Resurrection, the Magnificat (St. Luke 1:46-55), Te Deum if it wasn't done earlier, etc.

To help in the choice: Hymn 2 mentions Baptism; Hymn 3 is appropriate to the Hours of Midnight and Matins and is the original 42 verse "Kyrie eleison."

Rogation Processions

Rogation Days (Monday, Tuesday, and Wednesday before the Ascension of our Lord Jesus Christ).

Note: The Rogation days are marked by fasting and pilgrimage Processions to the Churches in the area, beginning with a Mass, and continuing with Litanies, Collects, and readings during the Processions to other Churches. In some cases, a Mass may be done at a destination Church. The Rogations do not begin Sunday evening, but Monday early morning. (The "giving up of Easter" is not in place of the Rogations.) According to footnotes by Dom Pierre Salmon in the Luxiel Lectionary, the Diocese of Arles took six hours to complete one day of the Rogations. Congregations of several Parishes in a Diocese walk together.

Some Gallican Missals give Rogation Collects for a few Saints: St. Peter, St. Paul, St. Stephen, St. Martin of Tours, and St. Gregory the Great.

The Order of Service for the Rogations is apparent when the Epistle readings are examined, and the Stowe-Lorrha Missal is familiar. The Epistle readings cover the General Epistles, and the books of Tobias, Judith, and Esther. Most of them are very long readings. This indicates that the Epistle readings were done during the Processions, and fit into an augmented Hour, or the Stowe-Lorrha Mass. There is a strict fast on these three days, so the need for stopping some place for dinner is not required. However, people should take water so they do not become ill, and rest-room stops must be provided. For health reasons, a light snack may be brought by those who need it. A head-covering is highly suggested for both men and women. This must be a quiet Procession, not a circus parade. A Cross, and Icons or banners should lead the Procession. The clergy remains vested during the journey. A cope should be worn over the other vestments.

If augmented Hours are done, a Mass is done for the entire Diocese before the Processions at the largest Church, after Matins (at the Second Hour), using the Stowe-Lorrha Missal. Immediately following that, the Third Hour Procession begins. All the people Process together to the various Churches. At each Hour:

Begin the Hour as in the Breviary, all walking quietly.

The Litany of the Saints from the Stowe-Lorrha Missal would be sung before or after the Psalms of that Hour (after the beginning of the Hour), and the congregation responds, while walking.

The Collects for the Rogation Saint(s) of the Church, Chapel or Shrine the Procession is going toward are sung after the Daily Collect of the Hour. The Procession stops and kneels or bows for the Collects.

Then the Epistle is sung loudly and enunciated clearly by a Reader or Deacon as the Procession continues walking quietly.

In place of the Gradual (after the Epistle, before the Litany of St. Martin), the Irish "Trisagion" Collects from Matins may be sung by all, while walking.

Then the Litany of St. Martin of Tours (from the Stowe-Lorrha Missal) is sung, and the congregation responds, while walking.

Next, before the Gospel, the people are censed without the words of the Offering of the Gifts, and the Book of the Gospels are Censed. The Procession halts while the Holy Gospel is sung loudly and clearly by the Deacon or Priest, and the people say after the Gospel, "Pray for us, and lift up the Gospel to us," and they are blessed with the Book of the Holy Gospels.

Then the Procession continues as the Prayer of the Community of the Brethren (long form) is read, not ending with the Creed and Our Father yet, and other supplicatory Litanies (in this Breviary) if the congregation has not yet arrived at its next destination. Finally, the Creed and Our Father are said.

At the destination Church, Chapel, or Shrine, the Priest or Bishop blesses the place, says the Collects of the Saints again, and all rest for a short while. Then they all continue. (If space allows, they all file into and out of the Church, Chapel or Shrine in an orderly way to pay their respects.)

At the end of the Rogations, after the Ninth Hour, they arrive for Vespers at the final destination, and sing Vespers together. The Priest or Bishop may end with the final Benediction from the Stowe-Lorrha Missal. This usage was probably usual. The Priest would lead his congregation on the entire pilgrimage, or a Bishop would lead his Diocese from Church to Church. There is no need to wait until the proper Hour to continue these Hours, because it is common in some Rites such as the Byzantine Rite to do prayers for an Hour in anticipation of that Hour, if the prayers will continue from a Mass.

If Masses were done at any destination Church, the Bishop or Priest who would be Celebrating the Mass would stay at that Church with a few Acolytes and congregation, and not travel from Church to Church. Deacons or other clergy could lead the Procession of the other congregations. The clergy who would be in the Procession begin the Mass as usual, but vest before the opening Litany of the Saints, and skip the opening Offering of the Gifts. Then they lead their congregation on the Procession to the first Church (agreed upon beforehand). Meanwhile, at the Church the Procession will be arriving at, at the same time the Procession begins, the Mass begins, including the Offering of the Gifts and all Collects. The Collects of the Saint are said just before the Epistle, and this would also be done in the Procession on the way to the Church. After the long Epistle and Gradual (Irish "Trisagion") is the Litany of Supplication of St. Martin of Tours, from the Stowe-Lorrha Mass, and if there is still some distance to walk, other supplicatory Litanies would be said (in Appendix V of this Breviary). The Celebrant at the destination Church also adds other supplicatory Litanies if needed, if the Procession has not arrived yet. As the Procession enters the destination Church, the Celebrant says the prayer before the censing. The people are censed, and hear the Holy Gospel and sermon in the destination Church, and the rest of the Mass (the Creed and Our Father are in the Mass). This method of doing the Procession would take much more time than the augmented Hours. The Byzantine Rite has some memory of its Trisagion Hymn being sung in a Procession that arrived at the main Cathedral just in time for the Great Entry, so there is precedent for this method, but the method most often used in Processions of the Western Rite in living memory followed the augmented Hours, and only one Mass for each day is given in the Gallican Missal. Although more than one Mass may be done in a day if there are separate Altars (as in visiting different churches in a procession), it is still not allowed to receive Holy Communion at all the churches visited, nor attend several Masses, except a Pascha or Christmas.

If more than one Mass is done in the day, only the Priest or Bishop of a Parish Celebrates the Mass at that Church. The congregation may receive Holy Communion once at the Church where their Confession has been heard. It is best to arrange these Masses so they are not done between the Sixth and Ninth Hours.

Rogation Collects for St. Peter, St. Paul, St. Stephen, St. Martin of Tours, and St. Gregory the Great.

These do not need to be done in a Church named after the Saint: in Irish custom, a Church or Chapel was often named after the patron or family who had built the Church, such as the Dowling Chapel in Clonmacnoise. The presence of a small Chapel dedicated to a Saint, or in a Church: an Icon, or relic of a Saint is sufficient for a Procession to a Church. A small outdoor Shrine dedicated to a Saint, such as a Shrine in a cemetary, is also sufficient for a Procession to it. The Collects for the following Saints are worthy to do. In this case, if visiting a Parish with another Titular, it is possible to supply Collects as well for the Titular Saint of their church from other sources.

Collect for St. Peter
O God, the refuge of the poor, the hope of the humiliated, and salvation of the miserable, clemently hear us, Thy kneeling suppliants: through Blessed Peter intervening for us, of the foundation of Thy Church, during this three day fast. And grant tranquillity from tribulations, and likewise from our enemies of these times, so that those who the justice of Thy scourgings rightly afflict, may be consoled with the abundance of Thy mercy, by the persistence of Blessed Peter himself, through Christ our Lord, Who reigneth with the Father and the Holy Spirit, throughout all ages of ages. **R.** Amen.

Collect after the Collect for St. Peter
Almighty and eternal God, Who to Blessed Peter the Apostle didst bestow, by the keys of the heavenly kingdom, the power to bind and loosen souls, and didst give [him] the Office of High Priest, hear our prayers of propitiation in this time of fasting, and by his intercession, we beseech Thee that we may be freed from deaths of our sins.* Through Christ our Lord, Who reigneth with the Father and the Holy Spirit, throughout all ages of ages. **R.** Amen. [* Romans 6:23.]

Collect for St. Paul
Behold, O Lord, we beseech Thee, our infirmities, and in these days of this fast, which are three in Consecration, three in number, by Thy interventing, Blessed Apostle Paul, quickly help us by faith, that those whom Thou dost correct with justice, Thou may console with mercy. Through Christ our Lord, Who reigneth with the Father and the Holy Spirit, throughout all ages of ages. **R.** Amen.

Another Collect for St. Paul
Hear O Lord, we beseech Thee, our cries in the days of fasting, which are three in number, of the Trinity, of the Holy; and by interceding, Blessed Paul our teacher and doctor, let offense of deliquencies depart, for Thy mercy is to always grant forgiveness, by tears of suppliants. Through Christ our Lord, Who reigneth with the Father and the Holy Spirit, throughout all ages of ages. **R.** Amen.

Collect for St. Stephen
Grant, we beseach Thee Almighty and merciful God, that by the weakness with which we are afflicted in these days of fasting, that the magnified, blessed Levite Stephen show forth aid of intervention, who has shown forth, an imitator of the Lord in suffering first in the blood of the martyrs; and may he ever be a perfect, supporting and swifty pardoning advocate. Through Christ our Lord, Who reigneth with the Father and the Holy Spirit, throughout all ages of ages. **R.** Amen.

Another Collect for St. Stephen
We beseech Thee, O Lord, that the prayer of Thy blessed Levite and martyr escort our extended prayers in this fast, so that Thy mercy may attend to our afflictions, and may we be encouraged by his prayers. Through Christ our Lord, Who reigneth with the Father and the Holy Spirit, throughout all ages of ages. **R.** Amen.

Collect for St. Martin of Tours
Stretch forth Thy right hand unto thy people praying for mercy in the time of their fast, that through interceding, Blessed Martin, that we may avoid imminent terrors, and receive the solace of immortal life, and grasp eternal joy. Through Christ our Lord, Who reigneth with the Father and the Holy Spirit, throughout all ages of ages. **R.** Amen.

Another Collect for St. Martin of Tours
O God, the author of fasting, the instiutor of abstinence, Who embracing the form of a fast cleared away the overabundence of gluttony, so that in us moral sobriety might reign. Look upon, and be favorable to, O Lord these suppliants who are empty during this three day fast of abstinence; and by the interceding, greatest of men, Blessed Martin, be won over and infuse the grace of Thy Blessing in all of us, so that as this fast was established unto the habit of fear of Thee, it may conquor gluttony of appetite. Thus may Thine illumination overcome the tinder of our sins in our senses. Through Christ our Lord, Who reigneth with the Father and the Holy Spirit, throughout all ages of ages. **R.** Amen.

Collect for St. Gregory the Great (the Dialogist)
Almighty, eternal God, fasting and satisfied by Thy Gifts, even perfected by the leanness which is pleasing to Thee, we suppliants appeal to Thy Majesty that the shadows of sins be expelled from our hearts in this time of fasting. Through our interceding, great and high Priest Gregory, create openness to the Divine Mysteries, and make us approach the True Light which is Christ. Through Christ our Lord, Who reigneth with the Father and the Holy Spirit, throughout all ages of ages. **R.** Amen.

Another Collect for St. Gregory the Great (the Dialogist)
Almighty, eternal God, by Whose order flesh is restrained from wantonness by the emptiness of fasting; may our flesh, disciplined by sobriety, know its Sower: through the intercessions of the highest Apostolic father, Gregory. In this fast, grant that all those who believe in Thee, the Spotless One, may practice the Faith so that they if they fast, they might strive against and escape the brambles. May Thy protection against these protect the virtuous, O Almighty Father, through Christ our Lord, Who reigneth with the Father and the Holy Spirit, throughout all ages of ages. **R.** Amen.

Rogation Monday (First Day of the Rogations.) *Strict Fast*
Matins (instead of the Gospel): Daniel 9:12-19
Third Hour (Augmented Hour or Mass): St. James (ALL); St. Matthew 5:17-26
Sixth Hour (Augmented Hour or Mass): I Peter 1:1 - 5:11; St. Matthew 7:1-12
Ninth Hour (Augmented Hour or Mass): Tobias (ALL); St. Matthew 6:1-13
Rogation Tuesday (Second Day of the Rogations.) *Strict Fast*
Matins (instead of the Gospel): Joel 1:13 - 2:11
Third Hour (Augmented Hour or Mass): II Peter (ALL); St. Matthew 13:1-23
Sixth Hour (Augmented Hour or Mass): I John (ALL); St. Luke 12:15-31
Ninth Hour (Augmented Hour or Mass): Judith (ALL); St. Matthew 5:31-48
Rogation Wednesday (Third Day of the Rogations.) *Strict Fast*
Matins (instead of the Gospel): Hosea 5:1 - 6:6
Third Hour (Augmented Hour or Mass): II John 1 - 11, III John 1-12;
   St. Matthew 4:13-17, 11:28-30
Sixth Hour (Augmented Hour or Mass): St. Jude (ALL); St. Matthew 21:28-32
Ninth Hour (Augmented Hour or Mass): Esther (ALL); St. Matthew 6:14-33

[There isn't space in this book for the Feasts of Ascension, Pentecost, Christmas, Epiphany, etc. Apply to Esp. Maelruain for the clergy book.]

Other Seasons' Processions or Special Hours

The Rogations just before the Ascension are traditional processions. In addition, there may be other penetential pilgrimage Processions. Although every Feast and Fast should not automatically require a pilgrimage Procession, these might be a good idea in places where the Feast is currently marked with a secular "parade." St. Patrick's day falls in Lent: it could have a Procession of augmented Hours after an early Mass, using the abecedarian Hymn to St. Patrick in place of the Gradual, and Collects and readings from his Mass and from that week in Lent (from the Book of Propers). If a Procession of this kind is especially large, it would be possible to have more than one group of readers among the people, so that all hear the prayers and readings. Several choirs could participate. Other Processions could occur at the beginning of Lent, and before the Irish beginning of Advent, on the Feast of St. Martin of Tours. Another Procession could occur on All Saints Day, or the Vigil, with Collects for the Saints and the Departed, and the Hymn "Altus Prosator," rather than the usual wearing of costumes. It is, however, traditional as a Christian way to eat sweets and pray for the dead at the time of All Saints Day.

Healing prayers from the Corrba Missal

For a [injured or diseased] eye. I venerate Bishop Ibar who heals [injuries] and illnesses of the eyes. May the blessing of God and [the intercession of] Christ's [servant, Ibar,] heal thine eye [and restore the] whole of thine eye.
Then the Priest spits on dirt and makes clay, and places it over the eyelids of him and says to him, Go and wash in the pool of Siloam, which is to be interpreted, sent. Do this and wash, and come forth seeing.

For a thorn. A splendid salve which binds a thorn: let it not be spot nor blemish, let it not be swelling nor illness, nor clotted gore, nor lamentable hole, nor enchantment. The sun's brightness heals the swelling, it smites the disease.

For disease of the urine. May [Almighty God cleanse] thy urine and put [His healing into thy soul] and into thy system and sustain thy body and restore thy health. May a cure of health heal thee!

The Blessing of Water
(Minor Blessing outside Baptism)

Bless, O Lord, this creature of water, that it may be a remedy unto the salvation of the human race. Grant, through the invocation of Thy Name through this creature of water, health of the body, protection of the soul, and a good defense, through our Lord Jesus Christ Who reigneth with the Father and the Holy Spirit, unto ages of ages. ℟. Amen.

The Exorcism of Water
(Minor Blessing outside Baptism)

I exorcise thee, impure spirit, by God the Father Almighty, Who made heaven, earth, and the seas, and all that are in them; that all power of the adversary, all the works of the devil, every assault, every phantasm of the enemy, may be eradicated, and be set to flight from this creature of water; that it may be Holy and Salvific; and a burning fire turned upon the snares of the enemy through the invocation of the Name of our Lord Jesus Christ, Who will come to judge the world by fire in the Holy Spirit. ℟. Amen.

✠

The Rite of Baptism

*[During the Vigil of the Resurrection on Pascha, do the entire Rite of Baptism, including the portions for Pascha. On Pascha at the Vigil of the Resurrection, **if there are NO Baptismal Candidates present and a Baptism will NOT be done**, do every prayer in the Rite of Baptism except for those which say, "Omit only if there is no candidate for Baptism on Pascha." **On the Vigil of the Resurrection at Pascha, with or without a candidate for Baptism, the water will be blessed using the Paschal Candle, and some of this water should be included, if possible, in all Baptismal water used through the year.**]*

[The Celebrant, Clergy, Congregation, Sponsors and person being Baptized, if able, say all Responses (℟.) together during the Rite of Baptism. Sponsors are Baptized and Confirmed Orthodox Christians in good standing in the Church.]

[Omit only if there is no candidate for Baptism on Pascha.]
O God, Who made Adam from the clay of the Earth: Although Adam sinned in Paradise, Thou didst not count that sin unto death, but through the Blood of Thine Only-Begotten Son, Thou wast pleased to redeem and lead back into Holy Glorious Jerusalem. For this reason, consider thy sentence O accursed one, and give honor to the living God, and depart from this servant of God, because my God and Lord was pleased to call this person to His Holy Grace and Mercy by Baptism through this Sign of the ✠ Cross which thou, devil, dare never cross out. Through our Lord Jesus Christ Who reigneth with His unoriginate Father and the Holy Spirit throughout ages of ages.
℟. Amen.

[The Celebrant, Clergy, Congregation, and person being Baptized say all "Amens" together during the Rite of Baptism.]

[Omit only if there is no candidate for Baptism on Pascha.]
O Lord, Holy Father, Almighty and eternal God, expel the devil and his kin from this person: from the head, from the hair, from the crown of the head, from the brain, from the brow, from the eyes, from the ears, from the nostrils, from the mouth, from the tongue, from beneath the tongue, from the throat, from the passages of the throat, from the neck, from the chest, from the heart, from the entire interior of the body, from the ribs, from the hands, from the feet, from all the members, from the joints of the members, from the thoughts, from the words, from the deeds, and from all developments now and in the future, through Thee, O Jesus Christ, Who reignest with Thy Father and the Holy Spirit throughout ages of ages. ℟. Amen.

[Always said:]
O God, Who for the Salvation of the human race didst institute the greatest Sacrament in the substance of the waters, be responsive to our invocation; and unto this element pour forth Thy Blessings, through many modes of purification, that this creature of water shall serve the Mystery unto the casting out of demons and expelling of diseases. May it put on Thy Divine Grace, so that whoever this stream shall splash both in this place, and in the houses of the faithful, may be without stain and be freed from fault. Do not let the destructive spirit remain, nor an air of corruption. Let all the hidden snares of the enemy be cut away, and if there is anything which has malice against the safety of those who dwell here or against those at peace, let it flee from the sprinkling of this water which is unto healing, through the invocation of Thy Name. Let it be a defense against every assault, through our Lord Jesus Christ Who reigneth with Thee and the Holy Spirit unto ages of ages. ℟. Amen.

[Always said:]

Consecration of Salt

O God, Who unto the salvation of men didst make a medicine through this health-giving salt, grant that this spirit be converted from the error of its kind and be redeemed, and that the Triune God act upon it, and it repel the devil by the renunciations and by the Sign of the ✠ Cross of our Lord Jesus Christ Who reigneth with the Father and the Holy Spirit unto ages of ages. ℟. Amen.

[Note that this is the only place in which the scribes have written this ending in full. It is from this model that all the other endings are derived.]

[Always said:]
Another Prayer

I exorcise thee, O creature of salt in the Name of God the Father Almighty and in the charity of our Lord Jesus Christ and in the power of the Holy Spirit. I exorcise thee by the Living God, by the True God, Who didst produce thee for the protection of mankind, and to be consecrated by His servants for the people coming unto the beginning of the Faith. Therefore we pray Thee, O Lord and our God, that this creature of salt ✠ In the Name of the Trinity may be made effective unto salvation, a Sacrament to put the enemy to flight which Thou, O Lord, let be ✠ sanctified unto sanctifying and ✠ blessed unto blessing, that it may be unto all that receive it a perfect medicine, remaining in their viscera in the Name of our Lord Jesus Christ, Who is coming to judge the living and the dead and the world by fire. **R.** Amen.

[Always said by everybody:]
The Renunciations.

Dost thou renounce Satan? **R.** I renounce him.
And all of his works? **R.** I renounce them.
And all of his pageantries? **R.** I renounce them.

[Always said by everybody:]
The Confessions

Dost thou believe in God, the Father Almighty?
[Catechumen or Sponsor] **R.** I believe [in one God, the Father Almighty, maker of heaven and earth and of all things visible and invisible].

[Always said by everybody:]
Dost thou also believe in Jesus Christ?
R. I believe [in one Lord Jesus Christ, the Only-Begotten Son of God Born of the Father before all ages. Light of light, true God of true God. Born, not made, of one Substance with the Father: through Whom all things were made. Who for us men, and for our Salvation descended from heaven. And was Incarnate of the Holy Spirit and the Virgin Mary: And was born man. And was crucified also for us: under Pontius Pilate; He suffered and was buried. And He rose on the third day, according to the Scriptures. And ascended into heaven: and sitteth at the right hand of God the Father. And He shall come again with glory to judge both the living and the dead: Whose Kingdom shall have no end.]

[Always said by everybody:]
Dost thou also believe in the Holy Spirit?
R. I believe [in the Holy Spirit, the Lord and Giver of life: Who proceedeth from the Father. Who with the Father and the Son together is worshipped and glorified: Who spake by the Prophets. And in one, Holy, Catholic, and Apostolic Church, one Baptism for the remission of sins, and the resurrection of the dead, and the life of the world to come.]

[Omit only if there is no candidate for Baptism on Pascha.]
The Priest breathes *and* touches him *[upon the head]*, then touches the breast and the back between the shoulder blades with the oil *[oil of Catechumens]*, *and thus anointing,* **says**:

[Omit only if there is no candidate for Baptism on Pascha.]
I anoint thee with the Oil of Sanctification in the Name of the Father and of the Son and of the Holy Spirit. Amen.

[Always said by everybody:]

Dost thou renounce Satan?	**R.**	I renounce him.
And all of his works?	**R.**	I renounce them.
And all of his pageantries?	**R.**	I renounce them.

[Omit only if there is no candidate for Baptism on Pascha.]
We pray Thee O Lord Holy Father almighty and eternal God to have mercy on Thy servant -N- whom Thou wast pleased to call to the beginning of Faith, expelling all blindness of the heart. Burst the snares of Satan by which he (she) was bound. Open unto him (her) the door of Thy Truth, that he (she) put on the ✠ Sign of Thy Wisdom, that he (she) be free of all the stenches of lust, and delight in the sweet odor of Thy precepts. May he (she) rejoice to serve Thee in the Church, and may he (she) progress day by day that he (she) may become sufficient unto the promise of Thy Grace, in the Name of the Father and of the Son and of the Holy Spirit unto ages of ages. **R.** Amen.

[Omit if there is no candidate for Baptism on Pascha.]

Prayer for a Sick Catechumen

This is to be used only if one of those who is to be Baptized is in immediate danger of Death:

I beg Thy intervention, O Lord, Holy Father Almighty and eternal God, Who came to the aid of those in danger and Who tempers the lashes, we humbly entreat Thee O Lord, by Thy holy visitation, raise Thy servant -N- from this illness, a temptation of the soul. As Thou didst for Job, set a limit and do not let the enemy triumph over this soul which is without the redemption of Baptism. Delay, O Lord departure unto death and extend this life. Make manifest that which Thou hast led unto the Sacrament of Baptism and do not bring harm by Thy redeeming act. Take away any opportunity of the triumph of the devil and preserve him (her) whom Thou hast willed to be joined to the Triumphant ones of Christ, that he (she) be reborn in Thy Church by the grace of Baptism and be made whole. This we ask through our Lord Jesus Christ Who reigneth with Thee and the Holy Spirit unto ages of ages. **R.** Amen.

[Always said:]

Exhortation

Nor let it escape thy notice O Satan, that punishment threatens thee, hell-fire threatens thee, on that day of judgment, on the day of eternal torture which is coming like a flaming hot fire, which hath been eternally prepared for thee and thine angels; and therefore for thy worthless damnation and damning: Pay homage to the Living God; Pay homage to Jesus Christ; Pay homage to the Holy Spirit, the Paraclete, by Whose power I admonish thee that in every way thou art a foul spirit, that thou shalt depart and move away from these servants of God, and that thou give back to God Himself those whom our Lord and God

Jesus Christ is pleased to call to His own grace and blessing, that they be made His Temple by the water of regeneration unto the remission of all sins in the Name of our Lord Jesus Christ Who is coming to judge the living and the dead and the world by fire.

℟. Amen.

[Omit only if there is no candidate for Baptism on Pascha.]
Salt is placed in the catechumen's mouth.
Effeta: that is 'be opened' Effeta.
It is an offering in honor of sweetness in the Name of God the Father and the Son and the Holy Spirit.

℟. Amen.

The catechumen bows.

[Omit only if there is no candidate for Baptism on Pascha.]
O Lord, Holy Father Almighty and eternal God, Who is, and Who was, and Who will come, and Who shall remain even unto the end, Whose origin is unknown and ending inconceivable: we supplicants invoke Thee, O Lord, upon this Thy servant -N-, whom Thou hast freed from the delusion of the Gentiles and from the most debased associations. Be pleased to hear him (her) who bows his (her) neck unto Thee. He (she) has approached the font of Baptism, that he (she) may be renewed by water and the Holy Spirit: polished and cleansed of the old man, putting on the new. Let him (her) who is fashioned in Thy likeness assume the incorrupt and spotless vestment. Let him (her) merit to serve Thee, our Lord, in the Name of our Lord Jesus Christ Who is coming to judge the living and the dead and the world by fire. ℟. **Amen.**

[Always said:]
O God, Who for the Salvation of the human race didst institute the greatest Sacrament in the substance of water, be responsive to our invocation, and by this element through various purifications, pour forth Thy Blessings: that this creature, in service unto Thy Mysteries, may put on Thy grace unto the casting out of demons and expelling of diseases. Let it be that whomsoever this stream shall splash both in this place, and in the houses of the faithful, may be without stain and be freed of fault. Do not let the destructive spirit remain nor any air of corruption. Let all the hidden snares of the enemy, if there are any, be cut away, because he has a grudge against the safety of those who dwell here and against those at peace. Let him flee from the sprinkling of this water which is unto healing through the invocation of Thy Name. Let this be unto defense against every assault, through our Lord Jesus Christ Who reigneth with Thee and the Holy Spirit unto ages of ages. ℟. Amen.

[Always said:]
Hear us, O Lord, Holy Father Almighty, eternal God, and be pleased to send Thy Holy angel from Heaven, who preserves, assists, shields, and attends to all those who dwell in the habitation of this Thy servant. ℟. Amen.

[Omit only if there is no candidate for Baptism on Pascha.]
Here the catechumen is **anointed with oil on the front and also between the shoulder blades on the back** *before being Baptized;* *[Up to now he or she is a catechumen.]*

[The Litany is always said:]
Then the Clergy, Catechumen and Sponsors process moving around the font *[counterclockwise], [while the Priest or other clergy] says: "Adferte" [folio 52v. The Litany of the Saints should be done, and Psalm 28, "Afferte Domino", afterwards.]*

The Litany of the Saints

Priest or Deacon: ✠ O God come to my assistance. **R.** O Lord make haste to help me. Glory be to the Father, and to the Son, and to the Holy Spirit, as it was in the beginning, is now, and ever unto ages of ages. **R.** Amen.

Deacon *(or Celebrant)*: We have sinned, O Lord, we have sinned: remit our sins and save us. Hear us, O Thou Who didst guide Noah upon the waves of the Flood, and didst recall Jonah from the abyss by Thy Word; free us. O Thou Who didst offer a hand to Peter as he was sinking; bear us up, O Christ, Son of God. Thou didst perform wonders among our fathers, O Lord: stretch forth Thy hand from on high to answer our necessities.

V. Free us, O Christ: **R.** Hear us, O Christ.
V. Hear us, O Christ: **R.** Hear us.
V. Kyrie eleison. [**R.** Christe eleison. **V.** Deo Gracias.]

Saint Mary	**R.** Pray for us.	*[Birthgiver of God]*
Saint Peter:	**R.** Pray for us.	*[Apostle of the 12, Holder of the Keys.]*
Saint Paul:	**R.** Pray for us.	*[Apostle called on the road to Damascus.]*
Saint Andrew:	**R.** Pray for us.	*[Apostle of the 12, First-called.]*
Saint James:	**R.** Pray for us.	*[Apostle of the 12, Greater, son of Zebedee.]*
Saint John:	**R.** Pray for us.	*[Apostle of the 12, Evangelist, Theologian.]*
Saint Bartholomew:	**R.** Pray for us.	*[Apostle of the 12, the Active.]*
Saint Thomas:	**R.** Pray for us.	*[Apostle of the 12, Didymus, the Twin.]*
Saint Matthew:	**R.** Pray for us.	*[Apostle of the 12, Evangelist, Levi.]*
Saint James:	**R.** Pray for us.	*[Apostle of the 12, Lesser, son of Alpheus.]*
Saint Thaddeus:	**R.** Pray for us.	*[Apostle of the 12, Brother of James.]*
Saint Matthias:	**R.** Pray for us.	*[Apostle of the 12, chosen after Pascha.]*
Saint Philip:	**R.** Pray for us.	*[Apostle of the 12, Trinity explained to him.]*
Saint Simon:	**R.** Pray for us.	*[Apostle of the 12, the Zealot.]*
Saint Mark:	**R.** Pray for us.	*[Evangelist.]*
Saint Luke:	**R.** Pray for us.	*[Evangelist.]*
Saint Stephen:	**R.** Pray for us.	*[Proto-Martyr.]*
Saint Martin:	**R.** Pray for us.	*[of Tours.]*
Saint Jerome:	**R.** Pray for us.	*[translator of the Bible from Greek to Latin.]*
Saint Augustine:	**R.** Pray for us.	*[of Canterbury.]*
Saint Gregory:	**R.** Pray for us.	*[the Dialogist, Pope, also claled Great.]*
Saint Hilary:	**R.** Pray for us.	*[of Poitiers.]*
Saint Patrick:	**R.** Pray for us.	*[of Ireland.]*
Saint Ailbe:	**R.** Pray for us.	*[of Emly.]*

Saint Finian:	℟. Pray for us.	*[of Clonard.]*
Saint Finian:	℟. Pray for us.	*[of Movilla.]*
Saint Keiran:	℟. Pray for us.	*[of Saigher.]*
Saint Keiran:	℟. Pray for us.	*[of Clonmacnoise.]*
Saint Brendan:	℟. Pray for us.	*[of Clonfert.]*
Saint Brendan:	℟. Pray for us.	*[of Birr.]*
Saint Columba:	℟. Pray for us.	*[of Iona.]*
Saint Columba:	℟. Pray for us.	*[of Terryglas.]*
Saint Comgall:	℟. Pray for us.	*[of Bangor.]*
Saint Cainnech:	℟. Pray for us.	*[of Kilkenny and Aghaboe.]*
Saint Finbarr:	℟. Pray for us.	*[of Gougane Barra in Cork.]*
Saint Nessan:	℟. Pray for us.	*[of Mungret.]*
Saint Fachtna:	℟. Pray for us.	*[of Rosscarberry in Cork.]*
Saint Lua:	℟. Pray for us.	*[of Lismore: 100 monasteries.]*
Saint Lacten:	℟. Pray for us.	*[of Friar's Island.]*
Saint Ruadhan:	℟. Pray for us.	*[of Lorrha.]*
Saint Carthage:	℟. Pray for us.	*[of Rahan and Lismore.]*
Saint Kevin:	℟. Pray for us.	*[of Glendalough.]*
Saint Mochon:	℟. Pray for us.	*[of Glendalough.]*
Saint Brigid:	℟. Pray for us.	*[of Kildare, Abbess.]*
Saint Ita:	℟. Pray for us.	*[of Killeedy, Abbess.]*
Saint Scetha:	℟. Pray for us.	*[virgin.]*
Saint Sinecha:	℟. Pray for us.	*[virgin.]*
Saint Samthann:	℟. Pray for us.	*[of Clonbroney, Abbess.]*

All you Saints: ℟. Pray for us.

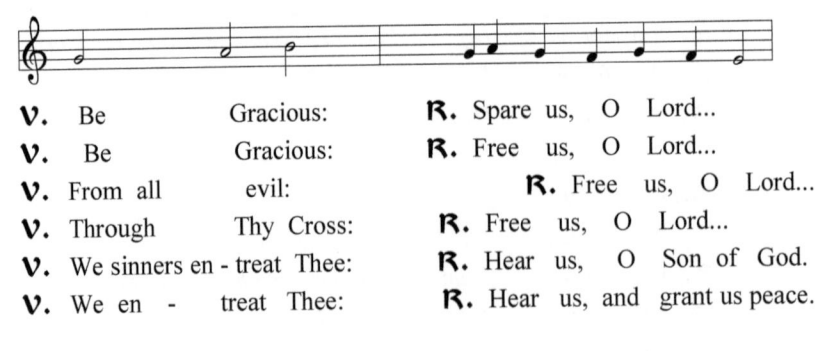

℣. Be Gracious:	℟. Spare us, O Lord...
℣. Be Gracious:	℟. Free us, O Lord...
℣. From all evil:	℟. Free us, O Lord...
℣. Through Thy Cross:	℟. Free us, O Lord...
℣. We sinners en-treat Thee:	℟. Hear us, O Son of God.
℣. We en-treat Thee:	℟. Hear us, and grant us peace.

℣. We en-treat Thee: ℟. Hear us.

V. O Lamb of God Who takest away the sins of the world:

R. Have mercy on us. **V.** Christ hear us: **R.** Christ hear us: **V.** Christ hear us.

[The Litany of the Saints is completed.]

Then read the Psalm verses:

[Always said:]   [Psalm 41:]
As the Hart panteth after the fountains of water; so my soul panteth after Thee O God. My soul hath thirsted after the strong living God.

[Always said: Verses from Psalm 28, Afferte Domino, or the whole Psalm. Folio 52v, Rite of Baptism.]
Bring to the Lord, O ye Children of God: bring to the Lord the offspring of rams.
Bring to the Lord glory and honor: Bring to the Lord glory to his Name: adore ye the Lord in His holy court. The Voice of the Lord is over the vast waters.

Then the **Blessing of the Font:**

[Always said:]
I exorcise thee, O creature of water, through the Living ✠ God, through the Holy ✠ God: through Him Who in the beginning by the Word separated thee from the dry land; through Him Whose Spirit moved upon thee; through Him Who commanded thee to flow out of paradise and to water the whole earth in four rivers; through Him Who produced thee from a rock that He might water the exhausted people He freed from Egypt; through Him Who sweetened thy bitterness by wood.

[Always said:]
I exorcise thee through Jesus ✠ Christ His Son, Who at Cana of Galilee as an admirable sign, by His power changed thee into wine; through Him Who walked with his feet upon thee and Who was Baptized by John in the Jordan, in thee; through Him Who shed thee with blood from His side; through Him Who commanded His disciples, saying: "Go forth and teach; teach all people, Baptizing them in the Name of the Father, and of the Son, and of the Holy Spirit."

[Always said:]
I command therefore, all impurity, all phantasm, all deception of the spirit to be rooted out and to flee from this creature of water, that for those who descend into it, may it be unto him (her) a well-spring effective unto eternal life. Therefore let it be made holy water, water blessed unto the regeneration of the sons of God the Father Almighty, in the Name of our Lord Jesus Christ Who is coming in the Holy Spirit to judge the world by fire.
R. Amen.

[Always said:]
I exorcise thee, O creature of water in the Name of God the Father ✠ Almighty and in the Name of our Lord Jesus ✠ Christ, His Son, and [in the Name] of the Holy ✠ Spirit that all the power of the adversary, all incursion of the devil, all phantasms be rooted out and flee from this creature of water that it become a well-spring unto eternal life, that whosoever is Baptized with it become the temple of the living God unto remission of sins, through our Lord Jesus Christ Who is coming to judge the world by fire. ℟. Amen.

[Always said:]
Almighty and eternal God, of Thy great affection, attend to Thy Mysteries: the Sacraments, and send forth a spirit of adoption to those becoming new people, those who this font of Baptism labors to bring forth unto Thee, that what is carried out through our humility may be filled with the effect of the power of Thy service, through our Lord Jesus Christ Who reigneth with Thee and the Holy Spirit, unto ages of ages. ℟. Amen.

[Always said:]
O God Who works marvelously by the unseen power of Thy Sacraments, let it be profitable and permissible for us to attain to the most cherished Mysteries. We are unworthy. Thou however dost not leave us bereft of the gift of Thy grace. Hear our prayer, through our Lord Jesus Christ Who reigneth with Thee and the Holy Spirit, unto ages of ages. ℟. Amen.

[Always said:]
O God Whose Spirit moved upon the waters in the midst of the primordial world, so that watery nature might take on the power of Sanctification; O God, Who prefigured the washing away of the reproach of those who are innocent of the world by cleansing waters of regeneration in the form of the surging of the Flood, so that by the service of that one and the same element there may be an end of pollution and beginning of virtues; look upon the face of Thy Church and multiply in her Thy generations which of grace flow from Thee. Gladden Thy besieged city and open the font of Baptism to the entire world. Yeah, open the font of renewal to the nations, that by the authority of Thy Majesty, he (she) may receive the race of Thine Only-Begotten: by the Holy Spirit,
[Here the Priest divides the water in the form of a Cross and his hand is immediately dried with a towel]
Who quickens this water of regeneration for humanity, which is prepared mysteriously by the admixture of His Illumination. By the Sanctification conceived of the immaculate womb of the divine font, let an offspring of Heaven emerge in this newly-regenerated creature. Although discerned by gender of the body or by age in time, the mother bears all into one childhood by grace. *[N.B.: The mother is the Church.]*

[Always said:]
Therefore, far away, O Lord command every unclean spirit to flee far away; that all worthless and diabolical delusion flee. Let nothing pervade this place contrary to virtue, nor lying in wait, nor hovering about, nor skulking to steal, nor corrupting to mar.
[The Priest touches the water with his hand]
Let this holy and innocent creature [the font] be free of all intrusion of assault, and be entirely purged and separated from all that is worthless. Let it be a font of life-regenerating water, a purifying stream, that all, by this cleansing, salvation-bearing bath through the Holy Spirit present in it, may attain the Pardon of perfect purification, through our Lord Jesus Christ Who reigneth with Thee and the Holy Spirit throughout all ages of ages. ℟. Amen.

[Always said:]
Therefore I bless thee, creature of water, by the Living ✠ God, by the Holy ✠ God; Who in the beginning by the Word separated thee from the dry land and commanded thee to water the earth in four rivers,

[The Priest divides the water in the form of a Cross and sprinkles the water to the four quarters]

Who sweetened thy bitterness in the desert to make thee drinkable, and for a thirsting people did produce thee from a rock. I bless thee through Jesus ✠ Christ His Son, our only Lord, Who in Cana of Galilee as a wonderous sign did convert thee to wine by His power, Who trod with His feet over thee, and was Baptized by John in the Jordan in thee, Who shed thee with blood from His side, and Who commanded His disciples that those who believe are to be Baptized in thee, saying, "Go forth and teach all nations, Baptizing them in the Name of the Father and of the Son and of the Holy Spirit."

[Always said:]
These are the commands to us Thy servants. O Thou, God almighty and clement, be present. Thou, Benign One, breath forth, Thyself, a blessing unto these simple waters by Thine own mouth, that they may have more that the purity of their nature which makes them suitable for the washing of bodies.

[Always said:]
[The Priest breathes on the water three times in the form of a Cross.]
Let them also be effective unto the purification of mind.

[On Pascha: *The Subdeacon, Deacon, or Celebrant takes the Paschal candle carefully from the stand, with the flame still lit, and the Celebrant immerses the lower end in the Water. Only the lower end of the Paschal candle enters the water.]*

[Always said:]
Let the entire power of the Holy Spirit descend into the entire substance of the font,

[The Priest breathes on the water three times in the form of a Ψ "

and the entire substance of this water may be fertile unto Regeneration. May all of this be effective unto the washing away of the stains of sin. May this nature fashioned in Thine own image be reshaped to its proper original honor, and be cleansed of the squalor of the Old Man, that all men who enter into this Sacrament of Regeneration may be reborn into the true innocence of a new infancy through our Lord Jesus Christ Who reigneth with Thee and the Holy Spirit throughout all ages of ages. ℟. Amen.

[Omit only if there is no candidate for Baptism on Pascha.]
The benediction having been completed, the **Priest pours Chrism in the form of a Cross into the Font.**

[On **Pascha,** *if there is no candidate for Baptism: The benediction having been completed, the* **Priest makes the Sign of the Cross over the Font (not pouring Chrism in the form of a Cross).** *Chrism is not used in the water if there are no candidates for Baptism. On Pascha, if there* **is** *a candidate for Baptism, Chrism is used as usual in the Rite of Baptism.]*

All the people present are sprinkled with the blessed water.

[Whether or not there is a candidate for Baptism on Pascha or any other time, the four directions in the Church and all members of the congregation are sprinkled. This sprinkling is not in place of Baptism, because a candidate for Baptism must be prepared to receive Baptism, the Celebrant must be aware of the candidate's desire, and the person must be Baptized by the Celebrant according to the complete Rite of Baptism.]

Who ever wishes, fills a flask with the Water of Benediction, and may bring the holy water home for the blessing of the house. ***
[On Pascha: Holy Water may be distributed, for order's sake, after the rest of the Mass is over.]

[On Pascha: *** Omit the rest of the Rite of Baptism ONLY if there is no candidate for Baptism on Pascha, and begin the rest of the Mass of the Resurrection IMMEDIATELY, page 178.]

+ + +

[If there IS a candidate for Baptism, at all times including Pascha, continue the Baptism:]

Baptism

Each one that is to be Baptized goes down into the Water and is immersed three times. [Immersion is preferred; or, if there is no font, pour an abundance of water; literally to toss water on them, as if to revive them, according to Celtic prayers. A shell may be used, and they are thoroughly drenched. The preferred form below is from Milan, requiring a response:]

Then, each candidate is asked individually by a Deacon: [The entire congregation says the responses together.]

Dost thou believe in God, the Father Almighty?
R. I believe.
The Servant of God **N.** is Baptized in the Name of the Father.
  The catechumen is immersed.

Dost thou also believe in Jesus Christ His Only-Begotten Son, our Lord, Who was born and died?
R. I believe.
The Servant of God **N.** is Baptized in the Name of the Son.
  The catechumen is immersed a second time.

Dost thou also believe in the Holy Spirit, the Catholic Church, Remission of sins, and the Resurrection of the flesh?
R. I believe.
The Servant of God **N.** is Baptized in the Name of the Holy Spirit.
  The catechumen is immersed a third time.

[Prayer completing the immersions, using the form of the Bobbio Missal:]

The Servant of God **N.** is Baptized in the Name of the Father, and of the Son, and of the Holy Spirit, Who have one Substance, that thou mayest have a part with the Saints unto life everlasting.

[OR: The Priest immerses him (her) in this manner (from Bobbio Missal): I Baptize thee in the Name of the Father **(immerse)**, and of the Son **(immerse)**, and of the Holy Spirit **(immerse)**, Who have one Substance, that thou mayest have a part with the Saints unto life everlasting.

Chrismation

[See notes. The Holy Chrism myrrh oil has been blessed by a Bishop on Holy and Great Thursday at the Bishop's Mass for the blessing of oils. A Priest may apply the Chrism, with Chrism blessed by a Bishop.]

[After the following prayer:] (Afterwards the one who was Baptized is anointed with the Holy Chrism.)

God Almighty, the Father of our Lord Jesus Christ, Who has regenerated thee by water and the Holy Spirit *[John 3:5]*, has given thee remission of all thy sins. He Himself Marks thee with the Chrism of Salvation in Christ.

Here the Chrismation is done upon the forehead, pouring it over the brow (as in a kingly anointing):

I anoint thee with the oil and the Chrism of Salvation and of Sanctification in the Name of the ✠ Father, and of the Son, and of the Holy Spirit, now and ever and unto ages of ages.   **R.** Amen.

Work, O creature of oil; work in the Name of God the Father Almighty, and the Son, and the Holy Spirit, and do not let an impure spirit remain here, nor in the members, nor in the interior, nor in the bones of the members, but may the Power of Christ, the Son of the living God most High, and the Power of the Holy Spirit, work in thee throughout all ages of ages.
R. Amen.

The Deacon gives him a white vestment over his head and covering the forehead. Meanwhile the Priest says:

Receive this holy and spotless white vestment which thou shalt wear before the tribunal of our Lord Jesus Christ.

Let him respond:
I accept it and I shall wear it.

And the Priest says:
Let the hand of the servant be opened.
Receive the Sign of the Cross of Christ ✠ in thy right hand and may it preserve thee unto eternal life.

Let him respond:
R. Amen.

Mandatum: The Foot Washing *(The Command)*
*A Towel is taken and the feet of him (her) that has just been
Baptized are washed [using plain water].*

Alleluia - Thy Word is a lamp unto my feet, O Lord. *[Ps 118:105]*
Alleluia - Help me O Lord, and I shall be saved. *[Ps. 118:117]*
Alleluia - Visit us with Thy Salvation, O Lord. *[Ps.105:4]*
Alleluia - Thou hast commanded Thy commandments to be kept most diligently
[Ps. 118:4]

Command Thy mercy, O Lord, O despise not the works of Thy hands. *[Ps. 137:8]*
If I then being your Lord and Master have washed your feet;
you also ought to wash one another's feet. For I have given you
an example that as I have done to you so you do also for others. *[John 13:14-15]*

Our Lord and Savior Jesus Christ, on the day before He suffered took the splendid, Holy and spotless towel, girded his limbs, and poured water into a bowl, and washed the feet of His disciples. Thou shalt do this in imitation of our Lord Jesus Christ to thy pilgrims and travelers.

> *[It was customary that the **parents retain the 'Feet Water' of their child** as a safeguard from undesirable visitor or influences. The newly Baptized person is pure, so they bless the foot water. This is similar to Christ entering the Jordan River at His Baptism, blessing the water when He entered, and signifies the Command that a Christian bless others in the world around them. They also receive the blessing to bless others by the foot washing.]*

> *[**On Pascha, or if immediately before a Mass:** The newly Baptized receives the Eucharist at the Mass which follows immediately. Infants and children who have been Baptized and Chrismated also receive Holy Communion at the Mass. Children and babes in arms may rest when they need to inside the Church; waking them gently at the time of Holy Communion. Omit the rest of the Rite of Baptism **ONLY** if there is a Mass immediately after the Rite of Baptism where the newly Baptized will receive Holy Communion.*

ON PASCHA: ** IMMEDIATELY begin the rest of the Mass of Resurrection page 178.]*

First Communion

[The newly Baptized receives the Eucharist from Pre-Sanctified Species retained for this purpose:]

The Body and Blood of our Lord Jesus Christ be to thee unto life eternal.

R. Amen.

Refreshed with spiritual nourishment and renewed with the food of heaven: by the Body and Blood of the Lord; let us return proper praise and thanks to our God and Lord Jesus Christ, as we pray for His inexhaustible mercy, so that we may have the divine gifts of the Sacraments unto the increase of Faith and perfection of eternal Salvation, through our Lord Jesus Christ Who reigneth with His unoriginate Father and the Holy Spirit, unto ages of ages. **R.** Amen.

Let us pray, dear brethren, for our brother (sister) -N- who has won the Grace of the Lord, that he (she) may bear the Baptism which he (she) has received, spotless and in its entirety before the tribunal of our Lord Jesus Christ, Who reigneth with His unoriginate Father and the Holy Spirit, unto ages of ages. **R.** Amen.

O God, we give Thee thanks, O Thou through Whom we have celebrated this Holy Mystery: and we beg of Thee a gift of Thy Sanctification, through our Lord Jesus Christ Who reigneth with Thee and the Holy Spirit, unto ages of ages. **R.** Amen.

Alleluia - Remember us, O Lord, in the favor of Thy people: visit us with Thy salvation.
[Ps. 105:4]
Alleluia - O Lord, save me: O Lord, give good success. *[Ps. 117:25]*
Alleluia - Shew us Thy mercy, O Lord, and grant us Thy Salvation. *[Ps. 84:8]*

Save us, O Jesus Who art mighty to save, O Thou Who gavest the soul and giveth salvation, through Thee our Lord, Who reigneth with Thine unoriginate Father and the Holy Spirit, unto ages of ages.
R. Amen.

[The Rites of Baptism and Chrismation are now completed.]

+ + +

Visitation of the Sick
(Ambrosian Rite, closest to Celtic)

Introduction:
The Lord said to His disciples, in my Name ye shall cast out demons, and ye shall lay thy hands upon the sick and they will become well.

Psalm 49:
The God of gods, the Lord hath spoken: and he hath called the earth. From the rising of the sun, to the going down thereof:
Out of Sion the loveliness of his beauty.
God shall come manifestly: our God shall come, and shall not keep silence.
A fire shall burn before him: and a mighty tempest shall be round about him.
He shall call heaven from above, and the earth, to judge his people.
Gather ye together his saints to him: who set his covenant before sacrifices.
And the heavens shall declare his justice: for God is judge.
Hear, O my people, and I will speak: O Israel, and I will testify to thee: I am God, thy God.
I will not reprove thee for thy sacrifices: and thy burnt offerings are always in my sight.
I will not take calves out of thy house: nor he goats out of thy flocks.
For all the beasts of the woods are mine: the cattle on the hills, and the oxen.
I know all the fowls of the air: and with me is the beauty of the field.
If I should be hungry, I would not tell thee: for the world is mine, and the fulness thereof.
Shall I eat the flesh of bullocks? or shall I drink the blood of goats?
Offer to God the sacrifice of praise: and pay thy vows to the most High.
And call upon me in the day of trouble: I will deliver thee, and thou shalt glorify me.
But to the sinner God hath said: Why dost thou declare my justices, and take my covenant in thy mouth?

Seeing thou hast hated discipline: and hast cast my words behind thee.
If thou didst see a thief thou didst run with him: and with adulterers thou hast been a partaker.
Thy mouth hath abounded with evil, and thy tongue framed deceits.
Sitting thou didst speak against thy brother, and didst lay a scandal against thy mother's son:
These things hast thou done, and I was silent. Thou thoughtest unjustly that I should be like to thee:
but I will reprove thee, and set before thy face.
Understand these things, you that forget God; lest he snatch you away, and there be none to deliver you.
The sacrifice of praise shall glorify me: and there is the way by which I will shew him the salvation of God.

Prayer:

Heal, O Lord, this Thy servant **N.** whose bones are troubled and whose spirit is greatly defiled. Please convert them and heal him (her) through Thy spiritual medicine and rescue his soul

Holy Unction (Anointing of the Sick, in the Corrha-Stowe Missal, for any sick person.)

[This is a Sacrament, not only for the dying, but for any sick person. This may be done at church or home with oil that has been blessed by a Bishop, and reserved Pre-Sanctified Eucharist.]

Bretheren, Let us pray to our Lord Jesus Christ for our brother (sister) -N- who has been beset by the cruel and pressing evil of languor, that the Charity of the Lord of the Heavens may be pleased to treat by these Medicines. May He be pleased, Who gave the soul and gives salvation, through our Lord Jesus Christ, Who reigneth with the same, His unoriginate Father and the Holy Spirit, unto ages of ages.

R. Amen.

Most beloved Brethren, let us pray in supplication for our sick brother (sister) unto the Loving and Almighty God, Who is quick to restore and strengthen, so that the creature may experience the Hand of the Creator: that either in the restoration or in the recovery, in His Name; the Affectionate Father may be pleased to restore His handiwork; through our Lord Jesus Christ, Who reigneth with the Same Father, and the Holy Spirit, unto ages of ages.

R. Amen.

Lord, Holy Father of the Universe, Almighty Founder, the Eternal God in Whom all live, Who vivifies the dead and brings those who are not, to become like unto those who are Thy original workmanship; O Thou Who art the great Builder, affectionately restore this Thy handiwork, through our Lord Jesus Christ Who reigneth with Thee and the Holy Spirit, unto ages of ages.

R. Amen.

Dearest Brethren, let us beseech God, in Whose hand is truly the breath of the living; Who is the life of the dying; that He might heal the ills of the body of this one, and grant Salvation to the soul; although we do not deserve it by our merits, the grace of mercy may be attained. May He grant our petitions through our Lord Jesus Christ, Who reigneth with the Father and the Holy Spirit, unto ages of ages.
R. Amen.

O Lord, Holy Father Almighty and eternal God, Thou Who art the Way and the Truth and the Life, hear and preserve Thy servant, -N- whom Thou hast enlivened and Redeemed by the precious great and Holy Blood of Thy Son, Who reigneth with Thee and the Holy Spirit, unto ages of ages.
R. Amen.

O God Who dost not desire the death of a sinner, but that he be converted and live, release this one unto Thyself, from a heart turned to sins, and grant the gift of continuing life through our Lord Jesus Christ Who reigneth with Thee and the Holy Spirit, unto ages of ages.
R. Amen.

O God Who, because of Thy love, dost ever offer Thyself for Thy creation, lovingly incline Thine ears to our supplications which we make unto Thee for Thy servant -N-, who labors under adverse health of body. Gently regard and visit him (her). In Thy Salvation and heavenly grace, grant relief, through our Lord Jesus Christ, Who reigneth with Thee and the Holy Spirit, unto ages of ages.
R. Amen.

The Gospel [Matthew 22:23, 29-33]

At that time, there came to Him the Sadducees who say there is no resurrection, and asked Him: And Jesus answering, said to them, 'You err, not knowing the Scriptures, nor the power of God. For in the resurrection they shall neither marry nor be married; but shall be as the angels of God in Heaven. And concerning the resurrection of the dead, have you not read that which was spoken by the Lord, saying to you: I am the God of Abraham, and the God of Isaac and the God of Jacob? He is not therefore the God of the dead but the God of the Living,' and the multitudes hearing it, were in admiration at His doctrine.

On that day Jesus said 'Immediately after the tribulation of those days, the sun shall be darkened and the moon shall not give her light, and the stars shall fall from heaven, and the powers of heaven shall be moved: and then shall appear the sign of the Son of man in heaven: and then shall tribes of the earth mourn: and they shall see the Son of man coming in the clouds of heaven with much power and majesty. And He shall send His angels with a trumpet, and a great voice: and they shall gather together his elect from the four winds, from the highest parts of the heavens to the utmost bounds of them.'

[Respond:
Pray for us and lift up the Gospel to us.]

The Anointing and Holy Communion

I anoint thee with the sanctified oil, that thou recover thy health: in the Name of the Father and of the Son and of the Holy Spirit, unto ages of ages. R. Amen.

O Lord, regard us Thy servants, that praying with confidence, we may be worthy to say:

Our Father, Who art in the Heavens, hallowed be Thy Name. Thy Kingdom come. Thy will be done on earth as it is in Heaven. Give us this day our daily bread and forgive us our debts as we forgive our debtors and lead us not into temptation but deliver us from evil.

[Priest:] Deliver us O Lord from every evil and preserve us in all good, O Jesus Christ, the Author of all that is good, Who reigneth unto ages of ages.
R. Amen.

We pray Thee, O Lord, for our brother (sister) -N- who is weighed down by his (her) infirmity. Let him (her) participate in the Act of Communion, that whenever the blots of this era attack him (her), or worldliness taint him (her), he (she) may be forgiven and cleansed by the Gift of Thy Faith, through our Lord Jesus Christ, Who reigneth with the Father and the Holy Spirit, unto ages of ages.
R. Amen.

[If Unction is served before a Mass, the Mass begins here in place of the ending.]

O Lord Holy Father, We faithfully beseech Thee, that by the reception of this Sacrosanct Eucharist of the Body and Blood of our Lord Jesus Christ, that as much as possible of the flesh and as much as possible of the soul may be made well, through our Lord Jesus Christ Who reigneth with Thee and the Holy Spirit, unto ages of ages.
R. Amen.

O Lord Jesus Christ, our God, hear us who pray for our sick brother (sister) that Thy Holy Eucharist may be his (her) protection, through Thee our Lord Jesus Christ, Who reigneth with Thine unoriginate Father and the Holy Spirit, unto ages of ages.
R. Amen.

The Peace and Charity of our Lord Jesus Christ and the Communion of His Saints be always with us.
Let him say:
R. Amen.

[The Eucharist is administered from reserved Pre-Sanctified Sacrament:]
May the Body and Blood of our Lord Jesus Christ, the Son of the living and most high God, be to thee unto life eternal.
R. Amen.

Having received our Saving food of the Divine Body, let us give thanks to Jesus Christ: because by the Sacrament of His Body and Blood He freed us from death, and is pleased to give a remedy to many of the bodies as well as the souls of the human race; Who reigneth with His unoriginate Father and the Holy Spirit, unto ages of ages.
R. Amen.

Let us give thanks to God the Father Almighty, Who, by the gift of His Sacrament, has quickened a change in us from our earthly origin and nature into heavenly nature, through our Lord Jesus Christ, Who reigneth with the same Father and the Holy Spirit, unto ages of ages.

R. Amen.

Convert us, O God our Salvation, and grant health to our sick ones. For He hath satisfied the empty soul and hath filled the hungry soul with good things - Alleluia, Alleluia. *[Ps 104:9]* Visit us, O God, in Thy Salvation - Alleluia. *[Ps 105:4]* The Lord is my strength and my praise, and He is become my Salvation - Alleluia. *[Ps 117:14]* I will take the Chalice of Salvation, and I will call upon the Name of the Lord - Alleluia. *[Ps 115:13]* Refreshed by the Body and Blood of Christ, may we ever say unto Thee, O Lord - Alleluia. O Praise the Lord, all ye nations, praise him all ye people. For His mercy is confirmed upon us and the truth of the Lord remaineth for ever. *[Ps 116]* Offer up the Sacrifice of justice and trust in the Lord. *[Ps 4:6]* O God, we give Thee thanks, O Thou through Whom we have celebrated the Holy Mysteries, and we claim the gift of Holiness from Thee Who reigneth unto ages of ages.

R. Amen.

The Benediction

[The Priest extends both hands, palms outwards, fingers forming the Sign ICXC over his head:]

May the Lord bless thee and protect thee. May the Lord reveal His face unto thee and have mercy. May the Lord turn His Face to thee and give thee peace.

And he responds:

R. Amen.

[The Priest] **Then signing him** *[with the right hand],* **saying:**

Thou art marked with the ✠ Sign of the Cross of Christ.
Peace be with thee unto life eternal.

And he responds:

R. Amen.

Thus ends the Order of Communion.

✠ ✠ ✠

Emergency Rites:

It is encouraged for people to dedicate their lives to Christ, and to receive the Sacraments of the Church through life. Unfortunately, sometimes this does not happen, but they express a wish to join the Church when dying.

Baptism in an emergency: Any Christian may do this. Pour any water, even spit, onto a person, saying and signing them with the Cross, "**I Baptize you in the Name of the Father, and the Son, and the Holy Spirit, Amen.**" (If they have a little time, before that moment, say, "Do you renounce Satan and all his works?" and they respond "I do." Also, then bless the water, making the Sign of the Cross over it. However, there may be no time.) A Priest must be present, with the proper Chrism oil, to add the Sacrament of **Chrismation**, but that may also be done simply, with crosses and "the seal of the Gift of the Holy Spirit." The Irish practiced Baptism of an unborn child in the case of a woman who went into very early labor. They had her swallow Baptismal water, and said the words of Baptism over her abdomen with the sign of the Cross, using a name for the child that would serve for either sex. (A name of an Archangel would do.) "**I Baptize this child (N.) in the Name of the Father, and the Son, and the Holy Spirit, Amen.**" If the child survives their extreme premature birth, they retain their name. (Names may be added later, but they retain this name as part of their name.) The full Sacrament of Baptism should be added after the child is born. A newborn child who is not expected to live may either have the emergency Baptism, or if there is time, may have the full Rite of Baptism and Chrismation with first Communion.

Confession may be heard silently in an emergency, holding a cross before the person and asking them to tell God all their sins. Then, the **Absolution** should be given by a Priest.

Holy Communion may be administered with Pre-Sanctified Gifts by a Priest if he is carrying them. A newborn receiving Holy Communion must have a very small Particle of the Body and Blood dissolved into blessed water, which is administered very carefully.

Marriage must be done by a Priest, and may be the simple form of asking each person if they are freely willing to marry the other, and having them each respond, "I do." then bless them in the Name of the Father, Son, and Holy Spirit, and pronounce them man and wife. (The marriage must also be recorded with the state, so two witnesses must be present to sign that they have witnessed the marriage, which the Priest must also sign, with the two being married. A physician might be needed to sign to indicate that the couple was of sound mind.) If they recover from their emergency, they are still married, although they may need to fulfill other paperwork. If they wish a Marriage Mass after that, they may do so. The Priest may say that the couple is married and asks for prayers from the church.

Monastic orders in an emergency may be done by a simple tonsure, and the person professing their intention and dedication to the task: see becoming a Cele De. If the person has no hair, that does not matter. They should kiss the Book of the Gospels or a Bible to seal their intention. However, if they recover from their emergency, they are still of the monastic order, which means that if they were married before orders, they are still married, but if they were not married before orders, they must remain celebate. It also was an alleged practice among some heretical groups to become monastic on the deathbed, and then to hasten the death, but such an horrific act would have the opposite effect, staining both the individuals and a group who would condone such a thing.

Prayers for the Dying and Funeral

Note: Use the Mass for the dead in the Celtic Missal, and the Propers for the dead in the Missal. The other materials which may be used, below, are from the Ambrosian Rite, which is the same as the Celtic Propers in all respects, and was derived from Celtic missions. A funeral service is found in the Bobbio Missal. The terms "servant" or "handmaid" may both be used in the case of a woman. Sing the Hymn to the Archangel Michael at the end of Unction, when the Soul goes forth from the Body, and as a Hymn at the Requiem Mass (included with the Hymns). Use the complete Psalms in the Psalter, in Greek - Latin numbering.

Prayers [before] the Soul Goes Forth from the Body

[Use these prayers with the Sacrament of Unction, and Holy Communion.]

The Lord said to His disciples, in my Name ye shall cast out demons, and ye shall lay thy hands upon the sick and they will become well.
 Psalm 49: The God of gods, the Lord hath spoken: and he hath called the earth...
[Use the text of the Psalm in the Psalter.]

Prayer:
Heal, O Lord, this Thy servant N. whose bones are troubled and whose spirit is greatly defiled. Please convert them and heal him (her) through Thy spiritual medicine and rescue his soul

(Use the Sacrament of Unction, which includes Anointing, Holy Communion, and Absolution.)

Office of Commending the Soul When it Goes Forth from the Body

+ Fare thee well in Christ. Peace be with thee. Amen.
As thy soul goes forth from this world, let it go forth in peace. In the Name of God the Father Almighty Who created thee. In the Name of Jesus Christ the Son of the Living God Who suffered for thee. In the Name of the Holy Spirit Who is poured forth in thee. In the Name of the Angels and Archangels, Patriarchs, Prophets, Apostles, Innocents, Martyrs, Confessors, Virgins, and all of the souls of the Saints who are pleasing to God. Today mayest thou be placed with them in peace, may thy place and habitation be in the Holy Heavenly Jerusalem. May Saint Michael the Archangel, who was meritorious to lead the heavenly armies, take thee up. May the Holy Angels lead thee and guide thee into the Heavenly Jerusalem. May Saint Peter the Apostle to whom the Lord handed down the keys to the heavenly kingdom, take thee up. Go forth in peace, in the Name of the Father, an of the Son, and of the Holy Spirit, Who will illuminate thee in life eternal and raise thee in the first resurrection in the newest Day. Lord Jesus Christ the Good Shepherd, receive the soul of Thy servant N. in peace, and forgive all of his (her) sins. Receive, O Lord, Thy servant in the good, and free his (her) soul from all the dangers of hell, and from the snares of punishments, and from all tribulations.
Free, O Lord, the soul of Thy servant, as Thou didst free Noah from danger.
Free, O Lord, the soul of Thy servant, as Thou didst free Elijah and Enoch from tasting death in the world.
Free, O Lord, the soul of Thy servant, as Thou didst free Abraham through faith and believing.
Free, O Lord, the soul of Thy servant, as Thou didst free Lot from Sodom and the flaming

fire.
Free, O Lord, the soul of Thy servant, as Thou didst free Isaac from the hand of his father Abraham.
Free, O Lord, the soul of Thy servant, as Thou didst free Jacob through the benediction of Thy majesty.
Free, O Lord, the soul of Thy servant, as Thou didst free Moses from the hand of Pharoah, king of the Egyptians.
Free, O Lord, the soul of Thy servant, as Thou didst free Job from his sufferings.
Free, O Lord, the soul of Thy servant, as Thou didst free Jonah from the belly of the whale.
Free, O Lord, the soul of Thy servant, as Thou didst free David from the hand of Saul the king, and Goliath, and from all of the chains of his sins.
Free, O Lord, the soul of Thy servant, as Thou didst free Daniel from the Lion's den.
Free, O Lord, the soul of Thy servant, as Thou didst free three youths, from the fiery furnace and the hand of the iniquitous king.
Free, O Lord, the soul of Thy servant, as Thou didst free Suzanna from false accusation.
Free, O Lord, the soul of Thy servant, as Thou didst free human race by Thy Passion.
Free, O Lord, the soul of Thy servant, as Thou didst free Peter and Paul from prison.
Free, O Lord, the soul of Thy servant, as Thou didst free Thecla from the three torments.
Thus be pleased to free, O Lord, the soul of this human being, and allow him (her) to dwell with Thee in the heavenly good things of Thy kingdom, Who with the Father and the Holy Spirit lives and reigns unto ages of ages. Amen.

Rite of Funeral
After the Soul has Gone Forth from the Body
Preparation of the Body
[Use the full text of the Psalms in the Psalter.]

With faithful affection of memory, dear brethren, let us implore the mercy of our Lord for the commemoration of our dear - **N.** - whom the Lord hath assumed from the temptations of this world so that He Himself may be pleased to bestow a resting place of peace and quiet, and remit all of the offenses of his slips of conscience, and grant him forgiveness of his sins. May the Lord wipe away and cleanse whatever guilt he (she) has in this world; through the wholeness of His unfathomable faith, and His loving kindness. Through our Lord Jesus Christ His Son, Who with Him lives and reigns God in unity with the Holy Spirit, through all ages of ages. Amen.

God, in Whom all live and by Whom our bodies are not lost by dying, but are changed for the better, Thee we suppliants beseech, that Thou command that the soul of Thy servant - **N.** - be lifted up by the hand of Thy Holy Angels, placed in the bosom of Thy friend Abraham the Patriarch, and resuscitated on the most new Day of the great Trial, and whatsoever fault they may have contracted because of the lying devil, do Thou, O faithful and merciful one, wash away with Thy forgiveness, through our Lord Jesus Christ, Thy Son, Who with Thee lives and reigns together with the Holy Spirit, through all ages of ages. Amen.

Receive, O Lord, the soul of Thy servant (or handmaid) - **N.** - which Thou wast pleased to free from the prison of this world, and free their soul from the principalities of darkness and a place of torment so that absolved of all of the chains of sin, they be born into eternal blessing of quiet and light, and deserve to be resuscitated among Thy Saints and elect in the glory of the Resurrection, through our Lord Jesus Christ, Thy Son, Who with Thee lives and reigns together with the Holy Spirit, through all ages of ages. Amen.

Do not enter into judgment with Thy servant, for before Thee, no man is justified, unless all of their sins have been granted forgiveness by Thee. Therefore we beseech Thee, that they do not bear Thy condemnation who are commended unto Thee by true supplication of the Christian faith, but sustained by Thy grace, may this one be worthy to evade the condemnation of vengeance, who lived marked with the Sign of the Trinity, through our Lord Jesus Christ, Thy Son, Who with Thee lives and reigns together with the Holy Spirit, through all ages of ages. Amen.

Pour forth Thy mercy on thy dead servant - **N.** - O Lord, that he not receive the condemnation unto punishments because of his works; he remembered Thy desires in prayers so that this true faith would join him to the crowd of the faithful and may Thy mercy join him to the Angelic chorus through our Lord Jesus Christ, Thy Son, Who with Thee lives and reigns together with the Holy Spirit, through all ages of ages. Amen.

After this, there is the continuous chanting of the Psalms, and the washing of the corpse.

1. Antiphon:
Lead me O Lord in Thy justice and direct my ways in Thy sight.

Psalm 1: Blessed is the man...

2. Antiphon:
Do not give him over to hell, O Lord, neither give his soul unto corruption.

Psalm 15: The inscription of a title to David himself. Preserve me, O Lord, for I have put trust in thee...

3. Antiphon:
See, O Lord, my humility, and forgive me all my sins.

Psalm 24: To thee, O Lord, have I lifted up my soul...

4. Antiphon:
Thou art, O Lord, my protector, into Thy hand I commend my spirit.

Psalm 30: In thee, O Lord, have I hoped, let me never be confounded:..

5. Antiphon:
My soul hath thirsted for the Living God: I will come forth and submit myself before the Face of God.

Psalm 41: As the hart panteth after the fountains of water;...

6. Antiphon:
Behold, God is my helper, and the Lord is the sustainer of my soul.

Psalm 53: Save me, O God, by thy name, and judge me in thy strength...

7. Antiphon:
Into Paradise may the Angels lead thee, and with glory may the holy Martyrs of God receive thee.

Psalm 61: Shall not my soul be subject to God? for from him is my salvation...

8. Antiphon:
Throughout my life I praised Thee, O Lord: give me rest with the Saints in the land of the living and save me.
Psalm 71: Give to the king thy judgment, O God: and to the king's son thy justice..:

9. Antiphon:
Remember O Lord that which is my lot, what man liveth who will not see death?

Psalm 82: O God, who shall be like to thee? hold not thy peace, neither be thou still, O God...

10. Antiphon: Lord, send Thine Angel, my protector who raiseth me from the dust of the earth so that I may be able to run to meet the Resurrection with Thy Saints.

Psalm Ps 91 It is good to give praise to the Lord: and to sing to thy name, O most High...

11. Antiphon:
Let our cry come unto Thee, O Lord.

Psalm 101 Hear, O Lord, my prayer: and let my cry come to thee...

12. Antiphon:
Uphold me according to thy word, and I shall live: and let me not be confounded in my expectation.

Psalm 118 Blessed are the undefiled in the way, who walk in the law of the Lord...

13. Antiphon:
This is my rest for ever and ever: here will I dwell, for I have chosen it.

Psalm 131 O Lord, remember David, and all his meekness...

14. Antiphon:
Thou art my hope, my portion in the land of the living. Bring my soul out of prison,

Psalm 141 I cried to the Lord with my voice: with my voice I made supplication to the Lord...

The body is sent in a coffin with and six candles set about the bier.

Wake for the Dead

Because of the necessity that the Psalms be sung and the three lessons read, then let the first watch read "fifty" psalms. With the Antiphon : **Guide me O Lord in Thy Justice.**
V. (Ps 1) Blessed is the man... Through Ps 52
Let the second read the next "fifty" Psalms with the Antiphon: **Behold God is my helper: and the Lord is the protector of my soul.** *Save me, O God, by thy name, and judge me in thy strength. ... through Ps 117*
Again let the third gathering read the next "fifty" with the Antiphon: **Uphold me according to thy word, and I shall live: and let me not be confounded in my expectation.** *Blessed are the undefiled in the way, who walk in the law of the Lord. ... until the end of Ps. 150*

Another set of Double Antiphons.
V. My Redeemer liveth and shall renew me
V. My bones shall be renewed and while in my flesh I will behold the Lord God.

Psalm 50 Have mercy on me, O God, according to thy great mercy...
V. Thou commandest that I be born, O Lord, fulfill Thy promise that I rise again
V. I come at Thy command, do not abandon me for Thou at Faithful.

Psalm 53   Save me, O God, by thy name, and judge me in thy strength...

V. I believe that the Lord will not abandon me nor condemn me when He cometh in judgement
V. But my Redeemer, the Faithful God, will be merciful to me.

Psalm 56:   Have mercy on me, O God, have mercy on me: for my soul trusteth in thee...

V. Thou created me, O Christ, I come at Thy command:
V. Forgive me O God; forgive me O Mighty free me from the hand of death.

Psalm 85: Incline thy ear, O Lord, and hear me: for I am needy and poo..r.

This Antiphon is for a Deacon or Priest:
V. I have become a stranger to my brethren as thou ordained.
V. Thou didst call me O God: behold, I come: accept me.

Psalm 68: Save me, O God: for the waters are come in even unto my soul...

Psalms for when the Body is carried to the Church:

A Sequence
1 We shall be filled with the good things of thy house;
V. For thy arrows are fastened in me : and thy hand hath been strong upon me.
2 Before I waste away
V. I am afflicted and humbled exceedingly : I roared with the groaning of my heart.
3 My flesh is endowed
V. For He will not change His mind
4 With but the few days
V. Hear, O Lord, my prayer: and let my cry come to thee.
6 Which Thou hast granted me
V. If I had been just, my mouth
7 I know, O Lord, that thy judgments are equity: and in thy truth thou hast humbled me.
V. Remember O Lord the work of Thy hand.
8 Free me
V. Have mercy on me O God, have mercy on me.
9 Does not God know?
V. Let the dead get up and arise.
10 I know because of
V. O God come to my assistance.
11. My desire
V. I am one who has spoken
12 Pour forth tears O eyes
V. I labored with sobbing.

13 My eyes are full of tears
V. O all of you who have passed over
14. The chains are loosened
V. Cleanse me entirely
15. Return to me
V. Unto Thee O Lord do I arise.
16. So that thou shalt not fear in spirit
V. May the Lord harken unto thee.
17. O Thou Who raised Lazarus
V. Grant eternal rest to him/her/them O Lord.
18 In Thy hand O Lord do I commend my spirit.
V. In Thee have I hoped, O Lord.

Chants for when the Body is carried to the Church:

I. I exalted Thee, O Lord, for Thou hast sustained me; lead my soul out of the inferno; Save me O Lord from among those descending into the lake.
II. Thou didst create me from the earth, endowed me with flesh: O Christ my Redeemer, revive me on the newest day.
III. Thy right hand, O Lord, sustained me; and taught me Thy discipline.
IV. With Christ our life appeared: so let it appear with Him in Glory.
V. Lord, Lord, when shall I come unto Thy judgement?
VI. I have soiled my soul set in flesh; before Thou shatter me: have mercy.
VII. O Lord, send forth thine Angel, my protector that he rouse me so that I may hasten to the resurrection with Thy Saints.

The coffin is placed at the foot of the altar with six candles about it. If the deceased is a Priest, the head is toward the altar and the face is covered with a chalice veil.

The Requiem Mass is Offered.

The Celtic Mass with the Propers of the Departed in the Missal, and these Lections and prayers:

Requiem: Epistle: I Corinthians. 15:51-58; Psalm: 138; Gospel: John 5:19-20; and 11:25-26; (Final Gospel below; said at the end of the Mass).
General Requiem Epistle: I Thess. 4:12-18; Psalm: 138; Gospel: John 5:19-20; and 11:25-26; (Final Gospel below; said at the end of the Mass).
Requiem for a Bishop Old Testament: Is. 26:2-20; Epistle: I Corinthians. 15:1-22; P: 138 or 139 or 147 (appropriate to the man) Gospel: John 6:48-59; 12:25-26; (Final Gospel below; said at the end of the Mass).

The final Gospel: The Passion Reading: [Matthew 26:17-29]

And on the first day of the Azymes, the disciples came to Jesus, saying: Where wilt thou that we prepare for thee to eat the pasch? But Jesus said: Go ye into the city to a certain man, and say to him: the master saith, My time is near at hand, with thee I make the pasch with my disciples. And the disciples did as Jesus appointed to them, and they prepared the pasch. But when it was evening, he sat down with his twelve disciples. And whilst they were eating, he said: Amen I say to you, that one of you is about to betray me. And they being very much troubled, began every one to say: Is it I, Lord? But he answering, said: He that dippeth his hand with me in the dish, he shall betray me. The Son of man indeed goeth, as it is written of him: but woe to that man by whom the Son of man shall be betrayed: it were better for him, if that man had not been born. And Judas that betrayed him, answering, said: Is it I, Rabbi? He saith to him: Thou hast said it. And whilst they were at supper, Jesus took bread, and blessed, and broke: and gave to his disciples, and said: Take ye, and eat. This is my body. And taking the chalice, he gave thanks, and gave to them, saying: Drink ye all of this. For this is my blood of the new testament, which shall be shed for many unto remission of sins. And I say to you, I will not drink from henceforth of this fruit of the vine, until that day when I shall drink it with you new in the kingdom of my Father.

V.. Redeem me O Lord
V. Unto to Thee O Lord, do I arise.

Prayer over the body (before leaving the church):
We implore Thy Mercy, Eternal Almighty God, Who wast pleased to create man in Thine image that the spirit and soul of Thy servant - **N.** - who at this time has been taken out of human things and Thou hast summoned to Thyself: receive him/her gently and mercifully. Do not let him/her be under the domination of the shadow of death nor let chaos or shadow of darkness hold him/her but rather may he/she be cleansed of the stains of all of their sins and gathered into the bosom of Abraham the Patriarch, and rejoice to have to a place of light and place of refreshment: and on the day of judgement may he/she stand forth and Thou command that he/she be revived with Thy Saints and Elect. Through O Lord Jesus Christ....

V. May the Chains be loosed   **R.** Cleanse me entirely

Following the Gospel according to Saint John (Chapter 6)
All that the Father giveth to me shall come to me; and him that cometh to me, I will not cast out. Because I came down from heaven, not to do my own will, but the will of him that sent me. Now this is the will of the Father who sent me: that of all that he hath given me, I should lose nothing; but should raise it up again in the last day. And this is the will of my Father that sent me: that every one who seeth the Son, and believeth in him, may have life everlasting, and I will raise him up in the last day.

Into Thy hand O Lord, I commend my spirit.
R. In Thee have I hoped, O Lord.

Chant while the body is taken from the Church to the tomb.

I. Throughout my life I praised Thee O Lord.
II. Remember what my substance is for hast thou made all the children of men in vain?
III. My soul sticks to the ground: vivify me O Lord according to Thy promise.
IV. Carry me into the land of the living: they await me.
V. See my humiliation and deliver me: for I have not forgotten the law.
VI. Thou didst command me to be born, O Lord.
VII. I believe that Thou shall not abandon me.
VIII. Thou didst create me O Christ.
IX. Truly my days shall be few: grant me rest with Thy Saints, O Lord.

At the tomb.

X. May Christ Who called thee, receive thee; may the Angels lead thee unto the bosom of Abraham.
XI. May this be my repose unto ages of ages.
XII. The Lord slays and restores to life: may He lead thee from the inferno and lead thee back.
XIII. May the Lord protect thee from all evil may the Lord preserve thy soul.
Psalm 120: I have lifted up my eyes to the mountains, from whence help shall come to me...

Psalm 22: The Lord shepherds me: and I shall want nothing...

Psalm 23: The earth is the Lord's and the fulness thereof: the world, and all they that dwell therein...

Psalm 24: To thee, O Lord, have I lifted up my soul...

Psalm 30: In thee, O Lord, have I hoped, let me never be confounded: deliver me in thy justice...

Psalm 31: Blessed are they whose iniquities are forgiven, and whose sins are covered...

Psalm 32: Rejoice in the Lord, O ye just: praise becometh the upright...

Psalm 40: Blessed is he that understandeth concerning the needy and the poor : the Lord will deliver him in the evil day...

Psalm 41: As the hart panteth after the fountains of water; so my soul panteth after thee, O God...

Psalm 50 Have mercy on me, O God, according to thy great mercy...

Psalm 53 Save me, O God, by thy name, and judge me in thy strength...

Psalm 56 Have mercy on me, O God, have mercy on me: for my soul trusteth in thee...

Psalm 66: May God have mercy on us, and bless us: may he cause the light of his countenance to shine upon us, and may he have mercy on us...

Psalm 69: O God, come to my assistance; O Lord, make haste to help me...

Psalm 70: In thee, O Lord, I have hoped, let me never be put to confusion:...

Psalm 85: Incline thy ear, O Lord, and hear me: for I am needy and poor...

Psalm 101: Hear, O Lord, my prayer: and let my cry come to thee...

Psalm 129: Out of the depths I have cried to thee, O Lord:...

Psalm 139: Deliver me, O Lord, from the evil man: rescue me from the unjust man...

Psalm 149: I have cried to the, O Lord, hear me: hearken to my voice, when I cry to thee...

Psalm 117:19-end Open ye to me the gates of justice: I will go into them, and give praise to the Lord. This is the gate of the Lord, the just shall enter into it.
I will give glory to thee because thou hast heard me: and art become my salvation.
The stone which the builders rejected; the same is become the head of the corner.
This is the Lord's doing: and it is wonderful in our eyes.
This is the day which the Lord hath made: let us be glad and rejoice therein.
O Lord, save me: O Lord, give good success.
Blessed be he that cometh in the name Lord. We have blessed you out of the house of the Lord.
The Lord is God, and he hath shone upon us. Appoint a solemn day, with shady boughs, even to the horn of the alter.

Thou art my God, and I will praise thee: thou art my God, and I will exalt thee. I will praise thee, because thou hast heard me, and art become my salvation.
O praise ye the Lord, for he is good: for his mercy endureth for ever.

Psalm 4:9
In peace in the selfsame I will sleep, and I will rest:
Let Thy Mercy, O Lord, be upon us, for we have hoped in Thee.
All that the Father has given unto me, comes unto me and I shall revive him on the newest day.
May the Lord preserve thee from all evil, may the Lord preserve thy soul.

Let us pray, dear brethren of the spirit of our beloved - **N.** - whom the Lord has been pleased to free from the snares of this world and age, whose body has been borne to the tomb: that the Faith of God please gather him/her into the bosom of Abraham, Isaac and Jacob and that when the day of judgement comes He make him/her to arise and be set among the Saints and elect at His right hand. May He grant this through our Lord Jesus Christ Who with the Father and the Holy Spirit, lives and reigns throughout all ages of ages. Amen.

Completing the required faithful office of the burial of the human body according to custom, let us faithfully implore God in Whom all live that He revive the body of our beloved - **N.** - which is interred by us in infirmity into the Order of the Saints and command his spirit to be gathered among the Saints and Faithful. Grant this through our Lord Jesus Christ Who with the Father and the Holy Spirit, lives and reigns throughout all ages of ages. Amen.

After the burial:

Unto Thee, O Lord, do we commend the soul of Thy servant N and he/she who is dead to the world may be alive unto Thee and that however he/she may have entered into sin through the fragility of mundane interaction, Thou blot out guilt because of Thy most merciful Faith. through our Lord Jesus Christ Who with the Father and the Holy Spirit, lives and reigns throughout all ages of ages. Amen.

O God, Thou art the eternal lover of human souls redeem from exile in all the torments of hell the soul of Thy Servant - **N.** - who while in body truly held to Thy Faith so that preserved from the confines of hell he/she may be called to associate with the Saints. through our Lord Jesus Christ Who with the Father and the Holy Spirit, lives and reigns throughout all ages of ages. Amen.

It is indeed arrogant for a human to dare to commend a human, for a mortal to dare to commend a mortal, for ashes to dare to commend ashes unto Thee O Lord our God, but since earth receives earth and sand is reduced again to sand, while all flesh is returned to its origin: we shall appeal tearfully unto Thy Faithfulness, O God Most Faithful Father and ask that Thou lead the soul of this Thy servant - **N.** - from the vile chasm of this world unto his/her native land. Receive him/her into the bosom of Abraham, Thy friend, and let a refreshing rain pour forth upon him/her. Let him/her be preserved from the fierce billowing flames of hell and allow him/her to participate in repose of the blessed. And whatever his/her sins might be, O Lord, release him/her from the punishments of his/her sins and forgive them by the extreme leniency of Grace: Do not let him/her receive the punishments due his/her sins, but let him/her experience the sweet goodness of Thy forgiveness: And when the end of the world dawns upon all of the high world, may he/she, gathered into the congregation of all the Saints, arise with the elect and be summoned unto Thy right hand. through our Lord Jesus Christ Who with the Father and the Holy Spirit, lives and reigns throughout all ages of ages. R.Amen.

May the Lord bless thee and protect thee. May the Lord reveal His face unto thee and have mercy. May the Lord turn His Face to thee and give thee peace.

R. Amen.
Eternal rest grant him/her, O Lord
R. And may perpetual light shine upon him/her.
And may his/her soul rest in peace.
R. Amen.

+ + + + + + + + + + + +

Litanies originally in Old Irish
Litanies

Prayers such as Litanies have always been done. The Litany of the Saints is in the Lorrha-Stowe Mass and may also be done in the Rite of Baptism. Each line of a Litany will ask different "Petitions," and will end with a response, such as "Lord have mercy" or, asking for intercession prayers from a Saint, "Pray for us." Some Litanies are traditional to say after an Hour, such as the "Litany of Confession" said after Matins on a Sunday Vigil, but Litanies may be said at any time of day.

The Rev. Charles Plummer accurately translated *Irish Litanies* from Old Irish that happen to be appropriate for Penitential seasons (London, 1925). A few short lines Rev. Plummer did not translate from Latin were translated into English by + Maelruain (Kristopher) Dowling.

The **Creed** (Credo) and the **Our Father** (Pater) should be said after completing a Litany. (These are written out at the end of this book.)

The Litany to Jesus in two parts seems to be one Litany, and the Litany of the Irish Saints in two parts seems to be one Litany (no Amen written between parts I and II).

The Litanies of the Virgin Mary (the Metrical Litany was composed by Colum cille, the other Litany was composed by Brogan of Clonast who died in 750) are very similar to parts of the Byzantine Akathist Hymn normally sung during Lent, and also the Byzantine Hymn to Mary, the "Champion Leader," which is sung only during Lent in the Byzantine usage.

The Litany of Confession praises God and the Saints, asks for forgiveness, and lists many sins. It is not a substitute for the Sacrament of Confession, but is part of preparation for that Sacrament, and may be said before Holy Communion. (A "Rite of Reconciliation," the Sacrament of Confession from St. Gall has been included in the beginning of the Stowe-Lorrha Missal.)

[The Rev. Plummer included some Litanies with later 15th century additions that are not in line with earlier Irish beliefs; unless a Litany seems to be of the same spirit as the Lorrha-Stowe Missal, the Antiphonary of Bangor, and other Orthodox texts, it is not included here.]

Litany of the Savior *[Praising Jesus and asking for Compunction.]*

O Savior of the human race;
O true physician of every disease, O heart-pitier and assister of all misery;
O fount of true purity, and of true knowledge;
O bestower of every treasure;
By the heavenly Father, by the Holy Spirit, and by Thine own Divinity;
By Thy great compassion, by Thy great affection to the human race from the beginning of the world to its end;
By Thy coming humbly from heavenly places in the form of a servant to help it and rescue it from the dominion of the devil;
By Thy Conception in the womb of Mary the Virgin;
By Thy Humanity which grew in unity of person with Thy Divinity;
By the loving mother from whom Thou didst receive it;
By Thy Birth of her, without opening of the womb;

By the offering and willing gift which Thou madest of Thyself to Cross and Passion for the sake of the human race;
By Thine ineffable compassion toward the seed of Adam;
By the deliverance that Thou broughtest to the just men of the five ages from the murk and darkness of hell;
By Thy Resurrection from the dead after three days;
By Thine Ascension into heaven in the presence of Thine Apostles and Thy disciples;
By the beauty and great glory in which Thou abidest eternally at the right hand of God the Father in heaven;
By Thy coming to the judgment of doom to gather together the just to dwell for ever in the eternal life, and to drive away the sinners to the sorrow and torments of hell;

Give to this wretched convicted sinner the grace of compunction of heart, and earnest repentance, that I may weep bitterly for every outrage, every contempt, and every provocation, that I have offered to the King of heaven and earth, and every harm that I have offered to myself up to this day, in word, in deed, in thought;

Grant me abstinence in place of gluttony, chastity in place of lust, compassion in place of greed, gentleness in place of wrath, spiritual joy in place of carnal sorrow, tranquillity in place of anxiety, silence in place of loquacity;

Impart to me Thy fear and Thy love around my heart and in my thought, that I may despise every carnal pleasure, and all vain glory of the present life;

That I may desire earnestly to meditate on Thee, to pray to Thee, and to praise Thee for ever;

That I may merit an abode of rest among the believing widows in the unity of the heavenly church in the presence of the Trinity unto the ages of ages. Amen.
[Creed and Our Father.]

Litany of the Virgin and All Saints
[A monastic Litany against future temptation and for chastity.]

May Mary, and John the youth, and John the Baptist, and all the Saints of the world intercede with the fount of true purity and true innocence, Jesus Christ, son of the Virgin, that the grace and compassion of the Holy Spirit may come to forgive us all our past sins, and to protect us from future sins, to subdue our fleshly lusts, and to check our unfitting thoughts;

To kindle the love and affection of the Creator in our hearts, that it may be He that our mind searches after and desires and meditates on for ever;

That our eyes may not be deceived by idle glances, and through the profitless beauty of perishable things;

That our hearing may not be perverted by idle songs, nor by the noxious persuasion of devils and evil men;

That our senses of taste may not be beguiled through dainties and many savors;

That He would free our tongues from reviling and insult and inept loquacity;

That we may not barter the true light and true beauty of the everlasting life for the deceitful phantasy of the present life;

That we may not forsake the pure wedlock and marriage of our husband and noble bridegroom, Jesus Christ, Son of the King of heaven and earth, for the impure wedlock of a slave of His, so that our soul and body may be a consecrated temple to the Holy Spirit, that we may accompany the blameless Lamb, that we may sing the song which only the virgins sing, that we may merit the crown of eternal glory in the unity of the company of heaven, in the presence of the Trinity, unto ages of ages. Amen.
[Creed and Our Father.]

The Litany of the Trinity

[This Litany is in three parts for the Holy Trinity, and asks for mercy.]

[A very important note: a manuscript from the British Museum dated from the 15th century added a portion during the Litany to the Father that is both heretical, denying the all-holy goodness of God the Father, but also resembles dabblings of that era in anti-Christian texts. Other manuscripts of this Litany do not have this inclusion. Historically, it is known that the Tudors in England did dabble in such things, and they may have added something to discredit an otherwise very reverent and beautiful prayer. No portion of that manuscript's inclusions has been included here.]

Mugrón, the coarb of Colum cille, composed these words concerning the Trinity.

Have mercy upon us, O God the Father Almighty *;
[* This may be repeated before each line.]

    O God of Hosts,
    O high God,
    O Lord of the world,
    O ineffable God,
    O Creator of the Elements,
    O invisible God,
    O incorporeal God,
    O God beyond all judgment,
    O immeasurable God,
    O impassible God,
    O incorruptible God,
    O immortal God,
    O immovable God,
    O eternal God,
    O perfect God,
    O merciful God,
    O wondrous God,
    O God we fear,
    O golden good,   *[the golden mean, i.e., the Commandments.]*
    O heavenly Father who art in heaven, Have mercy upon us.

Have mercy upon us, O Almighty God, Jesus Christ, Son of the living God *;
[* This may be repeated before each line.]

    O Son twice-born,
    O only-begotten of God the Father,
    O first-born of the Virgin Mary,
    O Son of David,
    O Son of Abraham,
    O beginning of all things,
    O completion of the world,
    O Word of God,
    O Way to the heavenly kingdom,
    O Life of all things,
    O everlasting Righteousness,
    O Image, O Likeness, O Form of God the Father,
    O Arm of God,
    O Hand of God,
    O Might of God,
    O Right-hand of God,
    O true Knowledge,
    O true Light of love, that lighteneth every darkness,

O guiding Light,
O Sun of righteousness,
O Morning star,
O Brightness of the Deity,
O Radiance of the eternal brightness,
O Intelligence of the mystic world,
O Mediator of all men,
O promised one of the Church,
O faithful Shepherd of the flock,
O Hope of the faithful,
O Angel of the great counsel,
O true Prophet,
O true Apostle,
O true Teacher,
O High Priest,
O Master,
O Nazarene,
O Bright-rayed,
O everlasting Satisfaction,
O Tree of life,
O true Heaven,
O true Vine,
O Rod of the stem of Jesse,
O King of Israel,
O Savior,
O Gate of life,
O choice Flower of the field,
O Lily of the Valleys,
O Rock of strength,
O Corner-stone,
O heavenly Zion,
O Foundation of the Faith,
O innocent Lamb,
O Diadem,
O gentle Sheep,
O Redeemer of the human race,
O very God,
O very Man,
O Lion,
O Calf,
O Eagle,
O Christ crucified,
O Judge of doom,   Have mercy upon us.
Have mercy upon us, O God Almighty, O Holy Spirit *;

[* This may be repeated before each line.]

O Spirit that art highest of all spirits,
O Finger of God,
O Protection of Christians,
O Comforter of the sorrowful,
O Clement one,
O merciful Intercessor,
O Imparter of true wisdom,
O Author of the Holy Scriptures,
O Ruler of speech,
O septiform Spirit,

O Spirit of wisdom,
O Spirit of understanding,
O Spirit of counsel,
O Spirit of strength,
O Spirit of knowledge,
O Spirit of affection,
O Spirit of fear,
O Spirit of love,
O Spirit of grace,
O Spirit from whom is ordered every lofty thing, [Have mercy upon us.]

[The rest of this manuscript is lost. One may add the Irish Trisagion Prayers from the Hour of Matins, below:]

(first time):
We adore Thee, eternal Father,
We call to Thee, eternal Son,
and we confess Thee O Holy Spirit, abiding the one Divine Substance.
Let us return due praise and thanks to Thee, one God in Trinity, that we may be worthy to praise Thee with unceasing voices, through eternal ages of ages. Amen.

(second time):
We adore Thee, eternal Father,
We call to Thee, eternal Son,
and we confess Thee O Holy Spirit, abiding the one Divine Substance.
Let us return due praise and thanks to Thee, one God in Trinity, that we may be worthy to praise Thee with unceasing voices, through eternal ages of ages. Amen.

Daily Collect during Great Lent: O God, Whom the army of heaven sings,
And Whom the Church of the Saints praises,
Whom the Spirit of the Universals hymns,
Have mercy, I beseech Thee, on all of us:
Who reignest unto ages of ages. Amen.

Collect for Monastic Vows and Tonsure: Let the Angels, Virtues, Thrones, and Powers praise Thee, O Lord, and let those who owe their origin to Thee rejoice in the office of Thy praise so that through harmony of the universe, expanding unto Thee in consonance, Thy will be done in Heaven and also on earth. We beseech Thee, O Lord, be at peace with Thy people that by Thy praises which are found in their mouths, there may remain, in every one of them, the defense of Thy Word, by which Thou doest teach and the Truth of our Life by which Thou doest ever regard us, and well-being by which Thou doest exalt the meek. For Thy many great deeds, we praise Thee, O Lord by thanks offerings of show of praise through the Psalms, mortification through the drum, by group worship through the chorus, exultation through the organ, jubilation through the cymbals that we deserve to have thy mercy, O Christ, Savior of the world.

(third time and ending):
We adore Thee, eternal Father,
We call to Thee, eternal Son,
and we confess Thee O Holy Spirit, abiding the one Divine Substance.
To Thee, O Trinity, we return praise and thanks
To Thee, O God, we recite unceasing praise
Thee, Father, unbegotten
Thee, Son, Only Begotten,
Thee O Holy Spirit from Father proceeding, we believe in our hearts.
We give Thee thanks inestimable, incomprehensible,
Almighty God, Who reignest unto the ages. Amen. [Creed and Our Father.]

Or, one may add the complete Byzantine Trisagion Prayers:
"Glory to Thee, our God, glory to Thee. O Heavenly King, Comforter, Spirit of Truth, Who art everywhere present and fillest all things, Treasury of good things and Giver of life: Come and dwell in us, and cleanse us of all impurity, and save our souls, O Good One."

"Holy God, Holy Mighty, Holy Immortal, have mercy on us."; *said three times.*

"Glory to the Father, and to the Son, and to the Holy Spirit, both now and ever, and unto ages of ages. Amen. O Most Holy Trinity, have mercy on us. O Lord, blot out our sins. O Master, pardon our iniquities. O Holy One, visit and heal our infirmities for Thy name's sake." *Then three times* "Lord have mercy," *another* Gloria *and the* Lord's Prayer.]

[The Stowe Missal ending from the Preface of the Trinity:
"[Thou] art not in one singularity of person but One Trinity of One Substance. Thee we believe; Thee we bless; Thee we adore; and we praise Thy Name unto eternity and unto ages of ages: Thou through Whom is the Salvation of the world; through Whom is the Life of men; through Whom is the Resurrection of the dead. [Amen.]"

One may also add the angelic ending of the Preface prayer, "Through Whom, unto Thy Majesty, the Angels give praise..." *and end with the Sanctus.]*
Then, Amen, Creed, and Our Father.

Litany of St. Michael
[Asking the Archangel St. Michael to pray to God for us at the time of death, in life on earth, and for freedom from the tyranny of sin. This Litany repeats the subject after the fifth verse and at the end.]

Maelisu O'Brolchan composed this.

O Angel!
Bear, O Michael of the mighty powers,
My cause before the Lord.

Hearest thou?
Ask of the forgiving God
Forgiveness for all my monstrous ill.

Delay not!
Bear my fervent longing
Before the King, the great King.

To my soul
Bring help, bring comfort,
In the hour of my departure from the earth.

In power,
To meet my waiting soul,
Come with many thousands of angels,
                            O Angel.

O warrior!
Against the crooked, foul, contentious world
Come to help me in very deed.

         Pour thou not
Contempt on what I say;
While I live, forsake me not.

         I choose Thee,
To free this soul of mine,
My reason, my sense, my flesh.

         O Advocate,
Triumphant, victorious in war,
O angelic slayer of Antichrist!
                              O Angel.

[Amen. Creed and Our Father.]

Litany of Jesus I *[A Litany in Two Parts]*
[Part I: An entreaty by the intercession of all the Saints to Jesus for protection.]

      I entreat Thee, O Holy Jesus, by Thy four Evangelists who wrote Thy Divine Gospels, to wit, Matthew, Mark, Luke, and John;

      I entreat Thee by Thy four chief Prophets who foretold Thy Incarnation, Daniel, and Jeremiah, and Isaiah, and Ezekiel;

      I entreat Thee by the nine Orders of the Church on earth, from Psalm-singer to Episcopate;

      I entreat Thee by all the intelligent ones who received these Orders from the beginning of the New Testament up till now; and who [shall] receive them from now till the Day of Judgment;

      I entreat Thee by the nine orders of the Church in heaven, to wit, Angels and Archangels, Virtues, Powers, Principalities, Dominions, Thrones, Cherubim, Seraphim;

      I entreat Thee by the twelve Patriarchs who foretold Thee through spiritual mysteries;

      I entreat Thee by the twelve minor Prophets who foreshadowed Thee;

      I entreat Thee by the twelve Apostles who loved Thee, and besought Thee, and followed Thee, and clave to Thee, and chose Thee above every one;

      I entreat Three by all Thy sons of true virginity throughout the whole world, both of the Old and New Testament, with John the youth, Thine own bosom-fosterling;

      I entreat Thee by all holy penitents with Peter the Apostle;

      I entreat Thee by all holy virgins throughout the whole world, with Mary Virgin, Thine own holy mother;

      I entreat Thee by all penitent widows with Mary Magdalene;

      I entreat Thee by all the folk of lawful marriage, with Job the suffering, on whom came trials;

      I entreat Thee by all the holy martyrs of the whole world, both of the Old and New Testament, from the beginning of the world, to Elijah and Enoch, who will suffer the last martyrdom on the brink of doom, with Stephen, Cornelius, Cyprian, Lawrence, George, Germanus;

      I entreat Thee by all the holy monks who warred for Thee throughout the whole world, with Elijah and Elisha in the Old Testament, with John and Paul and Antony in the New Testament;

      I entreat Thee by all those that had intelligence in the law of nature, with Abel, with Seth, with Elijah, with Enoch, with Noah, with Abraham, with Isaac, with Jacob;

      I entreat Thee by all those that had intelligence in the written law, with Moses, with Joshua, with Caleb, with Aaron, with Eleazar, with Jonah;

I entreat Thee by all those that had intelligence in the prophetic law, with Elijah, with Elisha, with David, and with Solomon;

I entreat Thee by all those that had intelligence in the law of the New Testament, with Thine own holy Apostles, and all Thy Saints to the end of the world;

I entreat Thee by all the holy Bishops who founded the ecclesiastical city in Jerusalem, with James of the knees,* Thine own holy brother;

> [* see Irish Biblical Apocrypha *by Máire Herbert and Martin McNamara MSC, Edinburgh, 1989 an important translation; about St. Joseph, St. James, and family. Also see the* Protoevangelium of St. James, *an early Greek Apocrypha, and the* Life of the Virgin Mary, the Theotokos *(Birthgiver of God): the life of Blessed Ever-Virgin Mary and the Holy Family.]*

I entreat Thee by all the holy Bishops who founded the ecclesiastical city in Rome, with Linus, and Cletus, and Clement;

I entreat Thee by all the holy Bishops who founded the ecclesiastical city in Alexandria, with Mark the Evangelist;

I entreat Thee by all the holy Bishops who founded the ecclesiastical city in Antioch, with Peter the Apostle;*

> [* *Traditionally, St. Peter founded the church at Antioch and was its first Bishop. After St. Peter, the Bishop of Antioch was St. Ignatius, the child who Jesus had allowed to hear Him. In Rome, St. Linus, its first Bishop, was consecrated by St. Paul. Of course, St. Peter was martyred in Rome and his holy relics are in St. Peter's Basilica. Constantinople was a Patriarchate at the time this Litany was written, but it had not been founded by an Apostle; not an Apostolic See. There may also have been political reasons why Constantinople was not included on this list: for example, Constantinople had claimed to be second to Rome in importance, instead of being after Alexandria, Jerusalem, and Rome. Alexandria, because of its secular importance and library, Christian college, monasticism, etc., was considered second to Rome at that time. A political fight between Constantinople and Alexandria was partly responsible for the promotion of heresies and strife in the Church.]*

I entreat Thee by all the holy infants of the whole world who endured the cross and martyrdom for Thy sake, with the two thousand one hundred and forty children who were slain by Herod in Bethlehem of Judah, and with the child Cyricus; [and the millions of children today martyred before they are born;]

I entreat Thee by all the hosts of the aged perfect and righteous men, who completed their old age and their perfection and their righteousness for Thy sake with Eli in the Old Testament; with the righteous and perfect aged senior, Simeon, in the beginning of the New Testament, who took Thee on his arms and knees and elbows, fondling Thee, and said: "Now Thou dost dismiss Thy servant, O Lord, according to Thy word, in peace; because my eyes have seen Thy salvation, which Thou hast prepared before the face of all peoples; a light to the revelation of the Gentiles and the glory of Thy people Israel."

I entreat Thee by all the holy Disciples who learned the spiritual sciences both of Old and New Testament, with the seventy-two Disciples;

I entreat Thee by all the perfect teachers who taught the spiritual meaning with Paul the Apostle;

That Thou wilt take me under Thy protection and defense and care, to preserve and protect me from demons and all their promptings, against all the elements of the world, against lusts, against transgressions, against sins, against the crimes of the world, against the dangers of this life, and the torments of the next, from the hands of enemies and every terror, against the fire of hell and doom, against shame before the face of God, against attacks [*lit.* seizures] of demons, that they may have no power over us at the entry of the other world; against the dangers of this world, against every man that God knows to have ill will towards us under the ten stars of the world;

May God keep far from us their rage, their violence, their anger, their cruelty, their craft;

May God kindle gentleness and love, and affection, and mercy, and forgivingness, in their hearts and in their thoughts, and in their souls, and in their minds and in their bowels.
[Amen. *If praying Part I alone, Creed and Our Father.*]

[This continues immediately with the Litany of Jesus II.]

Litany of Jesus II *[Continuation of the First Part]*
[Asking Jesus through His Life: for grace, righteousness, and being received into heaven.]

O holy Jesu;
O gentle friend;
O Morning Star;
O mid-day Sun adorned;
O brilliant flame of the righteous, and of righteousness, and of everlasting life, and of eternity;
O Fountain ever-new, ever-living, ever-lasting;
O heart's Desire of Patriarchs;
O Longing of Prophets,
O Master of Apostles and Disciples;
O Giver of the Law;
O Prince of the New Testament;
O Judge of doom;
O Son of the merciful Father without mother in heaven;
O Son of the true virgin maid, Mary, without father on earth;
O true and loving brother;
For the sake of Thy kindliness, hear the entreaty of this mean and wretched weakling for the acceptance of this sacrifice on behalf of all Christian churches, and on mine own behalf;
For the sake of the merciful Father, from whom Thou camest to us on earth;
For the sake of Thy Divinity, which that Father ordained for the reception of Thy Humanity;
For the sake of the pure and holy flesh which Thou didst take from the womb of the Virgin;
For the sake of the septiform Spirit, which co-ordained this flesh in union with Thyself and with Thy Father;
For the sake of the holy womb wherefrom Thou didst receive that flesh without loss of virginity;
For the sake of the holy stem and genealogy, from which Thou didst derive this flesh, from the flesh of Adam to the flesh of Mary;
For the sake of the seven things that were prophesied for Thee on earth, to wit Thy Conception, Thy Birth, Thy Baptism, Thy Crucifixion, Thy Burial, Thy Resurrection, Thy Ascension, Thy return to Judgment;
For the sake of the holy tree on which Thy sides were stretched;
For the sake of the truth-loving blood which was shed on us from that tree;
For the sake of Thine own Body and Blood which is offered on all holy altars that are in the Christian churches of the world;
For the sake of the whole scriptures in the setting forth of Thy Gospel;
For the sake of all righteousness in the setting forth of Thy Resurrection;

For the sake of Thy love, which is the head and summit of all commandments, as it is said: let charity magnify everything. [The greatest of these is charity... I Corinthians 13:13]

For the sake of Thy Kingdom with all its rewards and jewels and songs;

For the sake of Thy mercy, Thy forgivingness, Thy kindliness, and Thine own bounteousness, which is broader than any treasure, that I may have forgiveness and annulling of my past sins from the beginning of my life till this day, according to the word of David who said: "Blessed are they whose iniquities are forgiven: and whose sins are covered... [Psalm 31, 32 KJV];
that is,

Give and grant and impart Thy holy grace, and Thy Holy Spirit, to protect me and preserve me from all my sins present and future, and to kindle in me all righteousness, and to establish me in that righteousness to my life's end; and that He may receive me after my life's end into heaven, in the unity of Patriarchs and Prophets, in the unity of Apostles and Disciples, in the unity of Angels and Archangels, in the unity which excels every unity, that is, in the unity of the holy and exalted Trinity; Father, Son and Holy Spirit; for I have nothing unless I have it according to the word of the Apostle Paul: [Romans 7:24] "...who shall deliver me from the body of this death? The grace of God, by Jesus Christ our Lord," who reigns unto the ages of ages. Amen.

Finit. Amen. Finit.   [Credo et Pater.]

Litany of the Virgin
Composed by Brogan of Clonast, d. 750.
[Praising her and asking for intercession.]

O great Mary;   [R. **Pray for us.**]
O greatest of Marys;
O paragon of women;
O Queen of the Angels;
O Lady of heaven;
O Lady, full and overflowing with the grace of the Holy Spirit;
O blessed and more than blessed one;
O mother of the eternal glory;
O mother of the Church in heaven and earth;
O mother of affection and forgiveness;
O mother of the golden light;
O Honor of the ether;
O sign of gentleness;
O Gate of heaven;
O golden Casket;
O bed of kindness and compassion;
O Temple of the Deity;
O Beauty of virgins;
O Lady of the nations;
O Fountain of the gardens;
O cleansing of sins;
O washing of souls;
O mother of orphans;
O Breast of infants;
O consolation of the wretched;
O Star of the sea;
O Handmaid of God;
O Mother of Christ;
O Spouse of the Lord;
O beauteous as a dove;

O lovely as the moon;
O elect as the sun;
O repulse of Eve's reproach;
O renewal of life;
O Beauty of women;
O Chief of Virgins;
O Garden enclosed;
O true Fountain sealed;
O Mother of God;
O perpetual Virgin;
O holy Virgin;
O prudent Virgin;
O beauteous Virgin;
O chaste Virgin;
O Temple of the living God;
O Throne of the eternal King;
O Sanctuary of the Holy Spirit;
O Virgin of the stem of Jesse;
O Cedar of the hill of Lebanon;
O Cypress of the hill of Zion;
O crimson Rose of the land of Jacob;
O flourishing as a palm;
O fruitful as an olive-tree;
O glorious Son-bearer;
O light of Nazareth;
O glory of Jerusalem;
O beauty of the world;
O high-born of the Christian people;
O Queen of the world;
Hear the prayer of the poor;
Despise not the groans and sighs of the wretched;
Let our longing and our sighs be borne by thee to the presence of the Creator, for we are not worthy to be heard ourselves by reason of our ill-desert;
O mighty Lady of heaven and earth;
Cancel our guiltinesses and our sins;
Blot out our defilements and pollutions;
Raise the falls of the weaklings and the bound;
Release the enslaved;
Amend through thyself the assaults of our evil habits and vices;
Impart to us through thyself the flowers and adornments of good deeds and virtues;
Make the Judge propitious to us by thy prayers and intercessions;
For the sake of mercy abandon us not as a prey to our enemies;
Abandon not our souls to slavery;
And take us to thyself forever under thy protection;
We also pray and entreat thee, O holy Mary, through thy mighty intercession with thine only Son, Jesus Christ, Son of the living God, that God would protect us from all straits and temptations;
And request for us from the God of creation, that we may all receive from Him remission and forgiveness of all our sins and offences, and that we may obtain from Him also by thine intercession an eternal abode in the heavenly kingdom for ever and ever, in the presence of the Saints and holy virgins of the world.
May we merit it, may we inhabit it, unto ages of ages. Amen.
[Creed and Our Father.]

Metrical Litany of the Virgin Mary

[This Litany is similar to the Byzantine Akathist Hymn to the Blessed Virgin Mary, which also adds the Angelic Salutation. See Continuous Prayers. This Litany includes the Salutation in the content, yet it is focused on her Son and her intercessions for us to Him.] Colum cille composed this.

O Mary, kind gentle maid, give help to us;
O casket of the Lord's body, O shrine of mysteries!

O queen of all who reign, O holy virgin maid,
Pray for us that through thee our wretched transgression may be forgiven.

O compassion, O forgiving one, with the grace of the pure Spirit,
Entreat with us the true-judging King, Thy fair fragrant child.

O branch of the plant of Jesse, in the beauteous hazel wood,
Pray for me that I may have forgiveness of my foul guilt.

O Mary, great beauteous diadem, who didst free our race;
O Light most beauteous, O Garden of Kings.

O lustrous one, O shining one, with deed of white chastity,
O fair bright Ark of gold, O holy birth from heaven.

O Mother of righteousness, who didst excel all,
Pray with me thy First-born to save me at the Judgment.

O victorious, long-descended, host-attended, strong,
Entreat with us the mighty Christ, thy Father and thy Son.

O glorious star elect, O bush in bloom,
O strong choice torch, O sun that warmest all,

O ladder of the great fence whereby each holy one mounts,
Mayest thou be our protection towards the glorious palace.

O city fair and fragrant, thee the King did choose;
The great guest was in thy bosom for thrice three months.

O royal door elect, through which came into the body,
The shining choice Sun, Jesus, Son of the living God.

For the sake of the fair birth which was conceived in thy womb,
For the sake of the Only-begotten who is high king in every place;

For the sake of His Cross, which is above every cross,
For the sake of His Burial, who was buried in the rock;

For the sake of His Resurrection who arose before all,
For the sake of the holy household *[in the Age to come]* from every place to judgment;

Be thou our protection in the Kingdom of fair safety,
That we may go with Jesukin we pray while life lasts.
    O Mary. [Creed and Our Father.]

Litany of Irish Saints I *[Irish pronunciation of names necessary.]*
*[The Abecedarian Hymn, **Altus Prosator**, is used on All Saints Day, but this is a late Litany of Irish Saints. Parts one and two together tell of Irish Saints and ask for intercession in time of sickness. The Roman requirement for clergy to be celibate is late; St. Patrick Consecrated a married Bishop, following the Apostolic Canons.]*

Seven hundred and seventeen holy bishops of the people of the grace of the Lord in Corcach Mór with Bairre and Nessan, whose names are written in heaven,
> All of these I call to my aid.

Seven fifties of holy bishops with three hundred priests, whom Patrick ordained, with three hundred alphabets (which he wrote) when consecrating churches *, whereof was said:
> Seven fifties of holy reverend bishops
>   Did the venerable one ordain,
> With three hundred virgin priests
>   On whom he conferred orders.
>
> Three hundred alphabets he wrote,
>   Sweet was the good fortune of his hands,
> Three hundred fair churches he left,
>   He raised them from the ground.
> All of these I call to my aid.

> * *[An "abecedarian hymn," each letter of the alphabet beginning a verse, was used to consecrate churches. See the notes on abecedarian hymns, and the "Altus Prosator" by Colum cille.]*

Three fifties of holy bishops in Ailén arda Nemid;
> All of these I call to my aid.

Seven fifties of holy bishops, seven fifties of priests, seven fifties of deacons, seven fifties of subdeacons, seven fifties of exorcists, seven fifties of lectors, seven fifties of door-keepers, with all holy monks (endowed) with the grace of God at Loch Irci in the borders of Muscraige and Ui Eachach Cruada, as is said:
> The commemoration of Loch Irci
>   Wherein is a little bell melodious;
> many as leaves on branches,
>   Are the Saints that are therein.
> All of these I call to my aid.

Forty Saints in Glenn da Loch with Coemgen, noble priest; with Mochoe of Aired; with Maelanfis; Mochua of Cluain Dolcain; Morioc of Inis bó finne; Affinus (a Frank) priest; Cellach, a Saxon and archdeacon; Dagan (of Inber Daile); Moshenoc (of Mugna); Mochonoc (of Gailinne); Moshinu (of Glenn Munare); Mobai (mac hua Allae); Rufin (an anchorite); Mogoroc (of Dergne); Silan (a bishop); Darchell (an abbot); Molibba (son of Araide); Guaire (son of Dall); Glunsalach (of Slíab Fuait); Murdebur (brother of Caeman) sage and scribe; Corconutan (brother of Murdebur); Aedan (brother of Caeman) son of Congnad; Lochan of Cell Manach Escrach; and Enna; Petran (of Cell Lainne), and Menoc, etc.
> All of these I call to my aid.

Twenty-seven holy bishops in Cell Manach Escrach with Lochan and Enna;
> All of these I call to my aid.

Ten thousands and nine score hundreds (28,000) of priests in Cluain Mór with Maedoc and Mac ind Eicis (*i.e.* son of the poet);
> All of these I call to my aid.

Three thousands and three hundreds with Gerald the bishop and fifty saints of Luigne of Connaught who occupied Mag Eo of the Saxons;
> All of these I call to my aid.

Seventeen holy bishops in Cell Ailech of the Úi Echach; two holy bishops in Daurthech of the Úi Briuin Cualann; seven pilgrims of Imlech Mór;
> All of these I call to my aid.

Three fifties of holy bishops and twelve pilgrims with Sinchell the younger, the priest; and with Sinchell the elder, the bishop, and twelve bishops who occupy Cell Achid of Drummfota among the Úi Falge;
> All of these I call to my aid.

These are the names of the bishops at Cell Achid: Budoci (three), Conoci (three), Morgini (three), Uedgoni (six), Beuani (six), Bibi (six), Glomali (nine), Erconcini (nine), Grucinni (nine), Uennoci (twelve) Contumani (twelve) Anoci (twelve).

The Senchilli (were) Britons from Britain, the Cerrui from Armenia.

Litany of Irish Saints II *[Continued from part I.]*

Thrice fifty coracles of Roman pilgrims who landed in Erin with Ele, with Notal, with Neman the venerable, with Corconutain;
> Through Jesus [Christ, Thy Son our Lord, Who reigneth with Thee and the Holy Spirit, throughout all ages of ages.]

Three thousand anchorites who assembled with Mumu for one quest with Bishop Ibar, to whom the angels of God brought the great feast which St. Brigit made to Jesus in her heart;
> Through Jesus [Christ, Thy Son our Lord, Who reigneth with Thee and the Holy Spirit, throughout all ages of ages.]

Thrice fifty men or orders, true royal heroes each one of them, of the Gaels, who went on pilgrimage in one company with Abban Mac hÚi Chormaic;
> Through Jesus [Christ, Thy Son our Lord, Who reigneth with Thee and the Holy Spirit, throughout all ages of ages.]

Thrice fifty other pilgrims who went with Abban to Erin of men of Rome and Letha;
> Through Jesus [Christ, Thy Son our Lord, Who reigneth with Thee and the Holy Spirit, throughout all ages of ages.]

Seven hundred true monks who were hidden in Rathen before Mochuta went on his course of exile to Lesmór;
> Through Jesus [Christ, Thy Son our Lord, Who reigneth with Thee and the Holy Spirit, throughout all ages of ages.]

Eight hundred men who occupied Lesmór with Mochuta, each third one of them a man of the grace of God;
> Through Jesus [Christ, Thy Son our Lord, Who reigneth with Thee and the Holy Spirit, throughout all ages of ages.]

Thrice fifty true monks under the yoke of Bishop Ibar;
> Through Jesus [Christ, Thy Son our Lord, Who reigneth with Thee and the Holy Spirit, throughout all ages of ages.]

The monks of Fintan Mac Úi Echach; they fed on nothing but herbs of the earth and water. There is not room to enumerate them because of their multitude. Eight Fintans among them;

> Through Jesus [Christ, Thy Son our Lord, Who reigneth with Thee and the Holy Spirit, throughout all ages of ages.]

Four thousand monks with the grace of God under the yoke of Comgall of Benchor; *

> Through Jesus [Christ, Thy Son our Lord, Who reigneth with Thee and the Holy Spirit, throughout all ages of ages.]
>
> *[Benchor is also called Bangor.]*

Thrice fifty true martyrs under the yoke of Munnu son of Tulchan, on whom no man may be buried till doom;

> Through Jesus [Christ, Thy Son our Lord, Who reigneth with Thee and the Holy Spirit, throughout all ages of ages.]

Thrice fifty true pilgrims across the sea with Buite the bishop, and ten holy virgins with the grace of God;

> Through Jesus [Christ, Thy Son our Lord, Who reigneth with Thee and the Holy Spirit, throughout all ages of ages.]

The twelve pilgrims who went with Maedoc of Ferns across the sea;

> Through Jesus [Christ, Thy Son our Lord, Who reigneth with Thee and the Holy Spirit, throughout all ages of ages.]

Twelve youths who went to heaven with Molasse without sickness, the reward of their obedience;

> Through Jesus [Christ, Thy Son our Lord, Who reigneth with Thee and the Holy Spirit, throughout all ages of ages.]

Twelve youths who went with Columcille on pilgrimage to Alba;

> Through Jesus [Christ, Thy Son our Lord, Who reigneth with Thee and the Holy Spirit, throughout all ages of ages.]

The twelve pilgrims of whom Brendan found one man alive in the Cat's Island;

> Through Jesus [Christ, Thy Son our Lord, Who reigneth with Thee and the Holy Spirit, throughout all ages of ages.]

Three score men who went with Brendan to seek the land of promise;*

> Through Jesus [Christ, Thy Son our Lord, Who reigneth with Thee and the Holy Spirit, throughout all ages of ages.]
>
> *[Sites in North America show Irish Ogham alphabet, some pre-Christian, some with Christian prayers.]*

Thrice fifty true monks with the grace of God in Daire Connaid;

> Through Jesus [Christ, Thy Son our Lord, Who reigneth with Thee and the Holy Spirit, throughout all ages of ages.]

Four and twenty men of Munster who went with Ailbe on the ocean to revisit the land of promise, who are there alive till doom;

> Through Jesus [Christ, Thy Son our Lord, Who reigneth with Thee and the Holy Spirit, throughout all ages of ages.]

The anchorite whom Brendan found before him in the land of promise, with all the saints who fell in all the islands of the ocean (*i.e.,* the household of Patrick);

> Through Jesus [Christ, Thy Son our Lord, Who reigneth with Thee and the Holy Spirit, throughout all ages of ages.]

Colman Find (the white) with twelve men in Martra Corthea;

> Through Jesus [Christ, Thy Son our Lord, Who reigneth with Thee and the Holy Spirit, throughout all ages of ages.]

The Romans in Achad Galmae (in Úi Echach); the Romans in Letair Erca; the Romani and Cairrsech daughter of Brocan in Cell Achid Dallrach; Cuan the Roman in his church;

      Through Jesus [Christ, Thy Son our Lord, Who reigneth with
      Thee and the Holy Spirit, throughout all ages of ages.]
 The innocent boys in Cell Ailche, i.e. thrice fifty lads;
      Through Jesus [Christ, Thy Son our Lord, Who reigneth with
      Thee and the Holy Spirit, throughout all ages of ages.]
 Alfinus, the holy pilgrim, and Mochonoc, and Mochasco, and Anfegen with all the Saints in Tech na Commairgi;
      Through Jesus [Christ, Thy Son our Lord, Who reigneth with
      Thee and the Holy Spirit, throughout all ages of ages.]
 The Romans in Cluain Cain Cumni, the pilgrim in Cluain cain Mór;
      Through Jesus [Christ, Thy Son our Lord, Who reigneth with
      Thee and the Holy Spirit, throughout all ages of ages.]
 The Romans with Aedan in Cluain Dartada;
      Through Jesus [Christ, Thy Son our Lord, Who reigneth with
      Thee and the Holy Spirit, throughout all ages of ages.]
 The twelve Dogheads * with the two Sinchells in Cell Achid; the dogheaded ones with Manchan of Liath Mór,
      Through Jesus [Christ, Thy Son our Lord, Who reigneth with
      Thee and the Holy Spirit, throughout all ages of ages.]

      *[Doghead: in Greek "Reprobus" was the name of St. Christopher the Canaanite before Baptism, still an affectionate term for him in the East, referring to his ugliness, and a Latin play on the name of his country. There were probably twelve monks named Christopher in Cell Achid. St. Christopher, even though martyred in Lycia, was popular in Ireland, and Christopher is a popular Irish name.]

 Seven monks of Egypt in Disert Uilaig;
      Through Jesus [Christ, Thy Son our Lord, Who reigneth with
      Thee and the Holy Spirit, throughout all ages of ages.]
 The pilgrim with Mochua son of Luscu in Domnach Resen;
      Through Jesus [Christ, Thy Son our Lord, Who reigneth with
      Thee and the Holy Spirit, throughout all ages of ages.]
 The pilgrim in Belach Forcitail;
      Through Jesus [Christ, Thy Son our Lord, Who reigneth with
      Thee and the Holy Spirit, throughout all ages of ages.]
 The pilgrim in Cuil Ochtair;
      Through Jesus [Christ, Thy Son our Lord, Who reigneth with
      Thee and the Holy Spirit, throughout all ages of ages.]
 The foreigners in Saillide; the foreigners in Mag Salach;
      Through Jesus [Christ, Thy Son our Lord, Who reigneth with
      Thee and the Holy Spirit, throughout all ages of ages.]
 The foreigners in Achad Ginain;
      Through Jesus [Christ, Thy Son our Lord, Who reigneth with
      Thee and the Holy Spirit, throughout all ages of ages.]
 The Saxons in Rigair;
      Through Jesus [Christ, Thy Son our Lord, Who reigneth with
      Thee and the Holy Spirit, throughout all ages of ages.]
 The Saxons in Cluain Mucceda;
      Through Jesus [Christ, Thy Son our Lord, Who reigneth with
      Thee and the Holy Spirit, throughout all ages of ages.]
 The pilgrim in Inis Puinc;
      Through Jesus [Christ, Thy Son our Lord, Who reigneth with
      Thee and the Holy Spirit, throughout all ages of ages.]

The twelve pilgrims in Lethglas Mór;
> Through Jesus [Christ, Thy Son our Lord, Who reigneth with Thee and the Holy Spirit, throughout all ages of ages.]

The twelve men of the household of Finnia in Ard Brendomnaig;
> Through Jesus [Christ, Thy Son our Lord, Who reigneth with Thee and the Holy Spirit, throughout all ages of ages.]

Nine times fifty monks under the yoke of Mochoe of Noendruim;
> Through Jesus [Christ, Thy Son our Lord, Who reigneth with Thee and the Holy Spirit, throughout all ages of ages.]

Fifty men of the Britons with the son of Moinan in Land Léri;
> Through Jesus [Christ, Thy Son our Lord, Who reigneth with Thee and the Holy Spirit, throughout all ages of ages.]

Five pilgrim men in Suide Chail;
> Through Jesus [Christ, Thy Son our Lord, Who reigneth with Thee and the Holy Spirit, throughout all ages of ages.]

Thrice fifty pilgrims in Gair meic Moga;
> Through Jesus [Christ, Thy Son our Lord, Who reigneth with Thee and the Holy Spirit, throughout all ages of ages.]

Thrice fifty disciples with Manchan the Master;
> Through Jesus [Christ, Thy Son our Lord, Who reigneth with Thee and the Holy Spirit, throughout all ages of ages.]

Twelve men who went with Ailbe to death;
> Through Jesus [Christ, Thy Son our Lord, Who reigneth with Thee and the Holy Spirit, throughout all ages of ages.]

The three Úi Corras with their seven;
> Through Jesus [Christ, Thy Son our Lord, Who reigneth with Thee and the Holy Spirit, throughout all ages of ages.]

Twelve men with Morioc (i.e. Mac hÚi Laegde) across the sea;
> Through Jesus [Christ, Thy Son our Lord, Who reigneth with Thee and the Holy Spirit, throughout all ages of ages.]

The twelve boys in Daire Raibne;
> Through Jesus [Christ, Thy Son our Lord, Who reigneth with Thee and the Holy Spirit, throughout all ages of ages.]

The fifteen men who went with Ciaran of Saigir;
> Through Jesus [Christ, Thy Son our Lord, Who reigneth with Thee and the Holy Spirit, throughout all ages of ages.]

The folk that went with Patrick to Sliab Arnchin;
> Through Jesus [Christ, Thy Son our Lord, Who reigneth with Thee and the Holy Spirit, throughout all ages of ages.]

[Fifty-four men who went to martyrdom with Donnan of Egg to death;
> Through Jesus [Christ, Thy Son our Lord, Who reigneth with Thee and the Holy Spirit, throughout all ages of ages.]

Seven holy bishops of Druimm Urchailli; seven holy bishops of Cell Derc Daim; seven holy bishops of Tulach na nEpscop; seven holy bishops of Domnach Eochailli; seven holy bishops of Tulach Olcain; seven holy bishops in Dart;
> Through Jesus [Christ, Thy Son our Lord, Who reigneth with Thee and the Holy Spirit, throughout all ages of ages.]

Seven holy bishops of Cell Giallain; seven holy bishops of Miliue Fiaich;
> Through Jesus [Christ, Thy Son our Lord, Who reigneth with Thee and the Holy Spirit, throughout all ages of ages.]

Seven holy bishops of Mag Bolg; seven holy bishops of Mag Brechmaigi; seven holy bishops of Druimm Duin;
> Through Jesus [Christ, Thy Son our Lord, Who reigneth with Thee and the Holy Spirit, throughout all ages of ages.]

Seven holy bishops of Druimm Airbelaig; seven holy bishops of Raith Cungi; seven holy bishops in Dairi;

>Through Jesus [Christ, Thy Son our Lord, Who reigneth with Thee and the Holy Spirit, throughout all ages of ages.]

Seven holy bishops in Imlecha;

>Through Jesus [Christ, Thy Son our Lord, Who reigneth with Thee and the Holy Spirit, throughout all ages of ages.]

Seven holy bishops in Tamnacha;

>Through Jesus [Christ, Thy Son our Lord, Who reigneth with Thee and the Holy Spirit, throughout all ages of ages.]

Seven holy bishops of Domnach Ailmaigi; seven holy bishops of Domnach Iarlainni;

>Through Jesus [Christ, Thy Son our Lord, Who reigneth with Thee and the Holy Spirit, throughout all ages of ages.]

Seven holy bishops of Domnach Calliraigi; seven holy bishops of Domnach Lethan; seven holy bishops of Domnach Lini; seven holy bishops of Domnach Mor Chuti; seven holy bishops of Domnach Maigi Luadat; seven holy bishops of Domnach Aband Lifi;

>Through Jesus [Christ, Thy Son our Lord, Who reigneth with Thee and the Holy Spirit, throughout all ages of ages.]

Seven holy bishops of Domnach Mór Maigi Coba; seven holy bishops of Domnach Mór Damairni; seven holy bishops of Domnach Mór Findmaige; seven holy bishops of Domnach Mór Culae; seven holy bishops of Domnach Mór Alaith; seven holy bishops of Domnach Mór Tuammae; seven holy bishops of Domnach Mór Phile,

>Through Jesus [Christ, Thy Son our Lord, Who reigneth with Thee and the Holy Spirit, throughout all ages of ages.]

Seven holy bishops of Druimm Lethind; seven holy bishops of Druimm Airmedaig; seven holy bishops of Raith na nEpscop; seven holy bishops of Domnach Mór Echraid;

>Through Jesus [Christ, Thy Son our Lord, Who reigneth with Thee and the Holy Spirit, throughout all ages of ages.]

Seven holy bishops of Cluain Domail with Aedán; seven holy bishops of Cluain Eithne; seven holy bishops of Cluain Bainb; seven holy bishops of Cluain Airthir;

>Through Jesus [Christ, Thy Son our Lord, Who reigneth with Thee and the Holy Spirit, throughout all ages of ages.]

Seven holy bishops of Rigdond,

>Through Jesus [Christ, Thy Son our Lord, Who reigneth with Thee and the Holy Spirit, throughout all ages of ages.]

Seven holy bishops of Domnach Fairne; seven holy bishops of Domnach Ascaid; seven holy bishops of Domnach Fothirbe; seven holy bishops of Domnach Tamnaigi Buaidche; seven holy bishops of Tamnach Fiachrach;

>Through Jesus [Christ, Thy Son our Lord, Who reigneth with Thee and the Holy Spirit, throughout all ages of ages.]

Seven holy bishops of Coine; seven holy bishops of Cell Froich; seven holy bishops of Druimm Alad; seven holy bishops of Tuaimm Fobair; seven holy bishops of Cell Tine; seven holy bishops of Disert na nEpscop; seven holy bishops of Raith Baruu;

>Through Jesus [Christ, Thy Son our Lord, Who reigneth with Thee and the Holy Spirit, throughout all ages of ages.]

Seven holy bishops of Magh Itha; seven holy bishops of Dún Gaimin; seven holy bishops of Fothairbe Mór; seven holy bishops of Domnach Cule; seven holy bishops in Echaired; seven holy bishops in Troscad; seven holy bishops of Coilbda;

>Through Jesus [Christ, Thy Son our Lord, Who reigneth with Thee and the Holy Spirit, throughout all ages of ages.]

Seven holy bishops of Druimm Salaind; seven holy bishops of Cell Tuaiti; seven holy bishops of Domnach Mór, Maige Femin; seven holy bishops of Druimm Airthir;

seven holy bishops of Druimm Lias; seven holy bishops of Cluain Cae; seven holy bishops of Cluain Find[chaill]; seven holy bishops of Druimm Aiti;
> Through Jesus [Christ, Thy Son our Lord, Who reigneth with Thee and the Holy Spirit, throughout all ages of ages.]

Seven holy bishops of Cell Cuilind; seven holy bishops of Cell Belota; seven holy bishops of Coindera; seven holy bishops of hI (Iona); seven holy bishops of Cuil Carech;
> Through Jesus [Christ, Thy Son our Lord, Who reigneth with Thee and the Holy Spirit, throughout all ages of ages.]

Seven holy bishops of Domnach Mór Áine; seven holy bishops of Domnach Maige Fane; seven holy bishops of Domnach Mór Argarui; seven holy bishops of Domnach Mór Drothir Dremna; seven holy bishops of Domnach Mór Santlóir; seven holy bishops of Domnach Mór Assi; seven holy bishops of Domnach Dromma Cethig;
> Through Jesus [Christ, Thy Son our Lord, Who reigneth with Thee and the Holy Spirit, throughout all ages of ages.]

Seven holy bishops in Raith Scothgan; seven holy bishops of Bordgal; seven holy bishops of Cluain Muccada; seven holy bishops of Cluain Cain;
> Through Jesus [Christ, Thy Son our Lord, Who reigneth with Thee and the Holy Spirit, throughout all ages of ages.]

Seven holy bishops of Cell Inbir; seven holy bishops of Cell in Chluana; seven holy bishops of Cell Fini; seven holy bishops of Cathir Suibni; seven holy bishops of Ard-Chluain; seven holy bishops of Daire;
> Through Jesus [Christ, Thy Son our Lord, Who reigneth with Thee and the Holy Spirit, throughout all ages of ages.]

Seven holy bishops of Domnach na nEpscop; seven holy bishops of Tech Lonain; seven holy bishops in Raith Cind Slebi; seven holy bishops of Achad Ualind; seven holy bishops of Achad Nitt; seven holy bishops of Ross Roichbi;
> Through Jesus [Christ, Thy Son our Lord, Who reigneth with Thee and the Holy Spirit, throughout all ages of ages.]

Seven holy bishops of Domnach Mór Direthir; seven holy bishops in Etargabail; seven holy bishops of Tech Silain; seven holy bishops in Glenn Moronóc; seven holy bishops of Tír Cóicfhir;
> Through Jesus [Christ, Thy Son our Lord, Who reigneth with Thee and the Holy Spirit, throughout all ages of ages.]

Seven holy bishops in Domnach Nachain; seven holy bishops of Domnach Taulche; seven holy bishops of Domnach Ualand; seven holy bishops of Domnach Úa Fithis; seven holy bishops of Domnach Erobi; seven holy bishops of Domnach Bernsa; seven holy bishops of Sen-Domnach;
> Through Jesus [Christ, Thy Son our Lord, Who reigneth with Thee and the Holy Spirit, throughout all ages of ages.]

Seven holy bishops of Cell Forlochta; seven holy bishops of Cell Cunid; seven holy bishops of Cell Culi; seven holy bishops of Cell Onchon; seven holy bishops of Cell Aedloga; seven holy bishops of Cell Raisse; seven holy bishops of Cell Úa Carthind;
> Through Jesus [Christ, Thy Son our Lord, Who reigneth with Thee and the Holy Spirit, throughout all ages of ages.]

Seven holy bishops in Uthmana; seven holy bishops in Ucht Foraid, seven holy bishops of Raith meic Mella; seven holy bishops of Achad Glinni; seven holy bishops of Enach Duin; seven holy bishops of Tuaimm da Ualand;
> Through Jesus [Christ, Thy Son our Lord, Who reigneth with Thee and the Holy Spirit, throughout all ages of ages.]

Seven holy bishops of Tulach Labair; seven holy bishops of Tulach Craebain; seven holy bishops of Druimm meic Thail; seven holy bishops of Cúil Ferthigi; seven holy bishops of Ardachad Brechmaige;
> Through Jesus [Christ, Thy Son our Lord, Who reigneth with Thee and the Holy Spirit, throughout all ages of ages.]

Seven holy bishops of Raith Epscoip Comraide; seven holy bishops of Raith Fiachrach; seven holy bishops of Domnach Achaid Shetna;
> Through Jesus [Christ, Thy Son our Lord, Who reigneth with Thee and the Holy Spirit, throughout all ages of ages.]

Seven holy bishops of Cluain Emain; seven holy bishops of Cluain Airthir; seven holy bishops of Cluain Daim; seven holy bishops of Cluain Bini; seven holy bishops of Cluain Rathe; seven holy bishops of Cluain Talatho;
> Through Jesus [Christ, Thy Son our Lord, Who reigneth with Thee and the Holy Spirit, throughout all ages of ages.]

Seven holy bishops of Tech na Commairge; seven holy bishops in Rúscacha; seven holy bishops of Cell Ard; seven holy bishops of Cell Garbain; seven holy bishops of Findglass;
> Through Jesus [Christ, Thy Son our Lord, Who reigneth with Thee and the Holy Spirit, throughout all ages of ages.]

Seven holy bishops of Tech Áine; seven holy bishops of Cell Roiss; seven holy bishops of Cell Iae; seven holy bishops of Cluain Fota;
> Through Jesus [Christ, Thy Son our Lord, Who reigneth with Thee and the Holy Spirit, throughout all ages of ages.]

Seven holy bishops of Druimm Druith; seven holy bishops of Brúcas; seven holy bishops of Druimm Craebain; seven holy bishops of Druimm Crema; seven holy bishops of Carraic Mor;
> Through Jesus [Christ, Thy Son our Lord, Who reigneth with Thee and the Holy Spirit, throughout all ages of ages.]

Seven holy bishops of Cell Corbran; seven holy bishops of Cell Bratha; seven holy bishops in Land Lere; seven holy bishops of Uinnes Mór; seven holy bishops of Domnach Cairne;
> Through Jesus [Christ, Thy Son our Lord, Who reigneth with Thee and the Holy Spirit, throughout all ages of ages.]

Three hundred true monks who occupied Lethglenn, and twelve hundred of the servants of God with Molasse and the two Ernans; and Mar[tin] holy bishop of Lethglenn;
> All of these I call [to my aid]. [Amen. Credo et Pater.]

Recite this about the seven bishops: over water against boils, and jaundice, [any plague], and every [other] pestilence. Let the water be applied to the man. [and he heals well and the rest. Finit. Amen. Finit.]*

> *[Not from all sources. No ending is needed, as the last section is not a part of the Litany, but is a commentary on its use, and could be from a later date.]

Litany of the Virgins

[Asking many virgin Saints, the Lord God, and all Saints, for protection.]

I place myself under the protection,
Of Mary the pure Virgin,
Of Brigit, bright and glowing,
Of Cuach of great purity,
Of Moninna and Midnat,
Of Scire, Sinche, and Samchaine,
Of Caite, Cuach, Coemill,
Of Craine, Coipp, and Cocnat,
Of Ness the glorious of Ernaide,
Of Derbfalen (?) and Becnat,
Of Ciar, and Crone, and Caillann,
Of Lassar, Locha and Luaithrenn,
Of Rond, of Ronnat, of Rignach,
Of Sarnat, of Segnat, of Sodelb,

And of the virgins all together (in one place),
    North, South, East, West.
I place myself under the protection,
Of the excellent Trinity,
Of the Prophets, of the true Apostles,
Of the Monks, of the Martyrs,
Of the Widows and the Confessors,
Of the Virgins, of the Faithful,
Of the Saints and the Holy Angels;
To protect me against every ill,
Against demons and evil men,
Against thunder and bad weather,
Against sickness and false lips,
Against cold and hunger,
Against distress and folly,
Against vengeance and dishonor,
Against contempt and despair,
Against misfortune and wandering,
Against the plague of the tempestuous doom,
Against the evil of hell with its many monsters,
    And its multitude of torments.   [Amen. Creed and Our Father.]

Litany of Confession

[Praises God and the Saints, asks for forgiveness, and lists many sins. It is not a substitute for the Sacrament of Confession, but is part of preparation for Sacrament of Confession, and also of self examination.]

I have committed evil in all things in Thy Presence; I know my faults;
O King of Heaven, I have sinned by evil deeds against Thee alone.
Unto Thee I have tried to do what I am able: I recited my errors.
I say, O God, forgive everything I owe,
And let me call upon Thee first, but afterward I will state my crimes.

O Father, O Son, O Holy Spirit,
    Forgive me my sins.
O only-begotten Son of the heavenly Father,
    Forgive.
O one God, O true God, O chief God,
O (God) of one Substance,
O (God) only mighty, in three Persons, truly full of pity,
    Forgive.
O (God) the rewarder, forgiving, loving, pre-eminent, immense, vast, mysterious,
    Forgive.
O (God) above (all) gods,
O King about (all) kings,
O Man above (all) men,
    Forgive.
O World above (all) worlds,
O Power above (all) powers,
O Love above (all) loves,
O Cause above (all) causes,
O Fortress above (all) fortresses,
O Angel above (all) angels,
    Forgive.

O Archdeacon of heaven and earth,
                Forgive.
O High-priest of all creation,
O Archbishop of the seven heavens,
                Forgive.
O first Priest, O chief Priest,
O true Priest, O true Physician, O true Prophet, O true Friend,
                Forgive.
O only Sustainer of the threefold mansion,
O only Life of all created things,
O only Light of the seven heavens,
                Forgive.
O Subject of the Scriptures' meditation,
O Object of the chief prophets' search,
O Marrow of true wisdom,
O Father of true life,
O Voice of the congregation,
                Forgive.
O Abel, first martyr,
O Noah of the sacred ark,
O faithful Abraham,
O meek and gentle Moses,
O Aaron, first priest,
O noble David,
O mystic Solomon,
O corner (stone) of the Old Testament,
O pitiful Heart,
O honored Foster-father,
O Piercing of the heavy ground,
O blazing lamp,
O Jesu of Nazareth,
O Son of the sister,
O righteous brother,
                Forgive.

            De Confesione Scelerum. [About Confession of Evil Deeds.]
Come to help me, for the multitude of my inveterate sins have made dense my too guilty heart;

They have bent me, perverted me, have blinded me, have twisted me and withered me;

They have clung to me, have pained me, have moved me, have filled me;

They have humbled me, exhausted me, they have subdued me, possessed me, cast me down;

They have befooled me, drowned me, deceived me, and troubled me;

They have torn me, and chased me;

They have bound me, have ravaged me, have crucified me, rebuked me, sold me, searched me, mocked me;

They have maddened me, bewitched me, betrayed me, delayed me, killed me;
Forgive.

            Oratio. [Prayer.]
And according to the multitude of Thy mercies, blot out my iniquity.
O starry Sun,
O guiding Light,
O House of the planets,
O fiery wondrous Comet.   *[Literally. "hair," which people with better eyesight saw in comets.]*

O fruitful, billowy, fiery Sea,
>Forgive.

O fiery Glow,
O fiery Flame of doom,
>Forgive.

O holy Narrator, holy Scholar,
O full of holy grace, of holy strength,
O overflowing, loving, silent one,
O liberal thunderous bestower,
O rock-like warrior of hundred hosts;
O fair crowned one, victorious, skilled in battle,
>Forgive.

>De Confessione Oratio. [Prayer of Confession.]

For Thy Name's sake, forgive me my sins.
>Many and vast are my sins in their mass, through my heart and round about it like a net or a breast-plate;

>O King, they cannot be numbered;
>Despoil me of them, O God;
>Break, smite, and war against them;
>Ravage, bend, and wither them;
>Take away, repel, destroy them;
>Arise, scatter, defeat them;
>See, repress, waste them;
>Destroy, summon, starve them;
>Prostrate, burn, mangle them;
>Kill, slay and ruin them;
>Torture, divide, and purify them;
>Tear, expel, and raze them;
>Remove, scatter, and cleave them;
>Subdue, exhaust, and lay them low.

>Heavy then and bitter is
>The subdual and the piercing;
>The bond and the fetter;
>The confusion and the maddening;
>The disturbance and the raging;
>which the multitude of my sins brings upon me.
>By every disease Thou didst help;
>By every arm Thou didst comfort;
>By Thy conception in the womb of the Virgin Mary;
>By Thy birth in Bethlehem of Judea;
>By Thy pierced hands;
>By Thy royal Star;
>>Forgive.

>By the womb in which Thou wert;
>By the paps which Thou didst suck;
>>Forgive.

>By the breast which nurtured Thee;
>By every lip which kissed Thee;
>By every hand which touched Thee;
>By every foot which carried Thee;

By every ear which heard Thee;
By every eye which saw Thee;
By every heart which believed Thee;
> Forgive.

By Thy seven gifts;
By Thy seven orders;
By Thy seven heavens;
By Thy coming to earth into the womb of the Virgin Mary;
By Thy seven times with their saints;
> Forgive.

By Thy patience, by Thy lowliness;
By Thy humility, by Thy loftiness;
By Thy gentleness, by Thy dignity;
By Thy devotion, by Thy peacefulness;
By Thy uniqueness, by Thy nobleness;
By Thy holiness,
> Forgive.

By the arrest of Thee and the seizing;
By the smiting and the mocking;
By Thine acts,
> Forgive.

By the conspiracy, the crucifying, and the mangling;
> Forgive.

By Thy soul which harried hell, which filled heaven;
> Forgive.

By every soul Thou broughtest thence;
By Thy Resurrection from the dead;
> Forgive.

By Thine Ascension into heaven;
> Forgive.

By the Holy Ghost which came from heaven upon the Apostles,
> Forgive.

By every heart, by every body;
By every flesh, by every lip, by every eye;
By every creature whereon the Holy Spirit came, from the beginning of the world to the end;
By Thy coming again in the day of doom; (Grant) that I may be righteous and perfect, without great dread on me of hell or doom, without soreness or bitterness on Thy part towards me, O Lord;
For my sins are blazing through me and around me, at me and towards me, above me and below me.
Alas, Alas, Alas, forgive me, O God.

Every sin which I did, and took pleasure in doing;
Every sin which I did under compulsion, or not under compulsion;
> Forgive.

Every sin which I sought after, or did not seek after;
> Forgive.

Every evil that I did to any one, or that any one did to me;
> Forgive.

Every evil wherein any one took part, or did not take part with me;
> Forgive.

Every thing which I sought for, or did not seek for; found, or did not find;
> Forgive me.

Every one to whom I did good unjustly, or evil justly;
> Forgive.

Every good which I did, and marred; every evil which I did, and did not make good;
> Forgive.

Every provocation which I gave to God or man;
> Forgive me.

Every sitting down, every standing up; every movement, every stillness; every sleep, every sleeplessness; every forgetfulness, every remembrance; every carelessness, every carefulness; every longing, every desire, every lust; every thought, every love, every hate, which is, which was, which shall be mine, to my life's end;
> Forgive me.

Every will, every displeasure which I have harbored against God or man;
> Forgive me.

Every ill that I did, every good that I omitted, every sin within sin, every ill within good, every good within ill that I did;
> Forgive me for them. Amen.

From ears, from hands, from lips, from eyes; from heart, from sense; from limbs, from joints, from bowels; from intention, from desire; from secrecy, from concealment, from openness; from knowledge, from ignorance; from longing, from absence of longing; from inducement, from absence of inducement; from high, from low, from union, from disunion;

From little to great; from something to nothing; from youth to old age; from baptism to death;
> Forgive me, O God;

O Father, Son, and Holy Spirit, in spite of my sins.

O true God, I have sinned against Thee alone; forgive, forgive, forgive. Amen.

[Ending: Creed and the Our Father: the full text of the Creed and Our Father is at the end of this book.]

Notes on the Missal and Breviary
A Discussion of the Symbolism of the Mass
Treatise in the Original Manuscript of the Lorrha Missal

[This Treatise has been incorporated into the text of the Mass, to help in meditation and prayer. These notes are over a thousand years old, in old script, in the back of the Missal. The entire Treatise is in folios 65v continued through 67v.]

The Altar is the image of the inflicted persecution. The Chalice is the image of the Church which has been set and built upon the persecution of the Prophets and of others.

Water is first put into the Chalice while this is chanted: "I pray Thee, O Father; I ask intercession of Thee, O Son; I appeal to Thee, O Holy Spirit." This is an image of the People which are "poured into" the Church.

The setting of the Host upon the Altar is the His Conception. As this is done "Jesus Christ, Alpha and Omega. This is the First and the Last" is chanted. This is an image of Christ's Body which has been set in the linen sheet of Mary's womb.

Wine is then added to the water in the Chalice. this is Christ's Godhead with His humanity comes upon the People at the time of His Conception. While the Wine is poured "May the Father remit, may the Son pardon, may the Holy Spirit have mercy." is chanted.

All the text of the Mass which follows the preparation, the Introductory Collect, the fixed prayers and the additional Collects up to the Epistle and the Gradual is an image of the establishment of the Knowledge of Christ in the law of Nature through the Members of His Body and by His own deeds.

However, the portion of the Mass from the Epistle and Gradual to the half-uncovering of the Chalice is a recounting of the law Letter which prophesies Christ, but what is prefigured is not yet known.

The Gospel, Alleluia and prayers chanted from the half-uncovering of the Host and the Chalice until the prayer "May these gifts" is a recounting of the Law of the Prophets which specifically foretold Christ, but the significance of the Prophecy is unknown until His Incarnation.

The elevation of the Chalice, after the full uncovering during the prayer "May these gifts" is the commemoration of Christ's Birth and of His Glory through the signs and miracles.

When the prayer "Who, the day before He suffered, took Bread...." begins the Celebrant bows three time in repentance of his sins. He offers the Oblations to God and while this is done, the people kneel or prostrate, and there must be no other voice lest is disturb the priest for his mind must not separate from God while he chants this lesson. For this reason, its name is the Most Dangerous Prayer.

Later when the Celebrant and ministers step three steps backwards and three steps forward is the three ways in which everyone sins: in word, in thought, in deed. These are also the three means by which one is renovated and by which one is moved to Christ's Body.

The examination of the Chalice and Host and the effort with which the Celebrant attempts to break it is an image of the rejection and punches and lashings and the Arrest of Christ. The Host on the Paten is Christ's Flesh upon the tree of the Cross.

The Fraction of the Host upon the Paten is the breaking of Christ's Body with nails on the Cross.

The reunion of the two halves after the Fraction is the affirmation of the wholeness of Christ's Body after His Resurrection.

The submersion of the two halves in the Blood are an affirmation that at His Crucifixion, Christ's Body was covered in His Blood.

The Particle that is cut from the Bottom of the half which is on the priest's left hand is the wounding with the Lance in the Armpit of the right side; for Christ was facing Westward as He hung upon the Cross: Facing the City, and Longinus faced Eastward so what was left to Christ was right to him.

There are seven kind of Confraction, that is five Particles of the Daily Host as the image of the five senses of the soul; seven Particles of the Host of Saints and Virgins except the most important ones as the image of the Seven Gifts of the Holy Spirit; eight Particles of the Host of the Holy Martyrs as an image of the octonary New Testament; nine Particles of the Host of a Sunday [and also of the Proper Ferias of Lent] is an image of the nine Households of Heaven and the nine Grades of the Church; eleven Particles of the Host of the Apostles is an image of the incomplete number of the Apostles due to the Sin of Judas; twelve Particles of the Host of the Circumcision and of Holy Thursday are in memory of the complete number of the Apostles; thirteen Particles of the Host of Low Sunday and the Feast of the Ascension, is an image of Christ with His twelve Apostles, it is not usual to distribute from all thirteen Particles.

[The "octonary New Testament" has two meanings: 1) The Eighth Day of Creation; 2) The Eight Fold New Testament according to St. Athanasius:
4 Gospels; Acts and Epistles; Revelation; the Didache: Teaching of the Apostles; Pastor of Hermas. Since the time of this Missal, the last two have been deleted from the Bible.]

Added together, five, seven, eight, nine, eleven, twelve and thirteen come to sixty-five which is the number of Particles of the Host of Easter, Christmas and Pentecost. For all of them are comprised in Christ. All of the Confraction is set upon the Paten in the form of the Cross, and the upper Particle is moved down to the left side as reminder us that "Bowing His head, He gave up the ghost".

The arrangement of the Confraction at Easter and Christmas is: 14 Particles in the upright of the Cross, 14 Particles in the crosspiece, twenty Particles in its circlet: five pieces to each quarter; 16 pieces to the Crosses: 4 to each one. One Particle, for the Celebrant of the Mass is in the middle as the image of the Secrets kept in the heart. The upper part of the shaft of the Cross is for the Bishops, the left portion of the crosspiece is for Priests; the right portion of the crosspiece is to the grades lower than Priest; the lower portion of the stem is to monastics and penitents; the upper left quadrant is for young clerics; the upper right quadrant is to children; the lower left is for those who are truly repentant; the lower right is for those who are married and those who have never before received Communion.

This is what God has declared worthy, that the mind be upon the Symbols of the Mass, and that this be your mind: that portion of the Host which you receive is a portion of Christ from His Cross, and that there may be a Cross in the labor of each in his own life since it is that Cross which unites each one of us to the Crucified Body of Christ. It is not proper to swallow the Particle without having tasted it, just as it is improper to not bring savor into God's Mysteries. It is improper for it to be chewed by the back teeth for such an act symbolizes rumination over God's Mysteries, for it is by such rumination that heresy is increased. It is ended. Amen. Thanks be to God.

Notes on the Lorrha-Stowe Missal also called the Gospel of St. Maelruain
Notes on The Liturgy (Mass)

The Meaning of "Liturgy" and "Eternity"

Liturgy is a direct experience of the Presence of God. The Sacrifice or Offering of the Mass is identical to the Offering our Lord has made for us in His Incarnation, Death, and Resurrection. The term used by the Irish was "Offering," because it is one and the same Sacrifice that Christ asks us to remember always at the Last Supper. The term "Liturgy" means, in Greek, "the work of the people," or the praise and offering of all Christians through offering Holy Communion. The term "Mass" is from the Latin word that means "meal," because the Mass sustains us, giving us spiritual and physical nourishment in Holy Communion. The term "Missa" in Latin also means to send forth. The term "Eucharist" means "Thanksgiving," because it is in Holy Communion that we are thankful to God.

Jesus said, "This is my body" Mt 26:26, Mk 14:22, Lk 22:19, and "this is my blood" Mt 26:28, Mk 14:24, "the new testament in my blood" Lk 22:20, "which shall be shed for many unto remission of sins" Mt. 26:28, Mk 14:24, Lk 22:20. Greek interlinear Bible, Lk 22:19, "this do for my remembrance." ("touto poieite eis tyn emyn anamnysin.") In the Greek language's grammar, this is not a memory of a past thing, but the tense of the verb indicates a continuing, keeping in mind, an eternal reality, eternally present and not past. [Psalm 21:27-28, "shall remember, and shall be converted" is to keep in mind, but in the sense of the previous verse: that "the poor shall eat and shall be filled... their hearts shall live for ever and ever."] On Pascha, we say "Christ IS Risen." not "was," because the Resurrection is not past (Jn 11:25; 2 Tim. 2:18-19). If we do not participate in Christ's Passion and Resurrection, if we do not let Him directly enter our lives as present in time and eternity, even in our walking through daily activities, He has no part in us (Jn 13:8).

We believe these literal and eternal truths (Jn 3:16-21), because how could there be everlasting life if there is no eternity in the midst of time? (Mt 4:17; Mk 1:15; Lk 18:30; Jn 1:18; Jn 14:9; Mt 25:46, Mk 3:29, Jn 4:36, Jn 5:39; Jn 6:54; Jn 6:68; Jn 10:28; Jn 12:25; Jn 17:2-3; Rom 5:21, Rom 6:23, 2 Cor 4:17-18; Heb 9:12-15; 1 John 4:12; 1 John 5:20; Is 57:14-15, 20-21, Wis. 2:23, etc.) Christ, our high Priest, represents eternity in the midst of time for us. A Jewish reference to "eternity in the midst of time," that does not refer to Christ as our High Priest, but the Torah and the Priesthood, still shows a belief that runs through the Old Testament and New Testament in God, eternally present; from Jonathan Sacks, December 1997, chief Rabbi of the Brittish Commonwealth, "The issues never change, and the answers never change. I call this kind of *Torah* by a very ancient name, and that is *"Torat Kohanim"* because the *kohen*, the priest, was the first role model in Jewish history of the enduring structure of *kedusha;* the eternity in the midst of time. *Torah* as *chayei olam* -- eternal life-- in the midst of *chayei sha'ah* -- finite life." When we hear, "This IS my Body," "This IS my Blood," Christ is truly Present in the Eucharist. The term "Orthodox" means "right worship" of this eternal Reality. The term "Catholic" literally means the seat or foundation of truth, which is universal; Christ is the head of the

Church, not a replacement for Christ. The term "Christians" means "little Christs." To believe in the literal and fundamental Bible means to believe in the true Presence of Christ in the Eucharist, and to worship Him truly in Divine Liturgy.

Early Church Services, and the Mass

The Mass was not invented in Ireland. Predecessors of the Stowe-Lorrha Missal:

Early Christians originally participated in the services of the Synagogues and the Temple, notably St. James the Just who continued to preach in the Temple in Jerusalem until the time of his assassination. Synagogue services focused on reading of Scripture and teaching; this was not the "Temple sacrifice;" but prayer which a group of at least ten men could participate in wherever they lived. When the Temple was destroyed by the Romans in 70 A.D., the Synagogue worship survived among those who were scattered. (The "Hours," i.e. Psalms, were also read. See notes on the Hours.)

Among Christians, Agape occurred on nights before the Sabbath (Saturday). This was a communal meal which began with the lighting of lamps, the recitation of Psalms; in Apostolic times Epistles which were sent specifically to a community would be read, in later times these Epistles were replaced by the Epistles which were considered part of the Canon of Scripture (after St. Athanasius); and the reading of the Gospel. These were the meals at issue when the Apostles said that is is not fitting for us to wait tables, and St. Paul observed that some have nothing while others are drunk and gluttonous. To this day the Byzantine Rite celebrates an Agape service on the day of Pascha, because the primary Divine Liturgy of the day is the Vigil of the Resurrection, and in the morning the celebration continues with Hymns and prayers, but not the full Divine Liturgy in that Rite. Although some have called the Agape a "primitive Christian Liturgy," the focus on the Lord's Supper is not in the Agape.

The "Panikida" or lifting up of the blessed "All Holy" bread, essentially the same as the "Benediction" service in the Roman Catholic Church, was instituted in the Apostolic times by the Blessed Virgin Mary, according to Byzantine tradition. The "All Holy" Bread is in the shape of a triangle, representing the All Holy Trinity. In the East, the term "All Holy" and the triangular bread also became associated with the Blessed Virgin Mary as well. While the East tended to use blessed bread for this service instead of Eucharist, in the West a piece of the Eucharist was reserved for this service. (There are arguments about displaying reserved Eucharist this way; Orthodox reserve Eucharist, but do so for "Pre-Sanctified" Liturgies: so that the congregation may be with God, instead of viewing God at a distance. On the other hand, within the Divine Liturgy, there are times when the Eucharist is elevated for a moment, as part of our "keeping in mind" the Offering of God, as long as God is not seen as distant to us. The "Benediction" or "Panikida" has been done since the earliest Church.)

The Sacrifice of the Mass, also called the Lord's Supper, or the Divine Liturgy, is the primary Celebration (or Sacrifice), although it is an entering into the one Sacrifice of our Lord for all time and eternity, and therefore an "unbloody" Sacrifice, not a "re-enactment" or a "repeat" of the Sacrifice, but being there at the same time as Christ. Middle Eastern sources record the Liturgy of Hippolytus, which occur in the post-Apostolic Period. Also the Confession of Justin Martyr records such a Liturgy; so a Mass with full Consecration of the Eucharist has been practiced continuously since the very earliest Church. On Sunday this celebration represents the "Eighth Day of Creation," the Resurrection. (St. Gregory Nazianzus, the Theologian, born 325 or 329, died Jan 25 389, one of only a handful of recognized Theologians by the Eastern Orthodox churches, in his sermon on Pentecost, Oration XLI, part II, seventh volume of the Post-Nicene Fathers, states that although the number seven is a very important number, yet the eighth day of creation is the final day of the Resurrection, so eight becomes a symbol of something higher, an "octave" or the next step above the seven). In some places the Mass also takes place on Thursday which represents the day of the Institution of the Last Supper. The Mass was always accompanied with Psalmody, readings from Epistles and Gospels, homilies, but the center was always upon the real Presence of the Offering of Thanksgiving (the "Eucharist") of Jesus Christ Himself. All else is secondary. The

Sacrifice of the Mass is the same Temple sacrifice made perfect in Christ once for all time, eternally present, as it says in the eighth Hymn from the *Antiphonary of Bangor*, "Sancti Venite," which is sung "When the Clergy Communicates." Therefore, the Temple worship has not only survived the destruction of the Temple, but is fulfilled in Christ's own Body and Blood, Who died and is Risen from the dead.

Dating and history of the Lorrha-Stowe Missal, the Celtic Rite

Existing fragments of the earliest Liturgies are not complete. The Lorrha-Stowe Mass offers the earliest existing Liturgical usage that has complete Propers through the year. The Irish first received a Latin Mass, the "Missa Patricii," through St. Patrick, who had been kidnapped to Ireland where he was a slave as a boy, then escaped to the continent of Europe where he was trained and Ordained, and then Consecrated by Pope Celestius in 432, and given the Pallium to lead the Church in Ireland.

St. Mael Ruain was a devotee of St. Ruadhan (who died in 584). Ruadhan (Ruan) was one of the "twelve Apostles of Ireland," and was trained by Finian of Clonard. Ruadhan's monastery at Lorrha is in north Tipperary. Oengus calls him "Rodan, the lamp of Lorrha" (or Lothra, April 15/28). Ruadhan's famed curse of Tara, invoking all the Saints of Ireland, was not of the kings (there were others after his time at Tara), but of the Druid assemblies which ceased to meet there after the time of the king Diarmuid. The curse was due to the king taking a felon out of the sanctuary of the monastery at Lorrha.

The Lorrha-Stowe, or "Celtic Missal," is a translation from a Latin and Gaelic Missal, reputedly transcribed at Lorrha Monastery, the last commemoration added in the Ninth Century. The "Lorrha Missal" is known as the 'Stowe' Missal due to its acquisition by one of the Dukes of Buckingham for his Stowe Library. It is also known as the "Gospel of Mael Ruain," because it was bound together with the Gospel of St. John. The original is in the Royal Irish Academy, under "Stowe Missal" R.I.A. MS D ii 3: Cat. No. 1238, c. A.D. 792-803, Vellum: 15cm x 12cm (5 5/8" by 4 ½"), 67 leaves (incomplete, missing one "carpet" illuminated page). This "Missal" is more of a "Sacramentary" than a Mass book, because it contains four of the Sacraments bound together.

The form of the Liturgy and Services of Baptism and Unction found here reflect a true Celtic usage dating before 600 AD. It is uncertain how much of this form represents the usage brought to Ireland by St. Patrick in the early Fifth Century. One identifiable post-Patrician change is the late Fifth Century addition of the *Communicantes* of St. Gelasius in the Fourth Century Canon. That addition is the reason the Canon is attributed to him in the Lorrha Missal (*N.B.*: the *Communicantes* here is an earlier form than the modern Tridentine form which includes Leonine comments at the Ascension, and omits a few Feasts). Therefore the earliest possible date of the finalization of the form of the Lorrha Liturgy is the late Fifth Century. The presence in the Lorrha Liturgy of text that was specifically removed by St. Gregory the Great in most of Europe (such as the prayer against idols), sets the latest date of changes to the text at 600 A.D. The absence of the *Agnus Dei* mandated to be included in the Canon in the Roman usage by St. Sergius I in 690 further indicates the absence of Roman influence on the structure of this Missal after 600. Although the list of commemorations continues past that time, to the ninth century, that is not a modification of the structure or wording of prayers, but only an addition of names in a list. There were Irish who used the Lorrha-Stowe Mass through that time. Also, the Irish Propers and Hymns have many parallels with early Byzantine Hymns.

Dr. Bartholomew MacCarthy has demonstrated that the Mass contained within the volume is likely of the 6th century. From the 1913 *Catholic Encyclopedia*: "*The Stowe Missal*, perhaps his most celebrated work, published in the *Transactions of the Royal Irish Academy*, XXVII (1886), 135-268, in which he establishes the date of Moelchaich's recension as about 750 or at least the eighth century [who made an introductory prayer in Baptism], and proves that the so-called Middle Irish corruptions can be paralleled from old Irish MSS., none of which are later than the ninth century; he also separates the earlier portion of the text into a. the original Mass, dating from at least A.D. 500, called *Missa Patricii* in the *Book of Armagh* (A.D. 807), and, later augments and Roman contents." John MacErlean.

The book shrine, the "Cumdach" for the Lorrha Missal is from much later, about 1023-1052, commissioned by Donagh the son of Brian Boru, and it says it is the work of "Dunchad of the family of Cluain."

The Suppression of the Celtic Rite after 1171, the finding of the Missal

In the fifth century, St. Patrick had been taught by monasteries on the continent, but after his time, wars and barbarians in continental Europe reduced literacy there. Irish missionaries to Europe returned the light of literacy they had been given. However, in 1171 the Celtic Liturgy was suppressed by Norman invaders (under king Henry II of England) who acted with Papal support (a writ by Pope Adrian Breakspeare, who happened to be English). After 1172, non-Celtic church leaders rejected the Celtic Rite Liturgy and clergy. They felt the Faith had triumphed over all opposition, and that more pageantry and less instruction in dogma was required. They forgot that the Faithful must be watchful. Cults of idols are a threat to the spiritual health of every member of the Church; whether appearing in the form of false faiths, counterfeit forms of Christianity, or nationalism. This suppression occurred everywhere the faith had been kept alive, in Ireland and also in many missions of Irish Saints and their spiritual descendants on the continent of Europe. These included the monasteries of Luxeuil in France and Bobbio in Italy (founded by St. Columbanus), monasteries in Switzerland (founded by St. Gall), monasteries in Germany (founded by St. Killian), monasteries in the low countries (founded by St. Fursey), and many other Irish missions. (Note: interest in this form of the Liturgy has been continuously maintained in Milan, near Bobbio, because of the similarities of the Irish liturgics to the Ambrosian Rite, and also the power of the Patriarchate of Milan, almost equal to the Pope in Rome. Some other near-Celtic Rites have survived, such as Lyons in France. Books were not burned in the continent of Europe, even though the books were unused.) After 1172, the Irish in Ireland were not allowed to attend their own seminaries. Books were burned in England and Ireland. Other than Milan and Lyons, a complete Liturgy similar to the Celtic Rite was not used Liturgically from 1171 until this translation in 1996.

Some say that the Lorrha-Stowe Missal was found in the ruins of a wall of the O'Kennedy Castle at Lackeen a few miles away from Lorrha about 1735, another account says it had been in Austria in the Irish monastery at Ratisbon and into the possession of an Irish soldier in the Austrian army in 1784: John Grace, and from the Grace family into the possession of the Duke of Buckingham. Eventually it went back to Ireland in the Royal Irish Academy. (Irish served in the Austrian army and also the Russian army at that time, fighting the Turks. Those Irish who had protected all of Europe in that war were given gifts such as great horses, but had their possessions taken when they returned home to Ireland, because it was illegal for an Irishman to have great possessions; so the "donation" by the Grace family seems entirely possible.)

This Liturgy is Approved; the Orthodox Saints are always Saints

The Church is one and continuous, so this Missal is more than an effort at "Liturgical Archeology." Those Saints who used it and Bishops who approved it for many centuries are not dead, but alive in Christ. Their legacy to us should be given at least equal consideration with any prayer or hymn that is considered acceptable for use. We must confess our absolute faith that: just as He is One with the Father and the Holy Spirit, we of the True Church are One, and our Sacrament is One and the same; we are **one** Body of Christ. It is the same Eucharist that was and ever will be celebrated.

St. Basil the Great, who composed the Divine Liturgy of St. Basil (the first "Byzantine" Rite), was accused of innovating new prayers. In his Epistle 207, he says, "But, it is alleged, these practices were not observed in the time of the great Gregory. My rejoinder is that even the Litanies which you now use were not used in his time." The Celtic Rite was not influenced by Arian Liturgies; it is Orthodox, true worship, and does not neglect, hide, or change the truth; it was written before the Great Schism, before the re-writes of Alcuin, before any Carolingian Mass such as the Sarum Rite, before the practice of the mis-named, truly Carolingian, re-written "Gregorian" Rite. There was no need to re-write the Celtic Rite Mass as St. Basil had to do in the East, because the Celtic Rite was the complete and true Mass without heretical influence.

The Mass explains in graphic detail the redemptive acts of the Incarnation of Jesus Christ, His Birth, Death and Resurrection. The writer(s) assumes that those participating in the Mystery of the Eucharist seek to contemplate every detail. The study of the texts of this Liturgy and other offices provide a Catechism of the Faith, and an example of the "right" attitude for Christian worship of Almighty God. This is true even if one is only able to study these texts, but is unable to practice the Celtic Rite, due to unavailability of a church where this Liturgy is being done.

What Theological Problems Were Avoided by the Celtic Rite?

There is no room to list all the reductions of the truth over the centuries (in Greek: heresies). Some of the great Saints, such as the very early St. Irenaeus of Lyons, St. Gregory the Wonderworker (Thaumaturgis), St. Gregory of Nyssa, St. Gregory Nazianzus, St. Basil the Great, wrote treatises against many heresies. The Ecumenical Councils were called to uphold the faith against heresies, and named many of them. The Celtic Rite fights heresies, so a quick review is necessary. Considering that today many of these ideas are popular, prayers against these idols of the mind should not be cut from Liturgics. A review of some of these heresies might seem unnecessary, but such distorted views appear again and again, and it is necessary to guard against such heresies as these.

Heresies pertaining to the Nature of our Lord Jesus Christ and the Holy Trinity, reducing or blaspheming the fullness of Divinity. (Christ has both a divine and human nature and will, fully God and fully man; and the Holy Trinity is One God in Three Persons). Some of these heresies include: **Sabellianism**, **Modalism**, or **Monarchianism**, which stated that the Holy Trinity was a chimera sometimes appearing as Father, or Son, or Holy Spirit. God was said to have three "faces" or "masks" (Grk. *prosopa*); the Son and Holy Spirit only modes of the Father. "Monotheism" often has been interpreted this way, but Abraham understood one God in Three Persons in Genesis chapter 18. Genesis 1:1 refer to "Elohim," one word but plural. Modern counterparts of Sabellianism: Unitarianism, especially concerning the Holy Spirit. Unitarianism is more Arian concerning the Son. Universalism goes one step further, in a modalism similar to Origen, that all beings will be saved, no matter their beliefs or deeds, although they will be "refined" after death in a sort of "purgatory," another belief that is heretical. Another modalism which places Jesus Christ as the highest in the Holy Trinity is found among the "Jesus Only" movement, and also some Pentecostalists). **Arianism** and **Eunomianism**, which stated that Christ was not truly and completely God, but instead a created sort of superman. Although this heresy was condemned in the Council of Nicea, it appeared again soon afterwards. It was popular with emperors such as Valens, who saw Orthodoxy as a threat, and divided the Orthodox region of Cappadocia (Anatolia), into two parts, weakening the region so that in later centuries it was more susceptible to invasion (Anatolia is now Turkey). This heresy was similar to Greek and Roman pagan beliefs. St. Basil the Great argued successfully against Eunomius, and St. Gregory Nazianzus (called the Theologian), who wrote about time, nature, and God before the Creation, managed to convert Constantinople and all the East back to Orthodoxy. See their books in the Post Nicene Fathers (available on-line). (Modern counterpart: the mathematician Newton was Arian, and many modern scholars who combine agnosticism with their faith, also some sects such as Jehovah's Witnesses. Arians say "There was a time when He was not.") **Macedonianism** (named after a man, Macedonius, not a place), which was a further extension of Arianism, saying that the Father was greater than the Son, and the Son greater than the Holy Spirit, in a pagan-sort of emanation, reducing the Holy Spirit to a force without intelligence. (See Filioque below.) **Montanism**, a 2nd century heresy from Phrygia, in which Montanus, Prisca, and Maximilla, "the three," claimed to be incarnations of the Holy Spirit, and have ecstatic visions, Prisca also claiming that "I am word and spirit and power." In a 8th century (or so) Greek Acts of the Apostles, such persons were said to be possessed by demons who would often throw them from great heights to their deaths. This sect died out on its own. One of the followers of Montanus was Tertullian, a great legal writer, and therefore Montanism also emphasized extreme legalism, almost an Old Testament interpretation of harsh judgment of God. (Modern counterparts: Pentecostalism and the Charismatic movement, anyone who looks for signs and wonders more than the redemption of our Lord Jesus Christ, or who counts among its saints only those who are wonderworkers, and some aspects of modern Roman Catholicism which are very authoritarian, legalistic and also looking for signs; see "Filioque." **Filioque:** "And the Son," a phrase attached to the Creed: ("...I believe in the Holy Spirit, the Lord, the Giver of life, Who proceeds from the father" [and the Son]...). Invented in Toledo in 569, but added much later in the rest of Europe; enforced by Charlemagne after 800, and leading to the Great-Schism between the Eastern and Western Churches in 1054. The East interpreted this addition to the Creed as a form of Arianism or Macedonianism, reducing the Holy Spirit to an emanation. Those who had added the "Filioque" said that this fought Arianism because it elevated the position of Jesus Christ to Divine. The "Filioque" also had tendencies of Montanism. In the doctrine of "**infallibility**" of the Pope, since the Holy Spirit is said to reside in the Church, then the Pope was styled as divine, with more power than the keys of heaven, the "Vicar of Christ," i.e., "in place of Christ," or, the "Pontiff," "bridge between human and divine" (which was a term left over from pre-Christian Roman times). "By action of the Holy Spirit, the Pope is preserved from even the possibility of error" (Catholic Encyclopedia 1910... although "infallibility" did not become actual dogma in Rome until 1870). "Infallability" is connected to early heresies of Montanism and Manichaeism (dualism) because it placed the clergy above the rest of the faithful, making the clergy special conduits of the holy spirit, or dividing the faithful into two groups: the "pure-spiritual," and the "not-holy-canon-fodder." Rome and the Papacy became rigid and legalistic after the Great Schism. (Later heresies emphasized "the pure" such as the Cathar, etc., and some of the secret societies or attainment systems, including modern cults.) The term "ultramontanism" or "infallibility" of the Pope, has a derivation meaning "beyond the mountains," or support of the Pope of Rome by those beyond the Alps above Italy, but, nonetheless, has parallels to Montanism. In Orthodoxy, Jesus Christ is the Head of the Church, although the Apostles and Bishops have been sent out by Jesus Christ, given the keys of heaven, and are Sacramentally Consecrated. (St. Peter's Basilica in Rome has a Credo inscribed in the wall behind the high altar without the "Filioque," a sign of hope.) Emperor Charlemagne (800 A.D.) added a new idea, that he was a descendant of Jesus through children of St. Mary Magdalene, sealing the "divine right" of kings. It is easy to see how this form of Montanism creates divisions; it blasphemes the Offering made by Jesus Christ on the Cross for *all* of humanity, not just a few people or a nationalistic dynasty. **Marcionism** (or Markionism) , from 144 A.D., which stated that God the Father in the Old Testament was evil and not the same as God the Father in the New Testament, blaspheming the Father. This was written against by Tertullian, who was at the other extreme. St. Irenaeus of Lyons writes against many Gnostic heresies, including this. (Modern counterparts: the Medieval sect of Albigensians or Cathars revisited Marcionism in the 13th century, also Dominicans who argued against them but reviled the use of the Psalms or any use of the Old Testament, promoting the Rosary instead; Marcionism is found in some Protestant denominations and in modern cults who reject the Old Testament). **Monophysitism**, which stated that our Lord Jesus Christ was only divine, but put on His human nature only in appearance, or, in another version, that the "droplet" of human nature would be "swallowed" in the ocean of the Divinity of Christ, which led many away from the understanding of His great Offering: His suffering and death on the Cross as a man, leading to our salvation. (Modern counterpart: those who do not accept the humanity of Christ. Monophysitism sometimes becomes modalism.) **Nestorianism**, which stated that the two natures of Christ as both God and man were separate; also, that the human nature could achieve heaven by works alone, and that Christ was simply a human who had attained heaven. The heresy attacked the unity of the natures of Jesus Christ as God and man. Bishop Nestorius, Patriarch of Constantinople, had a chaplain Anastasius, who gave a sermon against the use of the word "Theotokos" or "Birthgiver of God," in Latin "Deigenitrix," applied to the Blessed Virgin Mary, also objecting to the dogma that she is truly the Mother of God (in Greek: Mater Theou) from the time of the conception of Christ at the Annunciation. Nestorius himself supported his chaplain, giving more sermons on the same theme. St. John Chrysostom was against Nestorius. News of the controversy came to Egypt, and the then Archbishop Theophilus of Alexandria, later St. Cyril of Alexandria added to the difficulties of St. John Chrysostom, in fact visiting Constantinople and causing more trouble for St. John Chrysostom with the emperor of Constantinople. Although St. Cyril was against the Nestorians and in favor of the use of the term "Theotokos" or "Birthgiver" to describe the Blessed Virgin Mary, otherwise he opposed St. John Chrysostom because of the political controversy between Alexandria and Constantinople as to which city should have the second place in primacy after Rome. (Treatises of St. Cyril were also used later to support the doctrines of the Monophysites. At first the treatises of St. Cyril were not considered extreme.) Other Patriarchates became involved, taking a stand against Nestorius, and the Roman Pope Celestine's Archdeacon Leo (later Pope St. Leo the Great) asked St. John Cassian, who was familiar with Greek and the East, to help write a treatise refuting the Nestorian heresy. The seven books by St. John Cassian, *On the Incarnation against Nestorius,* were published in haste before 430 A.D., before the Council of Ephesus. (St. John Cassian speaks of Nestorius as Bishop of Constantinople, and speaks of Augustine as though he were also still alive. Blessed Augustine died in 430 A.D.) St. John Cassian refers to Scripture, showing the unity of our Lord's Divinity and Person. He connects this new Nestorian heresy with the heresy of Pelagius, through the errors of Leporius of Treves, who had erroneously suggested that the Pelagian views of man's "sufficiency and strength" could be applied to our Lord, as if Christ were a mere man who used his free will to live without sin, and then at His Baptism He had been made Christ, as though after that time there were two Christs. St. John Cassian points to the connection between Pelagianism and Nestorianism, and underlines it in this work; the first writer to make this connection. He made this connection, and rejected both Nestorianism and Pelagianism, within the lifetime of Nestorius. The rejection of Nestorianism at the Council of Ephesus therefore also firmly rejected Pelagiansim. (Modern counterpart: many "attainment" systems, Pelagianism. There are also sects which divide the Holy Trinity into three separate gods, resembling the creator-preserver-destroyer model of Hinduism; such include Mormonism.) **Monothelitism**, which stated that Jesus Christ had two natures but one will, denying Gethsemane and also the fullness of the Sacrifice and Redemption offered by Christ (this led to the kidnapping and death of Pope St. Martin I and also St. Maximos the "Confessor" who should have been named Martyr.) Modern counterparts: Those sects denying both the full divinity and the full humanity of Jesus Christ; sects who confuse human desire with God's will, ascribing divine rights to individual people, i.e., the responsibility for and ability to order everything in the universe; those who refuse to say to God, "Thy will be done;" also those denying free will, or who would enslave or oppress others claiming that one group has a "divine right" to enslave, oppress, or judge others harshly.

Some Heresies pertaining to our Faith and Response to God

Nominalism: A God only for the few must also be a God who exists only in name. This means that the naming of something does not mean that it exists; this heresy blasphemed the truth of God, and has led to atheism and representationalism.

Representationalism: Representationalists do not believe in the Real Presence of the Body and Blood of Christ. God is remembered only as being in the past, not keeping God in mind in the eternal Presence (a misunderstanding of Greek grammar in Scripture). A faith that is only of a memory of the past and not a living Presence, is not faith in God.

Pelagianism: A form of Nestorianism which stated that works alone were sufficient to reach heaven, without the grace of God, attributed to Pelagius Britto. Such attainment systems break the unity of the faith. Blessed Augustine argued against this, but unfortunately, in many ways became what he argued against in his later years. The argument of Blessed Augustine of Hippo is another heresy called:

Radical Predestination: This states that Faith alone reaches heaven, but God creates some to go to heaven, and others to go to hell, denying the goodness of God and the goodness of God's creation. (This is often called "original guilt," which is different from "original sin.") Oddly, the result is the same as Pelagianism, because those who work hard and achieve material success are seen as being the chosen by God; therefore they achieve heaven by works alone. Later reforms such as Calvinism did not correct these views, but placed greater emphasis on work and materialism, replacing theology with "rational philosophy" with its new interpretations of Holy Scripture. Without theological and philosophical training and the Faith of the Apostles, they cannot agree on basic tenets of the Faith. The Realities themselves they said were "nominal," in name only, and not true. An example of the radical nature of this heresy: the followers of Augustine accused all monks of being "Semi-Pelagian" because of monks' works of labors and prayers; although labors and prayers had been directed by the Lord Jesus Christ.

Councils in Europe forbade discussion of some of the heresies or controversies such as the "**Immaculate Conception** of the Blessed Virgin Mary," which was not made dogma in the West until the mid-1800ds. Orthodox say we honor and venerate the Blessed Virgin Mary, but regard her as human and not conceived without sin, because Jesus Christ was fully human, fulfilling the law, not destroying it. However, Jesus Christ was the only-begotten Son of our Father in heaven, and He was conceived without sin.

Heresies such as these started and gained popularity in many regions, including both Byzantium and Europe; and there was never a time or place where the guard against heresy could be let down. Faith that Jesus Christ and the Father are one is often replaced by a belief that any ideology is acceptable, or belief may be rejected, or that salvation is through children, or may be postponed through reincarnation. Pride, the rejection of the love of God, causes a fall into damnation. An empty "zeitgeist" of whims and popularity can not replace the Holy Spirit. A superficial reading of Scripture can not replace the Last Supper eternally present, nor the spiritual truth of the meaning of the teaching of Christ.

The Celtic Rite Focuses on True Worship

The vital importance of correct belief is lost in modern Liturgies. The Celtic Mass is not "politically correct," but contains correct teaching leading us to salvation. The Celtic Rite states in clear terms:

Human nature of Christ, and the Offering Christ gives us of forgiveness of sins through His Cross: There is a place for admissions of personal inadequacy and the constant need for God's aid. The phrase "Yeah, in Thy sight not even those in Heaven are much more cleansed than we earthly humans, of whom, as the Prophet said of all our righteous acts: 'we are in comparison as unworthy as a menstrual rag.'" (Isaiah 64:6 in the Latin and Hebrew), is a strong statement, but it reminds us that Christ is also the Just Judge, but forgives us any deficiencies. The words "righteous acts" also may be read "justices." This opposes Pelagianism as well. The prayer of Saint Ambrose is reflected in the Sequence of the Requiem, *Dies Irae*, which says "who will answer for me if the just are barely saved?" i.e., we should ask the Saints to pray for us, but this states how unworthy we are of Salvation. Curiously, *Dies Irae* has also proved unpopular, and has been dropped from Roman funerals together with the vesture of penitence and petition.

Prayers against idols and for a "chain of charity": Only the Celtic Rite has retained, as part of the Gelasian Canon, "...rescue them and all of the people from the cult of idols and turn them unto Thyself, the True God, the Father Almighty." Only the Celtic Rite states in the Litany of St. Martin, "And the divine influence to remain with us, a holy chain of Charity..." These prayers directly ask for protection from heresy, and ask that we be connected to God and the Church through His Charity.

Unity of the Faith: References to the unity of the Eucharist in the whole world emphasize that the "Great Schism" and human policies could not break apart the divine unity of the Church as the Body of Christ in the universe, which is affirmed by every Priest who says, "With all those in the whole world who offer the Sacrifices in spirit unto God the Father, and the Son, and the Holy Spirit, our senior, the Priest, -N- *[Celebrant]* with the holy and venerable Priests, offers for himself, for his own, and for all the rest of the Catholic Church assembly..."

(The unity of the Eucharist and the prayers against idols are not an endorsement of the modern so-called "Ecumenical movement" which seeks a unity of administration but lacking all Christian doctrine, as though all beliefs are the same; that movement is an example of what happens when idols of the mind are not correctly understood, and education in the faith has fallen into the dark ages of ignorance. The true Body of Christ is for those who are in the true Body of Christ.)

A large Chalice and Paten fights the idea that God is only for extra pure ones, or clergy, or a very few chosen people. (The use of only Pre-Sanctified Eucharist for the congregation while the clergy always used the Paten and Chalice for themselves alone, also gave the impression that the Offering of the Mass was only for clergy, but everybody else only had crumbs, also dividing the clergy from other faithful, breaking unity in the Mass.) Since the Celtic Mass requires voluntary participation of the congregation, it is not radically Augustinian in its view of the voluntary nature of the Offering.

Prayers of the Fraction of the Eucharist are necessary to remind us of the Lord's suffering for the sake of all the world. The Fraction is before the Lord's Prayer.

The Eucharist is truly the Body and Blood and therefore the Real Presence of our God and Lord Jesus Christ for all time and in all of His actions in the world. The Lorrha-Stowe Mass proclaims Theosis, the obtaining of the Holy Spirit, through the Sacrament of the Eucharist in the words of the Fraction: "They have known the Lord - Alleluia - in the Fraction of the Bread - Alleluia... that which we now hold in hope, we may enjoy in truth by Heavenly fruition..." These phrases also fight the heresies of Pelagianism and Radical Predestination, because it is through the Body and Blood of Christ that the Lord is Known, not either works or faith alone. Also, the Fraction fights a tendency towards a rejection of the immanence of God. This tendency, not quite a heresy, is sometimes a problem for any person who studies so much that they no longer listen to the "still, small voice" of God.

The Confraction and the nine kinds of Communicants encourage Holy Communion for the congregation, an image of the whole Church.

Details on the Lorrha-Stowe Missal Manuscript: Folio Problems, Abbreviations

The Lorrha-Stowe Missal consists of the Gospel of St. John, followed by the Ordinary of the Mass, prayers ("Propers") to be inserted into the Mass for a few occasions (Masses for Apostles, Martyrs, Virgins, Living Penitents, and the Dead), the Rite of Baptism and Chrismation, some minor blessings and exorcisms of water, Holy Unction, and then a Treatise on the Mass, and a few prayers which are from a very torn page. Although the original manuscript places all the prayers to be substituted such as the general Propers for Apostles, Martyrs, Virgins, Living Penitents, and the Dead immediately after the Mass, our translation has placed these prayers in the order they would be encountered in the Mass so that these prayers would be seen and done.

Note the small size of the book, according to Warner on page ix of his introduction: "which measures 5 5/8 inches in height and 4 1/2 inches in width" (15cm x 12cm). This was a book made for traveling. The manuscript itself was written on vellum of irregular shape. It was bound in a haphazard fashion, not regular groups of a few pages sewn in neat "signatures." There were no page numbers in the original manuscript, all "folio" numbers were written in the Latin critical text in the order they were found when the manuscript was re-discovered (Latin critical text 1906). These folio pages have been numbered by leaf, and the back of each page with "v" for "verso."

A small section of folios is out of order. The haphazard binding included some folios which were one sheet folded and placed between two other pages in the manuscript: folios 30, 30v, 31, and 31v make sense toward the beginning of the manuscript, not at folio 30. The manuscript had been resewn at a later time than it was written. This problem was further compounded when some pieces of prayers were added later next to the wrong-order pages (the full prayers repeated elsewhere). Possibly, when the book was re-sewn it was spliced at a Litany which looked similar to another Litany of the Saints, because a second list of Saints happens to fall after the Words of Institution in the Commemoration of the Departed. The first Litany of the Saints is on folios 12, 30, 30v, and the beginning of folio 31. The prayer of St. Ambrose is on folio 31, 31v, and then folio 13; in the case of the Prayer of St. Ambrose, it seems as though there was an attempt to hide the prayer by breaking it into pieces The coherent prayer of St. Ambrose with its Scriptural quote proves the order in which the folios ought to be. There is a third possibility: that the beginning of the Litany of the Saints was memorized, but that folios 30, 30v, 31 and 31v, which are one continuous sheet of vellum, were able to be lifted out as an "Altar card" or palimpsest for the rest of the Litany of the Saints which could be put between pages into the Rite of Baptism, but that this was later sewn into the wrong place,

The order of the Mass is also discovered through the Treatise at the end of the Mass which was written contemporary with the rest of the Missal, and also some of the traditions which were handed down later which place the opening Litany of the Saints at the beginning of the Mass, and can be found in descriptions of the Roman Tridentine Liturgy by Fortesque. The folio order problem was noticed when the Latin critical text was made in 1906, but never corrected. [Latin critical text Edited by George F. Warner, M.A., D. Litt., Keeper of MSS. British Museum. Vol. I. Facsimile. London, 1906.] The Lorrha-Stowe Missal had five sections of signatures. Sections I, IV, and V were originally regular, meaning that a stack of velum was sewn down the center, and then folded, and sewn into the binding, in the same way as modern book "signatures" in hard-bound books. Sections II and III had several irregular sewn pages: as though they were sewn haphazardly first (perhaps due to an irregular shape of vellum) and then written on. Briefly, from Warner's notes and from a copy of a facsimile of the manuscript:

Section I: Eleven leaves: folios 1 through 11v of the Gospel of St. John, with the first page before torn away at the beginning. That first torn-away page is bordered the same as 11v, and was probably a full-page illumination. There are very few pages of illuminations. Folio 1 begins the Gospel of St. John with illuminated first letters. Folio 11v is a full page illumination of St. John.

Section II: Continued prayers prove the order: (Note the discussion above about folios 30, 30v, 31, and 31v.) Seventeen leaves: folios 12 through 28. Folio 14 is a narrow page insertion. Warner made careful illustrations and descriptions of this and the next section. The vellum for folio 12 folding at the center becomes folio 28, that is, the page on the other side of this signature. [Folio 30 and 31 should go next, inserted here.] The vellum for folio 13 folding at the center becomes folio 27 (regular). The vellum for folio 14 is an insertion, with a narrow page at 14 and only a short tail on the other side of the signature (this is the "Gloria" which is in the correct order, and then a short piece of a prayer that is misplaced but appears elsewhere again). The vellum for folio 15 folding at the center becomes folio 26 (regular). The vellum for folio 16 folding at the center becomes folio 21 (irregular). The vellum for folio 17 folding at the center becomes folio 20 (irregular). The vellum for folio 18 folding at the center becomes folio 19 (very irregular; these vellum pages are actually loose sheets, only slightly out of order with eachother because folio 19 is an "Altar Card" of the prayer of St. Gregory over the Gospel, done just before reading the Gospel. The Gospel extends from folio 18v to 20, proving that folio 19 is an insertion). The vellum for folio 22 folding at the center becomes folio 25 (irregular). The vellum for folio 23 folding at the center becomes folio 24 (irregular).

Section III: Continued prayers prove the order: Eighteen leaves: folios 29 through 46. (Note the discussion above about folios 30, 30v, 31, and 31v.) The vellum for folio 29 folding at the center becomes folio 46 (regular) (Note: folio 29 is just after the Words of Institution in the middle of a prayer, from "sacerdos tuus melchisedech", and folio 46v begins the Rite of Baptism.). The vellum for folio 32 folding at the center becomes folio 45 (regular). The vellum for folio 33 folding at the center becomes folio 44 (regular). The vellum for folio 34 folding at the center becomes folio 43 (regular). The vellum for folio 35 folding at the center becomes folio 36 (irregular). The vellum for folio 37 folding at the center becomes folio 42 (regular). The vellum for folio 38 folding at the center becomes folio 41 (regular). The vellum for folio 39 folding at the center becomes folio 40 (regular).

Section IV: Twelve leaves: folios 47 through 58, "original and regularly arranged" according to Warner. (This means that folio 47 is connected to folio 58; etc.)

Section V: Nine leaves: folios 59 through 67; with a tenth leaf pasted to the back cover. [Note: folio 59 is at Holy Communion within the Rite of Baptism.] Also "regular."

Ancient writers saved every scrap of vellum they could, which meant that instead of writing out all endings of prayers, they were more likely to say something such as "per..." which means "through...", which is similar to Byzantine Rite service books that say "Glory and Now" instead of the full endings of the Byzantine prayers: "*Glory* to the Father, and to the Son, and to the Holy Spirit, *Now* and ever and unto the ages of ages. Amen." When making a translation, for clarity it is necessary to write out all endings and "assumed" portions. This includes blessings at the end of the Liturgy, which were lifted from the Rite of Unction in the same Lorrha-Stowe Missal, and actual words used during Holy Communion which were lifted either from the Rite of Baptism or the Rite of Unction in the Lorrha-Stowe Missal; it was either assumed that the Priest would know these; or they were on a palimpsest insert or "Altar card" that could be lifted out for convenient use, but may have been later lost. Or, these prayers were written out once in Unction and that was considered sufficient; in the way that modern Byzantine service books assume that both the Priest and congregation are capable of turning pages to find repeated prayers, and that in an often-used book they would instantly know where to turn. What is strange is that the actual words of Baptism are not in the Rite of Baptism; this may have been a palimpsest that is lost; the words in the Rite of Baptism have been borrowed from the Irish Bobbio Missal.

Some specifics on the Mass: Liturgy of Word and Faith together

[Notes on the order of the Celtic Liturgy are in commentary in the Missal, folios 65v through 67v, and some specifics below.] The Celtic Liturgy is both glorious and concise. The actions concerning the Body and Blood of Christ occur throughout the Mass, forming a unity in the Mass and allowing no place where there appears to be a break: there is no separated "Liturgy of the Word" and "Liturgy of the Faithful." The Eucharist; the Word of God, the Holy Scriptures, the Body of Christ as both the Offering of Christ and the people of Christ or the Church, are always affirmed as one. The procession at the beginning of the Mass by the Celebrant to the Altar is the only "Entry," and is immediately followed by the beginning of the Offertory. The Word of God and the Sermon do not break the Mass into parts: there is a unity of the words of the Gospel with the Offeratory and prayers of the Mass in the Confraction, and a unity of the Sermon with the intentions of the Celebrant and the people throughout the Mass.

Correct Celtic Propers

'Propers' refer to the variable prayers inside of the Mass. The Propers and the Lectionary, the readings of Holy Scripture, vary with the day. Celtic Propers from the same period as this Mass should be used. Please do not use other Propers from other sources, such as Roman, Byzantine, or Anglican with this Missal. The Roman and Anglican Propers are post-schism, and the Byzantine Propers are not for the Divine Liturgy itself but for some of the Byzantine Hours such as Vespers or Matins. The Celtic Propers are the most complete in doctrine, have some of the most beautiful prayers ever composed, and match the Lectionary. Some general Propers are in the body of the text. The sources for Celtic Propers through the year are from the *Luxeuil Lectionary,* the *Bobbio Missal,* and the *Gothic Missal* and other texts such as the *Pontificale of Egbert.* These were produced by Irish scriptora, and the originals are in Latin dialects from the Fourth to Eighth centuries. (The *Martyrology of St. Oengus* which describes the Saints of each day in verse form, is in old Irish, translated into English by Whitely Stokes.) Although a complete translation of all the Propers through the year has been accomplished, this is in a separate book; apply to Bishop Maelruain.

The Bread

The bread used is leavened bread, as was once universal at the time the Church celebrated its unity and joy in the Resurrection of the dead and the life in the age to come. (Although Warren claims that unleavened bread was used, it would be impossible to perform the Immersion, Confraction, and Holy Communion as specified by the rubrics specifically given in the original text. Unleavened bread would either turn into mush that could not be broken into Particles and arranged on the Paten; or, it would not absorb the Precious Blood, shatter in the Confraction, not be cut with a knife, and need to be chewed with the molars.) Although the Host has been selected prior to the Mass, and blessed bread not used for Communion is divided into small pieces on a tray on the Credenza, the Host is not broken until the Fracture, nor divided into Particles until the Confraction; otherwise it could not be whole at the beginning of the Mass and broken in two at the Fracture. While the context of the Last Supper was the Passover; Christ eternally with us in the kingdom of heaven, the Church, is the leavening that is the kingdom of heaven (Mt

13:33), and His Pasch is one of thanksgiving, and an unbloody Sacrifice. The Host is round, and may be 3 to 6 inches in diameter (about 7 to 16 cm), but must be small enough to fit into the Chalice before the Fracture. It is made with yeast, plain flour, water, and a little salt, allowing the dough to rise a little. The top should be stamped with a Cross. The Host is one half inch to an inch thick (about 2 cm. thick), but not spherical.

Word Usage: Essential-Substantial

The term substantia in Latin (Substance), is not an assignment of physical characteristics of matter, nor is it just a name. It is the Being and central Reality: the 'substance' of a reality. (The use of the term "substance" to mean physical form is used by the Latins in other contexts.) The Latins did not happen to use the term 'essence' (ousion) as the Greeks did, only because ousion also signified 'odor' (its only meaning in modern Greek), a tentative suggestion and not reality to the Latins. To the Greeks, however, the term ousion also means the most essential and central, while the Greek term for substance (fusin) means only a physical manifestation. Such are the difficulties of translations from any one idiom to another. As this text is a translation from the Latin, the term 'Substance' is used in several places, but it is meant in the sense of the Latin use of the term substantia in context, which is identical to the Greek use of the term ousion in context. (The terms are substantially or essentially the same.) Idioms in this Missal were carefully checked to avoid errors in doctrine. (See John Cassian: Conference Chapter X with Abbot Daniel, a desert father. The term "flesh" sometimes means the physical body, sometimes the form of an idea, and may be good or bad in context.)

Word Usage: And the Holy Spirit

The Holy Spirit must be said to proceed from the Father alone, as the original Nicene Creed states, but some modern Roman Propers have an added "*Filioque*," [e.g.: 'and the Son'] in the Creed and also implied in endings of other prayers. Accordingly, the endings of most of the prayers in the Lorrha-Stowe Missal say, "and the Holy Spirit" rather than 'unity of the Holy Spirit." "Unity" is used only in Lorrha-Stowe Missal at the Examination and Fracture, "It is through Him, with Him, and in Him, within the unity of the Holy Spirit, that unto Thee, God the Father Almighty, is all honor and glory ..." in that context meaning the unity of belief, profession, and Sacrament which the Holy Spirit sustains in the Church.

Word Usage: Saints and their Examples

The original text of the Lorrha-Stowe Missal uses the term "*merita*" (attributes, accomplishments) as "examples" given by the Saints. The Bobbio Feast of St. John and St. James in Christmastide has a very different focus than later Propers: St. John is honored, but the readings and Propers reflect Christ's response concerning their seats and authority in heaven; faith and works together being correct doctrine, but pre-paid reservations for seats closer to Christ's right hand (through the "merits" of a Saint) not being correct.

Clergy in the Mass

The form of the Mass may use servers, readers, Subdeacon, Deacon, Priest, and Bishop. The sudden appearance of the Paten on the Altar suggests a Subdeacon. A Priest may serve alone, but this same Mass may be used where more clergy are present, although one "Senior" clergy leads the prayers and actions.

Rubrics (Gestures and Directions)

Rubrics are in italics. Those rubrics that were a result of research into inherited Western-Rite tradition are in brackets. **Rubrics found in the original text of the Lorrha-Stowe Missal do not have brackets around them**. The Celebrant, clergy, servers, and people should **study the rubrics** carefully before attempting to Offer this Mass. The rubrics (described by Fortesque) are drawn from the Roman Missal when they correspond with prayers or directions in the Lorrha text. Such rubrics were traditional before the time of Alcuin. Reasons for gestures of the later Tridentine and Byzantine Rites are clarified when this earlier setting is examined, such as the gestures at the Fracture in the Byzantine Rite. Commentaries on the images of the Mass from a later editor of the Lorrha Missal, but near the same time period, are also in italics, but not bracketed. These commentaries are included because they clarify the reasons for the actions and words of the Mass.

Penitential Prayers and Gestures
Penitential prayers are led by the Celebrant or a Deacon, and not chanted by the congregation. There are also penitential gestures specified in the Lorrha-Stowe text, such as the three steps backward and forward of the clergy just after the commemoration of the dead, remembering our sins of word, thought, and deed, and our restitution by these same means. Penitential prayers outside the Mass: Confession, the Hours, and Litanies.

Sounds of the Mass
During the Words of Institution hymns, Psalms, or other prayers may not be said, sung, etc. until the end of the Consecration; that is, possibly until the end of the Fraction. It is assumed that no musical instruments are used except a short ringing of bells, although early Irish illustrations show clergy carrying small harps, which may have been used as drones or for pitches, not necessarily to produce melodies. The music written out in this text is only for convenience and is drawn from Roman sources and some Irish chants.

The Irish claim that their music came from the Alexandrian school (through St. Patrick, who studied at Lerins, where monks who had studied with the Egyptian desert fathers taught). So-called "Gregorian" chant was much later than Pope St. Gregory, often borrowed. There are a few compositions left by the Greek St. Romanos the Melodist, and a handful of Russian compositions that are decipherable, but for the most part the earlier Byzantine and Slavonic musical "neumes" cannot be deciphered, and the music that we hear in Byzantine Churches is from the 18th and 19th centuries, composed to sound like the traditional melodies. The Ambrosian chant for the 13th century "Dies Irae" may have been borrowed from the Irish; at least the words were borrowed from some of the verses (after verse R) of the much earlier "Altus Prosator" of St. Columba. A few Irish chants were written down: the modern musical composition here (by Elizabeth Dowling) of Sancti Venite; in the last two verses, were direct quotes from ancient Irish chant. It is not certain how old the music for the "Deer's Cry" is. The "Te Deum" and some portions of chant within the Mass are standard "Gregorian" compositions. The "Gloria" here is a Scottish composition that fits the Lorrha-Stowe "Gloria" better than the Roman "Gloria."

Early Medieval music notation did not always write the "accidentals" (sharp and flat notes). In the "hexachord" system, the flats and naturals are left to the knowledge of the performer (but that "hexachord" system, based on the "Ut Re Mi" verses of a Vespers Hymn at the Nativity of St. John the Baptist, which itself is an earlier Roman composition by Horace, do not reflect all the European musical traditions which were often as dissonant as the troubadours, as complex as Machaut and the Spanish Mos-Arabic chant). The mode of the Roman Paschal Hymn of the Candle was probably the same as the similar Greek Hymn used at the same time in the Paschal Liturgy; the Gregorian composition may be used with or without the accidentals indicating the Greek Hypolydian mode (both versions are given here: the Greek version is more mysterious and glorious, but is unfamiliar or uncomfortable to some people; it follows the description of Boethius of Greek and contemporary fourth-century European musical modes).

Early composers claimed that their music was written by angels, and therefore composers would not write their names on their compositions, but research shows that most of the musical compositions of the Russians, Greeks, and Romans were re-written after about 1000 A.D. Therefore, there would be nothing wrong with writing music for Hymns and Psalms that are most often used, and also nothing wrong with using music that is for a piece with similar or condensed words (such as using the Byzantine composition for "The Bridegroom comes at Midnight" which is shorter than the Midnight Hymn from the Antiphonary of Bangor). The only limitation being that the music should reflect the beauty and grace found in the words, should not obscure the words with distractions, and should not slow the Liturgy down to the point where it takes twice as long. It may be possible to use six basic compositions for the Psalms: the weeks in Pentecost are in a cycle of six in the Celtic Propers, and the other two modes (together adding to the eight modes of the Alexandrian school) may be used during Holy Week and Paschaltide, and for Pentecost and Christmas. The modes used should reflect glory, peace and penitence, but not be so similar to each other that they all sound the same. Music may be the simplest of chant, but it would also be wonderful if more of the ancient melodies could be researched.

The Beginning of the Mass, Offering Not Before the Beginning

The opening prayers are for the entire congregation: "We have sinned, O Lord, we have sinned: remit our sins and save us. Hear us, O Thou Who didst guide Noah upon the waves of the Flood, and didst recall Jonah from the abyss by Thy Word; free us. O Thou Who didst offer a hand to Peter as he was sinking; bear us up, O Christ, Son of God. Thou didst perform wonders among our fathers, O Lord: stretch forth Thy hand from on high to answer our necessities." And, the first Litany of the Saints is done. The Celebrant vests in the middle of the Church. The Offertory begins the Mass, and does not precede the Mass: all the Church offering together with Christ. There are also Offertory prayers throughout the Mass, so that the "Liturgy of the Word" at the beginning of the Mass, and the "Liturgy of the Faithful" after the sermon are not divided from eachother.

Censing

For those with altar tables fixed against a wall, the pattern of **censing** should be as in Roman usage; the description in this Missal of the censing of an altar away from the wall is from Byzantine sources. (Descriptions of early Irish altars describe them away from the wall, but the Priest *faces* the Cross on the altar, i.e., faces east, the same direction as the congregation, and prays *with* the people, not facing the people.) The Roman manner of censing the Oblations matches the arrangement of sixty-five Particles on the Paten on special Feasts in this Mass: a Cross and circle, but the censing occurs before the Gospel, completing the Offertory, allowing a connection to the temple worship in the Old Testament where the use of only one censing was an Offering to God. Optional: a little censing may occur before the Gifts are covered, censing only the Veil and Gifts. This censing is part of the Offering, just before the [Old Testament and] Introductory Collects.

Gospel and Sermon

The Gospel must be read and Sermon must be given by the Celebrant or another Bishop, Priest, or Deacon, because this is not a lesson only for moral instruction, but it also is a lesson on the Word of God given in the presence of the Eucharist on the Altar and is for all time. Therefore, the subject of the Sermon must reflect on the words of the Gospel and Epistle, not on worldly subjects apart from that, or a reflection on the personality of the preacher. The Gospel is directly after Offertory prayers, and is itself part of the Offering. During the Sermon, people may sit. In early times, people brought folding chairs or rugs. Only the cook and doorwarden may be excused from the Sermon.

The Creed: Complete Nicene, and Two Other Apostolic Creeds

The Creed as set forth in the Liturgy of the Lorrha-Stowe Missal is the full Nicene Creed of the undivided Church, complete in doctrine. (The Latin use of "born," "natum ex patre ante omnia saecula" was used by the Irish to show Christ, generated rather than created; the Orthodox argument by St. Basil against Eunomius, "Do not press me with the questions: What is the generation? Of what kind was it? In what manner could it be effected? The manner is ineffable, and wholly beyond the scope of our intelligence; but we shall not on this account throw away the foundation of our faith in Father and Son. If we try to measure everything by our comprehension, and to suppose that what we cannot comprehend by our reasoning is wholly non-existent, farewell to the reward of faith; farewell to the reward of hope! If we only follow what is clear to our reason, how can we be deemed worthy of the blessings in store for the reward of faith in things not seen?" Adv. Eunomius ii 24. This is an good argument against Nominalism.) No alterations, omissions or additions were made to this Creed in the preparation of this translation, which is the Orthodox Creed of the Undivided Church and the Byzantine Rite.

In the Celtic Rite of Baptism there seem to be two occurrences of the Creed: the original text only gave the beginning of the responses, and therefore, upon further consideration, it was realized that the entire Nicene Creed is said as the proclamation of Faith required before Baptism, but at the immersion, only the response "I believe" is required. (The Bobbio Missal gives the Apostles' Creed at Baptism, which might have been written by later copiests to avoid any "Filoque"controversy, but the full Nicene Creed should be used always instead, especially in the Rite of Baptism. A longer "Creed of St. Athanasius" is in the Bishops' agreed statement.)

Always use the complete **Nicene Creed,** the Lorrha-Stowe Creed, translated from Latin:

I believe in one God, the Father Almighty, maker of heaven and earth and of all things visible and invisible. And in one Lord Jesus Christ, the Only-Begotten Son of God. Born of the Father before all ages. Light of light, true God of true God. Born, not made, of one Substance with the Father: through Whom all things were made. Who for us men, and for our Salvation descended from heaven. And was Incarnate of the Holy Spirit and the Virgin Mary: And was born man. And was crucified also for us: under Pontius Pilate; He suffered and was buried. And He rose on the third day, according to the Scriptures. And ascended into heaven: and sitteth at the right hand of God the Father. And He shall come again with glory to judge both the living and the dead: Whose Kingdom shall have no end. And I believe in the Holy Spirit, the Lord and Giver of life: Who proceedeth from the Father. Who with the Father and the Son together is worshiped and glorified: Who spake by the Prophets. And in one, Holy, Catholic, and Apostolic Church. I confess one Baptism for the remission of sins. And I look for the resurrection of the dead. + And the life of the world to come. Amen.

The text of the **Apostles' Creed from the Antiphonary of Bangor** (8th Century), given here for historical interest, as it is different from other "Apostles' Creeds." (Instead, the Nicene Creed above should always be used at all Masses and Hours.)

"I believe in God the Father Almighty, who is unseen, creator of all created things, visible and invisible. I believe in Jesus Christ, His only begotten Son, our Lord, God Almighty, who was conceived of the Holy Spirit, was born of the Virgin Mary, Suffered under Pontius Pilate, was crucified and buried. He descended into hell; on the third day He arose from the dead. He ascended into the Heavens and sitteth at the right hand of the God the Almighty Father. From there he will come to judge the living and the dead. I believe in the Holy Spirit, God Almighty, having one substance with the Father and the Son. [I believe] the Holy Church is Catholic [i.e. complete in doctrine], the forgiveness of sins, the Communion of the Saints, the resurrection of the Flesh. I believe in life after death, and life eternal in the glory of Christ. I believe all this in God. Amen."

In the **Bobbio Missal,** the following informative and typically Celtic essay is given, and is another **"Apostles' Creed."** Faith and its profession links us to the past and the future by God's Charity. This Creed shows the Apostles as "...the twelve hours of the day are illumined by the light of the Sun; unto whom Thou didst say 'ye are the light of the world'." (from a Collect before the Epistle, see meditations on the Hours, and the Lectionary assignments for the last twelve Gradual Psalms.)

"The Symbol of Faith was collected into 12 articles of the Apostles and assigned with caution:

"Peter said, 'I believe in God the Father Almighty.' John said, 'I believe in Jesus Christ, His only Son, God and our Lord.' James said, 'He was born of Mary, the Virgin, through the Holy Spirit.' Andrew said, 'He suffered under Pontius Pilate; was crucified and buried.' Philip said, 'He descended into hell.' Thomas said, 'He arose on the third day.' Bartholomew said, 'He ascended into Heaven, [and] sat at the right hand of God the Father Almighty.' Matthew said, 'From there He will come to judge the living and the dead.' James, the son of Alpheus, said: 'I believe in the Holy Spirit.' Simon Zelotes said: 'I believe in the Holy Church.' Judas, the brother of James, said: 'Through Holy Baptism [there is] remission of sins.' Matthias said, 'The resurrection of the flesh and eternal life. Amen.'

"This is what was collected and cautiously attributed to the 12 Apostles. For it is the Faith of the Saints in God. Unto the persons named, its name is the divine Gift of Faith. It is our Portion. This Faith unites God and man. This Faith joins the present and the future. Furthermore, Faith makes the invisible visible. After the grave, Faith opens the way to the Heavenly race, even to the Kingdom of Heaven. Therefore those who are constant in the confession of the Faith are not able to fear the wrath that is coming from on high."

Celtic Preface and Sanctus, a Masterpiece of Catechism and Praise

The Preface of the Trinity is always said, and precedes any other Preface for the season or Saint. (The term "Preface" is used in this Missal because it is a familiar term. The Lorrha-Stowe Missal calls this the "Dignum" indicating the first words of the prayer. The terms used in other Celtic Missals are noted in the text.) This Preface, with its ending of the praise of the angels and with the Sanctus, is the praise recorded in Revelation 4:8, "Holy, holy, holy, Lord God Almighty, Who was, and Who is, and Who is to come,". This Preface is a masterpiece of catechism and contemplation on God and His nature heard by the entire congregation, "...Holy Lord Almighty and eternal God. Thou Who with Thine Only-Begotten and the Holy Spirit, O God, art One and Immortal God, Incorruptible and Immutable God, Unseen and Faithful God, Marvelous and Praiseworthy God, Honorable and Mighty God, the Highest and Magnificent God, Living and True God, Wise and Powerful God, Holy and Exemplary God, Great and Good God, Terrible and Peaceful God, Beautiful and Correct God, Pure and Benign God, Blessed and Just God, Pious and Holy, not in one singularity of person but One Trinity of One Substance. Thee we believe; Thee we bless; Thee we adore; and we praise Thy Name unto eternity and unto the ages of the ages: Thou through Whom in the salvation of the world; through Whom is the life of men; through Whom is the resurrection of the dead." This praise of God is the kind that the angels continually give. It is worthy and just for us to say, but it has been removed from most modern liturgics so as not to offend the lukewarm, who think "glory and praise" is sufficient without mention of God's attributes, or that we are too unworthy to mention any attributes of God. It is worthy and right for us to give God this praise. Jesus Christ, God and man, has ascended into heaven raising the potential of our human nature higher than that of the angels, so we too may sing the Sanctus in the presence of the Holy Trinity in heaven. "Blessed is He Who cometh from heaven that He might enter the world, and didst become man unto the blotting out of the sins of the flesh, and became a Victim that through suffering He might give eternal life to those that believe..."

The Canon and Litanies in the Mass

Litanies include the Litany of St. Martin, Litanies of the Saints, and the Canon after the Sanctus. The Canon ("Therefore..."), a Litany without responses, prepares for the Words of Institution, and is necessary in every Liturgy. The term "Dominicus" (Lord) in the Lorrha-Stowe Missal title of the Canon does not mean "Dominicalis" which would mean Sunday. Concerning Litanies to the Saints: we can name many intentions, but we also ask the Saints to pray for us just as we would ask our friends to pray for us, especially so that we may be helped to pray to the infinite God and ask for His infinite mercy.

Consecration, Fraction, Epiklesis

The Epiklesis is an invocation of the Holy Spirit upon the gifts to effect the completion of the Consecration of the gifts so that they are the Body and Blood of our Lord Jesus Christ. There are many prayers woven into the text asking the Holy Spirit to make the Eucharist truly the Body and Blood of Christ, and affirming Christ's Presence in the Eucharist: the thrice repeated invocation of the Holy Spirit at the end of the Offertory, "Come, O Lord, the Almighty Sanctifier and bless this Sacrifice prepared unto Thee," is completed by other prayers: the Words of Institution called "The Most Dangerous Prayer" in the Lorrha Missal ("Take, eat, this is my Body..."), the Ascending Epiklesis immediately after that, the Fraction, the Proper Epiklesis from the Throne of St. Peter, and the prayers before and between the Psalms of the Confraction.

After the "Words of Institution" are said, the Western Rite "Ascending Epiklesis" is said, which is also a call for the Holy Trinity to have the Body and Blood of Jesus Christ. "...brought by the hands of Thy Holy Angel to Thy Altar on high, in the presence of Thy Divine majesty: that, as many of us as shall receive from the Altar of Sanctification the most sacred Body and Blood of Thy Son, may be fulfilled with all heavenly benediction and grace." (The consecration of an altar stone from the *Pontificale of Egbert*, said by the Bishop, cites Jacob's vision of the Ladder of the Angels and the Altar Jacob built where he had the vision: therefore anything set upon the Altar stone is at the base of the ladder traveled by Angels. Gen. 28:10-22.)

The words in this Mass at the Fraction are very powerful, a statement of *IS, Christ the Being*: "...The Bread which we break is the Body of our Lord Jesus Christ - Alleluia - The Chalice which we bless - Alleluia - is the Blood of our Lord Jesus Christ - Alleluia - in remission of our sins - Alleluia. Let Thy mercy be upon us - Alleluia - even as we have hoped on Thee..." The words of the Lorrha Fraction are missing from both the Roman and Byzantine Liturgies; their absence is felt by all acquainted with the prayers of the Lorrha Fraction. The prayers always said at the Fracture in the Lorrha Missal are valuable in focusing our minds and hearts on Christ and His Offering to us. The significance of the words of the Fraction are underlined by the prayer following the Fraction after the Celebrant has withdrawn the Host from the Chalice, placed it on the Paten and set it on the Corporal. This was adopted as the "*Post Secreta*" or "*Post Mysterium*" of the Fourth Sunday in the Gothic Missal: "We believe, O Lord. We believe we have been redeemed in this Fraction of the Body, and the pouring forth of the Blood; and we shall rely on the consumption of this Sacrifice for fortification: that which we now hold in hope, we may enjoy in truth by Heavenly fruition, through our Lord Jesus Christ Who reigneth with Thee and the Holy Spirit throughout all ages of ages."

The Gothic Missal had a Proper *Post Secreta* or *Post Mysterium* prayer in addition to, but not replacing, the other prayers. The prayers on the Dormition and Assumption of the Virgin and of the Throne of St. Peter are very similar to the Byzantine prayers, and therefore the Celtic Orthodox Christian Church always uses the Epiklesis prayer for the Throne of St. Peter as well as any other. Perhaps St. Peter may be the author of this first Epiklesis prayer, or it may have been inspired by the Blessed Virgin Mary who taught the Panikida (or Benediction) prayers. This prayer was written down by the Irish. (In the Byzantine Rite, it is claimed by some that, prior to Isabel Hapgood in the twentieth century, this prayer was not written down. This prayer is associated with the descent of the Holy Spirit at Pentecost at the Third Hour in Hapgood's translation. As a Proper prayer it is written as a variable prayer, but clergy would know to insert it always. In the Byzantine Rite, this prayer was probably later in the Liturgy than placed today, being associated closer with the Fraction and its meaning than the Words of Institution.) This prayer belongs just before the Lord's Prayer, after the Fraction, not earlier in the Liturgy: "We who serve, offer these prescribed Holy Gifts of our Salvation, that Thou may be pleased to send Thy Holy Spirit upon this Sacrifice so that it may be changed into a legitimate Eucharist for us in the Name of Thee, Thy Son and the Holy Spirit, in the transformation of the Body and Blood of our Lord Jesus Christ; and may it be unto us who eat and drink, Life eternal and the eternal Kingdom. Through Himself, Christ Our Lord who reigneth with Thee and the Holy Spirit throughout all ages of ages. Amen."

Both Species, Intinction

The unity of the Sacrament at the Elevation and Fraction is expressed by dipping the sacred Body of Christ into the sacred Chalice, as specified in the ancient Latin rubrics for the Lorrha-Stowe Mass. In this way, the Body of our Lord is not dissolved in His Blood, but is received as a distinct Particle infused with both Species. Perhaps the later habit of giving only the Body to the congregation as practiced in the post-schism Roman Church is a remnant of this dipping; that they still gave a Particle of the Body but no longer infused with the Blood. No Christian before the schism would consider themselves fully communicated without both Species (Body and Blood).

Unity, Eternity, the Mass in the Confraction and Litany of the Saints

There is both an element of eternity and also of the here and now: the eternal and the present the WAS, AND IS, AND EVER SHALL BE are one in this Mass. Everyone present at the Liturgy witnesses the Life of Christ in conjunction with the Saints of all ages. There are no directions to exclude Catechumens after a certain point. A comment by St. Bede that an un-Baptized king was refused Holy Communion indicates that after the Confraction, the doorwardens separated communicants from non-communicants, as practiced in most Orthodox Churches today, but did not remove non-communicants from the church. The opening Litany of the Saints is not for early arrivals at Church, but is for the entire congregation's participation; which was once true also of the later Roman and Sarum usages. We ask the Saints to pray for us at the beginning of the Mass, then in the

Commemoration for the Departed we pray for them as well as the souls of friends and family, in an acknowledgment that all in the Church pray for one another; even praying *for* the Saints, a doctrine of unity unique to the Celtic Rite. (We have inserted the places associated with these Saints next to them in the Litany of the Saints in Baptism.)

There is a unity in the use of one Host, and in the breaking into many Particles. The Confraction is the Gift of Christ to the gathering of the people, in the gathering of the Particles of the Lord's Sacrifice, reflecting the gathering in Ecclesia, the Church, or the Divine work of the people, Liturgy. The Lorrha Confraction, visualized, is the many Particles of the Lord's Body and Blood on the Paten in the form of a Cross; a different number of Particles for different observances. This is the Cross of victory, "By this Sign conquer," *One* Body and *One* Salvation. There may be evidence that the Byzantine Rite once followed the Lorrha practice in the Confraction and the Fraction: the fourteen inch sixth-century Syrian Greek Orthodox Paten with inscribed Cross and Greek dedication from Beth Misona, exhibit 50.381 in the Cleveland Museum of Art, would indicate this. During the Psalms of the Confraction before Holy Communion, the Celebrant has time to carefully remove Particles of the Lord's Body and place them on the Paten in the pattern required for the day, acknowledging the unity of the Body of Christ. The text of the Psalms are from the Douay-Rheims Bible; an excellent translation of the Septuagint Greek Old Testament and the Latin Vulgate Bible.

The sources for the Confraction illustrations are illuminations and stone carvings of Celtic sources. The notes on the Lorrha Missal tell us that the Confraction must be in the form of a Cross, but it only specifies the shape of the 65 Particles for Pascha, Christmas, and Pentecost. There is more than one possible shape for some of the numbers: illuminations and carvings of differing arrangements of Particles were found for the number 8, for example. The illustration in this text was found in the Lindisfarne Gospel, the Book of Kells, and the Book of Durrow. The upper-center Particle would be used for the Celebrant. Another arrangement on a stone carving showed a Roman-style Cross with a long bottom section. Another variant in the 8 Particles in the Book of Durrow showed six Particles similar to the 7 Particle Confraction, and the other two Particles in the upper corners. Larger Crosses would need a large Paten of about 14 inches in diameter (as found in the Greek Orthodox Syrian Paten from Beth Misona mentioned above). Even on a smaller Paten the general shape of the larger Crosses may be indicated using very small Particles, if great care is taken, but it would be very difficult to accomplish the arrangement for Pascha, Christmas, and Pentecost. (Glass is recorded as a material used for Patens and Chalices, and it is not difficult to find a suitable glass Paten and Chalice of a large enough size.) A Celebrant who does not have a large Paten should at least use the 9 Particles for Sundays and the 13 for the Ascension and on Low Sunday, but it is most important to obtain and bless a larger Paten before the major Feasts. It is suggested that the Priest practice breaking a piece of unconsecrated bread and arrange 65 pieces of it within a circle the same diameter as his Paten. The Host may be 3 to 6 inches in diameter, but must be small enough to fit into the Chalice before the Fracture.

Preparation Prayers before Communion at the Confraction affirm the Eucharist

Here are some of the powerful statements about Holy Communion found in this Mass at the Confraction, which affirm and complete the Epiklesis: "Whosoever eateth my Body and drinketh my Blood; such a one abideth in me and I in him... This is the Bread of Life which cometh down from heaven; whosoever eateth of it shall live unto eternity... The Lord gave the Bread of Heaven to them; man ate the Bread of the Angels... This sacred Body and Blood of the Lord and Savior; take you unto yourselves unto life eternal... Taste and see how sweet the Lord is..." Compare these to the quotes at the time of the Confraction chosen later by the Anglican Cranmer: "Come unto me all that travail and are heavy laden, and I will refresh you... So God loved the world that He gave His only-begotten Son, to the end that all that believe in Him should not perish but have everlasting life... This is a true saying, and worthy of all men to be received, that Christ Jesus came into the world, to save sinners... If any man sin, we have an Advocate with the Father, Jesus Christ the righteous, and He is the propitiation for our sins." These are lovely statements in the Gospels, but miss the point: these verses emphasize sin and the law of the Old Testament before the death and Resurrection of our Lord Jesus Christ rather than Christ and the greatest Mystery of His Life. These verses sadly avoid Christ's words of Offering at the Last Supper and teaching about His Offering on the Cross. The Lorrha Missal represents an older and truer form or Liturgy, which is very Orthodox, not a late reduction of the faith.

Corporate Holy Communion

In the receiving of Holy Communion, there is a corporate grouping of the people; receiving the Body and Blood of our Lord Jesus Christ is not an individual act apart from the Church. [Notes on Holy Communion itself are within the Mass, and also in the Discussion of the Symbols of the Mass which is part of the original manuscript.]

Dismissal and Final Gospel

The Dismissal prayers, including Thanksgiving and Benediction, are a necessary traditional close, considered to be after the Mass is ended, for the benefit of the entire congregation. ("The Mass is done," is a pun; in Latin, "Missa" also means to send forth, as the word Apostle also means "sent out.") The editors of the Lorrha Missal wrote these endings in the Sacraments of Baptism and Holy Unction, since Holy Communion in the form of Pre-Sanctified reserved Species was given at the end of both of these Sacraments. The Thanksgiving and Benediction after Unction is the most appropriate to use in a Mass, and has a final note in the original text after Unction saying "thus ends the Order of Communion," so these have been inserted after the Mass. Other Celtic Missals have special closing prayers on Festal days, which may be substituted. The Final Gospel is not bound in the end but at the beginning of the Lorrha text, possibly for the convenience of the Priest or Deacon who would have to find it after the Missal was closed at the end of the Liturgy. It would make sense for the Final Gospel of St. John (1:1-14, or 1-18) to be read by a Deacon, immediately before the Celebrant unvests in the middle of the church and before the congregation leaves, since, if the cooks and doorwardens were the only people excused from sermons, it would have been expected that the entire congregation be present from the opening Litany of the Saints until the final unvesting of the Priest: The people would stay because the implication of both cooks and doorwardens implies that the people would want to stay to eat together. Certainly the Final Gospel is one Irish tradition surviving in the Roman Rite that Alcuin did not change. Therefore that Gospel has been placed in the traditional place after the Dismissal in this edition of the Lorrha Missal. (Although the Byzantine Rite does not have a Final Gospel, they may have a sermon after the Liturgy rather than in the middle, implying that they also once had a Final Gospel.)

Notes on Baptism, Chrismation, First Communion and Command

As in the Liturgy, the Rite of Baptism of the Lorrha Missal is a teaching service. It teaches that the Church is our mother, giving birth to us into a life in Christ by the activity of the Holy Spirit, just as Jesus Christ was born into our humanity. Many of the prayers of this service can be found in the later Roman Ritual. However, based on other prayers in this text, it is clear that later Western understanding of some of the acts of Baptism differs from that of the time at which this Missal was last copied. Many of the prayers of Baptism seem to repeat; but each has its purpose. The opening from the exorcism prayers up to the first anointing with the Oil of the Catechumens suggest that these may be done outside the church building, and followed by the procession "around the font" (or to the font in the Church and then around it). Most churches probably did not have the luxury of a separate building to house the Baptistery; the font was probably inside the entrance of the Church itself. Therefore, the Litany of the Saints opens the portion taking place in the church, just as it does in the Mass. If the opening prayers before the procession are said in the church building, these prayers still form a distinct section of the Baptismal Rite. The complete Nicean Creed is said at the beginning of the Rite of Baptism; at the triple Immersion, the candidate says, "I believe." each time.

The multiple, lengthy exorcisms, the Blessings and Invocation of the Holy Spirit upon the water have the solemnity required of a Holy Sacrament, changing the water into Baptismal Water. The Priest breathes on the water in the form of a Cross and also the letter Psi, which stands for spirit. The formula of the immersion was not written down in the Lorrha text, so the wording from the *Bobbio Missal* has been inserted.

Chrismation is according to a kingly anointing, and seals the body with the prayer just after the Anointing, just as the prayer to exorcise each part of the body cleanses it at the beginning of the Baptism. Not until both the Baptism and the Chrismation have been completed is the "holy and spotless white vestment which thou shalt wear before the tribunal of our Lord Jesus Christ" given to the newly Baptized person who has put on Christ.

After the vesting, the hand of the newly-Baptized is consecrated to the making of the Sign of the Cross to bless themselves during prayer, while at Mass, and to bless their food or other items for personal use in the absence of a Priest.

Then the Foot-Washing, called the *Mandatum* (Command) occurs. The feet are washed (using plain water, not the Baptismal water), and Command given to the newly-Baptized to keep the Commandments, remain faithful to God, and to have mercy on their neighbor. This is not a further cleansing; the person has already been cleansed in Baptism; but it is another blessing of water by the newly-Baptized person, as Christ blessed the water when He entered the Jordan River (the newly-Baptized having just put on Christ). The Command is that the person not take Baptism and their Salvation for any selfish purpose, but immediately must be responsible for the Salvation of others as part of their Baptismal vows. "Thou shalt do this in imitation of our Lord Jesus Christ to thy pilgrims and travelers." In this way, Baptism leads a person into the corporate Church, with the responsibilities of membership in the Body of Christ, the responsibility to continue to learn and grow in Christ, and the responsibility to bring others to Christ. The Foot-washing is like a minor Ordination, as is the Byzantine Tonsure after Baptism, although the Foot-washing has a larger Command than the Tonsure. In the Mandatum, the action of the Priest and the responsibilities of the new member of the Body of Christ are clearly explained in terms of Scripture. The Foot-Washing as part of Baptism is missing in both the Byzantine and Roman Baptismal Rites.

The "foot water" is kept by the family as blessed water, to protect the child from undesirable visitors or influences, as recorded in Celtic folk tales. [In "The Horned Women," the foot-water "in which she had washed her child's feet" is put "outside the door on the threshold," reminiscent of the Passover blood on the door posts and lintels, to repel twelve witches who had planned to kill the family. From Lady Wilde's *Ancient Legends*, printed in *Celtic Fairy Tales* collected by Joseph Jacobs, a Dover republication of a book from 1892 published by David Nutt. International number 0-486-21826-0.] Christ washes His disciples' feet on the day which begins His Passover.

Then, having been Baptized, Confirmed, vested in the white garment, and the Command given in the Foot-Washing, the new member of the Body of Christ is given the Body and Blood of our Lord Jesus Christ. Prior to the change in Roman usage which set First Communion at age seven and Confirmation at puberty, it was generally understood that Baptism and Confirmation were prerequisites for participation in the Eucharist. Since the Rite of Baptism in this Missal contains First Communion, as does the Eastern usage, it is to be understood that Bishops of pre-tenth century Ireland considered the simple administration of Holy Chrism within the context of the many invocations of this Rite of Baptism sufficient as a Rite of Confirmation or Chrismation. Unlike the Mass, which mentions the Senior as Celebrant (Senior meaning the Bishop, Abbot, or Priest of highest rank), the Rite of Baptism specifically states in a few places that a Priest administers the entire Rite. He would have used oil and Holy Chrism Consecrated and supplied by the Bishop. (At the Mass of Holy Thursday in the Celtic Propers, the Bishop blesses Holy Chrism to be used by his entire diocese, which indicates that this Holy Chrism is to be distributed.) Furthermore, since the rubrics for the Confraction of the Eucharist of the Liturgy state that some portions were for children (as opposed to unmarried adults, i.e. postpubescents) it is clear that the ancient church of Ireland Baptized, Confirmed and Communicated very young children.

The Lorrha-Stowe Missal, a Chain of Charity

Together with the Rite of Holy Unction (Anointing of the Sick) the Missal contains four of the Sacraments as practiced by the Church of Ireland and its many missions scattered throughout the known world. For convenience, we have also included a fifth Sacrament, the Rite of Reconciliation from St. Gall. The Lorrha-Stowe Missal is the missionary Missal which converted skeptical pagans, brought Arians back to the faith, kept alive a tradition of incredible discipline and vitality. Details of its Sacramental rites are cited in Celtic literature, and are a vital part of the Celtic identity, and also of many other peoples on the continent of Europe in France, Italy, Switzerland, and Germany who were turned from Arianism and paganism. This Mass is bound together in a "chain of charity" and can revitalize our faith. May this Missal be a revelation to us all, and unite us to our Lord Jesus Christ, our hope and our Salvation.

English is used in this translation because it is the common language most in use today, and most useful as a missionary tool. At the time this Mass was written, Latin united the languages of the Pict, Briton, Irish, Anglo-Saxon, and many other languages on the continent. Although the translator has experience with spoken Ecclesiastical Medieval Latin, and has been very careful in this translation, he requests that anyone noting an error inform him of same. Note that some past translations of this Liturgy and accompanying Offices of the Sacraments did not correctly interpret Ecclesiastical idiom, whether of Latin with Medieval Gaelic sentence structures or Greek idiom of the Scriptures, which was familiar to the Celtic monks. Some translators have also "balderized," that is to say censored and tamed the Missal. Therefore, discrepancies between these and the present text are to be expected. Note that the folios of the text were bound incorrectly at a later period than they were copied (explained in a previous section). Therefore, other editions of this Mass may have the folios out of order from their original binding when the text was first copied.   +Maelruain

(What is not in the Missal: Marriage, Holy Orders, and a Few Services)

Only four of the major Sacraments are in the Lorrha-Stowe Missal, and we have also included a Confession and Absolution from St. Gallen, a fifth Sacrament. However, Marriage and Holy Orders are not here, because these had several forms.

Marriage originally involved a contractual agreement by the Irish legal system (Brehon law), and the marriage would be blessed by Christian clergy as well. There were several different blessings, although each blessing always joined the couple in and through Christ and the Church in a Sacrament. The vows of Betrothal are not the actual nuptial blessing. Betrothal is either an affirmation of "I do," "I will," or "Amen" in response to each being asked if they will promise to stay together. It is an assent given at the beginning of the ceremony. The Christian nuptial blessing itself is a prayer said over the couple, and may include an exchange of tokens such as rings, crowns, etc., and signifies the Sacrament of Marriage in union with God and eachother. (The Celtic Rites of Holy Matrimony usually would be combined with a Nuptial Mass, and would include some Propers for Martyrs as well. The Confraction verse for married persons, "The kingdom of Heaven tolerates sieges - Alleluia - and the forceful take it - Alleluia," is reminiscent of the hymn for Holy Martyrs sung in the Byzantine Nuptial Rite at the crowning, although the derivation of that Hymn may have been related to the Sacrament of Marriage as a minor Order. Or, that Hymn might be replaced by either Psalm 118 "Beati" or the Beatitudes, originally considered appropriate for Martyrs. Or use the entire long Community of the Brethren prayers which normally end the Hours.) There is a new copyrighted translation, not by Bishop Maelruain, of some Celtic marriage blessings; and because of the copyright, none of these blessings are included here.

Marriage may be a simple blessing by a Priest in an emergency (in case one of those being married has little time left to live), which is considered sufficient as a joining of a couple in Christ, with the proper legal forms (see emergency prayers). If a couple or their parents plan to have an elaborate wedding, it would be better to spend more time in prayer and a nuptial Mass rather than on garments, fancy foods, etc.; and spend more money to help the couple find suitable housing, and to give money to the poor.

Holy Orders is not a set of Proper prayers that would be in an ordinary Missal, since only a Bishop may perform an Ordination to a position of major clergy (Deacon, Priest, or Bishop; Bishop requiring more than one Bishop to do the Consecration). Appropriate Bishops' blessings and the Rites of Holy Orders are found in Egbert's *Pontificale* and other sources. A complete translation of these Proper prayers is in the book of Propers for clergy translated by Bishop Maelruain; apply to Bishop Maelruain. The Sacraments of Ordination have appropriate Propers and Lections in the Celtic Rite.

Other occasional services such as the Churching of a newborn (found in the Byzantine Rite) were not included in the Lorrha-Stowe Missal. Churching is related to the Feast of the Presentation or Purification February 2/15, because the Priest bows to the mother, and says to the baby, "Now let Thy servant depart in peace..." (the Canticle "Nunc Dimitis") since every child is made in the Image of God. After the Rite of Baptism, a child is brought to the church in a procession; the "Churching" would be just after the Celtic Rite "Mandatum," before "First Communion." (The feet are washed, and the child is commanded to do the will of God, just as they enter the Church.) There is nothing wrong with a Priest bowing to mother and child and saying the "Now let Thy servant..." prayer at the time the child is brought to the altar for their First Communion. If Baptism is done on the Vigil of the Resurrection of our Lord, after the Paschal candle has been lit, and the many people brought into the Church on this day (see the traditions, for example, in St. Basil's time), would have made it very difficult for individual "churchings" to occur. Before the Great Schism, although there were different Rites and practices, occasional prayers were often found copied into other usages, such as Byzantines using something like the Celtic Hymn of Midnight, and the Irish using something like the Byzantine Trisagion. Prayers may be supplied from other Orthodox sources for minor services in the Celtic Rite, but only when a Celtic Proper is not known. It is hoped that there will be much more research on the prayers and services of the Celtic Rite.

An Essay About the Cross in the Mass in Response to a Question:

The Cross is central to the Christian Faith. On traditional Gospel covers, a large Cross is central to the icons or symbols of the four Evangelists. Many early Patens had a Cross at their center, and the Altar table both East and West always has a Cross on it or immediately behind or above it. The Byzantine Rite and the Celtic Mass arrange the Particles on the Diskos or Paten in the form of a Cross. However, the Cross is more than a decorative motif that happens to be repeated in the Eucharist of both the Byzantine Rite and the Lorrha-Stowe (Celtic) Mass.

The Sign of the Cross was used by the Saints at the time of the Lorrha-Stowe Missal to test angels and even visions of the Lord Jesus Christ to see if they were indeed from heaven or an illusion from the tempter, because even the tempter may appear as an angel of light. (See *Vita Patrum, The Life of the Fathers* by St. Gregory of Tours, translated by Fr. Seraphim Rose and Paul Bartlett, the chapter on the life of St. Friardus the Recluse. Also the life of St. Martin of Tours by Sulpicius.) In the Confraction of the Lorrha-Stowe Mass, the Body and Blood of our Lord are already Consecrated, and are not an illusion sent by the tempter; but these are arranged in the form of the Cross because the Cross is pleasing to God, and also because contemplation of the Cross leaves no possibility for our *own* thoughts, words, or deeds to stray from Christ before us on the Paten and in the Chalice. For example, our thoughts must not be on the Priest; there must never be a personality cult.

After the great schism (after the Lorrha-Stowe Missal's use was suppressed), an heretical idea called *Nominalism* "denied the real being of universals on the ground that the use of a general word does not imply the existence of a general thing named by it," denying Platonic/Aristotelian Realism *(Encyclopaedia Britannica)* (later denying all metaphysical/spiritual reality and unity, calling them concepts and not necessarily realities). This led much later to the Protestant denial of the reality of the Eucharist; they identified the term "memory" with concept, instead of the Greek sense of keeping in mind or paying attention to. The purpose of keeping the Cross central in the Mass is to see Christ as the foundation, the cornerstone, keystone, rock of offense, scandalum which means rock or scandal, the Cross which not only keeps temptations and illusions away from us, but also gives us the courage to face Christ's life, death, resurrection, and our salvation as a fact, not just a name. We cannot dare to ask our heavenly Father for His Bread in the Lord's Prayer if we cannot dare to believe in Christ present in His Body and Blood, about which He Himself said, "I am the bread of life" (St. John 6:35), and "Take and eat." (Mt.26:26).

Each action of the Celebrant describes the Passion of our Lord, but the Mass has not abandoned His Resurrection. In the Celtic Mass, after the Fraction before the Lord's Prayer, the two halves are reunited to affirm the wholeness of Christ's Body after His Resurrection. Completing the Confraction, the Celebrant moves the upper Particle down to the left side signifying that "Bowing His head, He gave up the ghost." At that moment, the dead in Hades are freed (St. Matthew 27:50-53), sometimes called the "First Resurrection." Then, the Celebrant turns to the people, shows the people the precious Body of the Lord, saying, "Come forth and take possession of the kingdom of My Father - Alleluia - which hath been prepared for ye from the beginning of the world - Alleluia - Glory be to the Father and to the Son and to the Holy Spirit: Come forth! As it was in the beginning is now and ever unto ages of ages. Amen. Come forth!" At this moment the Celebrant proclaims Christ's Resurrection, and the future Final Resurrection, because in what other way may we take possession of the kingdom of our Father in heaven? We prepare by contemplating the Cross with peace and penitence, and now at His Resurrection we come forth to receive Communion with Faith and love.

Some may ask, then why not at all times replace the Cross with the Resurrection? Why think about our Lord suffering on the Cross every time we do the Mass, which may be as often as daily? Some Protestant churches today do not display the Cross at all, and in one Roman church the Altar Cross was replaced with a large stuffed globe. The tempter entices us to avoid our Lord's pain even though Christ suffers our sins daily, or the tempter suggests there is no tempter, even with all the evil in this world. The tempter hates the Cross because he was overcome by the Cross at the First Resurrection. We focus on the Passion and Cross of our Lord in the Mass before Holy Communion because:

First, Jesus Christ gave us His Body and Blood, "shed for many for the remission of sins." This is one Offering for eternity, and in eternity, we, the Saints, the entire Church has always celebrated the Mass as the Passion and Cross of the Lord. This is the tradition among the Orthodox and Roman Catholics as established by Jesus Christ, and carried out by the Church, Ecumenical Councils, Patriarchs, and Popes.

Second, it is only through the Cross that we may participate in the Resurrection, as Scripture tells us: St. Matthew 16:24-25, "...If any man will come after me, let him deny himself, and take up his cross, and follow me. For whosoever will save his life shall lose it: and whosoever will lose his life for my sake shall find it." St. John 12:32-33, "'And I, if I be lifted up from the earth, will draw all men unto me.' This he said, signifying what death he should die." We are drawn to Christ on His Cross and follow Him through His Resurrection and Ascension into the heavenly kingdom: the kingdom that is within us and among us in the Church (Romans 6:3-11).

Third, we cannot offer the sacrifice of praise and worship as unbloody unless we offer the perfect Sacrifice the Lord has given to us once for all time on the Cross. If we were to omit the Cross and Passion of the Lord, we would necessarily have to offer a bloody sacrifice of our own fabrication that would fall short of the Sacrifice offered by Christ; we would not offer anything to God but personalities, pride and opinion. But we know from Psalm 50 (or 51 KJV numbering), "For thou desirest not sacrifice; else would I give it: thou delightest not in burnt offering. The sacrifices of God are a broken spirit: a broken and a contrite heart, O God, thou wilt not despise." Instead of self-proclaimed wisdom (see Romans 1:18-25, I Corinthians 1:18-31), we must contemplate the Cross of Christ all through the Mass, and then we may receive Holy Communion in the joy of the Resurrection of our Lord Jesus Christ. - *Elizabeth Dowling*

The Celtic Lectionary in the Divine Liturgy and the Psalms in the Graduals and Alleluias

The Lectionary is the set Scripture readings on Sundays and the many Festival days of the year. *The Celtic Lectionary* uses representative Irish documents, parallels Bishop's Blessings in the *Pontificale of Egbert* (York), and reflects a more ancient, complete, dogmatic usage than Alcuin's Roman Lectionary ("Tridentine," or late Roman Rite). The earlier Lectionary of Treves (Trier) uses sequential Gospels through the Pentecost season, similar to the order of Lections in the Byzantine Rite, although using a different selection. Bishop Maelruain gathered Irish Lections and Propers from extant documents: Treves, Luxeuil, Bobbio, Bangor, Gothic Missal, Sélestat, Würzburg, etc. (A chart of many usages is found in the introduction to *Le Lectionnaire de Luxeuil* Paris, ms. lat. 9427, Dom Pierre Salmon, Abbé de Saint-Jerome, Rome, 1943.)

It was necessary to find Psalms for Graduals and Alleluias in the Mass. The Psalms in order happen to match Sunday Lections, and are prophetic about the life and teachings of Christ. Psalm 1 is the First Sunday in Advent. During the week following Christmas, the Psalms match the Saint days. Lent has many more Psalms since daily Lections in Lent are Old Testament; the Psalms on Lenten Sundays match the Gospels (continuing the sequential order). During Lent, Psalm 44, for the Annunciation, floats to that celebration. St. Columbanus himself said that Psalm 65 (Greek and Latin numbering, or 66 Hebrew numbering) "Jubilate Deo" "Shout with joy to God, all the earth..." is the Psalm of the Resurrection, and also corresponds to the sixty-five Particles in the Confraction in the Mass for Pascha. It happens that Psalm 65 is a continuation of the sequential order of Psalms. The sequential order continues through the Pentecost Season, and afterwards the last twelve of the fifteen Gradual Psalms match the designations of the Apostles' Creed in the Bobbio Missal for the Twelve Apostles, and the rest of the Psalms after those match the content of Feast days and Saint days. (Psalms assignments © 1996 by Elizabeth Dowling.)

The Lectionary begs for the Proper Prayers for the Masses through the year, which also offer great insight into the meaning of Scripture. For a translation from Latin of the full Propers through the year, contact Bishop Maelruain at www.CelticChristianity.org

Along with the Propers is the Life of the Saints, called "Life" in the singular (as explained by St. Gregory of Tours) because their Life is the sanctity given to them by the Holy Trinity. Every day of the year there are several Saints listed in the *Martyrology of Tallaght*, the *Speckled Book* of Oengus, Roman and Byzantine sources. The Celtic attitude towards these Saints is that a day with a large number of Saints is more important than a day with only one famous Saint, unless it is a Feast day of our Lord Jesus Christ or of the Blessed Virgin Mary, who is considered the first among the Saints. Longer histories of these Saints are available in many sources, such as Sulpicius for St. Martin of Tours; Secundinus for St. Patrick; St. Gregory of Tours; Pope St. Gregory the Dialogist (called "the Great" in the West, not to be confused with the very early St. Gregory the Wonderworker called "the Great" in the East); St. John Cassian and St. Athanasius who both wrote about desert fathers; Greek sources (8th century) such as books describing the Life of the Apostles; and modern sources such as Mary Ryan Darcy; Butler's Lives of the Saints; etc. When we ask for intercession prayers to God from the Saints, it is helpful to know more about them; they supported the faith when the Orthodox truth was in the minority (such as the case of St. Gregory Nazianzus the Theologian, who converted the city-state of Constantinople, the eastern capital of Rome, back to Orthodoxy); they wrote wonderful books supporting the faith and explaining Scripture, and they wrote about the history of the church. (Oengus's verses for each day, together with the *Martyrology of Tallaght,* the gloss explanation of Oengus's verses in the Speckled Book, and also other material from other sources, has been compiled and is another book available from Bishop Maelruain.)

Key: (Gospels, Epistles and Psalms are mostly in order, except for Saints' days.)
OT - Old Testament or replacement for Old Testament (Apocalypse same as Revelation.);
E - Epistles, Acts, or replacement for Epistle;
P - Psalms (**always in Greek numbering**), or replacement for Psalm (on one Sunday);
G - Gospels (St. Matthew, St. Mark, St. Luke, St. John).
Irish Lectionaries (From Continental Irish monasteries which continued ancient tradition):

[B] - Bobbio Missal (7th - 8thc);
[L] - Luxeuil Lectionary (7th - 8th c);
[C] - Paris (7th c).;
[T] - Treves Bible (Trier, 8th c.);
[S] - Sélestat Lectionary or Sélestat Epistle (7th -8th c);
[W] - Wurzburg Lectionary (8th c).
[*] - A few lections were supplied from other parts of the year or other traditional sources.
Advent starts in the week on or after November 13/26 (*Speckled Book*, Oengus).
I Advent   OT: Malachi 3:1-6 [B]; E: James 5:7-12,19, 20 [B]; P: 1; G: John 1:35-51 [C]
II Advent OT: Isaiah 35:1-10 [S]; E: Romans 8:3-6 [B]; P: 2; G: Matthew 24:15-44 [C]
Entrance into the Temple of the Blessed Virgin Mary at age three (Nov 21 or 22/ Dec 4 or 5) OT: Exodus 19:7-12; E: Eph 6:1-9; P: 146 ("Praise ye the Lord, becaue psalm is good..."); G: Luke 2:41-49
III Advent OT: Is 62:10-12; 45:8 [S]; E: Romans 11:30-36 [S]; P:3; G: Matthew 11:2-5 [C]
St. Andrew Nov. 30/ Dec. 13 (General for Apostles, see below, with these substitutions:) Vigil: E: Gal. 1:2 [*Vatican pericopes] Mass: E: I Cor. 4:9 [*Vatican pericopes]
IV Advent   OT: Isaiah 54:1-5 [S] E: I Thessalonians 2:19-3:8 [S]; P: 4; G: Luke 3:1-18 [T]
V Advent OT:Isaiah 40:1-10 [S]; E: I Thessalonians 3:9-13 [S]; P: 5; G: Matthew 3:1-12 [C] (may also add the theme from Advent I W: St. Matthew 11:4-5, Mt 20:29-34)
St. Thomas Dec. 21/ Jan 3 (General for Apostles, see below.) P: 127
VI Advent OT: Isaiah 11:1-10 [S]; E: Colossians 1:23-29 [S]; (P: 127 Psalm for St. Thomas, 127, usually repeated, or Christ entering Bethlehem Psalm 6 on Christmas Eve); G: Matthew 21:1-9 [C]
Christmas Eve (no room at the inn): E: Philippians 4:4-7 [B]; P: 6 G: Luke 12:35-37 [B]
Christmas (Dec 25/ Jan 7) Twelve Prophecies: I. Isaiah 62:10-63 [* from Advent]; II. Isaiah 6:1-13 [* from Advent]; III. Isaiah 7:1-8:22 [*]; IV. Isaiah 11:1-12:6 [* from Advent]; V. Isaiah 25:1-26:21 [*]; VI. Isaiah 35:1-10 [* from Advent]; VII. Isaiah 40:1-42:12 [L]; VIII . Isaiah 44:23-46:13 [L]; IX. "Augustine's" Sermon (not Augustine, but another written out) [L]; X. Isaiah 54:1-56:7 [L]; XI Malachi 3:1-4:6 [L]; XII.John 1:1-15 [L]; Mass: OT: Isaiah 9:1-7 [S]; Praises from the book of Daniel [L]; E: Hebrews 1:1-12 [L]; P: 148 and 150 (148: "Praise ye the Lord from the heavens..."); G: Luke 2:1-20 [L, C], (The Confraction uses 65 Particles.), Final Gospel: Matthew: entire Christmas narrative [B].
   Week of Christmas (specified OT, E and G, or later in the week use Christmas):
St. Stephen (Dec 26/ Jan 8) Matins: Jer. 17:7-18 [L]; E: Acts 6:1-8:2 [L]; P: 7; G: Matthew 17:23-18:11 [L]
Ss. John and James (Dec 27/ Jan 9) OT: Apoc 14:1-7 [L]; E: Acts 12:1-3 [B]; P: 9A&B and 123 and 130 (Psalm: day switched with Holy Innocents) ; G: Matthew 20:20-23 [B]
Holy Innocents (Dec 28/ Jan 10) OT: Jer 31:15-20 [L]; E: Apoc 6:9-11[B]; P: 8 (Psalm: day switched with Ss. John and James); G: Matthew 2: 11-23 [B]
St. Victor (and birds) (Dec 29/ Jan 11) P: 10 ("In the Lord I put my trust..."; Victor is St. Patrick's angel who appeared in the form of a bird. Instead of the hunt of the wren Jan. 1st.)
Mansuetus with virginal Ailbe (and the poor) (Dec 30/Jan 12) (Charity.) P: 11
St. Sylvester and end of Roman year (Dec 31/ Jan 13) P: 12 (End of year in the Psalm.)
Circumcision, (Jan 1/14) Animals, Fools, beginning of Roman year. Matins: Isaiah 44:24-45:7 [L]; OT: Isaiah 1:10-18 [L]; E: I Corinthians 10:14-31 [L]; P: 13; G: Luke 2:21-40 [L]
Sunday after Circumcision (if before Epiphany) OT: Ezechial 43:18-44:7 [L]; E: Ephesians 1:3-14 [L]; P: 14; G: Matthew 9:32-35 [L]
Epiphany (Jan 6/19) OT: Isaiah 60:1-16 [L]; E: Titus 2:11-13 [L]; P: 15; G: *All* of the following: Matthew 2:1-12 [T], Matthew 3:13-17 [L]; Luke 3:23 [L]; & John 2:1-11 [L]

295

Jesus' Lent (Jan 7/ 20)
First Sunday after Epiphany OT: Isaiah 6:1-10 [L]; E: I Corinthians 10:26-31 [L]; P: 16; G: Luke 4:16-31 [L,W both have Luke 4:16-22]
Coming out of Egypt of Mary's Great Son (Jan 11/24) E: (of the Sunday); P: 136; G: (of the Sunday)
Second Sunday after Epiphany (if before Jan 18/31) OT: Jer 16:9-15 [L]; E: I Corinthians 10:1-13 [L]; P: 17; G: Matthew 22:35-23:12 [L]
Throne of St. Peter and conversion of Constantine (Jan 18/31), OT: Osee 4:1-19 [*L for Sunday after]; E: Galatians 5:13 - 6:2 [*L for Sunday after] and Acts 12:1-17 [L]; P: 18 and 122; G: Matthew 16:13-19 [L,W], and John 21:15-19 [L] (Specific and General) (**Transfiguration** also uses Psalm 18, celebrated by the Irish on July 26/Aug. 8): OT: Mal 4:4-6 []; E:2 Peter 1:16-21 []; P: 18 and Ezekial 20-40-42a [*]; G: Mark 9:1-9 []
First Sunday after Throne of St. Peter (if before Pre-Lent) (OT, E, and P may be as on Throne of St. Peter) OT: Osee 4:1-19 [L]; E: Galatians 5:13 - 6:2 [L] and Acts 12:1-17 [*L];
P: 18; G: Matthew 17:1-9 [L] (Transfiguration, different reading than Throne of St. Peter)
Baptism of St. Paul (Jan 25/Feb 7) E: Romans 5:1-9 [] (and may read Acts 9:1-22); P: 141; G: Matthew 4:18-20 []; John 21:15-19 [] or Luke 6:6-19 [] (General Lections for Apostles)
Second Sunday after Throne of St. Peter (if before Pre-Lent) OT: Jer. 35:12-36:3 [L]; E: Eph. 5:3-21 [L]; P: 19; G: Luke 10:25-37 [L,W] (Good Samaritan)
Purification of the Virgin, Reception of Christ into the Temple, and blessing of candles OT: Is. 8:13-18 [*]; E: Heb 7:7-26 [*]; P: 135; G: Luke 2:22-40 [*]
Third Sunday after Throne of St. Peter (if before Pre-Lent) OT: Isaiah 49:8-26 [L]; E: Colossians 3:12-17 [L]; P: 20; G: Luke 14:1-15 [L]
The Devil Tempts Christ and flees from His Presence (Feb 15/28) (Same as Anathema Monday, the first Monday in Lent after Great Lent I).
Throne of St. Peter in Antioch (Feb 22/ March 7) E: Romans 5:1-9 []; P: 122; G: Matthew 4:18-20 []; John 21:15-19 [] or Luke 6:6-19 [] (For the Apostles.)
St. Matthias (Feb 23/ March 8) Same E and G as yesterday, P: 133;
Sexagesima (First Sunday of Pre-Lent in ancient times) E: II Corinthians 10:7-18 [S]; P: 21; G: Luke 8:4-15 [*B "Mass of the Fast"] (Parable of the Sower and Psalm 21, "O God my God, look uon me: whyhast Thou forsaken me?..." theme of Lent)
Quinquagesima (Second Sunday of Pre-Lent in ancient times) OT: Isaiah 55:6-12 [S]; E: Romans 12:1-16 [S]; P: 22; G: Luke 18:1-14 [*B "Another of the Fast"] (Widow and Judge, Publican and Pharisee)
Great Lent I OT in Matins: Genesis chapters 1, 2, 3; OT: Joel 2:12-14 [S]; E: IICor 6:2-10 [S, B, L: II Cor 6:2-16]; P: 23; G: Matthew. 6:1-8 [B, T] (alms and prayer in secret) Sunday of Orthodoxy "Anathama" Monday readings done in anticipation.
Monday in Lent I (During Great Lent, whole chapters from the Old Testament are read each day.) OT in Matins: Genesis 4; OT: Isaiah 58:1-14 [L]; E: II Corinthians 6:2-15 [L]; P: 24; G: Matthew 4:1-11 [B, T] (Same Lections as "The Devil Tempts Christ and flees from His Presence," which is the fixed date commemoration of this movable day.)
Tuesday in Lent I: OT in Matins: Genesis 5; Blessing of Babies and Catechumins: P: 25; G: Matthew 19:13 - [T]
Wednesday in Lent I: OT Genesis 6-8; Anointing with Oil; P: 26; G: Mark 7:24-30 [T]
Thursday in Lent I: OT: Genesis 11; P: 27
Friday in Lent I: OT: Genesis 12-15; P: 28
Saturday in Lent I: OT: Genesis 15-22; P: 29
Great Lent II OT in Matins: Genesis 37-41; OT: Proverbs 3:19-34 [S]; E: Ephesians 4:23-32 [*Vatican pericopes]; P: 30; G: Luke 15:11-24 [B, T, W] (Prodigal Son) During this week: Monday Genesis 42; P: 31; Tuesday Genesis 43; P:32; Wednesday Genesis 44; P:33; Thursday Genesis 45; P: 34; Friday Genesis 46-47; P: 35; Saturday Genesis 48-49-50; P: 36

Great Lent III OT in Matins: Exodus 14-15-16; OT: Isaiah 58:1-8 [S]; E: Colossians 2:4-17 [* Vatican pericopes]; P: 37; G: John 6:28-54 [B,T] ("I am the bread of life...") During this week: Monday Exodus 17 and 18; P: 38; Tuesday Exodus 19-20; P: 39; Wednesday Exodus 21 and 22; P: 40; Thursday Exodus 23; P: 41; Friday Exodus 24; P: 42; Saturday Exodus 32-33-34; P: 43.

Annunciation (March 25/ April 7) E: Heb 2:11-18 []; P: 44 (for the queen); G: Luke 1:26-38 []

Mid-Lent, Great Lent IV, Procession of the Cross OT in Matins: Numbers 22-23; OT: Zach. 8:19-23 [S]; E: Galatians 1:3-9 [* Vatican pericopes]; P: 45; G: John 6:71-7:30 [T-C] (Tabernacles, "I know Him, because I am from Him; and He hath sent me.") During this week: Monday Numbers 24; P: 46; Tuesday Numbers 25; P: 47; Wednesday OT: Numbers 26-27; P: 48; Thursday Numbers 28; P: 49; Friday Numbers 29, 31; P: 50; Saturday Numbers 32-33; P: 51.

Great Lent V OT in Matins: Osee (Hosea) 1-2-3; OT: Jer 18:13-23 [S]; E: Romans 6:17-23 [*Vatican Pericopes]; P: 52; G: John 11:47-56 [T] (Caiphas plots to kill Jesus, one man for the nation) During this week: Monday Osee 4; P: 53; Tuesday Osee 5; P: 54; Wednesday Osee 6-7; P: 55; Thursday Osee 8; P: 56; Friday Osee 9-10-11; P: 57; Saturday Osee 12-13-14; P: 58.

Great Lent VI, Palm Sunday OT in Matins: Jer. 31:31-34; The Traditio (opening of the ears) [L,B, T] and Blessing of Palms; OT: Jer.31:31-34 [L]; E: Hebrews 11:3-34 [L]; P: 59 (and can add Zach 9:9); G: John 12:1-26 [L, or T John 12:1-50] (Entrance into Jerusalem)

Holy Week Monday OT: Daniel 9:20-27 [L]; P: 60

Holy Week Tuesday OT: Jer 18:11-23, 20:7-13 [L]; P: 61

Holy Week Wednesday OT: Lamentations: 3:1-66 (it says 1-22, but all the Hebrew alphabet is implied) [L]; P: 62

Holy Thursday, Bishop's Blessing of Chrism, Footwashing OT in Matins: Exodus 19:1-20, 20:1-20 [L]; Matins Gospel: Matthew 26:2-16 [L]; Liturgy: OT: Exodus 12:1-24 [S, corrected]; E: I Corinthians 11:20-26 [B]; P: 62 and 63 (for the Institution of the Eucharist and also the betrayal); G: Matthew 26:17-35 [W-T-B]; Footwashing Gospel as the sermon: John 13:1-33 [T], and Beatitudes are sung during the footwashing: Matthew 5:3-12 [*]

Holy and Great Friday there is a harmony of the Passion Gospels with Old Testament readings (written out in Breviary). [* Source: *Antiphonary of Bangor* and other sources..]

Holy Saturday (modern Friday evening): P: 64; G: Matthew 27:61-66 [B], Cross Vigil prayers (in Breviary).

Vigil of The Resurrection of our Lord, Pascha (most important Liturgy of the year, see the special Resurrection Liturgy), Twelve Prophecies: I. Genesis 1:1-1:31,2:1-6 [W corrected]; II. Genesis 2:7-2:25,3:1-24 [W corrected]; III. Genesis 6:5-6:22,7:1-24,8:1-8:21 [W]; IV. Genesis 22:1-19 [L, W]; V. Genesis 27:1-40 [L,W]; VI. Exodus 12:1-50 [L]; VII. Exodus 13:18-13:22,14:1-14:31,15:1-15:21 [L]; VIII. Ezechial 37:1-11 [L]; IX. Isaiah 1:1-5:24 [L]; X. Josuah 3:1-3:17,4:1-4:25 [L]; XI. Jonah 1:1-3:10 [L]; XII. Daniel 3:1-100 [L]; E: I Corinthians 5:6-8 [B] and Romans 6:3-11 [L]; P: 65 (specified by St. Columbanus of Luxeuil) and 150; G: Matthew 28:1-20 [L,B,T] (Confraction uses 65 Particles.)

Dawn of the Resurrection: OT: Apoc 1:1-18 [B] (Apoc. means Apocalypse, or the Book of Revelation of St. John the Divine, this week instead of the Old Testament); E: Acts 1:1-8 [B]; P: 65 and 150; G: Luke 24:1-12 [B]

Monday of the Resurrection OT: Apoc.1:14-2:7 [L]; E: Acts 2:14-40 [L]; P: 65 and 150; G: Mark 15:47-16:11 [L]

Tuesday of the Resurrection OT: Apoc. 2:8-17 [L]; E: Acts 1:15-26 [L]; P: 65 and 150; G: Mark 16:12-20 [L]

Wednesday of the Resurrection OT: Apoc 5:1-13 [L]; E: I Corinthians. 15:47-58 [L]; P: 65 and 150; G: John 11:1-45 [L]

Thursday of the Resurrection OT: Apoc 14:1-7 [L]; E: Acts 3:1-19 [L]; P: 65 and 150; G: John 20:1-9 [L]
Friday of the Resurrection OT: Apoc 19:5-16 [L]; E: Act 5:17-41 [L]; P: 65 and 150; G: John 20:11-18 [L]
Saturday of the Resurrection OT: Apoc 21:1-8 [L]; E: I Corinthians 15, 31-45 [L]; P: 65 and 150; G: John 21:1-14 [L]
First Sunday after Pascha ("the Close of Easter" or "Low Sunday) OT: Isaiah 61:1-7 [L] ("acceptable year"); E: I Corinthians. 15:12-28 [L] ("first-fruits of them that sleep"); P: Daniel 3:1-45 [L sequence specified]; G: John 20:19-31 [W] (St. Thomas believes.)
Second Sunday after Pascha E: Acts 3:1-13 [S]; P: 66; G: John 3:16-24 [T] ("For God so loved the world...")
Third Sunday after Pascha E: Acts 2:22-28 [S]; P: 67; G: John 4:5-42 [T] (Christ offers "living water," woman at the well.)
Mid-Pascha, on the Wednesday E: Acts 4:31-35 [S]; P: 68; G: Luke 24:36-48 [T] (Theme of Pascha: Jesus eats with disciples.)
Fourth Sunday after Pascha E: Acts 4:36-5:11 [S]; P: 69; G: John 9:1-38 [W] (Christ cures man born blind.)
Fifth Sunday after Pascha E: Acts 16:19-36 [L]; P: 70; G: Mark 7:31-37 [L] (Christ cures deaf and dumb man.)

Rogation Processions (days before the Ascension) [all Lections from L]:
Rogation Monday Matins: Daniel 9:12-19; Third Hour: James (ALL); Matthew 5:17-26; Sixth Hour: I Peter 1:1 - 5:11; Matthew 7:1-12; Ninth Hour: Tobias (ALL); Mt 6:1-13
Rogation Tuesday Matins: Joel 1:13 - 2:11; Third Hour: II Peter (ALL); Matthew 13:1-23; Sixth Hour: I John (ALL); Luke 12:15-31; Ninth Hour: Judith (ALL); Mt 5:31-48
Rogation Wednesday Matins: Hosea 5:1 - 6:6; Third Hour: II John 1 - 11; III John 1-12; Matthew 4:13-17; 11:28-30; Sixth Hour: Jude (ALL); Matthew 21:28-32; Ninth Hour: Esther (ALL); Matthew 6:14-33
Ascension, the end of Paschaltide. Instead of OT: Acts 1:1-11 [L]; E: Ephesians 4:1-13 [L]; P: 71; G: John 13:33-35; 14:1-14 and Luke 24:49-53 [L] ("I shall go and prepare a place for you."... "the way, the truth, and the life").
Sunday after Ascension E: Acts 18:22 - 19:12 [L]; P: 72; G: John 17:1-26 [L] (Jesus's prayer for the whole world.)
Pentecost OT: Joel: 2:21-32 [L,W]; E: Acts 2:1-21 [L,S,]; P: 149 and 150 (149: "Sing ye to the Lord a new canticle: le His praise be in the church of the saints..."); G: John 14:15-29 [L] (The Confraction uses 65 Particles.)
First Sunday after Pentecost (one of the All-Saints' days) E: Gal.6:8-14 [L]; P: 147 ("Praise the Lord, O Jerusalem: praise thy God, O Sion..."); G: Matthew 16-24-27 [L]

In Pentecost season: All the Celtic Gospels have been arranged in sequential order. Old Testament Lections are from Sélestat, in the order they appear in that Lectionary; they match the Sunday Gospel. Epistles in Pentecost Season are supplied from the Byzantine Rite in sequential order [*]. The Celtic Gospels in order happen to fit the Epistles from the Byzantine Lectionary in order, but are not not the same Gospels that the Byzantine Lectionary uses. Most of these Gospels are from Treves, with five Gospels from Bobbio, and a few supplied from Wurzburg. Some Gospels from Treves had themes which repeated other Gospels at another time in the year; it was decided not to use these in Pentecost Season but instead Bobbio or Wurzburg those days, but they are noted here: Mk 9:1-13 - the Transfiguration, near that time, but a fixed date; Lk 10:25-37 Good Samaritan is the Second Sunday after Throne of Peter after Epiphany; Lk 12:32 - "Where your treasure is, there will your heart be also..." same as Matthew 6:19, which is Second Sunday after Pentecost; Lk 14:1-15 Healing on the Sabbath; take the lowest seat at a wedding; call the poor to a feast: this is on the Third Sunday after Throne of Peter after Epiphany; Lk 18:1-14 Unjust judge and widow, Publican and Pharisee:.this is on Quinquagesima in Pre-Lent.
Thursday after the first Sunday after Pentecost E: Romans 2:10-16 [*]; P: 73; G: Matthew 4:17-5:25 [T]

2nd (Sunday after) Pentecost OT: Is. 28:1-7 [S]; E: Rom 5:1-10 [*] (same as General Lection for Apostles) P: 74; G: Matthew 6:19-25 [W]
Thursday after 2nd Pentecost E: Romans 3:19-26 [*]; P: 75; G: Matthew 7:1-6 [W]
3rd Pentecost OT: Is. 40:28-41:4 [S]; E: Rom. 3:21-4:3 [*]; P:76; G: Matthew 7:7-11 [W]
Thursday after 3rd Pentecost E: Romans 4:4-12 [*]; P: 77; G: Matthew 7:12-21 [B]
4th Pentecost OT: Is. 41:8-14 [S]; E: Romans 6:1-11 [*]; P: 78; G: Matthew 9:18-26 [W]
Thursday after 4th Pentecost E: Romans 8:22-27 [*]; P: 79; G: Matthew 10:22-33 [W]
5th Pentecost OT: Is. 42:5-9 [S]; E: Romans 9:18-33 [*]; P: 80; G: Matthew 11:1-27 [T]
Thursday after 5th Pentecost E: I Corinthians 1:1-9 [*]; P: 81; G: Matthew 13:24-30 [B]
6th Pentecost OT: Is. 44:24-28 [S]; E: I Cor. 7:24-35 [*]; P: 82; G: Mt 15:10-28 [B,T]
Thurs. after 6th Pentecost E: I Cor. 12:27-13:3 [*]; P: 83; G: Matthew 19:16-30 [B]
7th Pentecost OT: Is. 49:8-13 [S]; E: II Cor. 1:12-20 [*]; P: 84; G: Matthew 22:23-33 [T]
Thurs. after 7th Pentecost E: II Corinthians 4:18-5:9 [*]; P: 85; G: Matthew 25:31-46 [B]
8th Pentecost OT: Jer. 16:19-21 [S]; E: II Cor. 12:20-13:2 [*]; P: 86; G: Mark 4:24-34 [T]
Thursday after 8th Pentecost E: II Corinthians 13:3-13 [*]; P: 87; G: Mark 4:36-41 [T]
9th Pentecost OT: Jer. 26:12-16 [S]; E: Galatians 1:1-10, 1:20-2:5 [*]; P: 88; G: Mark 5:1-17 [T]
Thursday after 9th Pentecost E: Galatians 2:21-3:7 [*]; P: 89; G: Mark 6:2-7 [T]
10th Pentecost OT: Is. 40:26-41:12 [S]; E: Gal. 3:8-14 [*]; P: 90; G: Mark 8:1-13 [*T]
Thursday after 10th Pentecost E: Galatians 3:15-22 [*]; P: 91; G: Mark 8:27-33 [T]
11th Pentecost OT: Ezekiel. 3:17-21 [S]; E: Galatians 3:23 - 4:5 [*]; P: 92; G: Mark 9:13-29 [T]
Thursday after 11th Pentecost E: Galatians 4:21-31 [*]; P: 93; G: Mark 10:1-15 [T]
12th Pentecost OT: Ezekiel. 5:5-12 [S]; E: Galatians 5 [*]; P: 95 (Psalm switched); G: Mark 10:17-31 [T]
Thurs. after 12th Pentecost E: Gal. 6:2-10 [*]; P: 94 (switched); G: Mark 10:42-45 [T]
13th Pentecost OT: Ezekiel 14:12-23 [S]; E: Ephesians 1:22-2:3 (2:13?) [*]; P: 96; G: Mark 10:46-end [T,W]
Thursday after 13th Pentecost E: Eph. 2:19-3:7 [*]; P: 97; G: Mark 11:12-19 [T,W]
14th Pentecost OT: Ezekiel 18:1-21 [S]; E: Ephesians 4:14-19 [*]; P: 98; G: Mark 11:27-33 [T]
Thursday after 14th Pentecost E: Ephesians 4:24-5:2 [*]; P: 99; G: Mark 12:28-34 [T]
15th Pentecost OT: Is. 63:15-64:4 [S]; E: Eph. 6:10-24 [*]; P: 100; G: Mark 13:14-37 [T]
Thursday after 15th Pentecost E: Philippians 1:8-14 [*]; P: 101; G: Luke 5:12-16 [T]
16th Pentecost OT: Ezekiel 37:1-14 [S]; E: Phil. 1:12-20 [*]; P: 102; G: Luke 5:27-32 [T]
Thursday after 16th Pentecost E: Philippians 1:20-27 [*]; P: 103; G: Luke 6:6-19 [T]
17th Pentecost OT: Ezekiel 37:21-25 [S]; E: Colosians 4:2-18 [*]; P: 104; G: Luke 9:57-62 [T]
Thursday after 17th Pentecost E: I Thess 2:1-8 [*]; P: 105; G: Luke 10:38-42 [T]
18th Pentecost OT: Joel 2:12-18 [S]; E: I Thess 2:9-19 [*]; P: 106; G: Luke 11:14-26 [T]
Thursday after 18th Pentecost E: I Thess 5:1-8 [*]; P: 107; G: Luke 11:27-54 [T]
19th Pentecost OT: Jer. 7:1-7 [S]; E: I Thess. 5:9-13, 24-28 (or without the skip in the Epistle) [*]; P:108; G: Luke 12:2-12 [T]
Thursday after 19th Pentecost E: II Thess 2:1-12 [*]; P: 109; G: Luke 12:54-13:17 [T]
20th Pentecost OT: Jer. 17:7-14 [S]; E: II Thess 2:13-3:5 [*]; P: 110; G: Lk 13:18-30 [T]
Thursday after 20th Pentecost E: I Timothy 1:1-14 [*]; P: 111; G: Luke 14:16-35 [T]
21st Pentecost OT: Is. 49:1-5 [S]; E: I Timothy 3:1-13 [*]; P: 112; G: Luke 16:1-13 [T] ("Praise the Lord, ye children...")
Thursday after 21st Pentecost E: I Timothy 3:14 - 4:8 [*]; P: 113 part B ("Not to us, O Lord, not to us: but to Thy name give glory...") (part A is on another day, see Greek numbering); G: Luke 16:19-31 [T]
22nd Pentecost OT: Is. 43:1-11 [S]; E: I Timothy 4: 9-16 [*]; P: 114; G: Luke 17:12-19 [T] ("I have loved, because the Lord will hear the voice of my prayer...")

Thursday after 22ⁿᵈ Pentecost E: I Timothy 5:1-10 [*]; P: 115; G: Luke 17:20-37 [T] ("I have believed, therefore have I spoken; but I have been humbled exceedingly...")
23ʳᵈ Pentecost OT: Is. 42:1-4 [S]; E: I Timothy 5:22-6:11 [*]; P: 113 part A and 116 as the Alleluia ("When Israel went out of Egypt..." and "O praise the Lord, all ye nations...") (see Greek numbering); G: Luke 18:15-30 [T,W]
Thursday after 23ʳᵈ Pentecost E: I Timothy 6:12-21 [*]; P: 117; G: Luke 18:35-43 - 19:1- end. [T] ("Give praise...")
24ᵗʰ Pentecost OT: Is. 42:18-21 [S]; E: Titus 1:5-2:1 [*]; P: 118 (the longest Psalm, or a few verses, such as verses 1-2, 175-176); G: Luke 20:9-19 [T]
Thursday after 24ᵗʰ Pentecost E: Titus 1:15-2:10 [*]; P: 119; G: Luke 20:20-40 [T]
25ᵗʰ Pentecost (no OT) E: Hebrews 4:1-13 [*]; P: 120; G: Luke 20:41-end [T]
26ᵗʰ or Last Sunday after Pentecost OT: Is. 33:2-9 [S]; E: Heb 7:1-6 [*]; P: 121; G: Lk 21:20-36 [T] [Always the last Sunday; skip Sundays just before this if Pascha is late.]

General Lections for theTwelve Apostles: (except as noted below) E: Rom 5:1-10 [B]; [Psalms as noted.] G: Matthew 4:18-20 [B] and John 21:15-19 [B]; or Luke 6:6-19 [*] Again, Psalms are in Greek Psalm numbering. Below is the Psalm, Apostles' daylight Hour, Bobbio Apostles' Creed assignment, specific Lections:

St. Peter P: 122 First Hour 'I believe in God the Father Almighty.' E: II Pet 1:12-21 [B]; G: Luke 22:31-32, and John 21:18-19, and Luke 21:12-17 [B] (See Ss. Peter & Paul.)
St. John P: 123 Second Hour 'I believe in Jesus Christ, His only Son, God and our Lord.'
St. James P: 124 Third Hour 'He was born of Mary, the Virgin, through the Holy Spirit.'
St. Andrew P: 125 Fourth Hour 'He suffered under Pontius Pilate; was crucified and buried.' (Nov 30/Dec 13) Vigil: E: Gal. 1:2 [*Vatican pericopes] Mass: E: I Cor. 4:9 [*Vatican pericopes]
St. Philip P: 126 Fifth Hour 'He descended into hell.'
St. Thomas P: 127 Sixth Hour 'He arose on the third day.' (Dec 21/Jan 3) E: Philippians 4: 10 - end - [*Vatican pericopes]
St. Bartholomew P: 128 Seventh Hour 'He ascended into heaven.'
St. Matthew P: 129 Eighth Hour 'From there He will come to judge the living and the dead.' G: Matthew 9:9- (13?) [T]
St. James son of Alphaeus P: 130 Ninth Hour 'I believe in the Holy Spirit.'
St. Simon Zelotes P: 131 Tenth Hour 'I believe in the Holy Church.'
St. Judas brother of James (not Iscariot) P: 132 Eleventh Hour 'Through Holy Baptism, remission of sins.'
St. Matthias P: 133 Twelfth Hour 'The resurrection of the flesh and eternal life. Amen.'

Entrance into the Temple of the Blessed Virgin Mary at age three (Nov 21 or 22/ Dec 4 or 5) OT: Exodus 19:7-12 [* General Lection for Feasts of the BVM]; E: Eph 6:1-9 [B General for Feasts of the BVM]; P: 146 ("Praise ye the Lord, because psalm is good..."); G: Luke 2:41-49 [B General for Feasts of the BVM] (Details of this Feast in The *Protevangelium of St. James.*)
Coming out of Egypt of Mary's Great Son (Jan 11/24) Psalm: 136, with the week.
Baptism of St. Paul, Jan25/ Feb 7 E: Romans 5:1-9 [General Lection,] (and may read Acts 9:1-22 [* narrative of his conversion]) for St. Paul: II Tim. 4:7 [*Vatican pericopes]; P: 141; G: Matthew 4:18-20; John 21:15-19 or Luke 6:6-19 (General Lections for Apostles)
Purification of the Virgin, Reception of Christ into the Temple, and blessing of candles OT: Is. 8:13-18 [*]; E: Heb 7:7-26 [*]; P: 135; G: Luke 2:22-40 [*]
The Devil Tempts Christ and flees from His Presence (Feb 15/28) (This is a fixed date, but the content is the same as Anathema Monday, the Monday immediately after the First Sunday in Lent. Note that the fixed date is the end of the "Jesus Fast" that starts Jan. 7th, after Epiphany. The "Jesus Fast" may actually stretch through to Pascha: see Fasting.)

Annunciation (March 25/April 7) E: Heb 2:11-18 [*]; P: 44 (queen); G: Luke 1:26-38 [*]
Finding the True Cross (May 3/ 16) E: Phil. 2:5-11 [B]; P: 134; G: Mt 13:44-50 [B]
St. Patrick (March 17 / 30) OT: Ezech 34:11-31 and Jer 3:14-15 [W]; E: Hebrews 12:28 - 13:21, *[L.] or* Corinthians II 5:11-20, Philippians 4:19-20. *[W.]*; P: 139; G: John 10:1-16, *[L.] or* Matthew 18:18-22, and Luke 10:1-20 *[W.]*
Ss. Peter and Paul (June 29/ Jul 12) readings specific for this day: E: Romans 8:15-27 [L]; P: (may do 77, along with 122 and 141); G: Matthew 5:1-16 [L]
Nativity of St. John the Baptist (June 24/ July 7) and **Conception of St. John the Baptist** (Sept 24/ Oct 7) OT: Isaiah 40:1-11 [L]; E: Acts 13:16-47 [L]; P: 140; G: St. Luke 1:5-80 [L]
Transfiguration also uses Psalm 18, celebrated by the Irish on July 26/Aug. 8): OT: Mal 4:4-6 []; E:2 Peter 1:16-21 []; P: 18 and Ezekial 20-40-42a [*ad libitum of chanter, choice for content]; G: Mark 9:1-9 []
The Macchabees   (August 1/14)   E: Romans 5:11-18 [*Clm], P: of the Sunday; G: of the Sunday
Passion of St. John the Baptist (Aug 29th/ Sept 11th.) OT: Is. 43:1-44 [L]: 5; E: Hebrews 11:33-12:7 [L]; P: 142; G: Matthew 14:1-14 [L]
Mass for New Fruits *(First Sunday in September after the Passion of St. John the Baptist, or Labor Day, if celebrated.)* OT: Joel 2:21-27 [L]; E: I Corinthians 9:7-15 [L]; P: of the Sunday; G: Matthew 12:1-8 [L] and John 4:35-38; 6:48-52 [L]
Dormition of the Blessed Virgin Mary (August 16th / August 29th, Celtic date.) OT: E: I Corinthians 7:25-40 [*L General Lection BVM] or Apoc 14:1-7 [B specific]; P:143 and P 4; G: Luke 1:39-56 [*L if conjoined to Throne of St. Peter in January 18th, the "announcement of the Dormition in Rome"] or Luke 10:38-42 [B specific for Dormition]
Feast of the Birth of the Virgin Mary, Birthgiver of God (Sept 8/21) OT: Exodus 19:7-12 [* General Lection for Feasts of the BVM]; E: Eph 6:1-9 [B General for Feasts of the BVM]; P: 144 and 100; G: Luke 2:41-49 [B General for Feasts of the BVM] ("I will extol thee, O God my king: and I will bless thy name for ever...") (Another set of General Lections for the BVM: E: I Cor 7:25-40 [L], Luke 1:39-56 [L])
Feast of the Dedication, Commemoration of the True Cross (Sept 15/ 28) OT: Gen. 28:10-22 [L,B]; E: I Corinthians. 3:9-17 [L,B]; P: 134; G: John 10:22-28 [L,B,T], and Luke 19:1-10 [L] (with the other Gospel for founders of a church.) (W has other lections.)
St. Michael the Archangel (May 9/22; Sept 29/Oct 12) E: Apoc 12:7-11 (Revelation) [B]; P: 137 and 102; G: Gospel: St Matthew. 17:1-9 [B] (Transfiguration)
All Saints (Nov 1/14, one of two All Saints) General Lections for Requiem E: I Thess. 4:12-18 [* Montpellier, Vatican pericopes]; P: 138; G: John 5:19-20; 11:25-26 [L,W] (General Requiem, or repeat the Propers of the First Sunday after Pentecost.)
St. Martin of Tours (Nov 11/24) OT: Jer. 17:7-14 [B]; E: II Timothy 3:16-4:8 [B]; P: 145; G: Matthew 25:14-21 [B] ("Praise the Lord, O my soul, in my life I will praise the Lord...")
Ordinary Lections for days of the week: [all from B:] Feria I: E: Romans G: Luke; Feria II: E: II Corinthians and Galatians G: Matthew; Feria III: E: Titus; G: Luke; Feria IV: E: Colosians; G: Luke and Mark; Feria V: E: Phil. G: John; "Other" G: John 14
For One Martyr OT Is. 60:4-16 [L]; E: II Timothy 2:3-3:12 [L], P: of the week and Ps 41:3b; G: John 15:17-16:4 [L]
For Many Martyrs OT Is. 65:13-66:2 [L]; E: Apoc. 6:9-7:17 [L]; G: Luke 21:9-19 [L]
For One Confessor E: II Timothy 3:16-4:8 [L]; P: of the week and, Ps 55:9; Ps 20:7; G: Matthew 25:14-23 [L]
For Many Confessors OT: Lamentations 3:25-42 [L]; E: I Timothy. 6:7-16 [L]; G: John 15:1-16 [L]
For a Bishop OT: Ezech 34:11-31 and Jer 3:14-15 [W]; E: Hebrews. 12:28-13:21 [L]; G: John 10:1-16 [L]

For Many Bishops OT: Ezech 34:1-31 [L]; E: I Peter 1:3-20; 5:1-15 [L]; G: Matthew 5:13-19 [L]
Requiem E: I Corinthians. 15:51-58 [L]; P: 138; G: John 5:19-29;11:25-26 [L,W]
General Requiem E: I Thess. 4:12-18 [* Montpellier, Vatican pericopes]; P: 138; G: John 5:19-29;11:25-26 [L,W]
Requiem for a Bishop OT: Is. 26:2-20 [L]; E: I Corinthians. 15:1-22 [L]; P: 138 or 139 or 147 (appropriate to the person) G: John 6:48-59; 12:25-26 [L]
Anniversary of a Church OT: Is. 54:1-56;7 [L]; E: Eph. 2:8-22 [L] P: of the week and Ps 86:1, and P: 134 (for the Feast of the Dedication, Sept. 15th); G: Matthew. 21:10-17 [L]
Professing of Virgins or for a Virgin Saint
OT: Is. 61:10-62:7 [L]; E: I Corinthians 7:25-40 [L]; G: Luke 1:39-56 [L]
or OT: Is. 61:10-62:7 [L]; E: Romans 7:24-8:4 [L]; G: Matthew 25:1-13 [L]
When the the Bishops ought to announce that the people pay a tenth OT: Mal. 1:6-11 [L]; E: I Corinthians. 9:7-12 [L]; G: Luke 20:45-21:5 [L] and Matthew 6:2-4 [L]
[Historical, but although each person should give of their substance, it should not oppress the poor.]
Ordination of Deacons OT:Ez. 44:15-16 [L]; E: I Timothy. 3:8-13 [L]; G: Lk 9:57-62 [L]
Ordination of Priests E: Titus 1:1-6 [L]; G: Luke 12:4-44 [L]
and/or OT: Ez 33:7-20 [W]; E: Hebrews. 12:28-13:21 [W]; P: Lev 2,2; G: John 10:1-30 [W]
Consecration of Bishops OT: Jer 1:4-19 [W]; E: I Timothy1:5; 3:1-7; 6:11 [W]; and II Timothy 2:15 [W]; and I Timothy 4:13-15; 5:22; 4:16; 3:13 [W]; P: Ps 106:32 ; G: John 21:15-17 [W]; and Luke 10:23 [W]; and Matthew 16:13-19 [W]
On Completion of a Pilgrimage E: I Timothy. 3:14-16 [L]; G: Lk 9:51-56; 12:35-37 [L]
On Returning from a Pilgrimage E: Romans 15:17-29 [L]; G: John 4:45-54 [L]
Psalms of Praise: P 146: Entrance into the Temple Nov. 21 or 22; P 147 First Sun. after Pentecost an All-Saints day; P 148 Christmas; P 149: Pentecost. P 150: the Alleluia at Pascha, Christmas, and Pentecost.)

Examples of Propers

All the Propers through the year are now translated: contact Bishop Maelruain. It was difficult to choose a few **Propers** for meditations. The Vigil of the Resurrection is a unique Mass, including much more than simple Propers integrated together, and although it is in this book, it is not an example of a usual Feast or Sunday and the use of its Propers.

The "Traditio" of Palm Sunday of St. Ambrose is also included in this book, since it is also a teaching for Catechumens. Kerubs from Ezekiel: St. Matthew - Man; St. Mark - Lion; St. Luke - Bull; St. John - Eagle; explained by the beginning of each Gospel.

The following are Propers for the Feast of the Finding of the True Cross, May 3/16, chosen because these include a devotion to the Holy Cross and music which may be done at several occasions through the year. Oengus says on this day, "The first finding of Christ's Cross with [its] many virtues: the death of Conlaed, a fair pillar: the great feast of the Virgin Mary." For the Finding of the True Cross, May 3rd, from *The Martyrology of Tallaght*: "Discovery of the Cross of Christ; the Conception of the Virgin Mary;..." On the Celtic calendar, the Annunciation coincides with the original date of the Crucifixion, (although the Crucifixion is always celebrated on the movable calendar), and therefore the Cross and the Blessed Virgin Mary are always commemorated together. (In the Byzantine Rite, the Annunciation is on the original date of the Resurrection, but the iconography of the Blessed Virgin Mary including icons of the Annunciation, require that there are circles under her eyes because of her sorrow. The Blessed Virgin Mary is also central in the Byzantine Hymns of Holy and Great Friday and the Akathist Hymns in Lent. In both the Byzantine and Western Rites, the sorrow of the Virgin Mary at the Crucifixion is honored through meditations such as the "Stabbat Mater" and "Ti Ipermaho.")

Feast of the Finding of the True Cross May 3 / 16

Introductory Collects

Beloved, let us glory in the Cross of our Lord Jesus Christ and let us rejoice with all our minds and with great reverence and joy of spirit celebrate the feast of this day because Our Lord and Savior Himself hung upon it and triumphed over the devil. Through this Cross the desires of concupiscence which evilly seduced by the allurement of the tree are checked by the bitterness of gall: that which deceived by the sweetness of the apple is restrained by the sharpness of vinegar, O Savior Who reigneth with Thee and the Holy Spirit throughout all ages of ages. Amen

Almighty and eternal God Who wast pleased by the joining of Thy Word to earthly members through truly venerable Mary, we beg for Thy immense clemency that we might proclaim by her veneration and achieve Thy satisfaction through Christ our Lord Who reigneth with Thee and the Holy Spirit, throughout all ages of ages. Amen.

Collects Before the Epistle

Grant us, O Almighty God, that through the Mystery of the Cross of Thine only-begotten Son the cup of venom of the old serpent which tries the faithful may pass by, through the healing which Christ commanded. May the Cross be able to purge from the breast of the faithful whatsoever transgression of the precepts might expel us from paradise and may the confession of the Name of Christ reform us unto paradise. our Lord Jesus Christ Who reigneth with Thee and the Holy Spirit throughout all ages of ages. Amen

Hear us O Lord Holy Father , Almighty God Who wast pleased to illumine the whole world from the shelter of the womb of blessed Mary. We suppliants pray to Thy Majesty that although we are not adequate in accomplishments by her Motherhood and Protection may we be deserving: We, Thy servants, beg Thee, O Lord, that we may enjoy the joys of Blessed Mary whose acts blots out the hand-writing of our sins through her child, Christ our Lord Who reigneth with Thee and the Holy Spirit, throughout all ages of ages. Amen.

Epistle Phil. 2:5-11, Psalm 134, "Praise ye the Name of the Lord...",

Gospel Matthew 13:44-50

Post Nomina

O Lord Jesus Christ Who wast suspended on the pillory of the Cross and in the likeness of a servant which Thou didst accept, Thou didst cry out unto the Father "Why hast Thou forsaken me?" and asked that He forgive Thy persecutors, we suppliants implore clemency that Thou may be pleased to grant that which was provided and demanded by the Father for the restoration of the humility of the flesh, now, by the same means, may endure by the power of Thy Divinity unto eternity, O Savior Who reigneth with Thee and the Holy Spirit throughout all ages of ages. Amen.

Ad Pacem

O Lord, may the Holy Spirit Who filled the viscera of blessed Mary with the truth of His splendor, be pleased to take up the gifts set forth upon Thine altar through our Lord Jesus Christ Who reigneth with Thee and the Holy Spirit throughout all ages of ages.

Dignum

It is worthy and just Almighty God to fulfill the debt of Sacrifice unto Thee and to raise unceasing praises of Thee and to set side by side the examples of Adam who dwelled in paradise and the Redeemer of the human race: Adam was indeed first but Christ is better: Adam was of earth; Christ is of Heaven: Adam was formed from Earth; Christ was conceived by a Word: Then, Eve was deceived by the tempting devil; Now, Mary is illumined by the Announcing Angel: Then, by the invidious serpent, Man who was created is bound; Now, through the beginning of mercy, man who endures is freed: Then, Man because of inattention is commanded to be banished from paradise: Now, the thief merits paradise for confessing Christ: Therefore we suppliants pray Thee O Most clement Father through the inexplicable Sacrament of the Cross and through the Kingship of Our Lord Jesus Christ Thy Son, that on this day on which we celebrate His Cross, we may celebrate with Spiritual joy and modest exultation and may He accept our humble voices in praise with the Powers saying:

Proper Blessing of the Day by a Bishop only if present

(Note: Although a Bishop might be rarely available, most of the Bishop's blessings offer insight into the Gospels and Epistles, and offer a reference for the preparation of a Sermon. For example, "length, breadth, etc." see Meditations on the Psalms, four layers of meaning: historical, and spiritual divided into allegorical, anagogical, and tropological. In Conferences of Abbot Isaac with St. John Cassian on prayer, he shows how the prayer of Jesus in chapter 17 of St. John's Gospel combines all four kinds of prayer:: supplication, prayer, intercession, thanksgiving (see the discussions of the "Our Father," layers of meaning, Kerubs). Also see the Hymn, "The Deers' Cry," which uses this image of "length, breadth, etc.")

V. KAL. Maii. Inventio Sanctae Crucis. Benedictio

May Almighty God Who restored the race of humanity through the Passion and gibbet of the Cross of His Only-Begotten Son Jesus Christ, bless you. Amen. And may He grant to you that with all the Saints may you, with devoted minds, be able to comprehend what the length, breadth, height and the depth of the same Cross may be. Amen.

To what extent you deny yourselves and bear the Cross, thus through the course of the present life you are able to follow our Savior, so that you may be worthy to be received among the chorus of angels after death. Amen.

May He Whose Dominion and Kingdom remain without end, be pleased to sustain us unto ages of ages. Amen.

May the blessing of God: the Father and the Son and the Holy Spirit and the peace of the Lord be ever with you. Amen.

> [Benedicat vos omnipotens deus qui per unigenti sui iesu christi domini nostri passionem. et crucis patibulum genus redemit humanum. Amen. Concedatque vobis ut cum omnibus sanctis qu[a]e sit eiusdem crucis. longitudo. latitudo. sublimitas et profundum. mente devota conprehendere possitis. Amen.
> Quatenus vosmetipsos abnegando. crucemque gestando. ita in presentis vite stadio redemptorem nostrum possitis sequi. ut ei inter choros angelorum post obitum mereamini adscisci. Amen.
> / Quod ipse. Amen. Benedictio.]

Post Communion Collects

Satisfied and refreshed with spiritual food let us venerate Almighty God the Father for all that has been done [for us] through our Lord Jesus Christ His Son Who reigneth and remaineth with Him with the Holy Spirit unto eternal ages of ages. Amen.

Hear us God the Almighty Father and grant what we ask: through our Lord Jesus Christ Who reigneth with Thee and the Holy Spirit thoughout all ages of ages. Amen.

Prayer During the Adoration of the Holy Cross, after the Mass of Finding of the True Cross

[Holy and Great Friday at the Sixth and Ninth Hours, Mid-Lent, Mid Pascha, Finding of the True Cross May 3, Dedication Sept. 14, and other devotions.]

℣. O Lord Jesus Christ Most Glorious creator of the world Who with Splendor of equal Glory to the Father and the Holy Spirit wast pleased to accept pure flesh and and permitted Thy most glorious palms to be nailed to the pillory of the Cross so that Thou might shatter the gates of hell and free the human race from death.

℟. Have mercy upon me who am miserable: who am borne down in my sins and sullied by an unclean lip: please do not abandon me O Glorious Lord but please absolve me for I have carried out evil deeds. Hear me, prostrate in the worship of Thy Life-giving Cross, so that in this holy solemn act I may be cleansed and worthy to attend Thee Who Livest and reignest with Thine unoriginate Father and the Holy Spirit throughout all ages of ages. Amen.

℣. O Lord Jesus Christ, I adore Thee ascending the Cross and bearing the Crown of Thorns:
℟. I beg Thee to liberate me from the angel of death.

℣. O Lord Jesus Christ I adore Thee wounded upon the Cross: Gall and vinegar Thy drink:
℟. I beg Thee that Thy death be my life.

℣. O Lord Jesus Christ, I adore Thee descending into hell freeing the captives:
℟. I beg Thee, do not let me go into the punishments of hell.

℣. O Lord Jesus Christ I adore Thee ascending into heaven and sitting at the right hand of the Father:
℟. I beg Thee have mercy upon me.

℣. O Lord Jesus Christ, I adore Thee coming in Judgement:
℟. I beg Thee that in Thy coming Thou dost not enter into judgement with me Thy sinful Servant but I beg Thee that Thou cast away my sins before Thou judge me. Amen.

When there is a special veneration of the Cross:
(During veneration: This Hymn is sung three times. Russian melody):

Be-fore Thy Cross, we bow down and wor - ship,
and Thy Re-sur-rec-tion we glor-i-fy.

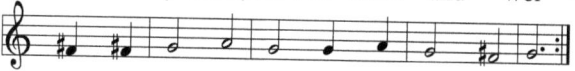

(Or the Greek melody below sung three times. Notes are natural unless flatted in this mode:)

Be-fore Thy Cross, Christ our Sav - ior, do we wor- ship and bow down, and Thy Re- sur- rec- tion we glor - i - fy.

Saint Patrick, Bishop (Apostle to the Irish)
March 17/March 30

St. Patrick, the Apostle to the Celtic people (including people of continental Europe who were brought back to knowledge after the dark ages by Irish monks; also the people of the American continents, as Old Irish Ogham writing has been found in West Virginia and elsewhere both before Christ and from later in the Christian era). The Psalm for today is almost a telling of the life of St. Patrick and what happened to his enemies through the hand of God, not the armies of men. If today is a Sunday, do each Proper and Lection for the Sunday in Lent first, but also do the commemorations and hymns for St. Patrick. In ancient Irish tradition, the fast is eased slightly today. Although on this day most of the Propers and Lections are only the General Propers for Apostles, it is probably one of the most requested Masses in the Celtic Rite.

>Use the **General Propers for Apostles, Martyrs, and Holy Virgins in the Celtic Missal,** with the day or week's Propers in Lent; for: the Collect Before the Epistle, the Dignum, the Post Sanctus (before the "Most Dangerous Prayer").

Old Testament
Ezech 34:11-31 and Jer 3:14-15 [Also do the Old Testament reading for today.]

Introductory Collect [Also, use the Introductory Collect for this week in Lent.]
O Lord God Almighty who dost answer the intercessions of the Saints for us, grant, we beseech Thee, that we may exult in the example of Saint Patrick, the confessor and High Priest and rejoice in his advocacy for us. Through Christ our Lord Who reigneth with Thee and the Holy Spirit throughout ages of ages. R. Amen.

Epistle Hebrews 12:28 - 13:21, *[Luxeiul] or* Corinthians II 5:11-20, Philippians 4:19-20. *[Wurzburg]*

Gradual Psalm 139 in Greek and Latin numbering entire, see the Psalter.
>(The Psalm for today in Lent should also be done.)

Alleluia *(The Alleluia may use the verses from the Speckled Book of Oengus:)*
Alleluia, Alleluia. The flame of a splendid sun, the Apostle of virginal Erin, may Patrick, with many thousands, be the shelter of our wretchedness. Alleluia.

Gospel John 10:1-16, *[Lux.] or* Matthew 18:18-22, and Luke 10:1-20 *[Wur.]*

Ad Pacem, (Secret, or Collect of the Preface) Always said aloud.
>[Use the first Ad Pacem from the Celtic Missal first. Then the following for St. Patrick. Then, for Lent.]

We beseech Thee Author of Blessings and Source of Sanctification that Thou be pleased to bless and sanctify this Sacrifice and by means of the intervention of the Blessed High Priest Patrick grant forgiveness of sins to us Thy servants. R. Amen.

Dignum, Contestatio, or Immolacio (Preface in the Roman Rite)
[Use the first Dignum, then for Martyrs and Apostles in the Celtic Missal, and then for this week in Lent.]

[ending from the Preface for the Apostles and All the Saints]:
...through our Lord Jesus Christ, by Whom all the Angels, Archangels, Prophets and Apostles, Martyrs and Confessors, Virgins, and All of the Saints, with a perpetual hymn and unwearied praises, with the four beasts and the twenty four elders *[Re.4:4-11, 5:8-14]* harmonize, saying: *[Sanctus, etc.]*

Proper Blessing of the Day by a Bishop only if present
(Note: A Bishop might be rarely available, but Bishop's blessings offer insight into Gospels and Epistles, and offer a reference for the preparation of a Sermon.)

In Natale Unius Apostoli [One Apostle, not specific to St. Patrick]
May God who granted you to be established in the Apostolic principles, be pleased to bless you through the intercessions and examples of His Apostle Patrick. Amen.

And may He who desires that you be adorned with the armor of their examples and writings, defend you from the snares of the Adversary through Apostolic protection. Amen.

So that you may come through to the inheritance of the eternal fatherland through their intercessions, and through whose doctrine you hold on to integrity of the faith. Amen.

May He Whose Kingdom and Dominion remain without end, be pleased to sustain us unto ages of ages. Amen.

May the blessing of God: the Father and the Son and the Holy Spirit and the peace of the Lord be ever with you. Amen.

> [Deus qui vos in apostolicis tribuit consistere fundamentis. benedicere vos dignetur beati apostoli sui ill. intercedentibus meritis. Amen.
> / Defendatque vos a cunctis adversis apostolicis persidiis [praesidiis]. qui vos eorum voluit ornari et munerari examplis et documentis. Amen.
> Quo per eorum intercessionem perueniatis ad aeterne patrie hereditatem. per quorum doctrinam tenetis fidei integritatem. Amen.
> Quod ipse prestare dignetur cuius regnum et imperium sine fine permanet in secula seculorum. Amen.
> Benedictio dei patris et filii. et spiritus sancti / et pax domini sit semper vobiscum. Amen.]

Confraction: 11 Particles for Holy Apostles

Hymns During Holy Communion: The Abecedarian Hymn "Audite omnes amantes" by St. Secundinus, a Breastplate, should be said in the three days of St. Patrick's Feast day (see contents). Also may be sung: The "Deer's Cry" by St. Patrick, which is another Breastplate.

Post Communion [Also use the Post Communion for this week in Lent.]
Grant we beseech Thee O Lord, that we be strengthened by Thy Life-Giving Sacrament and the prayers of the High Priest, Saint Patrick, Through Christ our Lord Who reigneth with Thee and the Holy Spirit throughout ages of ages. **R.** Amen.

The Traditio: Symbols of Gospels and Creed

Also called "The Opening of the Ears." A Catechism in preparation for Baptism. Palm Sunday after the blessing of Palms, for the whole congregation, every year. From the Bobbio Missal. (A longer version is in the Ambrosian Rite.)

STAND:
The ears of the Catechumens are anointed with Oil of Catechumens.
The Priest says to each: *"Effeta: that is, 'be opened,' Effeta." Then, to all present:*
Beloved, It is a divine joy to open the Gospel unto you. First we must explain in order, what the Gospel is and whence it cometh and whose words are set forth in it and why there are four who wrote these details and even who these four are, whom the prophet announced by the divine Spirit in symbols. Let this pass down without extreme methodical ordering which may even be a cause of confusion, so that, the ears of you who come to it might be opened and your senses may begin pounding away at it:

The Gospel is properly called the Good Announcement and particularly, it is the announcement/Annunciation of Jesus Christ our Lord: However, the Gospel is descended from Him because it announces and discloses these things which were spoken through His Prophets: He came in the flesh: as was written: I have said: Behold I am with you.

Briefly, this is an explanation of what is the Gospel: who are these four who were indicated by the Prophet? Now we assign figures and names to each based what was indicated by the Prophet Ezechial: "the aspects of those to the right, the first was like unto the Face of a man, the second like unto the face of a Lion ; of those the left the first was like the face of a bull and the second what that of an Eagle. " It is without a doubt that those four figures stand for these four Evangelists, but the names of those who wrote the Gospels are Matthew, Mark, Luke and John.

Hear the Gospel according to Matthew:
1 The book of the generation of Jesus Christ, the son of David, the son of Abraham:
2 Abraham begot Isaac. And Isaac begot Jacob. And Jacob begot Judas and his brethren.
3 And Judas begot Phares and Zara of Thamar. And Phares begot Esron. And Esron begot Aram.
4 And Aram begot Aminadab. And Aminadab begot Naasson. And Naasson begot Salmon.
5 And Salmon begot Booz of Rahab. And Booz begot Obed of Ruth. And Obed begot Jesse.
6 And Jesse begot David the king. And David the king begot Solomon, of her that had been the wife of Urias.
7 And Solomon begot Roboam. And Roboam begot Abia. And Abia begot Asa.
8 And Asa begot Josaphat. And Josaphat begot Joram. And Joram begot Ozias.
9 And Ozias begot Joatham. And Joatham begot Achaz. And Achaz begot Ezechias.
10 And Ezechias begot Manasses. And Manasses begot Amon. And Amon begot Josias.
11 And Josias begot Jechonias and his brethren in the transmigration of Babylon.
12 And after the transmigration of Babylon, Jechonias begot Salathiel. And Salathiel begot Zorobabel.
13 And Zorobabel begot Abiud. And Abiud begot Eliacim. And Eliacim begot Azor.
14 And Azor begot Sadoc. And Sadoc begot Achim. And Achim begot Eliud.
15 And Eliud begot Eleazar. And Eleazar begot Mathan. And Mathan begot Jacob.
16 And Jacob begot Joseph the husband of Mary, of whom was born Jesus, who is called Christ.
17 So all the generations, from Abraham to David, are fourteen generations. And from David to the transmigration of Babylon, are fourteen generations: and from the transmigration of Babylon to Christ are fourteen generations.
18 Now the generation of Christ was in this wise.

Beloved Brethren, let us explain to you why each one has its particular image and why Matthew is represented by the figure of a man: It is because the beginning of Matthew's Gospel gives nothing except the birth of the Savior: he tells us of the unabridged order of the generations.

Hear the Gospel according to Mark:
1 The beginning of the gospel of Jesus Christ, the Son of God.
2 As it is written in Isaias the prophet: Behold I send my angel before thy face, who shall prepare the way before thee.
3 A voice of one crying in the desert: Prepare ye the way of the Lord, make straight his paths.

Mark the Evangelist, bearing the figure of a Lion for the wilderness, begins saying "a voice crying in the wilderness prepare ye the way of the Lord". Further it is because the unconquerable One rules. We find examples of the many aspects of this Lion which are found in the saying: Judah my son is a lion's whelp: of my seed, lying thou dost sleep like a lion as just like a lion cub, who will awaken Him?

Hear the Gospel according to Luke:
1 Forasmuch as many have taken in hand to set forth in order a narration of the things that have been accomplished among us;
2 According as they have delivered them unto us, who from the beginning were eyewitnesses and ministers of the word:
3 It seemed good to me also, having diligently attained to all things from the beginning, to write to thee in order, most excellent Theophilus,
4 That thou mayest know the verity of those words in which thou hast been instructed.
5 There was in the days of Herod, the king of Judea, a certain priest named Zachary, of the course of Abia; and his wife was of the daughters of Aaron, and her name Elizabeth.
Luke, the Evangelist bears the aspect of a bull as his emblem: Our Savior is the Sacrifice and therefore Luke is compared to the bull. It is also because it contains the two horns of the two Testaments and the four feet of the four Gospels.

Hear the Gospel according to John:
1 In the beginning was the Word, and the Word was with God, and the Word was God.
2 The same was in the beginning with God.
3 All things were made by him: and without him was made nothing that was made.

John bears the likeness of an Eagle for he strives to the very heights. As David said of Christ: Thy youth shall be renewed like the Eagle's: it is Jesus Christ our Lord who rising from the dead ascends unto the Heavens whence soon, reigning he will come to us who hope that the Church may be glorified to spread new beginnings of Christian rule.

The giving of the Creed:

The divine Sacraments, dear Brethren, are not distributed as widely as is believing, neither is believing only but fearing nor can one hold the faith who is not grounded in the foundation of the fear of God. As Solomon said: the beginning Wisdom is fear of the Lord. One who fears the Lord in all things said by God is wise and faithful. This Symbol which you will hear today is that without which one can neither proclaim Christ nor hold the faith nor celebrate the grace of Baptism: The symbol in the seal of faith. the sacrament of the Eternal Catholic religion. May you be adequately prepared with all due reverence:

Hear the Symbol which the Holy Catholic Church bequeaths to you from the maternal mouth:

I believe in one God, the Father Almighty, maker of heaven and earth and of all things visible and invisible. And in one Lord Jesus Christ, the Only-Begotten Son of God. Born of the Father before all ages. Light of light, true God of true God. Born, not made, of one Substance with the Father: through Whom all things were made. Who for us men, and for our Salvation descended from heaven. And was Incarnate of the Holy Spirit and the Virgin Mary: And was born man. And was crucified also for us: under Pontius Pilate; He suffered and was buried. And He rose on the third day, according to the Scriptures. And ascended into heaven: and sitteth at the right hand of God the Father. And He shall come again with glory to judge both the living and the dead: Whose Kingdom shall have no end. And I believe in the Holy Spirit, the Lord and Giver of life: Who proceedeth from the Father. Who with the Father and the Son together is worshiped and glorified: Who spake by the Prophets. And in one, Holy, Catholic, and Apostolic Church. I confess one Baptism for the remission of sins. And I look for the resurrection of the dead. And the life of the world to come. Amen.

This explanation of the Symbol is repeated just as we said it so that is may be better implanted in your senses:
I believe in one God, the Father Almighty, maker of heaven and earth and of all things visible and invisible. And in one Lord Jesus Christ, the Only-Begotten Son of God. Born of the Father before all ages. Light of light, true God of true God. Born, not made, of one Substance with the Father: through Whom all things were made. Who for us men, and for our Salvation descended from heaven. And was Incarnate of the Holy Spirit and the Virgin Mary: And was born man. And was crucified also for us: under Pontius Pilate; He suffered and was buried. And He rose on the third day, according to the Scriptures. And ascended into heaven: and sitteth at the right hand of God the Father. And He shall come again with glory to judge both the living and the dead: Whose Kingdom shall have no end. And I believe in the Holy Spirit, the Lord and Giver of life: Who proceedeth from the Father. Who with the Father and the Son together is worshiped and glorified: Who spake by the Prophets. And in one, Holy, Catholic, and Apostolic Church. I confess one Baptism for the remission of sins. And I look for the resurrection of the dead. And the life of the world to come. Amen.

The Third time, as is said after the same manner so that in the future we may be able to arise by the more faithful course to the order of the composition of the Symbol:
I believe in one God, the Father Almighty, maker of heaven and earth and of all things visible and invisible. And in one Lord Jesus Christ, the Only-Begotten Son of God. Born of the Father before all ages. Light of light, true God of true God. Born, not made, of one Substance with the Father: through Whom all things were made. Who for us men, and for our Salvation descended from heaven. And was Incarnate of the Holy Spirit and the Virgin Mary: And was born man. And was crucified also for us: under Pontius Pilate; He suffered and was buried. And He rose on the third day, according to the Scriptures. And ascended into heaven: and sitteth at the right hand of God the Father. And He shall come again with glory to judge both the living and the dead: Whose Kingdom shall have no end. And I believe in the Holy Spirit, the Lord and Giver of life: Who proceedeth from the Father. Who with the Father and the Son together is worshiped and glorified: Who spake by the Prophets. And in one, Holy, Catholic, and Apostolic Church. I confess one Baptism for the remission of sins. And I look for the resurrection of the dead. And the life of the world to come. Amen.

I believe in one God, the Father [Pause] Almighty, maker of heaven and earth and of all things visible and invisible. And in one Lord Jesus Christ, the Only-Begotten Son of God. Born of the Father before all ages. Light of light, true God of true God. Born, not made, of one Substance with the Father: through Whom all things were made. Who for us men, and for our Salvation descended from heaven.

Behold, you have added "almighty" and truthfully added nothing which takes away from the promise, but watch securely: if you believe because He is omnipotent who makes the promise and in Jesus Christ His only begotten Son, our Lord. This is that sacrament by faith: unless one believes the Son of God with one's whole mind, they cannot confess the Father. Believe therefore in the Son of God: Only begotten of Unbegotten: living from living, true from true.

And was Incarnate of the Holy Spirit and the Virgin Mary
You hear the Holy Spirit, the author: yet you might doubt that the Virgin was able to conceive because the angel Gabriel spoke to Mary saying: The Holy Spirit cometh unto thee and the power of the Most High shall overshadow Thee. Why do you not believe he was formed a man in the womb of the Virgin Whom you believe formed man out earth? Neither should you doubt that the Virgin remained virgin after birth since many years before, the prophet Isaias blindly said: Behold a virgin shall conceive and bear a son. This divine statement is believing by authority.

And was crucified also for us: under Pontius Pilate; He suffered and was buried.
Let nothing confuse you concerning the trepidations and suffering of your Lord. Feel uneasy about nothing concerning the Cross, about nothing concerning the Tomb. Is it not in Him Who redeemeth you of the weakness of your fragility that there is the gift of faith? His Cross is your power. His death is your life.

And He rose on the third day, according to the Scriptures. And ascended into heaven: and sitteth at the right hand of God the Father.
If the three day burial of your Lord disturbs you, the eternal resurrection should lend all the more strength. The healing of every infirmity is in Christ. Therefore it is appropriate to marvel because He to Whom was due Heaven by attributes bore the Cross for you who are contemptible. If you believe the things you see and deny what you do not see, you are not capable of glory.

And He shall come again with glory to judge both the living and the dead: Whose Kingdom shall have no end.
Behold that He Who was judged of iniquities upon the earth, will come judging, seated in the Heavens. If you discern that any is guilty, then fear the Judge.

And I believe in the Holy Spirit, the Lord and Giver of life: Who proceedeth from the Father. Who with the Father and the Son together is worshiped and glorified: Who spake by the Prophets.
If, by faith, you have believed in the God the Father Almighty and in His Only begotten Son, it is necessary to confess the Holy Spirit. This is the same Holy Spirit Who proceedeth from the Father, of Whom the Savior said unto His blessed Apostles: Go forth and baptize all nations in the name of the Father and the Son and the Holy Spirit. One cannot recognize in quality, one whom one is not able to recognize in name.

And in one, Holy, Catholic, and Apostolic Church. I confess one Baptism for the remission of sins. And I look for the resurrection of the dead. And the life of the world to come.
If you do not believe in the Holy Church of God, then you are not capable of receiving the gifts from the Church of God because you are professed by this same with God the Father and the Son and the Holy Spirit so that through the Grace of Baptism you may be granted forgiveness of your sins. and your flesh may be renewed in the Resurrection unto eternity.
If you do not believe that your sins have been sent away from you, you cannot be absolved of sin.
If you do not believe that your flesh will be restored to you in the Resurrection, after death you will be unable to come to the fruition of life eternal. Amen.

Prayer: The Our Father, The Divine Prayer, The Lord's Prayer

What is Prayer, Abbot Isaac, and "Heavenly Sedulius" (St. Siadal)

In the two Conferences of Abbot Isaac with St. John Cassian, on Prayer, Abbot Isaac shows how the prayer of Jesus in chapter 17 of St. John's Gospel combines all four kinds of prayer: **supplication, prayer, intercession, thanksgiving,** in Chapter XVII of the first Conference of Abbot Isaac. (This entire Conference of Abbot Isaac is worthy to study.) Many Saints have commented on how to pray.

Then, concerning the Lord's Prayer, Abbot Isaac says, "And so there follows after these different kinds of supplication a still more sublime and exalted condition which is brought about by the contemplation of God alone and by fervent love, by which the mind, transporting and flinging itself into love for Him, addresses God most familiarly as its own Father with a piety of its own." In the next several chapters (XVIII through XXV) he discusses the "Our Father." This is an important meditation. Faith in God must be continuous, and therefore prayer must be continuous, and is needed to receive "Theosis," also understood as the "acquisition of the Holy Spirit," the pouring out of God's grace upon us. In Baptism and Chrismation this Enlightenment first comes to a new member of the Church, and may increase if a person loves God and prays continuously in Word, Thought, and Deed. Pope St. Leo the Great commented that at the Ascension of our Lord Jesus Christ, God came to earth, and in the Resurrection brought His humanity to heaven, so that we could rise to heaven with Him. Although that separates the natures of Christ perhaps too much, it gives humanity hope. Only a correct understanding of the Holy Trinity in the Orthodox Nicene Creed allows Enlightenment of the Holy Spirit, as is stated in the "Traditio." As the Celtic Missal says after the vesting, "Let our prayer ascend to the Throne of Thy Renown, O Lord, lest emptiness be returned to us in response to our petitions..."

Another commentary from the great Irish poet of the third century, Caelius Sedulius (the heavenly Siadal). His epic poem, the "Carmen Paschale" (Song of Pascha), is about the Life of Christ. This poem was completely translated into every European language but English, and was very popular throughout the Medieval era throughout Europe. It was plagiarized by Milton. (A century-old translation by Sigerson dropped half the lines; lines cut away included the title of Christ on the Cross, and lines about the True Eucharist; Sigerson may not have believed in Sacraments. A new translation has just been completed and may be more promising; we haven't seen it yet.) The Carmen Paschale has an analysis of the Lord's Prayer at the end of the second book. From Sigerson's awkward translation:

Now, therefore, showing swift Salvation's way,
The Judge benign His people taught to pray,
To briefly ask that they might quick obtain:
"Our Father" saying - ours, by Baptism's gain,
His own by right: His honor thus He gave,
What He alone possessed this all might have,
Rememb'ring God our Father is, in Him
We all should brothers be - not through the dim
Sad bond of Flesh original, but flame
Of spiritual Fire, to end our shame -
And don the new man lest we, who have been,
Through Christ, adopted sons of that serene
High Father, fall, degenerate, terrene.

Where hallowed should He be, Who every part
Has hallowed? Where, unless in the pure heard!
That we might hallowed by our worship grow
He first Himself permits, and orders so
That we bless Him Who blesses all below.

    His Kingdom come: that Kingdom all so fair!
Where end is none, nor Death is anywhere,
Nor changing times deplorable, nor Night
O'ermasters Day; where reigns our Prince of Light,
And Victor Victims throng rejoicing round,
Their noble brows with crowns eternal crowned!
    With constant vows, by noon, we pray, and night,
His Will be done on Earth as in the light Of Heaven -
Who no sin would have, nor fell
Assault of foe, malign, implacable:
Lest bodies now tow'rd Heaven drawn, anew
Revoked on Earth, might in the thralldom rue:-
Who, all things fostering with love, would even
Preserve the body with the soul 'twas given -
One part of earth we are, and one of Heaven!
    We hope the Food of Faith - our daily bread -
Lest that of Truth our minds be hungered,
And fast from Christ, Who feeds us with His Word and Body:
He, the Food, the Word - our Lord!
How cleaves His speech delectable, which comes
More sweet than honey in the honeycombs!
    We ask Forgiveness as we do not fail
Ourselves to pardon debts; He holds us bail,
Our word, His ward - more strictly bound if we
(Released ourselves) another will not free.
Should He - a thousand pounds forgiving - find
We nothing bate, but for a crown will grind
Some wretch; forthwith the Judgment falls, and cast
In dungeon dire we bide in bondage fast
Till all be paid, the uttermost and last.
    Our Lord - the Way of Light, of Peace the Path -
No tempter's snare will spread, but when He hath
Our evil left, He leaves us to - who loves
The world's soft lures, its pomp and pride, approves
Perdition's path: the Lover of all Good
Leaves him to go the downward way he would.
Let us step back, and seek ere it be late,
In heart, that rougher path which leads, though strait,
To climes celestial through the Narrow Gate!
    If man would Evil shun, advancing, we
Must follow Good - that fetters, this makes free,
This nourishes, that kills; remoter far
Than fire from water, light from darkness, star
From Earth, from discords peace, and all
Abounding Life from the sepulchral pall,
Is Good from Evil. Lo, before the eye
Two paths, to right and left diverging, lie:
One calls the Just unto the joys above -
Thy welcome, Abram! And thy breast of love -
One takes the guilty to their punishment.
God's Sole Will and good Liberty are meant
That all His Flock should, wolf-escaped, keep tryst
And live in joy amid the flocks of Christ.

Salve Sancta Parens (*another Hymn from the Carmen Paschale of Caelius Sedulius.*)
Hail, holy Mother, thou who'st born the King
Who Heav'n and Earth upholds and everything
Embracing, is Eternal, Infinite!
Thou, with a Virgin's honor, the delight
Of Motherhood hast owned: there hath not been
Thy like on earth, nor ever shall be seen,
Sole pleasing Christ, incomparable queen!

More verses about St. Mary from the Carmen Paschale:
As from sharp thorns there springs, all soft and pure
The Rose, which doth its mother's self obscure
With honor fair, so sacred Mary came
From stock of Eve and cleansed away her shame.

Meditations on Psalms and Hours

The purpose of prayer and the performance of formal Hours cannot be separated. The Dignum for the Ascension: "...Wherefore, rejoicing in the midst of Thine altars, O Lord of Virtues, we offer Thee sacrifices of praise..." There are many reasons to pray the Hours using the Psalms. The Psalms prophecy the Life of Christ. Christ and the Apostles continued the Old Testament tradition of singing Hymns, Mk 14:26. The Hours of the day and night help to focus on the struggle of the soul in the "arena" (sand where athletes wrestled). The following meditations on the Hours compare the writings of St. John Cassian: his Rule (Institutes), and also his Conferences with the desert fathers of Alexandria. (These meditations were compiled by Elizabeth Dowling.)

The Term "Sin" in the Psalms, Deficiency versus Active Sin

Since the words "sin" and "enemy" are mentioned very often in the Psalms, these terms should be defined. **'Amartyr'** in Greek means out of harmony. The Latin term **'Delicto'** means deficiency. Deficiencies are different than sins caused by deeds. Psalm 50 Greek numbering, or 51 Hebrew numbering, says in many English translations, "...in sins did my mother conceive me..." However, the Latin that the Irish used was 'delicto,' reading "...in deficiencies did my mother conceive me..." a very different concept. Not all sins are willful, but may be of neglect, ignorance, addiction, or even nature (although we were created good, we may have some natural tendencies that may distract us if used incorrectly). The Latin term: **'Peccata'** means sin done by choice, an active sin. The term "peccata" is used when asking God for forgiveness for sins, because forgiveness of a willed, active sin is asking more than asking forgiveness of ignorance or neglect, unless the ignorance or neglect is willful avoidance. The Augustinian presumption that sins are all willful also assumes that by the will alone the sins can be reversed, almost without God's help, almost Pelagian ("works" without faith or God's grace). Telling people to just "will" themselves to get better leads to harsh judgment of those who struggle with mental illness or stress caused by a trauma. Harsh judgment itself is prideful, and does not ask for or offer forgiveness, or healing, or prayer, or faith, i.e., is not Christian. Guilt is not the same as original sin: we inherit a tendency to sin from Adam and Eve, because we have the ability to explore and have free will, but we do not inherit the guilt of another.

"Flesh" and "Spirit" may be good or bad in context, not dual

The term "**flesh**" sometimes means the physical body, sometimes the form of an idea (St. John Cassian: Conference with Abbot Daniel Chapter X). See words "Essence" and "Substance" in the Mass notes. There is also a mistaken dualistic Augustinian (Manichaen) presumption that all flesh is evil but all spirit is good. Yet, the most dangerous sin is the pride of the devil, which is a sin of spirit. (St. John Chrysostom and Pope St. Gregory the Dialogist both place pride as the first of sins). Our Lord Jesus Christ's flesh is holy: both His physical Body, the Bread of Life; and the "flesh" of the bread of His teachings. Christianity is not a "dualist" religion of flesh versus spirit; these must be judged correctly.

Layers of Meaning in Scripture and Psalms, Nationalism is Not Correct

Overcoming "Enemies:" In the Psalms there are two layers of meaning, both present at the same time: **historical**, and **spiritual**. Within the spiritual meaning, there are also three layers of meaning: as explained in The First Conference of Abbot Nesteros to John Cassian, Chapter VIII. These three spiritual layers: **allegorical** finds parallels in events often in the present; **anagogical** is more prophetic of larger ideas, often in the future; and **tropological** offers a moral internal explanation so that we find a representation of a problem in the soul of a person, often from the past. "...practical knowledge is distributed among many subjects and interests, but theoretical is divided into two parts, i.e., the historical interpretation and the spiritual sense. Whence also Solomon when he had summed up the manifold grace of the Church, added, [Prov 31:21] 'for all who are with her are clothed with double garments.' But of spiritual knowledge there are three kinds, tropological, allegorical, anagogical, of which we read as follows in Proverbs: [22:20] 'But do you describe these things to yourself in three ways according to the largeness of your heart.' ...And so these four [including historical] previously mentioned figures coalesce, if we desire, into one subject, so that the same Jerusalem can be taken in four senses: **historically** as the city of the Jews; **allegorically** as the Church of Christ, **anagogically** as the heavenly city of God which is the mother of us all, **tropologically** as the soul of man, which is frequently subject to praise or blame from the Lord under this title..."

Note that many of the Psalms use terms such as "**enemies**" and "**nations**" to represent **tropological** meditations on our *own* faults as "enemies." We must not think the Psalms promote a nationalism which excludes others from coming to God in the same Holy Church that we are in [Is. 42:1, Mt 12:18]. Mt 12:21 "And in His name the Gentiles shall hope." Mt 24:14 "And this Gospel of the kingdom, shall be preached in the whole world, for a testimony to all nations, and then shall the consummation come." Psalm 21, "All the ends of the earth shall remember, and shall be converted to the Lord: And all the kindreds of the Gentiles shall adore in His sight. For the kingdom is the Lord's: and He shall have dominion over the nations." Psalm 95, "Declare His glory among the Gentiles: His wonders among all people... Bring ye to the Lord, O ye kindreds of the Gentiles, bring ye to the Lord glory and honor: bring to the Lord glory unto His Name. Bring up sacrifices, and come into His courts: Adore ye the Lord in His holy court."

Virtue overcoming sin through the Hours of Prayer, The Arch over the Heavens
Virtue Comes from God, Accepting God's Help

Rom 11:33 "O the depth of the riches of the wisdom and of the knowledge of God! How incomprehensible are His judgments, and how unsearchable His ways!" There are many lists of virtues. There is a warning against thinking that only doing any or all of the virtues alone will get a person into heaven, because all virtue comes from God, and accepting God's help is the first thing and the last thing (the Alpha and Omega) necessary to accomplish the goal of heaven.

The Holy Spirit gives the gifts of virtue, and the Holy Spirit must be honored through virtue. All virtue comes from God the Father, Son, and Holy Spirit. John 10:10 "The thief cometh not, but for to steal, and to kill, and to destroy. I am come that they may have life, and my have it more abundantly."

Mark 3:29 "But he that shall blaspheme against the Holy Spirit, shall never have forgiveness, but shall be guilty of an everlasting sin."

Matthew 25:40, 45-46 "...Amen I say to you, as long as you did it to one of these my least brethren, you did it to me. ...Amen I say to you, as long as you did not do it to one of these least, neither did you do it to me. And these shall go into everlasting punishment: but the just, into life everlasting."

Clement of Alexandria, in The Instructor. [Paedagogus.] "Virtue is Good, and comes from God." As Abbot Pinufius says to St. John Cassian, "Even if we have done all these things, they will not be able to expiate our offences, unless they are blotted out by the goodness and mercy of the Lord... [when He] supports our small and puny efforts with the utmost bounty." (Is. 43:25).

The Cross is the Greatest Sign of Virtue Which Comes From God

It is only necessary to attend the Hours of Holy and Great Friday to realize that all virtue comes from God, the Cross and Center of our spiritual life, and it is necessary to meditate on God. Especially at the Third, Sixth, and Ninth Hours, we contemplate the Holy Trinity in truth and not mocked in the Third Hour, and participate in His saving Grace in the Sixth Hour, and in the full impact of the completion of His Work and the beginning of Resurrection in the Ninth Hour, the "greatest Hour of the Crucifixion." (See "Continuous Prayers" earlier, and also prayer under the Virtue of Intercession of Saints below.)

God's Many Virtues together in the Church

Sin could not be overcome without virtue (from God), just as faith without works is dead according to the Epistles. Although we are justified by faith, the work of belief and of accepting God's help is necessary. Such work is difficult for one who is despondent, or limits their faith to their own limited experiences; mutual charity includes faith in others in the church who teach. (Paul to the Romans, 3:31, James 2:20, 1 Peter 4:8, "But before all things have a constant mutual charity among yourselves: for charity covereth a multitude of sins." 1 Peter 5:8 "Be sober and watch..." 1 John 2:3, "And by this we know that we have known Him, if we keep His commandments."

Although certain virtues are found more in one person than another (Rom 12:4-8 1 Cor 12:4-31), a superficial imitation of only one or two virtues will not lead to heavenly virtue. For example, those who concentrate on prayer and those who give much to others sometimes do not understand eachother, instead of grasping that both activities are necessary to follow virtue. Even the hermits pray for others, and those who are the almoners (charity givers) in a monastic community also live a prayer life. Even though different people have more strength in different virtues, all the virtues together, expressed by different people in a community, should be encouraged, because virtue itself is the Holy Spirit working in our lives.

Wisdom 9:16-19, "And hardly do we guess aright at things that are upon earth: and with labor do we find the things that are before us. But the things that are in heaven, who shall search out? And who shall know thy thought, except thou give wisdom, and send thy Holy Spirit from above: And so the ways of them that are upon earth may be corrected, and men may learn the things that please thee? For by wisdom they were healed, whosoever have pleased thee, O Lord, from the beginning."

The Gift of Virtue from the Holy Spirit (and the many kinds of virtue in the Church) is listed in Isaiah 11:1-6 and Galatians 5:18-26: "...wisdom, and of understanding, the spirit of counsel, and of fortitude, the spirit of knowledge, and of godliness..." "...charity, joy, peace, patience, benignity, goodness, longanimity, mildness, faith, modesty, continency, chastity..."

The Epistle of St. Polycarp to the Philippians, Chapter X -Exhortation to the Practice of Virtue. "[1] Stand fast, therefore, in these things, [2] and follow the example of the Lord, being firm and unchangeable in the faith, loving the brotherhood, [1 Pet. 2:17] and being attached to one another, joined together in the truth, exhibiting the meekness of the Lord in your intercourse with one another, and despising no one. [3] When you can do good, defer it not, because 'alms delivers from death.' [Tobit 4:10, 12: 9] [4] Be all of you subject one to another having your conduct blameless among the Gentiles,' [5] that ye may both receive praise for your good works, [6] and the Lord may not be blasphemed through you. [1 Pet. ii. 12] [7] But woe to him by whom the name of the Lord is blasphemed! [Isa. 52:5] [8] Teach, therefore, sobriety to all, and manifest it also in your own conduct." [The bracketed numbers, by Elizabeth Dowling, point to the order of eight principle faults being overcome by virtue; although not a direct correlation to the faults in all cases, these topics in this order are clearly more ancient than the fourth or fifth century. St. Polycarp was a direct disciple of St. John the Apostle.]

St. Justin Martyr in his First Apology, Chapter X, "And we have been taught, and are convinced, and do believe, that He accepts those only who imitate the excellences which reside in Him, temperance, and justice, and philanthropy, and as many virtues as are peculiar to a God who is called by no proper name." Chapter XXI, those made as "sons of God"... "And we have learned that those only are deified who have lived near to God in holiness and virtue..." The Didache also lists many virtues, quoting the Gospels.

Another list of virtues: Matthew 25:36-36, and Tobit chapters 4 and 12. "For I was hungry, and you gave me to eat; I was thirsty, and you gave me to drink; I was a stranger, and you took me in: naked, and you covered me; sick, and you visited me; I was in prison, and you came to me." (And Tobias adds to this list, burying the dead.)

Although there are lists of seven, for the "seven-fold Holy Spirit" (loosely attributed to Proverbs 9:1 which refers to seven pillars of wisdom); and twelve as gifts of the Holy Spirit in Galatians and Isaiah, God's gifts are all virtues, and as God is infinite, His virtues are also infinite. Therefore, in the middle of a list of seven qualities in a Byzantine prayer to the Holy Spirit, one of the qualities listed is "Treasury of blessings," because to list all the blessings would certainly number more than seven. Another list adds to fourteen, dividing these into "corporal" or physical, and "spiritual." As in the layers of meaning, historical, allegorical, anagogical, and tropological: any blessing, for example, the blessing of understanding, also has layers, and this means that there are many more than seven virtues.

(The later Europeans' seven "corporal acts of mercy" and seven "spiritual acts of mercy," a rather short list: Most of these are from Tobias 1:20, Tobias chapter 4, and Matthew 25:35-36. Corporal: (1) To feed the hungry, Matthew 25:35, Tobias 1:20, 1:7; 4:7-12; 4:17; (2) To give drink to the thirsty, Matthew 25:35; (3) To clothe the naked, Matthew 25:36, Tobias 1:20; Tobias 4:17; (4) To visit the imprisoned, (or earlier, to ransom captives) Matthew 25:36, Tobias 1:15; Isaiah 42:7, Is. 61:1; (5) To shelter the homeless, Matthew 25:35; (6) To visit the sick, Matthew 25:35; (7) To bury the dead, Matthew 25:40, Tobias 1:20-21, Tobias 2:3-9. Spiritual: (1) Admonish the sinner, Luke 15:7; (2) Instruct the ignorant, Mark 16:15; (3) Counsel the doubtful, John 14:27; (4) Comfort the sorrowful, Matthew 11:28; (5) Bear wrongs patiently, Luke 6:27-28; (6) Forgive all injuries, Matthew 6:12; (7) To pray for the living and the dead, John 17:24. One might add, from Tobias, to give the first-fruits to the temple, Tobias 1:6.)

Seven Steps also the Gift of Music: Psalms Curing the Wild Beast

The lists of sevens probably refer to the Holy Trinity present in the first "seven days" of creation, and a meditation on the inner meaning of creation. It would also refer to the seven steps in most scales of music. St. Basil talks about the music of the Psalms curing the savage beast, from the short preface to the Psalms before his commentary on Psalm 1, "...Let a man begin even to grow savage as some wild beast, and no sooner is he soothed by psalm-singing than straightway he goes home with passions lulled to calm and quiet by the music of the song...." this quote pre-dating other later writers who plagiarized St. Basil. St. Basil also mentions that music and the Psalms are from the Holy Spirit, "The Holy Spirit saw that mankind was hard to draw to goodness, that our life's scale inclined to pleasure, and that so we were neglectful of the right. What plan did He adopt? He combined the delight of melody with His teaching, to the end that by the sweetness and softness of what we heard we might, all unawares, drink the blessing of the words."

Names of God and the Virtues of Faith, Hope, and Charity

The virtue from God which is above is greater than all, and each one of God's virtues are infinite. From the Lorrha-Stowe Missal, at the "Dignum" or "Worthy" of the Holy Trinity, here is a list of God's virtues; even this list must be understood as a shortened list: "...Thou Who with Thine Only-Begotten and the Holy Spirit, O God, art One and Immortal God, Incorruptible and Immutable God, Unseen and Faithful God, Marvelous and Praise-worthy God, Honorable and Mighty God, the Highest and Magnificent God, Living and True God, Wise and Powerful God, Holy and Exemplary God, Great and Good God, Terrible and Peaceful God, Beautiful and Correct God, Pure and Benign God, Blessed and Just God, Pious and Holy, not in one singularity of person but One Trinity of One Substance... Thou through Whom is the Salvation of the world; through Whom is the Life of men; through Whom is the Resurrection of the dead...." In all, thirty four virtues on this list, and because each of them is infinite, more could be added, such as that the kingdom of God is near to us, or we are His offspring, Acts 17:24-29 or within us, Luke 17:21, or as the shining of lightning, Luke 17:24. Also, we should respond with virtues of prayer, from the Lorrha-Stowe Missal: "Truly it is worthy and just and right and unto Salvation for us now and here, always and everywhere to give thanks, through Christ our Lord, unto Thee, Holy Lord Almighty and Eternal God. ...Thee we believe; Thee we bless; Thee we adore; and we praise Thy Name unto eternity and unto ages of ages..."

Virtue is reflected in the Names of God. St. Gregory Nazianzus, Fourth Theological, the second concerning the Son, Oration XXX part XIX. "Of the other titles, some are evidently names of His Authority, others of His Government of the world, and of this viewed under a twofold aspect, the one before the other in the Incarnation. For instance the Almighty, the King of Glory, or of The Ages, or of The Powers, or of The Beloved, or of Kings. Or again the Lord of Sabaoth, that is of Hosts, or of Powers, or of Lords; these are clearly titles belonging to His Authority. But the God either of Salvation or of Vengeance, or of Peace, or of Righteousness; or of Abraham, Isaac, and Jacob, and of all the spiritual Israel that seeth God,-these belong to His Government. For since we are governed by these three things, the fear of punishment, the hope of salvation and of glory besides, and the practice of the virtues by which these are attained, the Name of the God of Vengeance governs fear, and that of the God of Salvation our hope, and that of the God of Virtues our practice; that whoever attains to any of these may, as carrying God in himself, press on yet more unto perfection, and to that affinity which arises out of virtues. Now these are Names common to the Godhead, but the Proper Name of the Unoriginate is Father, and that of the unoriginately Begotten is Son, and that of the unbegottenly Proceeding or going forth is The Holy Ghost [or Holy Spirit]. Let us proceed then to the Names of the Son, which were our starting point in this part of our argument..." [Note: this is similar to teaching in the "Traditio," belief in the Names of God.]

Our Response to the Virtues of Faith, Hope, and Charity

Note in the Names of God that Vengeance, Salvation, and Virtues reveal the three virtues of Faith, Hope, and Charity. These virtues are also listed in the First Conference with Abbot Chaeremon, Chapter VI. "There are three things which enable men to control their faults: either the fear of hell or of laws even now imposed; or the hope and desire of the kingdom of heaven; or a liking for goodness itself and the love of virtue..." In Tobias 4:23, three main virtues are listed, corresponding to faith, hope, and charity: "...fear God, depart from all sin, and do that which is good." These three virtues, (see St. Paul in 1 Corinthians chapter 13), sum up our attitudes towards virtue, which ultimately must be summed into charity, or the mutual love and giving of love and alms to God and to eachother, and to those who we have no hope of getting anything in return. (Virtue is more than obedience, it is an informed synergy and love with God.)

Word, Thought, and Deed of God and our Response

Note that in the Lorrha-Stowe Liturgy it gives three virtues of God, and how we may fall away from these. The description in the notes after the Mass: "Later when the Celebrant and ministers step three steps backwards and three steps forward is the three ways in which everyone sins: in word, in thought, in deed. These are also the three means by which one is renovated and by which one is moved to Christ's Body." The Word of God is before any finite thought, and thought is before the act or deed. Sins against these are sins against the Word which doubt, ignore, or turn against God, then sins against thought by unworthy plans or by inability to discern or by neglect of thought, and of course then sins of deeds or neglect to do what is right. Restoration by these means is listening to and believing in the Word, then discernment, planning and carrying out good deeds. The Irish also emphasize the "Holy Chain of Charity" (in the Lorrha-Stowe Mass), not an enslavement, but a connection to God, through the church, and through God's word, thought, and deed.

Two Commandments

Or, the two most important commandments of God, which can be applied to the virtues of love of God and charity: Matthew 22:37-40 Jesus said to him: Thou shalt love the Lord thy God with thy whole heart, and with thy whole soul, and with thy whole mind. This is the greatest and the first commandment. And the second is like to this: Thou shalt love thy neighbor as thyself. On these two commandments dependeth the whole law and the prophets. [From Deuteronomy 6:5 and Leviticus 19:18.] Tobias 4:16, "See thou never do to another what thou wouldst hate to have done to thee by another." Matthew 7:12, "All things therefore whatsoever you would that men should do to you, do you also to them. For this is the law and the prophets."

Twelve Virtues from St. Antony and Abbot Pinufius (St. John Cassian)

A list of some of the virtues, and relationships between them: (The following is only an abbreviated outline. It is equally possible to find other relationships between virtues, since God is the source of all virtue.) These writings about the virtues are from the Life of St. Antony by St. Athanasius (chapter 4), St. John Cassian on St. Antony, St. John Cassian in The Institutes Book V chapter 4, and Abbot Pinufius, Chapter 8 in the XX Conference of St. John Cassian. The order of the list of Abbot Pinufius is different from the first three sources, and uses different terms to describe the virtues, not exactly equivalent to eachother. However, the order of virtues of Abbot Pinufius' is very helpful, and he also gives Scriptural references for each one. Afterwards, he explains Martyrdom and Baptism in more detail. Most of the notes and Scriptural references below are consolidated from the Conference with Abbot Pinufius. These virtues complement the lists of the gifts of the Holy Spirit in Galatians 5:18-26, and 11:1-6. They also include the Sacraments within them, in virtues of word, thought, and deed.

(1) Baptism (the first of the Sacraments), responsibility as a Christian. Graciousness; grace of simplicity; chastity (having overcome sin). We should forget those things which are behind; when the sins are overcome, do not dwell on them more. Phil. 3:13 as Abbot Pinufius said to St. John Cassian, chapter IX, "...For it is impossible for the soul to continue in good thoughts, when the main part of the heart is taken up with foul and earthly considerations...;" "...wolf shall dwell with the lamb... and a little child shall lead them", Isaiah 11:6; "live in the Spirit, let us also walk in the Spirit," Gal. 5:25,. Romans 8:11, "And if the Spirit of him that raise up Jesus from the dead, dwell in you; he that raised up Jesus Christ from the dead, shall quicken also your mortal bodies, because of his Spirit that dewelleth in you." St. Gregory Nazianzus Oration XL on Holy Baptism, part VIII: "For, to say it all in one word, the virtue of Baptism is to be understood as a covenant with God for a second life and a purer conversation." St. Gregory Nazianzus states, in Oration XLV, the Second Oration on Easter, part XIII, that Christ takes away sin because He was tempted but did not Himself sin (from St. Paul). The Holy Spirit (or Holy Ghost) is described by St. John the Baptist, in Matthew 3:11-12, "I indeed baptize you in water unto penance, but he that shall come after me, is mightier than I, whose shoes I am not worthy to bear; he shall baptize you in the Holy Ghost and fire. Whose fan is in his hand, and he will thoroughly cleanse his floor and gather his wheat into the barn; but the chaff he will burn with unquenchable fire." (Also Luke 3:16-17). St. Athanasius on the life of St. Antony, part 20. "...Lord hath said, 'No man, having put his hand to the plough, and turning back, is fit for the kingdom of heavens.' And this turning back is nought else but to feel regret, and to be once more worldly-minded. But fear not to hear of virtue, nor be astonished at the name. For it is not far from us, nor is it without ourselves, but it is within us, and is easy if only we are willing... [Luke 17:21] 'The kingdom of heaven is within you.' Wherefore virtue hath need at our hands of willingness alone, since it is in us and is formed from us... [by God's gift of life to us, of course.] For this cause Joshua, the son of Nun, in his exhortation said to the people, 'Make straight your heart unto the Lord God of Israel,' [Joshua 24:14, 1 Kings (1 Sam) 7:3, Tobit 14:10] and St. John, 'Make your paths straight.' [John 1:23, Isaiah 40:3] For rectitude of soul consists in its having its spiritual part in its natural state as created. But on the other hand, when it swerves and turns away from its natural state, that is called vice of the soul... If we abide

as we have been made, we are in a state of virtue, but if we think of ignoble things we shall be accounted evil. If, therefore, this thing had to be acquired from without, it would be difficult in reality; but if it is in us, let us keep ourselves from foul thoughts. And as we have received the soul as a deposit, let us preserve it for the Lord, that He may recognise His work as being the same as He made it."

(2) Martyrdom and allowing God to cut away sin by examination ["martyr" means witness; here "cut away sin"also implies discernment of mind, a sword of truth, which must be practiced as well as prayer, so that the mind does not reject the truth of the words.] Study; flowers of knowledge; knowledge; modesty, crucified their flesh. [But see Psalm 50, an unbloody sacrifice, "...with burnt-offerings Thou wilt not be delighted. A sacrifice to God is an afflicted spirit: a contrite and humbled heart, O God, Thou wilt not despise..."] Phil. 3:8, "...I count all things to be but loss [except] for the excellent knowledge of Jesus Christ my Lord..." Matthew 16:24, "...If any man will come after me, let him deny himself, and take up his cross, and follow me." 1 Cor. 10:14-17, "...fly from the service of idols... The cup of benediction, which we bless, is it not the communion of the blood of Christ? And the bread, which we break, is it not the partaking of the body of the Lord? For we, being may, are one bread, one body, all that partake of one bread." Eph. 6:17 "And take unto you the helmet of salvation, and the sword of the Spirit which is the word of God." [The following quotes given by Abbot Pinufius must be taken in the interior, tropological meaning that reveals the soul, not in a physical or historical sense of flesh, as explained below by Cassiodorus: Heb 4:12, "For the word of God is living and effectual, and more piercing than any two edged sword; and reaching unto the division of the soul and the spirit, of the joints also and the marrow, and is a discerner of the thoughts and intents of the heart."; Heb 9:22 "And almost all things, according to the law, are cleansed with blood: and without shedding of blood there is no remission."; 1 Cor. 15:50 "Now this I say, brethren, that flesh and blood cannot possess the kingdom of God: neither shall corruption possess incorruption."; Jer 48:10 "Cursed be he that doth the work of the Lord deceitfully: and cursed be he that withholdeth his sword from blood."]

From the Latin Translation of Cassiodorus. (Sixth century Roman statesman who served Theodoric the Great, king of the Ostrogoths in Ravenna, lived a number of years in Constantinople, founded a monastery on his family estate in southern Italy called Vivarium, gathered a library, and wrote some exegetical works.) III.-Comments on the First Epistle of John. "Chap. 1 John 1:1. 'That which was from the beginning; which we have seen with our eyes; which we have heard.' Following the Gospel according to St. John, and in accordance with it, this Epistle also contains the spiritual principle. What therefore he says, 'from the beginning,' the Presbyter explained to this effect, that the beginning of generation is not separated from the beginning of the Creator. For when he says, 'That which was from the beginning,' he touches upon the generation without beginning of the Son, who is co-existent with the Father. There was; then, a Word importing an unbeginning eternity; as also the Word itself, that is, the Son of God, who being, by equality of substance, one with the Father, is eternal and uncreated. That He was always the Word, is signified by saying, 'In the beginning was the Word.' But by the expression, 'we have seen with our eyes,' he signifies the Lord's presence in the flesh, 'and our hands have handled,' he says, 'of the Word of life.' He means not only His flesh, but the virtues of the Son, like the sunbeam which penetrates to the lowest places,-this sunbeam coming in the flesh became palpable to the disciples. It is accordingly related in traditions, that John, touching the outward body itself, sent his hand deep down into it, and that the solidity of the flesh offered no obstacle, but gave way to the hand of the disciple. 'And our hands have handled of the Word of life; 'that is, He who came in the flesh became capable of being touched.' 1 John 2:1 '...Thus also Moses names the virtue of the angel Michael, by an angel near to himself and of lowest grade....' Ver. 1 John 3:20. He says, 'For God is greater than our heart;' that is, the virtue of God [is greater] than conscience, which will follow the soul. Wherefore he continues, and says, 'and knoweth all things.' Ver. 1 John 3:21. 'Beloved, if our heart condemn us not, it will have confidence before God.' Ver. 1 John 3:24. 'And hereby we know that He dwelleth in us by His Spirit, which He hath given us; 'that is, by superintendence and foresight of future events. Chap. 1 John 4:18. He says, 'Perfect love casteth out fear.' For the perfection of a believing man is love. Chap. v. 1 John 4:6. He says, 'This is He who came by water and blood;' and again,- Ver. 1 John 4:8. 'For there are three that bear witness, the spirit,' which is life, 'and the water,' which is regeneration and faith, 'and the blood,' which is knowledge; 'and these three are one.' For in the Saviour are those saving virtues, and life itself exists in His own Son."

(3) Fasting and repentence.; Fasting and sleeping on the ground; earnestness of work; strike the earth with the rod of his mouth, breath of his lips he shall slay the wicked; goodness. Acts 3:19, "Be patient, therefore, and be converted, that your sins may be blotted out." Matt. 3:2, "Do penance: for the kingdom of heaven is at hand." Psalm 101:10, "...the fear of the Lord is the beginning of wisdom. A good understanding to all that do it: his praise continues for ever and ever.", Acts 17:30 "And God indeed having winked at the times of this ignorance, now declareth unto men, that all should everywhere do penance." Psalm 108:24 "My knees are weakened through fasting: and my flesh is changed for oil."; Tobias 12:8 "Prayer is good with fasting and alms more than to lay up treasures of gold." Abbot Pinufius to St. John Cassian, "Even if we have done all these things, they will not be able to expiate our offences, unless they are blotted out by the goodness and mercy of the Lord... [when He] supports our small and puny efforts with the utmost bounty." (Is. 43:25). (Note below that both St. John Cassian and St. Mael Ruain of Tallaght strongly recommend moderation concerning fasting and kneeling. Prayer and fasting precede the Sacrament of Confession. Mt. 17:19-20; prayer and fasting also are needed first to bolster the faith, especially to remove demons.)

(4) Charity covering a multitude of sins, and also alms; Mutual love which animated all; magnanimity; wisdom; charity. 1 Peter 4:8, "But before all things have a constant mutual charity among yourselves: for charity covers a multitude of sins." Ecclus 3:33 "Water quenches a flaming fire, and alms resist sins", Tobias 4:7-12, 17 "Give alms out of your substance, and do not turn away your face from any poor person, for then the face of the Lord shall not be turned from you. According to your ability be merciful. For alms deliver from all sin, and from death, and will not allow the soul to go into darkness... Eat your bread with the hungry and needy, and with your garments cover the naked."; Tobias 12:9 "For alms delivereth from death, and the same is that which purgeth away sins, and maketh to find mercy and life everlasting." (Charity underlies all the virtues.)

(5) Shedding of tears over ones own sins; Long-suffering, silence, fear of the Lord; longanimity. Tobias 4:14 "Never allow pride to reign in your mind, or in your words: for from it all sin began."; Tobias 12:12 "When you did pray with tears, and did bury the dead... I offered your prayer to the Lord." Psalm 6:7, 9; "...for the Lord has heard the voice of my weeping." (This is not the shedding of tears of despondency, or loss of hope, or the result of doubts, but a gift of the Holy Spirit, experienced by some in their prayer life.)

(6) Confession and absolution from God. Watchfulness, continence, understanding. Ps 31:5 "I have acknowledged my sin to thee, and my injustice I have not concealed."; Ps 50:5-6 "For I know my iniquity, and my sin is always before me. To Thee only have I sinned, and have done evil before thee: that Thou mayst be justified in Thy words, and mayst overcome when Thou art judged."; Is. 43:24-26; "I am, I am he that blot out thy iniquities for my own sake, and I will not remember thy sins. Put me in remembrance, and let us plead together, tell if thou hast any thing to justify thyself." 1 John 1:9-10, "If we confess our sins, He is faithful and just, to forgive us our sins, and to cleanse us from all iniquity. If we say that we have not sinned, we make Him a liar, and His word is not in us." 2 Corinthians 11:30 and 12:5, "...but for myself I will glory nothing, but in my infirmities" 2 Cor 12:9 "...Gladly therefore will I glory in my infirmities, that the power of Christ may dwell in me." Sin means deficiency or lack of harmony (translating the Latin and Greek terms), not only sin of action or will, but also sin or neglect, ignorance, or silence giving consent to evil. Tobias 4:13 "And because thou wast acceptable to God, it was necessary that temptation should prove thee." Matthew

25:1-13, "...Watch ye therefore, because you know not the day nor the hour." Tobias 4:13, "Take heed to keep thyself, my son, from all fornication, and beside thy wife never endure to know a crime." (The Sacrament of Confession and Absolution helps us to be whole again, unburdened by sins which separate us from God.)

(7) Affliction of heart and body, as in humility and labor. Piety towards Christ; judge the poor with justice, reprove with equity for the meek; mildness. Psalm 24:15-18. "...for he shall pluck my feet out of the snare. Look thou upon me, and have mercy on me; for I am alone and poor... see my hard work and forgive all my sins." Christ's humility and labor for us: John 3:16, "For God so loved the world, as to give his only begotten Son; that whosoever believeth in him, may not perish, but may have life everlasting." ("Work" must be in moderation, remembering the "Rest" of the Lord on the seventh day, and that work should be for the things that are truly needed, Mt. 11:28-30, Mt. 6:28. Even so, work is recommended by St. Paul, a few examples: I Cor. 15:58, I Cor. 16:10, Eph. 2:10. Jesus who talks of those who harvest the fields of the faithful, Mt. 9:37. The Psalms speak of God's continuous work. Psalm 120:4-5 "Behold He shall neither slumber nor sleep, that keepeth Israel. The Lord is thy keeper, the Lord is thy protection upon thy right hand." This virtue goes with Amendment of Life, Meekness.)

(8) Amendment of life. Meekness; virtue of humility; godliness; benignity. Isaiah 1:16-18. "Wash yourselves, be clean, take away the evil... cease to do perversely, learn to do well, seek judgment, relieve the oppressed, judge for the fatherless, defend the widow. And then come, and accuse me, saith the Lord." John 3:21, "But he that doth truth, cometh to the light, that his works may be made manifest, because they are done in God." Matthew 25:35-36 "For I was hungry, and you gave me to eat; I was thirsty, and you gave me to drink; I was a stranger, and you took me in:" [Isa. 58:7; Ezech. 18:7; Ezech 18:16] "Naked, and you covered me: sick, and you visited me: I was in prison, and you came to me." [Eccli. 7:89] (Whether a person is a monk, unmarried laity, or married, it is necessary to practice humility all one's life. In the Lorrha-Stowe Mass, one of the Communion verses is, "the kingdom of Heaven tolerates sieges - Alleluia - and the forceful take it - Alleluia." Matt. 11:12, Latin and Greek. Modern English translations of this verse say "the kingdom of heaven suffereth violence... ," which does not make sense. It is the daily gift of meekness, laying "siege" to heaven, that allows the union of Marriage, and also allows any monastic contemplation.)

(9) Intercession of Saints , being anointed with oil, and praying for others. Unceasing prayer; vigils; fortitude; peace. 1 Thess. 5:17, "Pray without ceasing." 1 John 5:16, "He that knows his brother to sin a sin which is not to death, let him ask, and life shall be given to him.."; James 5:14-15, "...and the prayer of faith shall save the sick man: and the Lord shall raise him up: and if he be in sins, they shall be forgiven him."; Tobias 4:20, "Bless God at all times: and desire of God to direct thy ways, and that all thy counsels may abide in him."; Tobias 12:8 "Prayer is good with fasting and alms more than to lay up treasures of gold." Matthew 7:11, "If you then being evil, know how to give good gifts to your children: how much more will your Father who is in heaven, give good things to them that ask him?" "Kyrie eleison" or "Lord have mercy;" asks for God's anointing oil, one of the derivations of the Greek word "*eleison.*" (The Sacrament of Holy Unction, or Anointing, offers healing to the sick, but it also reminds us again and again of the wholeness that God gives to us, the spiritual health from God which comes to us with our cooperation. The Sacrament of Chrismation, which is part of the Rite of Baptism, brings us to the wholeness of the Holy Spirit. The Mandatum, or Command, tells us to pray and minister to others.)

Divinity, reached by the virtue of unceasing prayer is considered the center of all the virtues by the desert fathers interviewed by St. John Cassian. Without prayer, none of the other virtues are possible. XXIV Conference of Abbot Abraham, on Mortification, chapter VI, "Wherefore a monk's whole attention should thus be fixed on one point, and the rise and circle of all his thoughts be vigorously restricted to it; viz., to the recollection of God, as when a man, who is anxious to raise on high a vault of a round arch, must constantly draw a line round from its exact center, and in accordance with the sure standard it gives, discover by the laws of building all the evenness and roundness required. But if anyone tries to finish it without ascertaining its center though with the utmost confidence in his art and ability, it is impossible for him to keep the circumference even, without any error, or to find out simply by looking at it how much he has taken off by his mistake from the beauty of real roundness, unless he always has recourse to that test of truth and by its decision corrects the inner and outer edge of his work, and so finishes the large and lofty pile to the exact point..." Abbot Abraham also quotes Psalm 25, "I have loved the beauty of Thy house and the place of the dwelling of Thy glory." And the entire goal will not be met if continuous prayer is not the center of a person's life, "...but will without foresight raise in his heart a house that is not beautiful, and that is unworthy of the Holy Ghost, one that will presently fall, and so will receive no glory from the reception of the blessed Inhabitant, but will be miserably destroyed by the fall of his building." All virtue is in partnership with God, in unceasing prayer.

(10) Compassion and faith. Loving-kindness; pity; justice shall be the girdle of his loins, faith the girdle of his reins; faith. (Similar to amendment of life, and also charity.) Prov 15:27 "...By mercy and faith sins are purged away: and by the fear of the Lord every one declineth from evil."; Tobias 4:15 "If any man has done any work for you, immediately pay him his hire (money), and do not let the wages of your hired servant stay with you at all." (The highest justice, pity, and faith is the participation in and sharing of Holy Communion, the greatest Offering of our Lord Jesus Christ from us to God and God to us. Jesus Christ, through His Cross, has bought our Salvation)

(11) Warning and preaching to others covering a multitude of sins, and teaching. Endurance, methods of discretion; counsel; joy. James 5:20, "He must know that he who causes a sinner to be converted from the error of his way, shall save his soul from death, and shall cover a multitude of sins."; Tobias 4:19 "Seek counsel always of a wise man." (Holy Orders are not to "lord it over others as the Gentiles do," but to teach and minister, Mark 10:42-45. In the Mandatum, or Command, in Baptism, every Christian is told to pray for and minister to others, and this is similar to the tonsure at Baptism in the Byzantine Rite. Teaching is not reserved for a few, but wisdom must precede knowledge,. See fault 4, envy or coveteousness, below; also fault 8, pride. There are some cases where it is necessary to warn and teach, but other cases where teaching is prideful: a way to avoid the actual practice of what is preached. Luke 11:42, "But woe to you, Pharisees, because you tithe mint and rue and every herb; and pass over judgment, and the charity of God. Now these things you ought to have done, and not to leave the other undone." Luke 11:46, "But he said: Woe to you lawyers also, because you load men with burdens which they cannot bear, and you yourselves touch not the packs with one of your fingers." Luke 11:52, "Woe to you lawyers, for you have taken away the key of knowledge: you yourselves have not entered in, and those that were entering in, you have hindered."

The First Conference with Abbot Nesteros, Chapter XVI, explains the need to be freed from faults before explaining Scripture. Abbot Nesteros answers a question about why some people with great sin or confusion are able to quote Scripture, while some who seem almost perfect may be more simple-minded or illiterate. Only a few quotes are given here: "...One who does not carefully weigh every word of the opinions uttered cannot rightly discover the value of the assertion. For we said to begin with that men of this sort only possess skill in disputation and ornaments of speech; but cannot penetrate to the very heart of Scripture and the mysteries of its spiritual meanings... And the Psalmist also sees that this system ought to be followed, when he says: [Psalm 118 Greek or 119 Hebrew:] 'Blessed are they that are undefiled in the way: who walk in the law of the Lord. Blessed are they that seek His testimonies.' For he does not say in the first place: 'Blessed are they that seek His testimonies,' and afterwards add: 'Blessed are they that are undefiled in the way;' and by this clearly shows that no one can properly come to seek God's testimonies unless he first walks undefiled in the way of Christ by his practical life. ... Of those then who seem to acquire some show of knowledge or of those who while they devote themselves diligently to reading the sacred volume and committing the Scriptures to memory, yet forsake not carnal sins, it is well said in Proverbs: [Proverbs 11:22], 'Like as a golden ring in a swine's snout so is the beauty of an evil-disposed woman.' For what does it profit a man to gain the ornaments of heavenly eloquence and the most precious beauty of the Scriptures if by clinging to filthy deeds and thoughts he destroys it by burying it in the foulest ground, or defiles it by the dirty wallowing of his own lusts?... For [Ecclus. 15:9] 'from the mouth of a sinner praise is not comely;' as to him it is said by the prophet, [Ps. 49 Greek or 50 Hebrew] 'Wherefore dost thou declare My righteous acts, and takest My covenant in thy lips?' Of souls like this, who never possess in any lasting fashion the fear of the Lord of which it is said: [Prov. 15:33] 'the fear of the Lord is instruction and wisdom,' and yet try to get at the meaning of Scripture by continual meditation on them, it is appropriately asked in Proverbs: [Prov. 17:16] 'What use are riches to a fool? For a senseless man cannot possess wisdom.' But so far is this true and spiritual knowledge removed from worldly erudition, which is defiled by the stains of carnal sins, that we know that it has sometimes flourished most grandly in some who were without eloquence and almost illiterate. And this is very clearly shown by the case of the Apostles and holy men, who did not spread themselves out with an empty show of leaves, but were bowed down by the weight of the true fruits of spiritual knowledge: of whom it is written in the Acts of the Apostles: [Acts 4:13] 'But when they saw the boldness of Peter and John, and perceived that they were ignorant and unlearned men, they were astonished.'..." (And Abbot Nesteros gives many more examples. "Leaves" compared to "fruit" can also be taken to be pages of a codex as compared to fruits of charity; or it could mean a superficial reading of Scripture compared to the depth of tradition which includes Scripture and Sacraments. Scripture reference on spiritual blindness: Mt 6:22-23 "The light of thy body is thy eye. If thy eye be single, thy whole body shall be lightsome. But if thy eye be evil thy whole body shall be darksome. If then the light that is in thee, be darkness: the darkness itself how great shall it be!")

(12) Forgive others and be forgiven. Freedom from anger; dignity of patience; patience,   Matt. 6:12,14 "And forgive us our debts, as we also forgive our debtors... For if you will forgive men their offences, your heavenly Father will forgive you also your offences." Rom 6:14, "For sin shall not have dominion over you; for you are not under the law, but under grace." Gal 5:18, "But if you are led by the spirit, you are not under the law." [You have the power to forgive and receive forgiveness]. Is 11:9, "They shall not hurt, nor shall they kill in all my holy mountain... the earth is filled with the knowledge of the Lord...;" Tobias 4:16, "See thou never do to another what thou wouldst hate to have done to thee by another." Matthew 7:12, "All things therefore whatsoever you would that men should do to you, do you also to them. For this is the law and the prophets." Matthew 22:37-40 "Jesus said to him: Thou shalt love the Lord thy God with thy whole heart, and with thy whole soul, and with thy whole mind. This is the greatest and the first commandment. And the second is like to this: Thou shalt love thy neighbor as thyself. On these two commandments dependeth the whole law and the prophets." (These commandments in Deuteronomy 6:5 and Leviticus 19:18, are the beginning of forgiveness, because they acknowledge the reciprocal relationship between ourselves and our neighbors. Forgiveness is necessary before Confession and Absolution.)

List of Eight Sins and Virtues from an Irish Penitential

The eight sins listed by St. John Cassian are: Gluttony, Fornication, Covetousness, Anger, Dejection, Accidie, Vainglory, Pride. Although not in the same order, assigning the seven sins (other than gluttony) in Proverbs 6:16-19 to the sins listed by St. John Cassian and the Abbots of Egypt: Fornication: feet that are swift to run into mischief; Covetousness: a heart that deviseth wicked plots; Anger: hands that shed innocent blood; Accidie: a deceitful witness that uttereth lies; Despondency: him that soweth discord among brethren; Vain Glory: a lying tongue; and Pride: Haughty eyes. All of these are taken in the tropological, that is, their interior meaning within one person. Therefore, discord among the brethren may be interpreted as a person who is depressed and not able to trust, either in the help of others, their own positive thoughts, or God.

(These eight faults are ways in which many people fall; these are usually different from a falling away from the faith, or heresy, except for the faults of vain-glory and pride.)

The principal faults use symbols of the nations overcome by Moses and Joshua. Chapter XXIII of the Conference of Abbot Serapion: "...But as soon as these faults have been overcome by the people of Israel, i.e., by those virtues which war against them, then at once the place in our heart which the spirit of concupiscence and fornication had occupied, will be filled with chastity. That which wrath had held, will be claimed by patience. That which had been occupied by a sorrow that worketh death, will be taken by a godly sorrow and one full of joy. That which had been wasted by accidie, will at once be filled by courage. That which pride had trodden down will be ennobled by humility: and so when each of these faults has been expelled, their places (that is the tendency towards them) will be filled by the opposite virtues which are aptly termed the children of Israel, that is, of the soul that seeth God: and when these have expelled all passions from the heart we may believe that they have recovered their own possessions rather than invaded those of others." (Note: St. John Cassian's treatise, "On the Incarnation against Nestorius" explains that the name "Israel" meant "seeing God," because although it is true the Jacob wrestled with God, Jacob looked upon God and yet lived.)

Not only are virtues listed in the Life of Antony by St. Athanasius (paragraph 5), but also eight faults as the attacks of the devil he had to overcome (in a different order): Gluttony: the various pleasures of the table; Fornication: the other relaxations of life, then at length putting his trust in the weapons which are 'in the navel of his belly' (from Job) [which is his last temptation, because it takes the mind by surprise]; Covetousness: whispering to him the remembrance of his wealth, Anger: care for his sister, claims of kindred [because St. Antony was not prone to anger, but to care used as a distraction], Accidie: the difficulty of virtue and the labour of it; he suggested also the infirmity of the body and the length of the time; Despondency: in a word he raised in his mind a great dust of debate; Vain-glory: love of glory, Pride: first of all he tried to lead him away from the discipline.

From the Rule of St. Maelruain, which is the Rule of the Cele De. Several remedies were given for each fault, but it must be remembered that all these virtues together must be accomplished with God's help, and that continuous prayer is the center of these. The desert fathers said that all the power of virtue is needed to combat each fault.

1. Abstinence combats gluttony. Abstinence produces: spiritual joy, decency of body, purity of soul, silence till need (of speech), comprehension of wisdom, abundance of intelligence, application to the mysteries of God. Remedies for gluttony: moderate fasting, remorse of heart, rare meals, frequent self-questioning, watching, feasting the poor, solacing all the hungry, confinement at certain hours with a specified allowance, patience in regard to everything until it be considered. [Note: complete denial of food is not good, because food is a gift from God, but should be eaten in moderation, and shared with others. Gluttony, symbolized by the nation of Egypt, cannot be overcome, but kept in check, because God gives us the gift of food to strengthen us. The seven other nations that were overcome by the Israelites correspond to the other faults. See the "Rules of Fasting for Monastic and Lay Usage" in the beginning of this book. Fasting included not eating meat. Eating healthy foods and not eating foods without nutrition, also avoids gluttony. Being aware of the hunger of others, and actively trying to provide food to others, keeps the need for food in the correct perspective.]

2. Perseverance in chastity combats luxury [or fornication]. Perseverance in chastity produces: steadfastness of counsel, quiet discourse, steadfastness as opposed to fickleness, faithful promises, keeping of troth, meditation on God, modesty of nature, confirming of faith, hatred of this world, love of the world to come. Remedies against fleshly lust: subduing of gluttony, moderate meals, moderation in drink, avoidance of drunkenness, hatred of conviviality, mastering of nature, heedfulness in solitude, cheerfulness in company, attendance on elders, avoidance of young folk, a fixed measure of labor or reading or prayer, hatred of the rabble with unclean words, a stable mind with purity of conversation, desire of rewards so as to win them, contemplation of penalties so as to avoid them. [Abbot Chaeremon in the Conference on Chastity, chapter III, he names those things that St. Paul lists [Col 3:5] as fornication, uncleanness (inmunditia) of mind,

license (libido) meaning a person doing whatever they please, bad desire (concupiscentia mala) which includes all harmful desires in general or a corrupt will [Mt. 5:28], and finally avarice which is the next principal fault, and is the coveting not only of the goods of others but also of ones' own goods, and is the service of idols. Note: although marriage is a Sacrament, chastity is considered the highest state, because chastity overcomes distractions both physical and mental which can swiftly surprise a person. Most monks living alone as anchorites, or in a group as cenobites, are celibate. Yet, celibacy, or continency is the struggle; chastity is the goal which few achieve, because it is so pure, and so free of passion. But this is not a fault to dwell on. In the Second Conference of Abbot Chaeremon (on Chastity), Chapter III it is emphasized that anger may be overcome by placing ones self in situations that might provoke anger while practicing humility, but in the case of lust, it is best to avoid the idea, seek quiet solitude and seek to meditate, avoiding confrontation with it. In chapter V, Abbot Chaeremon says, "Besides, the desire for present things cannot be repressed or removed unless we replace the harmful things we want to remove with healthy ones. The soul cannot exist in any vital way without some feelings of desire or fear, or joy or sorrow. This must be turned to good account. If we chase carnal concupiscence from our hearts, we should immediately plant spiritual desires in their place so that our soul may always be occupied with them..." In chapter X Abbot Chaeremon reminds us that chastity is not achieved by vigilance and discipline alone, but by love and delight in purity itself. As long as adversity remains, you do not have chastity but continence. "But whatever is conquered through profound virtue, and not mixed with a trace of anxiety, will confer the continual firmness of peace on the victor." Even the eunuchs that are mutilated have carnal heat and the effect of lust, so even they must not relax from humility etc. It is also not by our own efforts, as said in chapter 15, "'Unless the Lord builds the house, they labor in vain who build it,.' Ps. 126 Greek numbering.]

3. Liberality with charity combats avarice. Liberality with charity produces: mercy with forgiveness, rectitude with truthfulness, bounty with gentleness, without pride, without hatred, without malice; compassion with eagerness, without treachery, without deceit, without cunning; benevolence without loquacity, without falsehood, without perjury, without insolence. Remedies for avarice: service of Christ's strangers, feasts for the poor, laboring for one's food, a mind set on poverty, trust in a blessing, prevision of punishment, hope of reward, expectation of judgment in presence of the Creator on the Day of Judgment. [Avarice is combined with coveteousness in earlier lists.]

3 (continued). Kindliness of heart without malice combats envy [coveteousness]. Kindliness of heart without malice produces: brotherly love, helpfulness to our neighbor, speaking well of everyone, hatred of reviling, rejection of murmuring, magnifying of everything good, rebuking of everything evil, kindly words, a mind compassionate to all men, save for aught that involves sin. The remedies for envy are: penance on bread and water for as long a time as there had been hatred in his heart. If evil has resulted from his envy, let him replace as much as was lost by his fault, if he have the wherewithal: if not, let him ask pardon tearfully and penitently... If it becomes a fixed habit with him, so that he does not remember to restrain himself, he is to be expelled from the church to a place of penance until he shall have given up that vice... Anyone who loves to hear [envious gossip], let him do penance.

b. There are, however, four cases in which it is right to find fault with the evil that is in a man who will not accept his cure by means of entreaty and kindness: either to prevent someone else from abetting him in this evil; or to correct the evil itself; or to confirm the good; for out of compassion for him who does the evil. [See the virtue 11 above, "warning and preaching to others."] But anyone who does not do it for one of these four reasons is a fault-finder, and does penance four days, or recites the hundred and fifty psalms for it, [i.e., is in danger of the sin of pride.]

[Coveteousness, or love of money, is often called the "root of all evil," I Tim 6:10 because it is a turning away of the mind, heart, and resources from God to a deadly end. St. Paul says, "the wages of sin is death." Rom. 6:23. Moliere made a play on this when the servant of the corrupt Don Juan screams "my wages, my wages," as Don Juan is taken to hell; the servant follows because he is looking for his money. St. John Cassian, in the Institutes, Book VII, Chapter I, describes covetousness or the love of money as a "foreign warfare," because it is outside of our nature and comes from a "corrupt and sluggish mind." Instead of going outside of ourselves towards God or charity towards other, money takes us outside of ourselves to become more selfish. It also develops from envy, Chapter IV: "the useless Cains of this world." And from "free choice of a corrupt and evil will." (Chapter V.)

In Chapters VII through X St. John Cassian illustrates a monk who finds all sorts of reasons, even within a monastery where all his needs would be cared for, that he might covet a little store of ready cash. "For with the increase of wealth the mania of covetousness increases." "With such strides then in a downward direction he goes from bad to worse, and at last cares not to retain I will not say the virtue but even the shadow of humility, charity, and obedience; and is displeased with everything, and murmurs and groans over every work; and now having cast off all reverence, like a bad-tempered horse, dashes off headlong and unbridled; and discontented with his daily food and usual clothing, announces that he will not put up with it any longer. He declares that God is not only in that place, and that his salvation is not confined to that place, where, if he does not take himself off pretty quickly from it, he deeply laments that he will soon die." And in this way, money causes a greater and greater panic. Chapter XXIV, "For the madness of this avarice is not satisfied with any amount of riches."

Chapter XIV: "And so this disease and unhealthy state is threefold... One feature is this, of which we described the taint above, which by deceiving wretched folk persuades them to hoard though they never had anything of their own when they lived in the world. Another, which forces men afterwards to resume and once more desire those things which in the early days of their renunciation of the world they gave up. A third, which springing from a faulty and hurtful beginning and making a bad start, does not suffer those whom it has once infected with this lukewarmness of mind to strip themselves of all their worldly goods, through fear of poverty and want of faith; and those who keep back money and property which they certainly ought to have renounced and forsaken, it never allows to arrive at the perfection of the gospel." (In handling money, these sought to possess it, return to it, and retain it.) Then St. John Cassian gives examples of these three deadly states: In Chapter XXV St. John Cassian discusses Judas Iscariot, who is called, in the Byzantine Rite, the "lover of money," (in all four Gospels, for example, Mt 26:14-16, 26:47-50, and 27:3-10). Ananias and Saphira also died because of this sin (Book of Acts chapter 5). Gehazi was given fatal leprosy and banished. (Chapter 5 of IV Kings, or in Bibles that are arranged with books of Samuel and Kings, Chapter 5 of II Kings), See the fault of Dejection: a deadly depression can also be caused by mentally dwelling on the state of finances. Gambling drains resources. Robbery also may lead to murder. In countries where a barter system has been replaced by loans and debt, people are forced to grow non-food crops while their families starve, and the nation becomes weaker.

In Chapter XV, St. James 1:8 is quoted, "A double-minded man is unstable in all his ways."... "No man can serve God and Mammon." [Mt 6:24] And "No man putting his hand to the plough and looking back is fit for the kingdom of God." [Lk 9:62]. In Chapter XXVII he reminds the monks that they have been instructed to "Go sell all that thou hast, and give to the poor, and thou shalt have treasure in heaven: and come follow me." [Mt. 19:21] Chapter XXX, "Above all, considering the state of our weak and shifty nature, let us beware lest the day of the Lord come upon us as a thief in the night and find our conscience defiled even by a single penny..." (from Mt. 24:42-44).]

4. Meekness and gentleness combats anger. Meekness and gentleness produce: soundness of heart, shunning of contention, gentle speech, repression of conceit, docility of nature, silence amid talkativeness, patience amid sufferings, hatred of reviling, zeal without chiding, benevolence without guile, munificence without malice. The remedy against anger, and all that springs from it is penance. (For serious crimes and offenses, this penance may take many years.) [In the Conference of Abbot John, Chapter XIV, "When then anyone discovers by those signs which we described above, that he is attacked by

outbreaks of impatience or anger, he should always practice himself in the opposite and contrary things, and by setting before himself all sorts of injuries and wrongs, as if offered to him by somebody else, accustom his mind to submit with perfect humility to everything that wickedness can bring upon him; and by often representing to himself all kinds of rough and intolerable things, continually consider with all sorrow of heart with what gentleness he ought to meet them. And, by thus looking at the sufferings of all the saints, or indeed at those of the Lord Himself, he will admit that the various reproaches as well as punishments are less than he deserves, and prepare himself to endure all kinds of griefs... How is it that even a gentle breeze has shaken that house of yours which you fancied was built so strongly on the solid rock?... One then who carefully considers these and other injuries of the same kind, will readily endure and disregard not only all kinds of losses, but also whatever wrongs and punishments can be inflicted by the cruellest of men, as he will hold that there is nothing more damaging than anger, nor more valuable than peace of mind and unbroken purity of heart, for the sake of which we should think nothing of the advantages not merely of carnal matters but also of those things which appear to be spiritual, if they cannot be gained or done without some disturbance of this tranquility." Conference of Abbot Theodore, Chapter X, "Seize the armor of patience to practice himself in virtue."]

    5 and 6. The remedies against despair are: a Spiritual joy with serenity of heart and mind against worldly sadness; b. Fervency of prayer, with fasting and watching, against sluggishness and torpor; c. Liberality with openness of mind toward God against inattention; d. A fixed measure of labor and prayer against idle volatility; e. Faith with works, joy with gentleness, against despair and malice of mind.

    [Despair: From the Irish Penitential: "But of worldly sadness there are three forms. The first is sadness and grief at parting with carnal friends for loss of their human affection, and for love and attachment to them; or because of parting with one's guilt and sins and fleshly lusts. Again, the second form of worldly sadness is the grief and despair that arise from every desire that a man desires, because he cannot satisfy it, save only the will of God. The third form of worldly sadness again is the grief and despair which arise from every good thing a man gets, through fear of its being taken away from him, and of its perishing, and through fear of parting with it, even later on, so that he is never free from grief and sadness while he lives, and he goes thereafter to find eternal grief, to everlasting torment without end." First Conference of Abbot Isaac, Chapter XXXII, a warning is given that despair, hesitation, and lack of confidence can impede prayer. Book IX of the Institutes, Chapter I, "... we have to resist the pangs of gnawing dejection: for it this, through separate attacks made at random, and by haphazard and casual changes, has secured an opportunity of gaining possession of our mind, it keeps us back at all times from all insight in divine contemplation, and utterly ruins and depresses the mind that has fallen away from its complete state of purity. It does not allow it to say its prayers with its usual gladness of heart, nor permit it to rely on the comfort of reading the sacred writings, nor suffer it to be quiet and gentle with the brethren; it makes it impatient and rough in all the duties of work and devotion: and, as all wholesome counsel is lost, and steadfastness of heart destroyed, it makes the feelings almost mad and drunk, and crushes and overwhelms them with penal despair." In Chapter II he quotes Proverbs 25:20, "...as the moth injures the garment, and the worm the wood, so dejection the heart of man." Chapter IV, "Sometimes it is found to result from the fault of previous anger, or to spring from the desire of some gain which has not been realized, when a man has found that he has failed in his hope of securing those things which he had planned. But sometimes without any apparent reason for our being driven to fall into this misfortune, we are by the instigation of our crafty enemy suddenly depressed with so great a gloom that we cannot receive with ordinary civility the visits of those who are near and dear to us; and whatever subject of conversation is started by them, we regard it as ill-timed and out of place; and we can give them no civil answer, as the gall of bitterness is in possession of every corner of our heart." Chapter VI, "For no one is ever driven to sin by being provoked through another's fault, unless he has the fuel of evil stored up in his own heart. Nor should we imagine that a man has been deceived suddenly..."

In Chapter VII St. John Cassian recommends that for this fault, because it is in ourselves and not others, that we should not give up our interactions with our brethren, but instead try to be patient with others and pacify any ill will.

Then, in Chapters IX he discusses danger of despair. In Chapter X "And so we must see that dejection is only useful to us in one case, when we yield to it either in penitence for sin, or through being inflamed with the desire of perfection, or the contemplation of future blessedness... 'The sorrow which is according to God worketh repentance steadfast unto salvation: but the sorrow of the world worketh death.'" (II Cor 7:10). Chapter XI, "But that dejection and sorrow which worketh repentance steadfast unto salvation is obedient, civil, humble, kindly, gentle, and patient, as it springs from a love of God, and unweariedly extends itself from desire of perfection to every bodily grief and sorrow of spirit; and somehow or other rejoicing and feeding on hope of its own profit preserves all the gentleness of courtesy and forbearance, as it has in itself all the fruits of the Holy Spirit...: 'love, joy, peace, forbearance, goodness, benignity, faith, mildness, modesty'" (Gal. 5:22-23 See these below under virtues.) "But the other is rough, impatient, hard, full of rancor and useless grief and penal despair, and breaks down the man on whom it has fastened, and hinders him from energy and wholesome sorrow, as it is unreasonable, and not only hampers the efficacy of his prayers, but actually destroys all those fruits of the Spirit of which we spoke, which that other sorrow knows how to produce." For this reason, a person suffering from depression should get help from both counseling and medicine immediately, because this fault can block our ability to respond to God's help. Although, one man did cry, "...Lord: help my unbelief." and was helped. St. Mark 9:23 This is because despair often leads to blasphemy, and turns away from help. If a person had a terminal illness, no expense would be spared to try to save them, but many people do not realize how dangerous depression is: depression can be fatal. Some specific remedies are given by St. John Cassian:

Chapter XII, "...all sorrow and dejection must equally be resisted, as belonging to this world, and being that which 'worketh death,' and must be entirely expelled from our hearts..." In Chapter XIII St. John Cassian suggests spiritual meditation, hope of the future, contemplation of promised blessedness. "...if, ever joyful with an insight into things eternal and future, and continuing immovable, we are not depressed by present accidents, or over-elated by prosperity, but look on each condition as uncertain and likely soon to pass away." The remedies in the Irish Penitential agree with these remedies.]

[5 and 6 continued: Note that Accidie, which may be equated with either sloth or a manic kind of wandering of attention is combined in the Irish Penitential with Despair. Courage is the opposite of Accidie, from Chapter XXIII of the Conference of Abbot Serapion. Conference with Abbot Serapion, chapter IX, "Dejection and accidie generally arise without any external provocation, like those others of which we have been speaking: for we are well aware that they often harass solitaries, and those who have settled themselves in the desert without any contact with other men, and this in the most distressing way. And the truth of this any one who has lived in the desert and made trial of the conflicts of the inner man, can easily prove by experience."

From Book X chapters I and II, of the Institutes, Accidie is "weariness or distress of heart. This is akin to dejection, and is especially trying to solitaries, and a dangerous and frequent foe to dwellers in the desert; and especially disturbing to a monk about the sixth hour [noon], like some fever which seizes him at stated times, bringing the burning heat of its attacks on the sick man at usual and regular hours. Lastly, there are some of the elders who declare that this is the 'midday demon' spoken of in the ninetieth Psalm... it produces dislike of the place, disgust with the cell, and disdain and contempt of the brethren who dwell with him or at a little distance, as if they were careless or unspiritual. It also makes a man lazy and sluggish about all manner of work which has to be done within the enclosure of his dormitory. It does not suffer him to stay in his cell, or to take any pains about reading, and he often groans because he can do no good while he stays there, and complains and sighs because he can bear no spiritual fruit so long as he is joined to that society; and he complains that he is cut off from spiritual gain, and is of no use in the place, as if he were one who, though he could govern others and be useful to a great number of people, yet was edifying none, nor profiting any one by his teaching and doctrine..." The description is both educational and entertaining, and shows how the monk is enticed to leave his cell, and stop the contemplation of God. The mention of this fault has been neglected in modern lists of "deadly sins."

In Book X of the Institutes, St. John Cassian quotes St. Paul concerning the fault and remedies for accidie: [I Thess. 4:9-13], "...And that you use your endeavor to be quiet, and that you do your own business, and work with your own hands, as we commanded you: and that you walk honestly towards them that are without; and that you want nothing of any man's..." John Cassian explains: "'And that you take pains to be quiet;' i.e., that you stop in your cells, and be not disturbed by rumors, which generally spring from the wishes and gossip of idle persons, and so yourselves disturb others. And, 'to do your own business,' you should not want in inquire curiously of the world's actions, or, examining the lives of others, want to spend your strength, not on bettering yourselves and aiming at virtue, but on depreciating your brethren. 'And work with your own hands, as we charged you;' to secure that which he had warned them above not to do; i.e., that they should not be restless and anxious about other people's affairs, nor walk dishonestly towards those without, nor covet another man's goods, he now adds and says, 'and work with your own hands, as we charged you.' For he has clearly shown that leisure is the reason why those things were done which he blamed above. For no one can be restless or anxious about other people's affairs, but one who is not satisfied to apply himself to the work of his own hands. He adds also a fourth evil, which springs also from this leisure, i.e., that they should not walk dishonestly: when he says: 'And that ye walk honestly towards those without.' He cannot possibly walk honestly, even among those who are men of this world, who is not content to cling to the seclusion of his cell and the work of his own hands; but he is sure to be dishonest, while he seeks his needful food, and to take pains to flatter, to follow up news and gossip, to seek for opportunities for chattering and stories by means of which he may gain a footing and obtain an entrance into the houses of others..." St. John Cassian emphasizes that this is considered a very grave fault by St. Paul [2 Thess. 3:6], "And we charge you... that you withdraw yourselves from every brother walking disorderly, and not according to the tradition which they have received of us."]

7 (and 8). The remedies against vain glory are: obedience without contumacy, humility with quietness, shunning of strife, smoothness without simulation, learning from the venerable, steadfastness of nature, a lowly mind, respect for God. [Vain-glory is concern about what others think about ones self, and also a concern about appearances.] Abbot Serapion, chapter XVI lists humility as the remedy against pride. Also note the remedies listed in the Irish Penitential under "envy."

(8.) Pride is a false belief that the center and origin of the universe is ones self. [Later than St. John Cassian the Europeans combined Vain-glory with Pride and reversed the order of the faults. St. Maelruain and the Irish maintained some of St. John Cassian's order of faults, but they reduced the list to seven faults; envy was separated from coveteousness; and accidie or sloth was not mentioned. St. John Cassian and the desert fathers say that gluttony is outside the other seven, not pride or sloth. The remedy against pride is very difficult, according to St. John Cassian, and includes an understanding that the universe is created by God, Who is infinitely greater than any individual person, and therefore we must obey God, not our own prideful whims. St. John Chrysostom, friend and mentor of St. John Cassian, discusses overcoming pride in his exegesis of the first Beatitude, "Blessed are the poor in spirit." Both St. John Chrysostom and Pope St. Gregory the Dialogist, also called the Great, list pride as the first of sins, because of the difficulty of overcoming it. Pope St. Gregory the Dialogist warned against Bishops taking on titles of divinity such as "Ecumenical" such as the Patriarch of Constantinople. Pope St. Gregory lived long before any Roman Bishop titled themselves "infallible." It is possible that pride was combined with vain-glory in the later Middle Ages to lessen the emphasis on the danger of pride, such as found in either the "divine right" of kings, or Bishops calling themselves infallible or representing the "Ecumen" or Body of Christ. See the note on the Hour of Vespers, below.]

    Vain-glory and pride (spiritual faults) are seen by St. John Cassian as paired and considered nearly impossible to overcome, just as mental wandering and despondency are paired (faults of mood, often called bi-polar), anger and covetousness are paired (faults of emotional desire), and gluttony and fornication or luxury are paired (the physical faults).

    Because later lists confused vain-glory and pride, here is more detail on pride:

    In the Conference of John Cassian with Abbot Serapion, Chapter VI, Abbot Serapion explains why three particular faults were used as a temptation for both Adam and Christ: "For it was right that He who was in possession of the perfect image and likeness of God should be Himself tempted through those passions, through which Adam also was tempted while he still retained the image of God unbroken, that is, through gluttony, vainglory, pride; and not through those in which he was by his own fault entangled and involved after the transgression of the commandment, when the image and likeness of God was marred. For it was gluttony through which he took the fruit of the forbidden tree, vainglory through which it was said "Your eyes shall be opened," and pride through which it was said "Ye shall be as gods, knowing good and evil." With these three sins then we read that the Lord our Saviour was also tempted; with gluttony when the devil said to Him: 'Command these stones that they be made bread;' with vainglory: 'If Thou art the Son of God cast Thyself down:' with pride, when he showed him all the kingdoms of the world and the glory of them and said; 'All this will I give to Thee if Thou wilt fall down and worship me' in order that He might by His example teach us how we ought to vanquish the tempter when we are attacked on the same lines of temptation as He was..." "...Nor could He who had vanquished gluttony be tempted by fornication, which springs from superfluity and gluttony as its root, with which even the first Adam would not have been destroyed unless before its birth he had been deceived by the wiles of the devil and fallen a victim to passion." "Yet according to Luke, who places last that temptation in which he uses the words 'If Thou art the Son of God, cast Thyself down,' we can understand this of the feeling of pride, so that the earlier one, which Matthew places third, in which, as Luke the evangelist says, the devil showed Him all the kingdoms of the world in a moment of time and promised them to Him, may be taken of the feeling of covetousness, because after His victory over gluttony, he did not venture to tempt Him to fornication, but passed on to covetousness, which he knew to be the root of all evils, and when again vanquished in this, he did not dare attack Him with any of those sins which follow, which, as he new full well, spring from this as a root and source; and so he passed on to the last passion: that is, pride, by which he knew that those who are perfect and have overcome all other sins, can be affected, and owing to which he remembered that he himself in his character of Lucifer, and many others too, had fallen from their heavenly estate, without temptation from any of the preceding passions..." "For to the one he said, 'Your eyes shall be opened;' to the other 'he showed all the kingdoms of the world and the glory of them.' In the one case he said 'Ye shall be as gods;' in the other, 'If Thou art the Son of God.'"

    In Chapter VII, Abbot Serapion reminds John Cassian how vainglory and pride "can be consummated even with the slightest assistance from the body. For in what way do those passions need any action of the flesh, which bring ample destruction on the soul they take captive simply by its assent and wish to gain praise and glory from men? Or what act on the part of the body was there in that pride of old in the case of the above mentioned Lucifer; as he only conceived it in his heart and mind, as the prophet tells us: [Is 14:13-14] 'Who saidst in thine heart: I will ascend into heaven, I will set my throne above the stars of God. I will ascend above the heights of the clouds, I will be like the most High.'..."

    Note in the virtue about "warning and preaching to others," one must be wary of pride; but also, one must be wary of the pride of having a great teacher, either because that can become a personality cult, or that the good teacher does not replace the disciple's need to understand and carry out the teachings themselves. Conference of Abbot Abraham, Chapter XVI, "...you must recognize that the rational part of your mind and soul is corrupt, that part namely from which the faults of presumption and vainglory for the most part spring. Further this first member, so to speak, of your soul must be healed by the judgment of a right discretion and the virtue of humility, as when it is injured, while you fancy that you can not only still scale the heights of perfection but actually teach others, and hold that you are capable and sufficient to instruct others, through the pride of vainglory you are carried away by these vain rovings, which your confession discloses. And these you will then be able to get rid of without difficulty, if you are established as I said in the humility of true discretion and learn with sorrow of heart how hard and difficult a thing it is for each of us to save his soul, and admit with the inmost feelings of your heart that you are not only far removed from that pride of teaching, but that you are actually still in need of the help of a teacher."

The Institutes Book V chapter IV, "For it is an ancient and excellent saying of the blessed Antony (the Great) that when a monk is endeavoring after the plan of the monastic life to reach the heights of a more advanced perfection, and, having learned the consideration of discretion, is able now to stand in his own judgment, and to arrive at the very summit of the anchorite's life, he ought by no means to seek for all kinds of virtues from one man, however excellent. For one is adorned with flowers of knowledge, another is more strongly fortified with methods of discretion, another is established in the dignity of patience, another excels in the virtue of humility, another in that of continence, another is decked with the grace of simplicity. This one excels all others in magnanimity, that one in pity, another in vigils, another in silence, another in earnestness of work. And therefore the monk who desires to gather spiritual honey ought like a most careful bee, to suck out virtue from those who specially possess it, and should diligently store it up in the vessel of his own breast; nor should he investigate what any one is lacking in, but only regard and gather whatever virtue he has. For if we want to gain all virtues from some one person, we shall with great difficulty or perhaps never at all find suitable examples for us to imitate. For though we do not as yet see that even Christ is made "all things in all," as the Apostle says [I Cor. 15:28], still in this way we can find Him bit by bit in all. For it is said of Him, "Who was made of God to you wisdom and righteousness and sanctification and redemption." [I Cor 1:30] While then in one there is found wisdom, in another righteousness, in another sanctification, in another kindness, in another chastity, in another humility, in another patience, Christ is at the present time divided, member by member, among all of the saints..."

The remedy against pride is humility (Conference of Abbot Serapion, chapter XVI). Where several of the Abbots do not try to match lesser virtues against faults, several of them list humility against pride, so humility is the greatest of the lesser virtues; the greatest virtue being contemplation of God.

Confession and Absolution overcomes the faults, but, according to an Irish Penitential, "There are four things for which no penance can be done in the land of Erin [or one's native land], namely, lying with a dead person; transgressing with a kinswoman (i. e.: sister or daughter) [or a child or an unwilling person]; falling into sin while holding higher Orders (i. e.: that of Bishop or Priest); and divulging a confession by saying 'this is what this man did.'" These require banishment from the land in which the sin was committed (from the country or continent) for at least twelve years, living the life of a penitent monastic. In addition, a pilgrimage from the land in which the sin was committed by water and foot to the Tomb of the Lord and immersion in the Jordan at the site of the Lord's Baptism are advisable as a sign of one's repentance.

Overcoming the Faults and Learning the Virtues in the Hours of Prayer

To review: God is the Cross or Center of all our prayer, the fountain of all Virtue, and without God, no Virtue is possible; this is emphasized in the Hours of the Crucifixion, especially the Third, Sixth, and Ninth Hour. If a compass is not used to make a center point, the arch will fall (see the virtue of continuous prayer under intercession of Saints. This is an early analogy made by Abbot Abraham to St. John Cassian.) Some faults are stronger in some people than others. While later writers such as the later Irish Penitential listed particular virtues that might combat particular sins, the earlier writers of the fifth century and earlier matched all virtue, that is, contemplation of Divinity together with the practice of many virtues together, as combating any and every sin, not dividing venial from mortal, and finding dangers in each. Examine each fault and pray to overcome it, go to Confession (Reconciliation), and truly repent (repair faults).

    The Hours focus on the days of the week and the Resurrection, and also help us to make war on the Eight Principal Faults described by St. John Cassian and the desert fathers of Egypt. Just as the Psalms of the Graduals and Alleluias in the Mass were found to match the Lectionary, it was also found that the virtues and faults to overcome could be assigned to the Hours of prayer, as a meditation; (one possible arrangement, by Elizabeth Dowling). Psalm 118:164 mentions seven times a day for prayer, and Proverbs 6:16-19 mentions seven major sins to be overcome. The Christian Egyptian desert fathers listed eight sins. Christians inserted the Ninth Hour at mealtime as an Hour of prayer. It is possible to find a correspondence of overcoming the principal faults to all eight Hours of prayer through the day and night.

    According to the Lorrha-Stowe Missal, in the Collect before the Epistle for the Mass of Apostles, Martyrs, and Holy Virgins, the twelve hours of daylight (half of a twenty-four hour day) correspond to the Twelve Apostles, and also to the twelve tribes of Israel, because Jacob (Israel) wrestled with God, saw God, and was not killed; the term "Israel" also applies to prayer and meditation, the "wrestling" with God, and also the ladder to heaven, the path, or Jesus Christ, Jn 14:6, the Way, Truth, and Life. "...We give Thee thanks O our Lord and God Jesus Christ, splendor of the Father's glory, and day of eternal clarity, for being pleased to illumine Thy twelve Apostles by the Fire of the Holy Spirit as the twelve hours of the day are illuminated by the light of the Sun...." The Virtues may be assigned to these twelve Hours of daylight. In the Bobbio Missal, there is an assignment of the Apostles to parts of an "Apostles' Creed," which may give an order through the day for these twelve hours of daylight. Although the virtues describe the Apostles' daylight vault of the heavens, there is no direct correlation between a particular sin and only one virtue; all virtues work together. The faults may also be assigned to be overcome; in the daylight Hours these may be assigned as: vain-glory, despondency, accidie, gluttony, and pride.

    The sins that may be assigned to be overcome at night (that is, anger, fornication, and covetousness) are combated directly by God alone. The verses of the Greek numbering Psalms 118, 119, 120, and 121 add to 200 verses, and seem to have a relationship with each other, or at least are useful for one hundred prostrations (or bows, in moderation) at every other verse at Cross Vigils. Psalm 118, the longest Psalm, mentions the Hours of prayer. Although the last three of these Psalms are not specified for the night Hours, these are important as Psalms of completion and of contemplation of God, who helps in distress (Psalm 119, note the treasury of prayers in the Hour of Matins), does not slumber nor sleep (Psalm 120, note that at Midnight we ask not to be as the foolish virgins who slept), and gives peace to Jerusalem (Psalm 121, note at the Beginning of Night we offer the prayer for peace).

    The cycle of Psalms that is read at the Beginning of Night and Midnight, covering the 150 Psalms in six days, left out a seventh day. On the seventh day it seems appropriate to do the Cross Vigil, which uses Psalms 118, 119, 120, and 121, with other Hymns (see the Cross Vigil). The arrangement of prayers from the Antiphonary of Bangor is partially described by St. Maelruain of Tallaght or Tamlactu, along with other commentary.

Hours, Virtues, Overcoming Faults

First Hour [7:00 A.M. at the cock crow.] [Bobbio Apostles' Creed:] Peter: 'I believe in God the Father Almighty.' Psalm 122 "To Thee have I lifted up my eyes; Who dwellest in heaven..." [Looking up to God in faith.] Virtue: [12] when we forgive others we are forgiven ourselves. [Although St. Peter is remembered as saying that charity covers a multitude of sins, he needed forgiveness first of all for his own sin of denial, at dawn. "Cock" also means Gaelic or Celtic, see Hymn 2 from the *Antiphonary of Bangor* by St. Hilary of Poitiers.]

Second Hour [8:00 A.M.] John: 'I believe in Jesus Christ, His only Son, God and our Lord.' Psalm 123 "...If it had not been that the Lord was with us, When men rose up against us; perhaps they had swallowed us up alive..." [St. John is the only Apostle who did not die a Martyr, but was put into boiling oil and survived it. He is also known as "O Theo Logos," because of his direct perception about God the Word; only a very few Saints are considered "Theologians" by the Byzantines. Also, the concept of the Divine and human natures of Christ, or of the kingdom of God within us, neither divine nor human natures "swallowing us up alive," nor swallowing the other; Theosis, which includes synergy or cooperation, not just affirmation or union, an insight that is discussed often in the Gospel of St. John.] Virtue: [11] the warning and preaching to others.

Second Hour of Prayer (after dawn, when the sun is fully up): Vainglory is combated, by prayers and collects of the morning, which steer us away from vanity. We are admonished not to look too hard in a mirror in the morning. In the "Second Hour," just after dawn, Psalms 50, 62, and 89 apply: "Have mercy on me, O God, according to Thy great mercy... In deficiencies did my mother conceive me..." "For thy mercy is better than lives... Thus will I bless Thee all my life long..." "Lord, Thou hast been our refuge: from generation to generation... From eternity and to eternity Thou art God.... In the morning man shall grow up like grass; in the morning He shall flourish and pass away: in the evening He shall fall, grow dry and wither... The days of our years in them are threescore and ten years. But if in the strong they be fourscore years: and what is more of them is labor and sorrow. For mildness is come upon us: and we shall be corrected..."
Third Hour [9:00 A.M.] James son of Zebedee, brother of St. John: 'He was born of Mary, the Virgin, through the Holy Spirit.'Psalm 124 "They that trust in the Lord shall be as mount Sion..." [Readings for Feasts of the Virgin Mary concern Mount Sion. She is seen as the "burning bush" at St. Catherine's monastery, because the power of the universe did not burn her alive. This James is confused with the James who was first Bishop of Jerusalem, "James of the Knees," the "brother of the Lord," but not related to the Virgin Mary, instead a step-son.] Virtue: [10] compassion and faith Prov 15:27, "...he that hateth bribes shall live. By mercy and faith sins are purged away: and by the fear of the Lord every one declineth from evil."

Third Hour of Prayer (9:00 A.M.): Despondency is fought. The Third Hour is the Hour of the descent of the Holy Spirit (Psalms 46, 53, and 114). Jesus asked His Father to send the Holy Spirit to the Apostles at Pentecost. This Hour combats despondency rather than pride which is an offense of the spirit. A prideful person should not "look down" on spiritual enemies, but this might help one who is despondent. "O clap your hands, all ye nations: shout unto God with the voice of joy..." [The nations represent overcoming the faults.] "Sing praises to our God, sing ye: sing praises to our King, sing ye. For God is the King of all the earth: sing ye wisely." "Save me, O God, by Thy Name, and judge me in Thy strength... "For Thou hast delivered me out of all trouble: and my eye hath looked down upon my enemies." "I have loved, because the Lord will hear the voice of my prayer... The sorrows of death have compassed me: and the perils of hell have found me. I met with trouble and sorrow: and I called upon the Name of the Lord... The Lord is the keeper of little ones: I was humbled, and He delivered me... I will please the Lord in the land of the living."

Fourth Hour [10:00 A.M.] Andrew: 'He suffered under Pontius Pilate; was crucified and buried.'Psalm 125 "...Going, they went and wept, casting their seeds. But coming, they shall come with joyfulness, carrying their sheaves." [Weeping, Death, and the promise of Resurrection. St. Andrew is the "first called," and the "first called" in the Resurrection were called from Hades at the time of the Crucifixion.] Virtue: [9] asking the intercession of Saints and being anointed with oil [meaning asking living and departed Saints for help, as one asks living and departed to help in curing sickness].

Fifth Hour [11:00 A.M.] Philip said, 'He descended into hell.' Psalm 126 "Unless the Lord build the house, they labor in vain that build it. Unless the Lord keep the city, he watcheth in vain that keepeth it..." [Hell was overthrown, because it was not kept by the Lord. Notice what the Lord said to St. Philip in St. John 14 verse 8 through chapters 15, 16, and 17, to St. Philip's question, "Lord, show us the Father, and it is sufficient for us." Chapter 14 begins, "In my Father's house are many mansions... I go to prepare a place for you..."] Virtue: [8] amendment of life. [only one of the virtues, not a replacement for all virtues.]

Sixth Hour [12:00 noon.] Thomas said, 'He arose on the third day.' Psalm 127 "Blessed are all they that fear the Lord: that walk in His ways..." [St. Thomas went the farthest in distance in missions. Notice the commentary in St. John 14:5-7, to St. Thomas's question, "how can we know the way?" In St. John 20:24-29, St. Thomas recognized the significance of the Resurrection, and learned faith.] Virtue: [7] affliction of the heart and body, or in other words, humility and labor.

At the Sixth Hour of Prayer (noon), Accidie is fought. Accidie is often associated with the noonday demon. The Lord Jesus Christ was lifted up on the Cross for all at noon. The daily Collect gives some insight into the event: "...[Thou] ascended the Cross and illumined the darkness of the world: Be pleased likewise to illumine our hearts..." Accidie is the wandering away from the truth, sometimes through sloth of mind, or sometimes through an active lack of attention, unlike our Lord who faced His suffering being nailed to the Cross. (This fault is paired with despondency, and it is said that it needs much courage, patience, labor, and prayer to overcome. Today we would call it the "manic" part of "bi-polar," "hyper-activity," or "attention-deficit.") The Psalms in Greek numbering for noon are Psalms 66, 69, and 115. "May God have mercy on us, and bless us: may He cause the light of His countenance to shine upon us; and may He have mercy on us. That we may know Thy way upon earth: Thy salvation in all nations..." "O God, come to my assistance, O Lord make haste to help me. Let them be confounded and ashamed that seek my soul. Let them be turned backward, and blush for shame that desire evils to me. Let them be presently turned away blushing for shame that say to me: Tis well, tis well..." "...I have believed, therefore have I spoken: but I have been humbled exceedingly. I said in my excess: Every man is a liar..."

Although not mentioned in the Hours listed by St. Brendan the Navigator (of Clonfert), there are two Psalms that directly mention noon, and also the wandering away from contemplation of Accidie: Greek numbering 36 and 90, or the opposite of Accidie as perseverence and courage and not wandering away. Psalm 36: "... Commit thy way to the Lord, and trust in Him: and he will do it. And He will bring forth thy justice as the light: and thy judgment as the noonday: be subject to the Lord and pray to Him. Envy not the man who prospereth in his way: the man who doth unjust things. Cease from anger, and leave rage: have no emulation to do evil. For evildoers shall be cut off: but they that wait upon the Lord, they shall inherit the land. For yet a little while, and the wicked shall not be: and thou shalt seek his place, and shalt not find it. But the meek shall inherit the land; and shall delight in abundance of peace... " Also, Psalm 90: "He that dwelleth in the aid of the most High shall abide under the protection of the God of Jacob. He shall say to the Lord: Thou art my protector and my refuge: my God, in Him will I trust. For He hath delivered me from the snare of the hunters: and from the sharp word. He will overshadow thee with His shoulders: and under His wings thou shalt trust. His truth shall compass thee with a shield: thou shalt not be afraid of the terror of the night. Of the arrow that flieth in the day, of the business that walketh about in the dark: of invasion, or of the noonday devil. A thousand shall fall at thy side, and ten thousand at thy right hand: but it shall not come nigh thee...   ...For He hath given His angels charge over thee: to keep thee in all thy ways. In their hands they shall bear thee up: lest thou dash thy foot against a stone. Thou shalt walk upon the asp and the basilisk: and thou shalt trample under foot the lion and the dragon..." In modern times, a meal is often served at noon, but in monastic tradition, the meal is at the Ninth Hour (around 3:00 P.M.)

Seventh Hour [1:00 P.M.] Bartholomew: 'He ascended into heaven.' Psalm 128 "Often they have fought against me from my youth..." [Bartholomew was called "the active" and his name means "son of Him Who suspends the waters" from notes on June 13th in Oengus the Cele De. Jesus Christ ascended into heaven as an active man while contemplating heaven. According to the Pope St. Leo the Great in the Paschal Vigil, the "happy fault" of Adam eventually allowed the coming to earth, death, Resurrection, and Ascension of our Lord. The Ascension emphasizes true worship of our Lord Jesus Christ, both Son of man and Son of God, and is a proof against the heresies of Nestorianism, Monophysitism, and others. Therefore, it is Confession of sins, and also the Confession of faith, which not only heals us but also opens us to Theosis, oneness with God without losing our identity.] Virtue: [6] confession of sins.

Eighth Hour [2:00 P.M.] Matthew: 'From there He will come to judge the living and the dead.' Psalm 129 "Out of the depths I have cried to Thee, O Lord: Lord, hear my voice..." [A Psalm usually for the departed. The Lord as Judge, but merciful to St. Matthew, who had been a tax-collector. His life is illustrated in the Parable of "the Publican and the Pharisee." The tax-collector asks, "Lord have mercy on me a sinner," and therefore is saved.] Virtue: [5] shedding of tears for the remembrance of sins, a blessing of the Holy Spirit, not the tears of despondency or depression.

Ninth Hour [3:00 P.M.] James, the son of Alpheus, the "less" (younger): 'I believe in the Holy Spirit.' Psalm 130 "Lord, my heart is not exalted: nor are my eyes lofty..." [Remembering St. James, and the gifts of the Holy Spirit as recorded in Isaiah 11:2 and also Galatians 5:22, which include humility. As St. John Chrysostom says, about the first Beatitude, it is necessary to be "poor in spirit," or humble, in order to receive the kingdom of heaven.] Virtue: [4] charity covering a multitude of sins, because the meaning of the word charity means grace from the Holy Spirit, and includes both spiritual generosity and also physical alms.

At the Ninth Hour of Prayer (3:00 P.M.), Gluttony is discussed, the traditional monastic time for meals in Ireland and also among the desert fathers of the Middle East. The Ninth Hour is the "Greatest Hour" of Holy and Great Friday, just as Matins is the Greatest Hour of the Resurrection. Christ gave up His life for us. Every time Christ gives us the Eucharist, it is eternally only the one Sacrifice of the Crucifixion, so that at mealtime it is also important to remember that Christ gives Himself to us. Also, the thief confessed and was promised Paradise at that time, so it is also a traditional time when Confession is heard, between the Ninth Hour and Vespers. Cornelius and the angel are also remembered at that time (Acts 10), with St. Peter and his vision of clean foods, and the mercy of God in letting the Gentiles into His Church. Many people do not have enough food, and we must take the gift of food seriously. The Psalms for the Ninth Hour are, in Greek numbering, Psalm 129, Psalm 132, and Psalm 147. Psalm 129 "Out of the depths I have cried to Thee, O Lord: Lord, hear my voice..." Egypt represents the nation of gluttony, and the Crucifixion was seen as the new Passover. Food is also a gift from God, and good in moderation, "Behold how good and how pleasant it is for brethren to dwell together in unity..." "Who hath placed peace in Thy borders: and filleth Thee with the fat of corn..."

Before or after the Hours are read, it is customary to sing the Magnificat and the Beatitudes with a hymn to St. Michael the Archangel, not skipped in daily practice. In a monastic community, this was common after the Ninth Hour or after the day's meal. The "Shrine of Piety" (from the end of Matins) may also end other Hours. In a strict ancient monastic community, if all one hundred and fifty Psalms were not read in a day, Psalm 118 was repeated after the Ninth Hour twelve times. (This Psalm includes 100 prostrations: add Psalms 119, 120, and 121 so that the verses number 200, a prostration after every other verse in the Cross Vigil. But St. Mael Ruain asks for moderation: this many prostrations ruin knees, and some monks were not able to pray in old age.)

Tenth Hour [4:00 P.M.] Simon Zelotes: 'I believe in the Holy Church.' Psalm 131 "...If I shall enter into the tabernacle of my house... This is my rest for ever and ever: here will I dwell, for I have chosen it.. Blessing I will bless her widow: I will satisfy her poor with bread. I will clothe her priests with salvation: and her saints shall rejoice with exceeding great joy...." [A Psalm about the Church. Simon is thought to be the bridegroom at the marriage at Cana.] Virtue: [3] fasting and repentance. Penitents sought admission to a monastic community, or re-admission to the church after apostasy under duress.

Eleventh Hour [5:00 P.M.] Judas, the brother of James: 'Through Holy Baptism [there is] remission of sins.' Psalm 132 "Behold how good and how pleasant it is for brethren to dwell together in unity: Like the precious ointment on the head, that ran down upon the beard, the beard of Aaron..." [Dwelling in the Church, and the anointing of Baptism. Baptism is into the Lord's death. This is the Judas people ask intercessions for lost causes, not the Iscariot.] Virtue: [2] Martyrdom: as described above, the white Martyrdom of working to attain knowledge. Or, switch this virtue with the virtue of the Twelfth Hour.

Twelfth Hour, [6:00 P.M.] Matthias: 'The resurrection of the flesh and eternal life. Amen.' Psalm 133 "Behold, now bless ye the Lord, all ye servants of the Lord: Who stand in the house of the Lord, in the courts of the house of our God..." [The Resurrection of the Dead and the Life in the age to come in the "courts of the house of our God." Matthias was the last called of the Twelve Apostles, in Acts 1:16-26, replacing Judas Iscariot.] Virtue: [1] Baptism [or, membership in the Church and taking responsibility. The foot-washing, or the "Mandatum" or "Command," is in the Lorrha-Stowe Baptism.]. [Note: St. Columbanus called the Hour of the Beginning of Night the "Twelfth Hour." This causes some confusion, because Vespers is before the Beginning of night, and elsewhere it says that the Hour of the Beginning of Night is "fully dark" even in summer, so it could not actually be the "Twelfth Hour" of daylight and before Vespers, unless that Hour was the equivalent to an Hour from another region, or indicating that the "Twelfth Hour" is also called "Compline," which means after eating, and eating takes place among the Irish after the Ninth Hour.]

The Hour of Vespers (sunset) combats Pride. Vespers uses Greek numbering Psalms 64, 103, and 112 with the Gloria and special Antiphons for the Gloria, the Angels' greeting to the shepherds. It is the traditional beginning of the Liturgical day (from Genesis, the evening and the morning were the first day, Gen. 1:5). "A Hymn, O God, becometh Thee in Sion: and a vow shall be paid to Thee in Jerusalem. O hear my prayer: all flesh shall come to Thee..." "Bless the Lord, O my soul: O Lord my God, Thou art exceedingly great. Thou hast put on praise and beauty: and art clothed with light as with a garment: Who stretchest out the heaven like a pavilion: Who coverest the higher rooms thereof with water. Who makest the clouds Thy chariot: Who walkest upon the wings of the winds. Who makest Thy angels spirits: and Thy ministers a burning fire..." "Praise the Lord, ye children: praise ye the Name of the Lord. Blessed be the Name of the Lord: from henceforth now and for ever... The Lord is high above all nations: and His glory above the heavens. Who is as the Lord our God, Who dwelleth on high, and looketh down on the low things in heaven and earth?... Who maketh a barren woman to dwell in a house; the joyful mother of children." God alone is glorious, and the good angels sing the praises of God. The bad angels fell from heaven out of pride. Nobody else is as great as God, and we should be content to dwell in a house, serving our spiritual children.

At the "Beginning of Night," Anger is combatted. (Or irritation caused by distractions.) (The Hour when fully dark, even in summer, in Latin "Compline" or "after dinner," but in the Irish and desert monasteries the dinner is at the Ninth Hour, and therefore the Irish call this Hour the Beginning of Night instead). The Beginning of Night asks God to pity those who beseech Him from the heart, or to preserve our hearts in the works of His statutes, and has the prayer for Peace. This Hour has a Psalm cycle through the week, and readings from

Acts and the Gospel of St. John, but there is an Antiphon read every night for peace. "...Abundant peace is for those who are attentive to Thy Law, O Lord, and there is no scandal in them." [From Psalm 118 Greek numbering or 119 Hebrew numbering, verse 165.] "May Thy peace, O Lord, King of Heaven, always pervade our vitals, so that we may not fear the terror by night..." The first Gradual Psalm, in Greek numbering 119, asks to overcome distress. "In my trouble I cried to the Lord: and He heard me.... With them that hate peace I was peaceable: when I spoke to them they fought against me without cause."

At the Beginning of Night, on alternate weeks, either the Gospel of St. John is read, or the Book of Acts of the Holy Apostles. The Gospel of St. John was bound together at the beginning of the Lorrha-Stowe Missal, the Lorrha-Stowe Missal is also called "The Gospel of St. Maelruain." In recent years a cohesive poetic style has been found in the Gospel of St. John, called "chiasm," in Greek: the outline of ideas follows A, B, C, B, A; or sometimes A, B, C, D, C, B, A; and the centers (C) also may follow a chiastic outline, etc. Several possible chiastic outlines and themes may be found based on the Greek text of St. John's Gospel, with several possible centers and supporting themes. The "lightning-flash of Divinity" (Byzantine Troparion Tone 2) implies connections going through each Gospel.

The Hour of Midnight combats Fornication and desire, in the Hymn of the Bridegroom and the ten virgins with their lamps. The Psalms are in a cycle through the week. Midnight has a hymn that remembers both the hour of Passover in Egypt, and the wise holy virgins going to meet the Bridegroom with one-pointed chaste mind. The daily Collect remembers that St. Peter was loosed from his chains at midnight, and before a Liturgy the Collect says that the Angels rejoiced at the Birth of Christ at midnight. (A shorter version of the Bridegroom Hymn appears in the Byzantine Rite in Holy Week). "This hour holds terror, thereon the destroying angel brought death to Egypt slaying the first-born." "The Bridegroom comes: the Maker of the heavenly Kingdom. Then Holy virgins hasten to attend the arrival bearing bright lamps." "Therefore let us watch soberly, bearing gleaming minds" "And at the time of Midnight both Paul and Silas, chained in prison praising Christ, were set free of bonds... Break the chains of our sins..." The second Gradual Psalm, in Greek numbering, Psalm 120, reminds us that God is always vigilant, and also we must remain vigilant. "I have lifted up my eyes to the mountains, from whence help shall come to me. My help is from the Lord, who made heaven and earth. May He not suffer thy foot to be moved: neither let Him slumber that keepeth thee. Behold He shall neither slumber nor sleep, that keepeth Israel... May the Lord keep thy going in and they going out; from henceforth now and for ever."

The Hour of Matins (after Midnight and before Dawn, around 3:00 A.M.) As one monk from Mt. Athos said, the quiet of the night when the world sleeps is especially free of distractions. Matins is the most important Hour of the Resurrection, and the longest Hour of Prayer. Matins combats Coveteousness with the better treasure of prayers. (Lay up not your treasure on earth, but in heaven. Mt 6:19-20. The "blessed law of divine commerce" in the "Dignum" of the Resurrection below rather than commercialism.) The daytime Hours may be completed in five to fifteen minutes, but Matins may take all night, with its many Psalms, Canticles, the Psalms of Praise (Psalms 148 through 150), Resurrection Gospels or Lenten readings, Hymns. This Hour compares life with death, the riches of heaven with the bankruptcy of earth, etc. If a person keeps riches for themselves, they do not gather together as the good shepherd or steward, but scatter as the thief and hireling of the sheep. Coveteousness causes death, which is the opposite of the purpose of Matins: the Hour of the Resurrection. The third Gradual Psalm, in Greek numbering 121, reminds us that God gives peace to Jerusalem as a city, or a gathering together the tribes (or, the Apostles as the virtues or treasures of heaven, or community of people). "For thither did the tribes go up, the tribes of the Lord: the testimony of Israel, to praise the Name of the Lord." At this time of night, Christ rescued souls from Hades and rose from the dead. At this time of night, our Lord prayed at the Garden of Gethsemane, not replacing the Crucifixion and Resurrection. His crucifixion is more than a physical reality or human death without spiritual meaning; His crucifixion is His Divine Offering (as in Psalm 50). Salvation through Christian prayer is more than thinking about God and our life and death. It is actively listening, battling against demons both internal and external, and receiving God. A life of prayer must include participation in the Holy Sacraments of the Church, with all the potency and potential that God gives us. Matins is more than an offering of prayers through the night; the night is now a holy time of meeting God, as explained in the "Dignum" said only in the Vigil Mass of the Resurrection:

"It is worthy and just, equal and just for us, here and everywhere to give Thee Thanks. To Thee we sing praises and offer sacrifice and trust in Thy mercy, O Lord Holy Father Almighty and eternal God, For Thou art great and dost wonderful things: Thou art God alone. Thou hast made the heavens in understanding. Thou didst form the land above the waters. Thou didst make great lights: the Sun to rule the day and the moon and stars to rule the night. Thou didst make us and not we, ourselves: despise not the works of thy hands. Thine is the day and Thine is the night. In the daytime hast Thou commanded Thy mercy; and in the nighttime Thou hast declared daily vigil. In the festival of this light we celebrate: This is the night of knowledge of the saving Sacraments: the night in which Thou dost grant forgiveness unto sinners: Thou doest make new from the old man: the mature with deluding senses Thou dost return as infants whom Thou dost bring forth, reborn in a new creature from the sacred font. This night a reborn people is conceived into eternal day. The halls of the heavenly kingdom are opened and humanity is transformed by the blessed law of divine commerce. This is the night which was made pleasures in which Thou delightest us, O Lord, in Thy works. This is the night in which hell was burst asunder, the night in which Adam was absolved, the night in which the groat that was lost is found, the night in which the lost sheep is laid upon the shoulders of the Good Shepherd, the night in which the devil was laid low, and the Sun of justice is arisen, and the bonds of hell being broken and the gates being shattered, many bodies of the Saints that had slept arose, and coming out of the tombs after the Resurrection came into the holy city. O truly blessed night which did merit to know the time and the hour when Christ rose, of which the prophet said in the Psalm: for the night shall be light as the day: the night in which the Resurrection unto eternity arose. Thee, therefore, Almighty God, the multitude of the heavenly creatures and the innumerable choirs of Angels proclaim without ceasing:" [then the Sanctus.]

Another Correspondence of the Apostles:
The Beatitudes, A Possible Inner Meaning of Ten Commandments

On the Feast day of Ss. Peter and Paul (June 29th, or Old Calendar July 12th), according to the Lectionary of Luxeiul and Bobbio arranged by St. Columbanus, the Gospel reading for the day is the Beatitudes, associated closely with all the Apostles; and the Proper Prayers for the Apostles include the prayer of the twelve hours of the day. Therefore, one may picture the Beatitudes as a list of virtues, also in this arch of the heavens. The Beatitudes, in reverse order, may also match the Ten Commandments. The Ten Commandments use the Hebrew word "La" which means not, or "do not" before each statement, rather than listing positive virtues. This is called the "Law" of God. [Exodus chapter 20]. From Hebrew: 1. No strange gods before me. 2. No graven thing. 3. Do not take the name of the Lord in vain. 4. Do not dishonor the Sabbath day. 5. Do not dishonor thy father and mother. 6. Do not kill. 7. Do not commit adultery. 8. Do not steal. 9. Do not bear false witness. 10. Do not covet.

The Beatitudes [St. Matthew 5:3-12] list virtues as positive blessings, in this order: "[1.] Blessed are the poor in spirit... [2.] Blessed are the meek... [3.] Blessed are they that mourn... [4.] Blessed are they that hunger and thirst after righteousness [or justice]... [5.] Blessed are the merciful... [6.] Blessed are the clean of heart... [7.] Blessed are the peacemakers... [8.] Blessed are they that are persecuted for righteousness [justice's] sake... [9.] Blessed are you when they shall revile you, and persecute you, and speak all that is evil against you untruly, for my sake... " The number and order of virtues in the Beatitudes are roughly in reverse order from the Ten Commandments. This is one possible assignment:

[9.] Blessed are you when they shall revile you, and persecute you, and speak all that is evil against you untruly, for my sake... " The last or ninth Beatitude blesses those who receive persecution caused by faithfulness to God. Faithfulness is the first three of the Ten Commandments: to have no strange gods before me, no graven thing, and not taking the name of the Lord in vain. Although the doctrine of the Holy Trinity is well developed in Christianity, sometimes prayers concerning these first Commandments have been taken away from modern Liturgies. (The doctrine of the Holy Trinity is also present in the Old Testament: see the Hebrew name "Elohim" used in Genesis 1:1, and Genesis chapter 18, among many examples.) Only the Lorrha-Stowe Missal has the following prayer: "Therefore we offer this oblation of our service and of Thy whole family, which we offer unto Thee in honor of our Lord Jesus Christ, and in commemoration of Thy blessed martyrs in this church, which Thy servants built in honor of Thy glorious Name. We beseech Thee graciously take it under Thy protection. Moreover, rescue them and all of the people from the cult of idols and turn them unto Thyself, the True God, the Father Almighty."

[8.] Blessed are they that are persecuted for righteousness [justice's] sake... The next-to-last or eighth Beatitude blesses those who hold on to justice, interpreted sometimes as doctrine and truth [as in the Rationale worn by the Priests described in Leviticus 8:8], and therefore is a Priestly function (we are all called to do), matching the commandment to "not dishonor the Sabbath day," which is interpreted by some desert fathers as continuous rest or Sabbath of silence and prayer, which should be done every day. (Conference of Abbot John Chapter VIII quoting Isaiah 58:13-14, about keeping silence and prayer on the Sabbath, and comparing the perfections of the Coenobite and Anchorite. Also, First Conference of Abbot Isaac, Chapter III, on keeping thoughts held on God in prayer, and Second Conference of Abbot Isaac, Chapter X.)

[7.] Blessed are the peacemakers... The seventh Beatitude is a reminder that our extended family, all of humanity, should be at peace, which is not dishonoring ones' father and mother (although there are times when this Beatitude is not followed: Mt 10:34-37 "Do not think that I came to send peace upon earth: I came not to send peace, but the sword. For I came to set a man at variance against his father, and the daughter against her mother..." and Lk 19:40 "To whom he said: I say to you, that if these shall hold their peace, the stones will cry out.") But also Christ says that the Apostles should bring peace, Mt. 10:12, and Christ gives peace at healings Mk 5:34, and as a blessing Lk 24:36, rebuking the wind Mk 4:39, and on honoring ones father and mother, that Mt 15:4-6 you should honor them more than the Pharisees, and that you should always honor your Father in heaven.

[6.] Blessed are the clean of heart... The sixth Beatitude goes with the sixth Commandment not to kill, and also means not to have anger in ones' heart. [Mt. 5:21-22 "You have heard that it was said to them of old: Thou shalt not kill. And whosoever shall kill shall be in danger of the judgment. But I say to you, and whosoever is angry with his brother, shall be in danger of the judgment..."]

[5.] Blessed are the merciful... The fifth Beatitude goes with the seventh Commandment, do not commit adultery, because of all the things people did that were unmerciful, allowing older women to beg for food was one of the worst, and indicated hardness of heart. [Mt. 19:7-9 "They say to him: Why then did Moses command to give a bill of divorce, and to put away? [Deut. 24:1] He saith to them: Because Moses by reason of the hardness of your heart permitted you to put away your wives: but from the beginning it was not so..."]

[4.] Blessed are they that hunger and thirst after righteousness [or justice]... The fourth Beatitude goes with the eighth Commandment not to steal, because stealing is the opposite of giving life, and every day we need to eat again, because life is stolen away from us. [John 10:10 "The thief cometh not, but for to steal, and to kill, and to destroy. I am come that they may have life, and may have it more abundantly." John 6:58 "As the living Father hath sent me, and I live by the Father; so he that eateth me, the same also shall live by me." John 4:13-14 "Jesus answered, and said to her: Whosoever drinketh of this water, shall thirst again; but he that shall drink of the water that I will give him, shall not thirst for ever: But the water that I will give him, shall become in him a fountain of water, springing up into life everlasting."]

[3.] Blessed are they that mourn... The third Beatitude goes with the ninth Commandment not to bear false witness, because it is truth in communication that brings joy, Christ as truth, the Word of God. Mourning here is for past sins, not personal grief. [John 16:22-24 "So also you now indeed have sorrow; but I will see you again, and your heart shall rejoice; and your joy no man shall take from you. And in that day you shall not ask me any thing. Amen, amen, I say to you: if you ask the Father any thing in my name, he will give it you. Hitherto you have not asked any thing in my name. Ask, and you shall receive; that your joy may be full."]

[2.] Blessed are the meek... and [1.] Blessed are the poor in spirit... The second Beatitude blessing those who are meek goes with the tenth Commandment to not covet, and refers to physical possessions. [Mt. 5:4 "Blessed are the meek: for they shall possess the land."]. The first Beatitude also refers to "do not covet." [Mt. 5:3 "Blessed are the poor in spirit: for theirs is the kingdom of heaven,"] referring to not only being meek in possessions, but also low in one's own pride, and thus being able to acquire the Holy Spirit. [Mt 11:28-30 "Come to me, all you that labor, and are burdened, and I will refresh you. Take up my yoke upon you, and learn of me, because I am meek, and humble of heart: and you shall find rest to your souls. For my yoke is sweet and my burden light."]

Conclusion, comparing the Desert Fathers to modernism, further study

The Beatitudes are in their own correct order, but it is the reverse order of other arrangements of sins and virtues such as the Ten Commandments. The desert fathers' order of faults gives an image of crossing the desert of principal faults into the promised land. When Pope St. Gregory the Dialogist arranged the number of "deadly sins" into seven, placing pride first, as St. John Chrysostom had placed pride as the first sin of the Beatitudes, St. Gregory may have been trying to reconcile the Beatitudes with the list of principal faults.

The eight paired faults: Gluttony/Fornication, Coveteousness/Anger, Despondency/Accidie, Vain-glory/Pride, are different from a modern list of seven deadly sins. The modern list: Pride, Envy, Anger, Sloth, Avarice, Gluttony and Lust. Notice that the modern "vain glory" has been replaced by envy, that "sloth" (or "accidie") and despondency are now not well understood and judged harshly, without compassion, as though a person could overcome these by their own will alone, replacing Orthodoxy with Pelagianism or Augustinianism (Manicheanism). There are many different lists of seven faults, all missing a fault (see the Irish Penitential above, closer to the desert fathers' list). The Virtues and Faults listed by the Desert Fathers is more complete.

St. John Chrysostom's commentary on the Beatitudes teaches about sin and virtue. St. Basil the Great "On the Holy Spirit" is very helpful in understanding the Orthodox attitudes toward the Holy Spirit, equal to the Father and the Son in Divinity. We must adore the Holy Spirit in truth, or else our finite understanding prevents us from reaching to heaven.

The Hours of Prayer, the Breviary
NOTES ON THE HOURS:

"How are we, mortals of the small word, to narrate anything which no one dares declare? We only pray this same maxim: O our eternal Lord, have mercy. Alleluia." (From *The Antiphonary of Bangor,* Hymn 3). Christians have always sung Hymns and Psalms. Our Lord and His Apostles prayed this way after the Last Supper before they went out to Gethsemane. St. Mark 14: 26 "And when they had sung a hymn they went forth to the Mount of Olives."

Prayer

There are many kinds of prayer. For more details, look under the headings: Continuous Prayer, Occasional Prayer, Litanies, Creed, the Divine Prayer (the Our Father), and Meditations on the Psalms and Hours. The Divine Liturgy, or Sacrifice of the Mass, is also prayer, as are the other Sacraments. An insight into the meaning of prayer is given in an explanation of the Our Father by the "Heavenly Sedulius," St. Siadal, because the Our Father contains all kinds of prayer. The Psalms were used as daily individual prayers, prayers in community, and for some as continuous prayers. Many Irish Saints memorized the entire Psalter, Gospels, and Epistles.

A note on the Psalm designations for Sundays, Saint days, and weekdays:

See the Celtic Lectionary: In the Lorrha-Stowe Missal, Psalms are used in the Gradual and Alleluia. Remnants of this practice in the Byzantine Rite are found in the Prokeimenon. Psalm assignments in the Mass, starting with Psalm 1 on the first Sunday in Advent, match the Lectionary and Propers of the Celtic Rite in content. The logical order of these Psalms telling the Life of Christ and the interior life of the soul is uncanny and prophetic;. (See the note about the Rosary under "Continuous Prayers;" the practice of the Rosary in Europe replaced the Psalms, adding meditations on the Life of Christ.)

Eight Times a Day

The Church arranged the reading of the Psalms and prayers into the Office of the Breviary, or the "Hours." The prayers of the Hours occur about every three hours through a twenty-four hour day. Psalm 118:164, "Seven times a day I have given praise to Thee, for the judgments of Thy justice." Christians added an eighth Hour, Matins, for the Resurrection, the "Eighth Day of Creation." Gregory Nazianzus, known as St. Gregory the Theologian, born 325 or 329, died Jan 25 389, one of only a handful of recognized Theologians by the Eastern Orthodox churches, in his sermon on Pentecost, Oration XLI, part II, seventh volume of the Post-Nicene Fathers, states that seven is a very important number as in the day of rest of the Lord, yet the Eighth Day of Creation [Sunday] is the final day of the Resurrection. Eight becomes a symbol of something higher, an "octave" or the next step above the seven. (See meditations on the Hours.)

What are the Psalms of the Hours?

The Hours are not a replacement for private prayers, but they are the watchfulness and prayer of a Christian community. In a monastic community, the all-night vigil was said in much the same way that an army or medical staff will keep watch, in shifts. Every verse of the Psalms would be sung antiphonally, which means to alternate verses. In shorter daytime Hours, it would be possible to repeat an Antiphon between verses. Psalms are sung in "choruses" of three Psalms together, then a rest if necessary. Often, they are sung seated.

The Hours of Prayer begin at sunset, "...and there was evening and morning one day" [Genesis 1:5], in both Byzantine and Western calendars. For example, "Sunday" Hours begin at sundown at Vespers (in modern times Saturday evening) about 6:00 P.M. at the Equinoxes, but the time varies according to the time of year and latitude. The next Hour is the Beginning of Night (when fully dark, even in summer, in Latin "Compline" or "after dinner," but in the Irish and desert monasteries of Egypt the dinner is at the Ninth Hour, and therefore the Irish call the Hour of prayer after Vespers the Beginning of Night instead). Then, Midnight at the hour of midnight. Matins is at about 3:00 A.M., or just prior to dawn, although to be able to sing all of Matins, the Psalms of Matins may actually start just after the Hour of Midnight is over. The daylight hours are numbered according to the number of hours of daylight, divided into twelve hours (with Hours of Prayer in the Breviary every three hours of the day). The first hour is normally dawn or 6:00 A.M.; but the Irish begin the day Hours at the Second Hour around 7:00 A.M., perhaps because of their northern latitude, or because they sang this Hour when the sky was fully light. The Third Hour is about 9:00 A.M. The Sixth Hour is noon. The Ninth Hour is about 3:00 P.M. (Note that Christ refers to evening as sunrise and morning as sunset: St. Matthew 16:2-3 "But He answered and said to them: When it is evening, you say, It will be fair weather, for the sky is red. And in the morning: Today there will be a storm, for the sky is red and lowering. You know then how to discern the face of the sky: and can you not know the signs of the times?" Christ is referring to a red sky in the west at sunset indicating a coming storm.)

Greater than a Local Irish Usage, Sources of Other Usages

The prayers and Canticles are numbered in the order they appear in the *Antiphonary of Bangor*, such as "AB 36", or they are culled from old Irish Rules or Irish documents. This Breviary represents more than a local Irish usage, and has prayers found throughout the ancient church, which are often shortened in other churches. (The Bridegroom Hymn AB 10, at Midnight in the Celtic Breviary, is abbreviated in the Byzantine Rite Bridegroom Hymn during Holy Week. "Fiery Creator of the Light giving Light" AB 9, is abbreviated in the Byzantine Hymn "Phos Hilarion." "The Hymn of the Apostles," AB 3, has forty verses that imply a response of "Kyrie eleison," other than the beginning and ending verses which end "Alleluia;" this may have become the "forty-fold Kyrie" which is sung only as the responses in the Byzantine Rite, and which became the "Kyrie" in the later Tridentine Roman Rite. The Greek "Kontakion" Hymns were originally Abecedarian Hymns, i.e., each letter of the alphabet began a new verse, but these are shortened to one verse in modern Byzantine practice. Irish Abecedarian Hymns pre-date the Byzantine Kontakion. The Irish Caelius Sedulius, or St. Siadal, taught poetry in Athens including Irish bardic forms.)

Blessing and Care of an Elder; the Sacraments; Word, Thought, and Deed

It is not necessary to be in any rank of clergy or a monastic to sing the Hours, although a blessing and guidance from a Priest is always a good idea. The more time put into a life of prayer, the more guidance is suggested; it is a very good idea to contact a spiritual Father who can be a guide for this life. (This may include a lay monk or nun, with the blessing of a Father Confessor who is able to give Absolution.) This can add wonderful experienced direction toward God, while protecting from delusions, distractions, and other pitfalls.

Prayer must be accompanied by participation in the Sacraments of the Orthodox Christian Church. We come to God, as the Irish fathers said, in Word, Thought, and Deed; the Word of God first, because God loves us first. We must not reject the Deed. God not only knows our words and thoughts, but also our deeds. Prayer is not said as a show, or psychological drama, but for our salvation which comes only from God. Therefore, prayer is not a replacement for the Sacraments of the Church, but a part of them. (See Liturgy notes).

How to Do the Hours and Prayers of the Church:
Melodies and Singing Aloud

The Breviary is not read silently. Psalm 50: "O Lord, Thou wilt open my lips: and my mouth shall declare Thy praise. For if Thou hadst desired sacrifice, I would indeed have given it: with burnt-offerings Thou wilt not be delighted. A sacrifice to God is an afflicted spirit: a contrite and humbled heart, O God, Thou wilt not despise." The words are sung instead of spoken because singing long prayers is more gentle to the voice, and has always been the way monks pray (see the section "Sounds in the Mass"). It is not necessary to know a melody. The simplest chant is on one note, going up or down a note or two at the end of a phrase. Simple Middle Eastern Christian chant uses a few notes or a scale in a mode, moving up and down one note at a time, and fits a phrase into that. (Russians tend to repeat notes, the Middle Eastern chant tends to use "neighbor notes" in a scale to sing the syllables.

"Melisma," or singing several notes on one syllable, may be beautiful, but it slows the singing.)

Originally, the Psalms each had a melody. The Irish were trained by monks who had studied long in the deserts near Alexandria in Egypt. There is some evidence that the chant of the Irish used modes and melodies also found in Ethiopian or Libyan music (theologically not the same doctrine at present, but the music of Ethiopia probably is the same as it originally was before their doctrinal shifts). The Ethiopian chant uses "Eight Tones" (modes) more chromatic than other modern Byzantine chants; much more chromatic than Gregorian chant. If a chanter wishes to study complex historical chant, it would be a beautiful offering, however, these prayers should be sung by anybody, and may be sung without embellishment.

Seasonal and Daily Collects and Prayers, Especially Matins

Collects and other prayers do change for the day of the week or Feast day. Only read all the Antiphons and Collects that apply to the day. For example, on a Sunday, read all the Sunday readings and special readings for Feasts if they fall on that day, but not the daily readings or readings for Feasts if they do not fall on that day. There are often two or three Sunday or daily prayers in a row. For example, do not read the Christmas reading in July just because it is printed on the page. A "Daily" Antiphon or Collect would be sung every day but the Vespers or Vigil of Sunday or Feast, or the daylight hours on Sunday or Feast. Sometimes there is a prayer for a day before or after a Canticle or Psalm, but not both before and after the Canticle: follow the directions that are given, especially in Matins, for these prayers. The reason for the placement of these prayers will become clear when doing them. The *Antiphonary of Bangor* titled most of its prayers as to where they should be placed. Other Antiphons and Collects without a day of the week, season, or special occasion noted on them, are sung at all times. These can appear before, between or after groups of seasonal Antiphons, so care must be taken to read them and not skip them.

Prayer of the Community of the Brethren, Long or Short

The Prayer of the Community of the Brethren ends each Hour. Read all the parts of the prayers, collects, and intercessory prayers. For example, if you do not have an abbot, still read the prayers for the abbot, but remember your Bishop or Priest who has blessed your prayer life, or remember all abbots and abbesses struggling to keep the Orthodox faith anywhere. If you do not know anybody that is impious, pray for those you haven't met who are, etc. Choose either the long form or the short form of the "Prayer of the Community of the Brethren." The short form does not offer as many intercessions, but is sometimes necessary if there is little time. (Both the long and short forms are given in the Antiphonary of Bangor.) After these prayers, the Creed and Our Father are sung.

The Creed and the Our Father in the Hours

The Creed and the Our Father are at the end of each Hour according to the Rule of St. Mael Ruain, and it is best to do the complete Nicene Creed as found in the Lorrha-Stowe Missal, because this is a complete statement of faith approved by Ecumenical Councils for use by all Christians. The Antiphonary of Bangor gives a version of the Apostles' Creed. Another Apostles' Creed in the Bobbio Missal illustrates the teachings of virtues of the Apostles in the order of the Creed, which may be matched to Psalms. (See "Creed" in the Missal notes, which has all three of these Creeds). There are longer Creeds, see the Bishops' statement of faith on our website: www.CelticChristianity.org (There isn't room for the entire Bishops' statement here, which is unfortunate, because it is a good catechism.)

The English translation given here of the Our Father only disagrees with modern translations influenced by German Bibles of the 15th century. The Pater Noster in the Lorrha-Stowe Missal and the Breviary is a half-century old English translation from Greek and Church Slavonic used in Orthodox Churches; it is exactly the same as St. Jerome's Latin and the New Testament Greek. The Douay translation of the Lord's Prayer does not agree with the Latin and Greek texts. See Prayer: "Our Father," an explanation of this greatest of prayers.

After the Creed and the Our Father, it is also traditional to sing Hymns, such as AB 2 (see the Cross Vigil), the Beatitudes, the Magnificat, and other Hymns.

The Psalms: Numbering, Rules, Gospels, Canticles, Psalm Names, the Psalms

Psalm Numbering in Greek among Early Christians, not Hebrew numbering

The numbering of the Psalms is found in the Septuagint (Greek Old Testament), the Latin Vulgate Bible, and the Douay-Rheims Bible (which is in English). These Psalms differ in numbering from most of the Psalms in the Hebrew and King James Version, Revised, and later English language texts, usually by one number. The Septuagint text was commonly available at the time our Lord Jesus Christ was teaching, and was the numbering used by the Apostles. This numbering has always been used by Christians, whether from Irish sources (in the *Antiphonary of Bangor*), Byzantine Orthodox Psalters, or Roman Catholic Breviaries. There are important word differences between the Greek Psalter (from the Septuigint, the accurate translation into Greek by Jewish scholars before Christ), and the Hebrew or King James Version of the Bible. The words may have been changed around 90 A.D. after the destruction of Jerusalem in 70 A.D. For example, the Hebrew Scripture available today is not exactly the same as the Hebrew Book of Isaiah found in the Dead Sea Scrolls. The controversial line, "A virgin shall conceive and bear a Son." is in the Dead Sea Scrolls, but the current Hebrew Scripture changed this to "a young girl" when several changes to the Hebrew were made around 90 A.D. For convenience sake, the Douay Psalter has been included in this book.

For those familiar with the Hebrew numbering, here is a number comparison:

Septuagint Greek, Latin, Douay:	Hebrew, King James Version, RSV:
Psalms 1 - 8	1 - 8 (same numbering).
9	9 and 10.
10 - 112	add a number.

(For example: Douay Psalm 22 is the same Psalm as KJV Psalm 23, except that the words and ideas have major differences between these versions in this Psalm; see the Psalms at the Confraction in the Mass, which need the Greek version.)

113	114 and 115.
114	116 verses 1-9.
115	116 verses 10-19.
116 - 145	add a number.
146	147 verses 1-11.
147	147 verses 12-20.
148 - 150	148 - 150 (same numbering).

Psalm Reading According to the Monastery of Bangor:

The daytime Hours have three set Psalms each, noted before Vespers.

At night, there are two separate cycles:

The arrangement by St. Mael Ruain of Tallaght for the Beginning of Night (9:00 P.M.), and the Hour of Midnight together, spreads the one hundred fifty Psalms over six days in one week. There are 12 or 13 Psalms in each of these two Hours, totaling 25 Psalms each night. The Cross Vigil may be done on the seventh day.

There are two other separate cycles of Psalms for Matins according to the Rule of St. Columbanus, separate from both the Daytime and also the Beginning of Night and Midnight Psalms. St. Columbanus's usage of Psalms in Matins varied from 75 Psalms on Saturdays and Sundays in winter during the longer nights, to 24 Psalms on weekdays in summer; with a variable number in spring and fall. There was a separate Rule for weekdays and for weekends in Matins according to St. Columbanus. The seasons marked by the Psalm arrangements of the Rule of St. Columbanus often coincided with the great Feasts.

In a large monastery, both the Rule of St. Columbanus for Matins, and the Rule of

St. Mael Ruain for Beginning of Night and Midnight, would be done. The method practiced at St. Mael Ruain's time (9th century) was to assign most of a monastic community to do Matins and the Daytime hours including Vespers, but the Beginning of Night and Midnight would be done by a few monks, rotating these monks on a regular basis. More monks would be present during Matins, since it is the Hour of the Resurrection, even though it is at night.

An "All-Night Vigil" using Beginning of Night and Midnight with Matins

It might be best to do a kind of "All-Night Vigil" by combining the Beginning of Night, Midnight, and, in anticipation by a few hours, Matins. This would be more similar to either the Benedictine Rule or the Byzantine Rule. Say the Psalms from St. Mael Ruain's Beginning of Night and Midnight Psalm table. This would shorten the entire night's services considerably, because Matins would not add an extra 24 to 75 Psalms on top of the 25 Psalms of Beginning of Night and Midnight, even though all the prayers from Beginning of Night, Midnight, and Matins would be done together. On Saturday (modern Friday night), the Cross Vigil would begin the All Night Hours. (Note that in Parish usage during Holy Week, an arrangement of this sort, combining the Hours of Vespers through Matins, may be done, and in the modern Byzantine Rite, the prayers during Holy Week are almost the same as the Celtic Hours, the only time during the year when the Hours are so similar.)

No Psalms on Holy and Great Friday, and Adjustments in Holy Week

On Holy and Great Friday, other readings are required. No Psalms are allowed that day. Holy Saturday and the Resurrection of our Lord Jesus Christ require other readings that would take up much time. Therefore, the Psalms normally read from Holy Thursday through the Vigil must be read earlier in Holy Week. (It would not be possible to do these Psalms all of Holy Saturday, because it would be too exhausting, taking strength and attention away from the Vigil of the Resurrection.) Doing more Psalms at the Beginning of Night and Midnight earlier in Holy Week is preferable to postponing the Psalms to the next week, because although one might be inclined to increase Psalms of praise, it would not be wise to add more prayers after all the rigors of Holy and Great Friday and the Vigil of the Resurrection. (St. Mael Ruain said in his community of Tallaght not to reduce readings, but these may be transferred to another day.) During the Paschal week (following Pascha), rest and moderation are needed. Those who are unable to do all the Psalm readings should still pray and attend the services on Holy Thursday, Holy and Great Friday through that evening (Holy Saturday), and the Vigil of the Resurrection on Holy Pascha.

A Few Solitaries Practice 150 Psalms in a Day, with Permission

Solitary Irish monastics often did all 150 Psalms every day, adding other prayers and hymns. If an individual finds the rigors of the Rule of St. Columbanus with the Psalms at Matins and the Rule of St. Mael Ruain with the Psalter recited in one week not enough for them, they may recite the entire one hundred and fifty Psalms every day. Reciting the entire Psalter has been done as recently as the nineteenth century by some Greek monks on Mt. Athos. In this case, the nine Canticles are inserted between these, and all the prayers are said through the day, as suggested by the groupings of Psalms and prayers of St. Mael Ruain and the *Antiphonary of Bangor*, but otherwise, Psalm tables from the Rule of St. Maelruain and the Rule of St. Columbanus are not used. St. Mael Rúain does suggest moderation, however, both to help a person to be attentive to their prayers, and also so that they do not become worn out physically and unable to do this all their lives. The Eastern Church also emphasizes that the Psalms are supposed to be broken up into small sections, according to the Ecumenical Councils. It would be necessary to have guidance in such practice, but we are also supposed to "pray without ceasing" (I Thess. 5:17), so if the Psalms are easier to say than reciting endless repetitive prayers every day, it might be useful to do the Psalms this way. [See *Contemporary Ascetics of Mount Athos, Volume II*, by Archimandrite Cherubim, appendix page 700. An individual monk practicing a daily recitation of 150 Psalms was taken from *The Life and Labors of Elder Hieroschemamonk Hilarion the Georgian* by Hieromonk Anthony of the Holy Mountain, Holy Trinity Monastery, Jordanville, NY 1985, pp. 68-73 in a letter of Fr. Sabbas to Fr. Denasius. Fr. Sabbas was following the instructions of his Elder Hilarion, a very traditional Orthodox Christian Byzantine monk without innovations.]

[Standing and sitting was alternated to relieve stress on the joints; and St. Maelruain chanted 150 Psalms in one week instead of one day. We recommend this method, for example, in the reading of the Gospel of St. John and the Book of Acts at the Beginning of Night: always stand for the Gospel, but one may sit during the reading of the Book of Acts, alternating weeks. It seems that a method of saying the Psalms which ends Friday Midnight, i.e., in one week, is being described, and St. Mael Ruain is also suggesting moderation in describing a man who couldn't bend his legs after doing 700 prostrations a day for a number of years. There wouldn't be time to do the one hundred and fifty Psalms in the evening, because in early monastic communities, only two monks were assigned in the oratory during Beginning of Night and Midnight, also leaving time for the reading of either three chapters of the Gospel of St. John or four chapters of the Book of Acts during the Beginning of Night. And, if one hundred fifty Psalms were done, also nine Canticles would be done. For example, the Paschal Vigil takes about five to six hours, with all the twelve Prophecies, Candle lighting, Baptism, Mass with Paschal Propers, etc.,; it takes a long time to read that many pages of prayers, and it was traditional to read prayers, including Psalms, out loud. And then the monks would have many labors during the day; and the daytime number of Psalms is set at a very low number in order to accommodate those labors. Therefore, the note about ending these on "Friday Midnight," indicating that they are spread over a week, makes the most sense. The treatise below is an attempt at a description about what St. Mael Ruain did, not a full description by St. Mael Ruain. It does not sound as if the writer fully understood the method of reading the Psalms that St. Mael Ruain employed. Other suggestions about reading the evening Psalms are given in St. Brendan's Navigatio, with an Antiphon to be said, and completing the twelve or thirteen Psalms with the Our Father, appropriate with the Creed at the end of the Hour.]

Beginning of Night and Midnight Céli Dé Psalter Arrangement According to the Rule of St. Mael Rúain

The day starts at Vespers, so that Sunday begins on sunset of Saturday. "...and there was evening and morning one day" (Genesis 1:5)

Greek, Latin, and Douay numbering:

		Beginning of Night	Midnight
Sunday	(modern Saturday night.)	Psalms 1-13	14-25
Monday	(modern Sunday night.)	26-37	38-50
Tuesday	(modern Monday night.)	51-63	64-75
Wednesday	(modern Tues. night.)	76-87	88-100
Thursday	(modern Wed. night)	101-112	113-124
Friday	(modern Thursday night)	125-137	138-150

This Cycle ends Friday Midnight according to St. Mael Rúain's rule. The Cross Vigil Psalms 118 through 121, the Hymns of the Cross Vigil, and the Shrine of Piety, may be done Saturday (modern Friday night). The Cross Vigil is especially appropriate after Holy and Great Friday, combined with the Psalm and Gospel of Holy Saturday Matins.

The Psalm table of St. Mael Ruain for the Beginning of Night and Midnight, which specified the Psalms by name:

I. The first fifty:

A. *Beatus vir* to *Domine quis habitabit.* 1-13 [13 Psalms]

   Then he made a genuflexion and said the *Pater Noster* and "O God come to my assistance, O Lord make haste to help me." and he said these versicles before each division [of twelve or thirteen].

B. *Domine quis habitabit* to *Dominus illuminatio*; 14-25 [12 Psalms] then the *Pater Noster,* etc. as above.

C. *Dominus illuminatio* to *Dixi custodiam,* 26-37 [12 Psalms] and then the *Pater Noster* and a genuflexion.
D. [From *Dixi custodiam* to the end of the first fifty, etc.] 38-50 [13 Psalms]

II. The second fifty:
A. *Quid gloriatur* to *Te decet,* 51-63 [13 Psalms] and then a *Pater Noster* and a genuflexion.
B. *Te decet* to *Voce.* 64-75 [12 Psalms]
C. *Voce* to *Misericordias.* 76-87 [12 Psalms]
D. *Misericordias* to the end. 88-100 [13 Psalms]

III. Third Fifty:
"The point at which he recited the canticle of the final division was while saying the Psalms which are **said at Midnight on Friday night**, for the last eight Psalms of this division were recited when Midnight was sung on Friday night."
A. *Domine exaudi* to *In exitu Israel.* 101-112 [12 Psalms]
B. *In exitu Israel* to *In convertendo.* 113-124 [12 Psalms]
C. *In convertendo* to *Domine probasti.* 125-137 [13 Psalms]
D. *Domine probasti* to the end. 138-150 [13 Psalms]

St. Mael Rúain's note for the final fifty Psalms: that the last Psalms fall on Midnight for Friday, indicates that these Psalms were said over the course of a week. Furthermore, there are twelve divisions, which cover only six days at two Hours of prayer. In the Rule of St. Columbanus, the Matins Psalms are a separate cycle.

The teaching of Mael Ruain on saying the Psalms and Hours, written out in full (translation from Old Irish, The Rule of Tallaght, *edited by Edward Gwynn, Dublin, 1927, pages 58-61, terms for the Hours corrected according to the Old Irish by Bishop. Maelrúan.)*

"His way of chanting the Psalms was this. He divided each fifty into four parts. His first division was from *Beatus vir* to *Domine quis habitabit.* Then he made a genuflexion and said the *Pater Noster* and *Deus in adiutorium meum intende* down to *festina* ["O God come to my assistance. O Lord make haste to help me."], and he said these versicles before each division. The second division was from *Domine quis habitabit* to *Dominus illuminatio;* then the *Pater Noster,* etc. as above. From *Dominus illuminatio* to *Dixi custodiam,* and then the *Pater Noster* and a genuflexion. [From *Dixi custodiam* to the end of the first fifty, etc.] The second fifty: from *Quid gloriatur* to *Te decet,* and then a *Pater Noster* and a genuflexion. From *Te decet* to *Voce.* From *Voce* to *Misericordias.* From *Misericordias* to the end.

"The point at which he recited the canticle of the final division was while saying the Psalms which are said at Midnight on Friday night , for the last eight Psalms of this division were recited when Midnight were sung on Friday night [modern Thursday night, according to the chart for Beginning of Night and Midnight]. The third fifty: from *Domine exaudi* to *In exitu Israel:* from *In exitu Israel* to *In convertendo:* from *In convertendo* to *Domine probasti:* from *Domine probasti* to the end. The point at which he recited the *Magnificat* was immediately after the *Beati.* He said one division sitting and the next standing, alternately. That is how he was wont to chant them.

His practice of saying the *Pater Noster* at the end of each division came to him from a holy person who lived at Coill Uaithne (he does not record his name). It was his custom not to rise without reciting the *Pater Noster* before sitting down. When he stood up to recite a division he said the *Pater Noster* before rising. When he had finished that division standing, he would sit down to recite the next, and he would say the *Pater Noster* as he sat down. hence it became the practice to say the *Pater Noster* at the end of each division.

Mael Dithruib said to Mael Ruain: 'I have heard,'said he, 'that it is Dublitir's custom to perform a vigil by saying the hundred and fifty Psalms standing, with the genuflexion after each psalm.' 'I do not recommend that practice to thee,' said Mael Ruain: 'that is not how we are accustomed to say the Psalter.' 'In what way should the canticles be recited?' asked Mael Dithruib. 'There are two methods of saying them. The first is, to say them all after the Psalms; or else to recite three of them after every fifty Psalms.' This latter was Mael Dithruib's practice.

"There was an anchorite in Clonard, whose labor was great. He used to make two hundred genuflexions at Matins, a hundred at each of the canonical hours, and a hundred at Midnight. Seven hundred genuflexions in all did he make in the twenty four hours. This was told to Mael Ruain. 'My word for it,' said he, 'there will be some space of time before his death when he will not be able to make a single genuflexion.' And this came true, for his legs became crippled, so that for a long while before his death he was unable to make a single genuflexion, by reason of the excessive number he had formerly made.*"

(* Although we hold up in our culture great athletic ability, the over-exertion of some people creates such diseases as severe arthritis. Moderation is recommended. However, the Cross Vigil with prostrations done once a week, or at times in penitential seasons, is a very good aerobic exercise, although it must be approached with caution.)

Page 73 of this Rule of St. Mael Rúain: monastic community:

"With the Celi De it is not the practice to sleep in the oratory. Their practice is that two of them should remain in the oratory until Midnight, and recite the hundred and fifty Psalms: [that is, usually broken up into the sets of 12 or 13 per night at the Beginning of Night] they dine in the afternoon and sleep until night, and sleep [again] from Midnight till Matins. Two others then remain from Midnight till Matins, and they also recite the hundred and fifty Psalms [again, usually broken up in the Rule of 12 or 13 Psalms for Midnight], and then sleep until Tierce [Third Hour] and say the office of Tierce in company with all the brethren.

"It is the practice of the Celi De that while they are at dinner one of them reads aloud the Gospels and the Rule and miracles of Saints, to the end that their minds may be set on God, not on the meal: and the man who preaches at that time has his dinner in the afternoon, and in the course of the [next] day they are questioned severally about the subject of the sermon, to see whether their minds were occupied with it on [the previous] night or not.

"He that has not attended Mass on Sunday must recite fifty [Psalms], standing, in a closed house, with his eyes signed with the Cross: this is the price he pays for the Mass. A hundred genuflections and a Cross-vigil, with the *Beati*, discharge his obligation.

"However much a man may suffer from thirst, he may not take a drink [before] Midnight. [He may drink between Midnight] and the office at bed time." *[It is best not to follow this advice due to modern medical knowledge, but St. Mael Ruain is suggesting that some people leave their prayers often to relieve themselves, and he is suggesting avoiding that. Also, before a Mass, water and food are not taken after Midnight, making this rule very difficult.]*

"The point at which he recited the *Magnificat* was immediately after the *Beati*. [after a few Psalms, such as Psalm 118, or possibly the Beatitudes, or both.]

"He said one division sitting and the next standing, alternately. That is how he was wont to chant them."

The Rule of Columbanus used only during Matins:
The Antiphonary of Bangor (Matins is also called Vigil):

When this Breviary was first printed, all the complicated Psalm tables for every day of the year of St. Columbanus for the Hour of Matins were included. However, even though it was specified that the tables of Psalms were used *only* in large communities where groups of monks recited the Psalms in shifts, some people assumed that an individual would be required to do all the Psalms of every Hour including Matins unassisted. Therefore, it would probably be best to direct interested people to a spiritual elder for further directions. The Rule of St. Columbanus is described without the tables here; if you wish to see all the tables for Matins for every day of the year, make a request to: www.CelticChristianity.org

Rule of St. Columbanus:
The Holy Nights (any night) preceding Saturday and Sunday:

This is a brief description of the Rule for Matins. In the Rule of Columbanus, the Matins Psalms on Saturday and Sunday together (the Hour of Matins alone) cover the complete Psalms during what they considered the winter months: between November 1st and January 31st. In the summer months, from May 1st to June 24th, Saturday and Sunday together cover 72 Psalms, almost half the Psalms. (The average for winter and summer Saturdays and Sundays together is an average of 111 Psalms). The Psalms in Matins on Saturday and Sunday for the months between winter and summer gradually increase or decrease.

From Nov 1-Jan 31: 75 Psalms. [each night: Sunday 75 and Saturday 75.]
From Feb 1-Apr 30: decrease 3 Psalms per week. [12 and a half weeks.]
From May 1- June 24: 36 Psalms.
From June 25-Oct 31: gradual increase from 36 to 75 Psalms. [18 weeks, increasing by a little more than two Psalm every week. If one is singing in groups of three, the numbers of Psalms will stay the same about every two weeks. The table lists changes in groups of three Psalms.]

Rule of St. Columbanus: On other nights in Matins (Monday to Friday):

The Rule of Columbanus also gives an outline of the Psalms read in the Hour of Matins during the week. The weekday Matins Psalms (Monday through Friday) in Matins alone cover the complete Psalter an *average* of once a week: in winter 180 Psalms, and in summer 120 Psalms, either 36 Psalms for five days of the week or 24 Psalms for five days of the week. (The average for winter and summer weekdays together is an average of 150 Psalms.) These numbers do not gradually decrease or increase, but jump suddenly from 36 to 24 Psalms:

From Sept 25-Mar 24: 36 Psalms. [Increase or decrease not mentioned.]
From Mar 25-Sept 24: 24 Psalms. [Increase or decrease not mentioned.]

The Feasts of the Conception of Our Lord Jesus Christ (the Annunciation) on March 25th and the Conception of St. John the Baptist (September 25th) were traditional Equinoxes in the Church, and the rest of the daily Matins Psalm calendar was derived from them.

For the summer months of the Saturday and Sunday Matins Psalm calendar: May 1 was the first day of Christ's preaching, according to the Irish calendar (when He went into the Temple and said, "This is the acceptable year of the Lord.") It is also the martyrdom of the Apostle Philip, who is called "highest" in the Martyrology of Oengus (indicating the start of summer; also, see the arrangement of the Psalms of the Apostles and the Hours; his is near to noon). Oengus also mentions St. James the brother of the Lord and the Apostle Matthew on this date, although this is an obscure reference. May 1 was known as "Lady day;" the Blessed Virgin Mary's official Birthday on September 8th, but an earlier celebration of it was in the beginning of May (without labeling it as a "nativity" celebration), for this reason: some calendars list "Lady Day" on May 3rd (which is also the celebration of the Finding of the True Cross during the reign of Constantine). In the Celtic Rite and early Martyrologies (calendars), the Annunciation (March 25th) was also the original date of the Crucifixion of our Lord, although the Crucifixion has always been celebrated on the movable calendar; and therefore any day on which is an adoration of the True Cross is also a day of commemoration of the Blessed Virgin Mary. The beginning of Christ's preaching ties in with the other important dates during this season:

the Feasts of Ascension and Pentecost. The birth of St. John the Baptist on June 24th ended this season.

For the winter months of the Saturday and Sunday Matins Psalm Calendar: the Celtic New Years is on November 1st, which became All Saints day because people always honored their departed at that time. The Octave of All Saints is soon before the Feast of St. Martin of Tours November 11th. November 13th began Advent in the Irish Church, which assured that there would be six Sundays in Advent before Christmas. Then, the Feasts of the Circumcision and Epiphany and its Octave filled half of January, and after that the Feast of St. Brigid and the Presentation of the Lord beginning February completed this season. November 1 to January 31 also are the darkest months of winter, and have the most night time for Psalms at night.

Note: in the Rule of St. Columbanus for Matins, sometimes the Psalms for a night might begin, for example, on Psalm 100, and 60 Psalms are to be read that night. In that case, read Psalms 100 to 150 and 1 to 10, which might be abbreviated 100 - 10. Unfortunately, the full table of Psalms for Matins in St. Columbanus's Rule is not included here, because we have found that outside of a large monastic community, most people are only confused by such a table. The full table is available at www.CelticChristianity.org

Alternate Psalm Usages:

(In the Byzantine usage, no Vigils are done Sunday evenings or on any Feast of the Lord. In the Celtic usage, St. Mael Rúain he ends his twelve divisions of Psalms of the Beginning of Night and Midnight on Friday Midnight (modern Thursday night). In the Rule of St. Columbanus, Matins has more Psalms and its own cycle. The Byzantine Psalms are not in order. The Psalm arrangement of the Celtic Churches is in order, not only in the Hours, but through the year in the Graduals and Alleluias of the Mass, and are prophecy of the life of Christ, Resurrection, Ascension, Pentecost, and the ages of ages. This chart illustrates the Byzantine arrangement of Psalms, and is to be used only within the context of Byzantine Hours, if practicing the Byzantine Rite:)

Byzantine Rule of Psalm Readings

The day starts at Vespers, so that Sunday begins on sunset of Saturday. "...and there was evening and morning one day" (Genesis 1:5)

Greek, Latin, and Douay numbering:	Beginning of Night	Midnight	Matins
Sunday	1-8	9-16,	17-23
Monday	***	24-31,	32-36
Tuesday	37-45	46-54,	55-63
Wednesday	64-69	70-76,	77-84
Thursday	85-90	91-100,	101-104
Friday	105-108	134-142,	143-150
Saturday	119-133	109-117,	118

Matins Sunday Resurrection Gospels in the Ten Week (Celtic) Cycle

There is a "Ten-Week Cycle" of Resurrection Gospels read in Sunday Matins; except not in Lent or Paschaltide. The Gospel of the Sunday Liturgy is repeated during Paschaltide. In the Celtic Rite, this ten-week cycle of Matins Gospels are not actually identified by Irish sources, as far as we know. Gospel Kerubs (angelic symbols), see the "Traditio" of St. Ambrose, read every Palm Sunday: St. Matthew - Man; St. Mark - Lion; St. Luke - Bull; St. John - Eagle. The symbols are from the beginning of the first chapters of the Gospels, as explained in the "Traditio," and show that the Gospel writers were inspired to write with slightly different perspectives. Gospels repeat events, these are from different viewpoints, all correct.

The Matins Resurrection Gospel is read by a Deacon or Priest [or Abbot, or rarely Abbess if blessed to do this outside of a Mass, see the hour of the Beginning of Night.]: Sunday begins at Vespers, on modern (secular) Saturday evening. On weekdays there is not a Matins Resurrection Gospel unless it is a Feast or titular.

During Lent and Paschaltide, there is an Old Testament or another reading in place of these Matins Gospels. (However, the reading of the Gospel of St. John at the Beginning of Night does not change, except at the end of Holy Week.)

Order of Gospels in Matins, first edition arrangement in the Breviary

Week I	St. John 20:1-18.	St. Mary Magdalene at the sepulchre.
Week II	St. Luke 24:1-12.	Women at the sepulchre.
Week III	St. Mark 16:9-20.	St. Mary Magdalene, Jesus with eleven.
Week IV	St. Luke 24:13-35.	Jesus and two on the road to Emmaus.
Week V	St. Matt. 28:1-10.	At the sepulchre: angel, guards, adoration.
Week VI	St. Mark 16:1-8.	Women at sepulchre, angel.
Week VII	St. Luke 24:36-53.	Eating with Jesus, disciples in temple.
Week VIII	St. John 20:19-31.	Eating with Jesus, doubts of St. Thomas.
Week IX	St. Matt. 28:11-20.	Disciples, mountain, baptize, Jesus with us.
Week X	St. John 21:1 to end.	Fishes, eating with Jesus, feed my sheep.

Variant Celtic Ten Week Matins Resurrection Gospels from Paschaltide

Some Gospels during Paschaltide have a direct theme of Resurrection. Some of these Gospels start and end at a different place than the previous list. The themes follow the Light of Christ in assurances, revelation, stating that Christ is Risen, that He is God, able to raise us from the dead, keep His promises, and then tells us to take our responsibilities to bring His teachings to others, continue to believe in Him, and be a part of receiving His heavenly banquet in His holy temple. The first edition Celtic arrangement seemed to match the prayers and Antiphons according to the Ten Commandments. However, these ten Paschal Gospels below may be better suited. Please let us know. *[Elizabeth Dowling, 2008]*

Week I: Vigil of The Resurrection of our Lord, Pascha Matthew 28:1-20 [L,B,T] At the sepulchre: angel, guards, adoration, disciples, mountain, baptize, Jesus with us.

Week II: Dawn of the Resurrection: Luke 24:1-12 [B] Women at the sepulchre. [may continue with Luke 24:13-35 Jesus and two on the road to Emmaus, not in the Celtic Paschal readings of the season, but worthy to read through the year at Matins,.]

Week III: Monday of the Resurrection: Mark 15:47-16:11 [L] Women at sepulchre, angel.

Week IV: Tuesday of the Resurrection: Mark 16:12-20 [L] Mary Magdalene, Jesus with eleven.

Week V: Wednesday of the Resurrection: John 11:1-45 [L] "I am the Resurrection." The raising of Lazarus from the dead.

Week VI: Thursday of the Resurrection: John 20:1-9 [L] St. Mary Magdalene at the sepulchre.

Week VII: Friday of the Resurrection: John 20:11-18 [L] St. Mary Magdalene at the sepulchre.

Week VIII: Saturday of the Resurrection: John 21:1-14 [L] [may read to verse 25.] Fishes, eating with Jesus, feed my sheep.

Week IX: First Sunday after Pascha: John 20:19-31 [W] Eating with Jesus, doubts of St. Thomas and faith of those who believe including those who have not seen Jesus.

Week X: Mid-Pascha, Wednesday after the Third Sunday after Pascha: Luke 24:36-48, [T] [may read to verse 53.] Theme of Pascha: Jesus eats with disciples. Disciples in temple.

ALL STAND FOR THE HOLY RESURRECTION GOSPEL. *[State before Gospel.]*
[The Gospels below have not been re-arranged, but the two lists above have been marked.]

        At the sepulchre: angel, guards, adoration. Week V St. Matt. 28:1-10.
        Variant order from Paschaltide: Week I St. Matthew 28:1-20

1 And in the end of the Sabbath, when it began to dawn towards the first day of the week, came Mary Magdalen and the other Mary, to see the sepulchre.
2 And behold there was a great earthquake. For an angel of the Lord descended from heaven, and coming, rolled back the stone, and sat upon it.
3 And his countenance was as lightning, and his raiment as snow.
4 And for fear of him, the guards were struck with terror, and became as dead men.
5 And the angel answering, said to the women: Fear not you; for I know that you seek Jesus who was crucified.
6 He is not here, for he is risen, as he said. Come, and see the place where the Lord was laid.
7 And going quickly, tell ye his disciples that he is risen: and behold he will go before you into Galilee; there you shall see him. Lo, I have foretold it to you.
8 And they went out quickly from the sepulcher with fear and great joy, running to tell his disciples.
9 And behold Jesus met them, saying: All hail. But they came up and took hold of his feet, and adored him.
10 Then Jesus said to them: Fear not. Go, tell my brethren that they go into Galilee, there they shall see me.

        Disciples, mountain, baptize, Jesus with us. Week IX St. Matt. 28:11-20.
        Variant order from Paschaltide: Week I St. Matthew 28:1-20 continued

11 Who when they were departed, behold some of the guards came into the city, and told the chief priests all things that had been done.
12 And they being assembled together with the ancients, taking counsel, gave a great sum of money to the soldiers,
13 Saying: Say you, His disciples came by night, and stole him away when we were asleep.
14 And if the governor shall hear of this, we will persuade him, and secure you.
15 So they taking the money, did as they were taught: and this word was spread abroad among the Jews even unto this day.
16 And the eleven disciples went into Galilee, unto the mountain where Jesus had appointed them.
17 And seeing him they adored: but some doubted.
18 And Jesus coming, spoke to them, saying: All power is given to me in heaven and in earth.
19 Going therefore, teach ye all nations; baptizing them in the name of the Father, and of the Son, and of the Holy Spirit.
20 Teaching them to observe all things whatsoever I have commanded you: and behold I am with you all days, even to the consummation of the world.

        Women at sepulchre, angel. Week VI St. Mark 16:1-8.
        Variant order from Paschaltide: Week III St. Mark 15:47 – 16:11.

15:47 And Mary Magdalen, and Mary the mother of Joseph, beheld where he was laid.
1 And when the Sabbath was past, Mary Magdalen, and Mary the mother of James, and Salome, bought sweet spices, that coming, they might anoint Jesus.
2 And very early in the morning, the first day of the week, they come to the sepulcher, the sun being now risen.
3 And they said one to another: Who shall roll us back the stone from the door of the sepulcher?
4 And looking, they saw the stone rolled back. For it was very great.
5 And entering into the sepulcher, they saw a young man sitting on the right side, clothed with a white robe: and they were astonished.

6 Who saith to them: Be not affrighted; you seek Jesus of Nazareth, who was crucified: he is risen, he is not here, behold the place where they laid him.
7 But go, tell his disciples and Peter that he goeth before you into Galilee; there you shall see him, as he told you.
8 But they going out, fled from the sepulcher. For a trembling and fear had seized them: and they said nothing to any man; for they were afraid.

    St. Mary Magdalene, Jesus and eleven. Week III St. Mark 16:9-20.

9 But he rising early the first day of the week, appeared first to Mary Magdalen, out of whom he had cast seven devils.
10 She went and told them that had been with him, who were mourning and weeping.
11 And they hearing that he was alive, and had been seen by her, did not believe.

    Variant order from Paschaltide: Week IV St. Mark 16:12-20.

12 And after that he appeared in another shape to two of them walking, as they were going into the country.
13 And they going told it to the rest: neither did they believe them.
14 At length he appeared to the eleven as they were at table: and he upbraided them with their incredulity and hardness of heart, because they did not believe them who had seen him after he was risen again.
15 And he said to them: Go ye into the whole world, and preach the gospel to every creature.
16 He that believeth and is baptized, shall be saved: but he that believeth not shall be condemned.
17 And these signs shall follow them that believe: In my name they shall cast out devils: they shall speak with new tongues.
18 They shall take up serpents; and if they shall drink any deadly thing, it shall not hurt them: they shall lay their hands upon the sick, and they shall recover.
19 And the Lord Jesus, after he had spoken to them, was taken up into heaven, and sitteth on the right hand of God.
20 But they going forth preached everywhere: the Lord working withal, and confirming the word with signs that followed.

    Women at the sepulchre. Week II St. Luke 24:1-12.
    Variant order from Paschaltide: Week II Luke 24:1-12, may add 24:13-35.

1 And on the first day of the week, very early in the morning, they came to the sepulcher, bringing the spices which they had prepared.
2 And they found the stone rolled back from the sepulcher.
3 And going in, they found not the body of the Lord Jesus.
4 And it came to pass, as they were astonished in their mind at this, behold, two men stood by them, in shining apparel.
5 And as they were afraid, and bowed down their countenance towards the ground, they said unto them: Why seek you the living with the dead?
6 He is not here, but is risen. Remember how he spoke unto you, when he was yet in Galilee.
7 Saying: The Son of man must be delivered into the hands of sinful men, and be crucified, and the third day rise again.
8 And they remembered his words.
9 And going back from the sepulcher, they told all these things to the eleven, and to all the rest.
10 And it was Mary Magdalen, and Joanna, and Mary of James, and the other women that were with them, who told these things to the apostles.
11 And these words seemed to them as idle tales; and they did not believe them.
12 But Peter rising up, ran to the sepulcher, and stooping down, he saw the linen cloths laid by themselves; and went away wondering in himself at that which was come to pass.

Jesus and two on the road to Emmaus. Week IV St. Luke 24:13-35.
Variant order from Paschaltide: Week II Luke 24:1-12, may add 24:13-35.

13 And behold, two of them went, the same day, to a town which was sixty furlongs from Jerusalem, named Emmaus.
14 And they talked together of all these things which had happened.
15 And it came to pass, that while they talked and reasoned with themselves, Jesus himself also drawing near, went with them.
16 But their eyes were held, that they should not know him.
17 And he said to them: What are these discourses that you hold one with another as you walk, and are sad?
18 And the one of them, whose name was Cleophas, answering, said to him: Art thou only a stranger in Jerusalem, and hast not known the things that have been done there in these days?
19 To whom he said: What things? And they said: Concerning Jesus of Nazareth, who was a prophet, mighty in work and word before God and all the people;
20 And how our chief priests and princes delivered him to be condemned to death, and crucified him.
21 But we hoped, that it was he that should have redeemed Israel: and now besides all this, today is the third day since these things were done.
22 Yea and certain women also of our company affrighted us, who before it was light, were at the sepulcher,
23 And not finding his body, came, saying, that they had also seen a vision of angels, who say that he is alive.
24 And some of our people went to the sepulcher, and found it so as the women had said, but him they found not.
25 Then he said to them: O foolish, and slow of heart to believe in all things which the prophets have spoken.
26 Ought not Christ to have suffered these things, and so to enter into his glory?
27 And beginning at Moses and all the prophets, he expounded to them in all the scriptures, the things that were concerning him.
28 And they drew nigh to the town, whither they were going: and he made as though he would go farther.
29 But they constrained him; saying: Stay with us, because it is towards evening, and the day is now far spent. And we went in with them.
30 And it came to pass, whilst he was at table with them, he took bread, and blessed, and brake, and gave to them.
31 And their eyes were opened, and they knew him: and he vanished out of their sight.
32 And they said one to the other: Was not our heart burning within us, whilst he spoke in the way, and opened to us the scriptures?
33 And rising up, the same hour, they went back to Jerusalem: and they found the eleven gathered together, and those that were with them.
34 Saying: The Lord is risen indeed, and hath appeared to Simon.
35 And they told what things were done in the way; and how they knew him in the breaking of bread.

Eating with Jesus, disciples in temple. Week VII St. Luke 24:36-53.
Variant order from Paschaltide: Week X St. Luke 24:36-.48, may read to 53.

36 Now whilst they were speaking these things, Jesus stood in the midst of them, and saith to them: Peace be to you; it is I, fear not.
37 But they being troubled and frightened, supposed that they saw a spirit.
38 And he said to them: Why are you troubled, and why do thoughts arise in your hearts?
39 See my hands and feet, that it is I myself; handle, and see: for a spirit hath not flesh and bones, as you see me to have.
40 And when he had said this, he showed them his hands and feet.

41 But while they yet believed not, and wondered for joy, he said: Have you here any thing to eat?
42 And they offered him a piece of a broiled fish, and a honeycomb.
43 And when he had eaten before them, taking the remains, he gave to them.
44 And he said to them: These are the words which I spoke to you, while I was yet with you, that all things must needs be fulfilled, which are written in the law of Moses, and in the prophets, and in the psalms, concerning me.
45 Then he opened their understanding, that they might understand the scriptures.
46 And he said to them: Thus it is written, and thus it behooved Christ to suffer, and to rise again from the dead, the third day: [Ps. 18:6]
47 And that penance and remission of sins should be preached in his name, unto all nations, beginning at Jerusalem.
48 And you are witnesses of these things. [Acts 1:8]
49 And I send the promise of my Father upon you: but stay you in the city, till you be endued with power from on high.
50 And he led them out as far as Bethania: and lifting up his hands, he blessed them.
51 And it came to pass, whilst he blessed them, he departed from them, and was carried up to heaven. [Acts 1:9]
52 And they adoring went back into Jerusalem with great joy.
53 And they were always in the temple, praising and blessing God. Amen.

Variant order from Paschaltide: Week V John 11:1-45 [L] The raising of Lazarus.
1 Now there was a certain man sick, named Lazarus, of Bethania, of the town of Mary and of Martha her sister.
2 (And Mary was she that anointed the Lord with ointment, and wiped his feet with her hair: whose brother Lazarus was sick.)
3 His sisters therefore sent to him, saying: Lord behold, he whom thou lovest is sick.
4 And Jesus hearing it, said to them: This sickness is not unto death, but for the glory of God: that the Son of God may be glorified by it.
5 Now Jesus loved Martha, and her sister Mary, and Lazarus.
6 When he had heard therefore that he was sick, he still remained in the same place two days.
7 Then after that, he said to his disciples: Let us go into Judea again.
8 The disciples say to him: Rabbi, the Jews but now sought to stone thee: and goest thou thither again?
9 Jesus answered: Are there not twelve hours of the day? If a man walk in the day, he stumbleth not, because he seeth the light of the world. [Apostles Collect, Lorrha-Stowe Missal]
10 But if he walk in the night, he stumbleth, because the light is not in him.
11 These things he said; and after that he said to them: Lazarus our friend sleepeth; but I go that I may awake him out of sleep.
12 His disciples therefore said: Lord if he sleep, he shall do well.
13 But Jesus spoke of his death; and they thought that he spoke of the repose of sleep.
14 Then therefore Jesus said to them plainly: Lazarus is dead.
15 And I am glad, for your sakes, that I was not there, that you may believe: but let us go to him.
16 Thomas therefore, who is called Didymus, said to his fellow disciples: Let us also go, that we may die with him.
17 Jesus therefore came, and found that he had been four days already in the grave.
18 (Now Bethania was near Jerusalem, about fifteen furlongs off.)
19 And many of the Jews were come to Martha and Mary, to comfort them concerning their brother.
20 Martha therefore, as soon as she heard that Jesus was come, went to meet him: but Mary sat at home.
21 Martha therefore said to Jesus: Lord, if thou hadst been here, my brother had not died.

22 But now also I know that whatsoever thou wilt ask of God, God will give it thee.
23 Jesus saith to her: Thy brother shall rise again.
24 Martha saith to him: I know that he shall rise again, in the resurrection at the last day.
25 Jesus said to her: I am the resurrection and the life: he that believeth in me, although he be dead, shall live:
26 And every one that liveth, and believeth in me, shall not die for ever. Believeth thou this?
27 She saith to him: Yea, Lord, I have believed that thou art Christ the Son of the living God, who art come into this world.
28 And when she had said these things, she went, and called her sister Mary secretly, saying: The master is come, and calleth for thee.
29 She, as soon as she heard this, riseth quickly, and cometh to him.
30 For Jesus was not yet come into the town: but he was still in that place where Martha had met him.
31 The Jews therefore, who were with her in the house, and comforted her, when they saw Mary that she rose up speedily and went out, followed her, saying: She goeth to the grave to weep there.
32 When Mary therefore was come where Jesus was, seeing him, she fell down at his feet, and saith to him: Lord, if thou hadst been here, my brother had not died.
33 Jesus, therefore, when he saw her weeping, and the Jews that were come with her, weeping, groaned in the spirit, and troubled himself,
34 And said: Where have you laid him? They say to him: Lord, come and see.
35 And Jesus wept.
36 The Jews therefore said: Behold how he loved him.
37 But some of them said: Could not he that opened the eyes of the man born blind, have caused that this man should not die?
38 Jesus therefore again groaning in himself, cometh to the sepulchre. Now it was a cave; and a stone was laid over it.
39 Jesus saith: Take away the stone. Martha, the sister of him that was dead, saith to him: Lord, by this time he stinketh, for he is now of four days.
40 Jesus saith to her: Did not I say to thee, that if thou believe, thou shalt see the glory of God?
41 They took therefore the stone away. And Jesus lifting up his eyes said: Father, I give thee thanks that thou hast heard me.
42 And I knew that thou hearest me always; but because of the people who stand about have I said it, that they may believe that thou hast sent me.
43 When he had said these things, he cried with a loud voice: Lazarus, come forth.
44 And presently he that had been dead came forth, bound feet and hands with winding bands; and his face was bound about with a napkin. Jesus said to them: Loose him, and let him go.
45 Many therefore of the Jews, who were come to Mary and Martha, and had seen the things that Jesus did, believed in him.

St. Mary Magdalene at the sepulchre. Week I St. John 20:1-18.
Variant order from Paschaltide: Week VI St. John 20:1-9.

1 And on the first day of the week, Mary Magdalen cometh early, when it was yet dark, unto the sepulcher; and she saw the stone taken away from the sepulcher.
2 She ran, therefore, and cometh to Simon Peter, and to the other disciple whom Jesus loved, and saith to them: They have taken away the Lord out of the sepulcher, and we know not where they have laid him.
3 Peter therefore went out, and that other disciple, and they came to the sepulcher.
4 And they both ran together, and that other disciple did outrun Peter, and came first to the sepulcher.
5 And when he stooped down, he saw the linen cloths lying; but ye he went not in.

6 Then cometh Simon Peter, following him, and went into the sepulcher, and saw the linen cloths lying,
7 And the napkin that had been about his head, not lying with the linen cloths, but apart, wrapped up into one place.
8 Then that other disciple also went in, who came first to the sepulcher: and he saw, and believed.
9 For as yet they knew not the scripture, that he must rise again from the dead.
10 The disciples therefore departed again to their home.

Variant order from Paschaltide: Week VII St. John 20:11-18

11 But Mary stood at the sepulcher without, weeping, Now as she was weeping, she stooped down, and looked into the sepulcher,
12 And she saw two angels in white, sitting, one at the head, and one at the feet, where the body of Jesus had been laid.
13 They say to her: Woman, why weepest thou? She saith to them: Because they have taken away my Lord; and I know not where they have laid him.
14 When she had thus said, she turned herself back, and saw Jesus standing; and she knew not that it was Jesus.
15 Jesus saith to her: Woman, why weepest thou? Whom seekest thou? She, thinking that it was the gardener, saith to him: Sir, if thou hast taken him hence, tell me where thou hast laid him, and I will take him away.
16 Jesus saith to her: Mary. She turning, saith to him: Rabboni (which is to say; Master).
17 Jesus saith to her: Do not touch me, for I am not yet ascended to my Father. But go to my brethren, and say to them: I ascend to my Father and to your Father, to my God and your God.
18 Mary Magdalen cometh, and telleth the disciples: I have seen the Lord, and these things he said to me.

Eating with Jesus, doubts of St. Thomas. Week VIII St. John 20:19-31.
Variant order from Paschaltide: Week IX St. John 20:19-31.

19 Now when it was late that same day, the first of the week, and the doors were shut, where the disciples were gathered together, for fear of the Jews, Jesus came and stood in the midst, and said to them: Peace be to you.
20 And when he had said this, he showed them his hands and his side. The disciples therefore were glad, when they saw the Lord.
21 He said therefore to them again: Peace be to you. As the Father hath sent me, I also send you.
22 When he had said this, he breathed on them; and he said to them: Receive ye the Holy Spirit.
23 Whose sins you shall forgive, they are forgiven them; and whose sins you shall retain, they are retained.
24 Now Thomas, one of the twelve, who is called Didymus, was not with them when Jesus came.
25 The other disciples therefore said to him: We have seen the Lord. But he said to them: Except I shall see in his hands the print of the nails, and put my finger into the place of the nails, and put my hand into his side, I will not believe.
26 And after eight days again his disciples were within, and Thomas with them. Jesus cometh, the doors being shut, and stood in the midst, and said: Peace be to you.
27 Then he saith to Thomas: Put in thy finger hither, and see my hands; and bring hither thy hand, and put it into my side; and be not faithless, but believing.
28 Thomas answered, and said to him: My Lord, and my God.
29 Jesus saith to him: Because thou hast seen me, Thomas, thou hast believed: blessed are they that have not seen, and have believed.
30 Many other signs also did Jesus in the sight of his disciples, which are not written in this book.
31 But these are written, that you may believe that Jesus is the Christ, the Son of God: and that believing, you may have life in his name.

Fishes, eating with Jesus, feed my sheep. Week X St. John 21:1 to end.
Variant order from Paschaltide: Week VIII St. John 21:1-14 or end.

1 After this, Jesus showed himself again to the disciples at the sea of Tiberias. And he showed himself after this manner.
2 There were together Simon Peter, and Thomas, who is called Didymus, and Nathanael, who was on Cana of Galilee, and the sons of Zebedee, and two others of disciples.
3 Simon Peter saith to them: I go a fishing. They say to him: We also come with thee. And they went forth, and entered into the ship: and that night they caught nothing.
4 But when the morning was come, Jesus stood on the shore: yet the disciples knew not that it was Jesus.
5 Jesus therefore said to them: Children, have you any meat? They answered him: No.
6 He saith to them: Cast the net on the right side of the ship, and you shall find. They cast therefore; and now they were not able to draw it, for the multitude of fishes.
7 That disciple therefore whom Jesus loved, said to Peter: It is the Lord. Simon Peter, when he heard that it was the Lord, girt his coat about him, (for he was naked), and cast himself into the sea.
8 But the other disciples came in the ship, (for they were not far from the land, but as it were two hundred cubits), dragging the net with fishes.
9 As soon then as they came to land, they saw hot coals lying, and a fish laid thereon, and bread.
10 Jesus saith to them: Bring hither of the fishes which you have now caught.
11 Simon Peter went up, and drew the net to land, full of great fishes, one hundred and fifty-three. And although there were so many, the net was not broken.
12 Jesus saith to them: Come, and dine. And none of them who were at meat, durst ask him: Who art thou? Knowing that it was the Lord.
13 And Jesus cometh and taketh bread, and giveth them, and fish in like manner.
14 This is now the third time that Jesus was manifested to his disciples, after he was risen from the dead.
15 When therefore they had dined, Jesus saith to Simon Peter: Simon, son of John, lovest thou me more than these? He saith to him: Yea, Lord, thou knowest that I love thee. He saith to him: Feed my lambs.
16 He saith to him again: Simon, son of John, lovest thou me? He saith to him: Yea, Lord, thou knowest that I love thee. He saith to him: Feed my lambs.
17 He said to him the third time: Simon, son of John, lovest thou me? Peter was grieved, because he had said to him the third time: Lovest thou me? And he said to him: Lord, thou knowest all things: thou knowest that I love thee. He said to him: Feed my sheep.
18 Amen, amen I say to thee, when thou wast younger, thou didst gird thyself, and didst walk where thou wouldst. But when thou shalt be old, thou shalt stretch forth thy hands, and another shall gird thee, and lead thee whither thou wouldst not.
19 And this he said, signifying by what death he should glorify God. And when he had said this, he saith to him: Follow me.
20 Peter turning about, saw that disciple whom Jesus loved following, who also leaned on his breast at supper, and said: Lord, who is he that shall betray thee?
21 Him therefore when Peter had seen, he saith to Jesus: Lord, and what shall this man do?
22 Jesus saith to him: So I will have him to remain till I come, what is it to thee? Follow thou me.
23 This saying therefore went abroad among the brethren, that that disciple should not die. And Jesus did not say to him: He should not die; but, So I will have him to remain till I come, what is it to thee?
24 This is that disciple who giveth testimony of these things, and hath written these things; and we know that his testimony is true.
25 But there are also many other things which Jesus did; which, if they were written every one, the world itself, I think, would not be able to contain the books that should be written.

Byzantine Eleven Matins Resurrection Gospels. In the Celtic Rite, the ten-week cycle is emphasized; the eleven-week cycle of the Byzantine Rite would not fit the Celtic Rite Matins, nor are the Byzantine Matins Resurrection Gospels complete. The skipped Resurrection Gospels of the Byzantine Rite include: Mt. 28:1-16, Jn 11:1-45 (Lazarus). These Byzantine Matins Gospels do not match the Byzantine Lections at Paschaltide, but they do use the last chapters of the four Gospels. This is the Byzantine eleven-week cycle: I Mt 28:16-20 (section 116); II Mark 16:1-8 (section 70); III Mark 16:9-20 (section 71); IV Luke 24:1-12 (section 112); V Like 24:13-35 (section 113); VI Luke 24:36=53 (section 114); VII John 20:1-10 (section 63); VIII John 20:11-18 (section 64); IX John 20:19-31 (section 65); X John 21:1-14 (section 66); XI John 21:15-25 (section 67).

Some Canticles:

In the Rule of St. Mael Ruain, all nine Canticles (including the *Magnificat*) would be sung during one week, not in one day, as in the Byzantine practice. As the Canticles are mentioned in the Rule of St. Mael Rúain, they could be sung during the Beginning of Night and Midnight, which do not vary in number from week to week. Outside of the singing of the Psalms, the *Magnificat* is sung after the Hours, or after meals, in addition to the singing of Canticles at the Psalms.

Traditionally, there are nine Canticles which are said during the reciting of the one hundred fifty Psalms, which may be spread out over a week, according to both Byzantine Typicons and also the Rules of Saints Columbanus and Mael Ruain. When counting the Biblical and other Canticles, however, there are many more than nine. Various arrangements of Canticles have been given through the centuries. In the Antiphonary of Bangor, some are specified during Matins, and some after other prayers. Some Canticles, even though they may not be commonly used, are still useful as prayers or meditation, and could be inserted into the daily Psalm cycle. Or, it is possible that nine Canticles were chosen which were most appropriate to the season. It is necessary to use a complete Douay-Rheims Bible for the Canticles; modern translations often reduce chapter 3 of the Book of Daniel, and leave out some of the other sources listed here. [The abbreviation "AB" means Hymns from the *Antiphonary of Bangor*, which are numbered from the beginning of that book.]

Canticles in the order of the Antiphonary of Bangor, and then other Canticles:

The First Canticle of Moses [Deuteronomy 32:1-43] AB 1 Matins Canticle on Sundays of Advent and the Feasts of the Circumcision and Epiphany.

The Antiphonary of Bangor Hymns 2 and 3 are the "Congregation of the Brethren" and the "Hymn of the Apostles," which are ancient Hymns, and may be used at various times. AB 2 by St. Hilary of Poitiers is specified as one of the Communion Hymns, and in the Cross Vigil. AB 3 is the ancient "Kyrie" as implied in the last verse, and has forty verses other than the two verses that end in "Alleluia." (Both the Western and Byzantine Rites have a remnant of the Kyrie: in the West it originally was reduced to nine verses; in the Byzantine Rite the verses were dropped and the prayer "Kyrie eleison" was repeated forty times.)

The Blessing of Saint Zacharias [St. Luke 1:68-80] AB 4 Matins Canticle used on other Sundays that the First Canticle of Moses is not done (most Sundays.).

The Magnificat [St. Luke 1:46-55] is given as an ending prayer for the Hours or after Holy Communion.

The Second Canticle of Moses [Exodus 15:1-19] AB 5 Always said in Matins.

The Prayer of the Three Youths is the Lection at the Sunday after Pascha. [Daniel 3:1-45] (This Lection misses the prayer which is from verses 51 through 56. In the Byzantine

Lection for this Canticle the context is missed, including verse 24, "And they walked in the midst of the flame, praising God and blessing the Lord." The Song of the Three Youths [Daniel 3:57-88a] AB 6, is sung during Matins, and more verses are sung at the Paschal Vigil and the Sunday after Pascha as the Gradual, as specified in the Lectionary of Luxeuil.

The "Te Deum" AB 7 is sung on Sundays in Matins (before the Sunday Liturgy).

Hymn AB 8: "Sancti Venite" is sung "When the Clergy Communicates" according to the Antiphonary of Bangor, but it continues during Holy Communion for the congregation. This is the main Communion Hymn of the Celtic Rite. (See Communion Hymns written out after the Mass.)

Hymn AB 9: "Fiery Creator of the Light giving Light," is one of the Matins blessings of the candle of the Resurrection, and therefore is in the Vigil of the Resurrection, including the themes of light, fire, and the honeycomb. The full text is in the Vigil of the Resurrection in this book. (It is possible that this Hymn has other uses such as at Sunday Vespers, modern Saturday evening; this Hymn being a much more joyful and complete Hymn than the Byzantine Hymn "Phos hilarion," because "Fiery Creator of the Light giving Light" is about the Resurrection. The Byzantine "Phos hilarion" or "Gladsome Light" was a Hymn from c. AD 200 or earlier, but the Celtic "Fiery Creator of the Light giving Light" could be equally old, or the Byzantine Hymn could be derived from it, "Fiery Creator..." is more clear.)

The Hymn of the Bridegroom (at Midnight) AB 10. (A shortened version of this Hymn appears in the "Bridegroom Services" of Holy Week in the Byzantine Rite, but in the Celtic Rite, this ancient hymn is sung every Midnight, especially before a Liturgy.)

Hymn and Procession to the Cross: AB 11 "Most Holy Martyrs of the Most high God..." Saturdays and Saints' Days in Matins

Hymn and Procession to the Cross: AB 12 "Spirit of Divine glorious Light, Look upon me, O Lord..." Sundays in Matins

The Irish "Trisagion" or Thrice-Holy Hymn [AB 123, 128, 125, 90 and 93] is sung in Matins. The "Gloria" [AB 116] with Antiphons is sung at Vespers and Matins (the Irish version is slightly different than the Roman or Byzantine versions). Since these are at the end of the Antiphonary of Bangor , they may have been later or borrowed. The Gloria is also in the Lorrha-Stowe Missal.

In the Celtic Rite, the Prophecy of Jonah is one of the Lections of the Prophecy at the Vigil of the Resurrection, as it is in the Byzantine Rite on Holy Saturday.

In the Celtic Rite, the Prayer of Isaiah [Is. 26:2-20] is used as the Old Testament Lection in a Requiem of a Bishop.

Canticle of Saint Simeon [Luke 2:29-32] "Nunc dimitis" "Now thou dost dismiss thy servant, O Lord, according to Thy word in peace; because my eyes have seen Thy salvation, which Thou hast prepared before the face of all peoples: a light to the revelation of the Gentiles, and the glory of thy people Israel." [This is used when a child is first brought to church, but not specified as a Canticle in the Celtic Rite.]

Canticle of Tobias [Tobias 13:23] A Hebrew version has been found of Tobit, but this book is listed as Deuterocanonical. It is in this book that the Archangel Raphael helps Tobias, and also is found the list of virtues found in St. Matthew 25:31-46, but including burying the dead.

Nine Odes of the Byzantine Rite

This is a possible list of nine Canticles. (Usually only eight of these are done in the Byzantine Rite.) These also are not all the possible Scriptural Canticles.
1. [Exodus 15:1-19] Moses in the Exodus.
2. [Deuteronomy 32:1-43] of Moses (only done in Tuesdays of Lent.)
3. [I Kings 2:1-10] Prayer of Anna, mother of the Prophet Samuel.
   [I Samuel 2:1-10 in the KJV Bibles.] Unique to the Byzantine Rite.
4. [Abb. 3:2-19] Abbacum the Prophet [Habbakuk]
5. [Is. 26:9-20] Prayer of Isiah the Prophet.
6. [Jonah 2:3-10] Prayer of Jonas the Prophet.
7. [Dan. 3:26-56] Prayer of the Three Youths
8. [Dan. 3:57-88] Song of the Three Youths
9. [Luke 1:46-55, and Luke 1:68-79] Magnificat of the Birthgiver of God, and the Prayer of Zacharias the father of St. John the Baptist (together).

The Russian Psalter adds a "151st" Psalm by the Prophet David, at the time David fought Goliath:

"I was the smallest among my brethren, and the youngest in the house of my father; I did shepherd the sheep of my father. My hands made an instrument, and my fingers fashioned a psaltery. And who shall tell my Lord? The Lord Himself, He Himself shall hearken. He sent forth His angel and took me from the flocks of my father, and anointed me with the oil of His anointing. My brethren were big and good, yet the Lord took not pleasure in them. I went forth to meet the alien, and he cursed me by his idols. But I drew his own sword and beheaded him, and took away the reproach from the sons of Israel."

Psalm Names

St. Mael Ruain states Psalms' Latin names in his list of Psalms to be said at the Beginning of Night and Midnight. The Psalms which follow this list have been grouped according to their use in the Hours of Beginning of Night and Midnight. Names of the 150 Psalms in Latin and English (in Septuagint Greek and Latin numbering):

1 (Hebrew 1) Beatus vir   Blessed is the man
2 (Heb. 2) Quare fremuerunt. Why have the Gentiles raged.
3 (Heb. 3) Domine quid multiplicati. Why, O Lord, are they multiplied
4 (Heb. 4) Cum invocarem. When I called upon Him
5 (Heb. 5) Verba mea auribus. Give ear, O Lord, to my words
6 (Heb. 6) Domine ne in furore. O Lord, rebuke me not in Thy indignation
7 (Heb. 7) Domine Deus meus. O Lord my God
8 (Heb. 8) Domine Dominus noster. O Lord our Lord
9 (Heb. 9&10) Confitebor tibi Domine. I will give praise to Thee O Lord
10 (Heb. 11) In Domino confido. In the Lord I put my trust
11 (Heb. 12) Salvum me fac. Save me, O Lord, for there is now no saint
12 (Heb. 13) Usquequo Domine. How long, O Lord, wilt thou forget
13 (Heb. 14) Dixit insipiens. The fool hath said in his heart
14 (Heb 15) Domine quis habitabit. Lord, who shall dwell in thy tabernacle
15 (Heb. 16) Conserva me Domine. Preserve me, O Lord
16 (Heb. 17) Exaudi Domine justitiam. Hear, O Lord, my justice

17 (Heb. 18) Diligam te Domine. I will love Thee, O Lord, my strength
18 (Heb. 19) Coeli enarrant. The heavens shew forth the glory of God
19 (Heb. 20) Exaudiat te Dominus. May the Lord hear thee
20 (Heb. 21) Domine in virtute. In Thy strength, O Lord
21 (Heb. 22) Deus Deus meus. O God, my God, look upon me
22 (Heb. 23) Dominus regit me. The Lord ruleth me
23 (Heb. 24) Domini est terra. The earth is the Lord's
24 (Heb. 25) Ad te Domini levavi. To Thee, O Lord, have I lifted up
25 (Heb. 26) Judica me Domine. Judge me, O Lord
26 (Heb. 27) Dominus illuminatio. The Lord is my light and my salvation
27 (Heb. 28) Ad te Domine clamabo. Unto Thee will I cry, O Lord
28 (Heb. 29) Afferte Domino. Bring to the Lord, O ye children of God
29 (Heb. 30) Exaltabo te Domine. I will extol Thee, O Lord
30 (Heb. 31) In te Domine speravi. In Thee, O Lord, have I hoped
31 (Heb. 32) Beati quorum. Blessed are they whose iniquities are forgiven
32 (Heb. 33) Exultate justi. Rejoice in the Lord, O ye just
33 (Heb. 34) Benedicam Dominum. I will bless the Lord at all times
34 (Heb. 35) Judica Domine nocentes me. Judge Thou, O Lord
35 (Heb. 36) Dixit injustus. The unjust hath said within himself
36 (Heb. 37) Noli aemulari. Be not emulous of evildoers
37 (H 38) Domine ne in furore. Rebuke me not, O Lord, in Thy indignation
38 (Heb. 39) Dixi custodiam. I said: I will take heed to my ways
39 (Heb. 40) Expectans expectavi. With expectation I have waited
40 (Heb. 41) Beatus qui intelligit. Blessed is he that understandeth
41 (H42) Quemadmodum desiderat. As the hart panteth after the fountains
42 (Heb. 43) Judica me Deus. Judge me, O God, and distinguish my cause
43 (Heb. 44) Deus auribus nostris. We have heard, O God, with our ears
44 (Heb. 45) Eructavit cor meum. My heart hath uttered a good word
45 (Heb. 46) Deus noster refugium. Our God is our refuge and strength
46 (Heb. 47) Omnes gentes plaudite. O clap your hands, all ye nations
47 (Heb. 48) Magnus Dominus. Great is the Lord
48 (Heb. 49) Audite haec omnes gentes. Hear these things, all ye nations
49 (Heb. 50) Deus deorum. The God of gods, the Lord hath spoken
50 (Heb. 51) Miserere. Have mercy on me, O God
51 (Heb. 52) Quid gloriaris. Why dost thou glory in malice
52 (Heb. 53) Dixit insipiens. The fool hath said in his heart
53 (Heb. 54) Deus in nomine tuo. Save me, O God, by Thy Name
54 (Heb. 55) Exaudi Deus. Hear, O God, my prayer
55 (Heb. 56) Miserere mei Deus. Have mercy on me, O God, for man
56 (Heb. 57) Miserere mei Deus. Have mercy on me, O God, have mercy
57 (Heb. 58) Si vere utique. If in very deed you speak justice
58 (Heb. 59) Eripe me. Deliver me from my enemies, O my God
59 (Heb. 60) Deus repulisti nos. O God, Thou hast cast us off
60 (Heb. 61) Exaudi Deus. Hear, O God, my supplication
61 (Heb. 62) Nonne Deo. Shall not my soul be subject to God?
62 (Heb. 63) Deus Deus meus ad te. O God, my God, to Thee do I watch

63 (Heb. 64) Exaudi Deus orationem. Hear, O God, my prayer
64 (Heb. 65) Te decet. A hymn, O God, becometh Thee in Sion
65 (Heb. 66) Jubilate Deo. Shout with joy to God (Pascha, Columbanus)
66 (Heb. 67) Deus misereatur. May God have mercy on us and bless us
67 (Heb. 68) Exurgat Deus. Let God arise
68 (Heb. 69) Salvum me fac Deus. Save, me, O God, for the waters
69 (Heb. 70) Deus in adjutorium. O God, come to my assistance
70 (Heb. 71) In te Domine. In Thee, O Lord, have I hoped
71 (Heb. 72) Deus judicium tuum. Give to the king Thy judgment, O God
72 (Heb. 73) Quam bonus Israel Deus. How good is God to Israel
73 (Heb. 74) Ut quid Deus. O God, why hast Thou cast us off unto the end
74 (Heb. 75) Confitebimur tibi. We will praise Thee, O God
75 (Heb. 76) Notus in Judea. In Judea God is known
76 (Heb. 77) Voce mea. I cried to the Lord with my voice
77 (Heb. 78) Attendite. Attend, O my people, to my law
78 (Heb. 79) Deus venerunt gentes. O God, the heathens are come
79 (Heb. 80) Qui regis Israel. Give ear, O Thou that rulest Israel
80 (Heb. 81) Exultate Deo. Rejoice to God our helper
81 (Heb. 82) Deus stetit. God hath stood in the congregation of gods
82 (Heb. 83) Deus quis similis. O God, who shall be like to Thee
83 (Heb. 84) Quam dilecta. How lovely are Thy tabernacles, O Lord
84 (Heb. 85) Benedixisti Domine. Lord, thou hast blessed Thy land
85 (Heb. 86) Inclina Domine. Incline Thy ear, O Lord, and hear me
86 (Heb. 87) Fundamenta ejus. The foundations thereof
87 (Heb. 88) Domine Deus salutis. O Lord, the God of my salvation
88 (Heb. 89) Misericordias Domini. The mercies of the Lord I will sing
89 (Heb. 90) Domine refugium. Lord, Thou hast been our refuge
90 (Heb. 91) Qui habitat. He that dwelleth in the aid of the most High
91 (Heb. 92) Bonum est confiteri. It is good to give praise to the Lord
92 (Heb. 93) Dominus regnavit. The Lord hath reigned
93 (Heb. 94) Deus ultionum. The Lord is the God to whom revenge
94 (Heb. 95) Venite exultemus. Come let us praise the Lord with joy
95 (Heb. 96) Cantate Domino. Sing ye to the Lord a new canticle
96 (H 97) Dominus regnavit. The Lord hath reigned, let the earth rejoice
97 (Heb. 98) Cantate Domino. Sing ye to the Lord a new canticle
98 (Heb. 99) Dominus regnavit. The Lord hath reigned, let the people
99 (Heb. 100) Jubilate Deo. Sing joyfully to God, all the earth
100 (Heb. 101) Misericordiam et judicium. Mercy and judgment
101 (Heb. 102) Domine exaudi. Hear, O Lord, my prayer
102 (Heb. 103) Benedic anima. Bless the Lord, O my soul; and let
103 (H 104) Benedic anima. Bless the Lord, O my soul, O Lord my God
104 (Heb. 105) Confitemini Domino. Give glory to the Lord, and call
105 (Heb. 106) Confitemini Domino. Give glory to the Lord, for He
106 (Heb. 107) Confitemini Domino... Give glory to the Lord...
107 (Heb. 108) Paratum cor meum. My heart is ready, O God
108 (H 109) Deus laudem meam. O God, be not Thou silent in my praise

109 (Heb. 110) Dixit Dominus. The Lord said to my Lord: Sit Thou
110 (Heb. 111) Confitebor tibi Domine. I will praise Thee, O Lord,
111 (Heb. 112) Beatus vir. Blessed is the man that feareth the Lord
112 (Heb. 113) Laudate pueri. Praise the Lord, ye children
113 (Heb. 114 & 115) In exitu Israel. When Israel went out of Egypt
114 (Heb. 116:1-9) Dilexi. I have loved, because the Lord will hear
115 (Heb. 116:10-19) Credidi. I have believed, therefore have I spoken
116 (Heb.117) Laudate Dominum. O praise the Lord, all ye nations
117 (Heb. 118) Confitemini Domino. Give praise to the Lord, for he is good
118 (Heb. 119) Beati immaculati. Blessed are the undefiled in the way
119 (Heb. 120) Ad Dominum. In my trouble I cried to the Lord
120 (Heb. 121) Levavi oculos. I have lifted up my eyes to the mountains
121 (Heb. 122) Laetatus sum in his. I rejoiced at the things that were said
122 (Heb. 123) Ad te levavi. To Thee have I lifted up my eyes
123 (Heb. 124) Nisi quia Dominus. If it had not been that the Lord was
124 (Heb. 125) Qui confidunt. They that trust in the Lord shall be
125 (Heb. 126) In convertendo. When the Lord brought back the captivity
126 (Heb. 127) Nisi Dominus. Unless the Lord build the house
127 (Heb. 128) Beati omnes. Blessed are all they that fear the Lord
128 (Heb. 129) Saepe expugnaverunt. Often have they fought against me
129 (Heb. 130) De profundis. Out of the depths I have cried to Thee
130 (Heb. 131) Domine non est. Lord, my heart is not exalted
131 (Heb. 132) Memento Domine. O Lord, remember David
132 (Heb. 133) Ecce quam bonum. Behold how good and how pleasant
133 (Heb. 134) Ecce nunc benedicite. Behold, now bless ye the Lord
134 (Heb. 135) Laudate nomen. Praise ye the Name of the Lord
135 (Heb. 136) Confitemini Domino. Praise the Lord, for He is good
136 (Heb. 137) Super flumina. Upon the rivers of Babylon, there we sat
137 (Heb. 138) Confitebor tibi. I will praise Thee, O Lord
138 (H 139) Domine probasti. Lord, Thou hast proved me, and known me
139 (Heb. 140) Eripe me Domine. Deliver me, O Lord, from the evil man
140 (Heb. 141) Domine clamavi. I have cried to Thee, O Lord, hear me
141 (Heb. 142) Voce mea. I cried to the Lord with my voice
142 (Heb. 143) Domine exaudi. Hear, O Lord, my prayer
143 (Heb. 144) Benedictus Dominus. Blessed be the Lord my God
144 (Heb. 145) Exaltabo te Deus. I will extol Thee, O God my king
145 (Heb.146) Lauda animas. Praise the Lord, O my soul
146 (Heb. 147:1-11) Laudate Dominum. Praise ye the Lord
147 (Heb. 147:12-20) Lauda Jerusalem. Praise the Lord, O Jerusalem
148 (Heb. 148) Laudate Dominum de caelis. Praise ye the Lord from the heavens
149 (Heb. 149) Cantate Domino. Sing ye to the Lord a new canticle
150 (Heb. 150) Laudate Dominum in sanctis. Praise ye the Lord in his holy places

The Psalms, Greek Numbering

Psalm Table of St. Mael Ruain: *Beatus vir* to *Domine quis habitabit*. 1-13
Sunday Beginning of Night (modern Saturday night).

---

1 (Hebrew 1) Beatus vir   Blessed is the man   (First Sunday in Advent)

　　　Blessed is the man who hath not walked in the counsel of the ungodly, nor stood in the way of sinners, nor sat in the chair of pestilence: But his will is in the law of the Lord, and on His law he shall meditate day and night. And he shall be like a tree which is planted near the running waters, which shall bring forth its fruit, in due season. And his leaf shall not fall off: and all whatsoever he shall do shall prosper. Not so the wicked, not so: but like the dust, which the wind driveth from the face of the earth. Therefore the wicked shall not rise again in judgment; nor sinners in the council of the just. For the Lord knoweth the way of the just: and the way of the wicked shall perish.

2 (Heb. 2) Quare fremuerunt   Why have the Gentiles raged   (Second Sunday in Advent)

　　　Why have the Gentiles raged and the people devised vain things? The kings of the earth stood up, and the princes met together, against the Lord and against His Christ. Let us break their bonds asunder: and let us cast away their yoke from us. He that dwelleth in heaven shall laugh at them: and the Lord shall deride them. Then shall He speak to them in His anger, and trouble them in His rage.

　　　But I am appointed king by Him over Sion His holy mountain, preaching His commandment. The Lord hath said to me: Thou art my Son; this day have I begotten Thee. Ask of me, and I will give Thee the Gentiles for Thy inheritance, and the utmost parts of the earth for Thy possession. Thou shalt rule them with a rod of iron and shalt break them in pieces like a potter's vessel.

　　　And now, O ye kings, understand: receive instruction, you that judge the earth. Serve ye the Lord with fear: and rejoice unto Him with trembling. Embrace discipline: lest at any time the Lord be angry, and you perish from the just way. When His wrath shall be kindled in a short time, blessed are all they that trust in Him.

3 (Heb. 3) Domine quid multiplicati   Why, O Lord, are they multiplied   (Third Sunday in Advent)

　　　　The psalm of David when he fled from the face of his son Absalom.

　　　Why, O Lord, are they multiplied that afflict me? Many are they who rise up against me. Many say to my soul: There is no salvation for him in his God. But Thou, O Lord, art my protector, my glory, and the lifter-up of my head. I have cried to the Lord with my voice: and He hath heard me from His holy hill. I have slept and have taken my rest: and I have risen up, because the Lord hath protected me. I will not fear thousands of the people surrounding me: arise, O Lord; save me, O my God. For Thou hast struck all them who are my adversaries without cause: Thou hast broken the teeth of sinners. Salvation is of the Lord: and Thy blessing is upon Thy people.

4 (Heb. 4) Cum invocarem When I called upon Him (Fourth Sunday in Advent)
Unto the end, in verses, a psalm for David.

When I called upon Him, the God of my justice heard me: when I was in distress, Thou hast enlarged me. Have mercy on me: and hear my prayer.

O ye sons of men, how long will you be dull of heart? Why do you love vanity, and seek after lying? Know ye also that the Lord hath made His Holy One wonderful: the Lord will hear me when I shall cry unto Him. Be ye angry, and sin not: the things you say in your hearts, be sorry for them upon your beds. Offer up the sacrifice of justice, and trust in the Lord: many say, Who sheweth us good things?

The light of Thy countenance, O Lord, is signed upon us: Thou hast given gladness in my heart. By the fruit of their corn, their wine, and oil, they are multiplied.

In peace in the selfsame I will sleep, and I will rest: For Thou, O Lord, singularly hast settled me in hope.

5 (Heb. 5) Verba mea auribus Give ear, O Lord, to my words (Fifth Sunday in Advent) Unto the end, for her that obtaineth the inheritance, a psalm for David.

Give ear, O Lord, to my words: understand my cry. Hearken to the voice of my prayer, O my King and my God. For to Thee will I pray: O Lord, in the morning Thou shalt hear my voice. In the morning I will stand before Thee, and will see: because Thou art not a God that willest iniquity.

Neither shall the wicked dwell near Thee: nor shall the unjust abide before Thy eyes. Thou hatest all the workers of iniquity: Thou wilt destroy all that speak a lie. The bloody and the deceitful man the Lord will abhor:

But as for me in the multitude of Thy mercy, I will come into Thy house: I will worship towards Thy holy temple, in Thy fear. Conduct me, O Lord, in Thy justice: because of my enemies, direct my way in Thy sight.

For there is no truth in their mouth: their heart is vain. Their throat is an open sepulchre: They dealt deceitfully with their tongues: judge them, O God. Let them fall from their devices: according to the multitude of their wickednesses cast them out: for they have provoked Thee, O Lord.

But let all them be glad that hope in Thee; they shall rejoice for ever: and Thou shalt dwell in them. And all they that love Thy Name shall glory in Thee. For Thou wilt bless the just. O Lord, Thou hast crowned us, as with a shield of Thy good will.

6 (Heb. 6) Domine ne in furore O Lord, rebuke me not in Thy indignation
(Christmas Eve) Unto the end, in verses, a psalm for David, for the octave.

O Lord, rebuke me not in Thy indignation, nor chastise me in Thy wrath. Have mercy on me, O Lord, for I am weak: heal me, O Lord, for my bones are troubled. And my soul is troubled exceedingly: but Thou, O Lord, how long? Turn to me, O Lord, and deliver my soul: O save me for Thy mercy's sake. For there is no one in death, that is mindful of Thee: and who shall confess to Thee in hell?

I have labored in my groanings, every night I will wash my bed: I will water my couch with my tears. My eye is troubled through indignation: I have grown old amongst all my enemies. Depart from me, all ye workers of iniquity: for the Lord hath heard the voice of my weeping. The Lord hath heard my supplication: the Lord hath received my prayer. Let all my enemies be ashamed and be very much troubled: let them be turned back and be ashamed very speedily.

7 (Heb. 7) Domine Deus meus O Lord my God   (St. Stephen, Dec. 26)
The psalm of David which he sung to the Lord, for the words of Chusi the son of Jemini.

O Lord my God, in Thee have I put my trust: save me from all them that persecute me, and deliver me. Lest at any time he seize upon my soul like a lion, while there is no one to redeem me, nor to save. O Lord my God, if I have done this thing, if there be iniquity in my hands: If I have rendered to them that repaid me evils, let me deservedly fall empty before my enemies. Let the enemy pursue my soul, and take it, and tread down my life on the earth, and bring down my glory to the dust. Rise up, O Lord, in Thy anger: and be Thou exalted in the borders of my enemies. And arise, O Lord my God, in the precept which Thou hast comanded: and a congregation of people shall surround Thee. And for their sakes, return Thou on high.   The Lord judgeth the people. Judge me, O Lord, according to my justice, and according to my innocence in me. The wickedness of sinners shall be brought to nought, and Thou shalt direct the just: the searcher of hearts and reins is God. Just is my help from the Lord: Who saveth the upright of heart. God is a just judge, strong and patient: is He angry every day? Except you will be converted, He will brandish His sword: He hath bent His bow, and made it ready. And in it He hath prepared the instruments of death: He hath made ready His arrows for them that burn.

Behold, he hath been in labor with injustice: he hath conceived sorrow, and brought forth iniquity. He hath opened a pit and dug it: and he is fallen into the hole he made. His sorrow shall be turned on his own head: and his iniquity shall come down upon his crown.

I will give glory to the Lord according to His justice: and will sing to the Name of the Lord the most high.

8 (Heb. 8) Domine Dominus noster O Lord our Lord (Holy Innocents, reverse order with Psalm 9, Dec 28) Unto the end, for the presses, a psalm for David.

O Lord our Lord, how admirable is Thy Name in the whole earth! For Thy magnificence is elevated above the heavens. Out of the mouth of infants and of sucklings Thou hast perfected praise, because of Thy enemies: that Thou mayest destroy the enemy and the avenger. For I will behold Thy heavens, the works of Thy fingers: the moon and the stars which Thou hast founded.

What is man that Thou art mindful of him? Or the son of man that Thou visitest him? Thou hast made him a little less than the angels: Thou hast crowned him with glory and honor: and hast set him over the works of Thy hands. Thou hast subjected all things under his feet; all sheep and oxen: moreover the beasts also of the fields. The birds of the air, and the fishes of the sea that pass through the paths of the sea. O Lord our Lord, how admirable is Thy Name in all the earth!

9 (Heb. 9&10) Confitebor tibi Domine I will give praise to Thee O Lord (A. St. John, and B. St. James of Jerusalem, according to the Celtic Rite, Dec. 27, reversed in date with Psalm 8. The conclusion of this Psalm is similar to Psalm 118, indicating a longer Psalm, and although there are two aspects of this Psalm, like 118 having twenty two aspects to it, this Psalm has the unity of one Psalm.)

> Note from the Douay-Rheims Version of 1955, after verse 21, the "late Hebrew doctors" meaning around 90 A.D.: "Here the late Hebrew doctors divide this psalm into two, making ver. 22 the beginning of Psalm 10. And again they join Psalms 146 and 147 into one, in order that the whole number of psalms should not exceed 150. And in this manner the psalms are numbered in the Protestant Bible." Title of this psalm: Unto the end, for the hidden things of the Son, a psalm for David.

9A I will give praise to Thee, O Lord, with my whole heart: I will relate all Thy wonders. I will be glad and rejoice in Thee: I will sing to Thy Name, O Thou most high. When my enemy shall be turned back: they shall be weakened and perish before Thy Face. For Thou hast maintained my judgment and my cause: Thou hast sat on the throne, Who judgest justice. Thou hast rebuked the Gentiles, and the wicked one hath perished: Thou hast blotted out their name for ever and ever. The swords of the enemy have failed unto the end: and their cities Thou hast destroyed. Their memory hath perished with a noise: but the Lord remaineth for ever.

He hath prepared His throne in judgment: and He shall judge the world in equity, He shall judge the people in justice. And the Lord is become a refuge for the poor: a helper in due time in tribulation. And let them trust in Thee who know Thy Name: for Thou hast not forsaken them that seek Thee, O Lord. Sing ye to the Lord, who dwelleth in Sion: declare His ways among the Gentiles: For requiring their blood He hath remembered them: He hath not forgotten the cry of the poor.

Have mercy on me, O Lord: see my humiliation which I suffer from my enemies. Thou that liftest me up from the gates of death, that I may declare all Thy praises in the gates of the daughter of Sion. I will rejoice in

Thy salvation: the Gentiles have stuck fast in the destruction which they prepared. Their foot hath been taken in the very snare which they hid. The Lord shall be known when He executeth judgments: the sinner hath been caught in the works of his own hands. The wicked shall be turned into hell, all the nations that forget God. For the poor man shall not be forgotten to the end: the patience of the poor shall not perish for ever. Arise, O Lord, let not man be strengthened: let the Gentiles be judged in Thy sight. Appoint, O Lord, a lawgiver over them: that the Gentiles may know themselves to be but men.

9B Why, O Lord, hast Thou retired afar off? Why dost Thou slight us in our wants, in the time of trouble? Whilst the wicked man is proud, the poor is set on fire: they are caught in the counsels which they devise. For the sinner is praised in the desires of his soul: and the unjust man is blessed. The sinner hath provoked the Lord: according to the multitude of his wrath he will not seek him: God is not before his eyes: his ways are filthy at all times. Thy judgments are removed from his sight: he shall rule over all his enemies. For he hath said in his heart: I shall not be moved from generation to generation, and shall be without evil. His mouth is full of cursing, and of bitterness, and of deceit: under his tongue are labor and sorrow. He sitteth in ambush with the rich in private places, that he may kill the innocent. His eyes are upon the poor man: he lieth in wait in secret like a lion in his den. He lieth in ambush that he may catch the poor man: to catch the poor, whilst he draweth him to him. In his net he will bring him down: he will crouch and fall, when he shall have power over the poor. For he hath said in his heart: God hath forgotten: he hath turned away His face not to see to the end.

Arise, O Lord God, let Thy hand be exalted: forget not the poor. Wherefore hath the wicked provoked God? For he hath said in his heart: He will not require it: Thou seest it, for Thou considerest labor and sorrow: that Thou mayest deliver them into Thy hands. To Thee is the poor man left: Thou wilt be a helper to the orphan. Break Thou the arm of the sinner and of the malignant: his sin shall be sought, and shall not be found. The Lord shall reign to eternity, yea, for ever and ever: ye Gentiles shall perish from His land. The Lord hath heard the desire of the poor: Thy ear hath heard the preparation of their heart. To judge for the fatherless and for the humble, that man may no more presume to magnify himself upon earth.

10 (Heb. 11) In Domino confido In the Lord I put my trust (St. Victor, Dec 29, St. Patrick's Angel, appearing as a bird; perhaps a protest of the wren hunt.)
Unto the end, a psalm for David.

In the Lord I put my trust: How then do you say to my soul, Get thee away from hence to the mountain like a sparrow? For, lo, the wicked have bent their bow; they have prepared their arrows in the quiver, to shoot in the dark the upright of heart. For they have destroyed the things which Thou hast made: but what has the just man done? The Lord is in His holy temple; the Lord's throne is in heaven: His eyes look on the poor man: His eyelids examine the sons of men. The Lord trieth the just and the wicked: but He that loveth iniquity hateth his own soul.

He shall rain snares upon sinners: fire and brimstone and storms of winds shall be the portion of their cup. For the Lord is just and hath loved justice: His countenance hath beheld righteousness.

11 (Heb. 12) Salvum me fac Save me, O Lord, for there is now no saint (St. Ailbe and the Poor, Dec. 30) Unto the end, for the octave, a psalm for David.

Save me, O Lord, for there is now no saint: truths are decayed from among the children of men. They have spoken vain things every one to his neighbor: with deceitful lips and with a double heart have they spoken. May the Lord destroy all deceitful lips, and the tongue that speaketh proud things. Who have said: We will magnify our tongue; our lips are our own. Who is Lord over us?

By reason of the misery of the needy and the groans of the poor, now will I arise, saith the Lord. I will set him in safety: I will deal confidently in his regard. The words of the Lord are pure words: as silver tried by the fire, purged from the earth, refined seven times. Thou, O Lord, wilt preserve us: and keep us from this generation for ever. The wicked walk round about: according to Thy highness, Thou hast multiplied the children of men.

12 (Heb. 13) Usquequo Domine How long, O Lord, wilt thou forget (St. Silvester, and end of year, Dec. 31) Unto the end, a psalm for David.

How long, O Lord, wilt Thou forget me unto the end? How long dost Thou turn away Thy face from me? How long shall I take counsels in my soul, sorrow in my heart all the day? How long shall my enemy be exalted over me? Consider, and hear me, O Lord my God. Enlighten my eyes that I never sleep in death: lest at any time my enemy say: I have prevailed against him.

They that trouble me will rejoice when I am moved: but I have trusted in Thy mercy. My heart shall rejoice in Thy salvation: I will sing to the Lord, Who giveth me good things: yea, I will sing to the Name of the Lord the most high.

13 (Heb. 14) Dixit insipiens The fool hath said in his heart (Feast of Circumcision and of Fools and Beasts, the Octave of Christmas, Jan 1.)
Unto the end, a psalm for David.

The fool hath said in his heart: There is no God. They are corrupt, and are become abominable in their ways: there is none that doth good, no, not one. The Lord hath looked down from heaven upon the children of men, to see if there be any that understand and seek God. They are all gone aside, they are become unprofitable together: there is none that doth good, no not one. Their throat is an open sepulchre: with their tongues they acted deceitfully: the poison of asps is under their lips. Their mouth is full of cursing and bitterness: their feet are swift to shed blood. Destruction and unhappiness in their ways: and the way of peace they have not known: there is no fear of God before their eyes. Shall not all they know that work iniquity, who devour my people as they eat bread? They have not called upon the Lord; there have they trembled for fear where there was no fear.

For the Lord is in the just generation; you have confounded the counsel of the poor man: but the Lord is his hope. Who shall give out of Sion the salvation of Israel? When the Lord shall have turned away the captivity of his people, Jacob shall rejoice and Israel shall be glad.

Psalm Table of St. Mael Ruain *Domine quis habitabit* to *Dominus illuminatio;* 14-25 [12 Psalms], Sunday Midnight (modern Saturday night).

---

14 (Heb 15) Domine quis habitabit Lord, who shall dwell in thy tabernacle (Sunday on or after Circumcision before Epiphany.) A psalm of David.

Lord, who shall dwell in Thy tabernacle? or who shall rest in Thy holy hill? He that walketh without blemish, and worketh justice: He that speaketh truth in his heart: who hath not used deceit in His tongue: Nor hath done evil to His neighbor: nor taken up a reproach against His neighbors. In His sight the malignant is brought to nothing: but He glorifieth them that fear the Lord.

He that sweareth to His neighbor, and deceiveth not; He that hath not put out his money to usury, nor taken bribes against the innocent: He that doeth these things shall not be moved for ever.

15 (Heb. 16) Conserva me Domine Preserve me, O Lord (Epiphany and the Baptism of Christ, Jan 6.) The inscription of a title to David himself.

Preserve me, O Lord, for I have put my trust in Thee. I have said to the Lord: Thou art my God, for Thou hast no need of my goods. To the saints, who are in His land, He hath made wonderful all my desires in them. Their infirmities were multiplied: afterwards they made haste. I will not gather together their meetings for blood-offerings: nor will I be mindful of their names by my lips.

The Lord is the portion of my inheritance and of my cup: it is Thou that wilt restore my inheritance to me. The lines are fallen unto me in goodly places: for my inheritance is goodly to me. I will bless the Lord Who hath given me understanding: moreover, my reins also have corrected me even till night. I set the Lord always in my sight: for He is at my right hand, that I be not moved. Therefore my heart hath been glad, and my tongue hath rejoiced: moreover, my flesh also shall rest in hope. Because Thou wilt not leave my soul in hell: nor wilt Thou give Thy holy one to see corruption.

Thou hast made known to me the ways of life: Thou shalt fill me with joy with Thy countenance: at Thy right hand are delights even to the end.

16 (Heb. 17) Exaudi Domine justitiam Hear, O Lord, my justice (First Sunday after Epiphany, within the week: January 6, 7, 8, 9, 10, 11, or 12.)
>The prayer of David.

Hear, O Lord, my justice: attend to my supplication. Give ear unto my prayer, which proceedeth not from deceitful lips.

Let my judgment come forth from Thy countenance: let Thy eyes behold the things that are equitable. Thou hast proved my heart, and visited it by night, Thou hast tried me by fire: and iniquity hath not been found in me. That my mouth may not speak the works of men: for the sake of the words of Thy lips, I have kept hard ways. Perfect Thou my goings in Thy paths: that my footsteps be not moved. I have cried to Thee, for Thou, O God, hast heard me: O incline Thy ear unto me, and hear my words. Shew forth Thy wonderful mercies; Thou Who savest them that trust in Thee. From them that resist Thy right hand keep me, as the apple of Thy eye. Protect me under the shadow of Thy wings. from the face of the wicked who have afflicted me. My enemies have surrounded my soul: they have shut up their fat: their mouth hath spoken proudly. They have cast me forth and now they have surrounded me: they have set their eyes bowing down to the earth. They have taken me, as a lion prepared for the prey; and as a young lion dwelling in secret places. Arise, O Lord, disappoint him and supplant him; deliver my soul from the wicked one: Thy sword from the enemies of Thy hand. O Lord, divide them from the few of the earth in their life: their belly is filled from Thy hidden stores. They are full of children: and they have left to their little ones the rest of their substance.

But as for me, I will appear before Thy sight in justice: I shall be satisfied when Thy glory shall appear.

17 (Heb. 18) Diligam te Domine I will love Thee, O Lord, my strength (Second Sunday after Epiphany, within the week: Jan 13, 14, 15, 16, or 17.)
>Unto the end, for David the servant of the Lord, who spoke to the Lord the words of this canticle, in the day that the Lord delivered him from the hands of all his enemies, and from the hand of Saul.

I will love Thee, O Lord, my strength: The Lord is my firmament, my refuge, and my deliverer. My God is my helper: and in Him will I put my trust. My protector and the horn of my salvation and my support. Praising, I will call upon the Lord: and I shall be saved from my enemies. The sorrows of death surrounded me: and the torrents of iniquity troubled me. The sorrows of hell encompassed me: and the snares of death prevented me. In my affliction I called upon the Lord: and I cried to my God: And He heard my voice from His holy temple: and my cry before Him came into His ears.

The earth shook and trembled: the foundations of the mountains were troubled and were moved, because He was angry with them. There went up a smoke in His wrath: and a fire flamed from His face: coals were kindled by it. He bowed the heavens, and came down: and darkness was under His feet. And He ascended upon the cherubim, and He flew; he flew upon the wings of the winds. And He made darkness His covert, His pavilion round about Him: dark waters in the clouds of the air. At the brightness that was before Him the clouds passed: hail and coals of fire. And the Lord thundered from heaven, and the Highest gave His voice: hail and coals of fire. And He sent forth His arrows, and He scattered them: He multiplied lightnings, and troubled them. Then the fountains of waters appeared, and the foundations of the world were discovered: At Thy rebuke, O Lord, at the blast of the spirit of Thy wrath.

He sent from on high, and took me: and received me out of many waters. He delivered me from my strongest enemies, and from them that hated me: for they were too strong for me. They prevented me in the day of my affliction: and the Lord became my protector. And He brought me forth into a large place: He saved me, because He was well pleased with me. And the Lord will reward me according to my justice; and will repay me according to the cleanness of my hands: Because I have kept the ways of the Lord; and have not done wickedly against my God. For all His judgments are in my sight: and His justices I have not put away from me. And I shall be spotless with Him: and shall keep myself from my iniquity. And the Lord will reward me according to my justice; and according to the cleanness of my hands before His eyes. With the holy, Thou wilt be holy; and with the innocent man Thou wilt be innocent. And with the elect Thou wilt be elect: and with the perverse Thou wilt be perverted. For Thou wilt save the humble people; but wilt bring down the eyes of the proud. For Thou lightest my lamp, O Lord: O my God, enlighten my darkness. For by Thee I shall be delivered from temptation; and through my God I shall go over a wall.

As for my God, His way is undefiled: the words of the Lord are fire-tried: He is the protector of all that trust in Him. For who is God but the Lord? Or who is God but our God? God who hath girt me with strength; and made my way blameless. Who hath made my feet like the feet of harts: and who setteth me upon high places. Who teacheth my hands to war: and Thou hast made my arms like a brazen bow. And Thou hast given me the protection of Thy salvation: and Thy right hand hath held me up: And Thy discipline hath corrected me unto the end: and Thy discipline, the same shall teach me.

Thou hast enlarged my steps under me; and my feet are not weakened. I will pursue after my enemies, and overtake them: and I will not turn again till they are consumed. I will break them, and they shall not be able to stand: they shall fall under my feet. And Thou hast girded me with strength unto battle; and hast subdued under me them that rose up against me. And Thou hast made my enemies turn their back upon me, and hast destroyed them that hated me. They cried, but there was none to save them, to the Lord: but He heard them not. And I shall beat them as small as the dust before the wind; I shall bring them to nought, like the dirt in the streets.

Thou wilt deliver me from the contradictions of the people: Thou wilt make me head of the Gentiles. A people which I knew not hath served me: at the hearing of the ear they have obeyed me. The children that are strangers have lied to me, strange children have faded away, and have halted from their paths.

The Lord liveth, and blessed be my God, and let the God of my salvation be exalted: O God, Who avengest me, and subduest the people under me, my deliverer from my enemies. And Thou wilt lift me up above them that rise up against me: from the unjust man Thou wilt deliver me. Therefore will I give glory to Thee, O Lord, among the nations: and I will sing a psalm to Thy Name. Giving great deliverance to His king, and shewing mercy to David His anointed: and to His seed for ever.

18 (Heb. 19) Coeli enarrant The heavens shew forth the glory of God (Throne of St. Peter also the conversion of St. Constantine Jan 18, and First Sunday on or after Throne of St. Peter. On the day of the Throne of St. Peter also do Psalm 122 for St. Peter. The Epiklesis for the Throne of Peter is also said through the year, and incorporated into the Ordinary of the Mass. Note that the earliest possible time for the beginning of Pre-lent is Sexagesima Sunday, so that the day of the Throne of St. Peter is always done before Pre-lent; the early Celtic Rite did not have a "Septuagesima Sunday" which would impede the Throne of St. Peter on some years. Psalm 18 is also used on the Transfiguration: Celtic date July 26.)

> [Compare to: Ezech 20:40-42a "In my holy mountain, in the high mountain of Israel, saith the Lord God, there shall all the house of Israel serve me; all of them, I say, in the land in which they shall please me. And there will I require your first-fruits and the chief of your tithes with all your sanctifications. I will accept of you for an odor of sweetness, when I shall have brought you out from the people and shall have gathered you out of the lands into which you are scattered: and I will be sanctified in you in the sight of the nations. And you shall know that I am the Lord."]
> Unto the end, a psalm for David.

The heavens shew forth the glory of God: and the firmament declareth the work of His hands. Day to day uttereth speech: and night to night sheweth knowledge. There are no speeches nor languages, where their voices are not heard. Their sound hath gone forth into all the earth: and their words unto the ends of the world.

He hath set His tabernacle in the sun: and He, as a bridegroom coming out of His bride-chamber, Hath rejoiced as a giant to run the way. His going out is from the end of heaven, And His circuit even to the end thereof: and there is no one that can hide himself from His heat.

The law of the Lord is unspotted, converting souls: the testimony of the Lord is faithful, giving wisdom to little ones. The justices of the Lord are right, rejoicing hearts: the commandment of the Lord is lightsome, enlightening the eyes. The fear of the Lord is holy, enduring for ever and ever: the judgments of the Lord are true, justified in themselves, More to be desired than gold and many precious stones: and sweeter than honey and the honeycomb. For Thy servant keepeth them: and in keeping them there is a great reward. Who can understand sins? From my secret ones cleanse me, O Lord: and from those of others spare Thy servant. If they shall have no dominion over me, then shall I be without spot: and I shall be cleansed from the greatest sin. And the words of my mouth shall be such as may please: and the meditation of my heart always in Thy sight. O Lord, my helper, and my redeemer.

19 (Heb. 20) Exaudiat te Dominus May the Lord hear thee (Second Sunday after Throne of St. Peter, if before Pre-lent) Unto the end, a psalm for David.
    May the Lord hear thee in the day of tribulation: may the Name of the God of Jacob protect thee. May He send thee help from the sanctuary: and defend thee out of Sion. May He be mindful of all thy sacrifices: and may thy whole burnt-offering be made fat. May He give thee according to thy own heart: and confirm all thy counsels.
    We will rejoice in Thy salvation: and in the Name of our God we shall be exalted.
    The Lord fulfill all thy petitions: now have I known that the Lord hath saved His anointed. He will hear him from His holy heaven: the salvation of His right hand is in powers. Some trust in chariots, and some in horses: but we will call upon the Name of the Lord our God. They are bound and have fallen: but we are risen and are set upright. O Lord, save the king: and hear us in the day that we shall call upon Thee.

20 (Heb. 21) Domine in virtute In Thy strength, O Lord (Third Sunday after Throne of St. Peter, if before Pre-lent) Unto the end, a psalm for David.
    In Thy strength, O Lord, the king shall joy: and in Thy salvation He shall rejoice exceedingly. Thou hast given him his heart's desire: and hast not withholden from him the will of his lips. For Thou hast prevented him with blessings of sweetness: Thou hast set on his head a crown of precious stones. He asked life of Thee: and Thou hast given him length of days for ever and ever. His glory is great in Thy salvation: glory and great beauty shalt Thou lay upon him. For Thou shalt give him to be a blessing for ever and ever: Thou shalt make him joyful in gladness with Thy countenance. For the king hopeth in the Lord: and through the mercy of the most High he shall not be moved.
    Let Thy hand be found by all Thy enemies: let Thy right hand find out all them that hate Thee. Thou shalt make them as an oven of fire, in the time of thy anger: the Lord shall trouble them in His wrath; and fire shall devour them. Their fruit shalt Thou destroy from the earth: and their seed from among the children of men. For they have intended evils against Thee: they have devised counsels which they have not been able to establish. For Thou shalt make them turn their back: in Thy remnants Thou shalt prepare their face.
    Be Thou exalted, O Lord, in Thy own strength: we will sing and praise Thy power.

21 (Heb. 22) Deus Deus meus O God, my God, look upon me
(Sexagesima, first Sunday of Pre-lent. There is no Septuagesima in the earlier Lectionary, so that the Throne of St. Peter is not skipped. The earliest possible date for Sexagesima might be Jan 25/Feb 7, using the modern calculation for the vernal Equinox, although the Celtic calendar placed the Vernal Equinox a few days earlier on March 17th, according to the earliest Roman practice. The latest date of Sexagesima might be Feb 27/March 12. The first Sunday in Pre-Lent begins the meditations on the Passion; the Gospel is the Sower.)

Unto the end, for the morning protection, a psalm of David.

O God, my God, look upon me: why hast Thou forsaken me? Far from my salvation are the words of my sins. O my God, I shall cry by day, and Thou wilt not hear: and by night, and it shall not be reputed as folly in me. But Thou dwellest in the holy place, the praise of Israel. In Thee have our fathers hoped: they have hoped, and Thou hast delivered them. They cried to Thee, and they were saved: they trusted in Thee, and were not confounded.

But I am a worm and no man: the reproach of men and the outcast of the people. All they that saw me have laughed me to scorn: they have spoken with the lips and wagged the head. He hoped in the Lord, let Him deliver Him: let Him save Him, seeing He delighteth in Him. For Thou art He that hast drawn me out of the womb: my hope from the breasts of my mother. I was cast upon Thee from the womb: From my mother's womb Thou art my God; depart not from me: For tribulation is very near: for there is none to help me.

Many calves have surrounded me: fat bulls have besieged me. They have opened their mouths against me, as a lion ravening and roaring. I am poured out like water: and all my bones are scattered. My heart is become like wax melting in the midst of my bowels. My strength is dried up like a potsherd, and my tongue hath cleaved to my jaws: and Thou hast brought me down into the dust of death. For many dogs have encompassed me: the council of the malignant hath besieged me. They have dug my hands and feet: they have numbered all my bones. And they have looked and stared upon me. They parted my garments amongst them: and upon my vesture they cast lots. But Thou, O Lord, remove not Thy help to a distance from me: look towards my defence. Deliver, O God, my soul from the sword: my only one from the hand of the dog. Save me from the lion's mouth: and my lowness from the horns of the unicorns. I will declare Thy name to my brethren: in the midst of the church will I praise Thee.

Ye that fear the Lord, praise Him: all ye the seed of Jacob, glorify Him. Let all the seed of Israel fear Him: because He hath not slighted nor despised the supplication of the poor man. Neither hath He turned away His face from me: and when I cried to Him he heard me. With Thee is my praise in a great church: I will pay my vows in the sight of them that fear Him. The poor shall eat and shall be filled: and they shall praise the Lord that seek Him: their hearts shall live for ever and ever. All the ends of the earth shall remember, and shall be converted to the Lord: And all the kindreds of the Gentiles shall adore in His sight. For the kingdom is the

Lord's: and He shall have dominion over the nations. All the fat ones of the earth have eaten and have adored: all they that go down to the earth shall fall before Him. And to Him my soul shall live: and my seed shall serve Him. There shall be declared to the Lord a generation to come: and the heavens shall shew forth His justice to a people that shall be born, which the Lord hath made.

22 (Heb. 23) Dominus regit me The Lord ruleth me (Quinquagesima. The Gospel is the Widow and Judge, and the Publican and the Pharisee.) A psalm for David.

The Lord ruleth me: and I shall want nothing. He hath set me in a place of pasture. He hath brought me up on the water of refreshment: He hath converted my soul.

He hath led me on the paths of justice, for His own Name's sake. For though I should walk in the midst of the shadow of death, I will fear no evils: for Thou art with me. Thy rod and Thy staff: they have comforted me.

Thou hast prepared a table before me, against them that afflict me. Thou hast anointed my head with oil: and my chalice which inebriateth me, how goodly is it! And Thy mercy will follow me all the days of my life: And that I may dwell in the house of the Lord unto length of days.

23 (Heb. 24) Domini est terra The earth is the Lord's (The First Sunday in Great Lent, The Head of the Fast, looking towards the Resurrection. Also see Monday of this week. The Gospel is about doing alms, praying, how to fast.)
On the first day of the week, a psalm for David.

The earth is the Lord's and the fullness thereof: the world and all they that dwell therein. For He hath founded it upon the seas: and hath prepared it upon the rivers.

Who shall ascend into the mountain of the Lord: or who shall stand in His holy place? The innocent in hands, and clean of heart, who hath not taken his soul in vain, nor sworn deceitfully to his neighbor. He shall receive a blessing from the Lord: and mercy from God his Savior. This is the generation of them that seek Him, of them that seek the face of the God of Jacob.

Lift up your gates, O ye princes, and be ye lifted up, O eternal gates: and the King of Glory shall enter in. Who is this King of Glory? The Lord Who is strong and mighty: the Lord mighty in battle.

Lift up your gates, O ye princes, and be ye lifted up, O eternal gates: and the King of Glory shall enter in. Who is this King of Glory? The Lord of hosts, He is the King of Glory.

24 (Heb. 25) Ad te Domini levavi To Thee, O Lord, have I lifted up (Christ overcoming temptations and rebuking the devil Feb 15, and also Monday, the first day in the Lenten Fast. The central theme is the same as the Synodikon.)
Unto the end, a psalm for David.

To Thee, O Lord, have I lifted up my soul: in Thee, O my God, I put my trust: let me not be ashamed. Neither let my enemies laugh at me: for none of them that wait on Thee shall be confounded. Let all them be confounded that act unjust things without cause.

Show, O Lord, Thy ways to me: and teach me Thy paths. Direct me in Thy truth, and teach me: for Thou art God my Savior, and on Thee have I waited all the day long. Remember, O Lord, Thy bowels of compassion: and Thy mercies that are from the beginning of the world. The sins of my youth and my ignorances do not remember. According to Thy mercy remember Thou me: for Thy goodness' sake, O Lord.

The Lord is sweet and righteous: therefore He will give a law to sinners in the way. He will guide the mild in judgment: He will teach the meek His ways. All the ways of the Lord are mercy and truth: to them that seek after His covenant and His testimonies. For Thy Name's sake, O Lord, Thou wilt pardon my sin: for it is great. Who is the man that feareth the Lord? He hath appointed him a law in the way he hath chosen. His soul shall dwell in good things: and his seed shall inherit the land.

The Lord is a firmament to them that fear Him; and His covenant shall be made manifest to them. My eyes are ever towards the Lord: for He shall pluck my feet out of the snare. Look Thou upon me, and have mercy on me: for I am alone and poor. The troubles of my heart are multiplied: deliver me from my necessities. See my abjection and my labor: and forgive me all my sins. Consider my enemies for they are multiplied, and have hated me with an unjust hatred. Keep Thou my soul, and deliver me: I shall not be ashamed, for I have hoped in Thee. The innocent and the upright have adhered to me: because I have waited on Thee. Deliver Israel, O God, from all his tribulations.

25 (Heb. 26) Judica me Domine Judge me, O Lord (Tuesday in the first week in Great Lent, Blessing of Babies and Catechumins.) Unto the end, a psalm for David.

Judge me, O Lord, for I have walked in my innocence: and I have put my trust in the Lord, and shall not be weakened. Prove me, O Lord, and try me: burn my reins and my heart. For Thy mercy is before my eyes: and I am well pleased with Thy truth.

I have not sat with the council of vanity: neither will I go in with the doers of unjust things. I have hated the assembly of the malignant: and with the wicked I will not sit. I will wash my hands among the innocent: and will compass Thy altar, O Lord. That I may hear the voice of Thy praise: and tell of all Thy wondrous works. I have loved, O Lord, the beauty of Thy house: and the place where Thy glory dwelleth.

Take not away my soul, O God, with the wicked: nor my life with bloody men: In whose hands are iniquities: their right hand is filled with gifts. But as for me, I have walked in my innocence: redeem me, and have mercy on me. My foot hath stood in the direct way: in the churches I will bless Thee, O Lord.

Psalm Table of St. Mael Ruain: *Dominus illuminatio* to *Dixi custodiam,* 26-37 [12 Psalms], Monday Beginning of Night (modern Sunday night).

---

26 (Heb. 27) Dominus illuminatio The Lord is my light and my salvation
(Wednesday in the first week in Great Lent, Anointing with Oil.)
    The psalm of David before he was anointed.

    The Lord is my light and my salvation; whom shall I fear? The Lord is the protector of my life; of whom shall I be afraid? Whilst the wicked draw near against me, to eat my flesh: My enemies that trouble me, have themselves been weakened, and have fallen. If armies in camp should stand together against me, my heart shall not fear. If a battle should rise up against me, in this will I be confident.

    One thing I have asked of the Lord, this will I seek after: that I may dwell in the house of the Lord all the days of my life: That I may see the delight of the Lord; and may visit His temple.

    For He hath hidden me in His tabernacle: in the day of evils, He hath protected me in the secret place of His tabernacle. He hath exalted me upon a rock: and now He hath lifted up my head above my enemies. I have gone round, and have offered up in His tabernacle a sacrifice of jubilation: I will sing, and recite a psalm to the Lord.

    Hear, O Lord, my voice, with which I have cried to Thee: have mercy on me and hear me. My heart hath said to Thee: My face hath sought Thee: Thy face, O Lord, will I still seek. Turn not away Thy face from me: decline not in Thy wrath from Thy servant. Be Thou my helper, forsake me not: do not Thou despise me, O God my Savior.

    For my father and my mother have left me: but the Lord hath taken me up. Set me, O Lord, a law in Thy way: and guide me in the right path, because of my enemies. Deliver me not over to the will of them that trouble me: for unjust witnesses have risen up against me, and iniquity hath lied to itself. I believe to see the good things of the Lord in the land of the living.

    Expect the Lord; do manfully: and let thy heart take courage; and wait thou for the Lord.

27 (Heb. 28) Ad te Domine clamabo Unto Thee will I cry, O Lord
(Thursday in the first week in Great Lent) A psalm for David himself.

    Unto Thee will I cry, O Lord: O my God, be not Thou silent to me; lest if Thou be silent to me, I become like them that go down into the pit. Hear, O Lord, the voice of my supplication: when I pray to Thee, when I lift up my hands to Thy holy temple. Draw me not away together with the wicked: and with the workers of iniquity destroy me not. Who speak peace with their neighbor: but evils are in their hearts. Give them according to their works: and according to the wickedness of their inventions. According to the works of their hands give Thou to them: render to them their reward. Because they have not understood the works of the Lord and the operations of His hands, Thou shalt destroy them, and shalt not build them up.

    Blessed be the Lord: for He hath heard the voice of my supplication. The Lord is my helper and my protector: in Him hath my heart confided, and I have been helped. And my flesh hath flourished again: and with my will I will give praise to Him. The Lord is the strength of His people: and the protector of the salvation of His anointed. Save, O Lord, Thy people and bless Thy inheritance: and rule them and exalt them for ever.

28 (Heb. 29) Afferte Domino Bring to the Lord, O ye children of God (Friday in the first week in Great Lent, also within the Rite of Baptism, Folio 52 v misspells this "Adferte.") A psalm for David, at the finishing of the tabernacle.

    Bring to the Lord, O ye children of God: bring to the Lord the offspring of rams. Bring to the Lord glory and honor; bring to the Lord glory to His Name: adore ye the Lord in His holy court.

    The voice of the Lord is upon the waters; the God of majesty hath thundered: the Lord is upon many waters. The voice of the Lord is in power: the voice of the Lord in magnificence. The voice of the Lord breaketh the cedars: yea, the Lord shall break the cedars of Libanus, And shall reduce them to pieces, as a calf of Libanus, and as the beloved son of unicorns. The voice of the Lord divideth the flame of fire: the voice of the Lord shaketh the desert: and the Lord shall shake the desert of Cades. The voice of the Lord prepareth the stags; and He will discover the thick woods: and in His temple all shall speak His glory.

    The Lord maketh the flood to dwell: and the Lord shall sit king for ever. The Lord will give strength to His people: the Lord will bless His people with peace.

29 (Heb. 30) Exaltabo te Domine I will extol Thee, O Lord (Saturday in the first week in Great Lent) A psalm of a canticle, at the dedication of David's house.

    I will extol Thee, O Lord, for Thou hast upheld me: and hast not made my enemies to rejoice over me. O Lord my God, I have cried to Thee: and Thou hast healed me. Thou hast brought forth, O Lord, my soul from hell: Thou hast saved me from them that go down into the pit.

    Sing to the Lord, O ye His saints: and give praise to the memory of His holiness. For wrath is in His indignation: and life in His good-will. In the evening weeping shall have place: and in the morning gladness. And in my abundance I said: I shall never be moved.

    O Lord, in Thy favor, Thou gavest strength to my beauty. Thou turndst away Thy face from me: and I became troubled. To Thee, O Lord, will I cry: and I will make supplication to my God. What profit is there in my blood, whilst I go down to corruption? Shall dust confess to Thee or declare Thy truth? The Lord hath heard, and hath had mercy on me: the Lord became my helper. Thou hast turned for me my mourning into joy: Thou hast cut my sackcloth and hast compassed me with gladness. To the end that my glory may sing to Thee, and I may not regret: O Lord my God, I will give praise to Thee for ever.

30 (Heb. 31) In te Domine speravi In Thee, O Lord, have I hoped (Second Sunday in Great Lent; the Gospel is the Prodigal son.)
Unto the end, a psalm for David, in an ecstasy.

In Thee, O Lord, have I hoped, let me never be confounded: deliver me in Thy justice. Bow down Thy ear to me: make haste to deliver me. Be Thou unto me a God, a protector, and a house of refuge, to save me. For Thou art my strength and my refuge: and for Thy Name's sake Thou wilt lead me and nourish me. Thou wilt bring me out of this snare which they have hidden for me: for Thou art my protector. Into Thy hands I commend my spirit: Thou hast redeemed me, O Lord, the God of truth.

Thou hast hated them that regard vanities to no purpose. But I have hoped in the Lord: I will be glad and rejoice in Thy mercy. For Thou hast regarded my humility: Thou hast saved my soul out of distresses. And Thou hast not shut me up in the hands of the enemy: Thou hast set my feet in a spacious place.

Have mercy on me, O Lord, for I am afflicted: my eye is troubled with wrath, my soul, and my belly. For my life is wasted with grief: and my years in sighs. My strength is weakened through poverty: and my bones are disturbed. I am become a reproach among all my enemies, and very much to my neighbors: and a fear to my acquaintance. They that saw me without fled from me: I am forgotten as one dead from the heart. I am become as a vessel that is destroyed: for I have heard the blame of many that dwell round about. While they assembled together against me, they consulted to take away my life.

But I have put my trust in Thee, O Lord: I said: Thou art my God; my lots are in Thy hands. Deliver me out of the hands of my enemies, and from them that persecute me. Make Thy face to shine upon Thy servant; save me in Thy mercy: Let me not be confounded, O Lord; for I have called upon Thee. Let the wicked be ashamed, and be brought down to hell. Let deceitful lips be made dumb; Which speak iniquity against the just, with pride and abuse. O how great is the multitude of Thy sweetness, O Lord, which Thou hast hidden for them that fear Thee! Which Thou hast wrought for them that hope in Thee, in the sight of the sons of men!

Thou shalt hide them in the secret of Thy face from the disturbance of men. Thou shalt protect them in Thy tabernacle from the contradiction of tongues. Blessed be the Lord: for He hath shewn His wonderful mercy to me in a fortified city. But I said in the excess of my mind: I am cast away from before Thy eyes. Therefore Thou hast heard the voice of my prayer when I cried to Thee. O love the Lord, all ye His saints: for the Lord will require truth and will repay them abundantly that act proudly. Do ye manfully, and let your heart be strengthened, all ye that hope in the Lord.

31 (Heb. 32) Beati quorum Blessed are they whose iniquities are forgiven
(Monday in the second week in Great Lent) To David himself, understanding.

Blessed are they whose iniquities are forgiven: and whose sins are covered. Blessed is the man to whom the Lord hath not imputed sin; and in whose spirit there is no guile.

Because I was silent my bones grew old; whilst I cried out all the day long. For day and night Thy hand was heavy upon me: I am turned in my anguish, whilst the thorn is fastened. I have acknowledged my sin to Thee: and my injustice I have not concealed. I said: I will confess against myself my injustice to the Lord: and Thou hast forgiven the wickedness of my sin. For this shall every one that is holy pray to Thee in a seasonable time. And yet in a flood of many waters they shall not come nigh unto Him.

Thou art my refuge from the trouble which hath encompassed me: my joy, deliver me from them that surround me. I will give thee understanding and I will instruct thee in this way, in which thou shalt go: I will fix my eyes upon thee. Do not become like the horse and the mule who have no understanding. With bit and bridle bind fast their jaws, who come not near unto thee.

Many are the scourges of the sinner; but mercy shall encompass him that hopeth in the Lord. Be glad in the Lord, and rejoice, ye just; and glory, all ye right of heart.

32 (Heb. 33) Exultate justi Rejoice in the Lord, O ye just (Tuesday in the second week in Great Lent) A psalm for David.

Rejoice in the Lord, O ye just: praise becometh the upright. Give praise to the Lord on the harp: sing to Him with the psaltery, the instrument of ten strings. Sing to Him a new canticle: sing well unto Him with a loud noise.

For the Word of the Lord is right; and all His works are done with faithfulness. He loveth mercy and judgment: the earth is full of the mercy of the Lord. By the word of the Lord the heavens were established: and all the power of them by the spirit of His mouth: Gathering together the waters of the sea, as in a vessel: laying up the depths in storehouses.

Let all the earth fear the Lord: and let all the inhabitants of the world be in awe of Him. For He spoke and they were made: He commanded and they were created. The Lord bringeth to nought the counsels of nations: and He rejecteth the devices of people, and casteth away the counsels of princes. But the counsel of the Lord standeth for ever: the thoughts of His heart to all generations. Blessed is the nation whose God is the Lord: the people whom He hath chosen for His inheritance.

The Lord hath looked from heaven: He hath beheld all the sons of men. From His habitation which He hath prepared, He hath looked upon all that dwell on the earth. He Who hath made the hearts of every one of them: Who understandeth all their works.

The king is not saved by a great army: nor shall the giant be saved by his own great strength. Vain is the horse for safety: neither shall he be saved by the abundance of his strength. Behold, the eyes of the Lord are on them that fear Him: and on them that hope in His mercy; To deliver their souls from death; and feed them in famine.

Our soul waiteth for the Lord: for He is our helper and protector. For in Him our heart shall rejoice: and in His Holy Name we have trusted.

Let Thy mercy, O Lord, be upon us: as we have hoped in Thee.

33 (Heb. 34) Benedicam Dominum   I will bless the Lord at all times
(Wednesday in the second week in Great Lent)
> For David, when he changed his countenance before Achimelech, who dismissed him, and he went his way.

I will bless the Lord at all times: His praise shall be always in my mouth. In the Lord shall my soul be praised: let the meek hear and rejoice.

O magnify the Lord with me: and let us extol His Name together. I sought the Lord, and He heard me: and He delivered me from all my troubles. Come ye to Him and be enlightened: and your faces shall not be confounded.

The poor man cried and the Lord heard him: and saved him out of all his troubles. The angel of the Lord shall encamp round about them that fear Him: and shall deliver them.

O taste, and see that the Lord is sweet: blessed is the man that hopeth in Him. Fear the Lord, all ye His saints: for there is no want to them that fear Him. The rich have wanted, and have suffered hunger: but they that seek the Lord shall not be deprived of any good. Come, children, hearken to me: I will teach you the fear of the Lord.

Who is the man that desireth life: who loveth to see good days? Keep thy tongue from evil: and thy lips from speaking guile. Turn away from evil and do good: seek after peace and pursue it.

The eyes of the Lord are upon the just: and His ears unto their prayers. But the countenance of the Lord is against them that do evil things: to cut off the remembrance of them from the earth. The just cried, and the Lord heard them: and delivered them out of all their troubles. The Lord is nigh unto them that are of a contrite heart: and He will save the humble of spirit. Many are the afflictions of the just: but out of them all will the Lord deliver them. The Lord keepeth all their bones: not one of them shall be broken. The death of the wicked is very evil: and they that hate the just shall be guilty. The Lord will redeem the souls of His servants: and none of them that trust in Him shall offend.

34 (Heb. 35) Judica Domine nocentes me   Judge Thou, O Lord   (Thursday in the second week in Great Lent)   For David himself.

Judge Thou, O Lord, them that wrong me: overthrow them that fight against me. Take hold of arms and shield: and rise up to help me. Bring out the sword, and shut up the way against them that persecute me: say to my soul: I am thy salvation. Let them be confounded and ashamed that seek after my soul. Let them be turned back and be confounded that devise evil against me. Let them become as dust before the wind: and let the angel of the Lord straiten them. Let their way become dark and slippery: and let the angel of the Lord pursue them. For without cause they have hidden their net for me unto destruction: without cause they have upbraided my soul. Let the snare which he knoweth not come upon him: and let the net which he hath hidden catch him: and into that very snare let them fall.

But my soul shall rejoice in the Lord: and shall be delighted in His salvation. All my bones shall say: Lord, who is like to Thee? Who deliverest the poor from the hand of them that are stronger than he: the needy and the poor from them that strip him.

Unjust witnesses rising up have asked me things I knew not. They repaid me evil for good: to the depriving me of my soul. But as for me, when they were troublesome to me, I was clothed with haircloth. I humbled my soul with fasting: and my prayer shall be turned into my bosom. As a neighbor and as an own brother, so did I please: as one mourning and sorrowful, so was I humbled. But they rejoiced against me, and came together: scourges were gathered together upon me, and I knew not. They were separated and repented not; they tempted me, they scoffed at me with scorn: they gnashed upon me with their teeth.

Lord, when wilt Thou look upon me? Rescue Thou my soul from their malice; my only one from the lions. I will give thanks to Thee in a great church; I will praise Thee in a strong people. Let not them that are my enemies wrongfully rejoice over me: who have hated me without cause and wink with the eyes. For they spoke indeed peaceably to me: and speaking in the anger of the earth they devised guile. And they opened their mouth wide against me: they said: Well done, well done, our eyes have seen it.

Thou hast seen, O Lord; be not Thou silent: O Lord, depart not from me. Arise, and be attentive to my judgment: to my cause, my God and my Lord. Judge me, O Lord my God, according to Thy justice; and let them not rejoice over me. Let them not say in their hearts: It is well, it is well, to our mind: neither let them say: We have swallowed him up. Let them blush and be ashamed together, who rejoice at my evils. Let them be clothed with confusion and shame, who speak great things against me.

Let them rejoice and be glad, who are well pleased with my justice: and let them say always: The Lord be magnified, who delights in the peace of his servant. And my tongue shall meditate Thy justice; Thy praise all the day long.

35 (Heb. 36) Dixit injustus The unjust hath said within himself (Friday in the second week in Great Lent) Unto the end, for the servant of God, David himself.

The unjust hath said within himself that he would sin: there is no fear of God before his eyes. For in His sight he hath done deceitfully: that his iniquity may be found unto hatred. The words of his mouth are iniquity and guile: he would not understand that he might do well. He hath devised iniquity on his bed: he hath set himself on every way that is not good; but evil he hath not hated.

O Lord, Thy mercy is in heaven: and Thy truth reacheth even to the clouds. Thy justice is as the mountains of God: Thy judgments are a great deep. Men and beasts Thou wilt preserve, O Lord: O how hast Thou multiplied Thy mercy, O God! But the children of men shall put their trust under the covert of Thy wings. They shall be inebriated with the plenty of Thy house: and Thou shalt make them drink of the torrent of Thy pleasure. For with Thee is the fountain of life: and in Thy light we shall see light.

Extend Thy mercy to them that know Thee; and Thy justice to them that are right in heart. Let not the foot of pride come to me: and let not the hand of the sinner move me. There the workers of iniquity are fallen: they are cast out, and could not stand.

36 (Heb. 37) Noli aemulari Be not emulous of evildoers (Saturday in the second week in Great Lent) A psalm for David himself.

Be not emulous of evildoers: nor envy them that work iniquity. For they shall shortly wither away as grass: and as the green herbs shall quickly fall. Trust in the Lord, and do good: and dwell in the land; and thou shalt be fed with its riches. Delight in the Lord: and He will give thee the requests of thy heart. Commit thy way to the Lord, and trust in Him: and he will do it. And He will bring forth thy justice as the light: and thy judgment as the noonday: be subject to the Lord and pray to Him.

Envy not the man who prospereth in his way: the man who doth unjust things. Cease from anger, and leave rage: have no emulation to do evil. For evildoers shall be cut off: but they that wait upon the Lord, they shall inherit the land. For yet a little while, and the wicked shall not be: and thou shalt seek his place, and shalt not find it. But the meek shall inherit the land; and shall delight in abundance of peace.

The sinner shall watch the just man: and shall gnash upon him with his teeth. But the Lord shall laugh at him: for he foreseeth that his day shall come. The wicked have drawn out the sword: they have bent their bow. To cast down the poor and needy: to kill the upright of heart. Let their sword enter into their own hearts: and let their bow be broken. Better is a little to the just than the great riches of the wicked. For the arms of the wicked shall be broken in pieces: but the Lord strengtheneth the just.

The Lord knoweth the days of the undefiled: and their inheritance shall be for ever. They shall not be confounded in the evil time; and in the days of famine they shall be filled: because the wicked shall perish. And the enemies of the Lord, presently, after they shall be honored and exalted: shall come to nothing and vanish like smoke. The sinner shall borrow, and not pay again: but the just sheweth mercy and shall live. For such as bless him shall inherit the land: but such as curse him shall perish.

With the Lord shall the steps of a man be directed: and he shall like well his way. When he shall fall he shall not be bruised: for the Lord putteth his hand under him. I have been young, and now am old: and I have not seen the just forsaken, nor his seed seeking bread. He sheweth mercy, and lendeth all the day long: and his seed shall be in blessing.

Decline from evil and do good: and dwell for ever and ever. For the Lord loveth judgment and will not forsake his saints: they shall be preserved for ever. The unjust shall be punished: and the seed of the wicked shall perish. But the just shall inherit the land: and shall dwell therein for evermore. The mouth of the just shall meditate wisdom: and his tongue shall speak judgment. The law of his God is in his heart: and his steps shall not be supplanted.

The wicked watcheth the just man: and seeketh to put him to death, But the Lord will not leave him in his hands: nor condemn him when he shall be judged. Expect the Lord and keep His way: and He will exalt thee to inherit the land: when the sinners shall perish thou shalt see. I have seen the wicked highly exalted, and lifted up like the cedars of Libanus. And I passed by, and lo, he was not: and I sought him and his place was not found.

Keep innocence, and behold justice: for there are remnants for the peaceable man. But the unjust shall be destroyed together: the remnants of the wicked shall perish. But the salvation of the just is from the Lord: and He is their protector in the time of trouble. And the Lord will help them and deliver them: and He will rescue them from the wicked, and save them: because they have hoped in Him.

37 (H 38) Domine ne in furore Rebuke me not, O Lord, in Thy indignation
(Third Sunday in Great Lent; the Gospel is, "I am the bread of life.")
A psalm for David, for a remembrance of the sabbath.

Rebuke me not, O Lord, in Thy indignation; nor chastise me in Thy wrath. For Thy arrows are fastened in me: and Thy hand hath been strong upon me. There is no health in my flesh, because of Thy wrath: there is no peace for my bones, because of my sins. For my iniquities are gone over my head: and as a heavy burden are become heavy upon me. My sores are putrified and corrupted, because of my foolishness. I am become miserable, and am bowed down even to the end: I walked sorrowful all the day long. For my loins are filled with illusions: and there is no health in my flesh. I am afflicted and humbled exceedingly: I roared with the groaning of my heart.

Lord, all my desire is before Thee: and my groaning is not hidden from Thee. My heart is troubled, my strength hath left me: and the light of my eyes itself is not with me. My friends and my neighbors have drawn near, and stood against me. And they that were near me stood afar off: And they that sought my soul used violence. And they that sought evils to me spoke vain things: and studied deceits all the day long.

But I, as a deaf man, heard not: and as a dumb man not opening his mouth. And I became as a man that heareth not: and that hath no reproofs in his mouth. For in Thee, O Lord, have I hoped: Thou wilt hear me, O Lord my God. For I said: Lest at any time my enemies rejoice over me: and whilst my feet are moved, they speak great things against me. For I am ready for scourges: and my sorrow is continually before me. For I will declare my iniquity: and I will think for my sin. But my enemies live, and are stronger than I: and they that hate me wrongfully are multiplied. They that render evil for good have detracted me: because I followed goodness.

Forsake me not, O Lord my God: do not Thou depart from me. Attend unto my help, O Lord, the God of my salvation.

Psalm Table of St. Mael Ruain: [From *Dixi custodiam* to the end of the first fifty, etc.] 38-50 [13 Psalms], Monday Midnight (modern Sunday night).
----

38 (Heb. 39) Dixi custodiam I said: I will take heed to my ways (Monday in the third week in Great Lent) Unto the end, for Idithun himself, a canticle of David.

I said: I will take heed to my ways: that I sin not with my tongue. I have set a guard to my mouth, when the sinner stood against me. I was dumb, and was humbled, and kept silence from good things: and my sorrow was renewed. My heart grew hot within me: and in my meditation a fire shall flame out. I spoke with my tongue: O Lord, make me know my end, And what is the number of my days: that I may know what is wanting to me.

Behold, Thou hast made my days measurable: and my substance is as nothing before Thee. And indeed all things are vanity; every man living. Surely man passeth as an image: yea, and he is disquieted in vain. He storeth up: and he knoweth not for whom he shall gather these things. And now what is my hope? Is it not the Lord? And my substance is with Thee.

Deliver Thou me from all my iniquities: Thou hast made me a reproach to the fool. I was dumb, and I opened not my mouth, because Thou hast done it: remove Thy scourges from me. The strength of Thy hand hath made me faint in rebukes: Thou hast corrected man for iniquity. And Thou hast made his soul to waste away like a spider: surely in vain is any man disquieted.

Hear my prayer, O Lord, and my supplication: give ear to my tears. Be not silent: for I am a stranger with Thee, and a sojourner as all my fathers were. O forgive me, that I may be refreshed, before I go hence, and be no more.

39 (Heb. 40) Expectans expectavi With expectation I have waited (Tuesday in the third week in Great Lent) Unto the end, a psalm for David himself.

With expectation I have waited for the Lord; and He was attentive to me. And He heard my prayers: and brought me out of the pit of misery and the mire of dregs. And He set my feet upon a rock: and directed my steps. And He put a new canticle into my mouth, a song to our God.

Many shall see and shall fear: and they shall hope in the Lord. Blessed is the man whose trust is in the Name of the Lord: and who hath not had regard to vanities and lying follies.

Thou hast multiplied Thy wonderful works, O Lord my God: and in Thy thoughts there is no one like to Thee. I have declared, and I have spoken: they are multiplied above number. Sacrifice and oblation Thou didst not desire: but Thou hast pierced ears for me. Burnt-offering and sin-offering Thou didst not require: then said I, Behold, I come.

In the head of the book it is written of me that I should do Thy will: O my God, I have desired it, and Thy law in the midst of my heart. I have declared Thy justice in a great church. Lo, I will not restrain my lips: O Lord, Thou knowest it. I have not hid Thy justice within my heart: I have declared Thy truth and Thy salvation. I have not concealed Thy mercy and Thy truth from a great council.

Withhold not Thou, O Lord, Thy tender mercies from me: Thy mercy and Thy truth have always upheld me. For evils without number have surrounded me; my iniquities have overtaken me, and I was not able to see. They are multiplied above the hairs of my head: and my heart hath forsaken me.

Be pleased, O Lord, to deliver me: look down, O Lord, to help me. Let them be confounded and ashamed together, that seek after my soul to take it away. Let them be turned backward and be ashamed, that desire evils to me. Let them immediately bear their confusion, that say to me: 'Tis well, 'tis well. Let all that seek Thee rejoice and be glad in Thee: and let such as love Thy salvation say always: The Lord be magnified. But I am a beggar and poor: the Lord is careful for me. Thou art my helper and my protector: O my God, be not slack.

40 (Heb. 41) *Beatus qui intelligit* Blessed is he that understandeth
(Wednesday in the third week in Great Lent) Unto the end, a psalm for David himself.

Blessed is he that understandeth concerning the needy and the poor: the Lord will deliver him in the evil day. The Lord preserve him and give him life, and make him blessed upon the earth: and deliver him not up to the will of his enemies. The Lord help him on his bed of sorrow: Thou hast turned all his couch in his sickness.

I said: O Lord, be Thou merciful to me: heal my soul, for I have sinned against Thee. My enemies have spoken evils against me: When shall he die and his name perish? And if he came in to see me, he spoke vain things; his heart gathered together iniquity to itself. He went out and spoke to the same purpose. All my enemies whispered together against me: they devised evils to me. They determined against me an unjust word: Shall he that sleepeth rise again no more? For even the man of my peace, in whom I trusted, who ate my bread, hath greatly supplanted me.

But Thou, O Lord, have mercy on me, and raise me up again: and I will requite them. By this I know that Thou hast had a good will for me: because my enemy shall not rejoice over me. But Thou hast upheld me by reason of my innocence: and hast established me in Thy sight for ever. Blessed be the Lord, the God of Israel, from eternity to eternity. So be it. So be it.

41 (H42) Quemadmodum desiderat As the hart panteth after the fountains
(Thursday in the third week in Great Lent, and also in the Rite of Baptism.) Unto the end, understanding for the sons of Core.

As the hart panteth after the fountains of water: so my soul panteth after thee, O God. My soul hath thirsted after the strong living God: when shall I come and appear before the face of God? My tears have been my bread day and night: whilst it is said to me daily: Where is thy God?

These things I remembered, and poured out my soul in me: for I shall go over into the place of the wonderful tabernacle, even to the house of God: With the voice of joy and praise: the noise of one feasting. Why art thou sad, O my soul? And why dost thou trouble me? Hope in God, for I will still give praise to Him: the salvation of my countenance, and my God.

My soul is troubled within myself: therefore will I remember Thee from the land of Jordan and Hermoniim, from the little hill. Deep calleth on deep, at the noise of Thy flood-gates. All Thy heights and Thy billows have passed over me.

In the daytime the Lord hath commanded His mercy: and a canticle to Him in the night. With me is prayer to the God of my life; I will say to God: Thou art my support; Why hast Thou forgotten me? And why go I mourning, whilst my enemy afflicteth me? Whilst my bones are broken, my enemies who trouble me have reproached me: Whilst they say to me day by day: Where is thy God? Why art thou cast down, O my soul? And why dost thou disquiet me? Hope thou in God, for I will still give praise to Him: the salvation of my countenance, and my God.

42 (Heb. 43) Judica me Deus Judge me, O God, and distinguish my cause
(Friday in the third week in Great Lent. Also, the last Psalm in the Confraction in the Mass.)

A psalm for David.

Judge me, O God, and distinguish my cause from the nation that is not holy; deliver me from the unjust and deceitful man. For Thou art God my strength: why hast Thou cast me off? And why do I go sorrowful whilst the enemy afflicteth me?

Send forth Thy light and Thy truth: they have conducted me, and brought me unto Thy holy hill, and into Thy tabernacles. And I will go in to the altar of God: to God Who giveth joy to my youth.

To Thee, O God, my God, I will give praise upon the harp: Why art thou sad, O my soul? And why dost thou disquiet me? Hope in God, for I will still give praise to Him: the salvation of my countenance, and my God.

43 (Heb. 44) Deus auribus nostris We have heard, O God, with our ears
(Saturday in the third week in Great Lent)

Unto the end, for the sons of Core, to give understanding.

We have heard, O God, with our ears: our fathers have declared to us. The work Thou hast wrought in their days: and in the days of old. Thy hand destroyed the Gentiles, and Thou plantedst them: Thou didst afflict the people and cast them out. For they got not the possession of the land by their own sword; neither did their own arm save them: But Thy right hand and Thy arm, and the light of Thy countenance: because Thou wast pleased with them.

Thou art Thyself my king and my God: Who commandest the saving of Jacob. Through Thee we will push down our enemies with the horn; and through Thy Name we will despise them that rise up against us. For I will not trust in my bow: neither shall my sword save me. But Thou hast saved us from them that afflict us: and hast put them to shame that hate us.

In God shall we glory all the day long: and in Thy Name we will give praise for ever. But now Thou hast cast us off, and put us to shame: and Thou, O God, wilt not go out with our armies. Thou hast made us turn our back to our enemies: and they that hated us plundered for themselves. Thou hast given us up like sheep to be eaten: Thou hast scattered us among the nations. Thou hast sold Thy people for no price: and there was no reckoning in the exchange of them. Thou hast made us a reproach to our neighbors; a scoff and derision to them that are round about us. Thou hast made us a byword among the Gentiles: a shaking of the head among the people. All the day long my shame is before me; and the confusion of my face hath covered me, At the voice of Him that reproacheth and detracteth me: at the face of the enemy and persecutor.

All these things have come upon us: yet we have not forgotten Thee: and we have not done wickedly in Thy covenant. And our heart hath not turned back: neither hast Thou turned aside our steps from Thy way. For Thou hast humbled us in the place of affliction; and the shadow of death hath covered us. If we have forgotten the Name of our God, and if we have spread forth our hands to a strange god: Shall not God search out these things? For He knoweth the secrets of the heart: Because for Thy sake we are killed all the day long: we are counted as sheep for the slaughter.

Arise, why sleepest Thou, O Lord? Arise, and cast us not off to the end. Why turnest Thou Thy face away and forgettest our want and our trouble? For our soul is humbled down to the dust: our belly cleaveth to the earth. Arise, O Lord, help us: and redeem us for Thy Name's sake.

44 (Heb. 45) Eructavit cor meum My heart hath uttered a good word
(The Annunciation of the Blessed Virgin Mary, March 25/April 7, fixed day, whenever that falls, with the other Psalm, Lections and services of that day.)
> Unto the end, for them that shall be changed, for the sons of Core, for understanding. A canticle for the Beloved.

My heart hath uttered a good word: I speak my works to the king. My tongue is the pen of a scrivener that writeth swiftly. Thou art beautiful above the sons of men; grace is poured abroad in thy lips; therefore hath God blessed thee for ever. Gird Thy sword upon Thy thigh, O Thou most mighty. With thy comeliness and thy beauty set out; proceed prosperously, and reign; Because of truth and meekness and justice: and thy right hand shall conduct thee wonderfully.

Thy arrows are sharp; under thee shall people fall, into the hearts of the king's enemies. Thy throne, O God, is for ever and ever: the sceptre of Thy kingdom is a sceptre of uprightness. Thou hast loved justice, and hated iniquity: therefore God, thy God, hath anointed thee with the oil of gladness above thy fellows. Myrrh and stacte and cassia perfume thy garments, from the ivory houses: out of which the daughters of kings have delighted thee in thy glory.

The queen stood on thy right hand, in gilded clothing: surrounded with variety. Hearken, O daughter, and see, and incline thy ear: and forget thy people and thy father's house. And the king shall greatly desire thy beauty: for He is the Lord thy God, and Him they shall adore. And the daughters of Tyre with gifts, yea, all the rich among the people, shall entreat thy countenance.

All the glory of the king's daughter is within in golden borders, clothed round about with varieties. After her shall virgins be brought to the king: her neighbors shall be brought to thee. They shall be brought with gladness and rejoicing: they shall be brought into the temple of the king. Instead of thy fathers, sons are born to thee: thou shalt make them princes over all the earth. They shall remember thy name throughout all generations. Therefore shall people praise thee for ever: yea, for ever and ever.

45 (Heb. 46) Deus noster refugium Our God is our refuge and strength
(Fourth Sunday in Great Lent, matching the Gospel, the Feast of Tabernacles and Christ preaching. Mid-Lent, the Adoration of the Cross of our Lord.)
Unto the end, for the sons of Core, for the hidden.

Our God is our refuge and strength: a helper in troubles, which have found us exceedingly. Therefore we will not fear when the earth shall be troubled: and the mountains shall be removed into the heart of the sea. Their waters roared and were troubled: the mountains were troubled with His strength. The stream of the river maketh the city of God joyful: the most High hath sanctified His own tabernacle.

God is in the midst thereof, it shall not be moved: God will help it in the morning early. Nations were troubled, and kingdoms were bowed down: he uttered His voice, the earth trembled. The Lord of armies is with us: the God of Jacob is our protector.

Come and behold ye the works of the Lord, what wonders He hath done upon earth: making wars to cease even to the end of the earth. He shall destroy the bow, and break the weapons: and the shield He shall burn in the fire.

Be still and see that I am God: I will be exalted among the nations, and I will be exalted in the earth. The Lord of armies is with us: the God of Jacob is our protector.

46 (Heb. 47) Omnes gentes plaudite O clap your hands, all ye nations
(Monday in the fourth week in Great Lent) Unto the end, for the sons of Core.

O clap your hands, all ye nations: shout unto God with the voice of joy, For the Lord is high, terrible: a great king over all the earth. He hath subdued the people under us: and the nations under our feet. He hath chosen for us his inheritance: the beauty of Jacob which He hath loved. God is ascended with jubilee: and the Lord with the sound of trumpet.

Sing praises to our God, sing ye: sing praises to our king, sing ye. For God is the king of all the earth: sing ye wisely. God shall reign over the nations: God sitteth on His holy throne. The princes of the people are gathered together, with the God of Abraham: for the strong gods of the earth are exceedingly exalted.

47 (Heb. 48) Magnus Dominus Great is the Lord (Wednesday in the fourth week in Great Lent, if following Old Testament Lections.)
A psalm of a canticle, for the sons of Core, on the second day of the week.

Great is the Lord, and exceedingly to be praised in the city of our God, in His holy mountain. With the joy of the whole earth is mount Sion founded, on the sides of the north, the city of the great king. In her houses shall God be known, when He shall protect her.

For, behold, the kings of the earth assembled themselves: they gathered together. So they saw; and they wondered, they were troubled; they were moved: trembling took hold of them. There were pains as of a woman in labor; with a vehement wind Thou shalt break in pieces the ships of Tharsis.

As we have heard, so have we seen, in the city of the Lord of hosts, in the city of our God: God hath founded it for ever. We have received Thy mercy, O God, in the midst of Thy temple. According to Thy Name, O God, so also is Thy praise unto the ends of the earth: Thy right hand is full of justice.

Let mount Sion rejoice, and the daughters of Juda be glad; because of Thy judgments, O Lord. Surround Sion, and encompass her: tell ye in her towers. Set your hearts on her strength: and distribute her houses, that ye may relate it in another generation. For this is God, our God unto eternity, and for ever and ever: He shall rule us for evermore.

48 (Heb. 49) Audite haec omnes gentes Hear these things, all ye nations
(Tuesday in the fourth week in Great Lent, if following Old Testament Lections.)
Unto the end, a psalm for the sons of Core.

Hear these things, all ye nations: give ear, all ye inhabitants of the world: All you that are earthborn, and you sons of men: both rich and poor together. My mouth shall speak wisdom: and the meditation of my heart understanding. I will incline my ear to a parable; I will open my proposition on the psaltery.

Why shall I fear in the evil day? The iniquity of my heel shall encompass me. They that trust in their own strength, and glory in the multitude of their riches, No brother can redeem, nor shall man redeem: he shall not give to God his ransom. Nor the price of the redemption of his soul: and shall labor for ever, and shall still live unto the end. He shall not see destruction, when he shall see the wise dying: the senseless and the fool shall perish together. And they shall leave their riches to strangers: and their sepulchres shall be their houses for ever. Their dwelling-places to all generations: they have called their lands by their names.

And man when he was in honor did not understand: he is compared to senseless beasts, and is become like to them. This way of theirs is a stumbling-block to them: and afterwards they shall delight in their mouth. They are laid in hell like sheep: death shall feed upon them. And the just shall have dominion over them in the morning: and their help shall decay in hell from their glory.

But God will redeem my soul from the hand of hell, when He shall receive me. Be not thou afraid when a man shall be made rich: and when the glory of his house shall be increased. For when he shall die he shall take nothing away: nor shall his glory descend with him. For in his lifetime his soul will be blessed: and he will praise thee when thou shalt do well to him. He shall go in to the generations of his fathers: and he shall never see light. Man when he was in honor did not understand: he hath been compared to senseless beasts, and made like to them.

49 (Heb. 50) Deus deorum The God of gods, the Lord hath spoken
(Thursday in the fourth week in Great Lent) A psalm for Asaph.

The God of gods, the Lord hath spoken: and He hath called the earth. From the rising of the sun, to the going down thereof: out of Sion the loveliness of His beauty.

God shall come manifestly: our God shall come, and shall not keep silence. A fire shall burn before Him: and a mighty tempest shall be round about Him. He shall call heaven from above: and the earth, to judge His people. Gather ye together His saints to Him: who set His covenant before sacrifices. And the heavens shall declare His justice: for God is judge.

Hear, O my people, and I will speak: O Israel, and I will testify to thee: I am God, thy God. I will not reprove thee for thy sacrifices: and thy burnt-offerings are always in my sight. I will not take calves out of thy house: nor he-goats out of thy flocks. For all the beasts of the woods are mine; the cattle on the hills, and the oxen. I know all the fowls of the air: and with me is the beauty of the field.

If I should be hungry, I would not tell thee: for the world is mine, and the fullness thereof. Shall I eat the flesh of bullocks? Or shall I drink the blood of goats? Offer to God the sacrifice of praise: and pay thy vows to the most High. And call upon me in the day of trouble: I will deliver thee, and thou shalt glorify me.

But to the sinner God hath said: Why dost thou declare my justices, and take my covenant in thy mouth? Seeing thou hast hated discipline: and hast cast my words behind thee. If thou didst see a thief thou didst run with him: and with adulterers thou hast been a partaker. Thy mouth hath abounded with evil: and thy tongue framed deceits. Sitting thou didst speak against thy brother, and didst lay a scandal against thy mother's son: these things hast thou done, and I was silent. Thou thoughtest unjustly that I should be like to thee: but I will reprove thee, and set before thy face.

Understand these things, you that forget God: lest He snatch you away, and there be none to deliver you. The sacrifice of praise shall glorify me: and there is the way by which I will shew him the salvation of God.

50 (Heb. 51) Miserere Have mercy on me, O God (Friday in the fourth week in Great Lent. This Psalm is the first Psalm of daylight for every Church: the Second Hour in the Celtic Hours, and the First Hour in the Byzantine Rite. In the phrase, "...And in sins did my mother conceive me...," "sins" is actually "deficiencies" or "delicto" in Latin, not willful sins or "peccata." This monastic Psalm focuses on the Holy Spirit.)
> Unto the end, a psalm of David, when Nathan the prophet came to him, after he had sinned with Bethsabee.

Have mercy on me, O God, according to Thy great mercy. And according to the multitude of thy tender mercies, blot out my iniquity. Wash me yet more from my iniquity: and cleanse me from my sin. For I know my iniquity: and my sin is always before me.

To Thee only have I sinned, and have done evil before Thee: that Thou mayest be justified in Thy words, and mayest overcome when Thou art judged. For, behold, I was conceived in iniquities: and in sins did my mother conceive me. For, behold, Thou hast loved truth: the uncertain and hidden things of Thy wisdom Thou hast made manifest to me.

Thou shalt sprinkle me with hyssop, and I shall be cleansed: Thou shalt wash me, and I shall be made whiter than snow. To my hearing Thou shalt give joy and gladness: and the bones that have been humbled shall rejoice.

Turn away Thy face from my sins: and blot out all my iniquities. Create a clean heart in me, O God: and renew a right spirit within my bowels. Cast me not away from Thy face: and take not Thy Holy Spirit from me. Restore unto me the joy of Thy salvation: and strengthen me with a perfect spirit.

I will teach the unjust Thy ways: and the wicked shall be converted to Thee. Deliver me from blood, O God, Thou God of my salvation: and my tongue shall extol Thy justice. O Lord, Thou wilt open my lips: and my mouth shall declare Thy praise. For if Thou hadst desired sacrifice, I would indeed have given it: with burnt-offerings Thou wilt not be delighted. A sacrifice to God is an afflicted spirit: a contrite and humbled heart, O God, Thou wilt not despise.

Deal favorably, O Lord, in Thy good-will with Sion: that the walls of Jerusalem may be built up. Then shalt Thou accept the sacrifice of justice, oblations and whole burnt-offerings: then shall they lay calves upon Thy altar.

Psalm Table of St. Mael Ruain: *Quid gloriatur* to *Te decet*, 51-63 [13 Psalms], Tuesday Beginning of Night (modern Monday night).

51 (Heb. 52) Quid gloriaris Why dost thou glory in malice (Saturday in the fourth week in Great Lent)
Unto the end, understanding for David, when Doeg the Edomite came and told Saul: David went to the house of Achimelech.

Why dost thou glory in malice, thou that art mighty in iniquity? All the day long thy tongue hath devised injustice: as a sharp razor, thou hast wrought deceit. Thou hast loved malice more than goodness: and iniquity rather than to speak righteousness. Thou hast loved all the words of ruin, O deceitful tongue. Therefore will God destroy thee for ever. He will pluck thee out, and remove thee from thy dwelling-place: and thy root out of the land of the living.

The just shall see and fear, and shall laugh at him, and say: Behold the man that made not God his helper: But trusted in the abundance of his riches: and prevailed in his vanity. But I, as a fruitful olive-tree in the house of God, have hoped in the mercy of God for ever: yea for ever and ever. I will praise Thee for ever, because Thou hast done it: and I will wait on Thy Name, for it is good in the sight of Thy saints.

52 (Heb. 53) Dixit insipiens The fool hath said in his heart (Fifth Sunday in Great Lent, warning against atheism, as in Psalm 13. The Gospel is Caiphas plotting against Jesus.) Unto the end, for Maeleth, understandings to David.

The fool said in his heart: There is no God. They are corrupted, and become abominable in iniquities: there is none that doth good.

God looked down from heaven on the children of men: to see if there were any that did understand, or did seek God. All have gone aside, they are become unprofitable together: there is none that doth good, no not one.

Shall not all the workers of iniquity know, who eat up my people as they eat bread? They have not called upon God: there have they trembled for fear, where there was no fear. For God hath scattered the bones of them that please men: they have been confounded, because God hath despised them.

Who will give out of Sion the salvation of Israel? When God shall bring back the captivity of His people, Jacob shall rejoice, and Israel shall be glad.

53 (Heb. 54) Deus in nomine tuo Save me, O God, by Thy Name (Monday in the fifth week in Great Lent)
Unto the end, in verses, understanding to David, when the men of Zion had come and said to Saul, is not David hidden with us?

Save me, O God, by Thy Name: and judge me in Thy strength. O God, hear my prayer: give ear to the words of my mouth. For strangers have risen up against me, and the mighty have sought after my soul: and they have not set God before their eyes.

For, behold, God is my helper: and the Lord is the protector of my soul. Turn back the evils upon my enemies: and cut them off in Thy truth.

I will freely sacrifice to Thee, and will give praise, O God, to Thy Name: because it is good: For Thou hast delivered me out of all trouble: and my eye hath looked down upon my enemies.

54 (Heb. 55) Exaudi Deus Hear, O God, my prayer (Tuesday in the fifth week in Great Lent) Unto the end, in verses, understanding for David.

Hear, O God, my prayer and despise not my supplication: be attentive to me and hear me. I am grieved in my exercise: and am troubled, at the voice of the enemy, and at the tribulation of the sinner. For they have cast iniquities upon me: and in wrath they were troublesome to me.

My heart is troubled within me: and the fear of death is fallen upon me. Fear and trembling are come upon me: and darkness hath covered me. And I said: Who will give me wings like a dove, and I will fly and be at rest? Lo, I have gone far off, flying away: and I abode in the wilderness. I waited for Him that hath saved me from pusillanimity of spirit and a storm.

Cast down, O Lord, and divide their tongues: for I have seen iniquity and contradiction in the city. Day and night shall iniquity surround it upon its walls: and in the midst thereof are labor and injustice. And usury and deceit have not departed from its streets. For if my enemy had reviled me, I would verily have borne with it. And if he that hated me had spoken great things against me, I would perhaps have hidden myself from him. But Thou a man of one mind: my guide, and my familiar: Who didst take sweet meats together with me: in the house of God we walked with consent.

Let death come upon them: and let them go down alive into hell. For there is wickedness in their dwellings: in the midst of them. But I have cried to God: and the Lord will save me. Evening and morning, and at noon, I will speak and declare: and He shall hear my voice. He shall redeem my soul in peace from them that draw near to me: for among many they were with me.

God shall hear: and the Eternal shall humble them. For there is no change with them, and they have not feared God: He hath stretched forth His hand to repay. They have defiled His covenant, they are divided by the wrath of His countenance: and His heart hath drawn near. His words are smoother than oil: and the same are darts.

Cast thy care upon the Lord, and He shall sustain thee: He shall not suffer the just to waver for ever. But Thou, O God, shalt bring them down into the pit of destruction. Bloody and deceitful men shall not live out half their days: but I will trust in Thee, O Lord.

55 (Heb. 56) Miserere mei Deus Have mercy on me, O God, for man
(Wednesday in the fifth week in Great Lent)

>Unto the end, for a people that is removed at a distance from the sanctuary, for David, for an inscription of a title (or pillar)when the Philistines held him in Geth.

Have mercy on me, O God, for man hath trodden me under foot: all the day long he hath afflicted me fighting against me. My enemies have trodden on me all the day long: for they are many that make war against me. From the height of the day I shall fear: but I will trust in Thee.

In God I will praise my words, in God I have put my trust: I will not fear what flesh can do against me. All the day long they detested my words: all their thoughts were against me unto evil. They will dwell and hide themselves: they will watch my heel. As they have waited for my soul, for nothing shalt Thou save them: in Thy anger Thou shalt break the people in pieces.

O God, I have declared to Thee my life: Thou hast set my tears in Thy sight. As also in Thy promise: then shall my enemies be turned back. In what day soever I shall call upon Thee, behold, I know Thou art my God. In God will I praise the word, in the Lord will I praise His speech: in God have I hoped, I will not fear what man can do to me.

In me, O God, are vows to Thee, which I will pay, praises to Thee: Because Thou hast delivered my soul from death, my feet from falling: that I may please in the sight of God, in the light of the living.

56 (Heb. 57) Miserere mei Deus Have mercy on me, O God, have mercy
(Thursday in the fifth week in Great Lent)

>Unto the end, destroy not, for David, for an inscription of a title, when he fled from Saul into the cave.

Have mercy on me, O God, have mercy on me: for my soul trusteth in Thee. And in the shadow of Thy wings will I hope, until iniquity pass away. I will cry to God the most High: to God Who hath done good to me. He hath sent from heaven and delivered me: He hath made them a reproach that trod upon me. God hath sent His mercy and His truth, and He hath delivered my soul from the midst of the young lions: I slept troubled. The sons of men, whose teeth are weapons and arrows: and their tongue a sharp sword.

Be Thou exalted, O God, above the heavens: and Thy glory above all the earth. They prepared a snare for my feet: and they bowed down my soul. They dug a pit before my face: and they are fallen into it. My heart is ready, O God, my heart is ready: I will sing, and rehearse a psalm. Arise, O my glory. Arise psaltery and harp: I will arise early. I will give praise to Thee, O Lord, among the people: I will sing a psalm to Thee among the nations: For Thy mercy is magnified even to the heavens; and Thy truth unto the clouds. Be Thou exalted, O God, above the heavens: and Thy glory above all the earth.

57 (Heb. 58) Si vere utique If in very deed you speak justice (Friday in the fifth week in Great Lent) Unto the end, destroy not, for David, for an inscription of a title.

If in very deed you speak justice: judge right things, ye sons of men. For in your heart you work iniquity: your hands forge injustice in the earth. The wicked are alienated from the womb; they have gone astray from the womb: they have spoken false things.

Their madness is according to the likeness of a serpent: like the deaf asp that stoppeth her ears: Which will not hear the voice of the charmers: nor of the wizard that charmeth wisely. God shall break in pieces their teeth in their mouth: the Lord shall break the grinders of the lions. They shall come to nothing, like water running down: He hath bent His bow till they be weakened. Like wax that melteth they shall be taken away: fire hath fallen on them, and they shall not see the sun. Before your thorns could know the brier: He swalloweth them up, as alive, in His wrath.

The just shall rejoice when he shall see the revenge: he shall wash his hands in the blood of the sinner. And man shall say: If indeed there be fruit to the just: there is indeed a God that judgeth them on the earth.

58 (Heb. 59) Eripe me Deliver me from my enemies, O my God (Saturday in the fifth week in Great Lent)

Unto the end, destroy not, for David, for an inscription of a title, when Saul sent and watched his house to kill him.

Deliver me from my enemies, O my God: and defend me from them that rise up against me. Deliver me from them that work iniquity: and save me from bloody men. For, behold, they have caught my soul: the mighty have rushed in upon me. Neither is it my iniquity, nor my sin, O Lord: without iniquity have I run, and directed my steps.

Rise up Thou to meet me, and behold: even Thou, O Lord, the God of hosts, the God of Israel; Attend to visit all the nations: have no mercy on all them that work iniquity. They shall return at evening, and shall suffer hunger like dogs; and shall go round about the city. Behold, they shall speak with their mouth, and a sword is in their lips: for, Who, say they, hath heard us? But Thou, O Lord, shalt laugh at them: Thou shalt bring all the nations to nothing.

I will keep my strength to Thee; for Thou art my protector: My God, His mercy shall prevent me. God shall let me see over my enemies; slay them not: lest at any time my people forget. Scatter them by Thy power: and bring them down, O Lord, my protector: For the sin of their mouth, and the word of their lips: and let them be taken in their pride.

And for their cursing and lying they shall be talked of when they are consumed: when they are consumed by Thy wrath; and they shall be no more. And they shall know that God will rule Jacob: and all the ends of the earth. They shall return at evening and shall suffer hunger like dogs: and shall go round about the city. They shall be scattered abroad to eat: and shall murmur if they be not filled.

But I will sing Thy strength: and will extol Thy mercy in the morning. For Thou art become my support and my refuge, in the day of my trouble. Unto Thee, O my helper, will I sing, for Thou art God, my defense: my God, my mercy.

59 (Heb. 60) Deus repulisti nos O God, Thou hast cast us off (Sixth Sunday in Great Lent, Palm Sunday. The Gospel is the Entrance into Jerusalem.)
>Unto the end, for them that shall be changed, for the inscription of a title, to David himself, for doctrine, when he set fire to Mesopotamia of Syria and Sobal; and Joab returned and slew of Edom, in the vale of the saltpits; twelve thousand men.

O God, Thou hast cast us off, and hast destroyed us: Thou hast been angry, and hast had mercy on us. Thou hast moved the earth, and hast troubled it: heal Thou the breaches thereof, for it has been moved.

Thou hast shewn Thy people hard things: Thou hast made us drink the wine of sorrow. Thou hast given a warning to them that fear Thee: that they may flee from before the bow: That Thy beloved may be delivered: save me with Thy right hand, and hear me.

God hath spoken in His holy place: I will rejoice, and I will divide Sichem: and will mete out the vale of tabernacles. Galaad is mine, and Manasses is mine: and Ephraim is the strength of my head. Juda is my king: Moab is the pot of my hope. Into Edom will I stretch out my shoe: to me the foreigners are made subject.

Who will bring me into the strong city? Who will lead me into Edom? Wilt not Thou, O God, Who hast cast us off? And wilt not Thou, O God, go out with our armies? Give us help from trouble: for vain is the salvation of man. Through God we shall do mightily: and He shall bring to nothing them that afflict us.

60 (Heb. 61) Exaudi Deus Hear, O God, my supplication (Monday in Holy Week, Sunday evening) Unto the end, in hymns, for David.

Hear, O God, my supplication: be attentive to my prayer. To Thee have I cried from the ends of the earth: when my heart was in anguish, Thou hast exalted me on a rock. Thou hast conducted me; for Thou hast been my hope; a tower of strength against the face of the enemy. In Thy tabernacle I shall dwell for ever: I shall be protected under the covert of Thy wings.

For Thou, my God, hast heard my prayer: Thou hast given an inheritance to them that fear Thy Name. Thou wilt add days to the days of the king: his years even to generation and generation. He abideth for ever in the sight of God: his mercy and truth who shall search? So will I sing a psalm to Thy Name for ever and ever: that I may pay my vows from day to day.

61 (Heb. 62) Nonne Deo Shall not my soul be subject to God? (Tuesday in Holy Week, Monday evening) Unto the end, for Idithan, a psalm of David.

Shall not my soul be subject to God? For from Him is my salvation: For He is my God and my Savior: He is my protector; I shall be moved no more. How long do you rush in upon a man? You all kill: as if you were thrusting down a leaning wall, and a tottering fence. But they have thought to cast away my price; I ran in thirst: they blessed with their mouth, but cursed with their heart.

But be thou, O my soul, subject to God: for from Him is my patience. For He is my God and my Savior: He is my helper, I shall not be moved. In God is my salvation and my glory: He is the God of my help, and my hope is in God. Trust in Him, all ye congregation of people: pour out your hearts before Him: God is our helper for ever.

But vain are the sons of men, the sons of men are liars in the balances: that by vanity they may together deceive. Trust not in iniquity, and cover not robberies: if riches abound, set not your heart upon them.

God hath spoken once. These two things have I heard: that power belongeth to God, and mercy to Thee, O Lord; for Thou wilt render to every man according to his works.

62 (Heb. 63) Deus Deus meus ad te O God, my God, to Thee do I watch (Wednesday in Holy Week, Tuesday evening. Repeated Holy Thursday.) A psalm of David, when he was in the desert of Edom.

O God, my God, to Thee do I watch at break of day. For Thee my soul hath thirsted. For Thee my flesh, O how many ways! In a desert land, and where there is no way and no water: so in the sanctuary have I come before Thee, to see Thy power and Thy glory. For Thy mercy is better than lives: Thee my lips shall praise. Thus will I bless Thee all my life long: and in Thy Name I will lift up my hands.

Let my soul be filled as with marrow and fatness: and my mouth shall praise Thee with joyful lips. If I have remembered Thee upon my bed, I will meditate on Thee in the morning: because Thou hast been my helper. And I will rejoice under the covert of Thy wings. My soul hath stuck close to Thee: Thy right hand hath received me. But they have sought my soul in vain; they shall go into the lower parts of the earth: They shall be delivered into the hands of the sword; they shall be the portions of foxes.

But the King shall rejoice in God; all they shall be praised that swear by Him: because the mouth is stopped of them that speak wicked things.

63 (Heb. 64) Exaudi Deus orationem Hear, O God, my prayer (Holy Thursday, and Wednesday evening. Note: there are no Psalms on Holy and Great Friday, but the Passion Gospels. See that section in the Breviary.) Unto the end, a psalm for David.

Hear, O God, my prayer, when I make supplication to Thee: deliver my soul from the fear of the enemy. Thou hast protected me from the assembly of the malignant: from the multitude of the workers of iniquity.

For they have whetted their tongues like a sword: they have bent their bow, a bitter thing, to shoot in secret the undefiled. They will shoot at him on a sudden, and will not fear: they are resolute in wickedness. They have talked of hiding snares: they have said: Who shall see them? They have searched after iniquities: they have failed in their search.

Man shall come to a deep heart: and God shall be exalted. The arrows of children are their wounds: and their tongues against them are made weak. All that saw them were troubled: and every man was afraid. And they declared the works of God: and understood His doings. The just shall rejoice in the Lord, and shall hope in Him; and all the upright in heart shall be praised.

Psalm Table of St. Mael Ruain: *Te decet* to *Voce.* 64-75 [12 Psalms], Tuesday Midnight (modern Monday night).

---

64 (Heb. 65) Te decet   A hymn, O God, becometh Thee in Sion (Holy and Great Saturday)

> To the end, a psalm of David, the canticle of Jeremias and Ezechiel to the people of the captivity, when they began to go out.

A hymn, O God, becometh Thee in Sion: and a vow shall be paid to Thee in Jerusalem. O hear my prayer: all flesh shall come to Thee.

The words of the wicked have prevailed over us: and Thou wilt pardon our transgressions. Blessed is He Whom Thou hast chosen and taken to Thee: He shall dwell in Thy courts. We shall be filled with the good things of Thy house: holy is Thy temple, wonderful in justice. Hear us, O God our Savior, Who art the hope of all the ends of the earth, and in the sea afar off. Thou Who preparest the mountains by Thy strength, being girded with power: Who troublest the depth of the sea, the noise of its waves.

The Gentiles shall be troubled, and they that dwell in the uttermost borders shall be afraid at Thy signs: Thou shalt make the outgoings of the morning and of the evening to be joyful. Thou hast visited the earth, and hast plentifully watered it: Thou hast many ways enriched it. The river of God is filled with water: Thou hast prepared their food: for so is its preparation. Fill up plentifully the streams thereof; multiply its fruits: it shall spring up and rejoice in its showers.

Thou shalt bless the crown of the year of Thy goodness: and Thy fields shall be filled with plenty. The beautiful places of the wilderness shall grow fat: and the hills shall be girded about with joy. The rams of the flock are clothed; and the vales shall abound with corn: they shall shout; yea, they shall sing a hymn.

65 (Heb. 66) Jubilate Deo Shout with joy to God (Pascha according to St. Columbanus of Luxeiul, with Psalm 150 as the Alleluia.)
>Unto the end, a canticle of a psalm of the resurrrection.

Shout with joy to God, all the earth: sing ye a Psalm to His Name: give glory to His praise. Say unto God: How terrible are Thy works, O Lord! In the multitude of Thy strength Thy enemies shall lie to Thee. Let all the earth adore Thee and sing to Thee: let it sing a Psalm to Thy Name.

Come and see the works of God: Who is terrible in His counsels over the sons of men. Who turneth the sea into dry land: in the river they shall pass on foot: there shall we rejoice in Him. Who by His power ruleth for ever; His eyes behold the nations: let not them that provoke Him be exalted in themselves.

O bless our God, ye Gentiles: and make the voice of His praise to be heard. Who hath set my soul to live: and hath not suffered my feet to be moved. For Thou, O God, hast proved us: Thou hast tried us by fire, as silver is tried. Thou hast brought us into a net; Thou hast laid afflictions on our back: Thou hast set men over our heads. We have passed through fire and water: and Thou hast brought us out into a refreshment.

I will go into Thy house with burnt-offerings: I will pay Thee my vows, which my lips have uttered, And my mouth hath spoken, when I was in trouble. I will offer up to Thee holocausts full of marrow, with burnt-offerings of rams: I will offer to Thee bullocks with goats.

Come and hear, all ye that fear God; and I will tell you what great things He hath done for my soul. I cried to Him with my mouth, and I extolled Him with my tongue. If I have looked at iniquity in my heart, the Lord will not hear me. Therefore hath God heard me, and hath attended to the voice of my supplication. Blessed be God, Who hath not turned away my prayer, nor His mercy from me.

66 (Heb. 67) Deus misereatur May God have mercy on us and bless us (Second Sunday after Pascha; Gospel is "For God so loved the world...". Note: First Sunday after Pascha uses part of the Song of the Three Youths instead of a Psalm.)
>Unto the end, in hymns, a psalm of a canticle for David.

May God have mercy on us, and bless us: may He cause the light of His countenance to shine upon us; and may He have mercy on us.

That we may know Thy way upon earth: Thy salvation in all nations.

Let people confess to Thee, O God: let all people give praise to Thee.

Let the nations be glad and rejoice: for thou judgest the people with justice and directest the nations upon earth.

Let the people, O God, confess to Thee: let all the people give praise to Thee: the earth hath yielded her fruit.

May God, our God bless us. May God bless us: and all the ends of the earth fear Him.

67 (Heb. 68) Exurgat Deus Let God arise (Third Sunday after Pascha; in the Gospel, Christ offers "living water," the woman at the well.)

Unto the end, a psalm of a canticle for David himself.

Let God arise, and let His enemies be scattered: and let them that hate Him flee from before His Face. As smoke vanisheth, so let them vanish away: as wax melteth before the fire, so let the wicked perish at the presence of God. And let the just feast and rejoice before God: and be delighted with gladness.

Sing ye to God; sing a psalm to His Name: make a way for Him Who ascendeth upon the west, The Lord is His Name. Rejoice ye before Him: but the wicked shall be troubled at His presence, Who is the Father of orphans, and the Judge of widows. God in His holy place: God Who maketh men of one manner to dwell in a house: Who bringeth out them that were bound in strength; in like manner them that provoke, that dwell in sepulchres.

O God, when Thou didst go forth in the sight of Thy people, when Thou didst pass through the desert: The earth was moved, and the heavens dropped at the presence of the God of Sina, at the presence of the God of Israel. Thou shalt set aside for Thy inheritance a free rain, O God: and it was weakened, but Thou hast made it perfect. In it shall Thy animals dwell: in Thy sweetness, O God, Thou hast provided for the poor. The Lord shall give the word to them that preach good things with great power.

The King of powers is of the beloved, of the beloved: and the beauty of the house shall divide spoils. If you sleep among the midst of lots, you shall be as the wings of a dove covered with silver, and the hinder parts of her back with the paleness of gold. When he that is in heaven appointeth kings over her, they shall be whited with snow in Selmon. The mountain of God is a fat mountain: A curdled mountain, a fat mountain. Why suspect, ye curdled mountains? A mountain in which God is well pleased to dwell: for there the Lord shall dwell unto the end.

The chariot of God is attended by ten thousands; thousands of them that rejoice: the Lord is among them in Sina, in the holy place. Thou hast ascended on high: Thou hast led captivity captive: Thou hast received gifts in men: Yea for those also that do not believe, the dwelling of the Lord God. Blessed be the Lord day by day: the God of our salvation will make our journey prosperous to us.

Our God is the God of salvation: and of the Lord, of the Lord, are the issues from death. But God shall break the heads of His enemies: the hairy crown of them that walk on in their sins. The Lord said: I will turn them from Basan; I will turn them into the depth of the sea: That thy foot may be dipped in the blood of thy enemies: the tongue of thy dogs be red with the same. They have seen Thy goings, O God, the goings of my God: of my king Who is in His sanctuary.

Princes went before joined with singers, in the midst of young damsels playing on timbrels. In the churches bless ye God the Lord, from the fountains of Israel. There is Benjamin a youth, in ecstasy of mind. The princes of Juda are their leaders: the princes of Zabulon, the princes of Nephthali. Command Thy strength, O God: confirm, O God, what Thou hast wrought in us. From Thy temple in Jerusalem, kings shall offer presents to Thee.

Rebuke the wild beasts of the reeds, the congregation of bulls with the king of the people; who seek to exclude them who are tried with silver. Scatter Thou the nations that delight in wars. Ambassadors shall come out of Egypt: Ethiopia shall soon stretch out her hands to God.

Sing to God, ye kingdoms of the earth: sing ye to the Lord: Sing ye to God, Who mounteth above the heaven of heavens, to the east. Behold, He will give to His voice the voice of power. Give ye glory to God for Israel; His magnificence, and His power is in the clouds. God is wonderful in His saints; the God of Israel is He Who will give power and strength to His people. Blessed be God.

68 (Heb. 69) Salvum me fac Deus Save, me, O God, for the waters (Mid-Pascha, Wednesday after the Third Sunday after Pascha; the Icon is often Christ teaching at age twelve in the temple, and in the Byzantine Rite the day is described as a meditation on the waters of Baptism in Paschaltide. The Gospel is Jesus eating with His disciples, the theme of Paschaltide.) Unto the end, for them that shall be changed, for David.

Save me, O God: for the waters are come in even unto my soul. I stick fast in the mire of the deep: and there is no sure standing. I am come into the depth of the sea: and a tempest hath overwhelmed me. I have labored with crying; my jaws are become hoarse: my eyes have failed, whilst I hope in my God. They are multiplied above the hairs of my head, who hate me without cause. My enemies are grown strong who have wrongfully persecuted me: then did I pay that which I took not away.

O God, Thou knowest my foolishness; and my offences are not hidden from Thee: Let not them be ashamed for me, who look for Thee, O Lord, the Lord of hosts. Let them not be confounded on my account, who seek Thee, O God of Israel. Because for Thy sake I have borne reproach; shame hath covered my face. I am become a stranger to my brethren: and an alien to the sons of my mother. For the zeal of Thy house hath eaten me up: and the reproaches of them that reproached Thee are fallen upon me. And I covered my soul in fasting: and it was made a reproach to me. And I made haircloth my garment: and I became a byword to them. They that sat in the gate spoke against me: and they that drank wine made me their song.

But as for me, my prayer is to Thee, O Lord; for the time of Thy good pleasure, O God. In the multitude of Thy mercy hear me, in the truth of Thy salvation. Draw me out of the mire, that I may not stick fast: deliver me from them that hate me, and out of the deep waters. Let not the tempest of water drown me, nor the deep swallow me up: and let not the pit shut her mouth upon me.

Hear me, O Lord, for Thy mercy is kind; look upon me according to the multitude of Thy tender mercies. And turn not away Thy face from Thy servant: for I am in trouble. Hear me speedily. Attend to my soul, and deliver it: save me because of my enemies. Thou knowest my reproach, and my confusion, and my shame. In Thy sight are all they that afflict me: my heart hath expected reproach and misery. And I looked for one that would grieve together with me, but there was none: and for one that would comfort me, and I found none. And they gave me gall for my food, and in my thirst they gave me vinegar to drink. Let their table become as a snare before them, and a recompense, and a stumbling-block. Let their eyes be darkened that they see not: and their back bend Thou down always. Pour out Thy indignation upon them: and let Thy wrathful anger take hold of them. Let their habitation be made desolate: and let there be none to dwell in their tabernacles. Because they have persecuted him whom Thou hast smitten; and they have added to the grief of my wounds. Add Thou iniquity upon their iniquity: and let them not come into Thy justice. Let them be blotted out of the book of the living: and with the just let them not be written.

But I am poor and sorrowful: Thy salvation, O God, hath set me up. I will praise the Name of God with a canticle: and I will magnify Him with praise. And it shall please God better than a young calf, that bringeth forth horns and hoofs. Let the poor see and rejoice: seek ye God, and your soul shall live. For the Lord hath heard the poor: and hath not despised His prisoners. Let the heavens and the earth praise Him; the sea, and every thing that creepeth therein. For God will save Sion: and the cities of Juda shall be built up. And they shall dwell there, and acquire it by inheritance. And the seed of His servants shall possess it; and they that love His Name shall dwell therein.

69 (Heb. 70) Deus in adjutorium O God, come to my assistance (Fourth Sunday after Pascha; in the Gospel, Christ cures a man born blind. The first line of this Psalm is repeated as a continuous prayer by the Desert Fathers of Sceti, and Irish monks.) Unto the end, a psalm for David, to bring to remembrance that the Lord saved him.

O God, come to my assistance: O Lord, make haste to help me.

Let them be confounded and ashamed that seek my soul: Let them be turned backward and blush for shame, that desire evils to me: Let them be presently turned away blushing for shame, that say to me: 'Tis well, 'tis well.

Let all that seek Thee rejoice and be glad in Thee; and let such as love Thy salvation say always: the Lord be magnified. But I am needy and poor: O God, help me. Thou art my helper and my deliverer: O Lord, make no delay.

70 (Heb. 71) In te Domine In Thee, O Lord, have I hoped (Fifth Sunday after Pascha; in the Gospel, Christ cures a deaf and dumb man.)
A psalm for David, of the sons of Jonadab, and the former captives.

In Thee, O Lord, I have hoped: let me never be put to confusion: deliver me in Thy justice, and rescue me. Incline Thy ear unto me, and save me. Be Thou unto me a God, a protector, and a place of strength: that Thou mayst make me safe. For Thou art my firmament and my refuge. Deliver me, O my God, out of the hand of the sinner, and out of the hand of the transgressor of the law and of the unjust: For Thou art my patience, O Lord: my hope, O Lord, from my youth. By Thee have I been confirmed from the womb: from my mother's womb Thou art my protector. Of Thee shall I continually sing: I am become unto many as a wonder: but Thou art a strong helper.

Let my mouth be filled with praise, that I may sing Thy glory: Thy greatness all the day long. Cast me not off in the time of old age: when my strength shall fail, do not Thou forsake me. For my enemies have spoken against me: and they that watched my soul have consulted together, Saying: God hath forsaken him, pursue and take him: for there is none to deliver him.

O God, be not Thou far from me: O my God, make haste to my help. Let them be confounded and come to nothing that detract my soul: let them be covered with confusion and shame that seek my hurt. But I will always hope, and will add to all Thy praise. My mouth shall shew forth Thy justice: Thy salvation all the day long. Because I have not known learning, I will enter into the powers of the Lord: O Lord, I will be mindful of Thy justice alone.

Thou hast taught me, O God, from my youth: and till now I will declare Thy wonderful works. And unto old age and grey hairs: O God, forsake me not, Until I shew forth Thy arm to all the generation that is to come: Thy power, and Thy justice, O God, even to the highest great things Thou hast done: O God, Who is like to Thee? How great troubles hast Thou shewn me, many and grievous: and turning Thou hast brought me to life, and hast brought me back again from the depths of the earth.

Thou hast multiplied Thy magnificence: and turning to me Thou hast comforted me. For I will also confess to Thee Thy truth with the instruments of psaltery: O God, I will sing to Thee with the harp, Thou holy one of Israel. My lips shall greatly rejoice, when I shall sing to Thee: and my soul which Thou hast redeemed. Yea and my tongue shall meditate on Thy justice all the day: when they shall be confounded and put to shame that seek evils to me.

71 (Heb. 72) Deus judicium tuum Give to the king Thy judgment, O God
(The Ascension into heaven of our Lord Jesus Christ, Thursday. Gospel: "I shall go and prepare a place for you."... "the way, the truth, and the life") A psalm on Solomon.

Give to the King Thy judgment, O God: and to the King's Son Thy justice: To judge Thy people with justice, and Thy poor with judgment.

Let the mountains receive peace for the people: and the hills justice. He shall judge the poor of the people: and He shall save the children of the poor: and He shall humble the oppressor. And He shall continue with the sun, and before the moon, throughout all generations. He shall come down like rain upon the fleece: and as showers falling gently upon the earth. In His days shall justice spring up, and abundance of peace, till the moon be taken away. And He shall rule from sea to sea: and from the river unto the ends of the earth.

Before Him the Ethiopians shall fall down: and His enemies shall lick the ground. The kings of Tharsis and the islands shall offer presents: the kings of the Arabians and of Saba shall bring gifts. And all kings of the earth shall adore Him: all nations shall serve Him. For He shall deliver the poor from the mighty: and the needy that had no helper. He shall spare the poor and needy: and He shall save the souls of the poor. He shall redeem their souls from usuries and iniquity: and their names shall be honorable in His sight. And He shall live, and to Him shall be given of the gold of Arabia. For Him they shall always adore: they shall bless Him all the day. And there shall be a firmament on the earth on the tops of mountains: above Libanus shall the fruit thereof be exalted. And they of the city shall flourish like the grass of the earth.

Let His Name be blessed for evermore: His Name continueth before the sun. And in Him shall all the tribes of the earth be blessed: all nations shall magnify Him. Blessed be the Lord, the God of Israel, Who alone doth wonderful things. And blessed be the Name of His majesty for ever: and the whole earth shall be filled with His majesty. So be it. So be it. The praises of David, the son of Jesse, are ended.

72 (Heb. 73) Quam bonus Israel Deus How good is God to Israel (Sunday after Ascension; Gospel St. John 17, Jesus' prayer for the whole world.) A psalm for Asaph.

How good is God to Israel: to them that are of a right heart! But my feet were almost moved; my steps had well nigh slipped. Because I had a zeal on occasion of the wicked, seeing the prosperity of sinners. For there is no regard to their death, nor is there strength in their stripes. They are not in the labor of men: neither shall they be scourged like other men. Therefore pride hath held them fast: they are covered with their iniquity and their wickedness. Their iniquity hath come forth, as it were from fatness: they have passed into the affection of the heart. They have thought and spoken wickedness: they have spoken iniquity on high. They have set their mouth against heaven: and their tongue hath passed through the earth. Therefore will my people return here: and full days shall be found in them.

And they said: How doth God know? And is there knowledge in the most High? Behold, these are sinners; and yet abounding in the world they have obtained riches. And I said: Then have I in vain justified my heart, and washed my hands among the innocent. And I have been scourged all the day; and my chastisement hath been in the mornings. If I said: I will speak thus; behold, I should condemn the generation of thy children. I studied that I might know this thing: it is a labor in my sight: Until I go into the sanctuary of God, and understand concerning their last ends. But indeed for deceits Thou hast put it to them: when they were lifted up Thou hast cast them down. How are they brought to desolation? They have suddenly ceased to be: they have perished by reason of their iniquity. As the dream of them that awake, O Lord; so in Thy city Thou shalt bring their image to nothing.

For my heart hath been inflamed, and my reins have been changed: and I am brought to nothing, and I knew not. I am become as a beast before Thee: and I am always with Thee. Thou hast held me by my right hand; and by Thy will Thou hast conducted me; and with Thy glory Thou hast received me.

For what have I in heaven? And besides Thee what do I desire upon earth? For Thee my flesh and my heart hath fainted away: Thou art the God of my heart, and the God that is my portion for ever. For behold, they that go far from Thee shall perish: Thou hast destroyed all them that are disloyal to Thee.

But it is good for me to adhere to my God, to put my hope in the Lord God: That I may declare all Thy praises, in the gates of the daughter of Sion.

73 (Heb. 74) Ut quid Deus O God, why hast Thou cast us off unto the end (Thursday after 1 Pentecost. Pentecost uses a different Psalm, and the first Sunday after Pentecost is an All-Saints Sunday, with a different Psalm.) Understanding for Asaph.

O God, why hast Thou cast us off unto the end? Why is Thy wrath enkindled against the sheep of Thy pasture?

Remember Thy congregation, which Thou hast possessed from the beginning: The sceptre of Thy inheritance which Thou hast redeemed: Mount Sion in which Thou hast dwelt.

Lift up Thy hands against their pride unto the end; see what things the enemy hath done wickedly in the sanctuary. And they that hate Thee have made their boasts, in the midst of Thy solemnity. They have set up their ensigns for signs, and they knew not both in the going out and on the highest top. As with axes in a wood of trees, they have cut down at once the gates thereof: with axe and hatchet they have brought it down. They have set fire to Thy sanctuary: they have defiled the dwelling-place of Thy Name on the earth. They said in their heart, the whole kindred of them together: Let us abolish all the festival days of God from the land. Our signs we have not seen; there is now no prophet: and he will know us no more. How long, O God, shall the enemy reproach? Is the adversary to provoke Thy Name for ever? Why dost Thou turn away Thy hand? And Thy right hand out of the midst of Thy bosom for ever?

But God is our king before ages: He hath wrought salvation in the midst of the earth. Thou by Thy strength didst make the sea firm: Thou didst crush the heads of the dragons in the waters. Thou hast broken the heads of the dragon: Thou hast given him to be meat for the people of the Ethiopians. Thou hast broken up the fountains and the torrents: Thou hast dried up the Ethan rivers. Thine is the day, and Thine is the night: Thou hast made the morning light and the sun. Thou hast made all the borders of the earth: the summer and the spring were formed by Thee.

Remember this, the enemy hath reproached the Lord: and a foolish people hath provoked Thy Name. Deliver not up to beasts the souls that confess to Thee: and forget not to the end the souls of Thy poor. Have regard to Thy covenant: for they that are the obscure of the earth have been filled with dwellings of iniquity. Let not the humble be turned away with confusion: the poor and needy shall priase Thy Name.

Arise, O God, judge Thy own cause: remember Thy reproaches with which the foolish man hath reproached Thee all the day. Forget not the voices of Thy enemies: the pride of them that hate Thee ascendeth continually.

74 (Heb. 75) Confitebimur tibi We will praise Thee, O God (Sunday 2 Pentecost) Unto the end, corrupt not, a psalm of a canticle for Asaph.

We will praise Thee, O God: we will praise, and we will call upon Thy Name. We will relate Thy wondrous works: when I shall take a time, I will judge justices.

The earth is melted, and all that dwell therein: I have established the pillars thereof.

I said to the wicked: Do not act wickedly: and to the sinners: Lift not up the horn. Lift not up your horn on high: speak not iniquity against God. For neither from the east, nor from the west, nor from the desert hills: for God is the judge.

One He putteth down, and another He lifteth up: for in the hand of the Lord there is a cup of strong wine full of mixture. And He hath poured it out from this to that: but the dregs thereof are not emptied: all the sinners of the earth shall drink.

But I will declare for ever: I will sing to the God of Jacob. And I will break all the horns of sinners: but the horns of the just shall be exalted.

75 (Heb. 76) Notus in Judea In Judea God is known (Thursday after 2 Pentecost) Unto the end, in praises, a psalm for Asaph: a canticle to the Assyrians.

In Judea God is known: His Name is great in Israel. And His place is in peace: and His abode in Sion: There hath He broken the powers of bows: the shield, the sword, and the battle.

Thou enlightenest wonderfully from the everlasting hills: All the foolish of heart were troubled.

They have slept their sleep: and all the men of riches have found nothing in their hands. At Thy rebuke, O God of Jacob, they have all slumbered that mounted on horseback. Thou art terrible, and who shall resist Thee? From that time Thy wrath. Thou hast caused judgment to be heard from heaven: the earth trembled and was still, When God arose in judgment, to save all the meek of the earth.

For the thought of man shall give praise to Thee: and the remainders of the thought shall keep holiday to Thee. Vow ye, and pay to the Lord your God: all you that are round about Him bring presents. To Him that is terrible; even to Him who taketh away the spirit of princes; to the terrible with the kings of the earth.

Psalm Table of St. Mael Ruain: *Voce* to *Misericordias*. 76-87 [12 Psalms], Wednesday Beginning of Night (modern Tuesday night).

---

76 (Heb. 77) Voce mea I cried to the Lord with my voice (Sunday 3 Pentecost) Unto the end, for Idithun, a psalm of Asaph.

I cried to the Lord with my voice: to God with my voice; and He gave ear to me. In the day of my trouble I sought God, with my hands lifted up to Him in the night: and I was not deceived. My soul refused to be comforted: I remembered God, and was delighted, and was exercised; and my spirit swooned away. My eyes prevented the watches: I was troubled, and I spoke not.

I thought upon the days of old: and I had in my mind the eternal years. And I meditated in the night with my own heart: and I was exercised, and I swept my spirit.

Will God then cast off for ever? Or will He never be more favorable again? Or will He cut off His mercy for ever, from generation to generation? Or will God forget to shew mercy? Or will He in His anger shut up His mercies?

And I said: Now have I begun: this is the change of the right hand of the most High. I remembered the works of the Lord: for I will be mindful of Thy wonders from the beginning. And I will meditate on all Thy works: and will be employed in Thy inventions.

Thy way, O God, is in the holy place: who is the great God like our God? Thou art the God that dost wonders. Thou hast made Thy power known among the nations: with Thy arm Thou hast redeemed Thy people, the children of Jacob and of Joseph.

The waters saw Thee, O God, the waters saw Thee: and they were afraid, and the depths were troubled. Great was the noise of the waters: the clouds sent out a sound. For Thy arrows pass: the voice of Thy thunder in a wheel. Thy lightnings enlightened the world: the earth shook and trembled. Thy way is in the sea, and Thy paths in many waters: and Thy footsteps shall not be known. Thou hast conducted Thy people like sheep, by the hand of Moses and Aaron.

77 (Heb. 78) Attendite Attend, O my people, to my law (Thursday after 3 Pentecost) Understanding for Asaph.

Attend, O my people, to my law: incline your ears to the words of my mouth. I will open my mouth in parables: I will utter propositions from the beginning. How great things have we heard and known, and our fathers have told us. They have not been hidden from their children, in another generation. Declaring the praises of the Lord, and His powers, and His wonders which He hath done. And He set up a testimony in Jacob: and made a law in Israel. How great things He commanded our fathers, that they should make the same known to their children: that another generation might know them.

The children that should be born, and should rise up and declare them to their children. That they may put their hope in God and may not forget the works of God: and may seek His commandments. That they may not become like their fathers, a perverse and exasperating generation; A generation that set not their heart aright: and whose spirit was not faithful to God. The sons of Ephraim who bend and shoot with the bow: they have turned back in the day of battle. They kept not the covenant of God: and in His law they would not walk. And they forgot His benefits, and His wonders that He had shown them.

Wonderful things did He do in the sight of their fathers: in the land of Egypt, in the field of Tanis. He divided the sea and brought them through: and He made the waters to stand as in a vessel. And He conducted them with a cloud by day: and all the night with a light of fire. He struck the rock in the wilderness: and gave them to drink, as out of the great deep. He brought forth water out of the rock: and made streams run down as rivers.

And they added yet more sin against Him: they provoked the most High to wrath in the place without water. And they tempted God in their hearts, by asking meat for their desires. And they spoke ill of God: They said: Can God furnish a table in the wilderness? Because He struck the rock, and the waters gushed out, and the streams overflowed. Can He also give bread, or provide a table for His people? Therefore the Lord heard, and was angry: and a fire was kindled against Jacob, and wrath came up against Israel. Because they believed not in God: and trusted not in His salvation.

And He had commanded the clouds from above, and had opened the doors of heaven. And had rained down manna upon them to eat; and had given them the bread of heaven. Man ate the bread of angels: He sent them provisions in abundance. He removed the south wind from heaven: and by His power brought in the southwest wind. And He rained upon them flesh as dust: and feathered fowls like as the sand of the sea. And they fell in the midst of their camp, round about their pavilions. So they did eat, and were filled exceedingly; and He gave them their desire: they were not defrauded of that which they craved.

And yet their meat was in their mouth: and the wrath of God came upon them. And He slew the fat ones amongst them: and brought down the chosen men of Israel. In all these things they sinned still: and they believed not for His wondrous works. And their days were consumed in vanity: and their years in haste. When He slew them, then they sought Him: and they returned, and came to Him early in the morning. And they remembered that God was their helper: and the most high God their redeemer. And they loved Him with their mouth: and with their tongue they lied unto Him. But their heart was not right with Him: nor were they counted faithful in His covenant.

But He is merciful, and will forgive their sins: and will not destroy them. And many a time did He turn away His anger: and did not kindle all

His wrath. And He remembered that they are flesh: a wind that goeth and returneth not. How often did they provoke Him in the desert: and move Him to wrath in the place without water! And they turned back and tempted God: and grieved the holy one of Israel. They remembered not His hand, in the day that He redeemed them from th hand of Him that afflicted them: How He wrought His signs in Egypt, and His wonders in the field of Tanis.

And He turned their rivers into blood: and their showers that they might not drink. He sent amongst them divers sorts of flies, which devoured them: and frogs which destroyed them. And He gave up their fruits to the blast: and their labors to the locust. And He destroyed their vineyards with hail: and their mulberry trees with hoarfrost. And He gave up their cattle to the hail: and their stock to the fire. And He sent upon them the wrath of His indignation: indignation and wrath and trouble: which He sent by evil angels. He made a way for a path to His anger. He spared not their souls from death: and their cattle He shut up in death.

And He killed all the firstborn in the land of Egypt: the firstfruits of all their labor in the tabernacles of Cham. And He took away His own people as sheep: and guided them in the wilderness like a flock. And He brought them out in hope, and they feared not: and the sea overwhelmed their enemies. And He brought them into the mountain of His sanctuary: the mountain which His right hand had purchased. And He cast out the Gentiles before them: and by lot divided to them their land by a line of distribution. And He made the tribes of Israel to dwell in their tabernacles.

Yet they tempted and provoked the most high God: and they kept not His testimonies. And they turned away, and kept not the covenant: even like their fathers they were turned aside as a crooked bow. They provoked Him to anger on their hills: and moved Him to jealousy with their graven things. God heard, and despised them: and He reduced Israel exceedingly, as it were to nothing. And He put away the tabernacle of Silo, His tabernacle where He dwelt among men. And He delivered their strength into captivity: and their beauty into the hands of the enemy. And He shut up His people under the sword: and He despised His inheritance. Fire consumed their young men: and their maidens were not lamented. Their priests fell by the sword: and their widows did not mourn. And the Lord was awaked as one out of sleep, and like a mighty man that hath been surfeited with wine. And He smote His enemies on the hinder parts: He put them to an everlasting reproach.

And He rejected the tabernacle of Joseph: and chose not the tribe of Ephraim. But He chose the tribe of Juda, Mount Sion which He loved. And He built His sanctuary as of unicorns, in the land which He founded for ever. And He chose His servant David, and took him from the flocks of sheep: He brought him from following the ewes great with young. To feed Jacob his servant, and Israel his inheritance. And he fed them in the innocence of his heart: and conducted them by the skilfulness of his hands.

78 (Heb. 79) Deus venerunt gentes O God, the heathens are come (Sunday 4 Pentecost) A psalm for Asaph.

O God, the heathens are come into Thy inheritance; they have defiled Thy holy temple: they have made Jerusalem as a place to keep fruit. They have given the dead bodies of Thy servants to be meat for the fowls of the air: the flesh of Thy saints for the beasts of the earth. They have poured out their blood as water, round about Jerusalem: and there was none to bury them. We are become a reproach to our neighbors: a scorn and derision to them that are round about us. How long, O Lord, wilt Thou be angry for ever? Shall Thy zeal be kindled like a fire? Pour out Thy wrath upon the nations that have not known Thee: and upon the kingdoms that have not called upon Thy Name. Because they have devoured Jacob: and have laid waste his place.

Remember not our former iniquities; let Thy mercies speedily prevent us: for we are become exceeding poor.

Help us, O God, our Savior: and for the glory of Thy Name, O Lord, deliver us: and forgive us our sins for Thy Name's sake: Lest they should say among the Gentiles: Where is their God? And let Him be made known among the nations before our eyes, by the revenging the blood of Thy servants, which hath been shed: let the sighing of the prisoners come in before Thee. According to the greatness of Thy arm, take possession of the children of them that have been put to death. And render to our neighbors sevenfold in their bosom: the reproach wherewith they have reproached Thee, O Lord.

But we Thy people, and the sheep of Thy pasture, will give thanks to Thee for ever: We will shew forth Thy praise, unto generation and generation.

79 (Heb. 80) Qui regis Israel Give ear, O Thou that rulest Israel (Thursday after 4 Pentecost)

Unto the end, for them that shall be changed, a testimony for Asaph, a psalm.

Give ear, O Thou that rulest Israel: Thou that leadest Joseph like a sheep. Thou that sittest upon the cherubims; shine forth before Ephraim, Benjamin, and Manasses: Stir up Thy might, and come to save us.

Convert us, O God, and shew us Thy face: and we shall be saved.

O Lord God of hosts, how long wilt Thou be angry against the prayer of Thy servant? How long wilt Thou feed us with the bread of tears, and give us for our drink tears in measure? Thou hast made us to be a contradiction to our neighbors: and our enemies have scoffed at us.

O God of hosts, convert us, and shew Thy face: and we shall be saved.

Thou hast brought a vineyard out of Egypt: Thou hast cast out the Gentiles and planted it. Thou wast the guide of its journey in its sight: Thou plantedst the roots thereof; and it filled the land. The shadow of it covered the hills: and the branches thereof the cedars of God. It stretched forth its branches unto the sea: and its boughs unto the river.

Why hast Thou broken down the hedge thereof: so that all they who pass by the way do pluck it? The boar out of the wood hath laid it waste: and a singular wild beast hath devoured it. Turn again, O God of hosts: look down from heaven, and see, and visit this vineyard: And perfect the same which Thy right hand hath planted: and upon the Son of man Whom Thou hast confirmed for Thyself.

Things set on fire and dug down shall perish at the rebuke of Thy countenance. Let Thy hand be upon the man of Thy right hand: and upon the Son of man Whom Thou hast confirmed for Thyself. And we depart not from Thee. Thou shalt quicken us: and we will call upon Thy Name. O Lord God of Hosts, convert us; and shew Thy face; and we shall be saved.

80 (Heb. 81) Exultate Deo Rejoice to God our helper (Sunday 5 Pentecost)
Unto the end, for the wine-presses, a psalm for Asaph himself.

Rejoice to God our helper: sing aloud to the God of Jacob. Take a psalm, and bring hither the timbrel: the pleasant psaltery with the harp. Blow up the trumpet on the new moon, on the noted day of your solemnity. For it is a commandment in Israel, and a judgment to the God of Jacob. He ordained it for a testimony in Joseph, when he came out of the land of Egypt: he heard a tongue which he knew not. He removed his back from the burdens: his hands had served in baskets.

Thou calledst upon me in affliction, and I delivered thee: I heard thee in the secret place of tempest: I proved thee at the waters of contradiction.

Hear, O my people, and I will testify to thee: O Israel, if thou wilt hearken to me, there shall be no new god in thee; neither shalt thou adore a strange god.

For I am the Lord thy God, who brought thee out of the land of Egypt: open thy mouth wide, and I will fill it. But my people heard not my voice: and Israel hearkened not to me. So I let them go according to the desires of their heart: they shall walk in their own inventions. If my people had heard me, if Israel had walked in my ways: I should soon have humbled their enemies, and laid my hand on them that troubled them. The enemies of the Lord have lied to Him: and their time shall be for ever.

And He fed them with the fat of wheat: and filled them with honey out of the rock.

81 (Heb. 82) Deus stetit God hath stood in the congregation of gods
(Thursday after 5 Pentecost) A psalm for Asaph.

God hath stood in the congregation of gods: and being in the midst of them He judgeth gods.

How long will you judge unjustly: and accept the persons of the wicked? Judge for the needy and fatherless: do justice to the humble and the poor. Rescue the poor: and deliver the needy out of the hand of the sinner. They have not known nor understood: they walk on in darkness: all the foundations of the earth shall be moved.

I have said: You are gods, and all of you the sons of the most High. But you like men shall die: and shall fall like one of the princes.

Arise, O God, judge Thou the earth: for Thou shalt inherit among all the nations.

82 (Heb. 83) Deus quis similis O God, who shall be like to Thee (Sunday 6 Pentecost) A canticle of a psalm for Asaph.

O God, who shall be like to Thee? Hold not Thy peace, neither be Thou still, O God.

For, lo, Thy enemies have made a noise: and they that hate Thee have lifted up the head. They have taken a malicious counsel against Thy people: and have consulted against Thy saints. They have said: Come and let us destroy them, so that they be not a nation: and let the name of Israel be remembered no more.

For they have contrived with one consent: they have made a covenant together against Thee, the tabernacles of the Edomites, and the Ismahelites: Moab, and the Agarens, Gebal, and Ammon and Amalec: the Philistines, with the inhabitants of Tyre. Yea, and the Assyrian also is joined with them: they are come to the aid of the sons of Lot. Do to them as Thou didst to Madian and to Sisara: as to Jabin at the brook of Cisson. Who perished at Endor: and became as dung for the earth. Make their princes like Oreb, and Zeb, and Zebee, and Salmana.

All their princes, who have said: Let us possess the sanctuary of God for an inheritance. O my God, make them like a wheel: and as stubble before the wind. As fire which burneth the wood: and as a flame burning mountains: So shalt Thou pursue them with Thy tempest: and shalt trouble them in Thy wrath. Fill their faces with shame: and they shall seek Thy Name, O Lord. Let them be ashamed and troubled for ever and ever: and let them be confounded and perish.

And let them know that the Lord is Thy Name: Thou alone art the most High over all the earth.

83 (Heb. 84) Quam dilecta How lovely are Thy tabernacles, O Lord (Thursday after 6 Pentecost) Unto the end, for the wine-presses, a psalm for the sons of Core.

How lovely are Thy tabernacles, O Lord of hosts! My soul longeth and fainteth for the courts of the Lord. My heart and my flesh have rejoiced in the living God.

For the sparrow hath found herself a house: and the turtle a nest for herself where she may lay her young ones: Thy altars, O Lord of hosts: my king and my God.

Blessed are they that dwell in Thy house, O Lord; they shall praise Thee for ever and ever. Blessed is the man whose help is from Thee: in his heart he hath disposed to ascend by steps, in the vale of tears, in the place which he hath set.

For the lawgiver shall give a blessing; they shall go from virtue to virtue: the God of gods shall be seen in Sion. O Lord God of hosts, hear my prayer: give ear, O God of Jacob. Behold, O God our protector: and look on the face of Thy Christ. For better is one day in Thy courts above thousands. I have chosen to be an abject in the house of my God: rather than to dwell in the tabernacles of sinners.

For God loveth mercy and truth: the Lord will give grace and glory. He will not deprive of good things them that walk in innocence: O Lord of hosts, blessed is the man that trusteth in Thee.

84 (Heb. 85) Benedixisti Domine Lord, thou hast blessed Thy land
(Sunday 7 Pentecost) Unto the end, for the sons of Core, a psalm.

Lord, Thou hast blessed Thy land: Thou hast turned away the captivity of Jacob. Thou hast forgiven the iniquity of Thy people: Thou hast covered all their sins. Thou hast mitigated all Thy anger: Thou hast turned away from the wrath of Thy indignation.

Convert us, O God our savior: and turn off Thy anger from us. Wilt Thou be angry with us for ever? Or wilt Thou extend Thy wrath from generation to generation? Thou wilt turn, O God, and bring us to life: and Thy people shall rejoice in Thee.

Shew us, O Lord, Thy mercy: and grant us Thy salvation. I will hear what the Lord God will speak in me: for He will speak peace unto His people. And unto His saints: and unto them that are converted to the heart. Surely His salvation is near to them that fear Him: that glory may dwell in our land.

Mercy and truth have met each other: justice and peace have kissed. Truth is sprung out of the earth: and justice hath looked down from heaven. For the Lord will give goodness: and our earth shall yield her fruit. Justice shall walk before Him: and shall set His steps in the way.

85 (Heb. 86) Inclina Domine Incline Thy ear, O Lord, and hear me
(Thursday after 7 Pentecost) A prayer for David himself.

Incline Thy ear, O Lord, and hear me: for I am needy and poor. Preserve my soul, for I am holy: save Thy servant, O my God, that trusteth in Thee. Have mercy on me, O Lord, for I have cried to Thee all the day. Give joy to the soul of Thy servant, for to Thee, O Lord, I have lifted up my soul. For Thou, O Lord, art sweet and mild: and plenteous in mercy to all that call upon Thee.

Give ear, O Lord, to my prayer: and attend to the voice of my petition. I have called upon Thee in the day of my trouble: because Thou hast heard me. There is none among the gods like unto Thee, O Lord: and there is none according to Thy works. All the nations thou hast made shall come and adore before Thee, O Lord: and they shall glorify Thy Name. For Thou art great and dost wonderful things: Thou art God alone.

Conduct me, O Lord, in Thy way, and I will walk in Thy truth: let my heart rejoice that it may fear Thy Name. I will praise Thee, O Lord my God, with my whole heart: and I will glorify The Name for ever: For Thy mercy is great towards me: and Thou hast delivered my soul out of the lower hell. O God, the wicked are risen up against me, and the assembly of the mighty have sought my soul: and they have not set Thee before their eyes. And Thou, O Lord, art a God of compassion, and merciful: patient, and of much mercy, and true.

O look upon me, and have mercy on me: give Thy command to Thy servant, and save the son of Thy handmaid. Shew me a token for good, that they who hate me may see, and be confounded: because Thou, O Lord, hast helped me and hast comforted me.

86 (Heb. 87) Fundamenta ejus The foundations thereof (Sunday 8 Pentecost)
For the sons of Core, a psalm of a canticle.

The foundations thereof are in the holy mountains: The Lord loveth the gates of Sion above all the tabernacles of Jacob. Glorious things are said of Thee, O city of God. I will be mindful of Rahab and of Babylon knowing me. Behold, the foreigners, and Tyre, and the people of the Ethiopians, these were there. Shall not Sion say: This man and that man is born in her: and the Highest Himself hath founded her?

The Lord shall tell in His writings of peoples and of princes: of them that have been in her. The dwelling in Thee is as it were of all rejoicing.

87 (Heb. 88) Domine Deus salutis O Lord, the God of my salvation (Thursday after 8 Pentecost)
A canticle of a psalm for the sons of Core, unto the end, for Mabeleth, to answer, understanding of Eman the Ezrahite.

O Lord, the God of my salvation: I have cried in the day and in the night, before Thee. Let my prayer come in before Thee: incline Thy ear to my petition.

For my soul is filled with evils: and my life hath drawn nigh to hell. I am counted among them that go down to the pit: I am become as a man without help, free among the dead. Like the slain sleeping in the sepulchres, whom Thou rememberest no more: and they are cast off from Thy hand. They have laid me in the lower pit: in the dark places, and in the shadow of death. Thy wrath is strong over me: and all Thy waves Thou hast brought in upon me. Thou hast put away my acquaintance far from me: they have set me an abomination to themselves. I was delivered up, and came not forth: my eyes languished through poverty. All the day I cried to Thee, O Lord: I stretched out my hands to Thee.

Wilt Thou shew wonders to the dead? Or shall physicians raise to life, and give praise to Thee? Shall any one in the sepulchre declare Thy mercy: and Thy truth in destruction? Shall Thy wonders be known in the dark: and Thy justice in the land of forgetfulness? But I, O Lord, have cried to Thee: and in the morning my prayer shall prevent Thee. Lord, why castest Thou off my prayer? Why turnest Thou away Thy face from me? I am poor, and in labors from my youth: and being exalted have been humbled and troubled. Thy wrath hath come upon me: and Thy terrors have troubled me. They have come round about me like water all the day: they have compassed me about together. Friend and neighbor Thou hast put far from me: and my acquaintance, because of misery.

Psalm Table of St. Mael Ruain *Misericordias* to the end [of the second fifty]. 88-100 [13 Psalms]. Wednesday Midnight (modern Tuesday night).

---

88 (Heb. 89) Misericordias Domini The mercies of the Lord I will sing (Sunday 9 Pentecost) Of understanding, for Ethan the Ezrahite.

    The mercies of the Lord I will sing for ever. I will show forth Thy truth with my mouth to generation and generation.

    For Thou hast said: Mercy shall be built up for ever in the heavens: thy truth shall be prepared in them. I have made a covenant with my elect: I have sworn to David my servant: thy seed will I settle for ever. And I will build up thy throne unto generation and generation.

    The heavens shall confess Thy wonders, O Lord: and Thy truth in the church of the saints. For who in the clouds can be compared to the Lord? Or who among the sons of God shall be like to God? God, who is glorified in the assembly of the saints: great and terrible above all them that are about Him.

    O Lord God of hosts, Who is like to Thee? Thou art mighty, O Lord, and Thy truth is round about Thee. Thou rulest the power of the sea: and appeasest the motion of the waves thereof. Thou hast humbled the proud one, as one that is slain: with the arm of Thy strength Thou hast scattered Thy enemies. Thine are the heavens, and Thine is the earth: the world and the fulness thereof Thou hast founded: the north and the sea Thou hast created. Thabor and Hermon shall rejoice in Thy Name: Thy arm is with might.

    Let Thy hand be strengthened, and Thy right hand exalted: justice and judgment are the preparation of Thy throne. Mercy and truth shall go before Thy Face. Blessed is the people that knoweth jubilation. They shall walk, O Lord, in the light of Thy countenance: and in Thy Name they shall rejoice all the day, and in Thy justice they shall be exalted. For Thou art the glory of their strength: and in Thy good pleasure shall our horn be exalted. For our protection is of the Lord: and of our king the holy one of Israel.

    Then Thou spokest in a vision to Thy saints, and saidst: I have laid help upon one that is mighty: and have exalted one chosen out of my people. I have found David my servant: with my holy oil I have anointed him. For my hand shall help him: and my arm shall strengthen him. The enemy shall have no advantage over him: nor the son of iniquity have power to hurt him. And I will cut down his enemies before his face; and them that hate him I will put to flight. And my truth and my mercy shall be with him: and in my Name shall his horn be exalted. And I will set his hand in the sea; and his right hand in the rivers. He shall cry out to me: Thou art my father: my God, and the support of my salvation: And I will make him my firstborn, high above the kings of the earth. I will keep my mercy for him for ever: and my covenant faithful to him. And I will make his seed to endure for evermore: and his throne as the days of heaven.

And if his children forsake my law: and walk not in my judgments: If they profane my justices: and keep not my commandments: I will visit their iniquities with a rod: and their sins with stripes. But my mercy I will not take away from him: nor will I suffer my truth to fail. Neither will I profane my covenant: and the words that proceed from my mouth I will not make void. Once have I sworn by my holiness: I will not lie unto David: his seed shall endure for ever. And his throne as the sun before me, and as the moon perfect for ever: and a faithful witness in heaven.

But thou hast rejected and despised: thou hast been angry with thy anointed. Thou hast overthrown the covenant of thy servant: thou hast profaned his sanctuary on the earth. Thou hast broken down all his hedges: thou hast made his strength fear. All that pass by the way have robbed him: he is become a reproach to his neighbors. Thou hast set up the right hand of them that oppress him: thou hast made all his enemies to rejoice. Thou hast turned away the help of his sword: and hast not assisted him in battle. Thou hast made his purification to cease: and Thou hast cast his throne down to the ground. Thou hast shortened the days of his time: Thou hast covered him with confusion.

How long, O Lord, turnest Thou away unto the end: shall Thy anger burn like fire?

Remember what my substance is: for hast Thou made all the children of men in vain? Who is the man that shall live, and not see death: that shall deliver his soul from the hand of hell? Lord, where are Thy ancient mercies, according to what Thou didst swear to David in Thy truth? Be mindful, O Lord, of the reproach of Thy servants (which I have held in my bosom) of many nations: Wherewith Thy enemies have reproached, O Lord: wherewith they have reporached the change of Thy anointed. Blessed be the Lord for evermore: So be it. So be it.

89 (Heb. 90) Domine refugium Lord, Thou hast been our refuge
(Thursday after 9 Pentecost) A prayer of Moses, the man of God.

Lord, Thou hast been our refuge: from generation to generation. Before the mountains were made, or the earth and the world was formed: from eternity and to eternity Thou art God.

Turn not man away to be brought low: and Thou hast said: Be converted, O ye sons of men. For a thousand years in Thy sight are as yesterday, which is past. And as a watch in the night; things that are counted nothing shall their years be. In the morning man shall grow up like grass; in the morning he shall flourish and pass away: in the evening he shall fall, grow dry, and wither. For in Thy wrath we have fainted away:

and are troubled in Thy indignation. Thou hast set our iniquities before Thy eyes: our life in the light of Thy countenance. For all our days are spent: and in Thy wrath we have fainted away. Our years shall be considered as a spider: the days of our years in them are threescore and ten years. But if in the strong they be fourscore years: and what is more of them is labor and sorrow. For mildness is come upon us: and we shall be corrected. Who knoweth the power of Thy anger: and for Thy fear can number Thy wrath? So make Thy right hand known: and men learned in heart, in wisdom. Return, O Lord: How long? And be entreated in favor of Thy servants.

We are filled in the morning with Thy mercy: and we have rejoiced, and are delighted all our days. We have rejoiced for the days in which Thou hast humbled us: for the years in which we have seen evils. Look upon Thy servants and upon their works: and direct their children. And let the brightness of the Lord our God be upon us, and direct Thou the works of our hands over us: yea, the work of our hands do Thou direct.

90 (Heb. 91) Qui habitat He that dwelleth in the aid of the most High
(Sunday 10 Pentecost) The praise of a canticle, for David.

He that dwelleth in the aid of the most High shall abide under the protection of the God of Heaven. He shall say to the Lord: Thou art my protector and my refuge: my God, in Him will I trust. For He hath delivered me from the snare of the hunters: and from the sharp word. He will overshadow thee with His shoulders: and under His wings thou shalt trust. His truth shall compass thee with a shield: thou shalt not be afraid of the terror of the night. Of the arrow that flieth in the day, of the business that walketh about in the dark: of invasion, or of the noonday devil. A thousand shall fall at thy side, and ten thousand at thy right hand: but it shall not come nigh thee. But thou shalt consider with thy eyes: and shalt see the reward of the wicked.

Because Thou, O Lord, art my hope: Thou hast made the most High Thy refuge. There shall no evil come to thee: nor shall the scourge come near thy dwelling. For He hath given His angels charge over thee: to keep thee in all thy ways. In their hands they shall bear thee up: lest thou dash thy foot against a stone. Thou shalt walk upon the asp and the basilisk: and thou shalt trample under foot the lion and the dragon.

Because he hoped in me I will deliver him: I will protect him because he hath known my Name. He shall cry to me, and I will hear him: I am with him in tribulation: I will deliver him, and I will glorify him. I will fill him with length of days: and I will show him my salvation.

91 (Heb. 92) Bonum est confiteri It is good to give praise to the Lord
(Thursday after 10 Pentecost) A psalm of a canticle, on the sabbath day.

It is good to give praise to the Lord: and to sing to Thy Name, O most High. To shew forth Thy mercy in the morning, and Thy truth in the night: Upon an instrument of ten strings, upon the psaltery: with a canticle upon the harp. For Thou hast given me, O Lord, a delight in Thy doings:

and in the works of Thy hands I shall rejoice.

O Lord, how great are Thy works! Thy thoughts are exceeding deep.

The senseless man shall not know: nor will the fool understand these things. When the wicked shall spring up as grass: and all the workers of iniquity shall appear: That they may perish for ever and ever: but Thou, O Lord, art most high for evermore. For, behold, Thy enemies, O Lord, for, behold, Thy enemies shall perish: and all the workers of iniquity shall be scattered.

But my horn shall be exalted like that of the unicorn: and my old age in plentiful mercy. My eye also hath looked down upon my enemies: and my ear shall hear of the downfall of the malignant that rise up against me.

The just shall flourish like the palm tree: he shall grow up like the cedar of Libanus. They that are planted in the house of the Lord shall flourish in the courts of the house of our God. They shall still increase in a fruitful old age: and shall be well treated, that they may show; That the Lord our God is righteous: and there is no iniquity in Him.

92 (Heb. 93) Dominus regnavit The Lord hath reigned (Sunday 11 Pentecost)
Praise in the way of a canticle, for David himself, on the day before the sabbath, when the earth was founded.

The Lord hath reigned, He is clothed with beauty: the Lord is clothed with strength, and hath girded Himself. For He hath established the world which shall not be moved.

Thy throne is prepared from of old: Thou art from everlasting. The floods have lifted up, O Lord: the floods have lifted up their voice. The floods have lifted up their waves, with the noise of many waters. Wonderful are the surges of the sea: wonderful is the Lord on high.

Thy testimonies are become exceedingly credible: holiness becometh Thy house, O Lord, unto length of days.

93 (Heb. 94) Deus ultionum The Lord is the God to whom revenge (Thursday after 11 Pentecost)
A psalm for David himself, on the fourth day of the week.

The Lord is the God to Whom revenge belongeth: the God of revenge hath acted freely. Lift up Thyself, Thou that judgest the earth: render a reward to the proud. How long shall sinners, O Lord: how long shall sinners glory? Shall they utter, and speak iniquity: shall all speak who work injustice?

Thy people, O Lord, they have brought low: and they have afflicted Thy inheritance. They have slain the widow and the stranger: and they have murdered the fatherless. And they have said: The Lord shall not see: neither shall the God of Jacob understand. Understand, ye senseless among the people: and, you fools, be wise at last. He that planted the ear, shall He not hear? Or He that formed the eye, doth He not consider? He that chastiseth nations, shall He not rebuke: He that teacheth man knowledge? The Lord knoweth the thoughts of men, that they are vain. Blessed is the man whom Thou shalt instruct, O Lord: and shalt teach him out of Thy law. That Thou mayest give him rest from the evil days: till a pit be dug for the wicked.

For the Lord will not cast off His people; neither will He forsake His own inheritance. Until justice be turned into judgment: and they that are near it are all the upright in heart.

Who shall rise up for me against the evildoers? Or who shall stand with me against the workers of iniquity? Unless the Lord had been my helper: my soul had almost dwelt in hell. If I said: My foot is moved: Thy mercy, O Lord, assisted me. According to the multitude of my sorrows in my heart: Thy comforts have given joy to my soul. Doth the seat of iniquity stick to Thee: Who framest labor in commandment? They will hunt after the soul of the just: and will condemn innocent blood.

But the Lord is my refuge: and my God the help of my hope. And He will render them their iniquity: and in their malice He will destroy them. The Lord our God will destroy them.

94 (Heb. 95) Venite exultemus Come let us praise the Lord with joy (Thursday after 12 Pentecost, reversed) Praise of a canticle, for David himself.

Come let us praise the Lord with joy: let us joyfully sing to God our Savior. Let us come before His presence with thanksgiving; and make a joyful noise to Him with psalms. For the Lord is a great God: and a great King above all gods.

For in His hand are all the ends of the earth: and the heights of the mountains are His. For the sea is His, and He made it: and His hands formed the dry land.

Come let us adore and fall down: and weep before the Lord that made us. For He is the Lord our God: and we are the people of His pasture and the sheep of His hand.

Today if you shall hear His voice, harden not your hearts: As in the provocation, according to the day of temptation in the wilderness: where your fathers tempted me, they proved me, and saw my works. Forty years long was I offended with that generation, and I said: These always err in heart. And these men have not known my ways: so I swore in my wrath that they shall not enter into my rest.

95 (Heb. 96) Cantate Domino Sing ye to the Lord a new canticle (Sunday 12 Pentecost) A canticle for David himself, when the house was built after the captivity.

Sing ye to the Lord a new canticle: sing to the Lord, all the earth. Sing ye to the Lord and bless His Name: show forth His salvation from day to day. Declare His glory among the Gentiles: His wonders among all people. For the Lord is great, and exceedingly to be praised: He is to be feared above all gods. For all the gods of the Gentiles are devils: but the Lord made the heavens. Praise and beauty are before Him: holiness and majesty in His sanctuary.

Bring ye to the Lord, O ye kindreds of the Gentiles, bring ye to the

Lord glory and honor: bring to the Lord glory unto His Name. Bring up sacrifices, and come into His courts: Adore ye the Lord in His holy court. Let all the earth be moved at His presence: say ye among the Gentiles: The Lord hath reigned. For He hath corrected the world, which shall not be moved: He will judge the people with justice.

Let the heavens rejoice, and let the earth be glad, let the sea be moved, and the fullness thereof: the fields and all things that are in them shall be joyful. Then shall all the trees of the woods rejoice before the Face of the Lord, because He cometh: because He cometh to judge the earth. He shall judge the world with justice, and the people with His truth.

96 (H 97) Dominus regnavit The Lord hath reigned, let the earth rejoice (Sunday 13 Pentecost) For the same David, when his land was restored again to him.

The Lord hath reigned, let the earth rejoice: let many islands be glad. Clouds and darkness are round about Him: justice and judgment are the establishment of His throne. A fire shall go before Him, and shall burn His enemies round about. His lightnings have shone forth to the world: the earth saw and trembled. The mountains melted like wax, at the presence of the Lord: at the presence of the Lord of all the earth. The heavens declared His justice: and all people saw His glory.

Let them be all confounded that adore graven things: and that glory in their idols. Adore Him, all you His angels: Sion heard, and was glad. And the daughters of Juda rejoiced, because of Thy judgments, O Lord.

For Thou are the most high Lord over all the earth: Thou art exalted exceedingly above all gods. You that love the Lord, hate evil: the Lord preserveth the souls of His saints, He will deliver them out of the hand of the sinner.

Light is risen to the just: and joy to the right of heart. Rejoice, ye just, in the Lord: and give praise to the remembrance of His holiness.

97 (Heb. 98) Cantate Domino Sing ye to the Lord a new canticle (Thursday after 13 Pentecost) A psalm for David himself.

Sing ye to the Lord a new canticle: because He hath done wonderful things. His right hand hath wrought for Him salvation: and His arm is holy. The Lord hath made known His salvation: He hath revealed His justice in the sight of the Gentiles. He hath remembered His mercy and His truth toward the house of Israel. All the ends of the earth have seen the salvation of our God.

Sing joyfully to God, all the earth: make melody, rejoice and sing. Sing praise to the Lord on the harp, on the harp, and with the voice of a psalm: with long trumpets, and sound of cornet. Make a joyful noise before the Lord our King: let the sea be moved and the fullness thereof: the world and they that dwell therein. The rivers shall clap their hands; the mountains shall rejoice together at the presence of the Lord: because He cometh to judge the earth. He shall judge the world with justice, and the people with equity.

98 (Heb. 99) Dominus regnavit The Lord hath reigned, let the people (Sunday 14 Pentecost) A psalm for David himself.

    The Lord hath reigned, let the people be angry: He that sitteth on the cherubims, let the earth be moved.

    The Lord is great in Sion: and high above all people. Let them give praise to Thy great Name, for it is terrible and holy: and the King's honor loveth judgment. Thou hast prepared directions; Thou hast done judgment and justice in Jacob.

    Exalt ye the Lord our God: and adore His footstool: for it is holy. Moses and Aaron among His priests: and Samuel among them that call upon His Name. They called upon the Lord, and He heard them: He spoke to them in the pillar of the cloud. They kept His testimonies and the commandment which He gave them. Thou didst hear them, O Lord our God: Thou wast a merciful God to them, and taking vengeance on all their inventions. Exalt ye the Lord our God, and adore at His holy mountain: for the Lord our God is holy.

99 (Heb. 100) Jubilate Deo Sing joyfully to God, all the earth (Thursday after 14 Pentecost) A psalm of praise.

    Sing joyfully to God, all the earth: serve ye the Lord with gladness. Come in before His presence with exceeding great joy. Know ye that the Lord He is God: He made us, and not we ourselves. We are His people and the sheep of His pasture: go ye into His gates with praise, into His courts with hymns: and give glory to Him. Praise ye His Name: for the Lord is sweet; His mercy endureth for ever, and His truth to generation and generation.

100 (Heb. 101) Misericordiam et judicium Mercy and judgment (Sunday 15 Pentecost) A psalm for David himself.

    Mercy and judgment I will sing to Thee, O Lord: I will sing, and I will understand in the unspotted way, when Thou shalt come to me. I walked in the innocence of my heart, in the midst of my house. I did not set before my eyes any unjust thing: I hated the workers of iniquities. The perverse heart did not cleave to me: and the malignant, that turned aside from me, I would not know. The man that in private detracted his neighbor, him did I persecute. With him that had a proud eye and an unsatiable heart, I would not eat.

    My eyes were upon the faithful of the earth, to sit with me: the man that walked in the perfect way, he served me. He that worketh pride shall not dwell in the midst of my house: he that speaketh unjust things did not prosper before my eyes. In the morning I put to death all the wicked of the land: that I might cut off all the workers of iniquity from the city of the Lord.

Psalm Table of St. Mael Ruain: *Domine exaudi* to *In exitu Israel*. 101-112 [12 Psalms]. Thursday Beginning of Night (modern Wednesday evening).

----

101 (Heb. 102) Domine exaudi Hear, O Lord, my prayer (Thursday after 15 Pentecost)

> The prayer of the poor man, when he was anxious, and poured out his supplication before the Lord.

Hear, O Lord, my prayer: and let my cry come to Thee. Turn not away Thy Face from me: in the day when I am in trouble, incline Thy ear to me. In what day soever I shall call upon Thee, hear me speedily. For my days are vanished like smoke: and my bones are grown dry like fuel for the fire. I am smitten as grass, and my heart is withered: because I forgot to eat my bread. Through the voice of my groaning, my bone hath cleaved to my flesh. I am become like to a pelican of the wilderness: I am like a night raven in the house. I have watched, and am become as a sparrow all alone on the house-top.

All the day long my enemies reproached me: and they that praised me did swear against me. For I did eat ashes like bread, and mingled my drink with weeping. Becuase of Thy anger and indignation: for having lifted me up Thou hast thrown me down. My days have declined like a shadow: and I am withered like grass.

But Thou, O Lord, endurest for ever: and Thy memorial to all generations. Thou shalt arise and have mercy on Sion: for it is time to have mercy on it, for the time is come. For the stones thereof have pleased Thy servants: and they shall have pity on the earth thereof. And the Gentiles shall fear Thy Name, O Lord, and all the kings of the earth Thy glory.

For the Lord hath built up Sion: and He shall be seen in His glory. He hath had regard to the prayer of the humble: and He hath not despised their petition. Let these things be written unto another generation: and the people that shall be created shall praise the Lord: Because He hath looked forth from His high sanctuary: from heaven the Lord hath looked upon the earth. That He might hear the groans of them that are in fetters: that He might release the children of the slain: That they may declare the Name of the Lord in Sion: and His praise in Jerusalem; When the people assemble together, and kings, to serve the Lord.

He answered him in the way of his strength: Declare unto me the fewness of my days. Call me not away in the midst of my days: Thy years are unto generation and generation. In the beginning, O Lord, Thou foundedst the earth: and the heavens are the works of Thy hands. They shall perish but Thou remainest: and all of them shall grow old like a garment: And as a vesture Thou shalt change them, and they shall be changed.

But Thou art always the selfsame: and Thy years shall not fail. The children of Thy servants shall continue: and their seed shall be directed for ever.

102 (Heb. 103) Benedic anima Bless the Lord, O my soul; and let (Sunday 16 Pentecost) For David himself.

Bless the Lord, O my soul: and let all that is within me bless His holy Name.

Bless the Lord, O my soul: and never forget all He hath done for thee. Who forgiveth all thy iniquities: Who healeth all thy diseases. Who redeemeth thy life from destruction; Who crowneth thee with mercy and compassion. Who satisfieth thy desire with good things: thy youth shall be renewed like the eagle's.

The Lord doth mercies, and judgment for all that suffer wrong. He hath made His ways known to Moses: His wills to the children of Israel. The Lord is compassionate and merciful: longsuffering and plenteous in mercy. He will not always be angry: nor will he threaten for ever. He hath not dealt with us according to our sins: nor rewarded us according to our iniquities. For according to the height of the heaven above the earth: He hath strengthened His mercy towards them that fear Him. As far as the east is from the west, so far hath He removed our iniquities from us.

As a father hath compassion on his children, so hath the Lord compassion on them that fear Him: for He knoweth our frame. He remembereth that we are dust. Man's days are as grass: as the flower of the field so shall he flourish. For the spirit shall pass in him, and he shall not be: and he shall know his place no more.

But the mercy of the Lord is from eternity and unto eternity, upon them that fear Him. And His justice unto children's children, to such as keep His covenant. And are mindful of His commandments to do them.

The Lord hath prepared His throne in heaven: and His kingdom shall rule over all. Bless the Lord, all ye His angels: you that are mighty in strength, and execute His word, hearkening to the voice of His orders. Bless the Lord, all ye His hosts: you ministers of His that do His will. Bless the Lord, all His works: in every place of His dominion, O my soul, bless thou the Lord.

103 (H 104) Benedic anima Bless the Lord, O my soul, O Lord my God (Thursday after 16 Pentecost) For David himself.

Bless the Lord, O my soul: O Lord my God, Thou art exceedingly great. Thou hast put on praise and beauty: and art clothed with light as with a garment. Who stretchest out the heaven like a pavilion: Who coverest the higher rooms thereof with water. Who makest the clouds Thy chariot: Who walkest upon the wings of the winds. Who makest Thy angels spirits: and Thy ministers a burning fire.

Who hast founded the earth upon its own bases: it shall not be moved for ever and ever. The deep like a garment is its clothing: above the mountains shall the waters stand. At Thy rebuke they shall flee: at the voice of Thy thunder they shall fear. The mountains ascend: and the plains descend into the place which Thou hast founded for them. Thou hast set a bound which they shall not pass over: neither shall they return to cover the earth. Thou sendest forth springs in the vales: between the midst of the hills the waters shall pass. All the beasts of the field shall drink: the wild asses shall expect in their thirst. Over them the birds of the air shall dwell: from the midst of the rocks they shall give forth their voices. Thou waterest the hills from Thy upper rooms: the earth shall be filled with the fruit of Thy works: Bringing forth grass for cattle, and herb for the service of men.

That Thou mayest bring bread out of the earth: and that wine may cheer the heart of man. That He may make the face cheerful with oil: and that bread may strengthen man's heart. The trees of the field shall be filled, and the cedars of Libanus which he hath planted: there the sparrows shall make their nests. The highest of them is the house of the heron: the high hills are a refuge for the harts: the rock for the irchins.

He hath made the moon for seasons: the sun knoweth his going down. Thou hast appointed darkness, and it is night: in it shall all the beasts of the woods go about: The young lions roaring after their prey, and seeking their meat from God. The sun ariseth, and they are gathered together: and they shall lie down in their dens. Man shall go forth to his work: and to his labor until the evening.

How great are Thy works, O Lord! Thou hast made all things in wisdom: the earth is filled with Thy riches. So is this great sea, which stretcheth wide its arms: there are creeping things without number: creatures little and great: there the ships shall go. This sea dragon which Thou hast formed to play therein: all expect of Thee that Thou give them food in season. What Thou givest to them they shall gather up: when Thou openest Thy hand, they shall all be filled with good. But if Thou turnest away Thy face, they shall be troubled: Thou shalt take away their breath, and they shall fail, and shall return to their dust. Thou shalt send forth Thy spirit, and they shall be created: and Thou shalt renew the face of the earth.

May the glory of the Lord endure for ever: the Lord shall rejoice in His works. He looketh upon the earth, and maketh it tremble: He toucheth the mountains, and they smoke.

I will sing to the Lord as long as I live: I will sing praise to my God while I have my being. Let my speech be acceptable to Him: but I will take delight in the Lord. Let sinners be consumed out of the earth, and the unjust, so that they be no more: O my soul, bless thou the Lord.

104 (Heb. 105) Confitemini Domino Give glory to the Lord, and call
(Sunday 17 Pentecost) Alleluia.

Give glory to the Lord, and call upon His Name: declare His deeds among the Gentiles. Sing to Him, yea, sing praises to Him: relate all His wondrous works. Glory ye in His holy Name: let the heart of them rejoice that seek the Lord. Seek ye the Lord, and be strengthened: seek His Face evermore.

Remember His marvellous works which He hath done: His wonders, and the judgments of His mouth. O ye seed of Abraham his servant; ye sons of Jacob His chosen. He is the Lord our God: His judgments are in all the earth. He hath remembered His covenant for ever: the word which He commanded to a thousand generations. Which He made to Abraham: and His oath to Isaac: And He appointed the same to Jacob for a law: and to Israel for an everlasting testament: Saying: To thee will I give the land of Chanaan, the lot of your inheritance.

When they were but a small number: yea very few, and sojourners therein: And they passed from nation to nation, and from one kingdom to another people. He suffered no man to hurt them: and He reproved kings for their sakes. Touch ye not my anointed: and do no evil to my Prophets. And He called a famine upon the land: and He broke in pieces all the support of bread. He sent a man before them: Joseph, who was sold for a slave. They humbled his feet in fetters: the iron pierced his soul, until His word came. The word of the Lord inflamed him: the king sent, and he released him; the ruler of the people, and he set him at liberty. He made him master of his house: and ruler of all his possession: That he might instruct his princes as himself: and teach his ancients wisdom.

And Israel went into Egypt: and Jacob was a sojourner in the land of Cham. And He increased his people exceedingly: and strengthened them over their enemies. He turned their heart to hate His people: and to deal deceitfully with his servants. He sent Moses his servant: Aaron, the man whom he had chosen. He gave them power to show His signs and His wonders, in the land of Cham. He sent darkness, and made it obscure: and grieved not his words. He turned their waters into blood: and destroyed their fish. Their land brought forth frogs, in the inner chambers of their kings. He spoke: and there came divers sorts of flies and sciniphs in all their coasts. He gave them hail for rain: a burning fire in the land. And he destroyed their vineyards and their fig trees: and He broke in pieces the trees of their coasts. He spoke, and the locust came, and the bruchus, of which there was no number. And they devoured all the grass in their land: and consumed all the fruit of their ground. And He slew all the firstborn in their land: the firstfruits of all their labor.

And He brought them out with silver and gold: and there was not among their tribes one that was feeble. Egypt was glad which they departed: for the fear of them lay upon them. He spread a cloud for their protection: and fire to give them light in the night. They asked, and the quail came: and He filled them with the bread of heaven. He opened the rock, and waters flowed: rivers ran down in the dry land. Because He remembered His holy word, which He had spoken to His servant Abraham.

And He brought forth His people with joy, and His chosen with gladness. And He gave them the lands of the Gentiles: and they possessed the labors of the people: That they might observe His justifications and seek after His law.

105 (Heb. 106)   Confitemini Domino   Give glory to the Lord, for He
(Thursday after 17 Pentecost)   Alleluia.

Give glory to the Lord, for He is good: for His mercy endureth for ever. Who shall declare the powers of the Lord? Who shall set forth all His praises? Blessed are they that keep judgment and do justice at all times. Remember us, O Lord, in the favor of Thy people: visit us with Thy salvation. That we may see the good of Thy chosen, that we may rejoice in the joy of Thy nation: that Thou mayest be praised with Thy inheritance.

We have sinned with our fathers: we have acted unjustly, we have wrought iniquity. Our fathers understood not Thy wonders in Egypt: they remembered not the multitude of Thy mercies. And they provoked to wrath going up to the sea, even the Red Sea. And He saved them for His own Name's sake: that He might make His power known. And He rebuked the Red Sea, and it was dried up: and He led them through the depths, as in a wilderness. And He saved them from the hand of them that hated them: and He redeemed them from the hand of the enemy. And the water covered them that afflicted them: there was not one of them left.

And they believed His words: and they sang His praises. They had quickly done, they forgot His works: and they waited not for His counsel. And they coveted their desire in the desert: and they tempted God in the place without water. And He gave them their request: and sent fulness into their souls. And they provoked Moses in the camp: Aaron the holy one of the Lord. The earth opened and swallowed up Dathan: and covered the congregation of Abiron. And a fire was kindled in their congregation: the flame burned the wicked. They made also a calf in Horeb: and they adored the graven thing. And they changed their glory into the likeness of a calf that eateth grass. They forgot God, Who saved them, Who had done great things in Egypt, wondrous works in the land of Cham: terrible things in the Red Sea.

And He said that He would destroy them, had not Moses His chosen stood before Him in the breach: To turn away His wrath, lest He should destroy them: and they set at nought the desirable land. They believed not His word, and they murmured in their tents: they hearkened not to the voice of the Lord. And He lifted up His hand over them, to overthrow them in the desert: And to cast down their seed among the nations, and to scatter them in the countries. They also were initiated to Beelphegor: and ate the sacrifices of the dead. And they provoked Him with their inventions: and destruction was multiplied among them.

Then Phinees stood up, and pacified Him: and the slaughter ceased. And it was reputed to Him unto justice: to generation and generation for evermore. They provoked Him also at the waters of contradiction: and Moses was afflicted for their sakes: because they exasperated His spirit: And He distinguished with His lips: they did not destroy the nations of which the Lord spoke unto them. And they were mingled among the heathens, and learned their works: and served their idols: and it became a stumblingblock to them. And they sacrificed their sons, and their daughters to devils. And they shed innocent blood: the blood of their sons and of their daughters which they sacrificed to the idols of Chanaan. And the land was polluted with blood, and was defiled with their works: and they went aside after their own inventions. And the Lord was exceedingly angry with His people: and He abhorred His inheritance. And He delivered them into the hands of the nations: and they that hated them had dominion over them.

And their enemies afflicted them: and they were humbled under their hands. Many times did He deliver them: But they provoked Him with their counsel: and they were brought low by their iniquities.

And He saw when they were in tribulation: and He heard their prayer. And He was mindful of His covenant: and repented according to the multitude of His mercies. And He gave them unto mercies, in the sight of all those that had made them captives.

Save us, O Lord, our God: and gather us from among the nations: That we may give thanks to Thy holy Name: and may glory in Thy praise. Blessed be the Lord, the God of Israel, from everlasting to everlasting: and let all the people say: So be it. So be it.

106 (Heb. 107) Confitemini Domino Give glory to the Lord... (Sunday 18 Pentecost) Alleluia.

Give glory to the Lord, for He is good: for His mercy endureth for ever. Let them say so that have been redeemed by the Lord: whom He hath redeemed from the hand of the enemy: and gathered out of the countries: From the rising and from the setting of the sun: from the north, and from the sea. They wandered in a wilderness, in a place without water: they found not the way of a city for their habitation. They were hungry and thirsty: their soul fainted in them. And they cried to the Lord in their tribulation: and He delivered them out of their distresses. And He led them into the right way: that they might go to a city of habitation.

Let the mercies of the Lord give glory to Him: and His wonderful works to the children of men. For He hath satisfied the empty soul: and hath filled the hungry soul with good things. Such as sat in darkness and in the shadow of death: bound in want and in iron. Because they had exasperated the words of God: and provoked the counsel of the most High: And their heart was humbled with labors: they were weakened, and there was none to help them. Then they cried to the Lord in their affliction: and He delivered them out of their distresses. And He brought them out of darkness and the shadow of death: and broke their bonds in sunder.

Let the mercies of the Lord give glory to Him: and His wonderful works to the children of men. Because He hath broken gates of brass and burst iron bars. He took them out of the way of their iniquity: for they were brought low for their injustices. Their soul abhorred all manner of meat: and they drew nigh even to the gates of death. And they cried to the Lord in their affliction: and He delivered them out of their distresses. He sent His word, and healed them: and delivered them from their destructions.

Let the mercies of the Lord give glory to Him: and His wonderful works to the children of men. And let them sacrifice the sacrifice of praise: and declare His works with joy. They that go down to the sea in ships, doing business in the great waters: These have seen the works of the Lord, and His wonders in the deep. He said the word, and there arose a storm of wind: and the waves thereof were lifted up. They mount up to the heavens, and they go down to the depths: their soul pined away with evils. They were troubled, and reeled like a drunken man: and all their wisdom was swallowed up. And they cried to the Lord in their affliction: and He brought them out of their distresses. And He turned the storm into a breeze: and its waves were still. And they rejoiced because they were still: and He brought them to the haven which they wished for.

Let the mercies of the Lord give glory to Him: and His wonderful works to the children of men. And let them exalt Him in the church of the people: and praise Him in the chair of the ancients. He hath turned rivers into a wilderness: and the sources of waters into dry ground: A fruitful land into barrenness: for the wickedness of them that dwell therein. He hath turned a wilderness into pools of waters: and a dry land into water springs. And hath placed there the hungry: and they made a city for their habitation. And they sowed fields, and planted vineyards: and they yielded fruit of birth. And He blessed them, and they were multiplied exceedingly: and their cattle He suffered not to decrease.

Then they were brought to be few: and they were afflicted through the trouble of evils and sorrow. Contempt was poured forth upon their princes: and He caused them to wander where there was no passing, and out of the way. And He helped the poor out of poverty: and made Him families like a flock of sheep. The just shall see, and shall rejoice: and all iniquity shall stop her mouth.

Who is wise, and will keep these things: and will understand the mercies of the Lord?

107 (Heb. 108) Paratum cor meum My heart is ready, O God (Thursday after 18 Pentecost) A canticle of a psalm for David himself.

My heart is ready, O God, my heart is ready: I will sing, and will give praise, with my glory. Arise, my glory; arise, psaltery and harp: I will arise in the morning early. I will praise Thee, O Lord, among the people: and I will sing unto Thee among the nations. For Thy mercy is great above the heavens: and thy truth even unto the clouds.

Be Thou exalted, O God, above the heavens, and Thy glory over all the earth: that Thy beloved may be delivered.

Save with Thy right hand and hear me: God hath spoken in His holiness. I will rejoice, and I will divide Sichem: and I will mete out the vale of tabernacles. Galaad is mine: and Manasses is mine: and Ephraim the protection of my head. Juda is my king: Moab the pot of my hope. Over Edom I will stretch out my shoe: the aliens are become my friends. Who will bring me into the strong city? Who will lead me into Edom? Wilt not Thou, O God, Who hast cast us off? And wilt not Thou, O God, go forth with our armies? O grant us help from trouble: for vain is the help of man.

Through God we shall do mightily: and He will bring our enemies to nothing.

108 (H 109) Deus laudem meam O God, be not Thou silent in my praise
(Sunday 19 Pentecost) Unto the end, a psalm for David.

O God, be not Thou silent in my praise: for the mouth of the wicked and the mouth of the deceitful man is opened against me. They have spoken against me with deceitful tongues; and they have compassed me about with words of hatred: and have fought against me without cause. Instead of making me a return of love, they detracted me: but I gave myself to prayer. And they repaid me evil for good: and hatred for my love.

Set Thou the sinner over him: and may the devil stand at his right hand. When he is judged, may he go out condemned: and may his prayer be turned to sin. May his days be few: and his bishopric let another take. May his children be fatherless: and his wife a widow. Let his children be carried about vagabonds, and beg; and let them be cast out of their dwellings. May the usurer search all his substance: and let strangers plunder his labors. May there be none to help him: nor any to pity his fatherless offspring. May his posterity be cut off; in one generation may his name be blotted out. May the iniquity of his fathers be remembered in the sight of the Lord: and let not the sin of his mother be blotted out. May they be before the Lord continually: and let the memory of them perish from the earth: because he remembered not to show mercy.

But persecuted the poor man and the beggar; and the broken in heart; to put him to death. And he loved cursing, and it shall come unto him: and he would not have blessing, and it shall be far from him. And he put on cursing, like a garment: and it went in like water into his entrails, and like oil in his bones. May it be unto him like a garment which covereth him; and like a girdle with which he is girded continually. This is the work of them who detract me before the Lord: and who speak evils against my soul.

But thou, O Lord, do with me for Thy Name's sake: because Thy mercy is sweet. Do Thou deliver me, for I am poor and needy: and my heart is troubled within me. I am taken away like the shadow when it declineth: and I am shaken off as locusts. My knees are weakened through fasting: and my flesh is changed for oil. And I am become a reproach to them: they saw me and they shaked their heads.

Help me, O Lord my God: save me according to Thy mercy. And let them know that this is Thy hand: and that Thou, O Lord, hast done it. They will curse and Thou wilt bless: let them that rise up against me be confounded: but Thy servant shall rejoice. Let them that detract me be clothed with shame: and let them be covered with their confusion as with a double cloak.

I will give great thanks to the Lord with my mouth, and in the midst of many I will praise Him: Because He hath stood at the right hand of the poor, to save my soul from persecutors.

109 (Heb. 110) Dixit Dominus The Lord said to my Lord: Sit Thou
(Thursday after 19 Pentecost) A psalm for David.

The Lord said to my Lord: Sit Thou at my right hand: Until I make thy enemies thy footstool. The Lord will send forth the sceptre of thy power out of Sion; rule thou in the midst of thy enemies. With thee is the principality in the day of thy strength, in the brightness of the saints: from the womb before the day-star I begot Thee.

The Lord hath sworn, and He will not repent: Thou art a priest for ever, according to the order of Melchisedech. The Lord at thy right hand hath broken kings in the day of His wrath. He shall judge among nations, He shall fill ruins: He shall crush the heads in the land of many. He shall drink of the torrent in the way: therefore shall He lift up the head.

110 (Heb. 111) Confitebor tibi Domine I will praise Thee, O Lord,
(Sunday 20 Pentecost) Alleluia.

I will praise Thee, O Lord, with my whole heart: in the council of the just, and in the congregation.

Great are the works of the Lord: sought out according to all His wills. His work is praise and magnificence: and His justice continueth for ever and ever. He hath made a remembrance of His wonderful works, being a merciful and gracious Lord: He hath given food to them that fear Him.

He will be mindful for ever of His covenant: He will show forth to His people the power of His works: That He may give them the inheritance of the Gentiles: the works of His hands are truth and judgment. All His commandments are faithful: confirmed for ever and ever, made in truth and equity.

He hath sent redemption to His people: He hath commanded His covenant for ever. Holy and terrible is His Name: the fear of the Lord is the beginning of wisdom. A good understanding to all that do it: His praise continueth for ever and ever.

111 (Heb. 112) Beatus vir Blessed is the man that feareth the Lord
(Thursday after 20 Pentecost) Alleluia, of the returning of Aggeus and Zacharias.

Blessed is the man that feareth the Lord: he shall delight exceedingly in His commandments. His seed shall be mighty upon earth: the generation of the righteous shall be blessed. Glory and wealth shall be in his house: and his justice remaineth for ever and ever.

To the righteous a light is risen up in darkness: He is merciful, and compassionate and just. Acceptable is the man that sheweth mercy and lendeth: he shall order his words with judgment, because he shall not be moved for ever.

The just shall be in everlasting remembrance: he shall not fear the evil hearing. His heart is ready to hope in the Lord, his heart is strengthened: he shall not be moved until he look over his enemies. He hath distributed, he hath given to the poor: his justice remaineth for ever and ever; his horn shall be exalted in glory.

The wicked shall see and shall be angry, he shall gnash with his teeth and pine away: the desire of the wicked shall perish.

112 (Heb. 113) Laudate pueri Praise the Lord, ye children (Sunday 21 Pentecost) Alleluia.

Praise the Lord, ye children: praise ye the Name of the Lord. Blessed be the Name of the Lord: from henceforth now and for ever. From the rising of the sun unto the going down of the same, the Name of the Lord is worthy of praise. The Lord is high above all nations: and His glory above the heavens.

Who is as the Lord our God, Who dwelleth on high, and looketh down on the low things in heaven and in earth? Raising up the needy from the earth: and lifting up the poor out of the dunghill: That He may place him with princes; with the princes of His people. Who maketh a barren woman to dwell in a house; the joyful mother of children.

Psalm Table of St. Mael Ruain: *In exitu Israel* to *In convertendo*. 113-124 [12 Psalms]. Thursday Midnight (modern Wednesday night).

---

113 (Heb. 114 & 115) In exitu Israel When Israel went out of Egypt (First Half: Sunday 23 Pentecost as the Gradual with Psalm 116 as the Alleluia for that day which is short. Second Half: Thursday after 21 Pentecost)

    A [First Part]

    Alleluia.

When Israel went out of Egypt, the house of Jacob from a barbarous people: Judea was made his sanctuary, Israel his dominion. The sea saw and fled: Jordan was turned back. The mountains skipped like rams: and the hills like the lambs of the flock. What ailed thee, O thou sea, that thou didst flee: and thou, O Jordan, that thou wast turned back? Ye mountains, that ye skipped like rams, and ye hills, like lambs of the flock?

At the presence of the Lord the earth was moved; at the presence of the God of Jacob: Who turned the rock into pools of water, and the stony hill into fountains of waters.

    B [Second Part]

Not to us, O Lord, not to us: but to Thy Name give glory. For Thy mercy, and for Thy truth's sake: lest the Gentiles should say: Where is their God? But our God is in heaven: He hath done all things whatsoever He would. The idols of the Gentiles are silver and gold, the works of the hands of men. They have mouths and speak not: they have eyes and see not. They have ears and hear not: they have noses and smell not. They have hands and feel not: they have feet and walk not: neither shall they cry out through their throat. Let them that make them become like unto them: and all such as trust in them.

The house of Israel hath hoped in the Lord: He is their helper and their protector. The house of Aaron hath hoped in the Lord: He is their helper and their protector. They that fear the Lord have hoped in the Lord: He is their helper and their protector. The Lord hath been mindful of us: and hath blessed us. He hath blessed the house of Israel: He hath blessed the house of Aaron.

He hath blessed all that fear the Lord, both little and great. May the Lord add blessings upon you: upon you, and upon your children. Blessed be you of the Lord: who made heaven and earth. The heaven of heaven is the Lord's: but the earth He has given to the children of men. The dead shall not praise Thee, O Lord: nor any of them that go down to hell. But we that live bless the Lord: from this time now and for ever.

114 (Heb. 116:1-9) Dilexi I have loved, because the Lord will hear (Sunday 22 Pentecost) Alleluia.

I have loved, because the Lord will hear the voice of my prayer. Because He hath inclined His ear unto me: and in my days I will call upon Him. The sorrows of death have compassed me: and the perils of hell have found me. I met with trouble and sorrow: and I called upon the Name of the Lord. O Lord, deliver my soul: the Lord is merciful and just, and our God sheweth mercy.

The Lord is the keeper of little ones: I was humbled, and He delivered me. Turn, O my soul, into thy rest: for the Lord hath been bountiful to thee. For He hath delivered my soul from death: my eyes from tears, my feet from falling. I will please the Lord in the land of the living.

115 (Heb. 116:10-19) Credidi I have believed, therefore have I spoken (Thursday after 22 Pentecost) Alleluia.

I have believed, therefore have I spoken: but I have been humbled exceedingly. I said in my excess: Every man is a liar. What shall I render to the Lord for all the things that He hath rendered to me? I will take the chalice of salvation: and I will call upon the Name of the Lord. I will pay my vows to the Lord before all His people: precious in the sight of the Lord is the death of His Saints. O Lord, for I am Thy servant: I am Thy servant, and the son of Thy handmaid. Thou hast broken my bonds: I will sacrifice to Thee the sacrifice of praise: and I will call upon the Name of the Lord.

I will pay my vows to the Lord in the sight of all His people: in the courts of the house of the Lord, in the midst of Thee, O Jerusalem.

116 (Heb.117) Laudate Dominum O praise the Lord, all ye nations (Short: Alleluia of Sunday 23 Pentecost; the Gradual is the first part of Psalm 113.) Alleluia.

O praise the Lord, all ye nations: praise Him, all ye people. For His mercy is confirmed upon us: and the truth of the Lord remaineth for ever.

117 (H 118) Confitemini Domino Give praise to the Lord, for he is good
(Thursday after 23 Pentecost) Alleluia.

Give praise to the Lord, for He is good: for His mercy endureth for ever. Let Israel now say, that He is good: that His mercy endureth for ever. Let the house of Aaron now say: that His mercy endureth for ever. Let them that fear the Lord now say: that His mercy endureth for ever.

In my trouble I called upon the Lord: and the Lord heard me, and enlarged me. The Lord is my helper: I will not fear what man can do unto me. The Lord is my helper: and I will look over my enemies.

It is good to confide in the Lord, rather than to have confidence in man. It is good to trust in the Lord, rather than to trust in princes.

All nations conpassed me about: and in the Name of the Lord I have been revenged on them. Surrounding me they compassed me about: and in the Name of the Lord I have been revenged on them. They surrounded me like bees, and they burned like fire among thorns: and in the Name of the Lord I was revenged on them. Being pushed I was overturned that I might fall: but the Lord supported me.

The Lord is my strength and my praise: and He is become my salvation. The voice of rejoicing and of salvation is in the tabernacles of the just. The right hand of the Lord hath wrought strength: the right hand of the Lord hath exalted me: the right hand of the Lord hath wrought strength.

I shall not die, but live: and shall declare the works of the Lord. The Lord chastising hath chastised me: but He hath not delivered me over to death. Open ye to me the gates of justice; I will go in to them, and give praise to the Lord: this is the gate of the Lord; the just shall enter into it. I will give glory to Thee because Thou hast heard me: and art become my salvation.

The stone which the builders rejected; the same is become the head of the corner. This is the Lord's doing: and it is wonderful in our eyes.

This is the day which the Lord hath made: let us be glad and rejoice therein. O Lord, save me: O Lord, give good success. Blessed be He that cometh in the Name of the Lord. We have blessed you out of the house of the Lord: the Lord is God, and He hath shone upon us. Appoint a solemn day, with shady boughs, even to the horn of the altar.

Thou art my God, and I will praise Thee: Thou art my God, and I will exalt Thee. I will praise Thee, because Thou hast heard me: and art become my salvation. O praise ye the Lord, for He is good: for His mercy endureth for ever.

118 (Heb. 119) Beati immaculati Blessed are the undefiled in the way
(Sunday 24 Pentecost. The longest Psalm, in the order of the Hebrew alphabet. (The first Psalm in the Cross Vigil. *The Cross Vigil has one hundred Prostrations, or bows: starting with the even verses of Psalm 118. The number of verses in Psalms 118, 119, 120, and 121 add to 200. St. Mael Ruain said to practice moderation; this many prostrations may damage joints, not a daily practice.)
Alleluia.

ALEPH

1 Blessed are the undefiled in the way, who walk in the law of the Lord.
2 Blessed are they that search His testimonies: that seek Him with their whole heart.
3 For they that work iniquity have not walked in His ways.
4 Thou hast commanded Thy commandments to be kept most diligently.
5 O that my ways may be directed to keep Thy justifications.
6 Then shall I not be confounded, when I shall look into all Thy commandments.
7 I will praise Thee with uprightness of heart, when I shall have learned the judgments of Thy justice.
8 I will keep Thy justifications: O do not Thou utterly forsake me.

BETH

9 By what doth a young man correct his way? By observing Thy words.
10 With my whole heart have I sought after Thee: let me not stray from Thy commandments.
11 Thy words have I hidden in my heart, that I may not sin against Thee.
12 Blessed art Thou, O Lord: teach me Thy justifications.
13 With my lips I have pronounced all the judgments of Thy mouth.
14 I have been delighted in the way of Thy testimonies, as in all riches.
15 I will meditate on Thy commandments: and I will consider Thy ways.
16 I will think of Thy justifications: I will not forget Thy words.

GIMEL

17 Give bountifully to Thy servant, enliven me: and I shall keep Thy words.
18 Open Thou my eyes: and I will consider the wondrous things of Thy law.
19 I am a sojourner on the earth: hide not Thy commandments from me.
20 My soul hath coveted to long for Thy justifications, at all times.
21 Thou hast rebuked the proud: they are cursed who decline from Thy commandments.
22 Remove from me reproach and contempt: because I have sought after Thy testimonies.
23 For princes sat, and spoke against me: but Thy servant was employed in Thy justifications.
24 For Thy testimonies are my meditation: and Thy justifications my counsel.

DALETH

25 My soul hath cleaved to the pavement: quicken Thou me according to Thy word.
26 I have declared my ways, and Thou hast heard me: teach me Thy justifications.
27 Make me to understand the way of Thy justifications: and I shall be exercised in Thy wondrous works.
28 My soul hath slumbered through heaviness: strengthen Thou me in Thy words.
29 Remove from me the way of iniquity: and out of Thy law have mercy on me.
30 I have chosen the way of truth: Thy judgments I have not forgotten.
31 I have stuck to Thy testimonies, O Lord: put me not to shame.
32 I have run the way of Thy commandments, when Thou didst enlarge my heart.

HÉ

33 Set before me for a law the way of Thy justifications, O Lord: and I will always seek after it.
34 Give me understanding, and I will search Thy law ; and I will keep it with my whole heart.
35 Lead me into the path of Thy commandments; for this same I have desired.
36 Incline my heart into Thy testimonies and not to covetousness.
37 Turn away my eyes that they may not behold vanity: quicken me in Thy way.
38 Establish Thy word to Thy servant, in Thy fear.
39 Turn away my reproach, which I have apprehended: for Thy judgments are delightful.
40 Behold I have longed after Thy precepts: quicken me in Thy justice.

VAU

41 Let Thy mercy also come upon me, O Lord: Thy salvation according to Thy word.
42 So shall I answer them that reproach me in any thing; that I have trusted in Thy words.
43 And take not Thou the word of truth utterly out of my mouth: for in Thy words, I have hoped exceedingly.
44 So shall I always keep Thy law, for ever and ever.
45 And I walked at large: because I have sought after Thy commandments.
46 And I spoke of Thy testimonies before kings: and I was not ashamed.
47 I meditated also on Thy commandments, which I loved:
48 And I lifted up my hands to Thy commandments, which I loved: and I was exercised in Thy justifications.

ZAIN

49 Be Thou mindful of Thy word to Thy servant, in which Thou hast given me hope.
50 This hath comforted me in my humiliation: because Thy word hath enlivened me.
51 The proud did iniquitously altogether: but I declined not from Thy law.
52 I remembered, O Lord, Thy judgments of old: and I was comforted.
53 A fainting hath taken hold of me, because of the wicked that forsake Thy law.
54 Thy justifications were the subject of my song in the place of my pilgrimage.
55 In the night I have remembered Thy Name, O Lord: and have kept Thy law.
56 This happened to me: because I sought after Thy justifications.

HETH

57 O Lord, my portion, I have said I would keep Thy law.
58 I entreated Thy Face with all my heart: have mercy on me according to Thy word.
59 I have thought on my ways: and turned my feet unto Thy testimonies.
60 I am ready, and am not troubled: that I may keep Thy commandments.
61 The cords of the wicked have encompassed me: but I have not forgotten Thy law.
62 I rose at midnight to give praise to Thee; for the judgments of Thy justification.
63 I am a partaker with all them that fear Thee; and that keep Thy commandments.
64 The earth, O Lord, is full of Thy mercy: teach me Thy justifications.

TETH

65 Thou hast done well with Thy servant, O Lord, according to Thy word.
66 Teach me goodness and discipline and knowledge; for I have believed Thy commandments.
67 Before I was humbled I offended; therefore have I kept Thy word.
68 Thou art good; and in Thy goodness teach me Thy justifications.
69 The iniquity of the proud hath been multiplied over me: but I will seek Thy commandments with my whole heart.
70 Their heart is curdled like milk: but I have meditated on Thy law.
71 It is good for me that Thou hast humbled me, that I may learn Thy justifications.
72 The law of Thy mouth is good to me, above thousands of gold and silver.

JOD

73 Thy hands have made me and formed me: give me understanding, and I will learn Thy commandments.
74 They that fear Thee shall see me and shall be glad: because I have greatly hoped in Thy words.
75 I know, O Lord, that Thy judgments are equity: and in Thy truth Thou hast humbled me.
76 O let Thy mercy be for my comfort, according to Thy word unto Thy servant.
77 Let Thy tender mercies come unto me, and I shall live: for Thy law is my meditation.
78 Let the proud be ashamed, because they have done unjustly towards me: but I will be employed in Thy commandments.
79 Let them that fear Thee turn to me: and they that know Thy testimonies.
80 Let my heart be undefiled in Thy justifications, that I may not be confounded.

CAPH

81 My soul hath fainted after Thy salvation: and in Thy word I have very much hoped.
82 My eyes have failed for Thy word, saying: When wilt Thou comfort me?
83 For I am become like a bottle in the frost: I have not forgotten Thy justifications.
84 How many are the days of Thy servant: when wilt Thou execute judgment on them that persecute me?
85 The wicked have told me fables: but not as Thy law.
86 All Thy statutes are truth: they have persecuted me unjustly, do Thou help me.
87 They had almost made an end of me upon earth: but I have not forsaken Thy commandments.
88 Quicken Thou me according to Thy mercy: and I shall keep the testimonies of Thy mouth.

LAMED

89 For ever, O Lord, Thy word standeth firm in heaven.
90 Thy truth unto all generations: Thou hast founded the earth, and it continueth.
91 By Thy ordinance the day goeth on: for all things serve Thee.
92 Unless Thy law had been my meditation: I had then perhaps perished in my abjection.
93 Thy justifications I will never forget: for by them Thou hast given me life.

94 I am Thine, save Thou me: for I have sought Thy justifications.
95 The wicked have waited for me to destroy me: but I have understood Thy testimonies.
96 I have seen an end of all perfection: Thy commandment is exceeding broad.

MEM

97 O how have I loved Thy law, O Lord! It is my meditation all the day.
98 Through Thy commandment, Thou hast made me wiser than my enemies: for it is ever with me.
99 I have understood more than all my teachers: because Thy testimonies are my meditation.
100 I have had understanding above ancients: because I have sought Thy commandments.
101 I have restrained my feet from every evil way: that I may keep Thy words.
102 I have not declined from Thy judgments: because Thou hast set me a law.
103 How sweet are Thy words to my palate: more than honey to my mouth!
104 By Thy commandments I have had understanding: therefore have I hated every way of iniquity.

NUN

105 Thy word is a lamp to my feet, and a light to my paths.
106 I have sworn; and am determined to keep the judgments of Thy justice.
107 I have been humbled, O Lord, exceedingly: quicken Thou me according to Thy word.
108 The free offerings of my mouth make acceptable, O Lord: and teach me Thy judgments.
109 My soul is continually in my hands: and I have not forgotten Thy law.
110 Sinners have laid a snare for me: but I have not erred from Thy precepts.
111 I have purchased Thy testimonies for an inheritance for ever: because they are the joy of my heart.
112 I have inclined my heart to do Thy justifications for ever, for the reward.

SAMECH

113 I have hated the unjust: and have loved Thy law.
114 Thou art my helper and my protector: and in Thy word I have greatly hoped.

115 Depart from me, ye malignant: and I will search the commandments of my God.
116 Uphold me according to Thy word, and I shall live: and let me not be confounded in my expectation.
117 Help me, and I shall be saved: and I will meditate always on Thy justifications.
118 Thou hast despised all them that fall off from Thy judgments; for their thought is unjust.
119 I have accounted all the sinners of the earth prevaricators: therefore have I loved Thy testimonies.
120 Pierce Thou my flesh with Thy fear: for I am afraid of Thy judgments.

AIN

121 I have done judgment and justice: give me not up to them that slander me.
122 Uphold Thy servant unto good: let not the proud calumniate me.
123 My eyes have fainted after Thy salvation: and for the word of Thy justice.
124 Deal with Thy servant according to Thy mercy: and teach me Thy justifications.
125 I am Thy servant: give me understanding that I may know Thy testimonies.
126 It is time, O Lord, to do: they have dissipated Thy law.
127 Therefore have I loved Thy commandments above gold and the topaz.
128 Therefore was I directed to all Thy commandments: I have hated all wicked ways.

PHE

129 Thy testimonies are wonderful: therefore my soul hath sought them.
130 The declaration of Thy words giveth light: and giveth understanding to little ones.
131 I opened my mouth, and panted: because I longed for Thy commandments.
132 Look Thou upon me and have mercy on me; according to the judgment of them that love Thy Name.
133 Direct my steps according to Thy word: and let no iniquity have dominion over me.
134 Redeem me from the calumnies of men: that I may keep Thy commandments.
135 Make Thy Face to shine upon Thy servant: and teach me Thy justifications.
136 My eyes have sent forth springs of water: because they have not kept Thy law.

SADE

137 Thou art just, O Lord: and Thy judgment is right.
138 Thou hast commanded justice Thy testimonies: and Thy truth exceedingly.
139 My zeal hath made me pine away: because my enemies forgot Thy words.
140 Thy word is exceedingly refined: and Thy servant hath loved it.
141 I am very young and despised; but I forget not Thy justifications.
142 Thy justice is justice for ever: and Thy law is the truth.
143 Trouble and anguish have found me: Thy commandments are my meditation.
144 Thy testimonies are justice for ever: give me understanding, and I shall live.

COPH

145 I cried with my whole heart: Hear me, O Lord: I will seek Thy justifications.
146 I cried unto Thee: Save me: that I may keep Thy commandments.
147 I prevented the dawning of the day, and cried: because in Thy words I very much hoped.
148 My eyes to Thee have prevented the morning: that I might meditate on Thy words.
149 Hear Thou my voice, O Lord, according to Thy mercy: and quicken me according to Thy judgement.
150 They that persecute me have drawn nigh to iniquity; but they are gone far off from Thy law.
151 Thou art near, O Lord: and all Thy ways are truth.
152 I have known from the beginning concerning Thy testimonies: that Thou hast founded them for ever.

RES

153 See my humiliation and deliver me: for I have not forgotten Thy law.
154 Judge my judgment and redeem me: quicken Thou me for Thy word's sake.
155 Salvation is far from sinners; because they have not sought Thy justifications.
156 Many, O Lord, are Thy mercies: quicken me according to Thy judgment.
157 Many are they that persecute me and afflict me; but I have not declined from Thy testimonies.
158 I beheld the transgressors, and I pined away: because they kept not Thy word.
159 Behold I have loved Thy commandments, O Lord: quicken me Thou in Thy mercy.

160 The beginning of Thy words is truth: all the judgments of Thy justice are for ever.

SIN

161 Princes have persecuted me without cause: and my heart hath been in awe of Thy words.
162 I will rejoice at Thy words, as one that hath found great spoil.
163 I have hated and abhorred iniquity; but I have loved Thy law.
164 Seven times a day I have given praise to Thee, for the judgments of Thy justice.
165 Much peace have they that love Thy law: and to them there is no stumbling block
166 I looked for Thy salvation, O Lord: and I loved Thy commandments.
167 My soul hath kept Thy testimonies: and hath loved them exceedingly.
168 I have kept Thy commandments and Thy testimonies: because all my ways are in Thy sight.

TAU

169 Let my supplication, O Lord, come near in Thy sight: give me understanding according to Thy word.
170 Let my request come in before Thee; deliver Thou me according to Thy word.
171 My lips shall utter a hymn: when Thou shalt teach me Thy justifications.
172 My tongue shall pronounce Thy word: because all Thy commandments are justice.
173 Let Thy hand be with me to save me: for I have chosen Thy precepts.
174 I have longed for Thy salvation, O Lord: and Thy law is my meditation.
175 My soul shall live and shall praise Thee: and Thy judgments shall help me.
176 I have gone astray like a sheep that is lost: seek Thy servant, because I have not forgotten Thy commandments.

119 (Heb. 120) Ad Dominum In my trouble I cried to the Lord
(Thursday after 24 Pentecost. *In the Cross Vigil: continuing prostrations.) A gradual canticle.

1 In my trouble I cried to the Lord: and He heard me.
2 O Lord, deliver my soul from wicked lips, and a deceitful tongue. *
3 What shall be given to thee, or what shall be added to thee, to a deceitful tongue?
4 The sharp arrows of the mighty, with coals that lay waste. *
5 Woe is me, that my sojourning is prolonged! I have dwelt with the inhabitants of Cedar:

6 my soul hath been long a sojourner. *
7 With them that hated peace I was peaceable: when I spoke to them they fought against me without cause.

120 (Heb. 121) Levavi oculos I have lifted up my eyes to the mountains
> (Sunday 25 Pentecost. * In the Cross Vigil: continuing prostrations.)
> A gradual canticle.

1 I have lifted up my eyes to the mountains, from whence help shall come to me. *
2 My help is from the Lord, who made heaven and earth.
3 May He not suffer thy foot to be moved: neither let Him slumber that keepeth thee. *
4 Behold He shall neither slumber nor sleep, that keepeth Israel.
5 The Lord is thy keeper, the Lord is thy protection upon thy right hand.*
6 The sun shall not burn thee by day: nor the moon by night.
7 The Lord keepeth thee from all evil: may the Lord keep thy soul. *
8 May the Lord keep thy coming in and thy going out; from henceforth now and for ever.

121 (Heb. 122) Laetatus sum in his I rejoiced at the things that were said
> (Last Sunday after Pentecost, or 26 Pentecost. * In the Cross Vigil: continuing prostrations.) A gradual canticle.

1 I rejoiced at the things that were said to me: We shall go into the house of the Lord. *
2 Our feet were standing in thy courts, O Jerusalem.
3 Jerusalem, which is built as a city, which is compact together. *
4 For thither did the tribes go up, the tribes of the Lord: the testimony of Israel, to praise the Name of the Lord.
5 Because their seats have sat in judgment, seats upon the house of David. *
6 Pray ye for the things that are for the peace of Jerusalem: and abundance for them that love thee.
7 Let peace be in thy strength: and abundance in thy towers. *
8 For the sake of my brethren, and of my neighbours, I spoke peace of thee.
9 Because of the house of the Lord our God, I have sought good things for thee. *

> [The Cross Vigil ends here. *During the Cross Vigil, in Psalms 118, 119, 120, and 121, prostrations may continue every other verse, 200 verses, 100 prostrations in all. Then continue with the Hymns of the Cross Vigil.]

122 (Heb. 123) Ad te levavi To Thee have I lifted up my eyes (St. Peter)
> Bobbio Missal designation for St. Peter in the Apostles' Creed: "Peter said, 'I believe in God the Father Almighty.'" A gradual canticle.

To Thee have I lifted up my eyes; Who dwellest in heaven. Behold, as the eyes of servants are on the hands of their masters; As the eyes of the handmaid are on the hands of her mistress: so are our eyes unto the Lord our God, until He have mercy on us. Have mercy on us, O Lord, have mercy on us: for we are greatly filled with contempt. For our soul is greatly filled: we are a reproach to the rich, and contempt to the proud.

123 (Heb. 124) Nisi quia Dominus If it had not been that the Lord was (St. John, writer of the fourth Gospel, designated as the Eagle in the "Traditio" of St. Ambrose.)
> Bobbio Missal designation for St. John in the Apostles' Creed: "John said, 'I believe in Jesus Christ, His only Son, God and our Lord.'" A gradual canticle.

If it had not been that the Lord was with us, let Israel now say: If it had not been that the Lord was with us, When men rose up against us; perhaps they had swallowed us up alive: When their fury was enkindled against us; perhaps the waters had swallowed us up. Our soul hath passed through a torrent: perhaps our soul had passed through a water insupportable. Blessed be the Lord, Who hath not given us to be a prey to their teeth. Our soul hath been delivered as a sparrow out of the snare of the fowlers: The snare is broken; and we are delivered. Our help is in the Name of the Lord, Who made heaven and earth.

124 (Heb. 125) Qui confidunt They that trust in the Lord shall be (St. James the Greater, the older James, son of Zebedee, brother of St. John. James and John were called Boanerges, the "Sons of Thunder.")
> Bobbio Missal designation for St. James in the Apostles' Creed: "James said, 'He was born of Mary, the Virgin, through the Holy Spirit.'" A gradual canticle.

They that trust in the Lord shall be as mount Sion: he shall not be moved for ever that dwelleth in Jerusalem. Mountains are round about it: so the Lord is round about His people, from henceforth now and for ever. For the Lord will not leave the rod of sinners upon the lot of the just: that the just may not stretch forth their hands to iniquity. Do good, O Lord, to those that are good, and to the upright of heart. But such as turn aside into bonds, the Lord shall lead out with the workers of iniquity: peace upon Israel.

Psalm Table of St. Mael Ruain: *In convertendo* to *Domine probasti*. 125-137 [13 Psalms]. Friday Beginning of Night (modern Thursday evening).

---

125 (Heb. 126) In convertendo When the Lord brought back the captivity (St. Andrew. Also "first-called" are those brought by Christ from Hades at the Crucifixion.)
> Bobbio Missal designation for St. Andrew in the Apostles' Creed: "Andrew said, 'He suffered under Pontius Pilate; was crucified and buried.'" A gradual canticle.

When the Lord brought back the captivity of Sion: we became like men comforted. Then was our mouth filled with gladness: and our tongue with joy. Then shall they say among the Gentiles: The Lord hath done great things for them. The Lord hath done great things for us: we are become joyful. Turn again our captivity, O Lord, as a stream in the south. They that sow in tears shall reap in joy. Going, they went and wept, casting their seeds. But coming, they shall come with joyfulness, carrying their sheaves.

126 (Heb. 127) Nisi Dominus Unless the Lord build the house (St. Philip)
> Bobbio Missal designation for St. Philip in the Apostles' Creed: "Philip said, 'He descended into hell.'")   A gradual canticle of Solomon.

Unless the Lord build the house, they labor in vain that build it. Unless the Lord keep the city, he watcheth in vain that keepeth it. It is vain for you to rise before light: rise ye after you have sitten, you that eat the bread of sorrow. When He shall give sleep to His beloved: behold, the inheritance of the Lord are children: the reward, the fruit of the womb.

As arrows in the hand of the mighty: so the children of them that have been shaken. Blessed is the man that hath filled the desire with them: he shall not be confounded when he shall speak to his enemies in the gate.

127 (Heb. 128) Beati omnes Blessed are all they that fear the Lord (St. Thomas, called Didymus, "twin," who traveled furthest, and learned to have faith in Christ after the Resurrection, celebrated the Sunday after Pascha. He also came latest after the Dormition of the Blessed Virgin Mary.)
> The Bobbio Missal designation of St. Thomas in the Apostles' Creed: "Thomas said, 'He arose on the third day.'" A gradual canticle.

Blessed are all they that fear the Lord: that walk in His ways. For thou shalt eat the labors of thy hands: blessed art thou, and it shall be well with thee. Thy wife as a fruitful vine, on the sides of thy house. Thy children as olive plants, round about thy table. Behold, thus shall the man be blessed that feareth the Lord. May the Lord bless thee out of Sion: and mayest thou see the good things of Jerusalem all the days of thy life. And mayest thou see thy children's children: peace upon Israel.

128 (Heb. 129) Saepe expugnaverunt Often have they fought against me (St. Bartholomew "the active.")
> Bobbio Missal designation for St. Bartholomew in the Apostles' Creed: "Bartholomew said, 'He ascended into Heaven, [and] sat at the right hand of God the Father Almighty.'" A gradual canticle.

Often have they fought against me from my youth, let Israel now say. Often have they fought against me from my youth: but they could not prevail over me: The wicked have wrought upon my back: they have lengthened their iniquity. The Lord Who is just will cut the necks of sinners: let them all be confounded and turned back that hate Sion. Let them be as grass upon the tops of houses: which withereth before it be plucked up: Wherewith the mower filleth not his hand: nor he that gathereth sheaves his bosom. And they that passed by have not said: The blessing of the Lord be upon you: we have blessed you in the Name of the Lord.

129 (Heb. 130) De profundis Out of the depths I have cried to Thee (St. Matthew, also called Levi, writer of the first Gospel, Kerub of the "Man" in the "Traditio.")
> Bobbio Missal designation for St. Matthew in the Apostles' Creed: "Matthew said, 'From there He will come to judge the living and the dead.'") A gradual canticle.

Out of the depths I have cried to Thee, O Lord: Lord, hear my voice: Let Thy ears be attentive to the voice of my supplication. If Thou, O Lord, wilt mark iniquities: Lord, who shall stand it? For with Thee there is merciful forgiveness: and by reason of Thy law I have waited for Thee, O Lord. My soul hath relied on His word: my soul hath hoped in the Lord. From the morning watch even until night: let Israel hope in the Lord. Because with the Lord there is mercy: and with Him plentiful redemption. And He shall redeem Israel from all his iniquities.

130 (Heb. 131) Domine non est Lord, my heart is not exalted (St. James the Less, the son of Alpheus; the younger Apostle James.)
> Bobbio Missal designation of St. James in the Apostles' Creed: "James, the son of Alpheus, said: 'I believe in the Holy Spirit.'" A gradual canticle of David.

Lord, my heart is not exalted: nor are my eyes lofty. Neither have I walked in great matters: nor in wonderful things above me. If I was not humbly minded; but exalted my soul: As a child that is weaned is towards his mother, so reward in my soul. Let Israel hope in the Lord: from henceforth now and for ever.

131 (Heb. 132) Memento Domine O Lord, remember David (St. Simon Zelotes, thought to be the young man at the wedding where the water was turned into wine.)
> Bobbio designation for St. Simon in the Apostles' Creed: "Simon Zelotes said: 'I believe in the Holy Church.'" A gradual canticle.

O Lord, remember David, and all his meekness. How he swore to the Lord, he vowed a vow to the God of Jacob: If I shall enter into the tabernacle of my house: if I shall go up into the bed wherein I lie: If I shall give sleep to my eyes, or slumber to my eyelids: Or rest to my temples: until I find out a place for the Lord, a tabernacle for the God of Jacob. Behold, we have heard of it in Ephrata: we have found it in the fields of the wood. We will go into His tabernacle: we will adore in the place where His feet stood. Arise, O Lord, into Thy resting-place: Thou and the ark, which Thou hast sanctified. Let Thy priests be clothed with justice: and let Thy saints rejoice. For Thy servant David's sake, turn not away the face of Thy anointed. The Lord hath sworn truth to David, and He will not make it void: Of the fruit of thy womb I will set upon thy throne. If thy children will keep my covenant, and these my testimonies which I shall teach them: Their children also for evermore shall sit upon thy throne. For the Lord hath chosen Sion: He hath chosen it for His dwelling. This is my rest for ever and ever: here will I dwell, for I have chosen it. Blessing I will bless her widow: I will satisfy her poor with bread. I will clothe her priests with salvation: and her saints shall rejoice with exceeding great joy. There will I bring forth a horn to David: I have prepared a lamp for my anointed. His enemies I will clothe with confusion: but upon him shall my sanctification flourish.

132 (Heb. 133) Ecce quam bonum Behold how good and how pleasant (St. Judas, brother of St. James, this is the good Judas, known as patron of lost causes.)
> Bobbio designations for St. Judas, the brother of James in the Apostles' Creed: "Judas, the brother of James, said: 'Through Holy Baptism [there is] remission of sins.'" A gradual canticle of David.

Behold how good and how pleasant it is for brethren to dwell together in unity: Like the precious ointment on the head, that ran down upon the beard, the beard of Aaron. Which ran down to the skirt of his garment: As the dew of Hermon, which descendeth upon mount Sion. For there the Lord hath commanded blessing, and life for evermore.

133 (Heb. 134) Ecce nunc benedicite Behold, now bless ye the Lord (St. Matthias, last called, just before Pentecost.)
> The Bobbio Missal designation for St. Matthias in the Apostles' Creed: "Matthias said, 'The resurrection of the flesh and eternal life. Amen.'" A gradual canticle.

Behold, now bless ye the Lord, all ye servants of the Lord: Who stand in the house of the Lord , in the courts of the house of our God. In the nights lift up your hands to the holy places, and bless ye the Lord. May the Lord out of Sion bless thee, He that made heaven and earth.

134 (Heb. 135) Laudate nomen Praise ye the Name of the Lord (Finding of the True Cross, May 3; Feast of Dedication of the first Church in Jerusalem and all Churches and of the Cross, Sept 14) Alleluia.

Praise ye the Name of the Lord, O you, His servants, praise the Lord: You that stand in the house of the Lord; in the courts of the house of our God. Praise ye the Lord, for the Lord is good: sing ye to His Name, for it is sweet. For the Lord hath chosen Jacob unto Himself: Israel for His own possession. For I have known that the Lord is great: and our God is above all gods. Whatsoever the Lord pleased He hath done, in heaven, in earth, in the sea, and in all the deeps.

He bringeth up clouds from the end of the earth: He hath made lightnings for the rain. He bringeth forth winds out of His stores: He slew the firstborn of Egypt from man even unto beast. He sent forth signs and wonders in the midst of thee, O Egypt: upon Pharaoh, and upon all his servants. He smote many nations: and slew mighty kings: Sehon king of the Amorhites, and Og king of Basan, and all the kingdoms of Chanaan. And gave their land for an inheritance: for an inheritance to His people Israel.

Thy Name, O Lord, is for ever: Thy memorial, O Lord, unto all generations. For the Lord will judge His people: and will be entreated in favor of His servants. The idols of the Gentiles are silver and gold, the works of men's hands. They have a mouth, but they speak not: they have eyes, but they see not. They have ears, but they hear not: neither is there any breath in their mouths. Let them that make them be like to them: and every one that trusteth in them.

Bless the Lord, O house of Israel: bless the Lord, O house of Aaron. Bless the Lord, O house of Levi: you that fear the Lord, bless the Lord. Blessed be the Lord out of Sion, Who dwelleth in Jerusalem.

135 (Heb. 136) Confitemini Domino   Praise the Lord, for He is good
(Purification, Feb 2) Alleluia.

Praise the Lord, for He is good: for His mercy endureth for ever. Praise ye the God of gods: for His mercy endureth for ever. Praise ye the Lord of lords: for His mercy endureth for ever.

Who alone doth great wonders: for His mercy endureth for ever. Who made the heavens in understanding: for His mercy endureth for ever. Who established the earth above the waters: for His mercy endureth for ever.

Who made the great lights: for His mercy endureth for ever. The sun to rule the day: for His mercy endureth for ever. The moon and the stars to rule the night: for His mercy endureth for ever.

Who smote Egypt with their firstborn: for His mercy endureth for ever. Who brought out Israel from among them: for His mercy endureth for ever. With a mighty hand and with a stretched-out arm: for His mercy endureth for ever. Who divided the Red Sea into parts: for His mercy endureth for ever. And brought out Israel through the midst thereof: for His mercy endureth for ever. And overthrew Pharaoh and his host in the Red Sea: for His mercy endureth for ever.

Who led His people through the desert: for His mercy endureth for ever. Who smote great kings: for His mercy endureth for ever. And slew strong kings: for His mercy endureth for ever. Sehon king of the Amorhites: for His mercy endureth for ever. And Og king of Basan: for His mercy endureth for ever. And He gave their land for an inheritance: for His mercy endureth for ever. For an inheritance to His servant Israel: for His mercy endureth for ever.

For He was mindful of us in our affliction: for His mercy endureth for ever. And He redeemed us from our enemies: for His mercy endureth for ever. Who giveth food to all flesh: for His mercy endureth for ever. Give glory to the God of heaven: for His mercy endureth for ever. Give glory to the Lord of lords: for His mercy endureth for ever.

136 (Heb. 137) Super flumina Upon the rivers of Babylon, there we sat (Coming out of Egypt of Jesus, Jan 11th) A psalm of David, for Jeremias.

Upon the rivers of Babylon, there we sat and wept: when we remembered Sion. On the willows in the midst thereof we hung up our instruments. For there they that led us into captivity required of us the words of songs. And they that carried us away said: Sing ye to us a hymn of the songs of Sion.

How shall we sing the song of the Lord in a strange land? If I forget Thee, O Jerusalem, let my right hand be forgotten. Let my tongue cleave to my jaws, if I do not remember thee: If I make not Jerusalem the beginning of my joy. Remember, O Lord, the children of Edom, in the day of Jerusalem: Who say: Rase it, rase it, even to the foundation thereof. O daughter of Babylon, miserable: blessed shall he be who shall repay thee thy payment which thou hast paid us. Blessed be he that shall take and dash thy little ones against the rock.

137 (Heb. 138) Confitebor tibi I will praise Thee, O Lord (St. Michael the Archangel) For David himself.

I will praise Thee, O Lord, with my whole heart: for Thou hast heard the words of my mouth. I will sing praise to Thee in the sight of the angels: I will worship towards Thy holy temple, and I will give glory to Thy Name. For Thy mercy, and for Thy truth: for Thou hast magnified Thy holy Name above all.

In what day soever I shall call upon Thee, hear me: Thou shalt multiply strength in my soul. May all the kings of the earth give glory to Thee: for they have heard all the words of Thy mouth. And let them sing in the ways of the Lord: for great is the glory of the Lord. For the Lord is high, and looketh on the low: and the high He knoweth afar off. If I shall walk in the midst of tribulation, Thou wilt quicken me: and Thou hast stretched forth Thy hand against the wrath of my enemies: and Thy right hand hath saved me. The Lord will repay for me: Thy mercy, O Lord, endureth for ever. O despise not the works of Thy hands.

Psalm Table of St. Mael Ruain: *Domine probasti* to the end. 138-150 [13 Psalms]. Friday Midnight (modern Thursday night).

---

138 (H 139) Domine probasti Lord, Thou hast proved me, and known me (All Saints/Souls Nov 1. One of the All-Saints days, see Sunday after Pentecost, Psalm 147. Verses 11-12 are quoted at Pascha: "...night shall be light as the day...")
Unto the end, a psalm of David.

Lord, thou hast proved me, and known me: Thou hast known my sitting down, and my rising up. Thou hast understood my thoughts afar off: my path and my line Thou hast searched out. And Thou hast foreseen all my ways: for there is no speech in my tongue.

Behold, O Lord, Thou hast known all things, the last and those of old Thou hast formed me, and hast laid Thy hand upon me. Thy knowledge is become wonderful to me: it is high, and I cannot reach to it.

Whither shall I go from Thy Spirit? or whither shall I flee from Thy face? If I ascend into heaven, Thou art there: if I descend into hell, Thou art present. If I take my wings early in the morning, and dwell in the uttermost parts of the sea: Even there also shall Thy hand lead me: and Thy right hand shall hold me.

And I said: Perhaps darkness shall cover me: and night shall be my light in my pleasures. But darkness shall not be dark to Thee, and night shall be light as the day: the darkness thereof, and the light thereof are alike to Thee. For Thou hast possessed my reins: Thou hast protected me from my mother's womb.

I will praise Thee, for Thou art fearfully magnified: wonderful are Thy works, and my soul knoweth right well. My bone is not hidden from Thee, which Thou hast made in secret: and my substance in the lower parts of the earth.

Thy eyes did see my imperfect being, and in Thy book all shall be written: days shall be formed, and no one in them. But to me Thy friends, O God, are made exceedingly honorable: their principality is exceedingly strengthened. I will number them, and they shall be multiplied above the sand: I rose up and am still with Thee.

If Thou wilt kill the wicked, O God: ye men of blood, depart from me: Because you say in thought: They shall receive Thy cities in vain. Have I not hated them, O Lord, that hated Thee: and pined away because of Thy enemies? I have hated them with a perfect hatred: and they are become enemies to me.

Prove me, O God, and know my heart: examine me, and know my paths. And see if there be in me the way of iniquity: and lead me in the eternal way.

139 (Heb. 140) Eripe me Domine Deliver me, O Lord, from the evil man (St. Patrick, Apostle to Ireland, March 17) Unto the end, a psalm of David.

Deliver me, O Lord, from the evil man: rescue me from the unjust man. Who have devised iniquities in their hearts: all the day long they designed battles. They have sharpened their tongues like a serpent: the venom of asps is under their lips.

Keep me, O Lord, from the hand of the wicked: and from unjust men deliver me: who have proposed to supplant my steps: the proud have hidden a net for me: And they have stretched out cords for a snare: they have laid for me a stumbling-block by the wayside.

I said to the Lord: Thou art my God: hear, O Lord, the voice of my supplication. O Lord, Lord, the strength of my salvation: Thou hast overshadowed my head in the day of battle. Give me not up, O Lord, from my desire to the wicked: they have plotted against me: do not Thou forsake me, lest they should triumph.

The head of them compassing me about: the labor of their lips shall overwhelm them. Burning coals shall fall upon them; Thou wilt cast them down into the fire: in miseries they shall not be able to stand. A man full of tongue shall not be established in the earth: evil shall catch the unjust man unto destruction.

I know that the Lord will do justice to the needy: and will revenge the poor. But as for the just, they shall give glory to Thy Name: and the upright shall dwell with Thy countenance.

140 (Heb. 141) Domine clamavi I have cried to Thee, O Lord, hear me (St. John the Baptist: Birth June 24; Conception, Sept. 24., at the time Zacharias burned incense in the Holy of Holies: St. Luke 1:9-23.) A psalm of David.

I have cried to Thee, O Lord, hear me: hearken to my voice, when I cry to Thee. Let my prayer be directed as incense in Thy sight: the lifting up of my hands, as evening sacrifice. Set a watch, O Lord, before my mouth: and a door round about my lips.

Incline not my heart to evil words: to make excuses in sins. With men that work iniquity; and I will not communicate with the choicest of them. The just man shall correct me in mercy, and shall reprove me: but let not the oil of the sinner fatten my head. For my prayer also shall still be against the things with which they are well pleased: their judges falling upon the rock have been swallowed up. They shall hear my words, for they have prevailed: as when the thickness of the earth is broken up upon the ground:

Our bones are scattered by the side of hell: but to Thee, O Lord, Lord, are my eyes: in Thee have I put my trust; take not away my soul. Keep me from the snare, which they have laid for me: and from the stumbling-blocks of them that work iniquity. The wicked shall fall in his net: I am alone until I pass.

141 (Heb. 142) Voce mea I cried to the Lord with my voice (St. Paul. Conversion Jan 25) Of understanding, for David, a prayer when he was in the cave.

I cried to the Lord with my voice: with my voice I made supplication to the Lord. In His sight I pour out my prayer: and before Him I declare my trouble.

When my spirit failed me, then Thou knewest my paths. In this way wherein I walked, they have hidden a snare for me. I looked on my right hand, and beheld: and there was no one that would know me. Flight hath failed me: and there is no one that hath regard to my soul.

I cried to thee, O Lord; I said: Thou art my hope, my portion in the land of the living. Attend to my supplication: for I am brought very low. Deliver me from my persecutors: for they are stronger than I. Bring my soul out of prison, that I may praise Thy Name: the just wait for me, until Thou reward me.

142 (Heb. 143) Domine exaudi Hear, O Lord, my prayer (Passion of St. John the Baptist) A psalm of David when his son Absalom pursued him.

Hear, O Lord, my prayer: give ear to my supplication in Thy truth: hear me in Thy justice. And enter not into judgment with Thy servant: for in Thy sight no man living shall be justified. For the enemy hath persecuted my soul: he hath brought down my life to the earth. He hath made me to dwell in darkness as those that have been dead of old: and my spirit is in anguish within me; my heart within me is troubled.

I remembered the days of old: I meditated on all Thy works: I meditated upon the works of Thy hands. I stretched forth my hands to Thee: my soul is as earth without water unto Thee. Hear me speedily, O Lord: my spirit hath fainted away. Turn not away Thy face from me: lest I be like unto them that go down into the pit. Cause me to hear Thy mercy in the morning: for in Thee have I hoped.

Make the way known to me, wherein I should walk: for I have lifted up my soul to Thee. Deliver me from my enemies, O Lord; to Thee have I fled: teach me to do Thy will, for Thou art my God. Thy good spirit shall lead me into the right land: for Thy Name's sake, O Lord, Thou wilt quicken me in Thy justice. Thou wilt bring my soul out of trouble: and in Thy mercy Thou wilt destroy my enemies. And Thou wilt cut off all them that afflict my soul: for I am thy servant.

143 (Heb. 144) Benedictus Dominus Blessed be the Lord my God (Dormition of the Blessed Virgin Mary, Aug. 15 and 16. See the *Protevangelium of St. James*.) A psalm of David against Goliath.

Blessed be the Lord my God, Who teacheth my hands to fight, and my fingers to war. My mercy, and my refuge: my support, and my deliverer. My protector, and I have hoped in Him: Who subdueth my people under me.

Lord, what is man, that Thou art made known to him? Or the son of man, that Thou makest account of him? Man is like to vanity: his days pass away like a shadow. Lord, bow down Thy heavens and descend: touch the mountains, and they shall smoke. Send forth lightning, and Thou shalt scatter them: shoot out Thy arrows, and Thou shalt trouble them. Put forth Thy hand from on high: take me out, and deliver me from many waters: from the hand of strange children. Whose mouth hath spoken vanity: and their right hand is the right hand of iniquity.

To Thee, O God, I will sing a new canticle: on the psaltery and an instrument of ten strings I will sing praises to Thee. Who givest salvation to kings: who hast redeemed Thy servant David from the malicious sword: deliver me, and rescue me out of the hand of strange children: whose mouth hath spoken vanity: and their right hand is the right hand of iniquity: whose sons are as new plants in their youth: their daughters decked out, adorned round about after the similitude of a temple: their storehouses full, flowing out of this into that: their sheep fruitful in young, abounding in their goings forth: their oxen fat. There is no breach of wall, nor passage, nor crying out in their streets.

They have called the people happy, that hath these things: but happy is that people whose God is the Lord.

144 (Heb. 145) Exaltabo te Deus I will extol Thee, O God my king (Nativity of the Blessed Virgin Mary, Sept. 8) Praise, of David himself.

I will extol Thee, O God my king: and I will bless Thy Name for ever; yea, for ever and ever. Every day will I bless Thee: and I will praise Thy Name for ever: yea, for ever and ever.

Great is the Lord, and greatly to be praised: and of His greatness there is no end. Generation and generation shall praise Thy works: and they shall declare Thy power. They shall speak of the magnificence of the glory of Thy holiness: and shall tell Thy wondrous works. And they shall speak of the might of Thy terrible acts: and shall declare Thy greatness. They shall publish the memory of the abundance of thy sweetness: and shall rejoice in Thy justice.

The Lord is gracious and merciful: patient and plenteous in mercy. The Lord is sweet to all: and His tender mercies are over all His works. Let all thy works, O Lord, praise Thee: and let Thy saints bless Thee. They shall speak of the glory of Thy kingdom: and shall tell of Thy power: To make Thy might known to the sons of men: and the glory of the magnificence of Thy kingdom. Thy kingdom is a kingdom of all ages: and Thy dominion endureth throughout all generations. The Lord is faithful in all His words: and holy in all His works. The Lord lifteth up all that fall: and setteth up all that are cast down. The eyes of all hope in Thee, O Lord: and Thou givest them meat in due season. Thou openest Thy hand: and fillest with blessing every living creature.

The Lord is just in all His ways: and holy in all His works. The Lord is nigh unto all them that call upon Him: to all that call upon Him in truth. He will do the will of them that fear Him: and He will hear their prayer, and save them. the Lord keepeth all them that love Him: but all the wicked He will destroy.

My mouth shall speak the praise of the Lord: and let all flesh bless His holy Name for ever; yea, for ever and ever.

145 (Heb.146) Lauda animas Praise the Lord, O my soul (St. Martin of Tours, Nov. 11th, the last Feast day before Advent.) Alleluia, of Aggeos and Zacharias.

Praise the Lord, O my soul: in my life I will praise the Lord: I will sing to my God as long as I shall be.

Put not your trust in princes: in the children of men, in whom there is no salvation. His spirit shall go forth, and he shall return into his earth: in that day all their thoughts shall perish.

Blessed is he who hath the God of Jacob for his helper, whose hope is in the Lord his God: Who made heaven and earth, the sea, and all things that are in them. Who keepeth truth for ever: who executeth judgment for them that suffer wrong: who giveth food to the hungry. The Lord looseth them that are fettered: the Lord enlighteneth the blind. The Lord lifteth up them that are cast down: the Lord loveth the just. The Lord keepeth the strangers; He will support the fatherless and the widow: and the ways of sinners He will destroy.

     The Lord shall reign for ever: Thy God, O Sion, unto generation and generation.

146 (Heb. 147:1-11) Laudate Dominum Praise ye the Lord (Entrance into the Temple of the BVM, Nov. 21. See the *Protevangelium of St. James*.) Alleluia.

     Praise ye the Lord, because psalm is good: to our God be joyful and comely praise.

     The Lord buildeth up Jerusalem: He will gather together the dispersed of Israel. Who healeth the broken of heart, and bindeth up their bruises. Who telleth the number of the stars: and calleth them all by their names.
Great is our Lord, and great is His power: and of His wisdom there is no number. The Lord lifteth up the meek, and bringeth the wicked down even to the ground.

     Sing ye to the Lord with praise: sing to our God upon the harp. Who covereth the heaven with clouds, and prepareth rain for the earth. Who maketh grass to grow on the mountains, and herbs for the service of men. Who giveth to beasts their food: and to the young ravens that call upon Him.
He shall not delight in the strength of the horse: nor take pleasure in the legs of a man. The Lord taketh pleasure in them that fear Him: and in them that hope in His mercy.

147 (Heb. 147:12-20) Lauda Jerusalem Praise the Lord, O Jerusalem (All Saints, Sunday after Pentecost, see Nov 1, Psalm 138 for the other Saints' day.) Alleluia.

     Praise the Lord, O Jerusalem: praise Thy God, O Sion. Because He hath strengthened the bolts of thy gates; He hath blessed thy children within thee.

     Who hath placed peace in thy borders: and filleth thee with the fat of corn. Who sendeth forth His speech to the earth: His word runneth swiftly. Who giveth snow like wool: scattereth mists like ashes. He sendeth His crystal like morsels: who shall stand before the face of His cold? He shall send out His word, and shall melt them: His wind shall blow, and the waters shall run.

     Who declareth His word to Jacob: His justices and His judgments to Israel. He hath not done in like manner to every nation: and His judgments He hath not made manifest to them. Alleluia.

148 (Heb. 148) Laudate Dominum de caelis Praise ye the Lord from the heavens (Christmas, and Matins Psalms of Praise.) Alleluia.

Praise ye the Lord from the heavens: praise ye Him in the high places. Praise ye Him, all His angels: praise ye Him, all His hosts. Praise ye Him, O sun and moon: praise Him, all ye stars and light. Praise Him, ye heavens of heavens: and let all the waters that are above the heavens praise the Name of the Lord. For He spoke, and they were made: He commanded, and they were created. He hath established them for ever, and for ages of ages: He hath made a decree, and it shall not pass away.

Praise the Lord from the earth: ye dragons, and all ye deeps: Fire, hail, snow, ice, stormy winds, which fulfil His word: Mountains and all hills: fruitful trees and all cedars: Beasts and all cattle: serpents and feathered fowls: Kings of the earth and all people: princes and all judges of the earth: Young men and maidens. Let the old with the younger praise the Name of the Lord: for His Name alone is exalted.

The praise of Him is above heaven and earth: and He hath exalted the horn of His people. A hymn to all His saints: to the children of Israel, a people approaching to Him. Alleluia.

149 (Heb. 149) Cantate Domino Sing ye to the Lord a new canticle (Pentecost, and Matins Psalms of Praise) Alleluia.

Sing ye to the Lord a new canticle: let His praise be in the church of the saints. Let Israel rejoice in Him that made him: and let the children of Sion be joyful in their king. Let them praise His Name in choir: let them sing to Him with the timbrel and the psaltery. For the Lord is well pleased with His people: and He will exalt the meek unto salvation.

The saints shall rejoice in glory: they shall be joyful in their beds. The high praises of God shall be in their mouth: and two-edged swords in their hands: To execute vengeance upon the nations: chastisements among the people: To bind their kings with fetters: and their nobles with manacles of iron: To execute upon them the judgment that is written: this glory is to all His saints. Alleluia.

150 (Heb. 150) Laudate Dominum in sanctis Praise ye the Lord in his holy places (Alleluia for Pascha, Christmas, and Pentecost, and Matins Psalms of Praise)

Alleluia.

Praise ye the Lord in His holy places: praise ye Him in the firmament of His power. Praise ye Him for His mighty acts: praise ye Him according to the multitude of His greatness. Praise Him with sound of trumpet: praise Him with psaltery and harp. Praise Him with timbrel and choir: praise Him with strings and organs. Praise Him on high sounding cymbals: praise Him on cymbals of joy: let every spirit praise the Lord. Alleluia.

Prayers Which End Most Hours:
(Long or Short Forms: Second, Third, Sixth, Ninth, Vespers, Matins Hours)
Prayer of the Community of the Brethren: Long form

Antiphon AB 40: Remember not our former iniquities; let Thy mercies speedily prevent us, for we have become exceedingly poor. (Ps 78:8)
Prayer: Help us, O God of our Salvation, for the Glory of Thy Name's sake.
Prayer: O Lord free us and forgive our sins because of Thy Name.
Prayer: Give not the soul of one who trusts in Thee over to the beasts.
Prayer: Forget not the souls of Thy poor ones unto the end.
Prayer: Respect Thy promises, O Lord: Who reignest unto the ages. Amen.

For Our Sins
Antiphon AB 40': O God, come to my assistance: O Lord, make haste to help me. (Ps. 69:2)
Prayer: Hasten, O Lord to free us from all of our sins: Who reignest unto the ages. Amen.

For the Baptized
Antiphon AB 41: Save, O Lord, Thy People and bless Thine inheritance: and rule them and exalt them for ever. (Ps. 27:9).
Prayer: Have mercy, O Lord, On Thy Catholic Church, which Thou didst ransom by Thy Holy Blood: Who reignest unto the ages. Amen.

For the Priests
Antiphon AB 41': Arise, O Lord into Thy resting place, Thou and Thine ark, which Thou hast sanctified. (Ps. 131:8)
Antiphon: Let Thy priests be clothed with justice and let Thy Saints rejoice. (Ps. 131:9)
Prayer: May all Thy Saints rejoice in Thee O Lord, they who hope upon Thee in all Truth: Who reignest unto the ages. Amen.

For the Abbot
Antiphon AB 42: The Lord preserve him and give him life, and make him blessed upon the earth. (Ps. 40:3a)
Antiphon: May the Lord keepeth thee from all evil: may the Lord keep thy soul. (Ps. 120:7)

Antiphon: May the Lord keep thy coming in and thy going out; from henceforth now and forever. (Ps. 120:8)

For the Brethren
Antiphon AB 43: Keep us, O Lord as the apple of Thine eye; protect us under the shadow of Thy wing. (Ps. 16:8b)
Prayer: Be pleased to protect and sanctify all of them, O Almighty God Who reignest unto the ages. Amen.

For the Brotherhood
Antiphon AB 44: Thou, O Lord wilt preserve us and keep us from this generation forever. (Ps. 11:8)
Prayer: Hear our prayers for our brethren, that Thou wilt have mercy upon them O God: Who reignest unto the ages. Amen.

For Peace of Peoples and Kingdoms
Antiphon AB 45: The Lord will give strength to His people: the Lord will bless His people with peace. (Ps. 28:11)
Prayer: Be pleased to grant peace to all, Almighty God: Who reignest unto the ages. Amen.

For Blasphemers
Antiphon AB 46: Thy mercy, O Lord, endureth forever: O despise not the works of Thy hands. (Ps. 137:8)
Prayer: O Lord God of Virtues, do not let those here remain in sin: Who reignest unto the ages. Amen.

For the Impious
Antiphon AB 47: Judge them, O God. Let them fall from their devices: according to the multitude of their wickednesses cast them out: for they have provoked Thee, O Lord. (Ps. 5:11b)
Prayer: May they who trust in themselves be confounded, O Lord, but not we who trust in Thee: Who reignest unto the ages. Amen.

For those who Journey (Ps. 117:25)
Antiphon AB 48: O Lord, save me: O Lord, give good success.
Prayer: Grant a successful journey to Thy servants: Who reignest unto the ages. Amen.

For Grace unto Pilgrims
Antiphon AB 49: Let all Thy works, O Lord, praise Thee, and let Thy Saints bless Thee. (Ps. 144:10)
Prayer: Our souls give Thee thanks for Thine innumerable good works, O Lord: Who reignest unto the ages. Amen.

For the Charitable (Ps 111:9)
Antiphon AB 50: He hath distributed, He hath given to the poor: His justice remaineth forever and ever. His horn shall be exalted in glory.
Prayer: O Lord, repay those who gave alms in this world in Thy Holy Kingdom: Who reignest unto the ages. Amen.

For the Infirm
Antiphon AB 51: And they cried to the Lord in their tribulation: and He delivered them out of their distresses. (Ps. 106:6)
Prayer: Grant, O Lord, Thy servants health of mind and body: Who reignest unto the ages. Amen.

For Captives
Antiphon AB 51': Arise, O Lord, help us and redeem us for Thy Name's sake. (Ps. 43:26)
Antiphon: Our help is in the Name of the Lord. (Ps. 123:8)
Prayer: Be pleased to save us through the invocation of Thy Name: Who reignest unto the ages. Amen.

For Martyrs
Antiphon AB 101: After fires and swords, crosses and beasts the Saints are borne with great triumph into the Kingdom and rest.
Antiphon AB 102: These are the ones who came forth in great tribulation and washed their stoles and made them white in the Blood of the Lamb.
Prayer AB 52: O God, Who hast bestowed the crown of martyrdom unto Thy Saints and Elect, we beseech Thee, O Lord, that through their examples, we who have not earned such glory may obtain forgiveness: Who reignest unto the ages. Amen.

For those who are in Tribulations
Antiphon AB 53: Unto Thee will I cry, O Lord; O my God, be not silent to me. (Ps. 27:1a) (Ps. 45:8)
Antiphon: The Lord of virtues is with us; the God of Jacob is our protector.
Prayer: O Our Helper, the God of Jacob, have mercy upon us, O Lord Who reignest unto the ages. Amen.
Collect AB 54: Holy among the Saints, the spotless Lamb: Glorious in the Heavens, Marvelous upon the Earth, grant us, O Lord, according to Thy Great Mercy that for which we petition and pray to Thee, O God: Who reignest unto the ages. Amen.

For Martyrs
Antiphon AB 103: In memory of Thy Martyrs, O Lord, harken to the prayer of Thy servants, O Christ.
Antiphon AB 104: In the invocation of Thy Holy Martyrs, have mercy, O God, upon Thy Suppliants.
Prayer AB 55: We pray the eternal Name of Thy Virtue, Almighty God, that Thou makest us to be equal to the Martyrs and all of Thy Saints: companions in example, similar in Faith, vigorous in devotion, alike in suffering, and fruitful in the Resurrection: Who reignest unto the ages. Amen.

For Penitents Antiphon AB 56: Have mercy on me, O God, according to Thy great mercy. (Ps. 50:3)
Prayer: Grant, O Lord, forgiveness to those who out of Faith are penitent unto Thee, according to Thy great mercy, O God: Who reignest unto the ages. Amen.

Credo   Complete Nicene Creed (Lorrha-Stowe Missal)

I believe in one God, the Father Almighty, maker of heaven and earth and of all things visible and invisible. And in one Lord Jesus Christ, the Only-Begotten Son of God. Born of the Father before all ages. Light of light, true God of true God. Born, not made, of one Substance with the Father: through Whom all things were made. Who for us men, and for our Salvation descended from heaven. And was Incarnate of the Holy Spirit and the Virgin Mary: And was born man. And was crucified also for us: under Pontius Pilate; He suffered and was buried. And He rose on the third day, according to the Scriptures. And ascended into heaven: and sitteth at the right hand of God the Father. And He shall come again with glory to judge both the living and the dead: Whose Kingdom shall have no end. And I believe in the Holy Spirit, the Lord and Giver of life: Who proceedeth from the Father. Who with the Father and the Son together is worshiped and glorified: Who spake by the Prophets. And in one, Holy, Catholic, and Apostolic Church. I confess one Baptism for the remission of sins. And I look for the resurrection of the dead. + And the life of the world to come. Amen.

The Divine Prayer   AB 36

Our Father, Who art in the Heavens, hallowed be Thy Name. Thy Kingdom come. Thy will be done on earth as it is in Heaven. Give us this day our daily bread and forgive us our debts as we forgive our debtors and lead us not into temptation but deliver us from evil. Amen.

Here Ends the Hour. *May do Beatitudes, Magnificat, Shrine of Piety.*

Prayer of Community of Brethren:
Short Form (AB 117-119)

AB 117 Antiphon 1: In Thee, O Lord, have I hoped, let me never be confounded: deliver me in Thy justice and rescue me. (Ps. 30:2)

An 2: O Lord my God: do not Thou depart from me, attend unto my help, the God of my Salvation. (Ps. 37:22b-23)

An 3: O God come to my assistance. O Lord make haste to help me.

Prayer: Hasten, O Lord to free us from all of our sins: Who reignest unto the ages. Amen.

For our Abbot

AB 118 Antiphon: The Lord preserve him and give him life, and make him blessed upon the earth. (Ps. 40:3a)

Antiphon: May the Lord keepeth thee from all evil: may the Lord keep thy soul. (Ps. 120:7)

Antiphon: May the Lord keep thy coming in and thy going out; from henceforth now and forever. (Ps. 120:8)

For the Brethren

AB 119 Antiphon: Keep us, O Lord as the apple of Thine eye; protect us under the shadow of Thy wing. (Ps. 16:8b)

Prayer: Be pleased to protect and sanctify all of them, Almighty God Who reignest unto the ages. Amen.

Complete Creed from The Lorrha-Stowe Missal

I believe in one God, the Father Almighty, maker of heaven and earth and of all things visible and invisible. And in one Lord Jesus Christ, the Only-Begotten Son of God. Born of the Father before all ages. Light of light, true God of true God. Born, not made, of one Substance with the Father: through Whom all things were made. Who for us men, and for our Salvation descended from heaven. And was Incarnate of the Holy Spirit and the Virgin Mary: And was born man. And was crucified also for us: under Pontius Pilate; He suffered and was buried. And He rose on the third day, according to the Scriptures. And ascended into heaven: and sitteth at the right hand of God the Father. And He shall come again with glory to judge both the living and the dead: Whose Kingdom shall have no end. And I believe in the Holy Spirit, the Lord and Giver of life: Who proceedeth from the Father. Who with the Father and the Son together is worshiped and glorified: Who spake by the Prophets. And in one, Holy, Catholic, and Apostolic Church. I confess one Baptism for the remission of sins. And I look for the resurrection of the dead. + And the life of the world to come. Amen.

The Divine Prayer (AB 36)

Our Father, Who art in the Heavens, hallowed be Thy Name. Thy Kingdom come. Thy will be done on earth as it is in Heaven. Give us this day our daily bread and forgive us our debts as we forgive our debtors and lead us not into temptation but deliver us from evil. Amen.

Here Ends the Hour. *May do Beatitudes, Magnificat, and Shrine of Piety.*